CONTEMPORARY ASIAN AMERICA

Contemporary Asian America

A Multidisciplinary Reader

THIRD EDITION

Edited by Min Zhou and Anthony C. Ocampo

NEW YORK UNIVERSITY PRESS
New York and London

NEW YORK UNIVERSITY PRESS
New York and London
www.nyupress.org

References to Internet websites (URLs) were accurate at the time of writing. Neither the author nor New York University Press is responsible for URLs that may have expired or changed since the manuscript was prepared.

Library of Congress Cataloging-in-Publication Data
Names: Zhou, Min, 1956– editor. | Ocampo, Anthony Christian, 1981– editor.
Title: Contemporary Asian America : a multidisciplinary reader /
edited by Min Zhou and Anthony C. Ocampo.
Description: Third edition. | New York : New York University Press, 2016. |
Includes bibliographical references and index.
Identifiers: LCCN 2015043568| ISBN 9781479829231 (cl : alk. paper) |
ISBN 9781479826223 (pb : alk. paper)
Subjects: LCSH: Asian Americans. | Asian Americans—Study and teaching.
Classification: LCC E184.06 C66 2016 | DDC 973/.0495—dc23
LC record available at http://lccn.loc.gov/2015043568

New York University Press books are printed on acid-free paper, and their binding materials are chosen for strength and durability. We strive to use environmentally responsible suppliers and materials to the greatest extent possible in publishing our books.

Manufactured in the United States of America

10 9 8 7 6 5 4 3 2 1

Also available as an ebook

From Min Zhou: For Philip Jia Guo and Lisa Phuong Mai, the children of Asian immigrants

From Anthony C. Ocampo: For my parents Myrtle and Chito Ocampo, immigrants from the Philippines

CONTENTS

LIST OF TABLES AND FIGURES

FIGURES

PREFACE TO THE THIRD EDITION

There was a time, not too long ago, when race in America was synonymous with the black-white dichotomy. But since the United States reformed its immigration policy and reopened its borders to newcomers, immigrants and their children have transformed the racial landscape of this country. In the past decade or so alone, the immigrant population has grown tremendously, from thirty million at the turn of the twenty-first century to over forty million today. The Pew Research Center's comprehensive study of Asian Americans, titled "The Rise of Asian Americans," surprised many by pointing out that Asian Americans, not Latinos, constituted the fastest growing racial group, and much of the growth is due to international migration. More than a third (36 percent) of the new immigrants who came to this country in 2010 were of Asian American or Pacific Islander descent, compared to 31 percent of Latino origin.

Over the past half century, Asian Americans grew from fewer than one million (or 0.6 percent of the total US population) in 1960 to more than nineteen million (or 6 percent of the US population) in 2013.[1] Although Asian Americans compose a tiny proportion of the US population, they form an increasingly visible racial minority group. Many Americans assume that Asian Americans congregate along the coastal states of the Pacific West, but in fact their numbers have increased most rapidly in new destinations of the US South, a region considered to be the "geographic center of black-white relations."[2] Asian Americans have now complicated Americans' notions of race. By virtue of their presence all over the country, it is now impossible for nineteen million people of Asian origins to remain unseen.

As the contributors of the following chapters demonstrate, Asian Americans have carved out niches and made themselves visible within many arenas of American life—schools and colleges, community-based organizations, suburbs and ethnoburbs, neighborhoods and "gayborhoods," political movements, and even professional sports leagues. Asian American immigrants and their children work in every echelon of the mainstream and ethnic labor markets—professional occupations, service sectors, hospitality industries, and health care and medicine—and have achieved measureable positive socioeconomic outcomes. Unlike the European and Asian immigrants of yesteryear, they excel in the education arena and fare well in American society on economic terms. They also have more resources and technology to intimately and economically tether themselves to the home countries they left behind. The emerging popularity of social media has helped democratize American pop culture, and Asian Americans have used the Internet to raise social consciousness (e.g., 18millionrising. com, *Hyphen* magazine), blog about Asian American racial injustices (e.g., Angry Asian Man), and build a fan base for their music and comedy (e.g., The Fung Brothers of Monterey Park, CA). Historically touted as "forever foreigners," Asian Americans throughout the United States are weaving themselves into the tapestry of American society and continue to be lauded as "the model minority."

Yet despite significant advances in social mobility, Asian Americans have yet to achieve a social status in the United States that is on par with that of their European counterparts of yesteryear. In spite of the widespread popularity of the "model minority" trope, there are Asian Americans who are poor and struggle to make ends meet, who barely make it into community colleges because of both academic and financial challenges, who live in the shadows because of their legal status, and who continue to be subject to overt and covert forms of racial discrimination on a daily basis. No matter what their levels of cultural and economic assimilation, they are still considered the racial other because of their phenotype, even those who are adopted by and raised in white families and communities for their entire lives. They continue to face a bamboo ceiling that blocks their mobility to leadership positions. Their representation in upper-level management in corporations, college and university administrations, Hollywood televisions and films, and even the US Congress remains negligible. Despite the fact that American society is more open than ever before, and an Asian American basketball player in the NBA has evolved into a national news sensation, Asian America is still on the margin of mainstream America. As French writer Jean-Baptiste Alphonse Karr famously declared, "The more things change, the more they stay the same."

Even the Pew Research Center report about the "rise" of Asian Americans was rife with controversy. To the credit of the organization, they consulted with several of the leading Asian American social scientists in the country; however, it was their *reporting* of the data that brought tremendous angst to Asian American leaders around the country. At its heart, the report seemed celebratory in nature—in total congruence with the model minority stereotype. In opting to highlight the successes, the report marginalized the segments of the community that were most in need. For every Asian American success story, there are many more Asian American families and communities who continue to suffer through the indignant effects of racism, sexism, homophobia, violence, and poverty. Given the scarcity of think tanks that address Asian American issues, the Pew Research Center report was a missed opportunity. In the eyes of many Asian American activists, scholars, and policymakers, they were "blindsided" by a one-dimensional depiction of what they know—and have proven with their life's work—to be a culturally and socioeconomically heterogeneous population.[3]

Like the Asian American population in the United States, *Contemporary Asian America* continues to evolve. We have enlisted an interdisciplinary group of sociologists, political scientists, psychologists, and ethnic studies scholars to contribute to this third edition new chapters that underscore the growing complexity of Asian American communities and social issues. Some of the chapters tackle new frontiers in Asian American studies. How is Latino immigration reshaping how Asian Americans think about race? How have gay Asian Americans carved out their agency in a time when LGBT individuals have reached unprecedented levels of acceptance? How has the age of Obama reshaped the political behaviors of Asian Americans? Other chapters address issues that Asian Americans continue to endure. How does race affect the everyday experiences of Asian American students and workers? What strategies do Asian Americans use to maintain their cultural and social ties to their home country? How do the historical, economic, and political relations of the United States across the Pacific affect Asian Americans' experiences in this country today? These are complicated questions, to which our book does not propose to provide a solution. Nonetheless, this third edition does hope to inspire a new generation of students—Asian American or not—to critically consider these issues, rather than reduce a population of nineteen million rising to mere Orientalist stereotypes.

As the coeditors, we are incredibly thankful to New York University Press (NYUP), who not only provided the initial spark to develop this reader into the new edition, but, as a publisher, has also made itself an important ally to the growing field of Asian American studies. We are grateful for their continued willingness to provide an important space for contemporary Asian American issues to be debated in a critical fashion. NYUP editor Jennifer Hammer has offered her unending support and enthusiasm for this project, as she did in the previous editions. We thank Eric Zinner for playing a key role in providing this important scholarly space for Asian American studies. We also thank Constance Grady and Dorothea Stillman Halliday, who have patiently guided us through the necessary steps in the publishing process, and Joseph Dahm, who is our meticulous copy editor.

We are grateful for our contributors, both old and new, who have not only helped make *Contemporary Asian America* a repository of the multifaceted experiences of Asian Americans, but also given us an important set of tools for understanding the current state and the future of this ever-evolving community. Their brilliant chapters shed new light on the history and current state of Asian America and inspire scholars and students of Asian American studies. When it comes to this extraordinary group of passionate scholars, "the past isn't dead; it's not even past," to invoke the words of the American writer William Faulkner.

This volume would not have been possible without the support of our past and present home institutions. We would like to express our gratitude for the institutional and funding support we have received from the School of Humanities and Social Sciences at Nanyang Technological University (NTU), Singapore; the Department of Sociology, Asian American Studies Department, Asian American Studies Center, and the fund from Walter and Shirley Wang Endowed Chair in US-China Relations and Communications at the University of California, Los Angeles; the Department of Psychology and Sociology at Cal Poly Pomona. We thank our home institutions for continuing to believe in the field of Asian American studies.

Finally, we would like to thank our wonderful colleagues, research assistants, students, friends, and family. Min would like to thank her colleagues and students in the Department of Asian American Studies at UCLA who have helped nurture her Asian American sensitivity and inspire her research in the field. Anthony would like to thank his colleagues at Cal Poly Pomona, the National Center for Faculty Development and Diversity, the Association of Asian American Studies, and the community of immigration, race, and gender scholars within the American Sociological Association, for their support. We thank our incredibly hardworking research assistants—Jin Lou, Jingyi Wen, and Hao Zhou from NTU and Audrey E. Aday, Sarine Aratoon, Irisa Charles, Joseph Cipriano, Jessica Galvan, and Milio Medina from Cal Poly Pomona. We appreciate the help from Antonio Ocampo for proofreading the manuscript. Min dedicates this book to her son Philip Jia Guo and daughter-in-law Lisa Phuong Mai. Anthony thanks his brothers and sisters from the UCLA sociology PhD program; his dearest friends both in and out of academia (especially Daniel Soodjinda and Elmer Manlongat); and his partner Joseph Cipriano. He dedicates this book to his mother and father, Maria Myrtle and Antonio "Chito" Ocampo, whose own migration story inspired him to pursue this profession.

Min Zhou, Singapore
Anthony C. Ocampo, Los Angeles
May 23, 2015

NOTES

1 Pew Research Center, "U.S. Hispanic and Asian Populations Growing, but for Different Reasons," http://www.pewresearch.org/fact-tank/2014/06/26/u-s-hispanic-and-asian-populations-growing-but-for-different-reasons/ (accessed May 23, 2015).

2 Monica McDermott, *Working Class White: The Making and Unmaking of Race Relations* (Berkeley: University of California Press, 2006), 1.

3 Karthick Ramakrishnan, "When Words Fail: Careful Framing Needed in Research on Asian Americans," *Hyphen Magazine*, June 27, 2012, http://www.hyphenmagazine.com/blog/archive/2012/06/when-words-fail-careful-framing-needed-research-asian-americans (accessed January 31, 2015).

PREFACE TO THE SECOND EDITION

It was no small coincidence that the US population hit the three-hundred-million mark just as we were putting the finishing touches on the second edition of *Contemporary Asian America* in October 2006. For most Americans, this unique historical moment was fairly anticlimactic. There were no visible signs of celebration—no parades with colorful floats and marching bands, no fireworks, not even a public gathering. President Bush—a politician who has an unusual way of speaking to the moment—delivered what can only be described as a tepid response to the demographic change. In a press release issued by the White House, the president lauded that people were "America's greatest asset," and praised the American people for their confidence, ingenuity, hopes and for their love of freedom. He concluded that "we welcome this milestone as further proof that the American Dream remains as bright and hopeful as ever."[1] This brief blip in the news cycle disappeared almost as suddenly as it came. To be certain, any celebrations that might have occurred were dampened by an ongoing debate in the United States about immigration and it impact on the environment, natural resources, public services, and quality of life.

By contrast, the arrival of the two-hundred-millionth American in November 1967 was a more splendid affair, marked by celebrations and extensive news coverage. Addressing the nation while standing before a giant census clock, President Lyndon Johnson delivered his own message of hope and caution for the future. As Haya El Nasser recounts, President Johnson's words were broken on several occasions by the sounds of applause from the crowd of onlookers who had converged on the Department of Commerce to hear the president speak.[2] Among the many events that celebrated the two-hundred-million mark was a contest of sorts, sponsored by *Life* magazine. The editors at *Life* sent teams of photographers to twenty-two cities across the United States, finding the baby who arrived closest to the hour appointed by the US Census Bureau when the two-hundred-millionth American would arrive. The winning baby was a fourth-generation Chinese American, Robert Ken Woo, Jr., born at Atlanta's Crawford Long Hospital at 11:03 AM, November 20, 1967, to Robert and Sally Woo. Woo's story was—to paraphrase the writer Gish Gen—"typically Asian American." Bobby's great-grandfather had come to Georgia after the Civil War to work on the Augusta Canal. His mother's family had fled the Communist Revolution in China and settled in Augusta in 1959 after several years of waiting for permission to emigrate. Both of parents were college graduates; his father worked as a certified public accountant in Georgia. Bobby Woo was one of a small number of Asian Americans growing up in the suburb of Tucker. He attended Harvard University as an undergraduate and as a law student. Today, he is a practicing attorney (and the first Asian American partner at King & Spalding, one of the most prestigious law firms in America), an advocate for immigrant rights, and the father of three children.

Woo's story is both fascinating and symbolically appropriate. Even though it was by happenstance, Woo's selection as the two-hundred-millionth American anticipated drastic changes that had altered the country's demographic, social, and political landscape since his ancestors first arrived in America nearly a hundred years before his birth. Woo's parents and Woo himself were beneficiaries of the growing educational and economic opportunities that were made available to them and other racial/ethnic minorities only within a relatively short span of time—the repeal of the Chinese Exclusion Act in 1943, the Immigration and Nationality Act of 1952 (also known as the McCarran-Walter Act), the Civil Rights Act of 1964, and subsequent changes in public policies and public attitudes toward racial/ethnic minorities as a result of the civil rights movement. The passage of the 1965 amendments to the Immigration and Nationality Act (Hart-Celler Act), two years before Woo's birth, made possible the coming of hundreds and thousands of immigrants from all over the world, especially from countries in Asia and Latin America that had legally been excluded. Consequently, the face of America has changed dramatically. Asian Americans, barely visible on the American scene in the 1960s, have experienced unparallel growth, largely through immigration, from 1.5 million in 1970 to 14.3 million as of today.

At a time when the United States is now the third most populous country on earth after China and India, one wonders what the future of Asian America will look like. With the exception of Woo's story, Asian Americans and their contributions to American life were hardly mentioned by the American public either at the two-hundred-million celebration in November 1967 or at the quiet passing of the three-hundred-million milestone during the third week of October 2006. This absence is a glaring one. Since the arrival of the first immigrants from Asia in the mid-nineteenth century, Asian Americans have played and will continue to play a critical role in this country's future. Their American stories need to be unfolded further and understood deeper. The second edition of *Contemporary Asian America: A Multidisciplinary Reader* grows out of this urgent need. We have thus worked assiduously to compile a new reader that delves into contemporary Asian America in its fullness and complexity; to assemble a selection of readings and documentary films that offer an excellent grounding for understanding many of the emerging trends, issues, and debates in the community and in Asian American studies; and to organize topics that lend insight into the future of this ethnically diverse Asian American community.

Listening to students, instructors, researchers, and others who have used the first edition of our reader for their studies, teaching, and research, we aimed to make the second edition of *Contemporary Asian America* more user-friendly by reducing its size and revamping it with the best and most up-to-date works that reflect contributions—and changes—that have occurred within the field of Asian American studies since 2000. Our goal proved challenging: How do you reduce the number of articles and yet retain the breath and depth? How do you retain the "classic" works most utilized by survey courses in Asian American studies and at the same time introduce new topics, concepts, and perspectives that are sensitive to the changing terrains of contemporary Asian America and essential for the continual development of Asian American studies today? We have addressed these questions rather substantively through a reconfiguration of certain sections from the original volume and the incorporation of original and recently published works that concern twenty-first-century Asian America, including the impact of September 11 on Asian American identity, citizenship, and civil liberties; globalization as a dynamic force shaping the contemporary Asian American community; theoretical debates that continue to inform Asian American studies; and an emphasis on diversity of Asian American experiences along lines of class, ethnicity, nativity, gender, and sexuality. Of particular importance to the new edition is the movement away from nation-centered models of identity formation (a core component of Asian American studies as it existed in the 1960s through the 1990s) to a model governed by fluidity, cosmopolitanism, and flexible identities rooted in global citizenship.

Of course, our interpretation of Asian American studies is just an interpretation, and perhaps a limited one at that. While no reader can be all things to all people, this new edition strives to achieve a balanced coverage with the range and depth that reflects our commitment to multiple interpretations of the Asian American experience(s) and the shared vision of the many possibilities and promises that is one of the defining features of Asian American studies. Along the way, we ask more questions than we answer, offering what we hope will be the framework for a larger discussion within and beyond the classroom. We believe that this second edition has met our intended goals. It also meets the growing expectations of our users. Instructors who have used the original edition of *Contemporary Asian America* should be able to comfortably adopt this new edition whether they choose to teach their courses the same way or differently. Those who have not used *Contemporary Asian America* before may now consider adopting it as it will surely stimulate much intellectual and personally reflexive discussion in classrooms.

We, as coeditors, are appreciative for the encouragement and support of so many individuals who made the original edition of *Contemporary Asian America* a great success and this second edition a real possibility. First and foremost, we thank our editor, Jennifer Hammer, at New York University Press (NYUP).

Hammer has been a champion of this edition. Her enthusiasm, encouragement, and editorial insight have made this project as intellectually challenging as fun. We thank Eric Zinner, the editor-in-chief at NYUP, for his steadfast support and for his vision of the possibilities of Asian American studies. We also thank our copy editor, Emily Wright, for her careful reading and meticulous editing of the entire manuscript. We are especially grateful to NYUP's anonymous reviewers who offered additional suggestions after carefully reading our second edition prospectus.

We are much indebted to many of our colleagues, friends, and students, who offered invaluable feedback, insightful comments, and thoughtful ideas, and copious suggestions for our second edition based on their own research and classroom experiences using the original edition of *Contemporary Asian America*. Among these are Christina Chin, Meera Deo, Lane Ryo Hirabayashi, Russell Leong, Valerie Matsumoto, Don Nakanishi, Kyeyoung Park, and Nancy Yuen at the University of California, Los Angeles; Robert Lee, Evelyn Hu-DeHart, Danielle Antoinette Hidalgo, and Karen Inouye at Brown University; Carl L. Bankston III, Yen Le Espiritu, Demetrius Eudell, Matt Guterl, Christopher Lee, Lynn Mie Itagaki, Elaine Kim, Susan S. Kim, Jennifer Lee, Sunaina Maira, Edward Melillo, Gary Okihiro, Rhacel Salazar Parreñas, Edward Park, John Park, Paul Spickard and his students, Leti Volpp, Ellen Wu, and Judy Wu at other institutions. We are extremely fortunate to work with our authors whose contributions were absolutely first-rate and whose cooperation was incredibly generous and timely. We thank Jason Gonzales, Ly P. Lam, Jesse Lewis, Ravi Shivanna, Tritia Soto, and Yang Sao Xiong who provided tremendous technical support and research assistance.

We would like to acknowledge the institutional support from the Department of Sociology, Department of Asian American Studies, and Asian American Studies Center at UCLA, and the Department of American Civilization and the Center for the Study of Race and Ethnicity in the Americas at Brown University. The Asian American Studies Center, the Social Sciences Division of the College of Letters and Sciences, and the Academic Senate at UCLA provided partial funding for the project. The Center for Advanced Studies in the Behavioral Sciences awarded a fellowship to Min Zhou during the academic year 2005–2006, which freed up much time for her to concentrate on developing this project.

Last—but certainly not least—we thank our wonderful families who continue to inspire us and our endeavors. Min Zhou dedicates this book to her husband Sam Nan Guo and son Philip Jia Guo. Jim Gatewood dedicates this book to his wife, Jules, to his mum, June Gatewood, and to his pugs, Boo and Moses.

Min Zhou and J. V. Gatewood
Los Angeles, October 2006

NOTES

1 Office of the Press Secretary, "Statement by the President on U.S. Reaching 300 Million Population Milestone" (News release, October 17, 2006), http://georgewbush-whitehouse.archives.gov/news/releases/2006/10/20061017–8.html (accessed September 12, 2015).

2 Haya El Nasser, "Little Fanfare Expected to Mark Population Milestone," *USA Today*, October 13, 2006, http://usatoday30.usatoday.com/news/nation/2006–10–12–population-milestone_x.htm (accessed September 12, 2015).

PREFACE TO THE FIRST EDITION

The purpose of this anthology is to provide undergraduate and graduate students and all those interested in the Asian American community with some of the most central readings informing Asian America and Asian American studies today. Of critical importance in selecting the readings is our goal of making the entire project a reflexive undertaking. The readings, while important in and of themselves to the evolution of Asian American studies and the development of the community, have been selected upon the basis of what they can tell our readers about themselves or their own lives and, essentially, about the ways in which our readers' experiences may resonate the larger framework of what we call "Asian American experience."

We feel that it is important at the outset to state the limitations of an anthology such as this one. No one reader can capture the diversity of voices, experiences, and people that constitute different Asian American communities today. In privileging one topic of discussion, we must necessarily exclude another. It would be disingenuous for us to state otherwise. One of the most noticeable absences readily apparent to students and teachers is that of literary works produced by Asian American authors—the novels, short stories, poetry, plays. These literary works have played a fundamental role in defining both the curriculum in Asian American studies and in providing a valuable window through which to evaluate identity formation within the community itself. Our decision not to include literary works as such is not by happenstance. Initially, we agreed to include these works, but found it extremely difficult to devise ways to excerpt pieces without losing sight of their original meaning and context. It is disingenuous to the writers of these literary works to break apart chapters in their books or even short stories in a selection that cannot be fully understood when isolated from its other parts. We feel that most of the excellent literary works that exist in Asian American studies should be read and experienced in their entirety. Another reason underlying our motivations is that this anthology is meant to accompany a college-level introductory course in Asian American studies. It has been our experience from teaching Asian American studies courses that many classes have almost always included a number of monographs and novels by Asian American authors that frame the discussion of certain historical, cultural, and social themes in the community. We thus decided to provide a focus that frames these discussions in a social science context.

Although there are a number of anthologies in the past that have focused on Asian American immigration, community development, and socialization, there are none that really attempt to integrate the intersection of these themes and their effects on the contemporary Asian American community. The basis on which each section of this anthology is devised has come about through our own introspection into those issues that students find meaningful in Asian American studies classes today. The issue of identity is a central concept in these classes, and we have made a conscious effort to include various abstractions of Asian American identity—abstractions that deal with the intersections between generation, class, gender, sexuality, religion, and the cultural reconstruction of identity. The sections are not meant to read as merely chronological, but rather as different themes framing the reflexive bent that we assume. To compromise on spatial limitations, we have also include in each section's suggested reading list a number of excellent works that have emerged in recent years as well as some of the "classic" readings in Asian American studies.

A project of this scope is never a solitary undertaking. We gratefully acknowledge the support and assistance of all those individuals who offered their precious time and invaluable help in shaping this anthology and making it better. First, we would like to thank Tim Bartlett, former editor at NYU Press, who initiated the project and pushed it through with his keen foresight and enthusiasm. Jennifer Hammer, our current editor at NYU Press, has graciously offered her unlimited support for this project as well as her own commitment to its underlying goals, which greatly facilitated our ability to make this project happen. We would also like to acknowledge the four anonymous reviewers who at an early stage read carefully and critiqued the works we originally selected and the manner in which we organized this reader. Their critical comments greatly strengthened the theoretical framework that we ultimately employed for the reader.

This project was partially supported by a research grant from the Asian American Studies Center at University of California, Los Angeles. We are particularly indebted to the Center Director, Don Nakanishi, who has always been committed to supporting faculty and students in teaching and research. We would like to thank our colleagues in both the Department of Sociology and Asian American Studies Center at UCLA for their insightful ideas, helpful comments, constructive critiques, and moral support; particularly we thank Shirley Hune, Yuji Ichioka, Jennifer Lee, Russell Leong, David Lopez, Valerie Matsumoto, Bob Nakamura, Don Nakanishi, Glenn Omatsu, Roger Waldinger, and Henry Yu. At other academic institutions, we specially thank Carlos Chan, Carla Tengan, and Horacio Chiong. We also thank our colleagues at the Japanese American National Museum for their support, specially Karin Higa, Darcie Iki, Sojin Kim, Eiichiro Azuma, Karen Ishizuka, Cameron Trowbridge, Debbie Henderson, Nikki Chang, Grace Murakami. A special thanks goes to Krissy Kim for her friendship and encouragement. We send a special note of appreciation to all the students in Asian American studies, among them Teresa Ejanda, Lakandiwa M. de Leon, Derek Mateo, Randall Park, Steven Wong, and many others, with whom we have worked and who gave us the incentive to compile this anthology. Diana Lee provided tremendous research and editorial assistance for this project.

Finally, we would like to express our deepest gratitude to our families who sacrificed a considerable amount of time with us to enable us to see this project through to completion.

Min Zhou
James V. Gatewood
Los Angeles, April 1999

Introduction

Revisiting Contemporary Asian America

MIN ZHOU, ANTHONY C. OCAMPO, AND J. V. GATEWOOD

As the new millennium unfolds, one cannot help but to notice dramatic changes that have transformed contemporary Asian America. Most significantly, the rapid pace of globalization and September 11 have altered the contours of our national identity while creating new challenges for Asian Americans. What is the current state of Asian America in the twenty-first century? How has it evolved and developed since the 1960s, a turbulent decade in America's history that witnessed the birth of the nation's ethnic consciousness movements? How have Americans of Asian ancestries constructed ethnic and national identities, and how has identity formation changed over time? To what extent has the Asian American community asserted itself socially and politically in American society? How are Asian Americans related to other racial/ethnic groups in the United States and to the people in their ancestral homelands and in other parts of the world? These are but a few of the questions posed by this anthology, an introductory reader for those interested in the urgent issues facing contemporary Asian America. We have selected a number of themes that critically inform the current state of the community. This anthology is meant to be personally meaningful to our readers, and to incorporate ideas that expose Americans to the struggles and triumphs of a racial minority group, to the evolution of Asian American studies, and to the broader social transformations in American society that have historically affected, and continue to affect, people of Asian ancestries and their communities.

Activism, the Movement, and the Development of Asian American Studies

For Asian Americans, these struggles profoundly changed our communities. They spawned numerous grassroots organizations. They created an extensive network of student organizations and Asian American studies classes. They recovered buried cultural traditions as well as produced a new generation of writers, poets, and artists. But most importantly, the struggles deeply affected Asian American consciousness. They redefined racial and ethnic identity, promoted new ways of thinking about communities, and challenged prevailing notions of power and authority.

—Glenn Omatsu (this volume)

The Legacy of Political Activism

The birth of the Asian American movement coincided with the largest student strike in the nation's history. At San Francisco State College, members of the Third World Liberation Front (TWLF), a coalition of African Americans, Latino Americans/Chicanos, Native Americans, and Asian Americans, launched a student strike in November 1968. The organizers made demands on the university for curricular reform, initially aimed at three specific goals. First, student strikers sought to redefine education and to make their curriculum at once more meaningful to their own lives, experiences, and histories and more reflective of the communities in which they lived. Second, they demanded that racial/ethnic minorities play a more active role in the decision-making process and that university administrators institute an admissions policy to give racial/ethnic minorities equal access to advanced education. Third, they attempted to effect larger change in the institutional practices by urging administrators to institutionalize ethnic studies at San Francisco State College. The strike, in which Asian Americans played an integral role, brought about significant institutional changes; in particular, it led to the establishment of the nation's first School of Ethnic Studies at San Francisco State College. More than just a token concession to the students, the School of Ethnic Studies began to implement the students' objectives of curricular reform and equal access to education.

In his seminal article, "The 'Four Prisons' and the Movements of Liberation" (this volume), Glenn Omatsu, a veteran activist of the movement, contends that the San Francisco student strike not only marked the beginning of the Asian American movement but also set the agenda for the articulation of an Asian American "consciousness." Omatsu argues that those involved in the movement were not simply seeking to promote their own legitimacy or representation in mainstream society. Rather, the movement raised questions about subverting ideals and practices that rewarded racial or ethnic minorities for conforming to white mainstream values. The active involvement of Asian Americans extended well beyond college campuses on which many of these issues were being raised; it reached the working-class communities from which many students originated. Omatsu highlights several emerging themes that exerted a profound impact on the Asian American struggles in the 1970s: (1) building a coalition between activists and the community, (2) reclaiming the heritage of resistance, (3) forming a new ideology that manifested in self-determination and the legitimization of oppositional practices as a means of bringing about change to the racist structures inherent to American society, (4) demanding equal rights and minority power, and (5) urging mass mobilization and militant action. For Omatsu, the Asian American movement was a grassroots working-class community struggle for liberation and self-determination.

The political activism of the 1960s unleashed shock waves that have continued to reverberate in the larger Asian American community today. As both Karen Umemoto and Glenn Omatsu recount in their pieces on the movement (this volume), the spirit that initially infused the period carried over into the next two decades, despite a changing political climate that marked the onset of what Omatsu (this volume) deems the winter of civil rights and the rise of neoconservatism. The movement has evolved to incorporate a broader range of diverse viewpoints and voices, helping frame the way in which many students approach Asian American studies today. Not only does the movement provide students with an understanding of the strategies employed by racial and ethnic minorities in their fight against racism and oppression in American society, it also suggests specific ways in which these strategies can be effectively used for minority empowerment.

Institutional Development

Shortly after the founding of the first ethnic studies program at San Francisco State College in 1968, other universities across the United States set to work on developing their own academic programs. According to a survey conducted by Don Nakanishi and Russell Leong in 1978, at least fourteen universities established Asian American Studies programs, including the Berkeley, Los Angeles, Davis, and Santa Barbara campuses of the University of California; the San Francisco, Fresno, San Jose, Sacramento, and Long Beach campuses of the California State University; the University of Southern California; the University of Washington; the University of Colorado; the University of Hawaii; and City College of New York. The programs at UC Berkeley and San Francisco State University had the largest enrollments, with fifteen hundred each, and offered sixty and forty-nine courses, respectively. The programs on other campuses offered four to sixty courses per academic year and enrolled one hundred to six hundred fifty students. All Asian American Studies programs, with the exception of UCLA's, listed teaching as their top priority, with community work and research ranked as second and third priorities. UCLA, in contrast, made research and publications as its primary goal, with teaching ranked second. By 1978, at least three universities, UCLA, San Francisco State University, and the University of Washington, offered graduate courses (Nakanishi and Leong 1978).

Since the movement of the later 1960s, Asian American studies has experienced unparalleled growth as Asian American student enrollment has increased at unprecedented rates at American universities. Today, Asian Americans account for 6 percent of the US population, but Asian American students are disproportionately overrepresented in prestigious public and private universities. In

1995, for example, Asian American students represented more than 10 percent of the student populations at all nine UC campuses and at twelve of the twenty CSU campuses, as well as at Harvard, Yale, MIT, Columbia, and other top-ranked universities. These regional and national enrollment trends have continued to grow with no signs of slowing down since the mid-1990s. The UC system, in particular, has seen its Asian American populations grow rapidly. For example, Asian Americans compose roughly 13 percent of California's population but make up more than one-third of the undergraduates enrolled in fall 2014 at the University of California system-wide, with 34 percent at Los Angeles, 39 percent at Berkeley, Davis, and Riverside, 44 percent at Irvine, and 45 percent at San Diego.[1] The nation's leading universities have also reported a dramatic increase in enrollment of Asian Americans, who made up 24 percent of the undergraduates at MIT, 20 percent at Stanford, 19 percent at Harvard, and 16 percent at Yale.[2] About 26 percent of Asian Americans are US-born, and nearly 50 percent of US-born Asian Americans aged twenty-five or older have at least a bachelor's degree—a rate more than 20 percentage points higher than that for average Americans (Pew Research Center 2012).

In response to these demographic changes, major public universities and a growing number of private universities in which Asian American student enrollments are disproportionately large have established Asian American studies departments or interdepartmental programs. Today, all the University of California and the California State University campuses have established Asian American studies programs, some of which have evolved into Asian American studies departments. Outside California, many universities and colleges have established similar programs, often in response to student protests, even hunger strikes, and pure enrollment numbers (Monaghan 1999). The current directory of the Association for Asian American Studies, complied at Cornell University, shows an incomplete count of thirty-two Asian American studies departments and interdepartmental programs, twenty Asian American studies programs within social sciences or humanities departments, and eighteen other universities and colleges that offer Asian American studies courses. These departments and interdepartmental or interdisciplinary programs offer a wide range of courses on the diversity of Asian American experiences and greatly enrich academic curricula on college campuses.[3]

Despite the current boom, however, institutional development has often met with obstacles, ranging from the loss of faculty and staff positions to the retirement of veteran or founding faculty to budget cuts arbitrarily imposed on relatively young but growing departments. Although continued expansion of programs and departments is not inevitable, and likely to be a matter of ongoing conflict, demographic pressures, the political weight of the Asian American community, and the continuing intellectual development of Asian American studies as a field make the prospects for growth very promising.

Asian American Studies as an Interdisciplinary Field

What is Asian American studies? Is it an academic field with its own unique perspective and with intellectually cohesive themes, or is it a field that brings together people of different disciplines who share common interests and who work on similar topics? According to the Association for Asian American Studies,

> Asian American Studies examines, through multidisciplinary lenses, the experiences of Asians in the United States. It is a field of study, creative and critical, interpretive and analytical, grounded in experience and theory. It is located in the academy and therewith shares some of the assumptions and values of intellectual production and pedagogy, but it is also rooted in the extra-academic community and therewith shares some of the assumptions and values of the prevailing and contested social and cultural relations. Its subject matter is the diverse (but united by "racial" construction, historical experience, political ends) peoples from Asia—from West to East Asia, South to Southeast Asia—who live(d) and work(ed) in the U.S. But its subject matter is also comparative and expansive, inclusive of America's Africans, Europeans, Latinos, and native peoples, and its geographic range is transnational, extending beyond the borders of the U.S.[4]

At the early stage of its development, Asian American studies understood itself as the offspring of the social movement from which it emerged. Thus, in its self-conceptualization, Asian American studies sought to reproduce central aspects of the broader movement for social change in which it started out as an oppositional orientation, preoccupied with refuting the prevailing theoretical paradigm of assimilation and fostering self-determination through a Third World consciousness (Nakanishi and Leong 1978; Omatsu, this volume; Umemoto, this volume). Both curricular development and research in the field focused on history, identity, and community (Tachiki et al. 1971). Meanwhile, Asian American studies explicitly served as an institutionalized training center for future community leaders, trying to connect scholars and students with grassroots working-class communities. Since the students and Asian American faculty of the 1960s and 1970s were mostly Japanese Americans and Chinese Americans, with a smaller number of Filipino Americans, most of the teaching and research focused on these ethnic populations.

Of course, the guiding theoretical principles and self-understanding of the founders, themselves still present and influential in the field, cannot be accepted without question. The founders' views carry the characteristic traces of the baby boom generation of which the founders are a part: namely, the sense of constituting a unique group whose actions mark a rupture with the past. Indeed, in the late 1960s and the 1970s, both the Asian American movement and the academic field were intent on distancing themselves from the traditional academic disciplines and the more established, or "assimilated," components of the Asian American community. For example, the ethnic consciousness movements of the 1960s fundamentally changed how historians and other social scientists interpreted Asian American history. The pre-movement historiography of the wartime incarceration of Japanese Americans tended to interpret this experience as a grave national mistake, but one that had been corrected by the postwar acceptance of Japanese Americans into American society. The movement challenged this established interpretation and influenced Japanese Americans and others to reexamine the internment experience within the context of the ongoing debate over past and present racism in American society. Although redress was successfully obtained, the issue of Japanese American internment continues to be linked with contemporary issues of racial justice.[5]

In retrospect, it is clear that contemporary Asian American studies stands in continuity with earlier attempts by Asian American intellectuals, within and outside the academy, to rethink their own experience and to link it to the broader sweep of American history. The connection is most evident in sociology: Paul Siu, Rose Hum Lee, and Frank Miyamoto, members of an older cohort, and Tamotsu Shibutani, Harry Kitano, James Sakoda, Eugene Uyeki, Netsuko Nishi, John Kitsuse, and many others, members of a younger cohort, have all made important contributions to the study of Asian America, as well as to broader areas in sociology. To the extent that Asian American studies involves activities that derive from an attempt at self-understanding, one also needs to point out the crucial literary, autobiographical, and polemical works of an earlier period: we note the writings of Jade Snow Wong, Monica Sone, Carlos Bulosan, Louis Chu, and John Okada, among others, a corpus that has now become the subject of considerable academic work within Asian American studies. Also noticeable is a small group of Euro-American researchers who work within the mainstream disciplines, but without the assimilatory, condescending assumptions that mar earlier work and who made significant contributions to the study of Asian America *prior* to the advent of the movement, providing notice to the disciplines that this was a topic worthy of their attention. The historians Alexander Saxton, Roger Daniels, and John Modell and the sociologist Stanford Lyman deserve particular mention.

In its recent iteration, Asian American studies is facing a new reality that is at odds with the Asian American community of the 1960s and 1970s. Asian American scholars have keenly observed several significant trends that have transformed Asian America, with attendant effects on Asian American studies within the academy: an unparalleled demographic transformation from relative homogeneity to increased diversity; an overall political shift from progressive goals of making societal changes toward more individualistic orientations of occupational achievements; unprecedented rates of socioeconomic mobility and residential de-segregation of native-born generations; and a greater separation between academia and the community (Fong 1998; Hirabayashi 1995; Kang 1998; Wat 1998). These trends mirror the broader structural changes that have occurred in American society since the late 1970s, which we shall discuss in greater detail shortly, and create both opportunities and challenges for the field.

To a large extent, Asian American studies has been energized by the interdisciplinary dynamism that exists not only in history, literature and literary works, and cultural studies, but also in anthropology, sociology, psychology, education, political science, social welfare, and public policy. The field has traditionally been guided by varying theoretical concerns—Marxism, internal colonialism, racial formation, postmodernism, and postcolonialism, among others—and has widened its purview of topics and subject matters. Interdisciplinary course offerings and research have touched on the daily experiences of the internally diverse ethnic populations: course subjects range from the histories and experiences of specific national origin groups to Asian American literature, film and art, and religion, as well as special topics such as gender studies, gay and lesbian studies, immigration, and health. The field has also expanded into comparative areas of racial and ethnic relations in America, diasporic experiences (including undocumented immigration), transnational communities, and the interconnectedness of Asians and Asian Americans, while maintaining a community focus through extensive internship and leadership development programs. These interdisciplinary and comparative approaches allow Asian American scholars and students to get beyond the simple assumption that, because people look similar, they must also share the same experiences, values, and beliefs. Asian American studies has also injected historical and ethnic sensibility into various academic disciplines and prevented itself from being trapped as an isolated elective subdiscipline.

On the academic front, however, there has been a debate over the relationship between theory and practice. Michael Omi and Dana Takagi voice a central concern over the lack of a sustained and coherent radical theory of social transformation, arguing that this absence may lead to a retreat to "more mainstream, discipline-based paradigmatic orientations." These scholars see the "professionalization" of the field at universities, the demands of tenure and promotion for faculty, and new faculty's lack of exposure to and experience of the movement of the earlier period as the main contributing factors to this trend of retreat. They suggest that the field should be "transdisciplinary" rather than "interdisciplinary" and that it should be revisited, rethought, and redefined according to three main themes—the scope and domain of theory, the definition of core theoretical problems and issues, and the significance of Asian American studies as a political project (Omi and Takagi 1995).

Meanwhile, some scholars and students express concern that Asian American studies is being diverted from its original mission of activism, oppositional ideology, and community-oriented practices (Endo and Wei 1988; Hirabayashi 1995; Kiang 1995; Loo and Mar 1985–1986). As the field gains legitimacy at universities, it is increasingly uprooted from the community. Although students have continued to involve themselves in community affairs, their activities tend to be framed in terms of service provision, since the social infrastructure in many Asian American communities is always almost in need of volunteers, as one might expect. But volunteering is all too often a part-time event, in which students may pass through the community and then ultimately maintain a distance from it. Lane Ryo Hirabayashi (1995) points out that the divergence goes beyond the institutional "reward structure" that prioritizes theoretical contributions over applied research. He alludes to the problems of essentialized notions of race and ethnicity, the presumed unity of the community, and the impacts of poststructural and postmodern critiques aiming at deconstructing academic dominance. He believes that these concerns can be effectively addressed by redefining the community as a multidimensional entity with ongoing internal class, generational, political, gender, and sexual divisions, reconceptualizing Asian American communities as a dynamic social construct, and incorporating new theories and methodologies into community-based research. Kent A. Ono points out that the risk of dissociation from community struggles is of particularly critical concern, because September 11 has fundamentally redefined race in America (Ono 2005). He argues that, in the post-9/11 context, Asian American studies must reconfigure itself to become more conversant about the connections with Arab and Arab American communities, Muslim communities, and other marginalized cultural communities.

Finding a common ground from which to approach issues in Asian American studies is a challenging task. Many scholars have made concerted efforts to develop alternative paradigms and perspectives to deal with issues confronting a new Asian America that has become more dynamic and diverse. For example, Lisa Lowe (this volume) reconceptualizes contemporary Asian America in terms of heterogeneity, hybridity, and multiplicity to capture the material contradictions among Asian Americans. L. Ling-chi Wang (1995) proposes a dual-domination model for understanding Asian American experiences that takes into account the diplomatic relations between the United States and Asian countries and the extraterritorial interaction between Asian American communities and their respective homelands. Sau-Ling C. Wong (1995) uses the term "denationalization" to address transnational concerns that have emerged from the intrinsic relations between Asia and Asian America. Sylvia Yanagisako (1995) advances the idea of contextualizing meanings, social relations, and social action and of liberalizing the confines of social borders that cut across nation, gender, ethnicity, kinship, and social class in Asian American history. Shirley Hune (2000) calls for the rethinking of race. She suggests that theoretical paradigms be shifted to articulate the multiplicity of racial dynamics that has moved the black-white dichotomy and that more attention be paid to the differential power and agency of minority communities in the United States and to the situation of Asian America in connection to disaporic communities around the globe.

Since the 1990s, Asian American studies as an academic field has flourished. While the *Amerasia Journal* made its debut in 1971 as the first major academic journal in Asian American studies, published by the Asian American Studies Center at UCLA, there has been a growing number of publication outlets for multidisciplinary works in the field, including *Journal of Asian American Studies*, the official journal of the Association for Asian American Studies (since 1998); *AAPI Nexus Journal: Policy, Practice, and Community* (since 2003), and *Asian American Journal of Psychology* (since 2009), as well as student-run journals, such as *Harvard Asian American Policy Review* (since 1990) and the *Stanford Journal of Asian American Studies* (online since 2008). Sucheng Chan's edited volume, *Remapping Asian American History* (2003), offers new theoretical perspectives and analytical frameworks, such as transnationalism, the politics of international migrations, and interracial/interethnic relations, and points to new directions in Asian American historiography. Other more recent works include *Asian American Studies Now: A Critical Reader*, edited by Jean Wu and Thomas Chen (2010), *The Color of Success: Asian Americans and the Origins of the Model Minority* by Ellen Wu (2013), *The Good Immigrants: How the Yellow Peril Became the Model Minority* by Madeline Hsu (2015).

While the ongoing discussion of goals and methodologies is at once refreshing and evidence of the field's continuing vitality, it also testifies to the degree to which intellectual and organizational tensions are built into the field. On the one hand, the very language of the debate, often filled with jargon and trendy concepts, stands in conflict with the self-professed orientation toward the community and its needs. On the other hand, there is a certain nostalgia among veteran activists, now mainly tenured professors, for the spirit of the 1960s and, to some extent, that yearning for the past ironically threatens to produce a divide between US-born (and/or US-raised) scholars and some of their Asian-born counterparts, especially those whose education in the United States was more likely to begin at the college and graduate level, and who may not share the same connections to a history that they never experienced.[6] Moreover, the ideological presuppositions of the scholars oriented toward the movement has the potential to create distance between them and the growing number of Asian American (often Asian-born) scholars who work on Asian American topics, but from the standpoint of the more traditional disciplines of history, sociology, demography, economics, political science, and so on. Of course, work in the traditional disciplines is by no means value-free, but the ideological presuppositions do not preclude the potential for expanding our understanding of the Asian American experience. Finally, we note the irony in the unspoken consensus about which groups are eligible for consideration as "Asian American," namely, everyone with origins east of Afghanistan. As Henry Yu has pointed out, the very definition of Chinese and Japanese as an "Asian American community" is itself the product of earlier externally imposed definitions of America's "Oriental Problem" (Yu 1998). The field initially organized itself around the study of peoples of East Asian descent, leaving others who were no less eligible on intellectual grounds, nor, for that matter, any less vulnerable to discrimination or stigmatization than the "official" Asian American categories, to different schools of "Oriental" studies.[7]

In our view, Asian American studies is best construed in the broadest possible terms, understood as that body of scholarship devoted to the study of Asian American populations, conducted from any number of standpoints, from within the frameworks most commonly found among scholars affiliated with Asian American studies as well as from a standpoint more closely connected to the traditional disciplines. Just as we reject the conventional disciplinary boundaries, we also opt for an expanded view of the field's geographical scope, in particular, emphasizing a transnational framework that enables us to "better understand the ways that flows of people, money, labor, obligations, and goods between nations and continents have shaped the Asian American experience" (Yanagisako 1995, 292; see also Lowe, this volume).

The first edition of *Contemporary Asian America* (2000) was the first anthology to integrate a broad range of multidisciplinary research in assessing the effects of immigration, community development, socialization, and politics on Asian American communities. It aimed to expose readers to contemporary developments in the field of Asian American studies and to highlight the changes that the field has undergone since its inception in the 1960s. The many issues—the Asian American movement, historical interpretations of the Asian American experience, immigration, family and community issues, religion, gender, sexuality, the construction of identity among Asian Americans, representation and the future direction of Asian American studies—that it covered are clearly of contemporary significance. It enjoyed great success precisely because of the range and depth of its coverage. In the second edition, we reaffirmed our commitment to providing historical readings on the birth and development of Asian American studies, Asian American community formation, new immigrant and refugee populations, queer Asian America, multiethnic Asian Americans, interracial and interethnic politics, and citizenship and identity, among many important topics. In this third edition, we have maintained the organizational structure of the anthology but revamped its contents by adding more recent works by young scholars. While it is impossible to cover every new and significant development of the entire field, we hope that the third edition continues to expose our readers to multiple interpretations of the multifaceted Asian American experience(s) and to serve as a valuable reference guide to illuminating some of the most groundbreaking scholarship in the history and contemporary development of the field.

The Contents of This Anthology

The chapters in the third edition vary in content and information. Some are meant to raise larger issues pertinent to Asian American studies and to provoke critical thinking, while others provide substantial data to enlighten students about the makeup of the community and its evolution over time. We hope that these two kinds of sources provide students with the background to raise their own questions, to respond to the readings, and to generally make up their own minds about the contemporary issues facing Asian America today. At the end of each section, we provide a list of reading response questions for use in conjunction with course material to enable students to seek out the most important information from each article and evoke other questions for discussion.

Claiming Visibility: The Asian American Movement

Part I presents two classic works on the genesis of Asian American studies and the underlying ideologies that are instrumental for political mobilization. Umemoto's piece surveys the history of the 1968 San Francisco State strike and offers an analysis of its importance to the development of Asian American movement. She shows the multifarious dimensions to which Asian Americans were part of the 1960s struggles. She argues that the student strike did not occur in a political vacuum, but rather was centrally informed by other ethnic consciousness movements and international Third World movements for liberation and self-determination. She asserts that the Asian American movement, specifically the outcome of the San Francisco State strike for Asian American students, left a legacy for the Asian American community and continued to influence Asian American student life on college campuses.

Framing his discussion in a much larger historical context, Omatsu underscores that the Asian American movement was a phenomenon centrally informed by the militant struggles against war, racism, and the multiple oppressions with which many Americans only began to grasp during the 1960s. He emphasizes that the Asian American movement was composed of diverse segments of the community and had one clear goal: liberation from oppression. He acknowledges the decline of the movement's vitality during the 1970s and 1980s with the rise of neoconservatism, but nonetheless argues that the future of Asian American studies hinges upon the community's ability to "forge a new moral vision, reclaiming the militancy and moral urgency of past generations and reaffirming the commitment to participatory democracy, community building, and collective styles of leadership."

Traversing Borders: Contemporary Asian Immigration to the United States

Part II examines the effects of contemporary Asian immigration on Asian American demographics and communities. Zhou, Ocampo, and Gatewood provide readers with an overview of the profound changes that have taken place in the past half century and a survey of the terrain that makes up contemporary Asian America. They locate their analysis as a mapping of ethnic diversity to raise issues on how the steady influx of Asian immigrants impact the Asian American community at present and in the future and what challenges the community currently faces as it is claiming America. They predict that as the community grows in number and heterogeneity, so too will its representation in the broader socioeconomic, cultural, and political milieu that is typified as "mainstream America."

Bankston and Hidalgo highlight unique aspects of international migration from Southeast Asia. By illustrating the unusual forces that bring refugees to the United States from Southeast Asia, the authors deftly suggest the differences—both subtle and overt—between refugees and their immigrant counterparts. Significant intragroup and intergroup differences exist among refugees from Vietnam, Laos, and Cambodia and nonrefugees from the Philippines and Thailand in the varied contexts of exit and reception. Bankston and Hidalgo argue that the differential starting points, especially the internal socioeconomic diversity of particular waves and "vintages" within the same nationalities over time, augur differential modes of incorporation and assimilation outcomes that cannot be extrapolated simply from the experience of earlier immigrant groups of the same nationality, let alone from immigrants as an undifferentiated whole.

Ties That Bind: The Immigrant Family and the Ethnic Community

Part III focuses on the family and the ethnic community. The chapter by Parreñas deals with transnational Filipino households, broadly defined as "famil[ies] whose core members are located in at least two or more nation-states." Drawing upon interviews with Filipina domestic workers in Los Angeles and Rome, Parreñas documents the formation and reproduction of transnational households among Filipino labor immigrants as one of many mechanisms available to immigrants as they cope with the exigencies of their new lives. She argues that transnational households have long existed among Filipino migrant workers who have historically faced legal and economic barriers to full incorporation into the host society. The recuperation of this immigrant tradition by contemporary Filipino immigrants is the result of intersecting structural and cultural forces.

Xiong's chapter focuses on the social and community relationships of Hmong immigrants and their descendants, a relatively small population on the opposite end of the socioeconomic spectrum. Hmong refugee communities face tremendous challenges adapting to life in the United States due to their lack of formal education, high rates of poverty, and earlier experiences of war prior to migration, all of which have lasting effects on their US-born children. Xiong highlights how their dispersed resettlement in this country has prompted transformations in the family structure of Hmong Americans, which in turn present unique obstacles to second-generation upward mobility—a notable contrast to the widespread stereotype that Asian Americans are all model minorities.

The chapter by Li, Skop, and Yu examines new patterns of community formation. Since the late 1960s, the combination of global economic restructuring, changing geopolitical contexts, and shifting American immigration policies has set in motion significant flows of new and diverse immigrant inflows from Asia to the United States. While family-sponsored immigrants continue to grow, record numbers of highly skilled, professional immigrants and wealthy investors have also joined the flow as result of the economic boom in China and other nations in Asia. As a result, patterns of immigrant settlement have also changed. The authors show that traditional inner-city enclaves still exist to receive newcomers but can no longer meet the social and economic needs of these newcomers. Affluent middle-class Asian immigrants tend to bypass inner-city ethnic enclaves to settle directly in suburbs that offer decent housing, high-performing schools, superior living conditions, and public amenities. As more and more immigrants settle away from urban enclaves, ethnoburbs have come into existence. The transformation of American suburbs into multiracial, multiethnic, multilingual, multicultural, and multinational communities challenges the widely accepted characterization of the suburbs as the citadel of the white middle class and the traditional notion of residential assimilation.

Struggling to Get Ahead: Economy and Work

Part IV delves into the question of how immigrants adapt to life in their new land. The chapter by Dhingra discusses the case of Indian Americans, an immigrant group whose educational attainment and income levels surpass those of nearly every other immigrant group in the country. Based on his extensive research of Indian American workers in various professional and entrepreneurial sectors, Dhingra shows that economic success does not always translate to full social incorporation into the American mainstream. As his research illustrates, Indian Americans have had to strategically navigate their different forms of cultural and ethnic capital to successfully achieve upward mobility in America.

Espiritu's chapter focuses on Filipina health care professionals, a much sought-after group among US immigrants. In Espiritu's view, US colonial training of nurses in the Philippines highlights the complex intersections of gender ideologies with those of race and class in shaping US colonial agendas and practices. The overrepresentation of health professionals among contemporary Filipino immigrants is not solely the result of contemporary global restructuring, the "liberalization" of US immigration rules, or individual economic desires, but rather is the product of historical outcomes of early twentieth-century US colonial rule in the Philippines. Espiritu also provides a detailed analysis of how migration processes, labor recruitment practices, and employment conditions have reconfigured gender and family relations. She shows that professional women, like most other working women, have to juggle full-time work outside the home with the responsibilities of child care and housework. In the context of migration, Filipina nurses often work in higher paid jobs, but lead lower status lives; their labor market advantage does not automatically or uniformly lead to more egalitarian relations in the family.

Eckstein and Nguyen address the working lives of Vietnamese immigrants working in American nail salons, which have emerged as a strong ethnic niche in and beyond the United States. As a result of their limited English proficiency and educational levels, Vietnamese manicurists have developed a foothold in the American beauty industry. Over the past few decades, Vietnamese immigrants, primarily women, have organically created a site in which they are able to develop strong professional networks and acquire important forms of career capital. Eckstein and Nguyen indicate that as the Vietnamese began to dominate the nail industry, they also began to diversify their services and transnationalize their clientele base all the way to Europe.

Sexuality in Asian America

Part V looks into an important subject area that has recently begun to receive its due attention in Asian American studies—the experiences of gay and lesbian Asian Americans. Nadal and Corpus, both counseling psychologists, examine how lesbian and gay Filipino Americans negotiate their sexual identity vis-à-vis the cultural norms of their ethnic community. Drawing on their qualitative research of lesbian and gay Filipinos throughout the country, their chapter addresses the unique factors that shape their social and emotional lives, including religion, family pressure, and race. They also discuss implications for how these findings can be incorporated into counseling programs geared toward lesbian, gay, bisexual, and transgender (LGBT) Asian Americans, their families, and their communities.

Han's chapter centers on the marginalized perspectives of gay Asian American men, who often encounter fetishization and racism within the mainstream, predominantly white gay spaces. Han dispels the idea that gay people, as an oppressed minority, are incapable of subordinating others. Instead, he draws on his analysis of LGBT publications to highlight how cultural representations of queer Asian Americans (and people of color) remain on the sidelines. Han shows how gay Asian American men face both overt and subtle forms of racism within a community that ironically portrays itself as accepting.

Race and Asian American Identity

Part VI examines issues of race and identity. The Asian American movement, inspired by the civil rights movement, has challenged the American racial stratification system and shaken its foundation. However, post-1965 Asian immigration has greatly complicated race relations. Janine Young Kim's chapter focuses on the (uneasy) relationship between the black/white paradigm and the Asian American civil rights agenda. Kim argues that the current race discourse oversimplifies the black/white paradigm and that the seemingly unproblematic discussion of the paradigm fails to articulate the full cost of its abandonment. She sees the black/white paradigm as retaining contemporary significance despite demographic changes in American society and as having direct relevance for the Asian American civil rights as well as for a deeper understanding of ever-changing and racially stratified society today.

Ocampo's chapter examines a new frontier in Asian American racialization. His study draws from surveys and interviews with second-generation Filipino Americans living in Southern California, a region where Latinos and Asian Americans now constitute a collective majority. Departing from the traditional black-white racial paradigm, his findings demonstrate that Filipinos most frequently negotiate their panethnic identity vis-à-vis Latinos and Asians. Specifically, he argues that the residual effects of Spanish and American colonialism have a deep influence on the way Filipinos develop (or do not develop) a sense of peoplehood with Latinos and other Asians. His chapter holds important implications for the direction of racial formation process as the United States becomes increasingly multiethnic.

Zhou's chapter takes another unique approach to Asian American racialization by asking the provocative question of whether Asian Americans are "becoming white." Asian Americans have been labeled a "model minority" for their high rates of socioeconomic achievement, and they appear on track to being accepted as "white." Zhou contends that the model minority stereotype serves to thwart other racial minorities' demands for social justice by pitting minority groups against one another while also setting Asian Americans apart from whites. She argues that, given the "foreigner" image Americans still have of Asians, whitening is both premature and misleading and can be a heavy burden upon Asian Americans themselves. Zhou shows that even though Asian Americans as a group have achieved parity with whites as measured by observable group-level socioeconomic characteristics such as education, occupation, and income, they are by no means fully viewed as "American," which is oftentimes synonymous to "white." In the end, whitening is a lived cultural phenomenon that has to do with the ideological dynamics of white America, rather than with the actual situation of Asian Americans. Speaking perfect English, effortlessly practicing mainstream cultural values, and even intermarrying members of the dominant group may help reduce this "otherness" at the individual level, but have little effect on the group as a whole. Like the model minority image that is imposed upon them, new stereotypes may unwhiten Asian Americans anytime and anywhere, no matter how "successful" and "assimilated" they have become.

Intermarriages and Multiracial Ethnicity

Part VII delves into the phenomenon of intermarriages and multiracial/ethnic identities. Lee and Bean's chapter adds another level of complexity into the current American population dynamics, calling attention to the increasing number of people who claim a multiracial background. Based on the analysis of the 2000 census data, the authors find that more than one out of every four Asian Americans intermarry and that one in eight Asian Americans is racially mixed, which is more than five times the national average in the United States. Today's high rates of Asian intermarriage would boost a substantial growth in the Asian multiracial population, which is projected to be at least one in three by 2050. Lee and Bean also discuss the implications for multiracial identification for America's changing color lines that revolve around a black-nonblack divide in the contexts of diversity and immigration.

Park Nelson's chapter approaches the question of ethnicity through the perspectives of transnational Korean adoptees. Korean adoption by American families is a phenomenon that has been occurring for the past fifty years, but it is only within the past decade that it has received attention within Asian American studies. Park Nelson addresses the challenges that Korean adoptees face in dealing with their racial experiences in the United States, given that many are raised by white parents, whose experience with race is obviously distinct. Moreover, she also addresses the strategies that Korean adoptees have used to explore their ethnic heritage, such as forming organizations specifically aimed at creating community among adoptees and their families and facilitating stronger connections between them and their country of birth.

Confronting Adversity: Racism, Stereotyping, and Exclusion

Part VIII touches on several aspects of adversity confronting Asian Americans—racism, stereotyping, and exclusion. Lisa Park's original chapter speaks to difficulties encountered by two sisters as they struggle to find their own place in American life. Confronting her sister's suicide in a meaningful way forces the narrator to consider the emotional toll that societal double standards wield on Asian Americans, especially those growing up in immigrant families. Park points out that racism, the perpetual drive to assimilate racial minorities to a white norm, the pressures placed upon the family and individual to live up to the model minority image, the family's frustration with downward mobility, and the community's reluctance to accept the mental health problem all play a part in her sister's suicide. She exposes the detrimental effects of the "model minority" stereotype—"Do you see what a lie it is and how it is used to reinforce the American Dream and punish those of us who don't 'succeed,' or who succeed 'too much'?" She suggests that the "model minority" image not only places unrealistic and harmful expectations on Asian Americans who do not characterize the affluence and success, but also extends to other racial minorities, specifically African Americans and Latino Americans, who are asked why they cannot do the same. At the twenty-fifth anniversary of her sister's suicide, Park writes another letter reflecting on her experiences as life moves on. She laments that there is "no such thing as progress" and that there is "no such thing as closure." Park's letters to her sister remind the readers that complacency inhibits process and that the fight against racism and social injustice demands constant vigilance, critical thinking, proactive attitude, and transformative action among Asian Americans.

Sunaina Maira lends her insights into the challenges faced by South Asian Americans in the wake of September 11. Drawing upon the experiences of young people in Boston, she assesses how racial stereotyping and the War on Terror have complicated identities and fostered an antagonism among men and women who see their opportunities constrained as a result of blatant stereotyping. The effect, Maira explains, is strengthened interethnic solidarity among Asians, but reduced desire for assimilation into mainstream American society.

Sue and his colleagues look at a form of racism that has become increasingly prevalent in the post–civil rights era—racial microaggressions. Racial microaggressions refer to the subtle messages that Asian Americans receive, both intentional and unintentional, that reinforce their sense of racial marginalization. Sue and his colleagues note that even supposed compliments such as "You speak such good English" or "You speak without accents" serve to remind Asian Americans of their forever foreigner status in this country. In this chapter, the authors use qualitative interview data to propose new metrics and surveys that can better measure these more covert forms of racial oppression that Asian Americans face in their everyday lives.

Behind the Model Minority

Part IX examines what lies behind the "model minority" stereotype. The publication of William Petersen's article on the virtues of Japanese American in *New York Times Magazine* in January 1966 marked a significant departure from the ways in which Asian immigrants and their succeeding generations had been traditionally depicted in popular culture. In December of the same year, another article similar in tone extolled Chinese Americans for their persistence and success. However, the celebration of the model minority buttresses the myth that the United States is devoid of racism and accords equal opportunity to all, and that those who lag behind do so because of their own poor choices and inferior culture (see Zhou, this volume).

The media circus that surrounded Jeremy Lin, the first major Asian American player in National Basketball Association (NBA), provided overwhelming evidence about the way American society was unable to comprehend that an Asian American man could become a star athlete. Leung chronicles how latent racist views of Asian American men came to the surface during the period of "Linsanity." Comments from sportscasters, news outlets, and coaches clearly demonstrated that American society (minus other Asians) was unable to "see past his Asian features" and acknowledge Lin's athletic prowess, despite his tremendous accomplishments as a high school and college basketball player. Ultimately, the attention that Lin received illustrated the incongruence of Asian bodies with an all-American pastime.

Lisa Sun-Hee Park's chapter demonstrates further that birthright does not necessarily bring about a complete sense of belonging into American society. Her interviews with second-generation Chinese and Korean Americans reveal a deep sense of need for Asian immigrants and their children to justify their presence in the United States. Park notes that these second-generation Americans understand their parents' migration story through an Orientalist lens that positions both them and their parents as foreigners in their adopted land. Against her own intuition, her analysis reveals that the migration stories that the second-generation Chinese and Koreans told were remarkably similar despite their age, gender, class background, and neighborhood. Such a trend reveals the tremendous impact of the racial stereotyping that Asian Americans confront.

Poon and Sihite's chapter illustrates the angst that some Americans exhibit when Asian Americans become *too* integrated into US institutions, particularly when it comes to elite colleges and universities. The authors provide an overview of the complicated relationship that Asian Americans have had with American higher education—being excluded by quotas, being targeted as taking the spots of "more deserving" applicants, and being portrayed as vigorous opponents to affirmative action policies. Within these conversations about Asian Americans and higher education, Poon and Sihite insert a necessary discussion of government divestment from institutions of higher learning, which serves to disenfranchise *all* students in the process, Asian Americans included.

Multiplicity and Interracial Politics

Part X discusses the complexity of citizenship and interracial politics. Lowe's chapter is a challenging piece to read in its entirety, since it may be open to multiple interpretations. Her purpose is twofold, first to disrupt the common tropes of generational conflict and filial relationships that permeate the Asian

American experience, and second to reconceptualize Asian American identity as an entity in a continual state of flux. The main point underlying her work is that Asian American culture is neither immutable nor vertically transmitted from one generation to the next. Asian American culture is as much a production of identities as a reception of traditions. As Lowe contends, "[t]he boundaries and definitions of Asian American culture are continually shifting and being contested from pressures both 'inside' and 'outside' the Asian-origin community." These shifting constructions of identity constitute the heterogeneity, hybridity, and multiplicity of contemporary Asian American community.

Nadia Kim's chapter adds a critique to the long-standing tendency of sociologists to equate socioeconomic integration with whitening. While Kim acknowledges that Asian Americans' racial experiences remain distinct from those of African Americans, she also notes that Asian Americans continually have their legal and social citizenship called into question more so than the latter. Kim argues that the deep historical and contemporary influence of US state relations with Asian nations functions as a necessary backdrop for developing a transnational framework for Asian Americans' racial subordination along the lines of citizenship.

Ng, Pak, and Hernandez look at the intersection of the perpetual foreigner and model minority stereotypes, specifically within the sphere of education. They point out the inherent contradictions in the Asian American educational experiences. On the one hand, Asian Americans have been applauded for their representation in institutions of higher learning; however, the threat of their presence has incited resentment among whites. Ng and her colleagues advocate for the disaggregation of Asian American students by nativity and ethnicity to better elucidate the heterogeneity of Asian American educational outcomes. The way Asian Americans are "framed," they argue, will have tremendous influence on their future in US higher educational institutions.

The chapter by Ramakrishnan and his colleagues draws from the 2008 National Asian American Survey about Asian American political behaviors, data they collected during the presidential primary and national elections. Their analyses show that race played a significant role in Asian Americans' support for Hillary Clinton over Barack Obama during the 2008 primaries. However, during the national election between Obama and Republican hopeful John McCain, race-based considerations became less important relative to party affiliation and issue preferences. Their findings have implications for how political candidates and movements must be framed in order to galvanize support from Asian American communities.

***

The chapters in this anthology taken as a whole illustrate the crucial prospects, possibilities, and problems currently faced by Asian Americans and their communities and by the field of Asian American studies. It is our hope that readers approach these issues in a critical and reflexive manner, one that draws heavily from their own experiences, histories, and interpretations. This anthology is by no means a definitive end to the complexity and range of issues confronting contemporary Asian America. In fact, it is only beginning to raise questions that may not necessarily have clear or definitive answers. For some people, the resolution may be simple. For many others, however, the solution may require compromise. We are excited by the prospects for the future of Asian American studies, but cast a tone of caution—one that is cognizant of how far the field has come from those early days at San Francisco State College. Our greatest successes—legitimacy in the academy, recognition by mainstream departments at universities across the United States, and publication of works by major university presses—seem to have distanced us further from the original goals of the Asian American movement. Nonetheless, we are moving forward in the new millennium. There are no clear answers, only prospects and possibilities.

NOTES

1 http://legacy-its.ucop.edu/uwnews/stat/ (accessed May 23, 2015).
2 http://www.princetonreview.com (accessed January 28, 2015).
3 http://www.aaastudies.org/list/index.html (accessed May 23, 2015).
4 http://www.aaastudies.org/aas/index.html (accessed May 23, 2015).
5 The author gained insight from Yuji Ichioka's comments. See also Yamamoto (1999) for detail.
6 See the special issue (vols. 1 and 2, 1995) of *Amerasia Journal* and part 2 of Hirabayashi (1995) for detail.
7 Indeed, all persons born in Asia, including those originating from that area arbitrarily (and Euro-centrically) designated as the Middle East, were excluded from citizenship until the 1952 Immigration Act. For details, see Haney-Lopez (1996).

REFERENCES

Chan, Sucheng, ed. 2003. *Remapping Asian American History.* Walnut Creek, CA: AltaMira Press.
Endo, Russell, and William Wei. 1988. "On the Development of Asian American Studies Programs." Pp. 5–15 in Gary Y. Okihiro, Shirley Hune, Arthur A. Hansen, and John M. Liu, eds., *Reflection on Shattered Windows: Promises and Prospects for Asian American Studies.* Pullman: Washington State University Press.
Fong, Timothy P. 1998. "Reflections on Teaching about Asian American Communities." Pp. 143–159 in Lane Ryo Harabayashi, ed., *Teaching Asian America: Diversity and the Problem of the Community.* Lanham, MD: Rowman & Littlefield.
Gupta, A., and J. Ferguson. 1992. "Beyond 'Culture': Space, Identity, and the Politics of Difference." *Cultural Anthropology* 7 (1): 6–23.
Haney-Lopez, Ian F. 1996. *White by Law: The Legal Construction of Race.* New York: New York University Press.
Hirabayashi, Lane Ryo. 1995. "Back to the Future: Re-framing Community-Based Research." *Amerasia Journal* 21: 103–118.

Hsu, Madeline Y. 2015. *The Good Immigrants: How the Yellow Peril Became the Model Minority.* Princeton: Princeton University Press.

Hune, Shirley. 2000. "Doing Gender with a Feminist Gaze: Toward a Historical Reconstruction of Asian America." Pp. 413–430 in Min Zhou and J. V. Gatewood, eds., *Contemporary Asian America: A Multidisciplinary Reader*, 1st ed. New York: New York University Press.

Kang, Laura Hyun Yi. 1998. "A Contending Pedagogy: Asian American Studies as Extracurricular Praxis." Pp. 123–141 in Lane Ryo Harabayashi, ed., *Teaching Asian America: Diversity and the Problem of the Community*. Lanham, MD: Rowman & Littlefield.

Kiang, Peter Nien-chu. 1995. "The New Waves: Developing Asian American Studies on the East Coast." Pp. 305–314 in Gary Y. Okihiro, Marilyn Alquizola, Dorothy Fujita Rony, and K. Scott Wong, eds., *Privileging Positions: The Sites of Asian American Studies.* Pullman: Washington State University Press.

Loo, Chalsa, and Don Mar. 1985–1986. "Research and Asian Americans: Social Change or Empty Prize?" *Amerasia Journal* 12 (2): 85–93.

Monaghan, Peter. 1999. "A New Momentum in Asian-American Studies: Many Colleges Create New Programs; Many Programs Broaden Their Courses and Research." *Chronicle of Higher Education*, March 29.

Nakanishi, Don T., and Russell Leong. 1978. "Toward the Second Decade: A National Survey of Asian American Studies Programs in 1978." *Amerasia Journal* 5 (1): 1–19.

Omi, Michael, and Dana Takagi. 1995. "Thinking Theory in Asian American Studies." *Amerasia Journal* 21 (1–2): xi–xv.

Ono, Kent A. 2005. "Asian American Studies after 9/11." Pp. 439–451 in Cameron McCarthy C. Richlow, Greg Dimitriadis, and Nadine Dolby, eds., *Race, Identity, and Representation in Education*, 2nd ed. New York: Routledge.

Pew Research Center. 2012. *The Rise of Asian Americans.* Washington, DC: Pew Research Center.

Tachiki, Amy, Eddie Wong, and Franklin Odo, with Buck Wong, eds. 1971. *Roots: An Asian American Studies Reader.* Los Angeles: UCLA Asian American Studies Center.

Wang, L. Ling-chi. 1995. "The Structure of Dual Domination: Toward a Paradigm for the Study of the Chinese Diaspora in the United States." *Amerasia Journal* 12 (1–2): 149–169.

Wat, Eric C. 1998. "Beyond the Missionary Position: Student Activism from the Bottom Up." Pp. 161–174 in Lane Ryo Harabayashi, ed., *Teaching Asian America: Diversity and the Problem of the Community*. Lanham, MD: Rowman & Littlefield.

Wong, Sau-Ling C. 1995. "Denationalization Reconsidered: Asian American Cultural Criticism at a Theoretical Crossroads." *Amerasia Journal* 21 (1–2): 1–27.

Wu, Ellen D. 2013. *The Color of Success: Asian Americans and the Origins of the Model Minority.* Princeton: Princeton University Press.

Wu, Jean Yu-Wen Shen, and Thomas Chen, eds. 2010. *Asian American Studies Now: A Critical Reader.* New Brunswick, NJ: Rutgers University Press.

Yamamoto, Eric. 1999. *Interracial Justice: Conflict and Reconciliation in Post–Civil Rights America.* New York: New York University Press.

Yanagisako, Sylvia. 1995. "Transforming Orientalism: Gender, Nationality, and Class in Asian American Studies." Pp. 275–298 in Sylvia Yanagisako and Carol Delaney, eds., *Naturalizing Power: Essays in Feminist Cultural Analysis.* New York: Routledge.

Yu, Henry. 1998. "The 'Oriental Problem' in America, 1920–1960: Linking the Identities of Chinese American and Japanese American Intellectuals." Pp. 191–214 in K. Scott Wong and Sucheng Chan, eds., *Claiming America: Constructing Chinese American Identities during the Exclusion Era.* Philadelphia: Temple University Press.

PART I

Claiming Visibility

The Asian American Movement

1

"On Strike!"

San Francisco State College Strike, 1968–1969: The Role of Asian American Students

KAREN UMEMOTO

The sixth of November, nineteen hundred and sixty-eight. Few thought this would mark the first day of the longest student strike in American history. Student leaders of the San Francisco State College Third World Liberation Front marched with their demands for an education more relevant and accessible to their communities. Their tenacity engaged the university, the police, and politicians in a five-month battle giving birth to the first School of Ethnic Studies in the nation. Batons were swung and blood was shed in the heat of conflict. But this violence was only symptomatic of the challenge made by activists to fundamental tenets of dominant culture as manifested in the university. African American, Asian American, Chicano, Latino, and Native American students called for ethnic studies and open admissions under the slogan of self-determination. They fought for the right to determine their own futures. They believed that they could shape the course of history and define a "new consciousness." For Asian American students in particular, this also marked a "shedding of silence" and an affirmation of identity.

The strike took place against the backdrop of nationwide Third World movements that had a profound impact on the culture and ideology of America. Never before had a convergence of struggles—civil rights, antiwar, women, student, and oppressed nationality—so sharply redefined the social norms of our society. Originating from the call for basic rights, protestors moved on to demand power and self-determination. When the state resisted, activists held to their convictions "by any means necessary." Though these movements did not produce major changes in the economic or political structure, they strongly affected popular ideology and social relations. They also resulted in the formation of mass organizations and produced a cadre of activists who would continue to pursue their ideals.

The San Francisco State strike was a microcosm of this struggle over cultural hegemony. The focus of the strike was a redefinition of education, which in turn was linked to a larger redefinition of American society. Activists believed that education should be "relevant" and serve the needs of their communities, not the corporations. The redefinition of education evolved from the early 1960s when students initiated programs to broaden the college curriculum and challenge admission standards. They supported the hiring and retention of minority faculty. They demanded power in the institution. When they were met with resistance, activists organized a campus-wide movement with community support for their demands. They built organizations, planned strategies and tactics, and published educational literature. Their activities were rooted in and also shaped more egalitarian relationships based on mutual respect. While this doctrine was not always fully understood nor always put into practice, it was the beginning of a new set of values and beliefs, a "New World Consciousness."

The emergence of this alternative vision is important to study today for several reasons. First, by understanding the beginnings of this vision, today's generation of students can revive certain "counterhegemonic" concepts that have been usurped and redefined by those in power. For example, campus administrators have revamped the concept of "self-determination" to the more benign ones of "diversity" and "cultural pluralism." Thus, the right of a group to decision-making power over institutions affecting their lives has been gutted to the level of "student input" by campus administrators.

Second, studying the strike can deepen our understanding of the process through which ideological currents develop among oppressed groups. Organizers are constantly trying to "raise political consciousness" among the people. But in what ways do the nature of the conflict, methods of organizing, strategy and tactics, propaganda and agitation, and historical factors influence mass consciousness within these movements?

This study analyzes the growth of political consciousness among Asian American students during the San Francisco State strike. I investigate the development of the strike in four stages from 1964 to 1969, defined according to dominant concepts within the movement: (1) 1964–1966—end of the civil rights era marked by the ideals of "racial harmony" and "participatory democracy"; (2) 1966–1967—implementation of programs under the banner of "serve the people" and "self-determination"; (3) fall 1968/winter 1969—struggle "by any means necessary"; and (4) spring/summer 1969—repression of protest and continued "commitment to the community." These concepts signify trends in ideological development and provide a means of understanding the strike as a seed of a revolutionary transformation in America.

1964–1966: "Racial Harmony" and "Participatory Democracy" and the Civil Rights Era

The civil rights era profoundly impacted the racial ideology of the nation, particularly Third World youth. The dreams of Martin Luther King, Jr. and unsung heroes inspired actions for equality, dignity, and self-respect. The African American movement clearly revealed the deep-rooted, institutionalized nature of racial oppression. Although protests resulted in reforms limited to the legal arena, their impact was felt in all other sectors of society.

Many Asian American students who were later to become active in the strike were moved by the protests. One Pilipino activist, R. Q., volunteered for a federal program on the East Coast:

> When I was in VISTA and worked in a black neighborhood. . . . They had riots in New Haven. . . . I came back to State College in '67, and the black students were at the forefront in wanting programs. . . . I think the black students and the Black Movement of the sixties made a major impact. They laid the groundwork, which made it a lot easier for us.[1]

The civil rights movement reshaped popular thinking about one's role in society. One student, B. I., described the impact on him:

> It had a very heavy impact because I found that to have anyone listen to you, you had to be forceful, expressing yourself, not being quiet. If you know you are in the right, you have every right to speak up and organize your people to a just cause. So that brought home to me the necessity of organized action, and to verbalize your feelings about what is going on.[2]

The protests forced President Kennedy to publicly support civil rights. His entrance into the historic March on Washington in 1963 lent federal legitimacy to the idea of racial harmony through integration. The enacting of legislation provided legal sanction for racial equality. Kennedy's slogan of a "New Frontier" also encouraged youth to participate in American democracy and transform society. This idealism contributed to formations of Students for a Democratic Society and Third World student organizations nationwide.[3] Faith in democracy led to initial acceptance of nonviolent protest and to the reform-oriented goals within mass movements.

This idealism manifested itself in experimentation in all aspects of life. What was called "counterculture" was indeed a reshaping of traditional goals, values, and behavior. One activist, I. C., explained this shift:

> There was all this emphasis on doing things for other people, such as the Peace Corps. All those ideas were instilled in us . . . "doing something, giving back to society." You couldn't just live for yourself. And I think that influenced my participation in the strike more than anything.[4]

Prior to 1963, student activism at San Francisco State centered around these themes. Students joined a 1960 walk to San Quentin prison against capital punishment, protested at the 1960 House Un-American Activities Committee

(HUAC) hearings, established an outdoor free speech area, joined the 1962 Freedom Rides, and organized lunch counter sit-ins at a local Mel's Drive-In. But 1963–1964 also saw the assassination of Medgar Evers, the murder of four black children in an Alabama church bombing, the murder of three Student Nonviolent Coordinating Committee (SNCC) workers, and preparation for an escalation in the war in Vietnam. These and other conflicts provided the context for a growing student movement.

Meanwhile, the slogan of racial harmony clashed with the reality of racial conflict. Asian Americans faced discrimination, especially in the areas of education, employment, and housing. A. S. described going to school in Stockton, California:

> I went to Franklin because of where I lived. But Edison was . . . [a] minority school, our kissing cousin school—many Chinese, Japanese, Filipinos, Mexicans, and Blacks. Franklin had more poor Whites. . . . You were told where to go. . . . There was a strict code that was enforced.[5]

For J. M., a growing awareness of racism caused conflicts within herself which altered life goals:

> I was going with a white man whom I met at Berkeley, whom I eventually married. And so I don't know how to explain this to you, it seems very disorganized and very chaotic, but at the same time I was aspiring to be White, wanting a white child, wanting to marry a white man, I was simultaneously being impacted by all of these events that were challenging me as an Asian woman.[6]

B. I. was like the vast majority of students at San Francisco State who came from the ranks of the working class. He was a farmworker while in high school:

> I spent some time in Fairfield, stoop labor, so I knew what they were saying about the low wages, and the twelve to fourteen-hour day. . . . I learned later on that Pilipinos were involved in organizing the first farmworkers' strike. And that made me very proud. . . . [7]

Several strike activists were with the US armed forces in Asia and faced racial hostilities. E. D. C., who became involved with Pilipinos in the strike, described an instance where he was used to "play an agent enemy, in other words, a gook or whatever."[8]

Although it is difficult to determine if those who understood racism were more disposed to strike involvement or if their involvement sensitized them to racial issues or both, it is clear that racial cleavages were at the center of the Asian American experience.

Student-Initiated Programs

The period 1964 to 1966 saw the development of student-run programs to address racial issues and other social concerns. These programs functioned within the university as alternative schools or "counterhegemonic sites" through which many students developed ideas running counter to prevailing paradigms.

The initial programs included the Fillmore Tutorial, the Community Involvement Program, the Experimental College, and the Work-Study Program. They were initiated with Associated Student government monies under its president, Tom Ramsey, a socialist, who wanted to use the $400,000 budget for community work.[9]

The Fillmore Tutorial was an African American–initiated program that tutored youth in the Fillmore District of San Francisco. The Community Involvement Program was an outgrowth of this. Students organized community activities including graphic arts workshops, a housing and job co-op, and support activities for the National Farmworkers Association and the Delano strike.[10]

The Experimental College offered alternative courses on topics including "Perspective on Revolution," "Urban Action," and "Competition and Violence." One outgrowth was the Work-Study Program, which was later renamed the Community Services Institute in 1968. A 1966 statement declared that education should be redefined to be relevant to community needs, to equip people to control their lives, and to teach that knowledge came from work in the community.[11]

These programs became increasingly popular. By fall 1966, the college had approximately fifteen courses with three hundred students; by spring 1967, there were sixty courses with eight hundred students;[12] and by fall 1968, nine experimental colleges existed in the eighteen-campus university system.[13]

A Master Plan for Future Confrontation

The foundation for growing contradictions between students and administrators was the 1960 Master Plan for Higher Education in California. The plan restructured education to meet the changing needs of industry and the growing student population. Projections estimated that by 1975, more than one million students would be enrolled in California higher education, nearly triple the full-time enrollment of 1958. Technically skilled and managerial workers were needed for developing high-tech and defense industries. The California Master Plan was preceded by the 1958 National Defense Education Act (NDEA), major federal legislation that provided aid to all levels of public and private education with particular support for the math, science, and foreign language fields. The linking of defense and education coincided with developments in the Cold War, including the 1957 Soviet liftoff of *Sputnik*, which launched the "space race."

The Master Plan established three tiers: University of California, California State College, and junior college systems, each with target student populations, specialized functions, and centralized governing boards. The UC system, for the top 12.5 percent of high school graduates, was provided "exclusive jurisdiction over training for professions and the sole authority in public higher education to award the doctor's degree."[14] The state college system was to provide "instruction in the liberal arts and sciences and in professions and applied fields ... and teacher education." Previously open to 70 percent of high school graduates, it was now reserved for the top 33 percent.[15] The junior colleges were to provide vocational training, general liberal arts background, and preparation for transfer to a four-year institution.

The Master Plan's "solution" to the increasing numbers of students was the "diversion" of students from state colleges and UC campuses to junior colleges.[16] To improve the "quality" of students, the UC system and state colleges were directed to develop new admissions requirements for the fall 1962.[17] Thus, instead of expanding the four-year institutions, the Master Plan restricted admissions. The net result was the decline of minority enrollments. At San Francisco State, African American enrollment dropped from an estimated 11 percent in 1960 to 3.6 percent by 1968.[18]

The Master Plan centralized decision making in the hands of business and political figures. A twenty-one-member Board of Trustees was established to govern the state college system, with the system-wide chancellor and board holding absolute control over all academic programs, distribution of allocated funds, and major personnel decisions.

Corporate spokespersons backed the Master Plan. In a 1969 speech titled "Business and Campus Unrest" to the Education Section Meeting in Sacramento, E. Hornsby Wasson, the board chairman of the Pacific Telephone and Telegraph Company, stated,

> The best we in business can do is to try and work with you ... furnishing the most clear-cut guidelines ... to produce the type of young man and woman we need to keep our state and our national economy moving in the years ahead. The interest stems from what I already have expressed: business depends on education *to produce young men and women capable of meeting the demands of our free enterprise system and thus living full, economically independent life.* (emphasis added)[19]

Business concerns received strong political support with Ronald Reagan's rise to the governorship in 1966. Under his leadership, a collision course was set with growing student radicalism on the issues of university access, relevancy, and control.

1966–May 1968: "Serve the People" and "Self-Determination"

As I got involved, I saw what happened [on campus] in terms of a microcosm . . . of what was going on in the city and the larger picture of inequality.
You can stay neutral and let it slide by you, or you can walk away from it and
deny those problems, or you can become a participant. To me, I was going to
become a participant.[20]
—B. L., student government and ICSA member

The process through which action gave rise to new ideas and new ideas shaped
action was dialectical. For Asian American students, this process took many
forms. Some were involved in the Experimental College, the Tutorial Program,
and other Associated Student activities. Some became involved through friendships or contact with other activists. Others literally walked into the strike.
Regardless of how they got involved, their actions led to greater questioning and
understanding, which in turn shaped later actions.

International events had profound impact on the Third World movements
in the United States. Anti-imperialist wars were raging in Asia, Africa, and
Latin America. Works of revolutionary intellectuals like Frantz Fanon, Amílcar Cabral, Che Guevara, and Mao Zedong were studied by activists in the
United States. The concept of "internal colonialism" became popular to depict
the oppressed status of minorities in America. For those who used the colonial analogy, liberation movements abroad suggested that freedom also could
be won at home. Anti-imperialism challenged fundamental tenets from the civil
rights era. Instead of racial integration, anti-imperialist movements argued for
national independence. Instead of nonviolence, they initiated armed struggle.
And instead of shared power, they called for "self-determination."

Events abroad were coupled with a growing discontent at the limitations of civil
rights programs. The discontent was felt most deeply by working-class sectors of
Third World communities, those least affected by legislation. An influential figure
who clearly represented this sector was Malcolm X, who was killed in 1963 but
whose message was popularized for years later. He called for African Americans
to control the resources and institutions of their communities "by any means necessary" and to identify their primary enemies as established institutions and those
who supported the status quo.[21] These themes are evident in the formation of
Asian American organizations during this period. Although these groups were
influenced by the African American movement, their development was unique
to their cultures and respective experiences in the United States. These groups
promoted pride in national heritage; they sought "self-determination" and "power
to the people." These slogans captured the diverse life experiences of the activists
who were conscious of racism and their lack of political power.

Intercollegiate Chinese for Social Action (ICSA)

ICSA was formed in October 1967 by Chinese students who were mainly interested in social, cultural, and community activities. They worked as volunteers for Chinatown social service agencies including the War on Poverty office, taught immigrant teenagers English language skills, and later solicited monies from the Associated Student government to expand the tutorial project and to study the Chinatown power structure.[22]

As campus conflicts intensified with a May 1968 sit-in, a new leadership arose and eventually steered ICSA toward the strike. By July 1968, the group established an office in Chinatown at 737 Clay Street. Though the organization was community-oriented from its founding, the new leadership was more militant. It immediately joined the Third World Liberation Front (TWLF). It also challenged the traditional Chinatown power brokers, particularly the Six Companies, over the use of Economic Opportunity Council monies and over problems of youth and working-class Chinese.

For the new ICSA leader, A. W., "power to the people" meant "a piece of the pie," since his experience showed him that poor people were rarely given anything. A. W. described himself as being a "playboy" and a "hippie." He accidentally walked into the May 1968 sit-in when he attempted to pay his fees in the administration building and "got busted" by the police.[23]

Following that incident, he and M. W. were approached by a member of the Black Students Union (BSU). They were impressed by the his militancy and suggested joining forces, but A. W. initially saw it as benefiting only African Americans. He described his change of mind:

> And I said, "Okay fine, you Blacks need to go to school, so you guys fight it, and I won't go against it. But I'm not for it because what am I getting out of this?" And he said, "What about all your Chinese who can't get into school?" . . . And I said, "Okay you convince me what you can give me and my people." . . . And he said, "We've got counseling, tutoring service, we have special admission." . . . So I said, "All right, I'm in." That was the first time in my life that somebody, not Asian, was willing to share with me their pot of gold. So I had nothing to lose, and all to gain, and then I got involved.[24]

Other ICSA members got involved through community issues. I. C. worked in Chinatown and was aware of the difficulties of immigrant youth. She helped to coordinate ICSA's tutorial program. In reflecting on the reasons for her involvement, she discussed the strong influence of her family who "taught you that you had to do what was right, do what was fair. And when you would see things that were not right, were not fair, [it] just upsets you."[25]

Others like J. C., who came from a middle-class family and grew up for most of his life in a predominately white Bay Area suburb, experienced a cultural and political awakening through his participation in ICSA. His involvement in the strike "was the process of constructing an identity."[26] In high school, he felt competition between peers over "who was whiter than who." But the strike was different:

> We came together, I think, a little more comfortable with who we were. . . . We found issues we felt [were] lack[ing] in our lives. So we could organize ourselves. We could socialize with one another. We could actually sacrifice part of our egos. So we could join a movement towards some objective that we all thought was correct. I think the one thing you can't do when you are trying to melt into the white world is to complain about it. But if you join with others of your own kind, you have the opportunity to trade stories . . . and articulate your hostility.[27]

This quest to validate the ethnic experience fit squarely with the ICSA demand for Chinese American studies under the authority of the people themselves.

M. W. and A. W. proceeded to involve the ICSA in the TWLF. M. W. described the conflict within ICSA:

> And so we had two factions. One faction that wanted to get more involved in the Third World group, because we figured that's where the power was. . . . There was another group that said, "No, we don't need that; we can go by ourselves" . . . and so we had elections, and all of a sudden I won . . . and we became part of the Third World Liberation Front, and became very active in the strike . . . which was radical for a lot of people at that time. They thought we were crazy.[28]

This was a major turning point for the organization and brought to power those who saw the importance of unity with other nationalities for the benefit of Chinese Americans.

Although joining with other Third World groups, the new ICSA leaders drew from figures in Chinese history, including Sun Tzu:[29]

> During the strike we read *The Art of War*. . . . All the Chinese in military history are raised on this . . . [which] says the main goal of war is to win . . . and the true leader doesn't lose lives. . . . The key to win victories is "know thyself."[30]

"Power to the people" for ICSA implicitly meant power to the working class of Chinatown. This is clear from their attacks on the landlords and power brokers, including the Six Companies. Frustrations had mounted over the latter's resistance to youth programs, including those of Leways and the Hwa Ching to develop jobs and programs. On August 17, 1968, ICSA members and community leaders including Reverends Larry Jack Wong, Ed Sue, and Harry Chuck led a peaceful march through Chinatown in support of "education, employment, health, housing, youth, senior citizens, and immigration."[31] ICSA members participated in a coalition called Concerned Chinese for Action and Change. The coalition held a press conference to present several demands, including those for a senior center, a full investigation of the Chinatown-North Beach Equal Opportunity Commission office, immediate action for a community youth center, and the future establishment of a multiservice center, educational program, and low-cost housing.[32] Students also attended many of the EOC meetings to demand seats on the board and programs to serve youth and low-income residents.

A. W. sat on a community board to the police department. He joined discussions about youth "problems" in the public schools. He pointed to the need for institutions to speak to the needs of immigrant youth:

> At that time, I think that Galileo [High School] was about 80 percent Chinese and 50 percent were non-English speaking. I said, "You need bilingual classes, and you need to give the students some pride." Their argument was that [the students] didn't want to participate. I said "How do you expect them to participate? . . . Give them something to be proud of and they will, in turn, turn Galileo into a good school." They thought it was horse shit. . . . Now they have all those things.[33]

Just as ICSA participation in Chinatown helped build opposition to the Six Companies, their increased understanding of Chinatown's problems strengthened their resolve to fight for ethnic studies. In a position paper, the group stated,

> Chinatown is a GHETTO. In San Francisco there are approximately 80,000 Chinese of whom the vast majority live in Chinatown. It is an area of old buildings, narrow streets and alleys and the effluvia of a great deal of people packed into a very small space. . . . Tuberculosis is endemic, rents are high and constantly rising . . . and space is at such a premium as to resemble the Malthusian ratio at its most extreme conclusion.[34]

The position paper advocated ethnic studies. It stated, "There are not adequate courses in any department or school at San Francisco State that even begin to deal with problems of the Chinese people in this exclusionary and racist environment."[35]

Community efforts converged with those of students. For example, G. W., who worked with Hwa Ching youth, returned to school after the strike began. He and others initiated the Free University for Chinatown Kids, Unincorporated, "to find ways to merge the college students and street kids together and hopefully share the best of their experiences."[36] The acronym, F.U.C.K.U., was a statement: "You guys [the university] don't like us? Well, we don't like you either."[37] F.U.C.K.U. met for several sessions with films, speakers, and discussion on problems and solutions for Chinatown youth.

An organization that actively supported the strike was Leways. Short for "legitimate ways," it set up a pool hall and soda fountain at 615 Jackson Street called the "Fountain of Youth." Leways member Alex Hing wrote, "Because the strike was aimed precisely at giving oppressed Third World people access to college, Leways became the staunchest supporters of the TWLF in Chinatown."[38] Leways assisted in educational, fund-raising, and picket activity during the strike. Through the strike and community involvement, Leways became increasingly political, and later some members formed the revolutionary Red Guards.

Supporters came from many political persuasions. Despite differences, important alliances were built over strike demands. The Equal Opportunity Council board in Chinatown, dominated by members of the Six Companies, held more conservative views as compared with those of strike organizers. However, they shared concern over educational access. G. W. described an exchange that began as a board member responded to students' appeal for support:

> "How dare you people make such a racket! My grandson's trying to apply for the university and couldn't get in!" I said in Chinese to him. "Read our demand carefully. We're doing this for your grandson. It is precisely people like your grandson who feel that they have been kept out ... and we want to get him in." And he said, "Oh, is that right? I'm for it!" And he turned around and looked at everybody. And since he's for it, the rest of the people said "for," and we got a majority. So we had EOC in Chinatown voting to support the San Francisco State Third World strike.[39]

Philippine-American Collegiate Endeavor (PACE)

PACE was established in spring 1968 by P. S. to organize and fight for the rights of Pilipino youth. He had learned about the efforts of Third World students through Professor Juan Martinez. PACE organized counseling programs, tutorial programs, tutor training, study centers, high school recruitment drives, newsletters, fund-raising dances, ethnic studies curricula, community outreach, and liaison with student government.

The backgrounds of PACE members were as diverse as those of other groups. However, most were foreign-born. A number came from military family backgrounds as well as farmworker families. A. S. remarked that "you had multidiverse types of Pilipinos who started PACE, which was really a miracle we even stuck together." But he added, "We had common backgrounds, we had common goals. And we really had a common thought ... that there really had to be something better in life than what we were used to."[40]

PACE saw the inequality they faced as rooted in racism. Members felt that uniting Third World people to create a new consciousness would enable them to control their own destinies. This viewpoint was expressed in the statement of goals and principles, which read,

> We seek . . . simply to function as human beings, to control our own lives. Initially, following the myth of the American Dream, we worked to attend predominantly white colleges, but we have learned through direct analysis that it is impossible for our people, so-called minorities, to function as human beings, in a racist society in which white always comes first. . . . So we have decided to fuse ourselves with the masses of Third World people, which are the majority of the world's peoples, to create, through struggle, a new humanity, a new humanism, a New World Consciousness, and within that context collectively control our own destinies.[41]

One of the ways this "New World Consciousness" would develop was through ethnic studies. These courses would educate people to the Pilipino American experience, thus lessening racist attitudes.

Some PACE members organized support for their demands within the community through explaining the concept of "self-determination" with concrete illustrations. P. S. explained,

> Self-determination was probably the closest [term] to making other people understand what we were trying to express. Because when you had to explain self-determination, you had to explain the other side, against what? . . . So that buzzword was just convenient to open up . . . discussions. . . . I thought it better to express how what we were doing was going to help. I would say it in different forms . . . how what we were doing would help kids get in school, get jobs . . . very visual things that they could relate to.[42]

Like ICSA members, PACE members saw "self-determination" as taking control over one's life. They initiated community programs through an off-campus office at 829 Cortland. The purpose was fourfold: to encourage and aid low-income Pilipino American students in the Mission area to enter college; to establish communication channels between youth organizations in the Bay Area; to research socioeconomic problems and their solutions; and to serve as a referral agency for employment, medical, housing, recreation, and counseling services.[43]

PACE worked with youth groups at schools and churches like Mission High School and St. Patrick's. One focus was to recruit Pilipino high school youth to college through the Educational Opportunity Program. Once in college, PACE worked with students to "make sure they stayed on campus" and completed their education. E. I. helped to recruit students and described,

Yeah, particularly on the south of Market . . . they played basketball to keep off the street. If they were out on the street, they would get busted . . . or they wound up in the Army. A lot of people got drafted. You know that the rank and file in the army was Third World. . . . So there was a better alternative: to get them onto campus.[44]

One issue in Manilatown and Chinatown concerned the eviction of elderly residents, community organizations, and small businesses from the International Hotel due to the encroaching financial district. Tenants and supporters resisted evictions for over ten years. Pilipino and other Asian students were active participants throughout the period of the campus strike. E. I. continued,

Sometime in November, mid-December, there were eviction notices posted on the International Hotel door. It said, "You who live here are hereby notified . . . that the Hotel is going to be demolished and you have to leave." . . . And I enlisted the support of [M. W.] and [G. W. of ICSA] and they marched with us. And we had 120 Pilipinos out there, senior citizens, residents of that building. We picketed down Montgomery. . . . These were elderly people, retired veterans. . . . I got appointed to the board of that association. And it was then becoming an issue that totally involved me, and I was a student.[45]

The community programs not only enabled a large number of students to participate in PACE, but also involved students in an implicit challenge to the individualistic pursuits promoted by the university. PACE's activities captured the sentiments of students to uplift their people. The membership roster included almost 70 out of an estimated 125 Pilipino students on campus.[46]

Asian American Political Alliance (AAPA)

AAPA was formed in late summer 1968 at San Francisco State College by mainly Japanese American women. It was a vehicle for students to share political concerns in a pan-Asian organization. One founder, P. N., had worked in the Experimental College and had participated in the May sit-in. During that summer, she met a woman whose brother was a member of AAPA at the University of California, Berkeley. She and others attended those meetings and by fall organized an AAPA at San Francisco State:

I felt a lot of need to do something about racism. Also, there was a need to do something about the lack of political involvement of Asians. . . . [There] was also this amorphous sense of wanting to build a sense of Asian American identity and . . . overcome what I saw as nationalistic kinds of trends. I wanted to see Asians from different ethnic backgrounds working together.[47]

The ideological development of San Francisco State AAPA was influenced by the movement at UC Berkeley. P. N. recalled that many of their concepts "were developed as a result of meetings and discussions, trying to get a sense of what AAPA should be and what its goals should be, what kinds of interests it should address."[48] In one of the first issues of the UC Berkeley AAPA newspaper in fall 1968, an article described the group as a "people's alliance to effect social and political changes."

> We believe that the American society is historically racist and is one which has systematically employed social discrimination and economic imperialism both domestically and internationally to exploit all people, but especially nonwhites.[49]

AAPA saw the problems facing Asian people as rooted in racism and imperialism; thus, it was important to build alliances based on race as well as common oppression; political organization should not only effect change but build new nonhierarchical social relationships; therefore, AAPA was only a transition to generate ideas "to effect fundamental social, economical, political changes." A parallel was drawn to the movements against imperialism in the Third World. "We Asian Americans support all oppressed peoples and their struggles for Liberation and believe that Third World People must have complete control over the political, economic, and educational institutions within their communities."[50]

At San Francisco State, AAPA attempted to organize political study that offered critical perspectives for its activity. One founding member stated that activists studied the "Red Book," which contained writings of Mao Zedong. They also read writings of Frantz Fanon and Black Power leaders, including the Black Panther Party newspaper. She described the impact of these readings:

> I think they helped to provide me with a conceptual framework within which I could look at how my involvement fit in with other events: the Vietnam War in particular and the connections between the strike, domestic issues, property, and international issues.[51]

Though AAPA did not have an off-campus office, there were informal gatherings at a house in the Richmond district, several miles west of Japantown. P. Y. explained how this house became a congregating point for AAPA activities, "like an extended family":

> Towards the end of the strike, they found us a big house on 4th and California, 4th and Cornwall actually. . . . They got the whole house, it was three stories, two big flats. There were about eight people living there, seven of them were AAPA members. And it became the meeting place. There was a [mimeo] machine in there, and all of our stuff was printed out of there, all the meetings were held there, all

the parties were held there. If anybody came in from out of town—a lot of people from L.A. used to come up—and that's where they would come. So that became a real home for AAPA.[52]

Cultural activities strengthened the closeness that P. Y. and many others spoke about during this period. One artist was Francis Oka, who was killed in an accident shortly after the strike. M. O. described his influence:

> We were like brother and sister. And he would always be the theoretical one; we kind of balanced each other off. And he was trying, struggling to be a writer and a poet and a songwriter. His idol was Dylan, Dylan Thomas . . . because of our friendship, he always opened my mind up and made me read things. . . . He was the foremost idealist in my life.[53]

The strike unleashed a creative spirit. AAPA member Janice Mirikitani became a leading figure in the Asian American arts movement. The strike provided a focus for her creative expression. She and others created the Third World Communications Collective and a Third World Women's Collective, and they published one of the first Asian American journals, *Aion*.

The appointment in late 1968 of S. I. Hayakawa as San Francisco State College president stirred up controversy in the Japanese American community. Public protest against Hayakawa challenged social codes within the community that discouraged confrontation. However, a minority of nisei publicly supported the students. The director of the YMCA office in Japantown, Y. W., explained this viewpoint:

> It could be that we had more contact with the younger generation in the course of our work. It could also be that we were far more interested in civil liberties, and in the question of freedom of speech, the freedom of assemblage. . . . It could also be that we really didn't feel that restrained to rock the boat, to challenge the status quo. I think it might have been the lessons learned from the evacuation. If there is a wrong, you don't keep quiet about it. . . . I think the evacuation was wrong, and this was one way to say so many years later.[54]

His sentiments may have been shared by some one hundred Japanese Americans who expressed support and even pride for striking students at a community meeting at Christ United Presbyterian Church on December 6, 1968. The program consisted of student presentations followed by discussion. A statement by an elderly woman marked a turning point as she expressed her joy that young people were standing up for their rights.

On the evening of February 21, 1969, 125 Japanese Americans picketed a dinner featuring Hayakawa as a speaker. The dinner was sponsored by the Community

Interest Committee of Nihonmachi, organized by several individuals affiliated with the Japanese American Citizen's League. AAPA members along with community leaders, including Yori Wada and Rev. Lloyd Wake of Glide Memorial Church, organized the protest and a press conference.

Third World Liberation Front (TWLF)

Closer relations among Third World students impacted the ideological development of Asian Americans by emphasizing the commonalities among "people of color" and creating a forum that facilitated a "cross-pollenization of ideas." The demands of the coalition set a foundation for unity and defined the political issues and struggles that occurred through the course of the strike. Due to the development of the African American movement and the participation of relatively experienced members of the BSU and Black Panther Party, African American students played an influential role in the TWLF.

One individual who was influential in the formation of the TWLF was Juan Martinez, a lecturer in the history department and the faculty advisor of the Mexican American Students Confederation (MASC). The TWLF coalition was formed with his encouragement in spring 1968. He had earlier encouraged P. S. to organize Pilipino students and when PACE was formed, it joined the TWLF. ICSA joined in spring. AAPA joined in summer 1968.

The themes of freedom and self-determination are evident in the "Third World Liberation Front Philosophy and Goals," which stated,

> The TWLF . . . has its purpose to aid in further developing politically, economically, and culturally the revolutionary Third World consciousness of racist oppressed peoples both on and off campus. As Third World students, as Third World people, as so-called minorities, we are being exploited to the fullest extent in this racist white America, and we are therefore preparing ourselves and our people for a prolonged struggle for freedom from this yoke of oppression.[55]

The TWLF saw immediate reforms in the context of radical, long-term change. A change in consciousness was seen as necessary to eliminate exploitation and racism.

Racism had been traditionally defined as a set of bigoted assumptions held by individuals. But in this period, racism was redefined as being "institutionalized" into all realms of society. The concept put emphasis on the structure of the economic and political system. Students began to deepen their analysis of society by merging this concept with their own life experiences.

In the immediate work, these ideas manifested themselves in three main demands made to the administration. First, the TWLF advocated the right of all Third World students to an education. They highlighted the existence of "institutionalized racism" as manifested in culturally biased "standardized" tests used as admissions criteria. They demanded open admissions and an expanded special admissions program.

In March and April 1968, TWLF members recruited many high school students to apply for admission to the university. On April 30, they sponsored an orientation at which several hundred students presented their applications to President Summerskill's office. They later called for the college to use all special admissions slots for disadvantaged students. In 1966 and 1967, the state colleges had admitted only 0.27 and 0.85 percent "disadvantaged" respectively, even though 2 percent were allowed through the "exception rule."[56]

Second, the TWLF challenged the fundamental purpose of education by demanding a School of Ethnic Area Studies. This demand stressed that education should be relevant to their lives and communities. Relevancy in education was clarified by students in their stated purpose of a School of Ethnic Area Studies:

> The school clearly intends to be involved in confronting racism, poverty and misrepresentation imposed on minority peoples by the formally recognized institutions and organizations operating in the State of California.[57]

This perspective represented a fundamental challenge to the underpinnings of the Master Plan. While the Master Plan called for restructuring the university based largely upon the priorities of the corporate sector, students advocated a redefinition of education to serve their communities. I. C., who was tutoring in Chinatown, stated that "the community had so many needs, and there were so few people that participated. We always hoped that when these courses came about, more people would be encouraged to go back and help the community."[58] PACE member R. Q. also stated, "I know nothing about my background, nothing historically about the people here in this country, and less about the Philippines."[59] Students wanted an education that would help them retrieve their historical legacy as well as contribute to social change in their communities.

Third, the TWLF demanded the right to have ethnic studies classes taught and run by Third World peoples. "Self-determination" meant that each nationality had the right to determine its own curriculum and hire its own faculty. Students argued that those who had lived a particular ethnic experience were best able to teach it to others. ICSA's M. W. added that "the winners are the ones who write the history books"[60] and that oppressed people had their own version of history. The TWLF also recognized that the existing criteria to evaluate ethnic studies and Third World faculty would be biased by racism. Thus, the TWLF demanded programmatic autonomy. The BSU had the most developed curricular philosophy. In their newspaper, *Black Fire*, they listed six goals for teaching:

(1) a cultural identity, because we live in a society that is racist, that degrades and denies cultural heritage of Third World people, specifically black people; (2) to educate our people to understand that the only culture we can have is one that is revolutionary (directed toward our freedom and a complete change in our living conditions), and that this will never be endorsed by our enemy; (3) to build a revolutionary perspective and to understand the need for using the knowledge and skills we have and get only for our liberation and the destruction of all the oppressive conditions surrounding us; (4) to educate ourselves to the necessity of relating to the collective and not the individual; (5) to strive to build a socialist society; (6) to redistribute the wealth; the knowledge, the technology, the natural resources, the food, land, housing, and all of the material resources necessary for a society and its people to function.[61]

The politics of the TWLF were not as overtly revolutionary as those of the BSU but nonetheless were influenced by them. For example, in the TWLF's demand for a School of Ethnic Area Studies, a similar rationale was put forward:

As assurance against the reoccurrence of education's traditional distortion and misrepresentation of Third World people's cultures and histories, the School of Ethnic Area Studies is to be developed, implemented, and controlled by Third World people. Whether an area study is at a developmental or a departmental level within the school, the people, of an area study will have sole responsibility and control for the staffing and curriculum of their ethnic area study.[62]

Resistance to the Challenge

DeVere Pentony, who had served as chairman of the Department of International Relations, dean of the School of Behavioral and Social Sciences, and deputy president at San Francisco State, wrote,

The more promising the programs became in exploring and modifying basic assumptions, the more resistance grew. As student programs moved away from strictly academic problems toward direct action, problems of budget, propriety, the role of the university and the place of students in the scheme of things came sharply into view.[63]

As early as June 1967, students had pushed the Council of Academic Deans to authorize a special "task force" to establish black studies, but nothing had resulted from it. And by summer 1968, there was still no black studies program. When President John Summerskill resigned after the May sit-in, Robert Smith took over the presidency. In his coauthored book, he attributes the delays in the establishment of black studies to the fact that "the college did not sense the urgency of the demand; the black students did not trust the world of the honkies."[64] In his view, both sides were being unreasonable; the strike could have been avoided. But he fails to recognize the fundamental contradictions underlying the conflict: student demands ran totally contrary to those who held greatest power in the university and the state. Smith's position was eventually overridden by the trustees; he was forced to resign after the strike began.

Some trustees objected to Experimental College courses and ethnic studies on the grounds that they were not "objective" or had introduced politics into the curriculum. Chancellor Dumke opposed partisan stands of students and faculty on social issues. "If the campus enters politics no force under heaven can keep politics from entering campus ... the university must remain pure and unsullied and above the battle." Nor did Dumke believe there was a need to expand special admissions. In a letter of transmittal on the question of expanding the 2 percent special admit limit, he stated that "programs for the disadvantaged are a relatively recent development, and that the actual number of students admitted as exceptions ... is not at present sufficient in itself to justify either expansion or maintenance of present limitations."[65]

The resistance by administrators and trustees led students to use different tactics. In May 1968, Third World students and the Students for a Democratic Society (SDS) staged a sit-in at President Summerskill's office. This resulted in the granting of 412 slots for Third World students over the next two semesters, the creation of at least ten faculty positions for Third World professors with student voice in the hirings, and the rehiring of Juan Martinez in the history department.[66] SDS's demand for ROTC to be expelled from campus was the only demand denied. During the May sit-in, police responded with their first major act of violence against student protesters. One policeman charged a woman. Terrence Hallinan, an attorney, intervened. He was clubbed on the head. Ten were injured and taken to the hospital and twenty-six were arrested.[67] Conflicts heightened when Summerskill resigned a few months later without fulfilling the promises he had made in a signed agreement with the students.

P. N., who participated in this sit-in and later founded AAPA, felt that the administration's resistance to students' demands was rooted in a racially biased understanding of history. "The hardest thing for a lot of administrators to comprehend was the notion [that] there was an existing deficit in the way history brings us [knowledge]—there are subjects we weren't taught." Institutional racism, she continued, "was a very, very difficult thing for people to comprehend, and not just white people."[68]

The resistance of the administration, along with police violence, led greater numbers of students to challenge traditional protest channels. The sentiment to use more militant tactics rose as frustration and anger mounted.

Structure and Organization of the TWLF

During this period, there were many efforts to split the ranks of the student coalition by administrators, media, and others. There were also efforts to learn from these events. In one instance, the TWLF issued a leaflet summing up the major lessons from the April 30, 1968, high school orientation. This was precipitated by mischaracterizations of the event in several news articles. Excerpts from the leaflet read,

> Members of TWLF, beware. What resulted after the April 30 event is exactly what emasculates any effort, actions or programs within an organization when the constituents blame one another for what the outside sources of media . . . take to slander and falsify charges against whatever an organization, like TWLF, stands for or does.[69]

Disunity emerged during the May sit-in. According to one account, the BSU was granted some concessions preceding the sit-in. Several members were still on probation from an earlier confrontation between BSU members and the *Gator* campus newspaper staff. BSU decided not to join the sit-in, and their refusal caused mistrust among some in the TWLF. Also, MASC and PACE were reported to have set up the SDS-TWLF joint action without formal approval of the TWLF coordinators. This upset the Latin American Students Association (LASO), which reportedly pulled out of the action a few days before the sit-in.[70]

Conflicts with the white left on campus also shaped the functioning of the TWLF. Self-determination was applied to the movement itself; white students were expected to respect the right of Third World organizations to lead their respective movements. Nationalism, which deemed one nationality's struggle as important above all other causes, influenced some Third World activists. However, this viewpoint was distinct from sentiments for national pride, identity, and self-determination which were held by the majority of activists. Some sectors of the white left failed to distinguish between narrow nationalism and national self-determination. Additionally, members of the Progressive Labor Party considered all nationalism to be reactionary.

Nationalism was a point of conflict within the TWLF. While most activists were committed to improving the conditions of their people, there was a growing suspicion that some were looking out only for themselves. As the movement faced setbacks, the administration encouraged divisions by offering settlements to each group individually.

To counteract divisions and to ensure internal accountability, the BSU developed an organizational structure that was to have great impact on the TWLF. BSU Central Committee member Terry Collins described this structure in a *Black Fire* article:

In the spring of 1968 the Black Students Union saw that there was a need for demo-cratic centralism. Before that time the Black Students Union had no formal struc-ture. Dominant personalities of two or three people tyrannically reigned over the other students. Factionalism was rampant, potential revolutionary brothers were disillusioned, sisters were used and abused in the name of "blackness." It was the era of the bourgeois cultural nationalism, a stage of evolution that all black stu-dents involved in the movement move through, but must shake quickly. Bourgeois cultural nationalism is destructive to the individual and the organization because one uses "blackness" as a criterion and uses this rationale as an excuse not to fight the real enemy when the struggle becomes more intense. That is why we presented a new structure to the people in the spring of 1968 and called for the election of a central committee.[71]

In the TWLF structure, each of the six organizations had two representatives to a Central Committee whose decisions were to be implemented by all groups.[72] Chairpersons would be alternated every four months to provide training and to share responsibilities. No one was authorized to speak for the coalition, negotiate with the administration, make statements to the media without the sanction of the TWLF.[73] Democracy was to be promoted by input through the respective organizations around three principles: fight against racism, fight for self-determination for Third World peoples, and support the TWLF demands.[74]

Strategy and Tactics

The BSU's approach toward strategy also influenced the TWLF. BSU members popularized the concept of "heightening contradictions" in order to educate people. Black studies professor Nathan Hare explained,

> For by heightening the contradictions, you prepare people for the confrontation which must come when they are fully sensitized to their condition. Rushing into confrontations without having heightened contradictions contrarily cripples the confrontation.[75]

Hare saw "heightening the contradictions" as a *strategy* to prepare people for confrontational *tactics*. The strategy was to educate the general student popula-tion about TWLF problems with the aim of involving them in confrontations to win demands. Violence was seen as a confrontational tactic rather than an organizing principle.

In contrast, P. N. of AAPA recalled a different interpretation:

> I guess the main reasons for using violent tactics . . . was . . . [to] heighten the contradictions, increase the level of confrontation. Because . . . the greater the

amount of pressure, the more incentive there is to resolve it. So by heightening the contradictions, or by heightening the level of tensions . . . there may be a faster resolution than if things stayed at a lower level of activity.[76]

This interpretation defined "heightening the contradictions" as a tactic. P. N. also observed that "there was a certain amount of macho that was also involved, as distinguished from looking at violence in a more analytical perspective as a tactical movement."[77] The "macho" attitude may have reflected a larger difference; some students may have viewed violence as a *strategy* to win their demands.

The idea of exposing contradictions between students and the administration was based on the assumption that underlying the conflict was a fundamental difference in values, beliefs, and, most of all, interests. Many students came to believe that racism, class, and political interests belied all rhetoric about the university as a neutral and objective entity.

1968–1969: "By Any Means Necessary"

The trustees are worried about a Black Studies department having an all-black faculty. They didn't mention that there are departments with all-white faculties. These people are scared of giving black people control over their own destinies. Does the college plan to do something about institutional racism or is it just going to fire Black Power advocates? I haven't seen anybody fired for being a racist.[78]
—Elmer Cooper, Dean of Student Activities

Students were angered by the refusal of the administration to act on their demands despite prior commitments. This period also saw police violence and political repression against mass movements, including the assassinations of Martin Luther King, Jr. and Robert Kennedy. Protesters at the Democratic National Convention were severely beaten. Many believed that substantive change would not be willingly given: it had to be won through force. Thus, they echoed the slogan of Malcolm X—"by any means necessary."

Many engaged in confrontational tactics after they had exhausted other channels. Some students had been seeking the expansion and institutionalization of ethnic studies and special admissions programs for four years. Promises had been made by Summerskill and others but were never implemented. Now, the administrators were using police to suppress student actions. Due to this repression, students began to understand that their demands represented a more fundamental challenge to the system. Although this understanding varied among students, it was widely shared and provided the basis for mobilizing hundreds in the confrontations with the administration. PACE's B. I. stated that even "the silence on the part of the administration [told me] that our demands were not relevant, told me that our contributions were not anything. So that's what led me to get more involved."[79]

Firing of George Murray Heightens Confrontation

BSU central committee member George Murray was fired from the English department for his political beliefs and activism in November. He had been hired in May to teach Educational Opportunity Program (EOP) courses. The Board of Trustees opposed his hiring due to his public statements challenging the racism of the university. Murray was also Minister of Education of the Black Panther Party. The alternative campus newspaper, *Open Process*, summarized the reason for his termination:

> Institutionalized racism is embedded in the status quo of American society; to challenge it with that in mind is to challenge the very foundations of society. George Murray was suspended not because he is black, but because as a member of the Black Panther Party he has challenged the institutions which have always enslaved black people including the educational system.[80]

The controversy over Murray's case reflected a polarization within the administration and faculty. Smith, like other liberals, argued that "if we are to continue as a nation ruled by law, we must give all citizens the benefit of *due process* and the protection of the law."[81] Chancellor Dumke was less concerned with due process than with the problem of "certain tiny groups of students . . . who have lost faith in our system, and are simply interested in overthrowing the establishment." He expressed his determination to suppress any disruption with whatever force necessary.[82]

One month after the publication of Dumke's statements, George Murray gave a speech at a rally at a trustees board meeting in Fresno. In his speech, he spoke about the betrayal of America by politicians.

> So you get people deceiving college students, deceiving the general populace in the United States . . . to manipulate you to the extent that you'll die for some nonfreedom in Viet Nam, that you'll die for some nonfreedom throughout Asia, Africa, and Latin America fighting people of color who have never victimized any American persons.[83]

He discussed the demands of African Americans, including the right of self-determination and exemption from the draft. Murray pointed to the examples of revolutionary struggles to win demands.

> We understand that the only way that we're going to get them [is] the same way which folks got theirs in 1776, the same way black people in Cuba got theirs in the 1950s . . . that is with guns and force. We maintain that political power comes through the barrel of a gun.[84]

After the *San Francisco Chronicle* reported Murray advocating "guns on campus," trustee opposition to his appointment increased. On November 1 the administration announced his suspension. Murray was later arrested during the first week of Hayakawa's administration, suspended again, and jailed without parole.

War of the Flea

On October 28, only days before Murray's suspension, the BSU called a rally to announce the strike and their demands.[85] In the following week, meetings were held by the BSU and TWLF, and the strike date was set as November 6. On the day before the strike, the TWLF held a general meeting attended by nearly seven hundred Third World students and community supporters. SNCC representative Stokeley Carmichael delivered a speech that raised the level of analysis of many students. He warned against trying to solve institutional racism simply by replacing white administrators with blacks. He said, "Now the way to insure that you get somebody ... who has the same political ideology that you have is to make sure that you can choose or you have control over that person." He also urged them to take the struggle seriously, stating, "do not start off with something you cannot maintain because in the long run you not only hurt yourself but movements to come." He concluded, "It is easier to die for one's people than it is to work and live for them, to kill for them, and to continue to live and kill for them."[86]

Following Carmichael, Benny Stewart presented the strategy of the "war of the flea." This strategy was adapted from the guerrilla war conditions facing many anticolonial movements in which the strength was based on mass support, familiarity with the terrain, and the advantage of elusiveness. He pointed to the failure of other campus movements after leaders had been arrested and argued for a new strategy for a prolonged struggle:

> We call it the war of the flea. .... What does the flea do? He bites, sucks blood from the dog, the dog bites. What happens when there are enough fleas on a dog? What will he do? He moves. He moves away. .... We are the people. We are the majority and the pigs cannot be everywhere. .... And where they are not, we are.[87]

One influential writer during this period was Frantz Fanon with his widely read book, *Wretched of the Earth*. He emphasized the role of revolutionary struggle by the oppressed to achieve liberation. Fanon and other Third World thinkers had great influence on student activists. At the same time, these ideas were integrated with the students' own experiences, both on campus and in American society. This period was marked by a rash of police incidents, including violence against the Panthers, assaults on Chicano youth in the Mission district, and the shooting of a Chinese woman in the eye by a drunk officer. Students also rallied at UC Santa Barbara, San Jose State, College of San Mateo, and throughout the nation. Student activity in Czechoslovakia, France, Italy, Spain, Japan, and China also received publicity. All of these events profoundly affected San Francisco State activists.

On November 6, mobile teams of Third World students entered buildings, dismissed classes, set trash cans on fire, and otherwise disrupted campus operations. Meanwhile, four hundred white students marched to President Smith's office in support of the TWLF demands. In contrast to characterizations of strikers as irrational youth, there was in fact a clear reasoning for actions based on a redefinition of violence.

Soon after the strike began, Smith called in the police and closed the campus. The next day, six hundred persons marched on the administration building during a noon rally. By the third day, the *Gator* reported a 50 percent drop in classroom attendance. By that time, students altered tactics and sent "educational teams" into classrooms to explain the strike issues.[88]

On November 13, the San Francisco police Tactical Squad beat several TWLF members. A rally was called and a thousand students gathered, ending in more police violence. By the end of the day, seven students had been arrested and eleven taken to the hospital for injuries.[89] Smith announced, "We'll keep classes closed until such time as we can reopen them on a rational basis."[90] The trustees gave Smith until November 20 to reopen the college. The faculty refused to resume classes and held "convocations" to try to resolve the problems. The BSU stated they would refuse to participate unless classes were canceled. When classes were not canceled on November 21, two thousand students rallied, and police again beat and arrested students. In the first two weeks of the strike, the police arrested 148 participants.[91] Though many Asian student activists participated in militant tactics, some were reluctant. AAPA member M. O. did not oppose the basic strategy because she believed that in order to gain ethnic studies, "the only answer at that time seemed to be: force them [administration]." However, she selectively chose not to participate in violent actions. "When I got to the point of throwing, I could pick it up, but I couldn't throw it. I thought, 'no, my involvement will have to be in other ways.'"[92] Another student opposed those tactics as he saw that the debris was cleaned up by Third World workers, including his father, who worked as a custodian on campus.

Winter–Spring 1968: Repression and Continued Community Commitment

On November 26, President Smith resigned, explaining his failure "to get from the chancellor and the trustees the resources and kinds of decisions I felt we needed. ... Further, we could not get them to look past serious provocative acts to basic problems."[93] However, underneath the "problems" were basic differences, which the trustees and California Governor Ronald Reagan clearly understood.

The silencing of liberals matched the rise of conservative national and state political figures. Following the election of Reagan as governor in 1966, Nixon became president in 1968. Republicans won the majority in both houses of the California state legislature. Through appointments, Reagan gained control of the state college Board of Trustees.[94] The naming of faculty member S. I. Hayakawa as president of the college was part of this political realignment. Hayakawa and colleagues in the Faculty Renaissance organization had courted Chancellor Dumke. They proposed to deliver ultimatums, restrict due process, suspend students, and fire disobeying faculty.[95] Hayakawa was a perfect choice, being of Japanese descent. He took a hard line against the student movement and served as a public spectacle for media consumption.

On December 2, fifteen hundred gathered after Hayakawa's ban on campus rallies. Hayakawa personally jumped onto the sound truck and ripped off the speaker cords. As the crowd was attempting to leave, several hundred police sealed off a section of campus and beat and arrested students, reporters, medics, and community supporters.[96] Hayakawa stated at a press conference, "This has been the most exciting day of my life since my tenth birthday, when I rode on a roller coaster for the first time!"[97]

On the evening of December 2, the American Federation of Teachers (AFT) held an emergency meeting and voted to request strike sanction from the San Francisco Central Labor Council. Their main concerns were faculty issues, including a nine-unit teaching requirement. On December 4, six thousand persons rallied on campus, and on December 6 a large rally was marked by police violence and arrests.[98] On December 11, the AFT set up an informal picket line in front of the administration building. And on December 13, Hayakawa announced an early Christmas recess.

TWLF leaders noted the tentativeness of their alliance with the AFT, whose strike began January 6. "We view it as positive that the AFT has finally gone on strike. It must be clear, however, that the AFT is, by their own admission, striking primarily for their own demands and only secondarily, under pressure, for the fifteen demands of TWLF."[99]

As students, faculty, and community supporters gained strength, the university prepared to take more repressive measures. On January 23, over 500 persons demonstrated on campus. Within five minutes, the police encircled the crowd and arrested 453 people.[100] Many spokespersons were incarcerated, leaving a void in the organized leadership. P. Y. of AAPA summarized this period:

We just didn't have the money or the time to deal with 400 arrests at one time. At that point a lot of energy went preparing for trials. . . . From that point on, the strike went downhill. A lot of EOP students and people who weren't directly involved in the day to day organization just stopped showing up. . . . A large part of the white student population that had supported the strike stopped going to school. . . . And everybody's court dates were starting to come up. . . . Some people were being pulled in for probation violation, for previous arrests. That's what happened to me, all of February. I don't know what happened during the last part of the strike because I was in jail.[101]

For the following months, much time was consumed in legal support efforts. Most trials took between four and six weeks, and by the year's end, 109 persons were convicted, and many served jail sentences.[102] Statewide, over 900 students and faculty were arrested on the state college campuses between November 1968 and March 1969.[103] This repression severely crippled the movement.

State repression impacted Asian students' understanding of the police in several ways. For AAPA member P. Y., this experience reinforced his developing understanding of society:

I think most kids have a real negative attitude [toward police]. What became clearer was that the political context they operated in . . . the role of the police [as] an internal army . . . against the working class and Third World people.[104]

P. Y. was indicted and served a jail sentence. In jail, he saw that the treatment in prison epitomized the status of poor and Third World people in society. From his four-month internment, he learned that "jail is like almost any other segment of society . . . class is such a determining thing on people's lives. For me that put into perspective a lot of the issues of the strike."[105] Meanwhile, Reagan, the trustees, and Hayakawa were able to distort the strike through the media and sway public support for their repressive measures. For example, Hayakawa described students as "a gang of goons, gangsters, con men, neo-Nazis, and common thieves."[106] Also, in a statement to the US Congress on February 3, 1969, he boasted about the use of police repression:

I believe that I have introduced something new to this business of preserving order on campuses. At most institutions the use of police is delayed as long as possible and when assistance is finally requested, the force is usually too small to handle the situation and new troubles develop. I went the other way. . . . The opposition has received my message. I think I have communicated successfully.[107]

B. L. stated his anger at the mischaracterization of the strike in the popular media:

Their main focus points were probably on Hayakawa and the so-called violence. Like maybe you break a window. But what about the inequity, the psychological damage inflicted on an individual and [the destruction] of their history. What about that kind of violence?[108]

Negotiation and Evaluation

The internal weaknesses of the student movement and the external repression of the state forced students into a position of negotiating the "nonnegotiable" demands. Their negotiating power was weakened when the AFT returned to work on March 5 after voting 112 to 104 to end the strike, despite an unsatisfactory compromise.[109] Meanwhile, to prevent public questioning of their repressive strategy, Hayakawa and Reagan felt pressure to reopen the campus.

After several attempts, Hayakawa recognized a "Select Committee" of faculty that "expected to act with the full authority of the president"[110] and negotiate with the TWLF. However, this committee was more liberal than Hayakawa, and it negotiated a compromise to his objection. On March 14, the committee met with Hayakawa to formalize the settlement. Since Hayakawa was to leave at 9 AM for a meeting with President Nixon, their meeting was set for 7:30 AM, at which time he was quoted as saying, "I'll give you a month. . . . If all is quiet by April 11, I'll consider your recommendations. Now, if you'll excuse me, I have to catch my plane for Washington. Good morning."[111] Hayakawa never signed the negotiated resolution. TWLF members and faculty proceeded to implement the resolution.

It is important to note the BSU's reasons for entering negotiations with the administration. BSU Central Committee member Leroy Goodwin outlined "major contradictions" in a May 1969 *Black Fire* article. A major reason to enter negotiations was "the determination and support of the people rapidly decreasing due to a low political level, communication gaps, and paranoia or fear of the Central Committee." Also, he pointed to five classifications of opportunism that plagued the movement: those who fronted as spokespersons and collected honorariums for themselves; those who left the struggle after the BSU secured their grades; spokespersons motivated by their personal prestige over the plight of the people; "shit slingers" who mainly criticized; and disruptiveness of the Progressive Labor Party.[112] He concluded, saying sarcastically, "But we came to grips with the reality that the struggle of oppressed people was more important than fourteen individuals walking around with the myth of the revolution going on in their minds. Imagine a flea worried about losing face."[113]

The BSU summation reflects demoralization and an emphasis on internal problems. Although there were internal contradictions, they existed within a context. This context included the alliance of conservative forces, popular sanction of police repression, racism in society including chauvinism in the white left, and the youthfulness of the movement, which, among other things, lacked more experience and theoretical grounding to sustain itself in an organized form.

Community Commitment

The lives of Asian student activists were changed in many ways. A common theme, however, voiced by all participants focused on a deep-rooted commitment to social change for the benefit of their communities. Some students stated that the strike may not have drastically altered their life. E. I., for example, felt he "would have wound up here anyway,"[114] working as a housing advocate and social worker. Others, like G. C., reflected upon the strike as a pivotal time in their lives:

> I think it changed my life in terms of providing some focus to the extent that my career wasn't that important to me. . . . Take a look at the decisions people made back then. It was what the community needed first; and what you could contribute emanated from that.[115]

P. N. stated that for her "what it means to be an Asian in American society" shaped her view of legal work:[116]

> I don't think I would have gone to law school if it hadn't been for the strike. . . . The reason why I did go to law school was to get some skills . . . to practice law, and look at law as a vehicle for social change.[117]

Others, including A. S., stated that student activism led them to utilize their skills in channeling resources to their communities "to build low-income housing, parks for the people."[118] A. W. stated that though most of the leadership went into the community, he "chose to stay [to teach] in the university."[119]

Many activists expressed a feeling of personal liberation. Speaking out and taking stands to the point of facing serious consequences instilled a boldness of character. P. N. added that she became "more adventurous, less looking for the safe way to do thing," while at the same time "more cautious" in dealing with the complexities of human nature.[120]

M. W. discussed the political ramifications:

> What it did is, I think, make me more politically conscious . . . when a person in administration, who is supposed to have authority, a title, . . . [you find that those] people use that [power] to put the pressure on you. Then after getting involved with bureaucrats and politicians, [you realize] that they are people like anyone else. I think that is one of the things I learned: not to be intimidated.[121]

Some activists left the campus with the view of reforming society. B. I. remarked, "I saw myself as a reformist working within the system, to try and get those things that would benefit poor people, regardless of whether you are Black, White or

Asian."[122] However, others like P. N. added, "I'd always felt since the strike that what was necessary to eliminate or alleviate racism was a major restructuring of our society, both economically and in eliminating barriers in terms of participation of Third World people in all walks of life."[123]

Conclusion: The Altered Terrain

Asian American students played a significant role in student movements of the sixties, as clearly demonstrated in the San Francisco State strike. The struggle was unique in that it was situated in an urban, multiethnic, liberal, working-class city. Perhaps that more closely tied the campus struggle to the respective national movements, while at the same time making bonds between them. In their challenge to the university, Asian students followed in the legacies of Pilipino farm labor organizers, International Hotel tenants, and concentration camp resisters. Their demand for a relevant and accessible education stemmed from the aspirations of peoples who had fought for justice and equality since their arrival in the United States. And, in many ways, it was this legacy that steeled the movement and today frames a context to understand the long-lasting significance of the strike.

The most obvious accomplishment was the establishment of the first School of Ethnic Studies in the nation. This school partially met the terms outlined in the TWLF demands, including the commitment of over twenty-two faculty positions, the establishment of a black studies department upon which the other ethnic studies departments were based, student participation in the committee to recommend the final plan for the school, and faculty power commensurate with that accorded other college departments. In addition, unused special admission slots were promised to be filled in spring 1969. Campus disciplinary action was recommended to be limited to suspension through fall semester 1969. Demands to retain or fire individual personnel were not met. Though negotiations fell short of meeting the demands in full, the school remains the largest national program in its faculty size and course offerings. The winning of these concessions set a precedent for other universities to follow. In fact, the organization and militancy shown by San Francisco State students led some administrators at other campuses to initiate minor concessions.

A less tangible, but equally significant, outcome of the strike was the emergence of a new generation of fighters who either remained on campus or entered their communities. Many took the concept of self-determination to establish self-help programs to continue political education and promote self-reliance. Many formed or joined organizations to define a collective approach to addressing problems. Some pursued advanced degrees to secure positions of influence within the system, while others concentrated on grassroots organizing to build progressive, community-based movements. Almost without exception, those interviewed affirmed a deep commitment to the basic values and beliefs forged during their days as students active in the strike; many traced their convictions to the period of the strike itself.

The legacy of the strike has also set the terrain for another generation of Asian students. Stemming from the post-1965 immigration, today's students have formed organizations based on the foundations set by an earlier generation. The institutionalization of ethnic studies and affirmative action programs has not only given students important support systems but also led to greater political influence for Asians in higher education.

These gains, however, have been increasingly contested. Then-governor Reagan launched his political career to become president of the United States, marking the rise of the New Right. The US economic decline has resulted in government cuts in education and social programs. Universities increasingly rely on private donations, defense-related contracts, and foundation grants, influencing the priorities of the university. Meanwhile, it is estimated that one-half of all ethnic studies programs have already been eliminated. Of those that remain, much of the emphasis has shifted away from the original intent for social change. Most programs have not enjoyed programmatic autonomy or student/community involvement in decision making, and many have lost relevance to community needs. Support for affirmative action has also waned. Since the landmark *Bakke* decision in 1978, minimum quotas for minority admissions have turned into invisible ceilings for Asians who are perceived as "overrepresented." The attention called to these unfair practices is now being used to question affirmative action for Chicanos, African Americans, and Native Americans. And Asians have been effectively eliminated from virtually all such programs. Tenure cases, particularly for minority faculty, have become battlegrounds over the definition of legitimate and relevant research. In short, the essence of the conflict in the San Francisco State strike remains central today.

The strike offers no blueprint for movements today. Its history, however, begins to reveal the nature of clashes between students and administrators. It reminds us that the existence of ethnic studies and special programs for oppressed groups has only been the result of hard-fought struggle. Students of today's movements can study this history as a benchmark to assess their own conditions. And, with that, democratic empowerment movements may set a new terrain for the next generation.

NOTES

Originally published in *Amerasia Journal* 15 (1): 3–41, 1989. ©1989 *Amerasia Journal*, reprinted by permission

1   R. Q., interview, September 11, 1985, San Francisco.
2   B. I., interview, September 5, 1985, San Francisco.
3   See also Kirkpatrick Sale, *SDS* (New York: Vintage, 1974) and Harry Edwards, *Black Students* (New York: Free Press, 1970).

4   I. C., interview, September 13, 1985, San Francisco.

5   A. S., interview, September 12, 1985, Fremont, CA.

6   J. M., interview, September 11, 1985, San Francisco.

7   B. I., interview, September 5, 1985, San Francisco.

8   E. D. C., interview, September 3, 1985, San Francisco.

9   William Barlow and Peter Shapiro, *An End to Silence: The San Francisco State College Student Movement of the 60s* (New York: Pegasus, 1971), 49.

10 Ibid., 68.

11 Robert Smith, Richard Axen, and DeVere Pentony, *By Any Means Necessary: The Revolutionary Struggle at San Francisco State* (San Francisco: Jossey-Bass, 1970), 39.

12 Ibid., 8.

13 DeVere Pentony, Robert Smith, and Richard Aven, *Unfinished Rebellions* (San Francisco: Jossey-Bass, 1971), 25.

14 Master Plan Survey Team, "A Master Plan for Higher Education in California, 1960–75" (Sacramento: California Department of Education, 1960), 43.

15 Ibid., 73.

16 Ibid., 60.

17 Ibid., 74.

18 Staff Report to the National Commission on the Causes and Prevention of Violence, prepared by William H. Orrick, Jr., "Shut It Down! A College in Crisis; San Francisco State College" (Washington, DC: National Commission on the Causes and Prevention of Violence, 1969), 75. Figures not available for other ethnic groups.

19 E. Hornsby Wasson, "Business and Campus Unrest" (speech delivered January 16, 1969), *Vital Speeches* 35, no. 11 (1969): 335.

20 B. L., interview, September 10, 1985, San Francisco.

21 For a discussion on the influence of Malcolm X on the African American student movement, see Edwards, *Black Students*.

22 Compiled from Barlow and Shapiro, *End to Silence*; Kuregiy Hekymara, "The Third World Movement and Its History in the San Francisco State College Strike of 1968–69" (doctoral diss., University of California, Berkeley, 1972).

23 A. W., interview, September 1985, San Francisco.

24 Ibid.

25 I. C., interview, September 13, 1985, San Francisco.

26 J. C., interview, September 1985, San Francisco.

27 Ibid.

28 M. W., interview, September 13, 1985, San Francisco.

29 See Sun Tzu, *The Art of War*, trans. and introduction by Samuel Griffith (London: Oxford University Press, 1963).

30 M. W., interview, September 13, 1985, San Francisco.

31 *East West*, August 28, 1968, 1, 4.

32 *East West*, September 4, 1968, 12.

33 A. W., interview, September 1985.

34 ICSA position paper, mimeographed, Special Collections Library, San Francisco State University.

35 Ibid.

36 G. W., interview, March 21, 1987, San Francisco.

37 Ibid.

38 Alex Hing, "'On Strike, Shut It Down!' Reminiscences of the S. F. State Strike," *East Wind* 2, no. 2 (Fall/Winter 1983): 42.

39 G. W., interview, March 21, 1987, San Francisco.

40 A. S., interview, September 12, 1985.

41 "Statement of the Philippine-American Collegiate Endeavor (PACE) Philosophy and Goals" (mimeograph).

42 P. S., interviews, May 14, June 6, 1986.

43 "PACE (Philippine-American Collegiate Endeavor) Program, S. F. State" (mimeographed).

44 E. I., interview, September 13, 1985, San Francisco.

45 Ibid.

46 Mimeographed roster of PACE members.

47 P. N., interviews, May 27, 1984, and September 11, 1985.

48 Ibid.

49 "AAPA Is," *Asian American Political Alliance Newspaper* 1 (UC Berkeley, late 1968): 4.

50 "AAPA Perspectives," *Asian American Political Alliance Newspaper* 1, no. 5 (UC Berkeley, fall 1969): 7.

51 P. N., interviews, May 27, 1984, and September 11, 1985.

52 P. Y., interviews, May 1984 and September 9, 1985.

53 M. O., interview, September 14, 1985, San Francisco.

54 Y. W., interview, September 4, 1985, San Francisco.

55 "Statement of the Third World Liberation Front Philosophy and Goals" (undated mimeo).

56 Coordinating Council for Higher Education, "California Higher Education and the Disadvantaged: A Status Report" (Sacramento, March 1968), table v.

57 Cited in Tsung Chi, *East Asian Americans and Political Participation: A Reference Handbook* (Santa Barbara, CA: ABC-CLIO, 2005), 200.

58 I. C., interview, September 13, 1985.

59 R. Q., interview, September 11, 1985.

60 M. W., interview, September 13, 1985.

61 Smith, Axen, and Pentony, *By Any Means Necessary*, 332.

62 "School of Ethnic Area Studies."

63 Pentony, Smith, and Aven, *Unfinished Rebellions*, 51.

64 Smith, Axen, and Pentony, *By Any Means Necessary*, 134.

65 Coordinating Council for Higher Education, "California Higher Education," 53.

66 Barlow and Shapiro, *End to Silence*, 167–170; "After the Strike: A Conference on Ethnic Studies Proceedings" (School of Ethnic Studies, San Francisco State University; Proceedings from the April 12–14, 1984, Conference), 14; Smith, Axen, and Pentony, *By Any Means Necessary*, 58–59.

67 Smith, Axen, and Pentony, *By Any Means Necessary*, 50–51.

68 P. N., interviews, May 27, 1984, and September 11, 1985.

69 *TWLF Newsletter*, n.d.

70 Barlow and Shapiro, *End to Silence*.

71 Smith, Axen, and Pentony, *By Any Means Necessary*, 140–141.

72 The six organizations within the TWLF were the Mexican American Student Confederation (MASC), Intercollegiate Chinese for Social Action (ICSA), Philippine American College Endeavor (PACE), Asian American Political Alliance (AAPA), Latin American Student Organization (LASO), and Black Students Union (BSU).

73 "By the Direction of the Third World Liberation Front" (mimeographed TWLF leaflet, n.d.).

74 Ibid.

75 Nathan Hare, "Two Black Radicals Report on Their Campus Struggles," *Ramparts* 8 (July 1969): 54.

76 P. N., interviews, May 27, 1984, and September 11, 1985.

77 Ibid.

78 Staff report to the National Commission on the Causes and Prevention of Violence, prepared by William H. Orrick, 52.

79 B. I., interview, September 5, 1985.

80 Quoted in Smith, Axen, and Pentony, *By Any Means Necessary*, 29.

81 Ibid., 113.

82 "Campus Violence—Crackdown Coming: Interview with Glenn S. Dumke Leading College Official," *U.S. News & World Report* 65 (September 23, 1968): 49.

83 Mimeographed copy of George Murray's speech (Fresno, CA, n.d.).

84 Ibid.

85 Barlow and Shapiro, *End to Silence*, 213–217.

86 Dikran Karagueuzian, *Blow It Up! The Black Student Revolt at San Francisco State College and the Emergence of Dr. Hayakawa* (Boston: Gambit, 1971), 100–102.

87 Quotes in Smith, Axen, and Pentony, *By Any Means Necessary*, 144–145.

88 Events compiled from Smith, Axen, and Pentony, *By Any Means Necessary*; Barlow and Shapiro, *End to Silence*; Karagueuzian, *Blow It Up!*; and various chronologies.

89 Barlow and Shapiro, *End to Silence*.

90 Smith, Axen, and Pentony, *By Any Means Necessary*, 166.

91 Ibid.

92 M. O., interview, September 14, 1985.

93 Smith, Axen, and Pentony, *By Any Means Necessary*, 187.

94 Ibid., 90.

95 Ibid., 207–208.

96 Barlow and Shapiro, *End to Silence*, 263–264.

97 Ibid., 264.

98 Ibid., 267–269, for a fuller account.

99 Quoted in Smith, Axen, and Pentony, 258–259.

100 Ibid.

101 P. Y., interviews, May 1984 and September 9, 1985.

102 Smith, Axen, and Pentony, *By Any Means Necessary*, 282.

103 Glenn S. Dumke, "Controversy on Campus: Need for Peace and Order" (speech, Town Hall of California, Los Angeles, February 18, 1969), *Vital Speeches* 35, no. 11 (March 15, 1969): 332–335.

104 P. Y., interview, May 1984 and September 9, 1985.

105 Ibid.

106 S. I. Hayakawa, "Gangsters in Our Midst," in *Crisis at SF State*, ed. Howard Finberg (San Francisco: Insight, 1969), 11.

107 "Statement by President S. I. Hayakawa, of San Francisco State College: Order on Campuses," *Congressional Record* 115 (February 3, 1969): 2462.

108 B. L., interview, September 10, 1985.

109 Smith, Axen, and Pentony, *By Any Means Necessary*, 229.

110 Ibid., 311.

111 Ibid.

112 *Black Fire* (San Francisco), May 1969.

113 Ibid.

114 E. I., interview, September 13, 1985, San Francisco.

115 G. C., interview, September 1985, San Francisco.

116 P. N., interviews, May 27, 1984, and September 11, 1985, San Francisco.

117 Ibid.

118 A. S., interview, September 12, 1985.

119 A. W., interview, September 1985, San Francisco.

120 P. N., interviews, May 27, 1984, and September 11, 1985, San Francisco.

121 M. W., interview, September 13, 1985, San Francisco.

122 B. I., interview, September 5, 1985, San Francisco.

123 P. N., interviews, May 27, 1984, and September 11, 1985, San Francisco.

2

The "Four Prisons" and the Movements of Liberation

Asian American Activism from the 1960s to the 1990s

GLENN OMATSU

According to Ali Shariati, an Iranian philosopher, each of us exists within four prisons.[1] First is the prison imposed on us by history and geography; from this confinement, we can escape only by gaining a knowledge of science and technology. Second is the prison of history; our freedom comes when we understand how historical forces operate. The third prison is our society's social and class structure; from this prison, only a revolutionary ideology can provide the way to liberation. The final prison is the self. Each of us is composed of good and evil elements, and we must each choose between them.

The analysis of our four prisons provides a way of understanding the movements that swept across America in the 1960s and molded the consciousness of one generation of Asian Americans. The movements were struggles for liberation from many prisons. They were struggles that confronted the historical forces of racism, poverty, war, and exploitation. They were struggles that generated new ideologies, based mainly on the teachings and actions of Third World leaders. And they were struggles that redefined human values—the values that shape how people live their daily lives and interact with each other. Above all, they were struggles that transformed the lives of "ordinary" people as they confronted the prisons around them.

For Asian Americans, these struggles profoundly changed our communities. They spawned numerous grassroots organizations. They created an extensive network of student organizations and Asian American studies classes. They recovered buried cultural traditions as well as produced a new generation of writers, poets, and artists. But most importantly, the struggles deeply affected Asian American consciousness. They redefined racial and ethnic identity, promoted new ways of thinking about communities, and challenged prevailing notions of power and authority.

Yet, in the two decades that have followed, scholars have reinterpreted the movements in narrower ways. I learned about this reinterpretation when I attended a class recently in Asian American studies at UCLA. The professor described the period from the late 1950s to the early 1970s as a single epoch involving the persistent efforts of racial minorities and their white supporters to secure civil rights. Young Asian Americans, the professor stated, were swept into this campaign and by later antiwar protests to assert their own racial identity. The most important influence on Asian Americans during this period was Dr. Martin Luther King, Jr., who inspired them to demand access to policymakers and initiate advocacy programs for their own communities. Meanwhile, students and professors fought to legitimize Asian American studies in college curricula and for representation of Asians in American society. The lecture was cogent, tightly organized, and well received by the audience of students—many of them new immigrants or the children of new immigrants. There was only one problem: the reinterpretation was wrong on every aspect.

Those who took part in the mass struggles of the 1960s and early 1970s will know that the birth of the Asian American movement coincided not with the initial campaign for civil rights but with the later demand for black liberation; that the leading influence was not Martin Luther King, Jr. but Malcolm X; that the focus of a generation of Asian American activists was not on asserting racial pride but reclaiming a tradition of militant struggle by earlier generations; that the movement was not centered on the aura of racial identity but embraced fundamental questions of oppression and power; that the movement consisted of not only college students but large numbers of community forces, including the elderly, workers, and high school youth; and that the main thrust was not one of seeking legitimacy and representation within American society but the larger goal of liberation.

It may be difficult for a new generation—raised on the Asian American code words of the 1980s stressing "advocacy," "access," "legitimacy," "empowerment," and "assertiveness"—to understand the urgency of Malcolm X's demand for freedom "by any means necessary," Mao's challenge to "serve the people," the slogans of "power to the people" and "self-determination," the principles of "mass line" organizing and "united front" work, or the conviction that people—not elites—make history. But these ideas galvanized thousands of Asian Americans and reshaped our communities. And it is these concepts that we must grasp to understand the scope and intensity of our movement and what it created.

But are these concepts relevant to Asian Americans today? In our community—where new immigrants and refugees constitute the majority of Asian Americans—can we find a legacy from the struggles of two decades ago? Are the ideas of the movement alive today, or have they atrophied into relics— the curiosities of a bygone era of youthful and excessive idealism?

By asking these questions, we, as Asian Americans, participate in a larger national debate: the reevaluation of the impact of the 1960s on American society today. This debate is occurring all around us: in sharp exchanges over "family values" and the status of women and gays in American society; in clashes in schools over curricular reform and multiculturalism; in differences among policymakers over the urban crisis and approaches to rebuilding Los Angeles and other inner cities after the 1992 uprisings; and in continuing reexaminations of US involvement in Indochina more than two decades ago and the relevance of that war to US military intervention in Iraq, Somalia, and Bosnia.

What happened in the 1960s that made such an impact on America? Why do discussions about that decade provoke so much emotion today? And do the movements of the 1960s serve as the same controversial reference point for Asian Americans?

The United States during the 1960s

In recent years, the movements of the 1960s have come under intense attack. One national bestseller, Allan Bloom's *Closing of the American Mind*, criticizes the movements for undermining the bedrock of Western thought.[2] According to Bloom, nothing positive resulted from the mass upheavals of the 1960s. He singles out black studies and affirmative action programs and calls for eliminating them from universities.

Activists who have continued political work provide contrasting assessments. Their books include Todd Gitlin's *The Sixties: Years of Hope, Days of Rage*; James Miller's *"Democracy Is in the Streets": From Port Huron to the Siege of Chicago*; Ronald Fraser's *1968: A Student Generation in Revolt*; Tom Hayden's *Reunion: A Memoir*; Tariq Ali's *Street Fighting Years*; George Katsiaficas's *The Imagination of the New Left: A Global Analysis of 1968*; and special issues of various journals, including *Witness*, *Socialist Review*, and *Radical America*.

However, as Winifred Breines states in an interesting review essay titled "Whose New Left?," most of the retrospects have been written by white male activists from elite backgrounds and reproduce their relationship to these movements.[3] Their accounts tend to divide the period into two phases: the "good" phase of the early 1960s, characterized by participatory democracy, followed by the post-1968 phase, when movement politics "degenerated" into violence and sectarianism.

"Almost all books about the New Left note a turning point or an ending in 1968 when the leadership of the movement turned toward militancy and violence and SDS [Students for a Democratic Society] as an organization was collapsing," Breines observes. The retrospects commonly identify the key weaknesses of the movements as the absence of effective organization, the lack of discipline, and utopian thinking. Breines disagrees with these interpretations:

> The movement was not simply unruly and undisciplined; it was experimenting with antihierarchical organizational forms. ... There were many centers of action in the movement, many actions, many interpretations, many visions, many experiences. There was no [organizational] unity because each group, region, campus,

commune, collective, and demonstration developed differently, but all shared in a spontaneous opposition to racism and inequality, the war in Vietnam, and the repressiveness of American social norms and culture, including centralization and hierarchy.[4]

Breines believes that the most important contributions of activists were their moral urgency, their emphasis on direct action, their focus on community building, and their commitment to mass democracy.

Similarly, Sheila Collins in *The Rainbow Challenge*, a book focusing on the Jesse Jackson presidential campaign of 1984 and the formation of the National Rainbow Coalition, assesses the movements of the sixties very positively.[5] She contends that the Jackson campaign was built on the grassroots organizing experience of activists who emerged from the struggles for civil rights, women's liberation, peace and social justice, and community building during the sixties. Moreover, activists' participation in these movements shaped their vision of America, which, in turn, became the basis for the platform of the Rainbow Coalition twenty years later.

According to Collins, the movements that occurred in the United States in the sixties were also part of a worldwide trend, a trend Latin American theologians call the era of the "eruption of the poor" into history. In America, the revolt of the "politically submerged" and "economically marginalized" posed a major ideological challenge to ruling elites:

> The civil rights and black power movement exploded several dominant assumptions about the nature of American society, thus challenging the cultural hegemony of the white ruling elite and causing everyone else in the society to redefine their relationship to centers of power, creating a groundswell of support for radical democratic participation in every aspect of institutional life.[6]

Collins contends that the mass movements created a "crisis of legitimation" for ruling circles. This crisis, she believes, was "far more serious than most historians—even those of the left—have credited it with being."

Ronald Fraser also emphasizes the ideological challenge raised by the movements due to their mass, democratic character and their "disrespect for arbitrary and exploitative authority." In *1968: A Student Generation in Revolt*, Fraser explains how these concepts influenced one generation of activists:

> [T]he anti-authoritarianism challenged almost every shibboleth of Western society. Parliamentary democracy, the authority of presidents . . . and [the policies of] governments to further racism, conduct imperialist wars or oppress sectors of the population at home, the rule of capital and the fiats of factory bosses, the

dictates of university administrators, the sacredness of the family, sexuality, bourgeois culture—nothing was in principle sacrosanct. ... Overall ... [there was]
a lack of deference towards institutions and values that demean[ed] people and a
concomitant awareness of people's rights.[7]

The San Francisco State Strike's Legacy

The retrospects about the 1960s produced so far have ignored Asian Americans.
Yet, the books cited above—plus the review essay by Breines—provide us with
some interesting points to compare and contrast. For example, 1968 represented
a turning point for Asian Americans and other sectors of American society. But
while white male leaders saw the year as marking the decline of the movement,
1968 for Asian Americans was a year of birth. It marked the beginning of the San
Francisco State strike and all that followed.

The strike, the longest student strike in US history, was the first campus uprising involving Asian Americans as a collective force.[8] Under the Third World Liberation Front—a coalition of African American, Latino, American Indian, and
Asian American campus groups—students "seized the time" to demand ethnic
studies, open admissions, and a redefinition of the education system. Although
their five-month strike was brutally repressed and resulted in only partial victories, students won the nation's first School of Ethnic Studies.

Yet, we cannot measure the legacy of the strike for Asian Americans only in
the tangible items it achieved, such as new classes and new faculty; the strike
also critically transformed the consciousness of its participants who, in turn,
profoundly altered their communities' political landscape. Through their participation, a generation of Asian American student activists reclaimed a heritage of
struggle—linking their lives to the tradition of militancy of earlier generations of
Pilipino farmworkers, Chinese immigrant garment and restaurant workers, and
Japanese American concentration camp resisters. Moreover, these Asian American students—and their community supporters—liberated themselves from the
prisons surrounding their lives and forged a new vision for their communities,
creating numerous grassroots projects and empowering previously ignored and
disenfranchised sectors of society. The statement of goals and principles of one
campus organization, Philippine-American Collegiate Endeavor (PACE), during
the strike captures this new vision:

> We seek ... simply to function as human beings, to control our own lives. Initially,
> following the myth of the American Dream, we worked to attend predominantly
> white colleges, but we have learned through direct analysis that it is impossible for
> our people, so-called minorities, to function as human beings, in a racist society
> in which white always comes first. ... So we have decided to fuse ourselves with
> the masses of Third World people, which are the majority of the world's peoples,

to create, through struggle, a new humanity, a new humanism, a New World Consciousness, and within that context collectively control our own destinies.[9]

The San Francisco State strike is important not only as a beginning point for the Asian American movement but also because it crystallizes several themes that would characterize Asian American struggles in the following decade. First, the strike occurred at a working-class campus and involved a coalition of Third World students linked to their communities. Second, students rooted their strike in the tradition of resistance by past generations of minority peoples in America. Third, strike leaders drew inspiration—as well as new ideology—from international Third World leaders and revolutions occurring in Asia, Africa, Latin America, and the Middle East. Fourth, the strike in its demands for open admissions, community control of education, ethnic studies, and self-determination confronted basic questions of power and oppression in America. Finally, strike participants raised their demands through a strategy of mass mobilizations and militant, direct action.

In the decade following the strike, several themes would reverberate in the struggles in Asian American communities across the nation. These included housing and anti-eviction campaigns, efforts to defend education rights, union organizing drives, campaigns for jobs and social services, and demands for democratic rights, equality, and justice. Mo Nishida, an organizer in Los Angeles, recalls the broad scope of movement activities in his city:

> Our movement flowered. At one time, we had active student organizations on every campus around Los Angeles, fought for ethnic studies, equal opportunity programs, high potential programs at UCLA, and for students doing community work in "Serve the People" programs. In the community, we had, besides [Asian American] Hard Core, four area youth-oriented groups working against drugs (on the Westside, Eastside, Gardena, and the Virgil district). There were also parents' groups, which worked with parents of the youth and more.[10]

In Asian American communities in Los Angeles, San Francisco, Sacramento, Stockton, San Jose, Seattle, New York, and Honolulu, activists created "serve the people" organizations—mass networks built on the principles of "mass line" organizing. Youth initiated many of these organizations—some from college campuses and others from high schools and the streets—but other members of the community, including small-business people, workers, senior citizens, and new immigrants, soon joined.

The *mass* character of community struggles is the least appreciated aspect of our movement today. It is commonly believed that the movement involved only college students. In fact, a range of people, including high school youth, tenants, small-business people, former prison inmates, former addicts, the elderly, and workers, embraced the struggles. But exactly who were these people, and what did their participation mean to the movement?

Historian George Lipsitz has studied similar, largely "anonymous" participants in civil rights campaigns in African American communities. He describes one such man, Ivory Perry of St. Louis:

> Ivory Perry led no important organizations, delivered no important speeches, and received no significant recognition or reward for his social activism. But for more than 30 years he had passed out leaflets, carried the picket signs, and planned the flamboyant confrontations that made the civil rights movements effective in St. Louis and across the nation. His continuous commitment at the local level had goaded others into action, kept alive hopes of eventual victory in the face of short-term defeats, and provided a relatively powerless community with an effective lever for social change. The anonymity of his activism suggests layers of social protest activity missing from most scholarly accounts, while the persistence of his involvement undermines prevailing academic judgments about mass protests as outbursts of immediate anger and spasmodic manifestations of hysteria.[11]

Those active in Asian American communities during the late 1960s and early 1970s know there were many Ivory Perrys. They were the people who demonstrated at eviction sites, packed City Hall hearing rooms, volunteered to staff health fairs, and helped with day-to-day operations of the first community drop-in centers, legal defense offices, and senior citizen projects. They were the women and men who took the concept of "serve the people" and turned it into a material force, transforming the political face of our communities.

The "Cultural Revolution" in Asian American Communities

But we would be wrong to describe this transformation of our communities as solely "political"—at least as our society narrowly defines the term today. The transformation also involved a cultural vitality that opened new ways of viewing the world. Unlike today—where Asian American communities categorize "culture" and "politics" into different spheres of professional activity—in the late 1960s they did not divide them so rigidly or hierarchically. Writers, artists, and musicians were "cultural workers" usually closely associated with communities, and saw their work as "serving the people." Like other community activists, cultural workers defined the period as a "decisive moment" for Asian Americans—a time for reclaiming the past and changing the future.

The "decisive moment" was also a time for questioning and transforming moral values. Through their political and cultural work, activists challenged systems of rank and privilege, structures of hierarchy and bureaucracy, forms of exploitation and inequality, and notions of selfishness and individualism. Through their activism in mass organizations, they promoted a new moral vision centered on democratic participation, cooperative work styles, and collective decision making. Pioneer poet Russell C. Leong describes the affinity between this new generation of cultural workers and their communities, focusing on the work of the Asian American Writers' Workshop, located in the basement of the International Hotel in San Francisco Chinatown/Manilatown:

> We were a post–World War II generation mostly in our twenties and thirties; in or out of local schools and colleges. . . . [We] gravitated toward cities—San Francisco, Los Angeles, New York—where movements for ethnic studies and inner city blocks of Asian communities coincided. . . . We read as we wrote—not in isolation—but in the company of our neighbors in Manilatown pool halls, barrio parks, Chinatown basements. . . . Above all, we poets were a tribe of storytellers. . . . Storytellers live in communities where they write for family and friends. The relationship between the teller and listener is neighborly, because the teller of stories must also listen.[12]

But as storytellers, cultural workers did more than simply describe events around them. By witnessing and participating in the movement, they helped to shape community consciousness. San Francisco poet Al Robles focuses on this process of vision making:

> While living and working in our little, tiny communities, in the midst of towering high-rises, we fought the oppressor, the landlord, the developer, the banks, City Hall. But most of all, we celebrated through our culture; music, dance, song and poetry—not only the best we knew but the best we had. The poets were and always have been an integral part of the community. It was through poetry—through a poetical vision to live out the ritual in dignity as human beings.[13]

The transformation of poets, writers, and artists into cultural workers and vision makers reflected larger changes occurring in every sector of the Asian American community. In education, teachers and students redefined the learning process, discovering new ways of sharing knowledge different from traditional, authoritarian, top-down approaches. In the social service sector, social workers and other professionals became "community workers" and under the slogan of "serve the people" redefined the traditional counselor/client relationship by stressing interaction, dialogue, and community building. Within community organizations, members experimented with new organizational structures and collective leadership styles, discarding hierarchical and bureaucratic forms where a handful of commanders made all the decisions. Everywhere, activists and ordinary people grappled with change.

Overall, this "cultural revolution" in the Asian American community echoes themes we have encountered earlier: Third World consciousness, participatory democracy, community building, historical rooting, liberation, and transformation. Why were these concepts so important to a generation of activists? What did they mean? And do they still have relevance for Asian American communities today?

Political analyst Raymond Williams and historian Warren Susman have suggested the use of "keywords" to study historical periods, especially times of great social change.[14] Keywords are terms, concepts, and ideas that emerge as themes of a period, reflecting vital concerns and changing values. For Asian Americans in the 1980s and 1990s, the keywords are "advocacy," "access," "legitimacy," "empowerment," and "assertiveness." These keywords tell us much about the shape of our community today, especially the growing role of young professionals and their aspirations in US society. In contrast, the keywords of the late 1960s and early 1970s—"consciousness," "theory," "ideology," "participatory democracy," "community," and "liberation"—point to different concerns and values.

The keywords of two decades ago point to an approach to political work that activists widely shared, especially those working in grassroots struggles in Asian American neighborhoods, such as the Chinatowns, Little Tokyos, Manilatowns, and International Districts around the nation. This political approach focused on the relationship between political consciousness and social change and can be best summarized in a popular slogan of the period: "Theory becomes a material force when it is grasped by the masses." Asian American activists believed that they could promote political change through direct action and mass education that raised political consciousness in the community, especially among the unorganized—low-income workers, tenants, small-business people, high school youth, and so on. Thus, activists saw political consciousness as rising not from study groups but from involving people in the process of social change—through their confronting the institutions of power around them and creating new visions of community life based on these struggles.

Generally, academics studying the movements of the 1960s—including academics in Asian American studies—have dismissed the political theory of that time as murky and eclectic, characterized by ultra-leftism, shallow class analysis, and simplistic notions of Marxism and capitalism.[15] To a large extent, the thinking was eclectic; Asian American activists drew from Marx, Lenin, Stalin, and Mao—and also from Frantz Fanon, Malcolm X, Che Guevara, Kim Il-sung, and Amílcar Cabral, as well as Korean revolutionary Kim San, W. E. B. Du Bois, Frederick Douglass, Paulo Freire, the Black Panther Party, the Young Lords, the women's liberation movement, and many other resistance struggles. But in their obsessive search for theoretical clarity and consistency, these academics miss the bigger picture. What is significant is not the *content* of ideas activists adopted but what activists *did* with the ideas. What Asian American activists *did* was to use the ideas drawn from many different movements to redefine the Asian American experience.

Central to this redefinition was a slogan that appeared at nearly every Asian American rally during that period: "The people, and the people alone, are the motive force in the making of world history." Asian American activists adapted a slogan originating in the Chinese revolution to the tasks of community building, historical rooting, and creating new values. Thus, the slogan came to capture six new ways of thinking about Asian Americans.

- Asian Americans became active participants in the making of history, reversing standard accounts that had treated Asian Americans as marginal objects.
- Activists saw history as created by large numbers of people acting together, not by elites.
- This view of history provided a new way of looking at our communities. Activists believed that ordinary people could make their own history by learning how historical forces operated and by transforming this knowledge into a material force to change their lives.
- This realization defined a political strategy: political power came from grassroots organizing, from the bottom up.
- This strategy required activists to develop a broad analysis of the Asian American condition—to uncover the interconnections in seemingly separate events, such as the war in Indochina, corporate redevelopment of Asian American communities, and the exploitation of Asian immigrants in garment shops. In their political analyses, activists linked the day-to-day struggles of Asian Americans to larger events and issues. The anti-eviction campaign of tenants in Chinatown and the International District against powerful corporations became one with the resistance movements of peasants in Vietnam, the Philippines, and Latin America—or, as summarized in a popular slogan of the period, there was "one struggle, [but] many fronts."
- This new understanding challenged activists to build mass, democratic organizations, especially within unorganized sectors of the community. Through these new organizations, Asian Americans expanded democracy for all sectors of the community and gained the power to participate in the broader movement for political change taking place throughout the world.

The redefinition of the Asian American experience stands as the most important legacy from this period. As described above, this legacy represents far more than an ethnic awakening. The redefinition began with an analysis of power and domination in American society. It provided a way for understanding the historical forces surrounding us. And, most importantly, it presented a strategy and challenge for changing our future. This challenge, I believe, still confronts us today.

The Late 1970s: Reversing Direction

As we continue to delve into the vitality of the movements of the 1960s, one question becomes more and more persistent: Why did these movements, possessing so much vigor and urgency, seem to disintegrate in the late 1970s and early 1980s? Why did a society in motion toward progressive change seem to suddenly reverse direction?

As in the larger left movement, Asian American activists heatedly debate this question.[16] Some mention the strategy of repression—including assassinations—US ruling circles launched in response to the mass rebellions. Others cite the accompanying programs of cooptation that elites designed to channel mass discontent into traditional political arenas. Some focus on the New Right's rise, culminating in the Reagan presidency. Still others emphasize the sectarianism among political forces within the movement or target the inability of the movement as a whole to base itself more broadly within communities.

Each of these analyses provides a partial answer. But missing in most analyses by Asian American activists is the most critical factor: the devastating corporate offensive of the mid-1970s. We will remember the 1970s as a time of economic crisis and staggering inflation. Eventually, historians may more accurately describe it as the years of "one-sided class war." Transnational corporations based in the United States launched a broad attack on the American people, especially African American communities. Several books provide an excellent analysis of the corporate offensive. One of the best, most accessible accounts is *What's Wrong with the U.S. Economy?*, written in 1982 by the Institute for Labor Education and Research.[17] My analysis draws from that.

Corporate executives based their offensive on two conclusions: First, the economic crisis in the early 1970s—marked by declining corporate profits—occurred because American working people were earning too much; and second, the mass struggles of the previous decades had created "too much democracy" in America. The Trilateral Commission—headed by David Rockefeller and composed of corporate executives and politicians from the United States, Europe, and Japan—posed the problem starkly: Either people would have to accept less, or corporations would have to accept less. An article in *Business Week* identified the solution: "Some people will obviously have to do with less. ... Yet it will be a hard pill for many Americans to swallow—the idea of doing with less so that big business can have more."

But in order for corporations to "have more," US ruling circles had to deal with the widespread discontent that had erupted throughout America. We sometimes forget today that in the mid-1970s a large number of Americans had grown cynical about US business and political leaders. People routinely called politicians—including President Nixon and Vice President Agnew—crooks, liars, and criminals. Increasingly, they began to blame the largest corporations for their economic problems. One poll showed that half the population believed that "big business is the source of most of what's wrong in this country today." A series of Harris polls found that those expressing "a great deal of confidence" in the heads of corporations had fallen from 55 percent in 1966 to only 15 percent in 1975. By the fall of 1975, public opinion analysts testifying before a congressional committee reported, according to the *New York Times*, "that public confidence in the government and in the country's economic future is probably lower than it has ever been since they began to measure such things scientifically." These developments stunned many corporate leaders. "How did we let the educational system fail the free enterprise system?" one executive asked.

US ruling elites realized that restoring faith in free enterprise could be achieved only through an intensive ideological assault on those challenging the system. The ideological campaign was combined with a political offensive, aimed at the broad gains in democratic rights that Americans, especially African Americans, had achieved through the mass struggles of previous decades. According to corporate leaders, there was "too much democracy" in America, which meant too little "governability." In a 1975 Trilateral Commission report, Harvard political scientist Samuel Huntington analyzed the problem caused by "previously passive or unorganized groups in the population [which were] now engaged in concerted efforts to establish their claims to opportunities, positions, rewards, and privileges which they had not considered themselves entitled to before." According to Huntington, this upsurge in "democratic fervor" coincided with "markedly higher levels of self-consciousness on the part of blacks, Indians, Chicanos, white ethnic groups, students, and women, all of whom became mobilized and organized in new ways." Huntington saw these developments as creating a crisis for those in power:

> The essence of the democratic surge of the 1960s was a general challenge to existing systems of authority, public and private. In one form or another, the challenge manifested itself in the family, the university, business, public and private associations, politics, the government bureaucracy, and the military service. People no longer felt the same obligation to obey those whom they had previously considered superior to themselves in age, rank, status, expertise, character, or talents.[18]

The mass pressures, Huntington contended, had "produced problems for the governability of democracy in the 1970s." The government, he concluded, must find a way to exercise more control. And that meant curtailing the rights of "major economic groups."

The ensuing corporate campaign was a "one-sided class war": plant closures in US industries and transfer of production overseas, massive layoffs in remaining industries, shifts of capital investment from one region of the country to other regions and other parts of the globe, and demands by corporations for concessions in wages and benefits from workers in nearly every sector of the economy.

The Reagan presidency culminated and institutionalized this offensive. The Reagan platform called for restoring "traditional" American values, especially faith in the system of free enterprise. Reaganomics promoted economic recovery by getting government "off the backs" of businesspeople, reducing taxation of the rich, and cutting social programs for the poor. Meanwhile, racism and exploitation became respectable under the new mantle of patriotism and economic recovery.

The Winter of Civil Rights

The corporate assault ravaged many American neighborhoods, but African American communities absorbed its harshest impact. A study by the Center on Budget and Policy Priorities measures the national impact:

- Between 1970 and 1980, the number of poor African Americans rose by 24 percent, from 1.4 million to 1.8 million.
- In the 1980s, the overall African American median income was 57 percent that of whites, a decline of nearly 4 percentage points from the early 1970s.
- In 1986, females headed 42 percent of all African American families, the majority of which lived below the poverty line.
- In 1978, 8.4 percent of African American families had incomes under $5,000 a year. By 1987, that figure had grown to 13.5 percent. In that year, a third of all African Americans were poor.[19]
- By 1990, nearly half of all African American children grew up in poverty.[20]

Manning Marable provides a stark assessment of this devastation in *How Capitalism Underdeveloped Black America*:

> What is qualitatively *new* about the current period is that the racist/capitalist state under Reagan has proceeded down a public policy road which could inevitably involve the complete obliteration of the entire Black reserve army of labor and sections of the Black working class. The decision to save capitalism at all costs, to provide adequate capital for restructuring of the private sector, fundamentally conflicts with the survival of millions of people who are now permanently outside the workplace. Reaganomics must, if it intends to succeed, place the onerous burden of unemployment on the shoulders of the poor (Blacks, Latinos and even whites) so securely that middle to upper income Americans will not protest in the vicious suppression of this stratum.[21]

The corporate offensive, combined with widespread government repression, brutally destroyed grassroots groups in the African American community. This war against the poor ripped apart the social fabric of neighborhoods across America, leaving them vulnerable to drugs and gang violence. The inner cities became the home of the "underclass" and a new politics of inner-directed violence and despair.

Historian Vincent Harding, in *The Other American Revolution*, summarizes the 1970s as the "winter" of civil rights, a period in which there was "a dangerous loss of hope among black people, hope in ourselves, hope in the possibility of any real change, hope in any moral, creative force beyond the flatness of our lives."[22]

In summary, the corporate offensive—especially its devastation of the African American community—provides the necessary backdrop for understanding why the mass movements of the 1960s seemed to disintegrate. Liberation movements, especially in the African American community, did not disappear, but a major focus of their activity shifted to issues of day-to-day survival.

The 1980s: An Ambiguous Period for Asian American Empowerment

For African Americans and many other people of color, the period from the mid-1970s through the Reagan and Bush presidencies became a winter of civil rights, a time of corporate assault on their livelihoods and an erosion of hard-won rights. But for Asian Americans, the meaning of this period is much more ambiguous. On the one hand, great suffering marked the period: growing poverty for increasing numbers of Asian Americans—especially refugees from Southeast Asia; a rising trend of racist hate crimes directed toward Asian Americans of all ethnicities and income levels; and sharpening class polarization within our communities—with a widening gap between the very rich and the very poor. But advances also characterized the period. With the reform of US immigration laws in 1965, the Asian American population grew dramatically, creating new enclaves—including suburban settlements—and revitalizing more established communities, such as Chinatowns, around the nation. Some recent immigrant businesspeople, with small capital holdings, found economic opportunities in inner-city neighborhoods. Meanwhile, Asian American youth enrolled in record numbers in colleges and universities across the United States. Asian American families moved into suburbs, crashing previously lily-white neighborhoods. And a small but significant group of Asian American politicians, such as Mike Woo and Warren Furutani, scored important electoral victories in the mainstream political arena, taking the concept of political empowerment to a new level of achievement.

During the winter of civil rights, Asian American activists also launched several impressive political campaigns at the grassroots level. Japanese Americans joined together to win redress and reparations. Pilipino Americans rallied in solidarity with the "People's Power" movement in the Philippines to topple the powerful Marcos dictatorship. Chinese Americans created new political alignments and mobilized community support for the prodemocracy struggle in

China. Korean Americans responded to the massacre of civilians by the South Korean dictatorship in Kwangju with massive demonstrations and relief efforts and established an important network of organizations in America, including Young Koreans United. Samoan Americans rose up against police abuse in Los Angeles; Pacific Islanders demanded removal of nuclear weapons and wastes from their homelands; and Hawaiians fought for the right of self-determination and recovery of their lands. And large numbers of Asian Americans and Pacific Islanders worked actively in the 1984 and 1988 presidential campaigns of Jesse Jackson, helping to build the Rainbow Coalition.

Significantly, these accomplishments occurred in the midst of the Reagan presidency and US politics' turn to the right. How did certain sectors of the Asian American community achieve these gains amid conservatism?

There is no simple answer. Mainstream analysts and some Asian Americans have stressed the "model minority" concept. According to this analysis, Asian Americans—in contrast to other people of color in America—have survived adversity and advanced because of their emphasis on education and family values, their community cohesion, and other aspects of their cultural heritage. Other scholars have severely criticized this viewpoint, stressing instead structural changes in the global economy and shifts in US government policy since the 1960s. According to their analysis, the reform of US immigration laws and sweeping economic changes in advanced capitalist nations, such as deindustrialization and the development of new technologies, brought an influx of highly educated new Asian immigrants to America. The characteristics of these new immigrants stand in sharp contrast to those of past generations and provide a broader social and economic base for developing our communities. Still other political thinkers have emphasized the key role played by political expatriates—both right-wing and left-wing—in various communities, but most especially in the Vietnamese, Pilipino, and Korean communities. These expatriates brought political resources from their homelands—e.g., political networks, organizing experience, and, in a few cases, access to large amounts of funds—and have used these resources to change the political landscape of ethnic enclaves. Still other analysts have examined the growing economic and political power of nations of the Asia Pacific and its impact on Asians in America. According to these analysts, we can link the advances of Asian Americans during this period to the rising influence of their former homelands and the dawning of what some call "the Pacific Century." Finally, some academics have focused on the significance of small-business activities of new Asian immigrants, arguing that this sector is most responsible for the changing status of Asian Americans in the 1980s. According to their analysis, Asian immigrant entrepreneurs secured an economic niche in inner-city neighborhoods because they had access to start-up capital (through rotating credit associations or from family members) and they filled a vacuum created when white businesses fled.[23]

Thus, we have multiple interpretations for why some sectors of the Asian American community advanced economically and politically during the winter of civil rights. But two critical factors are missing from the analyses that can help us better understand the peculiar shape of our community in the 1980s and its ambiguous character when compared to other communities of color. First is the legacy of grassroots organizing from the Asian American movement, and second is the dramatic rise of young professionals as a significant force in the community.

A stereotype about the movements of the 1960s is that they produced nothing enduring—they flared brightly for an instant and then quickly died. However, evidence from the Asian American movement contradicts this commonly held belief. Through meticulous organizing campaigns, Asian American activists created an extensive network of grassroots formations. Unlike similar groups in African American communities—which government repression targeted and brutally destroyed—a significant number of Asian American groups survived the 1980s. Thus far, no researcher has analyzed the impact of the corporate offensive and government repression on grassroots organizations in different communities of color during the late 1970s. When this research is done, I think it will show that US ruling elites viewed the movement in the African American community as a major threat due to its power and influence over other communities. In contrast, the movement in the Asian American community received much less attention due to its much smaller size and influence. As a result, Asian American grassroots formations during the 1970s escaped decimation and gained the time and space to survive, grow, and adapt to changing politics.

The survival of grassroots organizations is significant because it helped to cushion the impact of the war against the poor in Asian American communities. More important, the grassroots formations provided the foundation for many of the successful empowerment campaigns occurring in the 1980s. For example, Japanese Americans built their national effort to win reparations for their internment during World War II on the experiences of grassroots neighborhood organizations' housing and anti-eviction struggles of the early 1970s. Movement activists learned from their confrontations with systems of power and applied these lessons to the more difficult political fights of the 1980s. Thus, a direct link exists between the mass struggles of activists in the late 1960s and the "empowerment" approach of Asian Americans in the 1980s and 1990s.

But while similarities exist in political organizing of the late 1960s and the 1980s, there is one crucial difference: Who is being empowered? In the late 1960s and 1970s, activists focused on bringing "power to the people"—the most disenfranchised of the community, such as low-income workers, youth, former prisoners and addicts, senior citizens, tenants, and small-business people. In contrast, the "empowerment" of young professionals in Asian American communities marks the decade of the 1980s. The professionals—children of the civil rights struggles of the 1950s and 1960s—directly benefited from the campaigns for desegregation, especially in the suburbs; the removal of quotas in colleges and professional schools; and the expansion of job opportunities for middle-class people of color in fields such as law, medicine, and education.

During the 1980s, young professionals altered the political terrain in our communities.[24] They created countless new groups in nearly every profession: law, medicine, social work, psychology, education, journalism, business, and arts and culture. They initiated new political advocacy groups, leadership training projects, and various national coalitions and consortiums. They organized political caucuses in the Democratic and Republican parties. And they joined the governing boards of many community agencies. Thus, young professionals—through their sheer numbers, their penchant for self-organization, and their high level of activity—defined the Asian American community of the 1980s, shaping it in ways very different from other communities of color.

The emergence of young professionals as community leaders also aided mass political mobilizations. By combining with grassroots forces from the Asian American movement, young professionals advanced struggles against racism and discrimination. In fact, many of the successful Asian American battles of the past decade resulted from this strategic alignment.

The growing power of young professionals has also brought a diversification of political viewpoints to our communities. While many professionals embrace concerns originally raised by movement activists, a surprisingly large number have moved toward neoconservatism. The emergence of neoconservatism in our community is a fascinating phenomenon, one we should analyze and appreciate. Perhaps more than any other phenomenon, it helps to explain the political ambiguity of Asian American empowerment in the decade of the 1980s.

Strange and New Political Animals: Asian American Neoconservatives

Item: At many universities in recent years, some of the harshest opponents of affirmative action have been Chinese Americans and Korean Americans who define themselves as political conservatives. This, in and of itself, is not new or significant. We have always had Asian American conservatives who have spoken out against affirmative action. But what is new is their affiliation. Many participate actively in Asian American student organizations traditionally associated with campus activism.

Item: In the San Francisco newspaper *Asian Week*, one of the most interesting columnists is Arthur Hu, who writes about anti-Asian quotas in universities, political empowerment, and other issues relating to our communities. He also regularly chastises those he terms "liberals, progressives, Marxists, and activists." In a recent column, he wrote, "The left today has the nerve to blame AIDS, drugs, the dissolution of the family, welfare dependency, gang violence, and educational failure on Ronald Reagan's conservatism." Hu, in turn, criticizes the left for "tearing down religion, family, structure, and authority; promoting drugs, promiscuity, and abdication of personal responsibility."[25]

Item: During the militant, three-year campaign to win tenure for UCLA Professor Don Nakanishi, one of the key student leaders was a Japanese American Republican, Matthew J. Endo. Aside from joining the campus-community steering committee, he also mobilized support from fraternities, something that progressive activists could not do. Matt prides himself on being a Republican and a life member of the National Rifle Association. He aspires to become a CEO in a corporation but worries about the upsurge in racism against Asian Pacific peoples and the failure of both Republicans and Democrats to address this issue.

The Asian American neoconservatives are a new and interesting political phenomenon. They are new because they are creatures born from the Reagan-Bush era of supply-side economics, class and racial polarization, and the emphasis on elitism and individual advancement. And they are interesting because they also represent a legacy from the civil rights struggles, especially the Asian American movement. The neoconservatives embody these seemingly contradictory origins.

- They are proud to be Asian American. But they denounce the Asian American movement of the late 1960s and early 1970s as destructive.
- They speak out against racism against Asian Americans. But they believe that only by ending affirmative action programs and breaking with prevailing civil rights thinking of the past four decades can we end racism.
- They express concern for Asian American community issues. But they contend that the agenda set by the "liberal Asian American establishment" ignores community needs.
- They vehemently oppose quotas blocking admissions of Asian Americans at colleges and universities. But they link anti-Asian quotas to affirmative action programs for "less qualified" African Americans, Latinos, and American Indians.
- They acknowledge the continuing discrimination against African Americans, Latinos, and American Indians in US society. But they believe that the main barrier blocking advancement for other people of color is "cultural"—that, unlike Asians, these groups supposedly come from cultures that do not sufficiently emphasize education, family cohesion, and traditional values.

Where did these neoconservatives come from? What do they represent? And why is it important for progressive peoples to understand their presence?

Progressives cannot dismiss Asian American neoconservatives as simple-minded Republicans. Although they hold views similar at times to Patrick Buchanan and William Buckley, they are not clones of white conservatives. Nor are they racists, fellow travelers of the Ku Klux Klan, or ideologues attached to Reagan and Bush. Perhaps the group that they most resemble are the African American neoconservatives: the Shelby Steeles, Clarence Thomases, and Tony Browns of this period. Like these men, they are professionals and feel little kinship for people of lower classes. Like these men, they oppose prevailing civil rights thinking, emphasizing reliance on government intervention and social programs. And, like these men, they have gained from affirmative action, but they now believe that America has somehow become a society where other people of color can advance through their own "qualifications."

Neoconservative people of color have embraced thinkers such as the late Martin Luther King, Jr. but have appropriated his message to fit their own ideology. In his speeches and writings, King dreamed of the day when racism would be eliminated—when African Americans would be recognized in US society for the "content of our character, not the color of our skin." He called upon all in America to wage militant struggle to achieve this dream. Today, neoconservatives have subverted his message. They believe that racism in US society has declined in significance and that people of color can now abandon mass militancy and advance individually by cultivating the content of their character through self-help programs and educational attainment and retrieving traditional family values. They criticize prevailing "civil rights thinking" as overemphasizing the barriers of racism and relying on "external forces" (i.e., government intervention through social programs) to address the problem.

Asian American neoconservatives closely resemble their African American counterparts in their criticism of government "entitlement" programs and their defense of traditional culture and family values. But Asian American neoconservatives are not exactly the same as their African American counterparts. The growth of neoconservative thinking among Asian Americans during the past twenty-five years reflects the peculiar conditions in our community, notably the emerging power of young professionals. Thus, to truly understand Asian American neoconservatives, we need to look at their evolution through the prism of Asian American politics from the late 1960s to the early 1990s.

Twenty-five years ago, Asian American neoconservatives did not exist. Our community then had only traditional conservatives—those who opposed ethnic studies, the antiwar movement, and other militant grassroots struggles. The traditional conservatives denounced Asian American concerns as "special interest politics" and labeled the assertion of Asian American ethnic identity as "separatist" thinking. For the traditional conservative, a basic contradiction existed in identifying oneself as Asian American and conservative.

Ironically, the liberation struggles of the 1960s—and the accompanying Asian American movement—spawned a new conservative thinker. The movement partially transformed the educational curriculum through ethnic studies, enabling all Asian Americans to assert pride in their ethnic heritage. The movement accelerated the desegregation of suburbs, enabling middle-class Asian Americans to move into all-white neighborhoods. Today, the neoconservatives are mostly young, middle-class professionals who grew up in white suburbs apart from the poor and people of color. As students, they attended the elite universities. Their only experience with racism is name-calling or "glass ceilings" blocking personal career advancement—and not poverty and violence.

It is due to their professional status and their roots in the Asian American movement that the neoconservatives exist in uneasy alliance with traditional conservatives in our community. Neoconservatives are appalled by the violence and rabid anticommunism of reactionary sectors of the Vietnamese community, Chinese from Taiwan tied to the oppressive ruling Kuomintang party, and Korean expatriates attached to the Korean Central Intelligence Agency. They are also uncomfortable with older conservatives, those coming from small-business backgrounds who warily eye the neoconservatives, considering them as political opportunists.

Neoconservatives differ from traditional conservatives not only because of their youth and their professional status but, most important of all, their political coming of age in the Reagan era. Like their African American counterparts, they are children of the corporate offensive against workers, the massive transfer of resources from the poor to the rich, and the rebirth of so-called traditional values.

It is their schooling in Reaganomics and their willingness to defend the current structure of power and privilege in America that gives neoconservative people of color value in today's political landscape. Thus, Manning Marable describes the key role played by African American neoconservatives:

> The singular service that [they] . . . provide is a new and more accurate understanding of what exactly constitutes conservatism within the Black experience. . . . Black conservatives are traditionally hostile to Black participation in trade unions, and urge a close cooperation with white business leaders. Hostile to the welfare state, they call for increased "self-help" programs run by Blacks at local and community levels. Conservatives often accept the institutionalized forms of patriarchy, acknowledging a secondary role for Black women within economics, political life, and intellectual work. They usually have a pronounced bias towards organizational authoritarianism and theoretical rigidity.[26]

Marable's analysis points to the basic contradiction for African American neoconservatives. They are unable to address fundamental problems facing their community: racist violence, grinding poverty, and the unwillingness of corporate and government policymakers to deal with these issues.

Asian American neoconservatives face similar difficulties when confronted by the stark realities of the post-Reagan period:

- The neoconservatives acknowledge continuing discrimination in US society but deny the existence of institutional racism and structural inequality. For them, racism lies in the realm of attitudes and "culture" and not institutions of power. Thus, they emphasize individual advancement as the way to overcome racism. They believe that people of color can rise through merit, which they contend can be measured objectively through tests, grades, and educational attainment.
- The neoconservatives ignore questions of wealth and privilege in American society. In their obsession with "merit," "qualifications," and "objective" criteria, they lose sight of power and oppression in America. Their focus is on dismantling affirmative action programs and "government entitlements" from the civil rights era. But poverty and racism existed long before the civil rights movement. They are embedded in the system of inequality that has long characterized US society.
- The neoconservatives are essentially elitists who fear expansion of democracy at the grassroots level. They speak a language of individual advancement, not mass empowerment. They propose a strategy of alignment with existing centers of power and not the creation of new power bases among the disenfranchised sectors of society. Their message is directed to professionals much like themselves. They have nothing to offer to immigrant workers in sweatshops, the homeless, Cambodian youth in street gangs, or community college youth.
- As relative newcomers to Asian American issues, the neoconservatives lack understanding of history, especially how concerns in the community have developed over time. Although they aggressively speak out about issues, they lack experience in organizing around these issues. The neoconservatives function best in the realm of ideas; they have difficulty dealing with concrete situations.

However, by stimulating discussion over how Asian American define community problems, the neoconservatives bring a vibrancy to community issues by contributing a different viewpoint. Thus, the debate between Asian American neoconservatives and progressives is positive because it clarifies issues and enables both groups to reach constituencies that each could not otherwise reach.

Unfortunately, this debate is also occurring in a larger and more dangerous context: the campaign by mainstream conservatives to redefine civil rights in America. As part of their strategy, conservatives in the national political arena have targeted our communities. There are high stakes here, and conservatives regard the Asian American neoconservatives as small players to be sacrificed.

The high stakes are evident in an article by William McGurn titled "The Silent Minority," appearing in the conservative digest *National Review*.[27] In his essay, he urges Republicans to actively recruit and incorporate Asian Americans into party activities. According to McGurn, a basic affinity exists between Republican values and Asian American values: many Asian immigrants own small businesses; they oppose communism; they are fiercely prodefense; they boast strong families; they value freedom; and in their approach to civil rights, they stress opportunities, not government "set-asides." McGurn then chastises fellow Republicans for their "crushing indifference" to Asian American issues. He laments how Republicans have lost opportunities by not speaking out on key issues such as the conflict between Korean immigrant merchants and African Americans, the controversy over anti-Asian quotas in universities, and the upsurge in anti-Asian violence.

McGurn sees Republican intervention on these issues strategically—as a way of redefining the race question in American society and shifting the debate on civil rights away from reliance on "an increasingly narrow band of black and liberal interest groups." According to McGurn,

> Precisely because Asian Americans are making it in their adoptive land, they hold the potential not only to add to Republican rolls but to define a bona-fide American language of civil rights. Today we have only one language of civil rights, and it is inextricably linked to government intervention, from racial quotas to set aside government contracts. It is also an exclusively black-establishment language, where America's myriad other minorities are relegated to second-class citizenship.[28]

McGurn's article presages a period of intense and unprecedented conservative interest in Asian American issues. We can expect conservative commentaries to intensify black-Asian conflicts in inner cities, the controversy over affirmative action, and the internal community debate over designating Asian Americans as a "model minority."

Thus, in the coming period, Asian American communities are likely to become crowded places. Unlike the late 1960s, issues affecting our communities will no longer be the domain of progressive forces only. Increasingly, we will hear viewpoints from Asian American neoconservatives as well as mainstream conservatives. How well will activists meet this new challenge?

Grassroots Organizing in the 1990s: The Challenge of Expanding Democracy

Time would pass, old empires would fall and new ones take their place, the relations of countries and the relations of classes had to change, before I discovered if, that it is not quality of goods and utility which matter, but movement; not where you are or what you have but where you have come from, where you are going and the rate at which you are getting there.
—C. L. R. James, *Beyond a Boundary*[29]

On the eve of the twenty-first century, the Asian American community is vastly different from that of the late 1960s. The community has grown dramatically. In 1970, there were only 1.5 million Asian Americans, almost entirely concentrated in

Hawaii and California. By 1980, there were 3.7 million, and in 1990, 7.9 million—with major Asian communities in New York, Minnesota, Pennsylvania, and Texas. According to census projections, the Asian American population should exceed 10 million by the year 2000 and will reach 20 million by the year 2020.[30]

Moreover, in contrast to the late 1960s—when Chinese and Japanese Americans composed the majority of Asian Americans—today's community is ethnically diverse—consisting of nearly thirty major ethnic groups, each with a distinct culture. Today's community is also economically different from the 1960s. Compared to other sectors of the US population, there are higher proportions of Asian Americans who are very rich and very poor. This gap between wealth and poverty has created a sharp class polarization in our community, a phenomenon yet to be studied.

But the changes for Asian Americans during the past twenty-five years have not been simply demographic. The political landscape has also changed due to new immigrants and refugees, the polarization between rich and poor, and the emergence of young professionals as a vital new force. Following the approach of C. L. R. James, we have traced the origins of these changes. We now need to analyze where these changes will take us in the decade ahead.

Ideologically and politically, activists confront a new and interesting paradox in the Asian American community of the 1990s. On the one hand, there is a great upsurge of interest in the community and all things Asian American. Almost daily, we hear about new groups forming across the country. In contrast to twenty-five years ago, when interest in the community was minimal and when only progressive activists joined Asian American organizations, we now find a situation where many different groups—including conservatives and neoconservatives, bankers and business executives, and young professionals in all fields—have taken up the banner of Asian American identity.

On the other hand, we have not seen a corresponding growth in consciousness—of what it means to be Asian American as we approach the twenty-first century. Unlike African Americans, most Asian Americans today have yet to articulate the "particularities" of issues affecting our community, whether these be the debate over affirmative action, the controversy regarding multiculturalism, or the very definition of empowerment. We have an ideological vacuum, and activists will compete with neoconservatives, mainstream conservatives, and others to fill it.

We have a political vacuum as well. In recent years, growing numbers of Asian Americans have become involved in community issues. But almost all have come from middle-class and professional backgrounds. Meanwhile, vast segments of our community are not coming forward. In fact, during the past decade the fundamental weakness for activists has been the lack of grassroots organizing among the disenfranchised sectors of our community: youth outside of colleges and universities, the poor, and new immigrant workers. Twenty-five years ago, the greatest strength of the Asian American movement was the ability of activists to organize the unorganized and to bring new political players into community politics. Activists targeted high school youth, tenants, small-business people, former prison inmates, gang members, the elderly, and workers. Activists helped them build new grassroots organizations, expanding power and democracy in our communities. Can a new generation of activists do the same?

To respond to this challenge, activists will need both a political strategy and a new ideological vision. Politically, activists must find ways to expand democracy by creating new grassroots formations, activating new political players, and building new coalitions. Ideologically, activists must forge a new moral vision, reclaiming the militancy and moral urgency of past generations and reaffirming the commitment to participatory democracy, community building, and collective styles of leadership.

Where will this political strategy and new consciousness come from? More than fifty years ago, revolutionary leader Mao Zedong asked a similar question:

> Where do correct ideas come from? Do they drop from the skies? No. Are they innate in the mind? No. They come from social practice, and from it alone. . . . In their social practice, people engage in various kinds of struggle and gain rich experience, both from their successes and their failures.[31]

In the current "social practice" of Asian American activists across the nation, several grassroots organizing projects can serve as the basis for a political strategy and new moral vision for the 1990s. I will focus on three projects that are concentrating on the growing numbers of poor and working poor in our community. Through their grassroots efforts, these three groups are demonstrating how collective power can expand democracy, and how, in the process, activists can forge a new moral vision.

The three groups—the Chinese Progressive Association (CPA) Workers Center in Boston, Asian Immigrant Women Advocates (AIWA) in Oakland, and Korean Immigrant Worker Advocates (KIWA) in Los Angeles—address local needs. Although each organization works with different ethnic groups, their history of organizing has remarkable similarities. Each organization is composed of low-income immigrant workers. Each has taken up more than "labor" issues. And each group has fashioned very effective "united front" campaigns involving other sectors of the community. Thus, although each project is relatively small, collectively their accomplishments illustrate the power of grassroots organizing, the creativity and talents of "ordinary" people in taking up difficult issues, and the ability of grassroots forces to alter the political landscape of their community. Significantly, the focus of each group is working people in the Asian American community—a sector that is numerically large and growing larger. However, despite their numbers, workers in the Asian American community during the past decade have become voiceless and silent. Today, in discussions about community issues, no one places garment workers, nurses' aides, waiters, and secretaries at the forefront of the debate to define priorities. And no one thinks about the working class as the cutting edge of the Asian American experience. Yet, if we begin to list the basic questions now confronting Asian Americans— racism and sexism, economic justice and human rights, coalition building, and community empowerment—we would find that it is the working class, of all sectors in our community, that is making the most interesting breakthroughs on these questions. They are doing this through groups such as KIWA, AIWA, and the CPA Workers Center. Why, then, are the voices of workers submerged in our community? Why has the working class become silent?

Three trends have pushed labor issues in our community into the background during the past two decades: the rising power of young professionals in our community; the influx of new immigrants and refugees and the fascination of social scientists and policy institutes with the phenomenon of immigrant entrepreneurship; and the lack of grassroots organizing by activists among new immigrant workers.

Thus, although the majority of Asian Americans work for a living, we have relatively little understanding about the central place of work in the lives of Asian Americans, especially in low-income industries such as garment work, restaurant work, clerical and office work, and other service occupations. Moreover, we are ignorant about the role that labor struggles have played in shaping our history.[32] This labor history is part of the legacy that activists must reclaim.

In contrast to the lack of knowledge about Asian American workers, we have a much greater understanding about the role of young professionals, students, and, most of all, small-business people. In fact, immigrant entrepreneurs, especially Korean immigrants, are perhaps the most studied people of our community. However, as sociologist Edna Bonacich notes, the profile of most Asian immigrant entrepreneurs closely resembles that of workers, due to their low earning power, their long work hours, and their lack of job-related benefits. Thus, Bonacich suggests that while the world outlook of Asian immigrant entrepreneurs may be petit bourgeoisie, their life conditions are those of the working class and might better be studied as a "labor" question. Asian immigrant small businesses, she contends, play the role of "cheap labor in American capitalism."[33]

Other researchers have only begun to investigate the extent of poverty among Asian Americans and the meaning of poverty for our community. In California, the rate of poverty for Asian Americans rose from about 10 percent in 1980 to 18 percent in 1990. But, more important, researchers found that there are higher numbers of "working poor" (as opposed to "jobless poor") in the Asian American community than for other ethnic groups. Thus, in contrast to other Americans, Asian Americans are poor not because they lack jobs but because the jobs they have pay very low wages. According to researchers Dean Toji and James Johnson, Jr., "Perhaps contrary to common belief, about half of the poor work—including about a quarter of poor adults who work full-time and year-round. Poverty, then, is a labor question."[34]

Activists in groups such as KIWA, AIWA, and the CPA Workers Center are strategically focusing on the "working poor" in the Asian American community. KIWA—which was founded in 1992—is working with low-income Korean immigrants in Los Angeles Koreatown, including garment workers and employees in small businesses. AIWA—founded in 1983—organizes Chinese garment workers, Vietnamese garment and electronics workers, and Korean hotel maids and electronics assemblers. And the CPA Workers Center—which traces its roots to the landmark struggle of Chinese garment workers in Boston in 1985—is composed primarily of Chinese immigrant women. Although their main focus is on workers, each group has also mobilized students and social service providers to support their campaigns. Through these alliances, each group has carried out successful community organizing strategies.

The focus of the three groups on community-based organizing distinguishes them from traditional unions. Miriam Ching Louie of AIWA explains this distinction:

> AIWA's base is simultaneously worker, female, Asian, and immigrant, and the organization has developed by blending together several different organizing techniques. As compared to the traditional union organizing strategy, AIWA's approach focuses on the needs of its constituency. *Popular literacy/conscientization/transformation* [based on the teachings of Paulo Freire] is a learning and teaching method which taps into people's life experiences as part of a broader reality, source of knowledge, and guide to action. *Community-based organizing* takes a holistic view of racial/ethnic people and organizes for social change, not only so that the people can win immediate improvements in their lives, but so that they can also develop their own power in the course of waging the fight.[35]

AIWA's focus on grassroots organizing is illustrated by its "Garment Workers' Justice Campaign," launched in late 1992 to assist Chinese immigrant women who were denied pay by a garment contractor. AIWA organizers shaped the campaign to respond to the peculiar features of the garment industry. The industry in the San Francisco Bay Area is the nation's third largest—following New York and Los Angeles—and employs some twenty thousand seamstresses, 85 percent of them Asian immigrant women. The structure of the industry is a pyramid with retailers and manufacturers at the top, contractors in the middle, and immigrant women working at the bottom. Manufacturers make the main share of profits in the industry; they set the price for contractors. Meanwhile, immigrant women work under sweatshop conditions.

In their campaign, AIWA and the workers initially confronted the contractor for the workers' back pay. When they discovered that the contractor owed a number of creditors, they took the unusual step of holding the garment manufac-turer, Jessica McClintock, accountable for the unpaid wages. McClintock operates ten boutiques and sells dresses through department stores. The dresses—which garment workers are paid $5 to make—retail in stores for $175. AIWA and the workers conducted their campaign through a series of high-profile demonstra-tions at McClintock boutiques, including picket lines and rallies in ten cities by supporters. AIWA designed these demonstrations not only to put pressure on McClintock and educate others in the community about inequities in the struc-ture of the garment industry but also to serve as vehicles for empowerment for the immigrant women participating the campaign. Through this campaign, the women workers learned how to confront institutional power, how to forge alli-ances with other groups in the community, and how to carry out effective tactics based on their collective power.[36]

Thus, through its activities promoting immigrant women's rights, AIWA is expanding democracy in the community. It is bringing labor issues to the fore-front of community discussions. It is creating new grassroots caucuses among previously unorganized sectors of the community and forming new political alignments with supporters, such as students, young professionals, labor unions, and social service providers. Finally, AIWA is developing a cadre of politically sophisticated immigrant women and promoting a new leadership style based on popular literacy, community building, and collective power.

Similarly, in Boston, the CPA Workers Center is expanding democracy through its grassroots efforts around worker rights. The Center emerged out of the Chinese immigrant women's campaign to deal with the closing of a large garment factory in Boston in 1985.[37] The shutdown displaced 350 workers and severely impacted the local Chinese community due to the community's high concentration of jobs in the garment industry. However, with the assistance of the Chinese Progressive Alliance, the workers formed a labor-community-student coalition and waged an eighteen-month campaign to win job retraining and job replacement. Lydia Lowe, director of the CPA Workers Center, describes how the victory of Chinese immigrant women led to creation of the Workers Center, which, in turn, has helped other workplace campaigns in the Chinese community:

> This core of women activated through the campaign joined with community supporters from the CPA to found a community-based workers' mutual aid and resource center, based at CPA. . . . Through the Workers Center, immigrant work-ers share their experience, collectively sum up lessons learned, find out about their rights, and develop mutual support and organizing strategies. Today, the Workers Center involves immigrant workers from each of its successive organizing efforts, and is a unique place in the community where ordinary workers can walk in and participate as activists and decision-makers.[38]

Moreover, forming the Workers Center reshaped politics in the local Chinese community, turning garment workers and other immigrant laborers into active political players. "Previously the silent majority, immigrant workers are gaining increasing respect as a force to be reckoned with in the local Chinese community," states Lowe.

In Los Angeles, the formation of KIWA in March 1992—only a month before the uprisings—has had a similar impact. Through its programs, KIWA is bringing labor issues to the forefront of the Asian American community, educating labor unions about the needs of Asian American workers, and forming coalitions with other grassroots forces in the city to deal with interethnic tensions. KIWA is uniquely positioned to take up these tasks. Out of the multitude of Asian American organizations in Los Angeles, KIWA distinguishes itself as the only organization governed by a board of directors of mainly workers.

KIWA's key role in the labor movement and community politics is evident in the recent controversy involving the Koreana Wilshire Hotel.[39] The controversy began in late 1991 when Koreana Hotel Co. Ltd., a South Korean corporation, bought the Wilshire Hyatt in Los Angeles. The change in ownership meant that 175 unionized members, predominantly Latino immigrants, were out of jobs. Meanwhile, the new hotel management hired a new workforce, paying them an average of $1.50 per hour less than the former unionized workforce. The former workers, represented by Hotel Employees and Restaurant Employees (HERE) Local 11, called upon labor unions and groups from the Asian American, African American, and Latino communities to protest Koreana's union-busting efforts. Local 11 defined the dispute as not only a labor issue but a civil rights issue. With the help of groups such as KIWA and the Asian Pacific American Labor Alliance, Local 11 initiated a letter-writing campaign against Koreana, began a community boycott of the hotel, and organized militant actions outside the hotel, including rallies, marches, and a picket line, as well as civil disobedience at the nearby Korean consulate. In each of these actions, Local 11 worked closely with KIWA and members of the Asian American community. Due to the mass pressure, in late 1992 the Koreana management agreed to negotiate with Local 11 to end the controversy and rehire the union members.

Throughout the campaign, KIWA played a pivotal role by assisting Local 11 build alliances with the Asian American community. In addition, KIWA members promoted labor consciousness in the Korean community by urging the community to boycott the hotel. KIWA members also spoke at Local 11 rallies, mobilized for picket lines, and worked with the union in its efforts to put pressure on the South Korean government. By taking these steps, KIWA prevented the controversy from pitting the Korean community against Latinos and further enflaming interethnic tensions in Los Angeles.

Also, through campaigns such as this one, KIWA is educating Asian immigrants about unions; training workers around the tasks of political leadership;

and creating new centers of power in the community by combining the resources of workers, young professionals, and social service providers.

Thus, through grassroots organizing, KIWA—like AIWA and the CPA Workers Center—is expanding democracy in the Asian American community. Moreover, the three groups collectively are reshaping community consciousness. They are sharpening debate and dialogue around issues and redefining such important concepts as empowerment. What is their vision of empowerment, and how does it differ from prevailing definitions?

The Twenty-First Century: Building an Asian American Movement

[A] movement is an idea, a philosophy. . . . Leadership, I feel, is only incidental to the movement. The movement should be the most important thing. The movement must go beyond its leaders. It must be something that is continuous, with goals and ideas that the leadership can then build on.
—Philip Vera Cruz[40]

In the late 1960s, Asian American activists sought to forge a new approach to leadership that would not replicate traditional Eurocentric models—i.e., rigid hierarchies with a single executive at the top, invariably a white male, who commanded an endless chain of assistants. In their search for alternatives, activists experimented with various ideas borrowed from other movements, but most of all, activists benefited from the advice and guidance of "elders" within the Asian American community—women and men with years of grassroots organizing experience in the community, the workplace, and the progressive political movement. One such "elder" was Pilipino immigrant labor leader Philip Vera Cruz, then in his sixties. Vera Cruz represented the *manong* generation—the first wave of Pilipinos who came to the United States in the early twentieth century and worked in agricultural fields, canneries, hotels, and restaurants.

Now eighty-eight years old, Vera Cruz continues to educate a new generation of activists. His lifetime of experience in grassroots organizing embodies the historic themes of Asian American activism: devotion to the rights of working people, commitment to democracy and liberation, steadfast solidarity with all who face oppression throughout the world, and the courage to challenge existing institutions of power and to create new institutions as the need arises. These themes have defined his life and shaped his approach to the question of empowerment—an approach that is different from standard definitions in our community today.

Vera Cruz is best known for his role in building the United Farm Workers (UFW), a culmination of his many years of organizing in agricultural fields. In 1965, he was working with the Agricultural Workers Organizing Committee, AFL-CIO, when Pilipino farmworkers sat down in the Coachella vineyards of Central California. This sit-down launched the famous grape strike and boycott, eventually leading to the formation of the UFW. Many books and articles have told the story of the UFW and its leader Cesar Chavez. But, until recently, no one has focused on the historic role of Pilipinos in building this movement. Craig Scharlin and Lilia Villanueva have filled that vacuum with their new publication about Vera Cruz's life.

Following the successful grape boycott, Vera Cruz became a UFW vice president and remained with the union until 1977, when he left due to political differences with the leadership. He was critical of the lack of rank-and-file democracy in the union and the leadership's embrace of the Marcos dictatorship in the Philippines. Since 1979, Vera Cruz has lived in Bakersfield, California, and has continued to devote his life to unionism and social justice and to the education of a new generation of Asian American youth.

Vera Cruz's life experiences have shaped a broad view of empowerment. For Vera Cruz, empowerment is grassroots power: the expansion of democracy for the many. Becoming empowered means gaining the capacity to advocate not only for one's own concerns but for the liberation of all oppressed peoples. Becoming empowered means being able to fundamentally change the relationship of power and oppression in society. Thus, Vera Cruz's vision is very different from that of today's young professionals. For them, empowerment is leadership development for an elite. Becoming empowered means gaining the skills to advocate for the community by gaining access to decision makers. Thus, for young professionals, the key leadership quality to develop is assertiveness. Through assertiveness, leaders gain access to policymakers as well as the power to mobilize their followers. In contrast, Vera Cruz stresses the leadership trait of humility. For him, leaders are "only incidental to the movement"—the movement is "the most important thing." For Vera Cruz, empowerment is a process where people join to develop goals and ideas to create a larger movement—a movement "that the leadership can then build on."

Vera Cruz's understanding of empowerment has evolved from his own social practice. Through his experiences in the UFW and the AFL-CIO, Vera Cruz learned about the empty democracy of bureaucratic unions and the limitations of the charismatic leadership style of Cesar Chavez. Through his years of toil as a farmworker, he recognized the importance of worker solidarity and militancy and the capacity of common people to create alternative institutions of grassroots power. Through his work with Pilipino and Mexican immigrants, he saw the necessity of coalition building and worker unity that crossed ethnic and racial boundaries. He has shared these lessons with several generations of Asian American activists.

But aside from sharing a concept of empowerment, Vera Cruz has also promoted a larger moral vision, placing his lifetime of political struggle in the framework of the movement for liberation. Three keywords distinguish his moral vision: "compassion," "solidarity," and "commitment." Vera Cruz's lifetime of action represents compassion for all victims of oppression, solidarity with all fighting for liberation, and commitment to the ideals of democracy and social justice.

Activists today need to learn from Vera Cruz's compassion, solidarity, commitment, and humility to create a new moral vision for our community. In our grassroots organizing, we need a vision that can redefine empowerment—that can bring questions of power, domination, and liberation to the forefront of our work. We need a vision that can help us respond to the challenge of conservatives and neoconservatives, and sharpen dialogue with young professionals. We need a new moral vision that can help fill the ideological vacuum in today's community.

Nowhere is this ideological challenge greater than in the current debate over the model minority stereotype. The stereotype has become the dominant image of Asian Americans for mainstream society, and has generated intense debate among all sectors of our community. This debate provides an opportunity for activists to expand political awareness and, in the process, redefine the Asian American experience for the 1990s.

In the current controversy, however, activists criticize the model minority stereotype politically but not ideologically. Activists correctly target how the concept fails to deal with Asian American realities: the growing population of poor and working poor, the large numbers of youth who are not excelling in school, and the hardships and family problems of small-business people who are not "making it" in US society. Activists also correctly point out the political ramifications of the model minority stereotype: the pitting of minority groups against each other and growing interethnic tensions in US society. In contrast, conservative and neoconservative proponents of the model minority concept argue from the standpoint of both political realities and a larger moral vision. They highlight Asian American accomplishments: "whiz kids" in elementary schools; growing numbers of Asian Americans in business, politics, and the professions; and the record enrollment of youth in colleges and universities. Conservatives and neoconservatives attribute these accomplishments to Asian culture and tradition, respect for authority, family cohesion, sacrifice and toil, rugged individualism, and self-reliance—moral values that they root in conservative thinking. Conservatives and neoconservatives recognize that "facts" gain power from attachment to ideologies. As a result, they appropriate Asian culture and values to promote their arguments.

But is Asian culture inherently conservative—or does it also have a tradition of militancy and liberation? Do sacrifice, toil, and family values compose a conservative moral vision only—or do these qualities also constitute the core of radical and revolutionary thinking? By asking these questions, activists can push the debate over the model minority concept to a new, ideological level. Moreover, by focusing on ideology, activists can delve into the stereotype's deeper meaning. They can help others understand the stereotype's origins and why it has become the dominant image for Asian Americans today.

Historically, the model minority stereotype first arose in the late 1950s—the creation of sociologists attempting to explain low levels of juvenile delinquency among Chinese and Japanese Americans.[41] The stereotype remained a social-science construct until the 1960s, when a few conservative political commentators began to use it to contrast Asian Americans' "respect for law and order" to African Americans' involvement in civil rights marches, rallies, and sit-ins. By the late 1970s, the stereotype moved into the political mainstream, coinciding with the influx of new Asian immigrants into all parts of the United States. But the widespread acceptance of the stereotype was not simply due to the increase in the Asian American population or the new attention focused on our community from mainstream institutions. More importantly, it coincided with the rise of the New Right and the corporate offensive against the poor. As discussed earlier, this offensive economically devastated poor communities and stripped away hard-won political gains. This offensive also included an ideological campaign designed to restore trust in capitalism and values associated with free enterprise. Meanwhile, conservatives and neoconservatives fought to redefine the language of civil rights by attacking federal government "entitlement" programs while criticizing the African American "liberal establishment."

In this political climate, the model minority stereotype flourished. It symbolized the moral vision of capitalism in the 1980s: a celebration of traditional values, an emphasis on hard work and self-reliance, a respect for authority, and an attack on prevailing civil rights thinking associated with the African American community. Thus, the stereotype took on an ideological importance above and beyond the Asian American community. The hard-working immigrant merchant and the refugee student winning the local spelling bee have become the symbols for the resurrection of capitalist values in the last part of the twentieth century.

Yet, we know a gap exists between symbol and reality. Today, capitalism in America is not about small-business activities; it is about powerful transnational corporations and their intricate links to nation-states and the world capitalist system. Capitalist values no longer revolve around hard work and self-reliance; they deal with wealth and assets and the capacity of the rich to invest, speculate, and obtain government contracts. And the fruits of capitalism in the last part of the twentieth century are not immigrant entrepreneurship and the revival of urban areas; they are more likely to be low-paying jobs, unemployment, bankruptcies, and homelessness.

However, as corporations, banks, and other institutions abandon the inner city, the immigrant merchant—especially the Korean small business—emerges as the main symbol of capitalism in these neighborhoods. For inner-city residents, the Asian immigrant becomes the target for their wrath against corporate devastation of their neighborhoods. Moreover, as this symbol merges with other historical stereotypes of Asians, the result is highly charged imagery, which perhaps underlies the ferocity of anti-Asian violence in this period, such as the destruction of Korean small businesses during the Los Angeles uprisings. The Asian immigrant becomes a symbol of wealth—and also greed; a symbol of hard work—and also materialism; a symbol of intelligence—and also arrogance; a symbol of self-reliance—and also selfishness and lack of community concern. Thus, today the model minority stereotype has become a complex symbol through the confluence of many images imposed on us by social scientists, the New Right, and the urban policies of corporate and political elites.

Pioneer Korean immigrant journalist K. W. Lee—another of our Asian American "elders"—worries about how the melding of symbols, images, and stereotypes is shaping the perception of our community, especially among other people of color. "We are not seen as a compassionate people," states Lee. "Others see us as smart, hard-working, and good at making money—but not as sharing with others. We are not seen as a people who march at the forefront of the struggle for civil rights or the campaign to end poverty."[42] Like Philip Vera Cruz, Lee believes that Asian Americans must retrieve a heritage of compassion and solidarity from our past and use these values to construct a new moral vision for our future. Asian Americans must cast off the images imposed on us by others.

Thus, as we approach the end of the twentieth century, activists are confronted with a task similar to that confronting activists in the late 1960s: the need to redefine the Asian American experience. And, as an earlier generation discovered, redefining means more than ethnic awakening. It means confronting the fundamental questions of power and domination in US society. It means expanding democracy and community consciousness. It means liberating ourselves from the prisons still surrounding our lives.

In our efforts to redefine the Asian American experience, activists will have the guidance and help of elders like K. W. Lee and Philip Vera Cruz. And we can also draw from the rich legacy of struggle of other liberation movements.

Thus, in closing this chapter, I want to quote from two great teachers from the 1960s: Malcolm X and Martin Luther King, Jr. Their words and actions galvanized the consciousness of one generation of youth, and their message of compassion continues to speak to a new generations in the 1990s.

Since their assassinations in the mid-1960s, however, mainstream commentators have stereotyped the two men and often pitted one against the other. They portray Malcolm X as the angry black separatist who advocated violence and hatred against white people. Meanwhile, they make Martin Luther King, Jr. the messenger of love and nonviolence. In the minds of most Americans, both men—in the words of historian Manning Marable—are "frozen in time."[43]

But, as Marable and other African American historians note, both King and Malcolm evolved and became very different men in the years before their assassinations. Both men came to see the African American struggle in the United States in a worldwide context, as part of the revolutionary stirrings and mass uprisings happening across the globe. Both men became internationalists, strongly condemning US exploitation of Third World nations and urging solidarity among all oppressed peoples. Finally, both men called for a redefinition of human values; they believed that people in the United States, especially, needed to move away from materialism and embrace a more compassionate worldview.

If we, too, as Asian Americans, are to evolve in our political and ideological understanding, we need to learn from the wisdom of both men. As we work for our own empowerment, we must ask ourselves a series of questions. Will we fight only for ourselves, or will we embrace the concerns of all oppressed peoples? Will we overcome our own oppression and help to create a new society, or will we become a new exploiter group in the present American hierarchy of inequality? Will we define our goal of empowerment solely in terms of individual advancement for a few, or as the collective liberation for all peoples?

These are revolutionary times. All over the globe men are revolting against old systems of exploitation and oppression, and, out of the wombs of a frail world, new systems of justice and equality are being born. The shirtless and barefoot people of the land are rising up as never before. "The people who sat in the darkness have seen a great light." We in the West must support these revolutions. It is a sad fact that, because of comfort, complacency, a morbid fear of communism, and our proneness to adjust to injustice, the Western nations that initiated so much of the revolutionary spirit of the modern world have now become the arch antirevolutionaries. . . . Our only hope today lies in our ability to recapture the revolutionary spirit and go out into a sometimes hostile world declaring eternal hostility to poverty, racism, and militarism.[44]
—Martin Luther King, Jr.

I believe that there will ultimately be a clash between the oppressed and those who do the oppressing. I believe that there will be a clash between those who want freedom, justice, and equality for everyone and those who want to continue the system of exploitation. I believe that there will be that kind of clash, but I don't think it will be based on the color of the skin.[45]
—Malcolm X

NOTES

Originally published in *Amerasia Journal* 15 (1): xv–xxx, 1989. ©1989 *Amerasia Journal*, reprinted by permission.

1 Iranian philosopher Ali Shariati's four-prisons analysis was shared with me by a member of the Iranian Students Union, Confederation of Iranian Students, San Francisco, 1977.

2 Allan Bloom, *The Closing of the American Mind* (New York: Simon & Schuster, 1987).

3 Winifred Breines, "Whose New Left?," *Journal of American History* 75, no. 2 (September 1988): 528–545.

4 Ibid., 543.

5 Sheila D. Collins, *The Rainbow Challenge: The Jackson Campaign and the Future of U.S. Politics* (New York: Monthly Review Press, 1986).

6 Ibid., 16.

7 Ronald Fraser, *1968: A Student Generation in Revolt* (New York: Pantheon, 1988), 354–355.

8 Karen Umemoto, "'On Strike!' San Francisco State College Strike, 1968–69: The Role of Asian American Students," *Amerasia Journal* 15, no. 1 (1989): 3–41.

9 "Statement of the Philippine-American Collegiate Endeavor (PACE) Philosophy and Goals" (mimeograph), quoted in Umemoto, "'On Strike!,'" 15.

10 Mo Nishida, "A Revolutionary Nationalist Perspective of the San Francisco State Strike," *Amerasia Journal* 15, no. 1 (1989): 75.

11 George Lipsitz, "Grassroots Activists and Social Change: The Story of Ivory Perry," *CAAS Newsletter* (UCLA Center for Afro-American Studies, 1986). See also George Lipsitz, *A Life in the Struggle: Ivory Perry and the Culture of Opposition* (Philadelphia: Temple University Press, 1988).

12 Russell C. Leong, "Poetry within Earshot: Notes of an Asian American Generation, 1968–1978," *Amerasia Journal* 15, no. 1 (1989): 166–167.

13 Al Robles, "Hanging on to the Carabao's Tail," *Amerasia Journal* 15, no. 1 (1989): 205.

14 Warren J. Susman, *Culture as History: The Transformation of American Society in the Twentieth Century* (New York: Pantheon, 1973); and Raymond Williams, *Keywords: A Vocabulary of Culture and Society*, rev. ed. (New York: Oxford University Press, 1976).

15 John M. Liu and Lucie Cheng, "A Dialogue on Race and Class: Asian American Studies and Marxism," in *The Left Academy*, vol. 3, ed. Bertell Ollman and Edward Vernoff (Westport, CT: Praeger, 1986).

16 See Mary Kao, compiler, "Public Record, 1989: What Have We Learned from the 60s and 70s?," *Amerasia Journal* 15, no. 1 (1989): 95–158.

17 Institute for Labor Education and Research, *What's Wrong with the U.S. Economy? A Popular Guide for the Rest of Us* (Boston: South End, 1982), esp. chaps. 1 and 19.

18 Samuel Huntington, "The United States," in *The Crisis of Democracy: Report on the Governability of Democracies to the Trilateral Commission*, ed. Michel Crozier (New York: New York University Press, 1975).

19 Center on Budget and Policy Priorities, *Still Far from the Dream: Recent Developments in Black Income, Employment and Poverty* (Washington, DC: Center on Budget and Policy Priorities, 1988).

20 Center for the Study of Social Policy, *Kids Count: State Profiles of Child Well-Being* (Washington, DC: Center for the Study of Social Policy, 1992).

21 Manning Marable, *How Capitalism Underdeveloped Black America* (Boston: South End, 1983), 252–253.

22 Vincent Harding, *The Other American Revolution* (Los Angeles: UCLA Center for Afro-American Studies, and Atlanta: Institute of the Black World, 1980), 224.

23 For analyses of the changing status of Asian Americans, see Lucie Cheng and Edna Bonacich, eds., *Labor Immigration under Capitalism: Asian Workers in the United States before World War II* (Berkeley: University of California Press, 1984); Paul Ong, Edna Bonacich, and Lucie Cheng, eds., *Struggles for a Place: The New Asian Immigrants in the Restructuring Political Economy* (Philadelphia: Temple University Press, 1993); and Sucheng Chan, *Asian Americans: An Interpretive History* (Boston: Twayne, 1991).

24 For an analysis of the growing power of Asian American young professionals, see Yen Espiritu and Paul Ong, "Class Constraints on Racial Solidarity among Asian Americans," in Ong, Bonacich, and Cheng, *Struggles for a Place*.

25 Arthur Hu, "AIDS and Race," *Asian Week*, December 13, 1991.

26 Marable, *How Capitalism Underdeveloped Black America*, 182.

27 William McGurn, "The Silent Minority," *National Review*, June 24, 1991.

28 Ibid., p. 19.

29 C. L. R. James, *Beyond a Boundary* (New York: Pantheon Books, 1983), 116–117.

30 LEAP Asian Pacific American Public Policy Institute and UCLA Asian American Studies Center, *The State of Asian Pacific America: Policy Issues to the Year 2020* (Los Angeles: LEAP and UCLA Asian American Studies Center, 1993).

31 Mao Zedong, "Where Do Correct Ideas Come From?," in *Four Essays on Philosophy* (Beijing: Foreign Languages Press, 1966), 134.

32 See Glenn Omatsu and Edna Bonacich, eds., "Asian Pacific American Workers: Contemporary Issues in the Labor Movement," *Amerasia Journal* 18. no. 1 (1992).

33 Edna Bonacich, "The Social Costs of Immigrant Entrepreneurship," *Amerasia Journal* 14, no. 1 (1988).

34 Dean S. Toji and James H. Johnson, Jr., "Asian and Pacific Islander American Poverty: The Working Poor and the Jobless Poor," *Amerasia Journal* 18, no. 1 (1992): 85.

35 Miriam Ching Louie, "Immigrant Asian Women in Bay Area Garment Sweatshops: 'After Sewing, Laundry, Cleaning and Cooking, I Have No Breath Left to Sing,'" *Amerasia Journal* 18, no. 1 (1992): 12.

36 Miriam Ching Louie, "Asian and Latina Women Take on the Garment Giants," *CrossRoads*, March 1993.

37 Peter N. Kiang and Man Chak Ng, "Through Strength and Struggle: Boston's Asian American Student/Community/Labor Solidarity," *Amerasia Journal* 15, no. 1 (1989).

38 Lydia Lowe, "Paving the Way: Chinese Immigrant Workers and Community-Based Labor Organizing in Boston," *Amerasia Journal* 18, no. 1 (1992): 41.

39 Namju Cho, "Check Out, Not In: Koreana Wilshire/Hyatt Take-Over and the Los Angeles Korean Community," *Amerasia Journal* 18, no. 1 (1992).

40 Craig Scharlin and Lilia V. Villanueva, *Philip Vera Cruz: A Personal History of Filipino Immigrants and the Farmworkers Movement* (Los Angeles: UCLA Labor Center and UCLA Asian American Studies Center, 1992), 104.

41 For an overview of the evolution of the "model minority" stereotype in the social sciences, see Shirley Hune, *Pacific Migration to the United States: Trends and Themes in Historical and Sociological Literature* (New York: Research Institute on Immigration and Ethnic Studies of the Smithsonian Institution, 1977), reprinted in *Asian American Studies: An Annotated Bibliography and Research Guide*, ed. Hyung-chan Kim (Westport, CT: Greenwood, 1989). For comparisons of the "model minority" stereotype in two different decades, see "Success Story of One Minority Group in U.S.," *U.S. News & World Report*, December 26, 1966, reprinted in *Roots: An Asian American Reader*, ed. Amy Tachiki et al. (Los Angeles: UCLA Asian American Studies Center, 1971), and the essay by McGurn, "Silent Minority."

42 Author's interview with K. W. Lee, Los Angeles, October 1991.

43 Manning Marable, "On Malcolm X: His Message & Meaning" (Westfield, NJ: Open Magazine Pamphlet Series, 1992).

44 Martin Luther King, Jr., "Beyond Vietnam" (speech, Riverside Church, New York, April 1967).

45 Malcolm X, "Interview on Pierre Breton Show, January 19, 1965," in *Malcolm X Speaks*, ed. George Breitman (New York: Grove Press, 1966), 216.

STUDY QUESTIONS

(1) Trace the evolution of the San Francisco State College strike as outlined by Umemoto: What motivated the strike? Who was involved? In what ways did the strike transform the consciousness of its participants? What other struggles evolved out of the strike? What were the significant effects of the strike, and what legacy did it leave behind for Asian Americans?

(2) Omatsu contends that the 1970s signaled the ultimate disintegration of the social movements founded in the 1960s, specifically those movements centered on the liberation for racial/ethnic minorities. How did this process of disintegration contribute to what Omatsu calls "the winter of civil rights"? What implications were there for Asian American studies?

(3) How did the political landscape change for Asian Americans in the 1980s? Why was the 1980s an ambiguous period for Asian American empowerment? How does this period compare with the 1960s and 1990s? Are the concepts developed during the Asian American movement—self-determination, liberation, militant struggle—meaningful and relevant to Asian Americans today? Are the ideas of the movement alive today, or have they atrophied into relics—the curiosities of a bygone era of youthful and excessive idealism?

(4) In the aftermath of the radicalism within the Asian American movement emerged Asian American neoconservatives. What allowed neoconservative Asian Americans to become a vocal segment within the larger Asian American community? In what ways were they distinct from the radical leaders of the Asian American movement? What place would they have in the political mobilization of Asian Americans in the twenty-first-century United States?

(5) Asian American political organizing efforts often involve members of the same ethnic or panethnic group, but at other times they involve activists of other racial groups or even those from other parts of the globe. In what ways are ethnic-specific organizations distinct from those that are panethnic, interracial, or global? What are the advantages and disadvantages of these strategies for political organizing, respectively?

(6) Looking back at the Asian American movement historically, there have always been instances in which Asian American activists become politically engaged in injustices beyond the United States. What are some examples? How do these examples compare to some of the transnational social justice movements that Asian Americans are involved in today?

SUGGESTED READINGS

Chiang, Mark. 2010. *The Cultural Capital of Asian American Studies: Autonomy and Representation in the University*. New York: New York University Press.

Deutsch, Nathaniel. 2001. "'The Asiatic Black Man': An African American Orientalism?" *Journal of Asian American Studies* 4 (3): 193–208.

Fujino, Diane. 2012. *Samurai among Panthers: Richard Aoki on Race, Resistance, and a Paradoxical Life*. Minneapolis: University of Minnesota Press.

Gee, Emma, ed. 1976. *Counterpoint: Perspectives on Asian America*. Los Angeles: UCLA Asian American Studies Center.

Ho, Fred. 2000. *Legacy to Liberation: Politics & Culture of Revolutionary Asian/Pacific America*. New York: AK Press.

Hune, Shirley. 1989. "Opening the American Mind and Body: The Role of Asian American Studies." *Change* 21 (6): 56–60, 62–63.

Kibria, Nazli. 1998. "The Racial Gap: South Asian American Racial Identity and the Asian American Movement." Pp. 69–78 in Lavina Dhingra Shankar and Rajini Srikanth, eds., *A Part Yet Apart: South Asians in Asian America*. Philadelphia: Temple University Press.

Lien, Pei-Te. 2001. *The Making of Asian America through Political Participation*. Philadelphia: Temple University Press.

Ling, Susie. 1989. "The Mountain Movers: Asian American Women's Movement in Los Angeles." *Amerasia Journal* 15 (1): 51–67.

Maeda, Daryl. 2012. *Rethinking the Asian American Movement.* New York: Routledge.

Nakanishi, Don. 1995/1996. "Linkages and Boundaries: Twenty-Five Years of Asian American Studies." *Amerasia Journal* 21 (3): xvii–xxv.

Narasaki, Karen, and June Han. 2004. "Asian American Civil Rights Advocacy and Research Agenda after 9/11." *AAPI Nexus* 2 (1): 1–17.

Okamoto, Dina G. 2006. "Institutional Panethnicity: Boundary Formation in Asian-American Organizing." *Social Forces* 85 (1): 3–25.

Ono, Kent A. 2004. *Asian American Studies after Critical Mass.* New York: Blackwell.

Prashad, Vijay. 2000. *The Karma of Brown Folk.* Minneapolis: University of Minnesota Press.

———. 2001. *Everybody Is Kung Fu Fighting: Afro-American Connections and the Myth of Cultural Purity.* Boston: Beacon.

Saito, Leland T., K. Geron, E. De La Cruz, and J. Singh. 2001. "Asian Pacific Americans Social Movements and Interest Groups." *PS: Political Science and Politics* 34 (3): 619–624.

Tachiki, Amy, Eddie Wong, and Franklin Odo, with Buck Wong, eds. 1971. *Roots: An Asian American Reader.* Los Angeles: UCLA Asian American Studies Center.

Wang, L. Ling-Chi. 1996. "Asian Americans and Debates about Affirmative Action." *Asian American Policy Review* 6: 49–57.

Wei, William. 1993. *The Asian American Movement.* Philadelphia: Temple University Press.

FILMS

Choy, Curtis (producer/director). 1993. *The Fall of the I-Hotel* (58-minute documentary).

Ding, Loni (producer/director). 1991. *Claiming a Voice: The Visual Communications Story* (60-minute documentary).

Lee, Grace (producer/director). 2013. *American Revolutionary: The Evolution of Grace Lee Boggs* (90-minute documentary).

Shiekh, Irum (director/producer). *On Strike! Ethnic Studies, 1969–1999* (30-minute documentary).

Tajima-Peña, Rene (director, coproducer). *My America (Or Honk if You Love Buddha)* (87-minute documentary).

Tajiri, Rea, and Pat Saunders (directors/producers). 1993. *Yuri Kochiyama: Passion for Justice* (57-minute documentary).

Winn, Robert (director). 2005. *Grassroots Rising* (60-minute documentary).

PART II

Traversing Borders

Contemporary Asian Immigration to the United States

3

Contemporary Asian America

Immigration, Demographic Transformation, and Ethnic Formation

MIN ZHOU, ANTHONY C. OCAMPO, AND J. V. GATEWOOD

Anyone who rides the subway in New York, drives on the freeway in California, or walks into any urban classroom will immediately feel the impact of contemporary immigration. Large-scale, non-European immigration to the United States began in the late 1960s after a long hiatus due to restricted immigration and has accelerated at rapid speeds since the early 1990s. Between 1980 and 1999, more than 16 million immigrants immigrated into the United States, more than the total number of immigrants who arrived during first two decades of the twentieth century (14.6 million admissions between 1900 and 1919) when immigration was at its peak.[1] From 2000 to 2012, another 13.4 million immigrated legally to the United States as permanent residents. Unlike turn-of-the-twentieth-century immigrants, today's newcomers have come predominantly from non-European countries. Since the 1980s, 78 percent of the immigrants admitted to the United States have come from the Americas (excluding Canada) and Asia, only 12 percent from Europe, compared to more than 90 percent at the earlier peak. The share of immigrants from Asia as a proportion of the total admissions grew from a tiny 5 percent in the 1950s to 11 percent in the 1960s and to 33 percent the 1970s, and has remained at around 35 percent since 1980.[2] The Philippines, China, India, Korea, and Vietnam have been on the list of top ten sending countries since 1980. What caused this massive human movement in recent years, particularly from Asia? Who are these newcomers? How does the host society receive them? How do they affect US-born peoples of Asian descent who share their cultural heritage and their communities, and how are they affected by the natives and their new homeland? These questions are of central importance, as they will certainly determine the future of Asian America.

The Driving Forces behind Contemporary Immigration from Asia

US immigration legislation has always appeared humanitarian in principle and democratic in ideology. However, beginning with the Chinese Exclusion Act of 1882, Congress passed various laws to restrict immigration from the "barred zone" (known as the Asia-Pacific Triangle) and to single out Asian immigrants for exclusion. Asian immigrants were not only barred from reentering the country, but also denigrated "aliens ineligible to citizenship," were consequently deprived from owning land, attaining professional occupations, sending for their family members, marrying white Americans, and becoming equal participants in American society. World War II marked a watershed for Asian Americans since their homelands, Japan excepted, were allies of the United States. Congress repealed the Chinese Exclusion Act in 1943 and other Asian exclusion acts at the end of the war and passed the War Brides Act in 1945 to allow American GIs to reunite with their Asian wives in the United States. The public began to shift its perception of Asian Americans as "yellow peril" to "model minorities." This change in perception included Japanese Americans, whose population—some 120,000 at its peak—languished in American-style concentration camps for the duration of World War II. Two-thirds of these prisoners were American citizens. In 1952, Congress passed the McCarran-Walter Act, making all national origin groups eligible for naturalization. While this act eliminated race as a barrier to immigration, it maintained the national origins quota system in immigration policy that limited migrants from specific regions to token numbers up until the late 1960s.

During the 1960s, at the time when the United States was entangled in an unpopular war against Vietnam while also in the throes of the civil rights movement, both international and domestic crises pushed Congress to clean up the remaining discriminatory immigration legislation. Meanwhile, labor market projections showed that an acute shortage of engineering and medical personnel would soon materialize unless the United States opened its door to foreign labor. In response, Congress passed the Hart-Celler Act in 1965. This landmark piece of legislation abolished the national origins quota system and strived toward two goals: to reunite families and to meet the labor market demand for skilled labor. Since the law went into effect in 1968, immigration from Asia and the Americas has accelerated rapidly, with little sign of slowing down. Between 1970 and 2012, a total of 11.4 million Asians were admitted into the United States as legal immigrants (not counting the thousands of refugees who began to arrive in the mid-1970s and the estimated one million Asian immigrants who remain undocumented).[3] The majority of contemporary Asian immigrants were either family-sponsored migrants (more than two-thirds) or employer-sponsored skilled workers (about one-fifth). The Hart-Celler Act of 1965 has impacted Asian immigration, but the main driving forces are beyond the scope of US immigration policy. Recent changes worldwide—global economic restructuring, rapid economic development in Asia, and increasing US political, economic, and military involvement in Asia—have all combined to perpetuate Asian immigration to the United States.

The globalization of the US economy in the postindustrial era, particularly since World War II, has forged an extensive link of economic, cultural, and ideological ties between the United States and many developing countries in the Pacific Rim. Globalization at this stage has perpetuated emigration from developing countries in two significant ways. First, direct US capital investments into developing countries transform the economic and occupational structures in these countries by disproportionately targeting production for export while taking advantage of raw material and cheap labor. Such twisted development, characterized by the robust growth of low-skilled jobs in export manufacturing, draws a large number of rural, and particularly female, workers into the urban labor markets. Increased rural-urban migration, in turn, causes underemployment and displacement of the urban workforce, creating an enormous pool of potential emigrants (Sassen 1989). Second, economic development following the American model in many developing countries stimulates consumerism and consumption and raises expectations regarding the standard of living. The widening gap between consumption expectations and the available standards of living within the structural constraints of the developing countries, combined with easy access to information and migration networks, in turn create tremendous pressure for emigration (Portes and Rumbaut 2014). Consequently, US foreign capital investments in developing countries have resulted in the paradox of rapid economic growth and high emigration from these countries to the United States.

On the US side, unprecedented growth in capital-intensive, high-tech industries and in services forecasts a severe shortage of skilled workers. American businesses and policymakers believed that importing skilled labor was the quickest solution. Since the 1980s, about one-third of the engineers and medical personnel in the US labor market have come from abroad—mostly from India, China, Taiwan, and the Philippines. However, the shortage of skilled labor is not a sufficient explanation for the trends in highly skilled migration, since skilled immigration disproportionately originates from selected countries in Asia (almost two-thirds of the total skilled immigration in 2012). It is the global integration of higher education and advanced training in the United States in interaction with the opportunity structure in the homelands that have set in motion the highly skilled immigration. The infusion of the educational systems with globalization in many developing countries—notably India, Korea, the Philippines, and Taiwan—has given rise to a sizable professional class within these countries. Many members of this emerging middle class are frustrated by the uneven economic development and lack of mobility opportunities at home that devalue their education and skills, and, in some cases, they also feel powerless to make changes because of repressive political systems in their homelands. They therefore actively seek emigration as a preferred alternative, and the change in US immigration policy has facilitated this move (Liu and Cheng 1994). Also, the emergence of the United States as the premier training ground for international students has been instrumental in supplying the US economy with needed skilled labor (Ong, Cheng, and Evans 1992). Many foreign students have found permanent employment in the United

States after completing their studies or practical training. For example, in 1995, close to 40 percent of the immigrants from mainland China were admitted under employment-based preferences. Almost all of them had received higher education or training in the United States.

In addition, Southeast Asian refugees constitute a significant share of contemporary Asian immigration. Since 1975, more than one million refugees have arrived from Vietnam, Laos, and Cambodia as a direct result of the failed US intervention in Southeast Asia. The United States originally had little economic interest in Southeast Asia but was drawn in because of the threat of communist takeovers in the region. The development of the communist bloc dominated by the former Soviet Union, the communist takeover in China in the late 1940s, and the direct confrontation with communist troops in the Korean War prompted a US foreign policy aimed at "containing" communism, which ultimately dragged Americans into Indochina. The Vietnam War, its expansion into Southeast Asia, and political turmoil in the region left millions of people living in poverty, starvation, and constant fear, while forcing many others to flee from their homelands. One ironic consequence of the US involvement in Indochina is that sizable parts of the populations of Vietnam, Laos, and Cambodia are now in America (Rumbaut 1995). By 1996, more than 700,000 refugees from Vietnam, 210,000 from Laos, and 135,000 from Cambodia had been admitted to the United States. Since then, Southeast refugee inflows have declined, but such decrease has been accompanied by a rapid increase of family-sponsored migrants from the region. As a result, these communities have experienced significant growth. According to the 2010 census, there are now 1.7 million Vietnamese, 232,000 Laotians, and 277,000 Cambodians living in the United States (US Census Bureau 2012).

Southeast Asian refugees fled their countries in different waves. Although Saigon, Vientiane, and Phnom Penh fell to the communist forces roughly at the same time in 1975, only the Vietnamese and a small number of the Hmong resistance force had the privilege of being "paroled" (being allowed under special provision of the law) into the United States immediately after the war. Approximately 130,000 Vietnamese refugees and only 3,500 Hmong refugees landed on US soil in 1975 (Chan 1994), while the majority of Hmong resistance forces, Laotian royalists, and Cambodians sought refuge in Thailand. During what is known as the second wave, a large refugee exodus occurred at the end of the 1970s when thousands fled Vietnam. About a quarter of a million Vietnamese refugees went to China, while some half a million floated in the open sea to be rescued by the national guards of whichever country they happened to be near. Almost half of the "boat people" were reported to have perished at sea, and the remaining half ended up in camps in Thailand, Indonesia, Malaysia, Singapore, the Philippines, and Hong Kong. Thousands of refugees also fled Laos and Kampuchea (formerly Cambodia) on land to seek refuge in crowded camps along the Thai border. Despite harsh repatriation efforts by the Thai government, about 600,000 Cambodians (15 percent of the country's population) and some 100,000 Hmong and 200,000 lowland Laotians (10 percent of the country's population) fled on land to Thailand, awaiting resettlement in a third country (Chan 1991). The refugee exodus continued in large numbers in the early 1980s. Although the newly established governments in Southeast Asia did not plunge the three countries into a bloodbath as so many had once feared, continuing political and religious repression, economic hardship, incessant warfare, and contacts with the outside world led many Southeast Asians to escape in search of a better life (Zhou and Bankston 1998).

Once set in motion, international migration is perpetuated by extensive and institutionalized migration networks. Networks are formed by family, kinship, and friendship ties, facilitating and perpetuating international migration because they lower the costs and risks of movement and increase the expected net returns to such movement (Massey et al. 1987). US immigration policy has been instrumental in sustaining and expanding family migration networks. The Hart-Celler Act of 1965 and its subsequent amendments give preference to family reunification, providing immediate relatives of US citizens with unlimited visa numbers and other relatives with the majority of visa allocations subject to the numerical cap. More than two-thirds of the legal immigrants admitted to the United States since the 1970s have been family-sponsored immigrants. Even among employer-sponsored migrants and refugees, the role of networking is crucial. Family, kin, and friendship networks also tend to expand exponentially, serving as a conduit to additional and thus potentially self-perpetuating migration. Immigration from Asia is expected to continue at its high volume because many recent immigrants and refugees will have established citizenship status and will become eligible sponsors who can send for family members to reunite in the United States. In fact, in 2012 the Pew Research Center reported that Asians surpassed Hispanics as the largest immigrant population in the United States. According to the report, Asian Americans are the fastest growing minority group in the country.[4]

Overall, contemporary immigration has been influenced and perpetuated not simply as a result of the Hart-Celler Act but also by the interplay of a complex set of macro- and micro-structural forces. Understanding its dynamics requires a reconceptualized framework that takes into account the effects of globalization, uneven political and economic developments in developing and developed countries, the social processes of international migration, and the role of the United States in world affairs. One significant implication arising from these processes is that high levels of immigration will continue to remain an inseparable part of Asian American life for years to come.

The New Face of Asian America

Immigration is transforming Asian America in ways unanticipated by longtime Asian immigrants and their US-born children. Although Asian Americans as a group are relatively few in number, making up 6 percent of the U. S. population, they have aggressively asserted their presence in the American milieu, fighting their way, with varied success, into mainstream economic, social, and political institutions. Before the immigration surge in the late 1960s, the Asian American population was a tiny fraction of the total US population—about a third of one percent in 1900 and 0.7 percent in 1970—and was composed mainly of three national-origin groups—Japanese, Chinese, and Filipinos. Figure 3.1 shows the percentage distribution of the Asian American population from 1900 to 2010 (Barringer, Gardner, and Levin 1993; US Census Bureau 2012). Prior to 1930, Asians in America were mainly either Chinese or Japanese, mostly immigrants. Between 1930 and 1970 the number of Filipinos increased significantly. Filipinos were mostly brought into the United States to fill the labor shortage caused by anti-Asian legislation and the restrictive National Origins Act of 1924. By 1970, Japanese Americans were the largest national origin group, making up 41 percent of the Asian American population, followed by Chinese Americans (30 percent) and Filipino Americans (24 percent). Members of other national origin groups (mostly Koreans) represented less than 5 percent of the total.

As Figure 3.1 shows, however, the heterogeneity of Asian American ethnicities increased tremendously by the end of the twentieth century. As of the latest census, Japanese compose less than a tenth of the Asian population. While Chinese and Filipino Americans remain the two largest Asian American groups, their proportion of the total Asian population decreased to 23 percent and 19 percent, respectively. While Japanese, Chinese, and Filipinos once dominated the Asian population, they constitute only about half of Asians today, due mainly to the exponential rise of the Korean, Asian Indian, and Vietnamese populations.

Pre–World War II immigrants from Asia represented less than 5 percent of the total new arrivals admitted to the United States, a direct result of anti-Asian prejudice and various restrictive immigration laws. Most of the earlier Asian immigrants came from China and Japan, with a smaller number from the Philippines, India, and Korea. These earlier immigrants, like "the tired, huddled masses" from Europe, were typically poor and uneducated peasants, and many of them intended to make a quick fortune to bring back to their homelands. Because of the drastic differences in migration histories among the earlier Asian-origin groups, only Japanese immigrants were able to develop family-based communities with a significant US-born population in the pre–World War II period. Chinatowns, the rather dispersed Filipino enclaves, and other Asian immigrant communities were primarily bachelor societies with single adult males overrepresented and with few women, children, and families (Chan 1991; Takaki 1989; Zhou 1992).

The distorted population growth in Asian American communities is living evidence of decades of legal exclusion and discrimination. From the time of their arrival, Asian immigrants were subject to laws that served to exclude them from the social and economic opportunities available to most white immigrants.

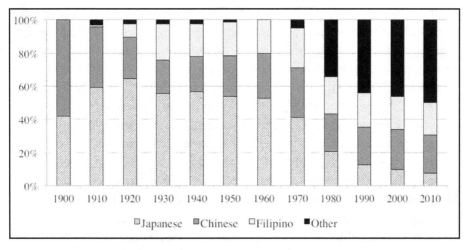

Figure 3.1. Percentage Distribution of Asian American Population, 1900–2010. *Source:* 1900–1970: Barringer, Gardner, and Levin (1993, 42); 1980–2010: US Census Bureau (1983, 1993, 2002, 2012).

Despite the eventual repeal of the laws that excluded Asian immigrants and barred them from the rights of naturalization, the Asian American population grew very slowly, making up barely half a percent of the total US population by 1950. The number of people in some Asian-origin groups was so miniscule, in fact, that the US census did not even categorize them until 1980 (Nash 1997).[5] Nonetheless, the relaxation of immigration legislation during the early 1940s and 1950s, combined with a postwar baby boom, did give rise to a notable US-born youth cohort, most of whom lived on the West Coast. This group, comprising mostly Japanese and Chinese Americans, came of age in the late 1960s to form the core force of the Asian American movement at college campuses on the West Coast and in the Northeast.

The diversity of the Asian American population started to take shape during the 1970s. The dramatic increase in Asian immigration marked the beginning of contemporary Asian America. In sheer numbers, the US Asian and Pacific Islander population grew from a total of 1.4 million in 1970, to 7.3 million in 1990, to 12 million in 2000, to over 19 million in 2013 (in contrast to 205,000 in 1900), an impressive twelvefold increase in just four decades. Much of this growth is attributed to immigration, which has accounted for more than two-thirds of the total population growth. The population of most of the new national-origin groups—Indians, Koreans, Vietnamese, Cambodians, Laotians, and the Hmong—grew at spectacular rates, almost entirely because of immigration (Pew Research Center 2012). It was estimated that, if the current levels of net immigration, intermarriage, and ethnic affiliation hold, the size of the Asian population will increase from 12 million in 2000 to 34 million in 2050, growing from 4 to over 8 percent of the total US population (Smith and Edmonston 1997).

The recency of Asian immigration highlights two distinct demographic characteristics of the Asian American population: a disproportionately large foreign-born component and a general decline of the foreign-born component in all national-origin groups. As indicated in Figure 3.2, the foreign-born component dominates all Asian American groups, except for Japanese Americans. However, there is a large percentage drop in the proportion of the foreign-born (about 15 percent) for every group except for the Vietnamese. This demographic trend is a strong indication of a growing second generation—US-born children of foreign-born parentage. The great majority of the foreign-born is of working age. By contrast, the US-born Asian American population is an extremely young group. More than half of US-born Asian Americans are under eighteen years of age. One implication about this emerging new second generation is that it will grow up in an era of continuously high immigration, joined by a sizeable foreign-born youth cohort—the 1.5 generation—whose members are far more diverse in ethnic backgrounds, the timing of immigration, degrees of acculturation, orientation, and outlooks. This is a situation quite distinct from that which faced the second generation of immigrants in the 1950s and 1960s, because of restrictive immigration.

Diverse National Origins

The dramatic growth in absolute numbers of Asian immigrants has been accompanied by the increasing ethnic diversity within the Asian American population itself. As of 2010, the US census recorded thirteen national-origin or ethnic groups with populations exceeding 150,000, as revealed in Table 3.1. Since 1980, no single group has accounted for more than one-quarter of the Asian American population. While major national-origin groups—Japanese, Chinese, Filipino, Korean, Indian, and Vietnamese—were proportionally represented in 2000, other national-origin or ethnic groups—Cambodian, Laotian, the Hmong, Pakistani, and Thai—marked their presence in Asian America only very recently since the late 1970s. Because of the unique migration patterns in each of the originating countries, national origins are strongly associated with the type of legal admission (family-sponsored, employer-sponsored, or refugees) and with the skill levels of immigrants. For example, many Filipino immigrants to the United States are college graduates with transferable job skills; many are physicians and nurses sponsored by US employers in the health care industry. Indian immigrants are mostly employed as physicians and computer programmers, as well as small-business entrepreneurs (Dhingra, this volume). Koreans are predominantly middle-class professionals but tend to be disproportionately self-employed in small-scale retail trade. Chinese immigrants are more mixed, including fairly even proportions of rural peasants, urban workers, and the highly skilled. Southeast Asian refugees, in contrast, were pushed out of their

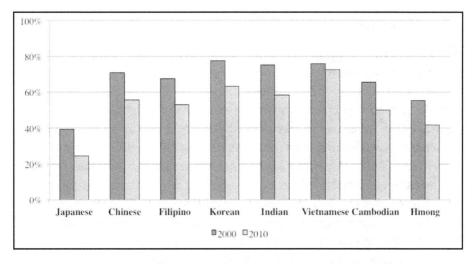

Figure 3.2. Asian American Population: Percentage Foreign-Born, 1900–2010. *Source:* US Census Bureau (2002, 2012).

homelands by force and suffer tremendous postwar trauma and social displacement, compounded by a lack of education and professional skills, which negatively affect their resettlement (Bankston and Hidalgo, this volume).

TABLE 3.1. Asian American Population, 1980–2000 (Thousands)

	1990	% Total	2000	% Total	2010	% Total
Chinese	1,545	22.8	2,858	24.1	4,010	23.2
Filipino	1,407	20.8	2,385	20.1	3,417	19.7
Japanese	848	12.5	1,152	9.7	1,304	7.5
Indian	815	12.0	1,856	15.7	3,183	18.4
Korean	799	11.8	1,227	10.3	1,706	9.8
Vietnamese	615	9.1	1,212	10.2	1,737	10.0
Cambodian	149	2.2	213	1.8	277	1.6
Pakistani	—	—	209	1.8	409	2.4
Laotian	147	2.2	197	1.7	232	1.3
Hmong	94	1.4	185	1.6	260	1.5
Thai	91	1.3	150	1.3	237	1.4
Other Asian	265	3.9	215	1.8	548	3.2
Total	6,775	100.0	11,859	100.0	17,320	100.0

Source: US Census Bureau (1993, 2002, 2012).

Diverse Socioeconomic Backgrounds

Another distinguishing characteristic of contemporary Asian America is the tremendous heterogeneity in diverse socioeconomic status. The 2012 Pew Research Center report attests to the vast differences in Asian Americans' levels of education, occupation, and income by national origins. In the aggregate, about half of all Asian Americans over the age of twenty-five have earned a college degree or higher, however educational attainment varies widely by ethnicity. For example, 70 percent of Indian American adults (aged twenty-five years or older) reported having attained bachelor's degrees or more, and more than 45 percent of Chinese, Filipino, Korean, and Japanese Americans reported so, but only 26 percent of Vietnamese Americans and fewer than 15 percent of Cambodian, Laotian, and Hmong Americans (compared to 28 percent of average American adults). While there has been a significant increase in the educational attainment levels of all groups over the past decade, the disparities are still strong.

Among employed workers (age sixteen years or older), about 60 percent of Indian Americans and more than half of Chinese and Japanese Americans held managerial or professional occupations, but about a quarter of Vietnamese and fewer than 20 percent reported so (compared to 34 percent of average American workers). Furthermore, Indian and Filipino Americans reported a median family income of more than $70,000, and Chinese and Japanese Americans, more than $60,000, but Korean and Southeast Asian families reported a median family income around or significantly below the national average of $50,000. Poverty rates for Asian Americans ranged from a low of 6 percent for Filipinos and 10 percent for Indians and Japanese to a high of more than 38 percent for the Hmong and 29 percent for Cambodians (compared to about 12 percent for average American families) (Reeves and Bennett 2004).

Diverse Settlement Patterns

A third salient feature of contemporary Asian America is the diverse geographic settlement patterns of immigrants and their offspring. Historically, most Asian immigrants in the United States have been concentrated in Hawaii and in states along the Pacific Coast, with a small number of Chinese moving east to settle in New York. Within each area of settlement, they have been highly segregated in ethnic enclaves, such as Chinatowns, Little Tokyos, and Little Manilas. Today, geographic concentration continues to be significant as newcomers follow the footsteps of their predecessors to settle on the West Coast in disproportionate numbers (Zhou 2009; Zhou, Tseng, and Kim 2008). California remains the preferred destination for immigrants from Asian countries and has just over 30 percent of the nation's Asian American population, though this is a significant decline from 40 percent back in 2000. Tables 3.2 and 3.3 show the geographic distribution of Asian Americans by metropolitan areas (PMSAs or MSAs),[6] further confirming historical and contemporary patterns of ethnic concentration. Nonetheless, the Asian American presence in other parts of the mainland United States is growing—about 21 percent of Asian Americans live in the US South, another 20 percent in the Northeast, and about 10 percent in the Midwest.[7]

TABLE 3.2. Top Ten Metro Areas with Largest Asian American Population, 2010

	Total Population (Thousands)	Asian American Population (Thousands)	% Asian American
New York, NY	8,175	1,135	13.9
Los Angeles, CA	3,793	484	12.8
San Jose, CA	946	327	34.6
San Francisco, CA	805	289	35.9
San Diego, CA	1,307	241	18.4
Honolulu, HI	337	230	68.2
Chicago, IL	2,696	167	6.2
Houston, TX	2,099	140	6.7
Fremont, CA	214	117	54.7
Philadelphia, PA	1,526	107	7.0
Seattle, WA	609	101	16.6
Sacramento, CA	466	99	21.2
United States	281,421	17,320	4.6

Source: US Census Bureau (2012).

TABLE 3.3. Largest Asian American Population Growth, by Region and State, 2000–2010

	2000 (Thousands)	2010 (Thousands)	Percentage Increase
Region			
South	2,267	3,835	69.2
Midwest	1,393	2,054	47.5
Northeast	2,368	3,429	44.8
West	5,870	8,003	36.3
Top 10 states			
Nevada	112	243	116.0
Arizona	119	231	94.6
North Carolina	136	253	85.4

TABLE 3.3. (*cont.*)

	2000 (Thousands)	2010 (Thousands)	Percentage Increase
North Dakota	5	9	85.1
Georgia	200	365	82.9
New Hampshire	19	35	79.6
Delaware	19	34	77.9
Arkansas	25	45	76.9
Indiana	73	127	74.0
Texas	644	1,111	72.4
United States	11,898	17,320	45.6

Source: US Census Bureau (2012).

Nonetheless, the Asian American population has begun to disperse throughout the Northeast, the Midwest, and the South. For example, sizeable ethnic communities are found in New Orleans (Vietnamese), Houston (Vietnamese and Chinese), and Minneapolis (the Hmong), cities that traditionally received few Asian immigrants. Although there is still evidence of clustering along national or ethnic lines at the local level, there are very few examples of the large and distinctly monoethnic enclaves that were common in the past. In San Francisco, Los Angeles, and New York, there are no new Chinatowns where more than half of the residents are coethnics; Koreatowns in New York and Los Angeles, and Little Saigon in Orange County are no exception. Filipinos Americans and Indian Americans are comparatively more spread out across the urban landscape with few identifiable ethnic enclaves. For example, as of 2000, only 2 percent of Los Angeles County's Chinese Americans lived in Chinatown (decreased from 12 percent in 1990), 7.4 percent of Korean Americans lived in Koreatown (decreased from 22 percent in 1990), and a tiny number of Japanese Americans (fewer than 700) lived in Little Tokyo. A recent report by the *Huffington Post* noted that urban ethnic enclaves have "wane[d] as Asians head to the suburbs."[8] Overall, trends of spatial integration (moving into white middle-class neighborhoods) and suburbanization among Asian Americans have been particularly strong in recent years, resulting in decreasing levels of residential segregation even in areas of high concentration.

Identity, Emerging Ethnicity, and the Assimilation Problem

"Who Am I?"

We ABC [American-born Chinese] were ridiculed by the old immigrants as "Bamboo Stick" for not being able to speak Chinese and not being accepted as "white people." We are not here. We are not there. . . . We are different. Most of us are proud of the Chinese cultural heritage, but due to the pressure to assimilate and the lack of opportunity, we don't know much about the Chinese way.[9]

The issue of identity has always occupied a central place in the minds of Asian Americans. Changing demographics and residential mobility in contemporary Asian America make it more salient than ever before. However, this issue has concerned native-born generations more than the first generation, because native-born generations are caught in the insider/outsider divide: they suffer from the paradoxical experience of being in America but not fully a part of it. Both immigrants and their US-born children encounter this paradoxical experience, yet their feelings about it are different.

Mainstream American society pressures all immigrants to "fit in" and "not rock the boat." The society also expects immigrants, however diverse or initially disadvantaged they may be, to assimilate into the mainstream as quickly as possible. Behind this ideology of assimilationism, however, there is an invisible force for inclusion and exclusion. Writing in 1782, J. Hector St. John de Crevecoeur described an American as "either an European or the descendant of an European." More than a century later, Israel Zangwill (1914) characterized an American as an "immaculate, well-dressed, accent-free Anglo." These kinds of definitions of "American," widely if often unconsciously held, make it hard, if not impossible, for people to feel fully American if they happen to be nonwhite, including those whose ancestors settled on this land long before the first Europeans reached American shores. The 1790 National Origin Act prohibited all but free white persons from becoming US citizens. Thus, not all outsider groups were afforded the privilege of becoming American. A second-generation Chinese American in her sixties explained her isolation from mainstream American society and her socially imposed otherness in these words:

> The truth is, no matter how American you think you are or try to be, you do not look "American." If you have almond-shaped eyes, straight black hair, and a yellow complexion, you are a foreigner by default. People will ask where you come from but won't be satisfied until they hear you name a foreign country. And they will naturally compliment your perfect English.[10]

Immigrants are deemed "outsiders," and they tend to cope with their alienation from the immigrant perspective. Historically, people of Asian descent were considered members of "inferior races" and were negatively portrayed as the "indispensable enemy" and as the "yellow peril." No matter how hard they tried to accommodate to American ways, Asian immigrants and Americans of Asian ancestry were considered undesirable and unassimilable aliens (Chan 1991). The Chinese Exclusion Act of 1882, the first immigration act in US history to exclude an entire category of immigrants purely on the basis of national origin, is a prime example. The forced removal and incarceration of Japanese Americans during World War II is another case in point. The federal government, under provision of President Franklin D. Roosevelt's Executive Order 9066, justified these actions as a "military necessity" vital to the national defense of the United States (despite the fact of evidence confirming the loyalty of Japanese Americans). In contrast, no such categorical treatments were imposed on German Americans and Italian Americans.

As a reactive strategy to resist subjugation and discrimination, Asian immigrants retreated into their own ethnic communities, rebuilding ethnic institutions that resembled those found in the homeland and relying on one another for moral and practical supports (Zhou 2009). Extreme adversity allowed them to develop a clear sense of their position in the host society as "foreigners" and to maintain tangible ties to their ethnic community and their homeland, which became internalized as part of their shared experience. Since most Asian immigrants chose to come to the United States to seek better opportunities either for themselves or for their children, their shared experience of marginalization reinforced their determination to push their children into the mainstream by choosing a path of least resistance (Kitano 1969). For example, prewar issei (first generation) drew on extensive ethnic resources in developing trade and business associations to negotiate favorable arrangements with the larger economy and to support their children's education (Matsumoto 1993; Nishi 1995). War-traumatized Japanese American parents or grandparents were reluctant to share wartime memories with their children and grandchildren for fear of hurting their children's chances of social integration (Takezawa 2000). Post-1965 Korean immigrants pushed their children toward prestigious universities because they looked to their children to regain the social status the parents had lost in the host society (Zhou and Kim 2006).

Unlike most members of the first generation who tend to avoid arousing antagonism by subscribing to the dominant society's mode of behavior—hard work, education, delayed gratification, nonconfrontational attitudes in the face of injustice—their offspring, American citizens by birth, are likely to fully embrace the principles of freedom, equality, and civil liberties on which citizenship is based. They are unlikely to think of their parents' home country as a place to which they might return, nor do they use it as a point of reference by which to assess their progress in the new land. Rather, their expectations are governed by the same standards to which other Americans aspire, and it is by those standards that US-born Asian Americans assess themselves and are assessed by others. However, American society is not color-blind, and the phenotypes of the second generation subject them to the same types of discrimination and injustice faced by the first generation regardless of how long they have been in the United States. A third-generation Japanese American from Monterey Park, California, expressed frustration at being objectified as a "foreigner":

> Asian Americans fought for decades against discrimination and racial prejudice. We want to be treated just like everybody else, like Americans. You see, I get real angry when people come up to me and tell me how good my English is. They say: "Oh, you have no accent. Where did you learn English?" Where did I learn English? Right here in America. I was born here like they were. We really hated it when people assume that just because Asian Americans look different we were foreigners. It took us a long time to get people to see this point, to be sensitized to it. Now the new immigrants are setting us back. People see me now and they automatically treat me as an immigrant. I really hate that. The worst thing is that these immigrants don't understand why I am angry. (Cheng and Yang 1996, 305)

An examination of today's Asian American populations highlights the demarcation between the different generations. Because of the recency of immigration, this group remains primarily an immigrant group, in which the first generation makes up more than two-thirds of the total Asian American population.[11] It is only among Japanese Americans and Chinese Americans that we notice a sizeable third or fourth generation. Among Asian American children under eighteen years of age, more than 90 percent are either foreign-born or children of foreign-born parents. Growing up in the context of an immigrant family is extremely difficult for Asian American children. Parents often place multiple pressures on their children to "do and say the right things" or to "act white" as a means of moving into the mainstream and accessing resources typically reserved for "insiders." In the process of growing up, the children often find themselves vacillating between the outsider's world from which they came and an insider's world into which they were born; they are increasingly ambivalent about their conflicting identities.

Many second-generation Asian Americans of the 1960s and 1970s went through a period of profound confusion, feeling trapped by the ironies of being in America but not a part of it. In the wake of the Asian American movement, young Asian Americans who entered American institutions of higher education began to confront these identity issues. The movement forged a space in which these young people not only shared their own personal experiences of racism and suffering in American society but also began to articulate an Asian American consciousness and to refashion their own identities in ways that were meaningful to their experiences—an Asian American identity. At a time when Asian Americans began to empower themselves across panethnic lines and to raise an ethnic consciousness to a new level for future generations, it is ironic that much of the shame and frustration that previously engulfed the second generation has resurfaced among the children of contemporary immigrants from Asia. Some of the children, especially those who live in suburban, white, middle-class neigh-borhoods, internalize the negative stereotypes that society imposes upon their parents' generation and have undergone traumatic, even suicidal, identity crises, in which they feel ashamed of who they are, try to become who they are not, and end up being neither, as so vividly described in "A Letter to My Sister" (Park, this volume). A Chinese American college student, born in the early 1980s, reveals her confusion as a teenager:

> As a child, I had a very difficult time coping with my ethnic identity. I was hesitant to call myself American because as I perceived it, American meant all the beauti-ful Anglo children in my classes. Yet I was also hesitant to call myself Chinese for two reasons. First, I had no clear concept of what Chinese was besides the fact that my parents were from China. [Second,] I did not feel Chinese. I did not want to be Chinese. I wanted to be White . . . I tried to hide my identity. I buried it deep within my subconscious, became oblivious to it. Yet every so often, it would be invoked. . . . Perhaps the most notorious manifestation of my shame was my inability to answer the simple question, "What are you?" . . . When I was con-fronted with questions concerning my racial background, I found myself unable to answer. . . . Unable to utter the simple words, "I am Chinese." I just could not do it. It was too painful for some reason. The words seemed too dissonant and distaste-ful. So many times I simply shrugged and said: "I don't know."[12]

The pressure to assimilate and the conditional acceptance by mainstream soci-ety takes a heavier toll on the second generation growing up in suburban white middle-class neighborhoods than on those who live in inner-city ethnic enclaves (Sung 1987). Within the enclave, the homeland is transplanted, ancestral culture and values are honored and practiced as a way of life, and ethnic pride is invigo-rated. Outside the enclave, ethnicity is subject to the rank order of the racial stratification system, operating under the assumption that ethnic traits should be abandoned in order to become "American." In the midst of an identity crisis, US-born children who are seemingly assimilated structurally may find that they lack a homeland on which they can fall back and an ethnic space in which they can express their fear and anxieties. This explains in part why so many Asian American college students demand ethnic studies classes. These ethnic studies classes do not merely serve to disseminate information or transport knowledge but provide a space in which Asian Americans address the issue of identity, allowing them to release negative feelings about themselves as well as inner ten-sions and anxieties. These classes let them rebuild a sense of self-worth and a group identity as a means of ethnic empowerment.

The Salience of Ethnicity

Identity crises are not uncommon among adolescents as they grow into adulthood, but they are not necessarily defining experiences for all members of native-born generations. Since the birth of the Asian American movement, a vibrant and multifaceted ethnic culture has emerged and been reconstructed among US-born Asian Americans in their attempt to reclaim their identity. This culture is neither mainstream American nor clearly associated with the immigrant generation. It is a hybrid form that has come to assume tremendous significance among Asian Americans as a viable means of resistance and compromise within the existing power structure. This phenomenon indicates the fluid nature of ethnicity.

The sociologist William Yancey and his colleagues argue that the emergence of an ethnic culture has relatively little to do with the country of origin but more to do with the structure of opportunity in America. Instead of viewing the transplanted cultural heritage as the principal defining characteristic of an ethnic group, these scholars suggest that the development and persistence of ethnicity is a paradoxical process. On the one hand, it is defined in the context of frequent association and interaction with others of common origins and cultural heritage. On the other hand, it is dependent on structural conditions that characterize the positions of groups in American society and create common experiences and interests, thereby setting the potential for collective mobilization around shared goals. Ultimately, it is "a manifestation of the way populations are organized in terms of interaction patterns, institution, personal values, attitudes, lifestyle, and presumed consciousness of kind"—the result of a process that continues to unfold (Yancey, Juliani, and Erikson 1976, 400). Drawing on this reasoning, we see that Asian Americans develop different patterns of ethnic identification according to the length of time in the United States, internal group dynamics, and structural situations that the particular immigrant group and its descendants have encountered.

As we have discussed, identity formation varies across generations and national origin groups. The immigrant generation generally reaffirms its ethnic identity on the basis of homeland cultures and life experiences not only through ethnic practices but also through memories of its lived experiences in the homeland or during the process of movement. For example, Southeast Asian refugees share the common experience of having lived through internal power struggles in their home countries, the horrors of war, and the ordeal of exile and death. These life-threatening experiences become the basis for ethnic solidarity. Drastic cultural changes and adverse societal treatments or disadvantages associated with immigrant status in the host society can reinforce ethnic identity, as in the case of ethnic enclaves where transnational ties and kinship networks remain strong and homeland cultures are often frozen in time as the result of a collective, concerted effort to preserve them.

US-born Asian Americans and those who arrived in the United States as infants or as school-age children, in contrast, usually do not seize on traditional cultural symbols as a mode of defining their ethnicity. Rather, they tend to build their identities largely on the basis of mediating *interpretive memories* of homeland cultures in which they have never personally lived, and their own diverse life experiences in the United States. Living in immigrant families and in (or close to) ethnic communities has made life in the homeland a continuing reality because parents often communicate to children with a strong sense of determination and instill in them a sense of origin. Close proximity to kinship networks and ethnic enclaves certainly exerts an important effect on the US-born, providing an infrastructure that keeps alive the memories of homeland cultures. The collective memory of Chinese exclusion, the US colonization of the Philippines, and the incarceration of Japanese Americans serve as pivotal organizational principles for ethnic identity among US-born Chinese Americans, Filipino Americans and Japanese Americans, respectively. The support of Asian American donors to the Museum of the Chinese in the Americas in New York and the Japanese American National Museum in Los Angeles is living proof that even the most "assimilated" of Asian Americans clearly retain vital links to their ethnic culture and to the community that sustains it.

Often, however, actual experiences in American society outweigh memories. Transplanted cultural heritage is no longer the requirement or the defining characteristic of ethnicity for the native-born. Rather, the emergence and persistence of ethnicity depends on the structural conditions of the host society and the position that the immigrant groups occupies in that social structure. The treatment of Asian Americans as foreigners, the glass ceiling, and racially motivated hate crimes all serve to reaffirm ethnic identity. However, this ethnic identity, even when it is affiliated with a national origin, differs for the first generation and its native-born offspring in that the ethnicity of the first generation has a taken-for-granted nature, whereas that of native-born generations is derived both from the collective memory of the historical experience and from the native-born generations' actual experience in a more self-conscious, reflexive way.

This vibrant emergent ethnic culture transcends the spatial boundaries of ethnic enclaves as well as the symbolic meaning of ethnicity. It is a culture characterized by structures that promote cooperation among coethnics while adopting activities and organizations (e.g., ethnic churches, sports clubs, trade guilds, political organizations) as a means of resistance (Espiritu 1992; Tuan 1999). Yet, what ethnicity means, stands for, or symbolizes differs from region to region, city to city, and town to town in the vast expanse of the United States. Being Japanese American in Hawaii or Chinese American in Monterey Park or Vietnamese

American in Little Saigon is not the same as having those identities in New York, Houston, or New Orleans.

Is this emergent ethnicity symbolic? The sociologist Herbert Gans asserts that "as the functions of ethnic cultures and groups diminish and identity becomes the primary way of being ethnic, ethnicity takes on an expressive rather than instrumental function in people's lives, becoming more of a leisure-time activity" (Gans 1979, 9). Among the features of symbolic ethnicity is that it does not carry with it material consequences and does not serve to enhance group solidarity. Indeed, ethnic identity associated with a homeland has become blurred among the second or third generations, who have lost their ancestral languages, have intermarried at rates far exceeding the national average, and no longer involve themselves with their ethnic communities on a daily basis, making their ethnicity "symbolic." Our argument about interpretive memories of homeland culture points to the importance of symbolic ethnicity. Clearly, ethnicity is not an either/or matter but rather a variable outcome that varies in its intensity. As we have noted earlier, Asian Americans, both foreign-born and US-born, experience high levels of educational attainment, occupational mobility, and residential integration, have high rates of intermarriage, and rapidly lose facility in the native language; hence, much of Asian ethnicity may be optional. As they climb up the socioeconomic ladder in American society, many established Asian Americans may have more choices as to whether they want to be Asian and how Asian they should be when they want to.

At the societal level, however, we argue that the notion of symbolic ethnicity does not always apply well to Asian Americans or to other racial minority groups, since being non–ethnic American is still not an option for them, as it is for most European immigrants and their offspring (Takezawa 2000; Waters 1990). The outcry that "America does not include me, only a part of me" is heard from many US-born, "well assimilated" Asian Americans. This suggests that unless the whole racial perception of Americans changes and includes other groups as Americans, emergent ethnicity, often in the form of panethnicity, will continue to remain instrumental for the excluded social groups. Such emergent panethnicity serves as both a defense mechanism against racism and an empowering mechanism for unity and solidarity.

Ethnicity is situational and structurally conditioned. Under certain circumstances, it can evolve into panethnicity, a form of ethnic aggregation typically oriented toward achieving certain material ends and empowerment. In thinking about panethnicity, we draw on the work of the sociologists David Lopez and Yen Espiritu, who link it to a set of cultural and structural preconditions: shared cultural values and life experiences in American society, imposed societal perception and treatment as one phenotypical group, and the internal need for political mobilization to fight for minority rights and to protect group interests (Lopez and Espiritu 1990). We add that rapid language switch to English and increasing interethnic and interracial marriages also contribute to the formation of panethnicity. Today, Asian Americans intermarry extensively with members of other racial or ethnic groups. In Los Angeles County, for example, about one-third of Asian Americans, and about half of all second-generation Asian Americans marry outside their ethnic groups. Ambiguous phenotype may ease social constraints imposed by the existing racial stratification system while fostering a strong sense of panethnicity among multiracial or multiethnic Americans.

However, lumping together all peoples of Asian ancestry complicates the notion of ethnicity and its subsequent application to a particular ethnic group, because panethnicity accounts neither for regional or national differences nor for the historical legacies of intergroup conflicts. At this juncture, the term "Asian American," in and of itself, assumes a political agenda for those who subscribe to it, and panethnicity remains a political identity for instrumental purposes. The Asian American community today is, and continues to be, marked by tremendous diversity in the era of high immigration. Diverse languages and religions and differing historical legacies of domination and colonization in Asia make it unlikely that a panethnic coalition will develop in the near future. Differences in class background among the immigrant generation and divergent modes of incorporation of that generation can also deter the formation of panethnicity. The success of Asian Americans' integration into American society as individuals can both enhance and weaken their ability to act collectively. Also, while it is true that discrimination and violence against one Asian group serve to unite Asian Americans, they can also create intragroup conflict. During World War II, the US government singled out Japanese Americans as enemies and targets for incarceration. Fearing similar treatment, some Chinese Americans found themselves constantly invoking their Chinese ethnicity and even wore buttons with derogative anti-Japanese words to distinguish themselves. The negative stereotypes about welfare dependency and gang violence among Southeast Asians also cause some Asian American groups to distance themselves from them and even blame them for their plight.

The Assimilation Problem

The issue of assimilation has been the core of a classic scholarly debate on immigration, and racial and ethnic relations. Classical assimilation theory predicts a linear trajectory toward structural integration into the mainstream of society. In this view, the children and the grandchildren of the immigrants move beyond the status of the first generation and progressively become less distinct from other Americans. This particular perspective shares a series of assumptions: outsider groups, however diverse and initially disadvantaged, all absorb a common culture and gain equal access to the opportunity structure; they do so in a more or less natural way, gradually deserting old cultural and behavioral patterns in favor of new ones; and the whole process, once set in motion, moves inevitably and irreversibly toward the dissolution of the original group. Consequently, observable ethnic differences are largely a function of time and generational status in the United States. In some cases, the time span for assimilation may be prolonged, but, in the end, distinctive ethnic characteristics eventually fade, retaining only some symbolic importance (Alba and Nee 2003; Gans 1979; Gordon 1964; Warner and Srole 1945).

Assimilation theories arose as an abstraction from the experience of earlier European immigration. The theoretical reflections developed largely while the process of immigrant adaptation was under way. Now that it is over, one can safely conclude that the descendants of the 1880 to 1920 wave have overcome earlier disadvantages, achieving parity with, if not outdistancing, "white" Americans of English ancestry, or what Milton Gordon calls the "core cultural group" (Gordon 1964). Unfortunately, assimilation theories provide no account of why this outcome should have transpired—unless one subscribes to that variant of the modernization theory that most earlier writers embraced but many contemporary social scientists have now challenged. Most important, past success may be due to the specific circumstances encountered by earlier immigrants and their offspring—the fact that between the 1920s and the 1950s, America experienced a long period of restricted immigration, which almost certainly weakened immigrants' attachment to their culture and patterns of group affiliation. Should this be the case, the past is unlikely to prove a useful guide to the future, since we appear to be headed for more, not less, immigration in the years to come.

Assimilationism—the ideology that imposes the dominant core culture on all immigrants to American society—is highly exclusive. The "melting pot" does not wholeheartedly embrace non-European immigrants. The experiences of African Americans are a case in point. Nathan Glazer (1993) shows how racism serves to exclude African Americans from assimilating or sharing in the opportunities of economic and social mobility. Racism and prejudice have also affected the situation of Asian Americans, although to a different degree. Examples are ample, but we point out three of the most obvious.

First, the perception of Asian Americans as "foreigners" has imposed and perpetuated the "otherness" on the group. As we have discussed in detail in the previous section, it is the socially imposed category based on phenotype, rather than acculturation and social mobility, that governs how group members are received and treated in American society. Speaking perfect English, effortlessly practicing mainstream cultural values, and even intermarrying members of the dominant group may help reduce this "otherness" at the individual level but have little effect on the group as a whole, given the relatively small size of the third or later generations of the Asian American population (only 10 percent of the total) and the high levels of recent immigration.

Second, the image of "the yellow peril," although largely repudiated in the post–World War II period, has repeatedly resurfaced throughout American history, especially in situations when the United States is at odds with immigrants' ancestral homelands in Asia. The bombing of Pearl Harbor during World War II turned Japanese immigrants and Americans of Japanese ancestry into enemies who were forcibly exiled from their homes and put into internment camps. The communist takeover of China in the late 1940s and the subsequent Cold War made Chinese Americans of the 1950s prime suspects of treason and espionage. The perceived economic threat from Japan in the 1980s led to the murder of Vincent Chin, a Chinese American, mistaken for a Japanese, who was beaten to death by disgruntled unemployed autoworkers in Detroit. The renewed spy stereotype is currently manifested in the case of a Taiwan-born scientist, Wen Ho Lee, who was convicted of stealing nuclear secrets for China in the court of public opinion before even appearing in a court of law. This litany of examples is endless.

Third, the "model minority" stereotype has reinforced the "otherness" of Asian Americans. It is important to note that this stereotype derives from a larger political agenda, serving the ideological function of delegitimizing African American (in particular) claims for equalization of outcomes as opposed to equalization of opportunities. Although Asian Americans as a group are above average on just about any socioeconomic indicator that counts, the "model minority" stereotype obscures the very real problems that many highly "successful" Asians encounter. In particular, highly skilled professionals, who are most definitely part of the middle, if not the upper-middle, class, are not doing quite as well as their non-Hispanic white counterparts; they experience disproportionately underemployment because of overqualification and overwork (Zhou and Kamo 1994). Furthermore, the stereotype paints a one-sided picture of the Asian American population, obscuring the plight of those who are not doing well and thus further absolving the broader society of any responsibility for redress. There are immigrant workers who are doing poorly, some subjected to severe exploitation. Some groups—Laotians, Hmong, and Cambodians—are still struggling at the very bottom of the social ladder, facing the risk of being trapped in the urban underclass, and others—perhaps the Filipinos—may be stuck in the lower middle class, showing trends of downward mobility (Oropesa and Landale 1997).

In sum, the notion of assimilation, whether it is manifested in a straight line or bumpy line, seems to clearly imply a *single* line—an idea that is very difficult to reconcile with the historical record of large and significant differences in the rate at which various groups move ahead in American society. Because of the complexity of the reality with its multifaceted and dynamic nature, it is difficult to comprehend the experiences of today's racial minorities, Asian Americans included, within the assimilationist framework that makes explicit or implicit Anglo-conformist assumptions. Assimilationism may still be a social or moral

imperative imposed on immigrants by the dominant culture, but it may not necessarily be the imperative toward which all immigrant groups and their succeeding generations are striving.

Discussion and Conclusions

Diversity is the hallmark of contemporary Asian America. The influx of Asian
immigrants in response to the 1965 Hart-Celler Act and broader economic,
social, and geopolitical factors has brought new challenges for the adaptation of
new immigrants and their children into society. As the community continues to
grow in number, so too will their representation in the broad cultural, social, and
economic milieu that we typify as "mainstream American society."

The implications of the dramatic changes in contemporary Asian America
that we have just described are particularly relevant for the development of
a coherent vision for future Asian America. First and foremost, diversity in
national origins produces stark disparities within the Asian American community. National origins evoke drastic differences in homeland cultures, such
as languages, religions, foodways, and customs; histories of international relations; contexts of emigration; reception in the host society; and adaptation patterns. Such differences persist most significantly in the private domain, affecting
not only the immigrant generation, but also the native-born generations. For
some national origin groups, such as the Chinese and Indians, internal differences in languages or dialects and religions are quite substantial. While ethnic
diversity among the second and third generations may be blurred because of
rapid switch to English and high rates of out-marriages, it is extremely difficult
to group everybody under a pan-Asian umbrella at the individual level. While
increasing differences within an emerging Asian America may create obstacles
for panethnic coalitions, the connections between children of Asian immigrants
and those of Latin American and other national origins can create new possibilities for racial formations in a society that is no longer defined by the black-white
racial paradigm and is becoming increasingly multiracial and multiethnic. For
example, Latin American immigration is reshaping the incorporation processes
of Asian children of immigrants as well as influencing the mechanisms of Asian
American panethnic consciousness (Ocampo, this volume).

Second, socioeconomic diversity gives rise to diverse mobility patterns. New
immigrants may continue to follow the traditional bottom-up route to social
mobility, starting their American life in isolated urban enclaves, but some segment of this urban population may be permanently trapped in poverty with dim
prospects for the future. Those with sufficient social and economic resources
may simply bypass the bottom starting line, moving directly into mainstream
labor markets and settling directly into suburban middle-class communities
(Portes and Zhou 1993). These trajectories to social mobility not only affect

life chances of the first generation but also have profound social implications for the new second generation, since the current state and future prospects of immigrant offspring are related to the advantages or disadvantages that accrue through parental socioeconomic status.

Socioeconomic diversity leads to divergent destinies, creating a bifurcated distribution of the Asian American population along class lines. Some national origin groups, such as the Chinese, Filipino, Japanese, Koreans, and Asian Indians, have converged with the general US population, with the rich and the poor on the ends and an ever-growing affluent class in the middle. But, many others, especially the most recent refugee groups, are struggling in the most underprivileged segment of US society. Consequently, class bifurcation toward two ends of society's class spectrum will likely lead to fragmentation of the larger Asian American community, creating new obstacles for political mobilization and ethnic solidarity. Bifurcation also affects the new second generation. Unlike the second generation of the 1960 and 1970s, most of whom grew up in segregated urban enclaves, a visible proportion of today's second generation is growing up in affluent Euro-American neighborhoods in suburbia. Members of the suburban middle class maintain little contact with their working-class coethnics in urban enclaves and show limited interest in working-class issues.

Moreover, socioeconomic diversity leads to divergent destinies, creating a bifurcated distribution of the Asian American population along class lines. Some Asian immigrant groups have converged with middle-class American, but many others, especially the most recent refugee groups, are struggling in the most underprivileged segment of American society. Consequently, class bifurcation toward both ends of society's class spectrum will likely lead to fragmentation of the larger Asian American community, which will hinder political mobilization and panethnic solidarity. Bifurcation also likely affects the second generation. Unlike the second generation of the 1960s and 1970s, most of whom grew up in segregated urban enclaves, a visible proportion of today's second generation is growing up in affluent white middle-class suburbs. Members of the suburban middle-class coethnics may have fewer ties to their working-class coethnics in urban enclaves and show limited interest in working-class community issues.

Third, diverse settlement patterns also have long-term implications for the development of a cohesive Asian American community. Those who are currently segregated in the inner city are confronted with a reality more daunting than the one faced by their earlier counterparts. Today, the United States has an emerging "hourglass" economy in which movement from bottom to top has gotten progressively more difficult. Those newcomers who are poorly educated and lack marketable skills may find themselves stalled or, even worse, stumbling beneath the ranks of the lower working class, either because they are unable to obtain employment or because the jobs they do obtain do not pay a decent family wage. Consequently, they and their children may become trapped in poverty and isolated from mainstream American society. While successful structural integration may not automatically lead to social acceptance, those who have achieved residential mobility are undoubtedly more privileged, enjoying comfortable homes, safe neighborhoods, quality schools, and more channels to mobility.

Last but not least, immigration complicates intergenerational relations and ethnic solidarity. US-born Asian Americans, especially those assumed to be "assimilated," have been rudely reawakened with renewed images of being "foreigners." Stereotyped images of "American" create both psychological and practical problems for native-born Americans who phenotypically resemble the new arrivals. One frequently hears of the harassment of US-born Mexican Americans suspected of being undocumented immigrants and of comments about third-generation Japanese Americans' "good English." The children, born in the United States and similar to other American children, suffer from persistent disadvantages merely because they look "foreign" (US Commission on Civil Rights 1992, 1998). While they are infuriated by their unfair treatment as foreigners, US-born Asian Americans are also caught between including immigrants in their struggle for racial equality and excluding them. Similar to other Americans in speech, thought, and behavior, US-born Asian Americans often hold values about labor rights, individualism, civil liberty, and, ultimately, the ideology of assimilationism that are different from those of their foreign-born counterparts. These differences, intertwined with the acculturation gap between immigrant and native-born generations, have impeded ethnic coalition, ideological consensus, and collective action (Zhou 2001).

Negotiating differences and coalition building within this very heterogeneous ethnic community will continue to remain the foremost priority in the twenty-first century. Policies reflecting the interests and needs of Asian Americans must develop a flexible framework to incorporate the diversity that characterizes the contemporary community. New generations of Asian Americans will have to vie for their own place within their respective communities and challenge stereotypes that serve to denigrate their agency in mainstream American society. Although Asian Americans will continue to rally (as they have historically) around issues that unite them on the basis of a shared sense of racial identity—ethnic stereotyping, hate crimes, economic and political scapegoating, and the glass ceiling—specific national and cultural interests espoused by Asian American ethnic groups will demand innovative approaches to promoting the continued development of pan-Asian coalitions while reflecting interethnic differences.

NOTES

1 The number includes 1.6 million formerly unauthorized aliens and 1.1 million special agricultural workers who were granted permanent resident status under the provisions of the Immigration Reform and Control Act of 1986 (Zhou 2001).

2 The number of Asian immigrants excludes those from Iran, Israel, and Turkey, except for 1991, when the Asian share dropped to 18 percent due to the sudden increase in the legalizees under IRCA, most of whom were Mexicans or Central Americans.

3 *Yearbook of Immigration Statistics: 2012*, http://www.dhs.gov/sites/default/files/publications/ois_yb_2012.pdf (accessed January 10, 2015).

4 Pew Research Center (2012).

5 A small number of Asian Indians were present at the time. They were, however, classified as "Hindu" in the 1920, 1930, and 1940 censuses, as "white" in 1950 and 1960, and as "Asian or Pacific Islander" since 1970 (Nash 1997).

6 As defined by the US Bureau of the Census, PMSA stands for primary metropolitan statistical area and MSA for metropolitan statistical area, terms that generally refer to central cites.

7 US Asian American Population map, http://www.pewsocialtrends.org/asianamericans-graphics/st_12-06-17_aa_map/ (accessed January 27, 2015).

8 Hope Yen and Ben Nuckols, "Urban Chinatowns Wane as Asians Head to the Suburbs," *Huffington Post*, January 19, 2012, http://www.huffingtonpost.com/2012/01/19/urban-chinatowns-decline_n_1217122.html (accessed January 27, 2015).

9 Originally quoted in Bernard Wong (1982, 33). Also cited in Morrison G. Wong (1995, 86).

10 Personal communication with a retired Chinatown activist in New York.

11 The detailed generation breakdown among Asian Americans is as follows: 65 percent belong to the first generation (foreign-born), 25 percent the second generation (US-born of foreign-born parentage), and 10 percent the third or later generations (US-born of US-born parentage), compared to 9 percent, 11 percent, and 80 percent, respectively, in the general US population. Figures are from the 2000–2002 Current Population Survey of the US Census Bureau.

12 Class discussion on ethnic identity, UCLA, March 1999.

REFERENCES

Alba, Richard, and Victor Nee. 2003. *Remaking the American Mainstream: Assimilation and Contemporary Immigration*. Cambridge, MA: Harvard University Press.

Barringer, Herbert, Robert B. Gardner, and Michael J. Levin. 1993. *Asian and Pacific Islanders in the United States, p. 42, table 2.5*. New York: Russell Sage Foundation.

Chan, Sucheng. 1991. *Asian Americans: An Interpretive History*. New York: Twayne.

———. 1994. *Hmong Means Free: Life in Laos and America*. Philadelphia: Temple University Press.

Cheng, Lucie, and Philip Q. Yang. 1996. "Asians: The 'Model Minority' Deconstructed." Pp. 305–344 in Roger Waldinger and Mehdi Bozorgmehr, eds., *Ethnic Los Angeles*. New York: Russell Sage Foundation.

de Crevecoeur, J. Hector St. John. 1904 [1782]. *Letters from an American Farmer*. New York: Fox and Duffield.

Espiritu, Yen Le. 1992. *Asian American Panethnicity: Bridging Institutions and Identities*. Philadelphia: Temple University Press.

Gans, Herbert J. 1979. "Symbolic Ethnicity: The Future of Ethnic Groups and Cultures in America." *Ethnic and Racial Studies* 2: 1–20.

Glazer, Nathan. 1993. "Is Assimilation Dead?" *Annals of the American Academy of Political and Social Sciences* 530: 122–136.

Gordon, Milton M. 1964. *Assimilation in American Life: The Role of Race, Religion, and National Origins*. New York: Oxford University Press.

Kitano, Harry. 1969. *Japanese Americans: The Evolution of a Subculture*. Englewood Cliffs, NJ: Prentice Hall.

Liu, John M., and Lucie Cheng. 1994. "Pacific Rim Development and the Duality of Post-1965 Asian Immigration to the United States." Pp. 74–99 in Paul M. Ong, Edna Bonacich, and

Lucie Cheng, eds., *The New Asian Immigration in Los Angeles and Global Restructuring*. Philadelphia: Temple University Press.

Lopez, David, and Yen Espiritu. 1990. "Panethnicity in the United States: A Theoretically Framework." *Ethnic and Racial Studies* 13: 198–224.

Massey, Douglas S. Rafael Alarcon, Jorge Durand, and Humberto Gonzalez. 1987. *Return to Azlan: The Social Process of International Migration from Western Mexico*. Berkeley: University of California Press.

Matsumoto, Valerie. 1993. *Farming the Homeplace*. Ithaca, NY: Cornell University Press.

Nash, Philip Tajitsu. 1997. "Will the Census Go Multiracial?" *Amerasia Journal* 23 (1): 17–27.

Nishi, Setsuko Matsunaga. 1995. "Japanese Americans." Pp. 95–133 in Pyong Gap Min, ed., *Asian Americans: Contemporary Trends and Issue*. Thousand Oaks, CA: Sage.

Ong, Paul M., Lucie Cheng, and Leslie Evans. 1992. "Migration of Highly Educated Asians and Global Dynamics." *Asian and Pacific Migration Journal* 1 (3–4): 543–567.

Oropesa, R. S., and N. S. Landale. 1997. "Immigrant Legacies: Ethnicity, Generation and Children's Family and Economic Lives." *Social Science Quarterly* 78 (2): 399–416.

Pew Research Center. 2012. *The Rise of Asian Americans*. http://www.pewsocialtrends. org/2012/06/19/the-rise-of-asian-americans/.

Portes, Alejandro, and Rubén G. Rumbaut. 2014. *Immigrant America: A Portrait*. 4th ed. Berkeley: University of California Press.

Portes, Alejandro, and Min Zhou. 1993. "The New Second Generation: Segmented Assimilation and Its Variants among Post-1965 Immigrant Youth." *Annals of the American Academy of Political and Social Science* 530: 74–98.

Reeves, Terrance J., and Claudette E. Bennett. 2004. *We the People: Asians in the United States*. 2000 Census Special Report, CENSR-17. Washington, DC: US Census Bureau.

Rumbaut, Rubén G. 1995. "Vietnamese, Laotian, and Cambodian Americans." Pp. 232–270 in Pyung Gap Min, ed., *Asian Americans: Contemporary Trends and Issues*. Thousand Oaks, CA: Sage.

Sassen, Saskia. 1989. "America's Immigration Problems." *World Policy Journal* 6 (4): 811–832.

Smith, James P., and Barry Edmonston, eds. 1997. *The New Americans: Economic, Demographic and Fiscal Effects of Immigration*. Washington, DC: National Academy Press.

Sung, Betty Lee. 1987. *The Adjustment Experience of Chinese Immigrant Children in New York City*. Staten Island, NY: Center for Migration Studies.

Takaki, Ronald. 1989. *Strangers from a Different Shore: A History of Asian Americans*. New York: Penguin.

Takezawa, Yasuko I. 2000. "Children of Inmates: The Effects of the Redress Movement among Third-Generation Japanese Americans." Pp. 299–314 in Min Zhou and J. V. Gatewood, eds., *Contemporary Asian American: A Multidisciplinary Reader*, 1st ed. New York: New York University Press.

Tuan, Mia. 1999. *Forever Foreign or Honorary White? The Asian Ethnic Experience Today*. New Brunswick, NJ: Rutgers University Press.

US Census Bureau. 1983. *1980 General Population Characteristics, United States Summary*. Washington, DC: Government Printing Office. http://www2.census.gov/prod2/decennial/documents/1980/1980censusofpopu8011u_bw.pdf.

———. 1993. *1990 Census of Population: Asians and Pacific Islanders in the United States* (1990 CP-3-5). Washington, DC: Government Printing Office. https://www.census.gov/prod/cen1990/cp3/cp-3-5.pdf.

———. 2002. *The Asian Population, 2000* (2000 Census Briefs) https://www.census.gov/prod/2002pubs/c2kbr01-16.pdf.

———. 2012. *The Asian Population, 2010* (2010 Census Briefs) https://www.census.gov/prod/cen2010/briefs/c2010br-11.pdf.

US Commission on Civil Rights. 1992. *Civil Rights Issues Facing Asian Americans in the 1990s: A Report*. Washington, DC: Government Printing Office.

———. 1998. *The Economic Status of Americans of Asian Descent: An Exploratory Investigation*. Washington, DC: Clearing House Publications.

Warner, W. Lloyd, and Leo Srole. 1945. *The Social Systems of American Ethnic Groups*. New Haven, CT: Yale University Press.

Waters, Mary C. 1990. *Ethnic Options: Choosing Identities in America*. Berkeley: University of California Press.

Wong, Bernard. 1982. *Chinatown: Economic Adaptation and Ethnic Identity of the Chinese*. New York: Holt, Rinehart and Winston.

Wong, Morrison G. 1995. "Chinese Americans." Pp. 58–94 in Pyong Gap Min, ed., *Asian Americans: Contemporary Trends and Issues*. Thousand Oaks, CA: Sage.

Xie, Y., and K. A. Goyette. 2004. *The American People, Census 2000: A Demographic Portrait of Asian Americans*. New York: Russell Sage Foundation.

Yanagisako, Sylvia. 1995. "Transforming Orientalism: Gender, Nationality, and Class in Asian American Studies." Pp. 275–298 in Sylvia Yanagisako and Carol Delaney, eds., *Naturalizing Power: Essays in Feminist Cultural Analysis*. New York: Routledge.

Yancey, William, Richard Juliani, and Eugene Erikson. 1976. "Emergent Ethnicity: A Review and Reformulation." *American Sociological Review* 41 (3): 391–403.

Yu, Henry. 1998. "The 'Oriental Problem' in America, 1920–1960: Linking the Identities of Chinese American and Japanese American Intellectuals." Pp. 191–214 in K. Scott Wong and Sucheng Chan, eds., *Claiming America: Constructing Chinese American Identities During the Exclusion Era*. Philadelphia: Temple University Press.

Zangwill, Israel. 1914. *The Melting Pot: Drama in Four Acts*. New York: Macmillan.

Zhou, Min. 1992. *Chinatown: The Socioeconomic Potential of an Urban Enclave*. Philadelphia: Temple University Press.

———. 2001. "Contemporary Immigration and the Dynamics of Race and Ethnicity." Pp. 200–242 in Neil Smelser, William Julius Wilson, and Faith Mitchell, eds., *America Becoming: Racial Trends and Their Consequences*. Washington, DC: National Academy Press.

———. 2009. *Contemporary Chinese America: Immigration, Ethnicity, and Community Transformation*. Philadelphia: Temple University Press.

Zhou, Min, and Carl L. Bankston. 1998. *Growing Up American: How Vietnamese Children Adapt to Life in the United States*. New York: Russell Sage Foundation.

Zhou, Min, and Yoshinori Kamo. 1994. "An Analysis of Earnings Patterns for Chinese, Japanese and Non-Hispanic Whites in the United States." *Sociological Quarterly* 35 (4): 581–602.

Zhou, Min, and Susan S. Kim. 2006. "Community Forces, Social Capital, and Educational Achievement: The Case of Supplementary Education in the Chinese and Korean Immigrant Communities." *Harvard Educational Review* 76 (1): 1–29.

Zhou, Min, Yen-fen Tseng, and Rebecca Y. Kim. 2008. "Rethinking Residential Assimilation through the Case of Chinese Ethnoburbs in the San Gabriel Valley, California." *Amerasia Journal* 34 (3): 55–83.

4

The Waves of War

Refugees, Immigrants, and New Americans from Southeast Asia

CARL L. BANKSTON III AND DANIELLE ANTOINETTE HIDALGO

Southeast Asia stretches from the northern borders of Laos and Vietnam through the southern islands of Indonesia. It includes Myanmar (Burma), Thailand, and Cambodia, as well as Malaysia and the Philippines. The overwhelming majority of Southeast Asian Americans, who made up about one-third of the total Asian American population at the beginning of the twenty-first century, came from the Philippines, Vietnam, Laos, Cambodia, and Thailand. There is a great deal of diversity among these nations. The people of the Philippines, for example, speak mostly non-tonal, grammatically complex languages related to Malay and Indonesian. Most Filipinos are Catholic, although a substantial minority is Muslim, and their culture is deeply influenced by a Spanish colonial history (Ocampo 2014). The Vietnamese speak a tonal language and have received cultural influences from China, including Confucianism and the Mahayana Buddhism common in other parts of East Asia. Vietnam also has a large number of Catholics, as a result of French colonial domination. Thailand, Laos, and Cambodia have had close historical and cultural ties with each other. Most people in all three practice the Theravada Buddhism of Southeast Asia, and the three nations have had long cultural ties to India, the source of their writing systems. The Thai and the Lao speak closely related tonal languages, while the Cambodians (also known as the Khmer) speak an unrelated non-tonal language. All of these nations also have significant internal variation, with large minority groups, such as the Hmong from the mountains of Laos.

While there is diversity among the ancestral homelands of America's Southeast Asian population, there is also similarity. All have maintained traditional societies based on wet-rice farming. More important for their immigration history, all of them came into contact with the United States as a result of the American military interventions from the end of the nineteenth through the end of the twentieth centuries. War created the paths of migration between North America and Southeast Asia. The timing of the wars, and the parts played by the Southeast Asians in these wars, shaped many of the conditions of migration and the processes of adaptation to the new homeland. Filipinos, the first to be affected by America's rise to global dominance, developed a deep, but complicated familiarity with American society. The war in Indochina brought new nationalities to the United States as refugees, but it also affected nonrefugee migration from both the Philippines and Thailand, where the United States had military bases during the second half of the twentieth century.

American foreign policy in the form of military activities created connections between the United States and the nations of origin of major Southeast Asian American groups. American immigration and refugee policies then played a great part in determining who would arrive in the United States from this distant part of the world and what opportunities and barriers they would find.

War, Occupation, and Migration from the Philippines

The Philippines was a Spanish colony from the second half of the sixteenth century until the end of the nineteenth, when Filipino independence forces rose against the colonial power. The United States was an expanding industrial force, and some American leaders believed that the United States needed a strong navy and overseas stations for it, as well as new resources. At the beginning of the Spanish-American War in 1898, as a strategic move against Spain and as a tactic for expanding the international role of the United States, Assistant Secretary of the Navy Theodore Roosevelt secretly ordered a US fleet to attack Spanish forces at Manila, the chief city of the Philippines. The Spanish were ill prepared for the American attack and were quickly defeated. Instead of turning the island colony over to the Filipino rebel forces, the United States made arrangements with Spain and placed the Philippines under American rule (Bankston 2006).

For several years Filipino forces struggled with the new occupying power. Scholars have estimated that two hundred thousand to five hundred thousand Filipinos died in the fight against American colonization (San Juan 1998). After putting down the Filipino independence fighters, the United States began to attempt to remake the Philippines according to American concepts. The Americans created an extensive public school system and founded the University of the Philippines on the model of US research universities. The new colonists constructed roads and public buildings. The Americans created a US-style government and encouraged the growth of political parties.

The American occupation of the Philippines marked the first movement of the United States into Southeast Asia. As the English language and familiarity with North American ways began to spread through the Philippines, the contact established by war also promoted migration from the Philippines to the United States and its territories. From 1903 to 1938, the Pensionado Act passed by the US Congress provided funds for Filipino students to study in the United States. Following the example of these Pensionados, or sponsored students, other unsponsored Filipinos entered American schools and universities, creating the movement of people and ideas between the two nations.

From 1910 to 1920, the Filipino American population increased from under three thousand to over twenty-six thousand (Bankston 2006). During the 1920s, this population grew even more rapidly as a result of the demand for agricultural workers in Hawaii and California. Canneries in Alaska and other locations also began to draw Filipino workers. Filipinos found work at sea, as well, working in the American merchant marine until 1936 and in the US Navy, where they were typically assigned as mess stewards.

As Figure 4.1 shows, the American occupation and control of the Philippines, together with American demand for Filipino labor, led the number of Filipinos in the United States to grow from under twenty-seven thousand in 1920 to over a hundred thousand ten years later. After the United States established the Philippine Commonwealth and placed the Philippines on the track to independence in 1934, migration went down and the Philippine American population even decreased slightly by 1940. The Tydings-McDuffie Act, which created the Commonwealth, redefined Filipinos as aliens, rather than US nationals, and gave Filipinos an admission quota of only fifty individuals per year (Bankston 2006). However, another war changed relations between the two nations once again.

Following the attack on Pearl Harbor, the Japanese invaded and occupied the Philippines in 1942. Some Filipinos at first saw the Japanese as liberators from the Americans. Others joined with the Americans against the new invaders. Opposition to the Japanese soon intensified pro-American feelings among many Filipinos (Bankston 2003).

The United States recognized Philippine independence in 1946, but the Americans kept large military bases in the Philippines. These major centers of the US armed forces in Southeast Asia became one of the most important sources of migration. By one estimate, about half of all the immigrants who came to the United States between 1946 and 1965 arrived as wives of US military personnel (Reimers 1985). Postwar immigration policies also helped foster an expanding Filipino American population. The Luce-Celler Bill of 1946 increased the quota of Filipino migrants to the United States to one hundred per year, and spouses of US citizens were entirely outside the quota. The Education Exchange Act of 1946 began what would later become one of the most important sources of Filipino migration to the United States: nurses. This act enabled foreign nurses to spend two years in the United States for study and professional experience. The difference between living standards in the two countries encouraged many nurses to stay after the two years, and the demand for nurses in the United States made it relatively easy for them to find work. Once again, national relations shaped by war were followed by immigration policies to direct flows of migrants. During the post Word War II period, though, the bases in the Philippines became staging points for the next great involvement of the United States in Southeast Asia, the Vietnam War. Migrant flows were to become waves.

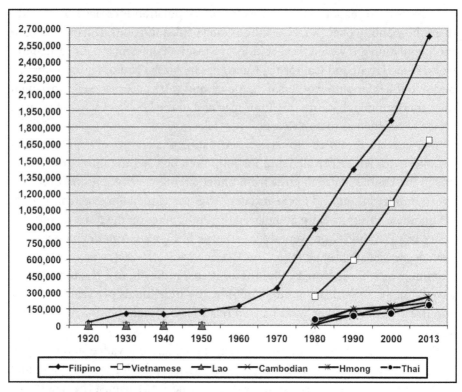

Figure 4.1. Major Southeast Asian Populations in the United States, 1920–2013. *Source:* US Census Bureau (1970, 1983, 1993, 2002, 2012, 2014).

Although Filipino Americans are the oldest Southeast Asian group in the United States, their population grew most rapidly during the same period of time that other Southeast Asians began to arrive. The growth of the Filipino American population, though, began a few years earlier than that of other Southeast Asian American groups. In 1965, the United States greatly amended its immigration policy. The new immigration law replaced a national origins quota system that allotted places mainly to Europeans with caps for each hemisphere and a system of preferences to be used in allocating places in overall quotas. Spouses, unmarried children under 18, and parents of US citizens could enter the United States without numerical restriction. Adult family members of US citizens had first preference; and spouses and unmarried adult children of resident aliens had second preference. Professionals and people with special abilities had third preference. In the descending system of preferences, family connections became the primary basis for acceptance and professional and job skills became a secondary basis. Because the US occupation of the Philippines had created complex, long-standing ties between the two nations, Filipinos were poised to take advantage of the 1965 change in immigration laws. Largely educated in English and familiar with North American culture, Filipinos had skills that were in demand in the United States. High-skilled professionals made up a large segment of the post-1965 migrants from the Philippines. Before 1960, fewer than 2 percent of the people of Filipino ancestry residing in the United States had professional occupations, compared to 6 percent of all Americans. By 1980, though, about a quarter of Filipinos in the United States were professionals, and twenty years later this had gone up to nearly a third (Bankston 2006). The American demand for medical workers, and the fact that the American occupation had established American training and standards for Filipino medical professionals, accounted for the overrepresentations of nurses, physicians, and medical technicians who immigrated from the Philippines. Nurses, who had already begun moving from the Philippines to the United States following the 1948 Education Exchange Act, emigrated in even greater numbers following the passage of the Health Professions Assistance Act in 1976. This piece of legislation required professional immigrants to have job offers from American employers, and it was followed by active cooperation of immigration officials with American hospitals in recruiting nurses. Again, the connections between the United States and the Philippines created by the invasion and long occupation meant that the Philippines was training nurses ready for work in the United States and it was therefore an ideal setting for recruitment (Bankston 2006).

Spouses of American service personnel who had served in the Philippines continued to make up a substantial portion of the post-1965 immigration, with much of this due to the American buildup in Southeast Asia during the Vietnam War. In 1980, one out of every four married Filipino American women had husbands who had served in the US military during the Vietnam War period. The popular identification of the Philippines as a source of wives also expanded into civilian American society, so that marriages arranged by mail between women in the Philippines and men in the United States had become fairly common by the 1970s. By the early 1990s, an estimated 19,000 "mail-order brides" were leaving the Philippines each year to join husbands and fiancés abroad, with the United States as the primary destination (Bankston 1999, 2006).

As the Filipino American population grew, there were more people in the United States with immediate relatives in the Philippines. Because the 1965 change in immigration law had made family reunification the category that allowed the most immigrants, this meant that each immigrant opened the way for others, resulting in an exponential growth in the Filipino American population throughout the end of the twentieth century (Bankston 2006).

While the post-1965 Filipino immigrants were fairly widely dispersed around the nation, they did have some centers of settlement, promoted by the family reunification emphasis of US immigration law. By 2013, just under half of all Filipinos in the United States (46 percent) lived in California. Los Angeles County in Southern California was the single largest concentration, since it was home to an estimated 320,600 Filipino Americans, or 12 percent of all Filipinos in the United States (US Census Bureau 2014).

The Vietnam War and New Sources of Migration

Following World War II, the Cold War between the United States and the communist nations of the Soviet Union and China led America to extend its involvement in Southeast Asia beyond the Philippines. Communists, headed by former Soviet Comintern agent Ho Chi Minh, led the struggle for the independence of the French colony of Vietnam. Unable to reestablish control over Vietnam, France accepted a peace agreement in 1954 that divided Vietnam into a communist-dominated northern portion and a southern portion, where the French at first hoped to maintain some influence. Anticommunist, disproportionately Catholic, groups established themselves in South Vietnam. North Vietnam, together with dissidents in the South, sought to reunify the country. With this Cold War setting as the backdrop, the United States saw the conflict in Vietnam as critical to prevent the spread of communism. By 1965, the US effort to maintain the South Vietnamese government led the United States to send huge numbers of their own troops.

The Vietnam War brought the United States into closer contact with other nations in the region of Vietnam. As early as 1950, the Americans forged ties with Thailand as a response to the Korean War (Randolph 1986). Thailand began to receive substantial foreign aid and military assistance from the United States. With direct American intervention in Vietnam, these ties grew even closer and stronger. Following the American lead, Thailand sent troops into Vietnam. Even more important for the future Thai American population, by the height of the Vietnam War in the early 1970s, "Thailand harbored more than 750 U.S. aircraft actively involved in operations over Indochina and served as temporary home to some 50,000 American servicemen" (Randolph 1986). As part of the Vietnam War activities, the United States established seven major US air bases in Thailand (Bishop and Robinson 1998), which have been described as "highly sexualized" zones promoting interaction between American men and local Thai women (Enloe 2000, 231). Even more American servicemen passed temporarily through Thailand from Vietnam and other parts of the region for "R&R" (rest and recreation). Aside from purely military activities, the United States also provided Thailand with a wide array of programs from the US Agency for International Development (USAID), the US Information Service (USIS), and other acronymic organizations during this period (Randolph 1986).

American war efforts from Thailand moved into Laos, as well as Vietnam. In Laos, the guerilla forces known as the Pathet Lao ("Lao Nation") were allies of the North Vietnamese, and the "Ho Chi Minh Trail," North Vietnam's main supply route to its troops in the South, ran the length of eastern Laos. The United

States began massive bombing in Laos, conducted from Thailand, and recruited a secret army among the Laotian minority group known as the Hmong.

The war also spread into Cambodia, which had been part of French Indochina along with Vietnam and Laos. Cambodia had its own communist-led insurgents known as the Khmer Rouge. It was also used by communist Vietnamese forces as a sanctuary and a base for launching attacks into South Vietnam. In the late 1960s, Cambodia's leader Prince Norodom Sihanouk allowed the Americans to engage in bombing the Cambodian countryside in order to drive the Vietnamese forces out. The prince's cooperation was limited, though, and the Americans acquiesced when the Cambodian military, under General Lon Nol, staged a coup, establishing the Khmer Republic. The coup caused Sihanouk to flee to the Khmer Rouge and to urge his supporters to take up arms against the new Cambodian government.

With Lon Nol in power, there were no limits on American bombing. Eager to force the North Vietnamese to accept a peace that would enable American troops to withdraw from a highly unpopular war, the Americans dropped an estimated 539,129 tons of bombs on the small country. This was about three and a half times the amount of bombs dropped on Japan during all of World War II. Social disruption, together with the political appeal of Sihanouk, greatly increased the power of the radical Khmer Rouge. After the Khmer Rouge took power in 1975, they forced the populace out of the cities and into concentration camps, where millions of Cambodians died from sickness, starvation, and executions.

Although the Philippines was separated from the events in Thailand, Cambodia, Laos, and Vietnam by the South China Sea, relations between this former US colony and the US government were also affected by the Vietnam War. Under pressure from the Americans, the Philippines sent a modest number of troops to fight in Vietnam. More importantly, though, "the United States was vastly increasing its use of Philippine and Thai facilities in its war" (Thompson 1975, 87). As in Thailand, this expansion of military facilities brought an increase in the military personnel stationed in Philippine bases.

In 1973, with growing unwillingness among the American people for continuing the war in Vietnam, the United States withdrew nearly all of its forces from Vietnam, Cambodia, and Laos. In the spring of 1975, South Vietnam fell to the forces of the North and Cambodia fell to the Khmer Rouge. The Royal Government of Laos allowed the Pathet Lao into a coalition government, and the Pathet Lao rapidly took over the country.

The United States continued to have dwindling numbers of troops in Thailand until the summer of 1976, after negotiations with the Thai government failed to renew agreements for a US military presence (Randolph 1986). By that time, though, well over thirty thousand Thai people had left for the United States. Thailand had become a familiar place to many Americans, and a clear migration route had been established. The bases in the Philippines, product of the first

American military intervention in Southeast Asia and central locations for the intervention in Vietnam, closed in 1991.

Refugees from Vietnam, Cambodia, and Laos

In 1965, the same year that the United States began sending significant numbers of troops to Vietnam, the United States changed its immigration laws, removing discriminatory national origins quotas that opened the gates to immigrants from Asia. As Figure 4.1 shows, the Filipino American population grew rapidly in the years following 1970 and other Southeast Asian groups became significant parts of the nation during this time. The change in immigration laws also set the stage for the growth of the Southeast Asian population, in particular, by formalizing refugee policy and creating a special type of visa for refugees, known as the "seventh preference" visa category.

This new visa category for refugees should be understood in terms of the global foreign policies that led to American involvement in the Vietnam War. The Refugee Relief Act of 1953, one of the earliest pieces of refugee legislation in the United States, resulted from President Harry Truman's appeal to Congress to authorize visas for escapees from the communist-dominated nations of Eastern Europe. The Hungarian Refugee Adjustment Act of 1958 was designed to help Hungarian refugees remain in the United States as permanent residents following the Hungarian uprising against Soviet control. The most energetic US governmental efforts on behalf of refugees prior to the mid-1970s were products of the Cuban Refugee Program, established in the early 1960s to help those fleeing from Fidel Castro's Cuba. Many of the voluntary agencies and even individuals who would later become active in resettling Southeast Asian refugees were earlier involved with resettling Cuban refugees. American refugee policy, like American defense policy, was almost entirely concerned with communism during the second half of the twentieth century.

Ten years after the new immigration policy in 1965, US involvement in the war in Vietnam led to a refugee program that entirely overshadowed Cuban resettlement. In the spring of 1975, the US-supported governments of South Vietnam, Laos, and Cambodia fell to communist forces. As North Vietnamese forces took control of what had been South Vietnam, hundreds of thousands of South Vietnamese, many formerly associated with the American war effort, fled by boat into the China Sea. The United States rapidly created a program known as Operation New Life, which moved refugees to American military bases to prepare them for temporary resettlement in the United States. In this way, 126,000 Vietnamese, most of whom were well educated and fairly familiar with the American way of life, became the first wave of Southeast Asian refugees to settle in the United States.

During the late 1970s, Vietnamese continued to leave their country by boat, or on foot across Cambodia to Thailand. Cambodians and Laotians also continued to flee, most of them into Thailand. In 1977, Attorney General Griffin Bell used his parole authority, his power to admit emergency cases into the country temporarily, to allow thousands of people from the three Indochinese countries of Cambodia, Laos, and Vietnam to resettle in the United States. That same year, President Carter signed legislation that permitted the Indochinese to become permanent residents, establishing a path to eventual citizenship.

When tensions between Vietnam and Cambodia led to the Vietnamese invasion of Cambodia in December 1978, Vietnam was attacked by Cambodia's ally, China. These events resulted in an outpouring of refugees from both Cambodia and Vietnam, including many ethnic Chinese living in Vietnam. In response to the refugee crisis, Congress passed the most comprehensive piece of refugee legislation in American history, the Refugee Act of 1980. In place of the "seventh preference category" established in 1965, which admitted refugees as part of the total number of immigrants allowed into the United States, the Refugee Act provided for an annual number of admissions for refugees. This amount was to be independent of the number of immigrants permitted, and it was to be established each year by the president in consultation with Congress.

Refugees began entering the United States in unprecedented numbers. The Orderly Departure Program was created in 1980 by an agreement between the American and Vietnamese governments. This program enabled Vietnamese political prisoners and Amerasians (half-Vietnamese children of American soldiers) to leave Vietnam legally for resettlement in the United States (Zhou and Bankston 1998).

The vast majority of those allowed into the United States by Operation New Life in 1975 were Vietnamese. In the spring of that year, the United States brought in 4,600 Cambodians and 800 people from Laos, as well as the 126,000 from Vietnam. At the end of 1975, though, the US Congress agreed to accept more of the people from Laos who were languishing in refugee camps in Thailand. During the following year, the United States brought in 10,200 refugees from Laos who had been living in the Thai border camps. Most of those admitted at that time were members of families headed by people who had been employed by USAID, USIS, or the US embassy in the Laotian capital of Vientiane.

In the late 1970s, the numbers of those arriving from Laos diminished again, to 400 in 1977, and then rose to 8,000 in 1978. At the end of the 1970s, war between Vietnam and Cambodia created new, highly publicized waves of refugees to Southeast Asia, bringing increased public attention to the region and creating a favorable environment for the admission of new Southeast Asian refugees. Refugee resettlement in the United States of people from Laos grew to 30,200 in 1979, 55,500 in 1980, and 19,300 in 1981, or about 105,000 individuals during this three-year period. Admissions from Laos reached the high point in 1980 and then gradually slowed to a trickle over the course of the twentieth century. These admissions included both ethnic Lao, frequently families of soldiers associated with the former Kingdom of Laos, and members of the Hmong secret army that had been recruited by American intelligence. Seen as enemies by the new government of the Lao People's Democratic Republic, people in these two groups fled across the border into Thailand. The Thai government responded by pressuring the Americans to accept more refugees.

Large-scale refugee movement from Cambodia to the United States began in the year of the 1980 Refugee Act. In 1981, over 38,000 Cambodian refugees reached the United States. By the end of the 1980s, numbers of Cambodian refugees began to decline. With the withdrawal of Vietnam from Cambodia in the late 1980s, the flow of refugees came to an end. In the second half of the 1990s, the movement of 1,000 to 2,000 legal immigrants per year replaced the refugee movement from Cambodia (Bankston and Hidalgo 2006). By the 2000s, the flow of refugees from Cambodia had essentially stopped. Between 2002 and 2011, only 84 individuals of Cambodian nationality were admitted to the United States (Bankston 2014a).

None of the Southeast Asian groups except Filipinos appear before 1980 in Figure 4.1 because there were no significant numbers of any of these other groups. However, in 1980, the first year the other Southeast Asians appeared, there were already over a quarter of a million Vietnamese and close to 68,000 people from Cambodia and Laos in the United States. These new arrivals had come onto the American scene so suddenly because the US government was coordinating their resettlement and they were connected to the United States through the American military engagement in their nations. The government coordination of resettlement also had important implications for the ways in which the members of the new groups would fit into American society.

Concerned about the social and political impact of its refugee policy, the US government at first attempted to scatter people from Vietnam, Laos, and Cambodia around the nation. The government pursued its resettlement efforts by working through voluntary agencies, such as religion-based charities and social service groups. Refugees settled in locations where voluntary agencies were available to find housing and organize support. Both the initial attempt to scatter refugees and the use of voluntary agencies tended to create relatively small Southeast Asian communities throughout the country, so that members of the Southeast Asian refugee groups were neither dispersed as individuals, nor concentrated entirely into single large ethnic enclaves (Zhou and Bankston 1998).

By the second decade of the twenty-first century, the largest concentrations of Southeast Asian refugee groups were primarily in Southern California. However, other communities of Vietnamese, Cambodians, Lao, and Hmong were widespread. The ethnic Lao were the least concentrated of the groups, often forming small communities around the United States. Texas was home to the largest number of these, with a population of about 13,000 Lao Americans in the early 2010s, mainly in the Dallas-Fort Worth and Houston-Brazoria Areas

(Bankston 2014a). Minnesota had almost as many Lao Americans as Texas in the early 2010s (about 12,000), living primarily in Saint Paul and Minneapolis, drawn by the support programs that also served the Hmong (Bankston 2014d).

By 2012, Los Angeles County was home to nearly 34,000 Cambodians and almost 7,000 lived in neighboring Orange County. Within Los Angeles County, the city of Long Beach had the greatest concentration of Cambodians, home to about 17,000 people of this ethnicity in 2012 (Ruggles et al. 2010), although some Cambodian American spokespersons maintained that these estimates were dramatically low and that the actual number of Cambodian Americans in Long Beach was probably closer to twice that many (Bankston 2014a). As early as the mid-1980s, the area along Tenth Street in Long Beach had become known among Cambodian Americans as the "New Phnom Penh," after the capital of Cambodia.

Nearby Los Angeles also had a significant population of Cambodians of at least 4,250. Stockton, California, had the second largest Cambodian community, numbering at least 10,000. Outside of California, the greatest number of Cambodian Americans were found in Massachusetts, where over 14,000 lived. About half of the Massachusetts Cambodians lived in the city of Lowell. Other states with large Cambodian populations include Texas (at least 6,000), Pennsylvania (at least 5,500, located mostly in Philadelphia), Virginia (at least 4,000), New York (at least 4,000, over two-thirds of whom lived in New York City), Minnesota (at least 4,000), and Illinois (over 3,000) (Bankston 2014a; Ruggles et al. 2010).

Many Hmong were initially resettled by voluntary agencies in Minnesota. As a result, the city of Saint Paul became a magnet, and by the end of the twentieth century Hmong was the single largest non-English language in Saint Paul's public schools. By 2010, the Minneapolis-Saint Paul area was home to 53,000 Hmong. Other Hmong sought to concentrate in the warmer climate of California, seeking relatively rural areas. By the mid-1980s, an estimated 20,000 Hmong had resettled in the three California Central Valley Counties of Merced, San Joaquin, and Fresno. By the 2010s, Fresno and Sacramento were each home to 24,000 to 26,000 Hmong. Other Northern California metropolitan areas with large Hmong populations included Stockton (6,900), Merced (6,300), and Chico (3,300) (Bankston and Hidalgo 2006; Bankston 2014b).

The Vietnamese, largest of the refugee groups, began to establish their most notable ethnic community in Southern California during the 1980s. By 1990 California's Orange County had become home to "Little Saigon" in the city of Westminster. With its Vietnamese-style shop fronts and Vietnamese language signs, Little Saigon could easily be confused with an upscale neighborhood in its Asian namesake. One fourth of the Vietnamese people in the United States had settled in the Los Angeles–Orange County–San Diego metropolitan area by 2000 (Rumbaut 2006). In the early 2010s the Vietnamese American populations of the cities of Westminster and adjacent Garden Grove numbered nearly 88,000 people (Bankston 2014e).

Still, the original government policy of scattering refugees around the nation, together with sponsorship by geographically dispersed voluntary agencies, continued to have consequences for the settlement of the Vietnamese. Montana, North Dakota, and Wyoming were the only states in the United States to hold fewer than one hundred Vietnamese at the beginning of the twenty-first century, and identifiable Vietnamese communities could be found around the country. Outside of California, Texas, Florida, Washington, and Virginia had the largest Vietnamese American populations by the 2010s.

Movement from Vietnam to the United States shifted from a refugee basis to an immigrant basis in the twenty first century, as Vietnamese Americans established transnational links between the two countries. During the decade 2004 to 2013, only slightly over 1,000 people per year entered the United States from Vietnam as refugees, but an average of 31,500 arrived each year as legal permanent residents (US Department of Homeland Security 2014). Most of this immigration was due to family connections between people in the United States and in Vietnam (Bankston 2014c).

Migration from Thailand

Until the late 1960s, Thailand was a distant and unfamiliar land for most Americans, and very few Thai people reached American shores. The new post-1965 immigrants from Thailand to the United States generally fell into two categories: professional jobseekers and Thai spouses of American service personnel (Cadge and Sangdhanoo 2002; Footrakoon 1999). The path to migration for the professionals had been opened both by the change in immigration law and by the American military presence in Thailand that facilitated contact and movement between the two countries.

The migration path of the spouses was, of course, even more directly linked to US military intervention in Southeast Asia, and it was a path taken by many new arrivals from Thailand. The 1980 US census showed that nearly 30 percent of all Thai immigrants and 40 percent of all female Thai immigrants were married to veterans of the US military. By that census year, a majority of married Thai American women (57 percent) had husbands who had been Vietnam era veterans. Migration through marriage led to a predominance of women among the Thai in America. According to US census data, women made up 62 percent of the Thai American population in 1980, 63 percent in 1990, and just over 60 percent in 2000 (Hidalgo and Bankston 2011). In their overview of the development of Thai Buddhism in America, Cadge and Sangdhanoo (2002) remark that "largely as a result of marriages between Thai women and American men who served in Vietnam, more women than men born in Thailand have and continue to live in the United States." Marriage and family remained the primary route for migration from Thailand. From 2004 through 2013, 83,792 people from Thailand were admitted to the United States as legal permanent residents. In the representative year 2013, 8 out of 10 nonrefugee immigrant admissions were immediate relatives of US citizens (a category made up mostly of spouses) and another 8 percent came in under family-sponsored preferences (Bankston and Hidalgo 2006; US Department of Homeland Security 2014).

As Figure 4.1 shows, the Thai American population established during the Vietnam War years continued to grow throughout the twentieth century and into the twenty-first, so that the American Community Survey of the US census counted 186,333 people of Thai origin by 2013. This figure may lose substantial numbers of undocumented immigrants from Thailand, smuggled into the country as workers by coethnics or arriving on tourist and student visas and remaining after visa expiration. Since so many of the legal immigrants were professionals or spouses of US citizens, Thai Americans had settled in various locations throughout the country. Nevertheless, they had established some notable ethnic concentrations by the end of the century. The Los Angeles area was also home to over one-third of the Thai American population in 2013, with about 25,600 residing in Los Angeles County itself according to census estimates. At the beginning of the year 2000, the section of Hollywood Boulevard between Western and Normandie Avenues was officially designated as Thai Town. Other fairly large Thai concentrations were located in New York City and Chicago (Bankston and Hidalgo 2006; US Census Bureau 2014).

Variations in Patterns of Immigrant Adaptation

The Vietnamese, Lao, Hmong, and Cambodians have generally differed somewhat from the Thai and Filipinos in their processes of adaptation to life in the United States. The first four groups arrived in America in mass waves of refugees, resettled by agencies and available for assistance on arrival. Although some members of these groups, particularly in the first wave of Vietnamese refugees, had high levels of education and professional experience in their own countries, they generally had little familiarity with life in the United States. By contrast, the Filipinos and the Thai came as individual immigrants, frequently with professional qualifications that could be fairly readily put to use or with marital or family connections that could ease their entry into US society (Bankston 2014c).

The five Southeast Asian groups also differ in a number of other respects, aside from their connections to refugee status. Cambodians and Hmong often arrived in the United States with serious disadvantages. Cambodian society had been torn apart during the Khmer Rouge years, and Cambodian Americans often had to recover from horrific personal tragedies while they sought to adapt to life in the United States. The Hmong had lived in a largely illiterate, rural culture in the mountains of Laos, and North America was an utterly strange world to many of them. Although Filipinos and Thai shared many characteristics as immigrant groups, the long familiarity of the Filipinos with American ways distinguished them from the Thai, as well as from the other Southeast Asians. Below, we look briefly at the patterns and processes of adaptation of each of the Southeast Asian national groups.

Filipino Americans

In general, people of Filipino ancestry in the United States are well-educated, tend to work at white-collar jobs, and move fairly easily through American society. As shown in Table 4.1, at the close of the twentieth century, Filipino Americans were more likely than others in the United States to work at management and professional jobs, showed rates of English proficiency similar to the rest of the American population, and had higher percentages of high school graduates and college graduates than other Americans did. While only 54 percent of traditionally college-aged young adults in the United States were enrolled in institutions of higher education, fully two-thirds of Filipinos in this age group were attending such institutions.

As a result of their relatively advantaged overall socioeconomic positions, Filipinos were less likely to be unemployed or receive public assistance than the rest of the US population, and they were markedly less likely than others to be poor. Their median per capita income was slightly higher than that of the nation at large, but they enjoyed substantially larger household incomes. The most probable explanation of this discrepancy is that Filipino American households tended to contain more workers than other households, an explanation that is consistent with the somewhat larger family sizes of Filipinos. Filipino Americans had rates of home ownership only slightly below those of other Americans and their homes were generally worth much more than those of other Americans. Their highly valued homes were probably only partly a result of their professional jobs and high household incomes. As with many other Asian groups, highly valued homes also reflect the high housing prices on the West Coast.

Filipino Americans were similar to the nation in general in family structure. This partly reflects their high degree of socioeconomic assimilation and partly reflects the fact that the families of Filipino Americans often did include other Americans. Filipinos in the United States continue to have very high rates of marriage to members of other racial and ethnic groups (Hidalgo and Bankston 2010).

The high degree of out-marriage among Filipino Americans naturally meant that to outward appearance many of them were completely absorbed in mainstream American society. It also meant that the ethnic identification of the children of Filipino Americans was often unclear. Data from the American Community Survey enable us to estimate that there were over one million people

TABLE 4.1. Socioeconomic and Family Characteristics of the US Population and of Major Southeast Asian Groups in the United States, 2010–2012

	All US	Filipino	Thai	Vietnamese	Cambodian	Lao	Hmong
% in management & professional jobs	29.4	32.9	29.1	22.4	16.0	14.6	15.6
% speaking English well or very well	96.2	94.7	82.2	71.1	76.0	78.0	81.7
% high school graduates (over 25)	86.1	92.2	83.9	69.7	64.2	68.2	63.8
% college graduates (over 25)	28.6	48.3	44.1	25.4	15.3	12.0	14.7
% enrolled in higher education (aged 19–22)	54.3	66.3	70.2	77.6	47.1	48.9	53.2
% unemployed	9.6	8.0	7.4	9.2	12.2	11.7	14.9
% in poverty	17.4	7.3	17.6	16.9	22.4	18.6	30.0
% on public assistance income	19.2	15.9	11.5	21.2	23.1	22.5	34.4
Median household income ($)	63,500	92,679	63,661	63,800	56,736	59,212	51,578
Median per capita income	29,245	30,825	28,800	23,373	20,500	25,000	23,476
Home ownership (%)	69.0	65.5	57.9	68.9	55.9	61.0	52.3
Median home value ($)	180,000	300,000	250,000	240,000	200,000	150,000	130,000
Average family size	3.02	3.80	2.86	3.92	4.13	4.04	5.90
% single-mother households	14.2	14.5	13.8	13.0	21.1	22.2	16.8
% single-father households	5.0	5.6	7.0	8.4	13.9	11.5	13.5

Source: Ruggles et al. (2010).

of mixed Filipino ancestry in the United States during the years 2011 through 2013, or about 28 percent of all Americans with a Filipino background (US Census Bureau 2014). The complex historical heritage of Filipino Americans also complicates their ethnic identification. The Spanish colonial background of the Philippines has resulted in cultural and linguistic influences that can encourage identification with Latino groups in the United States, as well as with white and black Americans (Ocampo 2014).

Despite their apparent absorption into various streams of the larger American society, though, Filipino Americans do generally retain a sense of belonging to a distinctive group. Even Filipinos married to non-Filipinos have often formed networks of Filipino friends. Filipino American clubs often sponsor events such as beauty pageants and celebrations of Philippine national holidays to maintain the sense of connection to the ancestral land (Bankston 2014c).

Vietnamese Americans

The Vietnamese, largest of the refugee groups and second largest Southeast Asian nationality in the United States, were less well represented in management and professional jobs than the Filipinos or Thai; nearly 30 percent of Vietnamese Americans spoke English less than well by the years 2010 through 2013, as seen in Table 4.1. However, while Vietnamese Americans had proportionately fewer adult high school and college graduates than other Americans or nonrefugee Southeast Asian groups, a higher percentage of traditionally college-aged Vietnamese were enrolled in higher education than young people in any of the other categories.

The participation of young Vietnamese in college-level institutions reflects their striking educational success in American schools. Some scholars have attributed this success to cultural values brought from Vietnam (Caplan, Choy, and Whitmore 1991). Zhou and Bankston (1998) have argued that the Vietnamese communities dispersed around the nation have been the source of much of this success. Their studies indicate that the Vietnamese developed high levels of ethnic solidarity in response to resettlement, often in low-income neighborhoods, in an alien society. The ethnic solidarity, frequently centered on Vietnamese Catholic churches or Vietnamese Buddhist temples, provided social controls and encouragement for young people to concentrate on education as a means of bypassing disadvantaged environments to jump into the American middle class. This ethnic solidarity, together with a generation gap between young people growing up in America and their elders, also produced alienation from Vietnamese adult society on the part of a substantial portion of Vietnamese youth. The two trends of educational success and alienation, according to Zhou and Bankston (1998), have been the sources of the competing stereotypes of Vietnamese young people as "delinquents" or "valedictorians." Returning to the location of their original study a decade after drawing this conclusion, Zhou and Bankston (2006) found further validation of this bifurcation of Vietnamese American youth, resulting from relationships to the ethnic community.

Although during the years of refugee settlement Vietnamese Americans had relatively high poverty rates and high rates of participation in public assistance, by 2012 these rates were similar to those of the general population, as were their unemployment rates. In home ownership, also this refugee-origin population had caught up with other Americans. Again, the high valuation of homes owned by Vietnamese Americans probably reflects their large numbers on the West Coast. With somewhat larger families than other Americans, the native-born part of the Vietnamese American population was likely to grow rapidly over the first part of the twenty-first century.

One of the consequences of the planting of Vietnamese communities around the United States is that Vietnamese Americans have frequently maintained close ties among widely distributed ethnic concentrations. On the negative side, this has meant that members of Vietnamese youth gangs have been able to move relatively easily from one location to another. On the positive side, it has meant that Vietnamese in one place can often seek help from those in another. When Hurricane Katrina devastated New Orleans at the end of August 2005, for example, residents of the Vietnamese neighborhoods of that city were able to seek refuge in the Vietnamese community of Houston (Bankston 2014c).

Cambodian Americans

Despite the decades that have passed since the Khmer Rouge era, some Cambodians in the United States have continued to be haunted by events in their homeland. Their stress had psychological and physical consequences. Settled in low-income, urban neighborhoods in the United States, Cambodians often suffer from violence and hostility. During the 1980s and 1990s, Cambodian youth gangs developed in several of these neighborhoods. Adults often had trouble finding work, since most of them had been farmers in their native land and had few skills that were relevant to life in the United States. In recent years, though, evidence suggests that a new generation of Cambodian Americans has been making significant progress in American society.

As seen in Table 4.1, Cambodians were still underrepresented in professional and management jobs by the second decade of the twenty-first century. While their English fluency remained lower than that of other Americans, three-quarters spoke English well. It is notable that although Cambodians over twenty-five were markedly less likely than most Americans to be high school or college graduates, Cambodians aged nineteen through twenty-two were only slightly less likely to be attending college, indicating intergenerational educational progress.

Although in earlier years Cambodians had been much less well situated economically than other Americans, by 2012 they had unemployment rates, poverty rates, and rates of participation in public assistance that were only a few percentage points higher than those of other Americans. In an edition of this chapter, we reported that the median per capita income of Cambodian Americans was only about half that of the nation as a whole (Bankston and Hidalgo 2007). By 2012, Cambodians still had lower incomes ($20,500, compared to $29,245), but the gap had narrowed considerably. The gap was even narrower in household incomes, probably as a result of having more earners per family in Cambodian American households. The comparatively high home values of those who owned their own homes, again, are most likely due to the fact that so many were located in California.

While Cambodian Americans had larger family sizes than any of the groups shown in this table, except for Hmong, single-parent families were also common among Cambodians. About one-fifth of the families in this group were mother-only and over one-third were headed by a single mother or single father. This family structure reflects both the continuing influence of the refugee experience and the remaining socioeconomic challenges of Cambodian Americans.

Despite the challenges, Cambodians have established strong communities in many locations in the United States. Cambodian cultural organizations have been active in the United States, and by 2009 there were at least 109 Cambodian Buddhist temples around the nation. Members of this group have also become connected to Americans from other backgrounds. By 2010, one-fourth of married Cambodian American women and 13 percent of married Cambodian American men had spouses from another group, most often white Americans. Cambodians in California and Texas also frequently live close to Mexican Americans, and Cambodians in these locations frequently learn Spanish and adopt some Mexican American customs (Bankston 2014a).

Lao Americans

Like most of the other refugee nationalities, the ethnic Lao in the United States live mostly in cities, although they come from mainly rural locations in Laos. The Lao, as seen in Table 4.1, have been the least likely of all the Southeast Asian nationalities to work at professional or management occupations. This is primarily a reflection of the tendency of the Lao to work at blue-collar trades, rather than an indication of the lack of adaptation to American society. In our earlier look at the socioeconomic situation of the Lao, we observed the unemployment rate of the Lao was double that of other Americans in 2000 (Bankston and Hidalgo 2007). By 2012, though, the unemployment, poverty, and public assistance participation rates of the Lao were only slightly higher than those of the general American population.

The educational backgrounds of the Lao were similar to those of the Cambodians, with limited formal education among those over twenty-five. However, also like the Cambodians, college attendance rates in the nineteen through twenty-two age group were only a few percentage points lower than similarly aged people throughout the American population, indicating rapid intergenerational progress in education.

Families tend to be close in Laos, where all family members need to work together to produce rice harvests and care for the elderly. In the United States, the Lao retain this emphasis on family life, although many adults worry about their Americanized children drifting away from their families. Partly as a result of the importance of family, Lao Americans continue to have larger families than most Americans do.

Although the Lao have generally experienced less difficulty in adapting to American society than the Cambodians or the Hmong, they have faced their share of challenges. Often living in relatively low-income neighborhoods, they face all the difficulties presented by these environments, particularly those of rearing children in strange and sometimes dangerous settings. Lao youth gangs have formed in a number of ethnic communities, and the generation gaps between parents and children are often great. The relatively high rates of single-parent families, similar to those of Cambodian Americans, reflect the continuing challenges of Lao communities in the United States.

Hmong Americans

The Hmong have faced great challenges in adapting to life in the United States, coming as they do from a largely illiterate society in a mountainous region of Laos. Nevertheless, considering the great cultural differences between the mountains of Laos and American cities, the Hmong have dealt with their transition with strength and resilience. They have developed self-help organizations and many have achieved rapid upward mobility, especially among members of the younger generation.

Of all the Southeast Asian groups, the Hmong experienced some of the most serious problems in adapting to American society and have had to deal with some of the most negative reactions from other Americans. A number of localities objected to the arrival of the Hmong. Concerned about the influx of Hmong to Minnesota, in 1986 Republican Senator Dave Durenberger asked the US State Department to restrict the number of Hmong sent to that state, believing that the Hmong had few prospects for employment and were difficult to assimilate. High rates of reliance on public assistance rendered the Hmong vulnerable to changes in American domestic policies. The welfare reform bill that the US Congress passed in 1996 denied several forms of public assistance to Hmong families, and in 1997 the Department of Agriculture began cutting off food stamps to some of the Hmong.

The controversial Hmong practice of "bride capture" placed a number of them in conflict with American authorities. This practice involves the ritual seizure of a bride by a prospective husband. In the 1985 *People v. Moua* case, bride capture became a legal issue when a Hmong bride with an American upbringing and perspective charged a suitor with kidnapping and rape.

Other cultural differences have also led to conflicts between the Hmong and other Americans. In 2004, Chai Soua Vang, a truck driver, made national news when he shot eight people, killing six of them. Vang had been hunting deer on private land and apparently got into an argument with other hunters who asked him to leave. Some accounts suggest that he did not understand that hunting can be forbidden on open land and that he saw the other hunters as threatening and disrespectful (Bankston 2014b).

By the second decade of the twenty-first century many challenges remained. As shown in Table 4.1, like the Cambodians and the Lao, the Hmong had low representation in managerial and professional occupations. Among all the groups, the Hmong had the highest unemployment, poverty, and public assistance participation rates, as well as the lowest median household income, the lowest rates of home ownership, and the lowest home values among those who were home owners. However, they also showed definite indications of adaptation to American society. Although those over twenty-five showed low levels of high school and college completion, young Hmong in the traditional college-age group were about as likely as the general population to be enrolled in higher education.

Hmong families remain large by American standards, as shown in Table 4.1. These large families contribute to the rapid growth of the Hmong American population, and they also result in a young population. In 2010, half the Hmong population of the United States was less than twenty years old (Bankston 2014b). Given the educational progress among young Hmong, this bodes well for this growing American ethnic minority.

Thai Americans

Since many contemporary Thai arrive in the United States as professionals or as students, they have relatively high occupational and educational levels. As of 2012 Thai Americans showed about the same representation as other Americans in professional and managerial jobs, and they had very high rates of college completion and current enrollment in higher education (see Table 4.1). They also had median per capita and household incomes only slightly lower than those of the general American population. These indicators of socioeconomic position may be a bit misleading with regard to Thai immigrants, who tend to be either relatively prosperous or disadvantaged in American society (Cadge and Sangdhanoo 2002; Bankston and Hidalgo 2006). Nevertheless, the Thai in the United States had lower unemployment rates and lower rates of public assistance participation than most Americans did.

Despite Thailand's rapid economic rise in the late twentieth century, it still has many desperately poor people, and this has led to a largely unrecognized problem of low income Thai being smuggled into the United States. This problem came to national attention in August 1995, when US immigration officials staged a raid on a garment factory in El Monte, California. Surrounded by barbed wire, the factory held seventy-two workers from Thailand, kept in virtual slavery by coethnic employers. In a number of other cases, immigration officials in the United States have found Thai women brought illegally to the United States and forced to work as prostitutes (Bankston and Hidalgo 2006).

The fact that so many Thai Americans who are legally in the United States are married to non-Thai means that they tend to be highly assimilated in many respects. Although English is not widely spoken in Thailand, 82 percent of Thai Americans spoke English well by 2012, as shown in Table 4.1. As in the case of Filipinos, out-group marriage by the Thai has also meant a heavily mixed-race native-born population. In 2013, nearly one-third of all those in the United States with a Thai ethnic heritage were of mixed ancestry (US Census Bureau 2014).

Despite the apparent assimilation of many Thai Americans, they often retain strong ethnic identities. As the Thai American population has grown, these identities have frequently been expressed through Thai Buddhist temples. According to Wendy Cadge, a scholar specializing in Thai American Buddhism, about eighty-seven Thai temples have been established in twenty-nine states across the United States. These temples help to maintain transnational connections, since the monks have generally been trained in Thailand and the temples sometimes receive financial assistance from the Thai government. Furthermore, Thai American children's participation in cultural events at the *wat* (temple) serves as an important link to networks in Thailand and their cultural heritage (Cadge 2004). Thai temples also frequently serve as ways of connecting non-Thai spouses to Thai culture (Perreira 2004).

Conclusion

As the United States rose to global power at the end of the nineteenth century, North America came into close contact with different parts of the world. Southeast Asia played an important part in this American rise to power. The Philippines became the site of the earliest American military activities outside of the Western Hemisphere as it was conquered and occupied by the United States. American involvement in mainland Southeast Asia during the 1960 later became one of the central episodes of the Cold War.

The American military movement into Southeast Asia resulted in waves of migration. The time and nature of this movement in turn shaped the time and nature of the migration. The Philippines, with its long connection to the United States, became the source of one of the largest Asian American populations. Spouses of soldiers were one of the big categories of immigrants from the Philippines. Often English-speaking, educated in American-style institutions, and familiar with American culture, other immigrants from these islands flowed into the United States after the liberalization of American immigration laws. The Vietnam War stimulated more immigration from the Philippines, location of American bases, and put American service personnel into Thailand. The increased contact with Thailand resulted in more migration from that nation, disproportionately in the form of spouses of American citizens, but also in the form of new professional migration. The end of the Vietnam War led to the massive relocation of refugees from Vietnam, Cambodia, and Laos.

US immigration and resettlement policies, often shaped by the same global concerns that produced US military intervention in Southeast Asia, followed the international connections produced by war. These policies helped to select who in the Philippines, Thailand, Vietnam, Cambodia, and Laos would move to the United States and to direct patterns of settlement and adaptation around the nation.

REFERENCES

Bankston, Carl L. III. 1999. "Mail-Order Brides." Pp. 866–869 in Carl L. Bankston III and R. Kent Rasmussen, eds., *Encyclopedia of Family Life*. Pasadena, CA: Salem Press.

———. 2003. "The Philippines." Pp. 441–459 in Carl L. Bankston III, ed., *World Conflicts: Asia and the Middle East*. Pasadena, CA: Salem Press.

———. 2006. "Filipino Americans." Pp. 180–205 in Pyong Gap Min, ed., *Asian Americans: Contemporary Trends and Issues*, 2nd ed. Thousand Oaks, CA: Pine Forge Press.

———. 2014a. "Cambodian Americans." In *Gale Encyclopedia of Multicultural America*, 3rd ed. Farmington Hills, MI: Gale Research.

———. 2014b. "Hmong Americans." In *Gale Encyclopedia of Multicultural America*, 3rd ed. Farmington Hills, MI: Gale Research.

———. 2014c. *Immigrant Networks and Social Capital*. London: Polity Press.

———. 2014d. "Lao Americans." In *Gale Encyclopedia of Multicultural America*, 3rd ed. Farmington Hills, MI: Gale Research.

———. 2014e. "Vietnamese Americans." In *Gale Encyclopedia of Multicultural America*, 3rd ed. Farmington Hills, MI: Gale Research.

Bankston, Carl L. III, and Danielle Antoinette Hidalgo. 2006. "Southeast Asia: Laos, Cambodia and Thailand." Pp. 624–640 in Mary Waters and Reed Ueda, eds., *The New Americans: A Guide to Immigration since 1965*. Cambridge: Harvard University Press.

———. 2007. "The Waves of War: Immigrants, Refugees, and New Americans from Southeast Asia." Pp. 139–157 in Min Zhou and James V. Gatewood, eds., *Contemporary Asian America*, 2nd ed. New York: New York University Press.

Bishop, Ryan, and Lillian S. Robinson. 1998. *Night Market: Sexual Cultures and the Thai Economic Miracle*. New York: Routledge.

Cadge, Wendy. 2004. *Heartwood: The First Generation of Theravada Buddhism in America*. Chicago: University of Chicago Press.

Cadge, Wendy, and Sidhorn Sangdhanoo. 2002. "Thai Buddhism in America: A Historical and Contemporary Overview." Paper presented at the annual meeting of the Society for the Scientific Study of Religion, Salt Lake City, UT.

Caplan, N. H., M. H. Choy, and J. K. Whitmore. 1991. *Children of the Boat People: A Study of Educational Success*. Ann Arbor: University of Michigan Press.

Enloe, Cynthia. 2000. *Maneuvers: The International Politics of Militarizing Women's Lives*. Berkeley: University of California Press.

Footrakoon, Orapan. 1999. "Lived Experiences of Thai War Brides in Mixed Thai-American Families in the United States." Doctoral dissertation, University of Minnesota.

Hidalgo, Danielle Antoinette, and Carl L. Bankston III. 2010. "Blurring Racial and Ethnic Boundaries in Asian American Families: Asian American Family Patterns, 1980–2005." *Journal of Family Issues* 3: 280–300.

———. 2011. "The Demilitarization of Thai-American Marriage Migration, 1980–2000." *Journal of International Migration and Integration* 12: 85–99.

Ocampo, Anthony C. 2014. "Are Second-Generation Filipinos 'Becoming' Asian American or Latino? Historical Colonialism, Culture, and Panethnicity." *Ethnic and Racial Studies* 37: 425–455.

Perreira, Todd. 2004. "Sasana Sakon and the New Asian American: Intermarriage and Identity at a Thai Buddhist Temple in Silicon Valley." Pp. 313–337 in Tony Carnes and Fenggang Yang, eds., *Asian American Religions*. New York: New York University Press.

Randolph, R. Sean. 1986. *The United States and Thailand: Alliance Dynamics, 1950–1985*. Berkeley: University of California Press.

Reimers, David M. 1985. *Still the Golden Door: The Third World Comes to America*. New York: Columbia University Press.

Ruggles, Steven, Matthew Sobek, Trent Alexander, Catherine A. Fitch, Ronald Goeken, Patricia Kelly Hall, Miriam King, and Chad Romander. 2010. *Integrated Public Use Microdata Series: Version 3.0. 5% PUMS Samples*. Minneapolis: Historical Census Projects, University of Minnesota.

Rumbaut, Ruben. 2006. "Vietnamese, Laotian, and Cambodian Americans." Pp. 262–289 in Pyong Gap Min, ed., *Asian Americans: Contemporary Trends and Issues*, 2nd ed. Thousand Oaks, CA: Pine Forge Press.

San Juan, Epifanio. 1998. "One Hundred Years of Producing and Reproducing the 'Filipino.'" *Amerasia Journal* 24 (2): 1–33.

Thompson, W. Scott. 1975. *Unequal Partners: Philippine and Thai Relations with the United States, 1965–75*. Lexington, MA: D.C. Heath.

US Census Bureau. 1970. *Census of Population and Housing, 1970 [United States]* (Summary Statistic File 4A). Washington, DC: Government Printing Office.

———. 1983. *1980 Census of Population and Housing* (Summary File 4). Washington, DC: Government Printing Office.

———. 1993. *1990 Census of Population: Asians and Pacific Islanders in the United States* (1990 CP-3-5). Washington, DC: Government Printing Office. https://www.census.gov/prod/cen1990/cp3/cp-3-5.pdf.

———. 2002. *The Asian Population, 2000* (2000 Census Briefs). https://www.census.gov/prod/2002pubs/c2kbr01-16.pdf.

———. 2012. *The Asian Population: 2010* (2010 Census Briefs). Washington, DC: US Department of Commerce, Economics and Statistics Administration.

———. 2014. *American Community Survey* (2013 3 year survey). http://factfinder2.census.gov/faces/nav/jsf/pages/searchresults.xhtml?refresh=t&keepList=t (accessed November–December 2014).

US Department of Homeland Security. 2014. *Yearbook of Immigration Statistics: 2013*. Washington, DC: US Department of Homeland Security.

Zhou, Min, and Carl L. Bankston III. 1998. *Growing Up American: How Vietnamese Children Adapt to Life in the United States*. New York: Russell Sage Foundation.

———. 2006. Delinquency and Acculturation in the Twenty First Century: A Decade's Change in a Vietnamese American Community." Pp. 117–139 in Ramiro Martinez, Jr. and Abel Valenzuela, Jr., eds., *Immigration and Crime: Ethnicity, Race, and Violence*. New York: New York University Press.

(1) In what ways did the passage of the 1965 Immigration Act (Hart-Celler Act) remedy the litany of anti–Asian immigration legislation passed in the years leading up to World War II? How did the 1965 Immigration Act alter the preference system? Why did so many well-educated Asians immigrate into the United States after the passage of this act? What impact has Asian immigration had upon the ethnic composition of the US labor force? To what extent will Asian immigrants continue to enter the United States in the twenty-first century? Drawing upon evidence presented by the authors, make a case that Asian immigrants will continue to come to the United States at a steady pace, slow down significantly, or halt altogether. What factors might promote immigration among this group, and what factors might stem its tide?

(2) Diversity is the hallmark of contemporary Asian America. How did the 1965 Immigration Act (Hart-Celler) contribute to the diversity of Asian Americans in the United States? What are some of the key differences (e.g., socioeconomic status, national origin, regional settlement) between Asians living in the United States during the early twentieth century versus those after the 1965 Immigration Act? What challenges do these differences present for the cohesion of Asian American communities and organizations?

(3) How does generational status affect how people conceptualize Asian American identity? What other factors might shape how immigrant-, second-, and later-generation Asian Americans understand their ethnicity? What are the different social, cultural, and economic factors that affect their assimilation trajectory in the United States?

(4) One of the defining features of Southeast Asia as a region is its long-standing history of war. What role has American foreign policy—including the US legacy of colonialism—played in the migration histories of Southeast Asians? In what ways have armed struggles in the region shaped international migration? How does the legacy of war continue to shape the fortunes of Southeast Asians once resettled in the United States? How do Southeast Asian refugees differ from refugees from Cuba, the former Soviet Union, and other regions of Asia?

(5) Bankston and Hidalgo chronicle the historical involvement of the United States throughout Southeast Asia. How has this affected Southeast Asian migration to the United States? What were the different pathways that Southeast Asian immigrants took to get to the United States? How did these pathways affect their incorporation into US society?

(6) Bankston and Hidalgo note that diversity is one of the defining characteristics of Southeast Asians who come to the United States. How is each of the subgroups similar or different? What factors have shaped the patterns of settlement and secondary migration that later emerged? What occupational and economic progress has been made by immigrant/refugee populations? To what extent have members of the refugee groups made use of public assistance programs? Why have some groups—Filipino and Thai—adapted to life in the United States more successfully than their counterparts from the same general region?

SUGGESTED READINGS

Baldoz, Rick. 2011. *The Third Asiatic Invasion: Migration and Empire in Filipino America, 1898–1946*. New York: New York University Press.

Chan, Sucheng. 1991. *Asian Americans: An Interpretive History*. Boston: Twayne.

Choy, Catherine Ceniza. 2003. *Empire of Care: Nursing and Migration in Filipino American History*. Durham, NC: Duke University Press.

Danico, Mary, and Anthony C. Ocampo, eds. 2014. *Asian American Society: An Encyclopedia.* Thousand Oaks, CA: Sage.

Daniels, Roger. 1997. "United States Policy towards Asian Immigrants: Comparative Developments in Historical Perspective." Pp. 73–89 in Darrell Y. Hamamoto and Rudolfo D. Torres, eds., *New American Destinies: A Reader in Contemporary Asian and Latino Immigration.* New York: Routledge.

Dirlik, Arif. 1996. "Asians on the Rim: Transnational Capital and Local Community in the Making of Contemporary Asian America." *Amerasia Journal* 22 (3): 1–24.

Freeman, James, ed. 1989. *Hearts of Sorrow: Vietnamese American Lives.* Stanford, CA: Stanford University Press.

Hing, Bill Ong. 2004. *Defining America through Immigration Policy.* Philadelphia: Temple University Press.

Hsu, Madeline Y. 2015. *The Good Immigrants: How the Yellow Peril Became the Model Minority.* Princeton: Princeton University Press.

Liu, J., P. Ong, and C. Rosenstein. 1991. "Filipino Immigration to the United States." *International Migration Review* 25: 487–513.

Maira, Sunaina. 2002. *Desis in the House: Indian American Youth Culture in New York City.* Philadelphia: Temple University Press.

Min, Pyong Gap. 2011. "The Immigration of Koreans to the United States: A Review of 45 Year (1965–2009) Trends." *Development and Society* 40 (2): 195–224.

Ngai, Mae. 2005. *Impossible Subjects: Illegal Aliens and the Making of Modern America.* Princeton: Princeton University Press.

Park, Jung-Sun. 2004. "Korean American Youth and Transnational Flows of Popular Culture across the Pacific." *Amerasia Journal* 30 (1): 147–169.

Rodriguez, Robyn. 2010. *Migrants for Export: How the Philippine State Brokers Labor to the World.* Minneapolis: University of Minnesota Press.

San Juan, E. 1998. *From Exile to Diaspora: Veterans of the Filipino Experience in the United States.* Boulder, CO: Westview.

Schlund-Vials, Cathy. 2012. *War, Genocide, and Justice: Cambodian American Memory Work.* Minneapolis: University of Minnesota Press.

Shukla, Sandhya. 2003. *India Abroad: Diasporic Cultures of Postwar America and England.* Princeton: Princeton University Press.

Takaki, Ronald. 1989. *Strangers from a Different Shore.* Boston: Little, Brown.

Verghese, Abraham. 1997. "The Cowpath to America." *New Yorker*, June 23 and 30, 70–88.

Yang, Philip. 2011. *Asian Immigration to the United States.* Cambridge: Polity.

Zhou, Min. 2009. *Contemporary Chinese America: Immigration, Ethnicity, and Community Transformation.* Philadelphia: Temple University Press.

FILMS

Chiang, S. Leo (producer/director). 2009. *A Village Called Versailles* (67-minute documentary; 15-minute condensed version).

Coffman, Tom (producer/director). 2000. *Arirang: The Korean American Journey/The Korean American Dream* (55-/56-minute documentary).

De Castro, Naomi (director). 1988. *In No One's Shadow: Filipinos in America* (28-minute documentary).

Ding, Loni (producer/director). 1998. *Chinese in the Frontier West: An American Story* (60-minute documentary).

Lowe, Felicia (producer/director). 1988. *Carved in Silence* (45-minute docudrama).

Meerman, Marije (director). 2001. *The Chain of Love* (50-minute documentary).

Ohama, Corey (producer/director). 1997. *Double Solitaire* (20-minute documentary).

Razvi, Raeshma, and G.A.P. (producers). 2002. *One Family* (10-minute documentary).

Siegel, Taggart (director). 2001. *Split Horn: The Life of a Hmong Shaman in America* (56-minute documentary).

Vargas, Jose Antonio (producer/director). 2013. *A Film by an Undocumented American* (90-minute documentary).

Wehman, John (producer/director). 1994. *Filipino Americans: Discovering Their Past for the Future* (54-minute documentary).

PART III

Ties That Bind

The Immigrant Family and the Ethnic Community

5

New Household Forms, Old Family Values

The Formation and Reproduction of the Filipino Transnational Family in Los Angeles

RHACEL SALAZAR PARREÑAS

Much like other immigrant groups in the United States, Filipino migrants turn to the family for support against the social and economic pressures that they encounter upon settlement. They use the family in myriad ways. For example, Filipino migrants are known to have preserved various cultural practices to secure the use of the family as a source of support in settlement. They create fictive kinship, enforce a keen sense of obligation among kin, and use an extended as opposed to a nuclear base for the family (Almirol 1982; Agbayani-Siewart and Revilla 1995). In general, Filipino migrants preserve various cultural practices so as to secure from the community mutual support for the economic mobility of the family and assistance in difficult periods of adjustment in settlement.

In my own observations, Filipinos use the family in other ways. The family is a social institution that adapts strategies variably in response to structural, cultural, and ideological forces in society. Concomitantly, Filipinos have taken advantage of this flexibility by incorporating various strategies of household maintenance. For example, multiple nuclear families may reside in one household so as to decrease expenses and in some cases may go as far as to purchase a house collectively. They also share tasks such as child care across households. These examples show that Filipino families are neither monolithic nor static but instead consist of diverse household forms.

This chapter presents one strategy of household maintenance utilized by Filipino migrants for easing their settlement into the United States. In particular, I document the formation and reproduction of the Filipino transnational household. By transnational family or household, I refer to a family whose core members are located in at least two or more nation-states. In such a family, a migrant settles in the host society, while his or her family—spouse, children, and/or parents—stays in the Philippines. The purpose is to explain how and why transnational households form and reproduce among contemporary Filipino migrants in Los Angeles. Thus, I elaborate on the *structural factors* propelling Filipinos into transnational households as well as the *cultural factors* to which Filipinos turn in order to form such households.

Background

The data are derived from a comparative study of migrant Filipina domestic workers in Rome and Los Angeles. I rely primarily on interviews conducted with twenty-six Filipina domestic workers in Los Angeles. I supplement these data with interviews that I had gathered with fifty-six domestic workers in Rome and ten children who had grown up in transnational households. Transnational households are in fact the dominant strategy of household maintenance for migrant Filipina domestic workers. Of the twenty-six women interviewed in Los Angeles, twenty maintain transnational households. Of these twenty women, fourteen have dependent children living in the Philippines, one lives apart from her husband in the Philippines, and five are single women whose monthly remittances sustain the day-to-day living expenses of their families.

Before I proceed with my discussion of the transnational household, I need to first acknowledge the limitation in my data. The sample of domestic workers does not represent the wide range of occupations held by Filipino migrants in the United States and correspondingly does not reflect the varying demands imposed on the family by different work routines. Because live-in work arrangements are still common among Filipina domestic workers, they can more or less be expected to turn to transnational household structures. Responsibilities for the families of employers prevent them from meeting the demands of child care and other reproductive labor in their own families. As a result, they send their children to the Philippines or leave them there, where a wide kin network inclusive of blood and affinal relations may provide care for dependents.

However, professional Filipino women such as nurses are also known to maintain transnational households in the community. They do so to balance their work inside and outside the home. Immigrant Filipinas have one of the highest rate of labor force participation, reaching 83 percent in 1980 among married immigrant women (Espiritu 1997). In 1990, immigrant Filipino women also held the highest employment ratio among women in Los Angeles, with 83 percent of the working-age population gainfully employed (Ong and Azores 1994a). Confronted with a wage gap, Filipina immigrants often maximize their earnings by working extended hours (Yamanaka and McClelland 1994; Espiritu 1997). For example, it is common for Filipina nurses in Los Angeles to hold two full-time jobs (Ong and Azores 1994b). Despite their high rate of labor force participation, Filipina women are still expected to do most of the housework and child care in their families. Consequently, long hours at work coupled with their continued responsibility for domestic chores may lead even professional women to send their children back to the Philippines. They usually do so only for a short period of time, during infancy, when child care demands are greatest. They also usually do so because of their preference for child care to be provided by kin instead of strangers in child care facilities in the United States.

Notably, the formation of transnational households is not exclusive to Filipino labor migrants. Various studies document its formation among contemporary migrants from the traditional sending countries of Haiti and Mexico.[1] Transnational families are also not particular to present-day migrants. They have historically been a common form of household maintenance for temporary labor migrants in various regions of the world. The earliest Chinese migrant workers in the United States, "guest workers" in Western Europe, and Mexican *braceros* in the southwestern United States, to name a few examples, adapted "split households" because of the disparate levels of economic development in the sending and the receiving countries and the legal barriers to the integration of migrants in the United States (Glenn 1983); these conditions continue today.

We can also speculate that it was not uncommon for Filipino migrants in the pre–World War II period to adopt such households. Prior to World War II, the Filipino community was composed mostly of single men. The cost of bringing women to the United States, coupled with the uncertainty of life for migrant farm workers, discouraged the migration of women. In 1930, women composed only 16.6 percent of the population (Espiritu 1995). Yet, this skewed gender composition does not reflect the distribution of marital status in the community. In 1930, the number of married Filipino men (7,409) far exceeded the number of Filipino women (1,640) on the US mainland (Parreñas 1998a). This strongly suggests that Filipino migrants, as they were subject to antimiscegenation laws, adapted transnational households when wives could not join them because of either economic uncertainties or legal restrictions barring the entry of Filipinos into the United Status.[2]

Yet, while split households in earlier migrant communities were homogeneous and composed primarily of a male income producer living apart from female and young dependents in the sending country, contemporary split households, for example, those from the Philippines and the Caribbean (Basch, Schiller, and Blanc 1994), include income-producing female migrants. Unlike in the past, with the split households of male migrants, traditional gender roles are contested in today's transnational families of female migrants, with women acting as the breadwinner of the family.

How and why do transnational households form among contemporary Filipino migrants? This is the question I answer in this chapter. My discussion of the transnational household is divided into three sections. In the first section, I describe the structural forces propelling the formation of transnational households. Then, in the second section, I enumerate the cultural practices enabling the formation of such households. The third and final section proceeds to describe the Filipino transnational family. In this section, I present two vignettes that illustrate the difficulties and sacrifice entailed in the reproduction of the transnational family.

Global Capitalism: Structural Factors of Transnational Household Formation

Global capitalism and its resulting processes within sending and receiving communities of migration propel the formation of transnational households. Migrants form transnational households to mediate the following structural forces: the unequal level of economic development in sending and receiving nations; legal barriers that restrict their full incorporation into the host society and polity; and the rise of anti-immigrant sentiments. Transnational households result from a conglomeration of contemporary social realities. However, these constitutive features are not particular to global capitalism. Instead, they are old practices—long-standing realities—that are merely being redeployed with greater speed and force with the advent of globalization.

As structural forces in society spur the formation of transnational households, they are not uncommon strategies of household maintenance for low-wage migrant workers, such as Filipina domestic workers. While affording their families a comfortable, middle-class lifestyle in the sending country, the meager wages of low-paid migrant workers do not provide a comparable lifestyle in receiving countries. The lesser costs of reproduction in sending countries such as the Philippines enable migrant laborers to provide greater material benefits for their children, including comfortable housing, as opposed to the cramped living quarters imposed on migrants by high rents in "global cities," burgeoning economic centers that rely on the "routine" services of low-wage immigrant laborers (Sassen 1988, 1994). Finally, the family can expedite the achievement of its goals of accumulating savings and property by forming transnational households. Thus, migrants create transnational households as a strategy to maximize resources and opportunities in the global economy. The migrant family transcends borders and the spatial boundaries of nation-states to take advantage of the lower costs of reproducing—feeding, housing, clothing, and educating—the family in the "Third World." Its spatial organization is in direct response to the forces of global capitalism as the geographical split of the family coincides with the uneven development of regions and the unequal relations between states in the global economy.

Restrictions against the integration of immigrants in postindustrial nations today also fuel the formation of transnational families. The displacement of workers and loss of stable employment for middle-income "native" workers have led to the scapegoating of immigrants, particularly Latinos in the United States (Perea 1997; Feagin 1997). The resulting enforcement of barriers against the integration of migrant laborers and especially their families promotes the maintenance of transnational households. In the United States, lawmakers are entertaining the promotion of temporary labor migration and the elimination of certain preference categories for family reunification, including the preference categories for adult children and parents of US citizens and permanent residents—the trend being to preserve the labor provided by migrants but to discontinue support for their reproduction (Chavez 1997). Moreover, nativist grassroots organizations (e.g., Americans for Immigration Control, Stop the Out-of-Control Problems of Immigration Today) aimed at the further restriction and exclusion of immigration have sprouted throughout the United States.[3] With anti-immigrant sentiments brewing in the United States, migrant parents may not want to expose their children to the racial tensions and anti-immigrant sentiments fostered by the social and cultural construction of low-wage migrants as undesirable citizens (Basch, Schiller, and Blanc 1994; Ong 1996). Yet, among my interviewees, many had been caught in the legal bind of being either undocumented or obtaining their legal status only after their children have reached adult age, when children are no longer eligible for immediate family reunification. Hence, while they may have wanted to sponsor the migration of their children to the United States, they have legally been unable to do so.

"Receiving" societies such as the United States most likely support the formation of transnational households. This is because such households guarantee them the low-wage labor of migrants without forcing them to accept responsibility for their reproduction. By containing the costs of reproduction in sending countries, receiving countries can keep to a minimum the wages of immigrant workers. Thus, while receiving countries need the low-wage labor of migrants, they want neither the responsibilities nor the costs of the reproduction of these workers. This is particularly shown by the passage of Proposition 187, the 1995 California state referendum that bars undocumented immigrants from receiving any tax-supported benefits, including education, health, and social services (Martin 1995). Thus, the formation of transnational households, though a strategy of resistance in globalization, maintains the inequalities of globalization. Receiving countries benefit from the minimized wage demands of a substantial proportion of their workforce. Such economic benefits translate to increased production activities, leading to growth and profits for the higher-tier workers of receiving countries.

The formation of transnational households further enforces the limited integration of low-wage migrant workers. The separation of the migrant family stunts the incorporation of the migrant into the host society, since it is often the children whose greater ability to acculturate paves the way of integration in settlement (Portes and Rumbaut 1996). The consideration of the workings of border politics in transnational households also illustrates the enforcement of limited integration in this process of household formation. On the one hand, the operation of transnational households transcends territorial borders, with the family acting as a conduit between localized communities in separate nation-states. Transcendence, however, does not signify elimination of barriers (i.e., borders). Transnational households should not be praised as a small-scale symbol of the migrant's agency against the larger forces of globalization, because the formation of transnational households marks an enforcement of "border control" on migrant workers. If transnational households can be seen as representing transcendence, they also signify segregation. Transnational households form from the segregation of the families of immigrant workers in sending countries. Thus, they form from the successful implementation of border control, which makes families unable to reunite. Border control further aggravates the experience of transnational families by making return migration difficult for undocumented workers. In turn, family separation is often prolonged and may even extend to a span of a life cycle. Among my interviewees, for example, the length of separation between mothers and their now adult children in transnational families is as long as sixteen years.

The Persistence of Familism: Cultural Factors of Transnational Household Formation

Transnational households emerge in response to the global labor market but also form because of strong kinship ties (Basch, Schiller, and Blanc 1994). However, in the Philippines, transnational households have come to signify the decline and disintegration of family values and consequently "the destruction of the moral fabric" of society (Tadiar 1997, 171). Because they fail to fulfill the ideological notion of a traditional Filipino family, transnational households are considered "broken homes."

Filipino families are traditionally nuclear in structure. Members carry a strong sense of solidarity and obligation to members of their nuclear family and, to a lesser extent, to their larger kin group inclusive of consanguineal (i.e., parent and sibling), affinal, and fictive kin (Medina 1991). The kinship base on which Filipinos may rely is extended by the multilineal and bilateral descent system in the Philippines. Filipinos maintain an equal sense of allegiance to maternal and paternal kin. Moreover, they extend their kinship network by including in their families fictive kin, kin obtained spiritually (e.g., *compadrazgo* system), and cross-generational and cousin ties.

Transnational households are considered "broken" for a number of reasons. First, the maintenance of this household form diverges from traditional expectations of cohabitation among spouses and children. Second, transnational households do not meet the traditional division of labor in the family, as transnational mothers do not maintain the social expectation that women to perform domestic chores. Notably, this expectation still stands despite the high labor force participation of women in the Philippines (Medina 1991). Third, they diverge from traditional practices of socialization in the family. While the socialization of children is expected to come from direct supervision and interaction with parents as well as other adults, the geographic distance in transnational households inhibits the ability of mothers to provide direct supervision to their children.

Yet, the formation of these households depends on the persisting cultural value of *pakikisama*, meaning mutual cooperation or familism, that is, sentiments of collectivism and mutual obligation among kin. Transnational households would not be able to form and reproduce without the cultural value of *pakikisama*, and the mechanisms strengthening such an allegiance including (1) mutual assistance, (2) consanguineal responsibility, (3) "generalized family exchange networks" (Peterson 1993), and (4) fosterage. Transnational households have come to show the resilience of the Filipino family in the advent of globalization.

The operation of transnational households rests on the strength of mutual assistance among extended kin in the Philippines. In transnational households, the migrant shoulders the responsibility of providing for primary and extended kin by remitting funds regularly. In fact, not one of my interviewees has failed to provide consistent financial assistance to her family. Notably, most single migrants send remittances to elderly parents on a monthly basis. Only those with relatives (e.g., brothers and sisters) working outside the Philippines do not send money regularly since they are able to share the responsibility of financial support.

Another mechanism on which transnational families rely is consanguineal responsibility, that is, the extension of responsibility to parents, siblings, and even nieces and nephews for those without children. The high level of interdependency in extended families of Filipina domestic workers is first illustrated by the tremendous responsibility women have for their extended kin in the Philippines. Many single domestic workers shoulder the financial costs of reproduction of the extended family by investing in the education of younger generations. While married domestic workers with children usually cover the schooling only of their own children, those who migrated as single women support extended kin prior to marriage. Besides sending remittances to cover the day-to-day living expenses of their parents and other relatives, Pacita Areza and Letty Xavier, for example, covered the costs of the college education of at least four nieces and nephews before getting married in the United States.

> I sent my sisters to school. . . . One finished a degree in education and the other one in commerce. One only finished high school. . . . Until now, I still help my nieces and nephews. I am sending them to school. With one of my brothers, I am helping him send his two children to college. One just graduated last March and one has two more years to go. With one of my sisters, she has two children and she does not have a job and she is separated from her husband. I help her out—I am helping by paying for their schooling. Once all my nieces and nephews are done with their schooling, I can go back to the Philippines. (Pacita Domingo Areza, married with no children, domestic worker in Los Angeles)

From the start, when I started working in the Philippines, I have helped my family significantly. My nieces and nephews, I sent them to school. . . . One of the first nephews I sent to school is a civil engineer. . . . The second one is a midwife, and the third one is a teacher. The next two sisters are also in education, and they are all board passers. My dreams have come true through them. Right now, one is in nautical school, and he is going overseas soon. Right now, I have stopped supporting them. Those I sent to school, I want them to be the ones supporting their younger brothers and sisters. They are their responsibilities already. I think I have done my part. (Letty Xavier, married, domestic worker in Los Angeles)

Of thirteen migrant workers who at one point had been single women in Los Angeles, five women sent at least three or more nieces and nephews to college. Others provided valuable financial support to their families. Besides subsidizing the everyday living expenses of elderly parents, some purchased the house where their parents and siblings, including those with children, now live and sent at least one younger relative to college. As Gloria Diaz, a domestic worker in Rome with a sister in the United States, explains, they would feel guilty if they did not provide for their relatives in need: "When I don't send money, I feel guilty because my mother is alone, and it is my obligation to help."

Often, the primary contribution of migrant domestic workers to the "kin work" of the extended family is the education of younger generations. In acknowledgment of their extensive support, younger members of their extended family often consider the migrants second mothers. Nieces and nephews refer to them as "Mama" or "Nanay" (Mom) as opposed to just the customary reference of "Tita" (Aunt). For domestic workers, their financial assistance to the family provides them the most tangible reward for their labor. Because of a cultural system based on an economy of gratitude, the immense generosity of migrant workers, especially adult single migrants, guarantees them a well-established kinship base if they choose to return to the Philippines. This economy of gratitude is premised on the value of *utang na loob*, literally, debt of the soul, in which favors are returned with lifelong debt.

The cooperation of sending younger members of the extended family to college also operates on the system of generalized family exchange among kin (Peterson 1993). In such a system, the success of one member of the family represents the success of the family as a collective unit. Peterson defines this family exchange system as entailing an open reciprocal exchange: "Generalized exchanges are those in which A gives to B, B gives to C, C gives to a D, and D gives to an A" (1993, 572). By sending one or more persons to college, domestic workers assume that those that they send to school will reciprocate by later supporting their younger siblings and relatives through school. These younger relatives are then culturally expected to provide care and support for the domestic worker once she chooses to return and retire in the Philippines.

The high level of interdependency among extended families is also reflected in the reliance of migrant parents on grandparents, aunts, and other relatives for the care of dependents left in the Philippines. In the Philippines, it is not uncommon for families to take in extended family members whose own immediate families may not be able to provide as much material or emotional security. Fosterage of children is in fact a common practice among extended kin in the Philippines (Peterson 1993). For example, Cecilia Impelido, a street vendor in Rome, was raised by her grandmother for fourteen years. The arrangement, she claims, strengthened kinship ties to her maternal grandmother in the province even as it eased the financial costs of reproduction for her parents in Manila. Transnational families are embedded in the cultural practice of fosterage. Parents outside the Philippines rely on other relatives to act as "guardians" of their children. In exchange, the remittances sent by parents to dependents in the Philippines benefit the "guardians." The reciprocal bond of dependency between migrant parents and guardians keeps the family intact: migrant parents usually rely on female kin—grandmothers, aunts, and other relatives—to care for the children they have left behind in the Philippines, while caregiving relatives are more than likely ensured a secure flow of monthly remittances.

Inasmuch as their maintenance is aided by relations with extended kin, transnational households strengthen extended family kinship, with children (and also elderly parents) acting as the enduring embodiment of the bond of interdependency. Migrants rely on extended kin to care for their dependents, while extended kin raise their standard of living with the financial support provided by migrant workers. The extended family bolsters the option of migration for individuals otherwise bound by duties and responsibilities to dependents in the Philippines. Thus, transnational households depend on the resilience of extended family bonds in the Philippines. They form not solely from the limits imposed by the structures of globalization and the manipulation of these structures by migrants. The persisting cultural value of familism assists with the formation of transnational households as much as the structural forces of globalization.

A Description of the Filipino Transnational Family

In this section, I describe the Filipino transnational family by presenting vignettes of the two most common forms of transnational households in the Filipino diaspora. Transnational households can be divided into three subcategories: one-parent-abroad transnational households, two-parent-abroad transnational households, and adult-child(ren)-abroad transnational households. One-parent-abroad transnational households are families with one parent—a mother or a father—producing income abroad as other members carry out the functions of reproduction, socialization, and the rest of consumption in the Philippines. In two-parent-abroad transnational households, both the mother and the father are migrant laborers, while the children usually reside together in the Philippines under the care of other relatives. Finally, adult-children-abroad transnational households are families in which the earnings of adult children as migrant laborers provide necessary or additional financial support to relatives (e.g., parents, brothers and sisters) in the Philippines.

The two most common forms of transnational households are one-parent-abroad and adult-children-abroad households. Among my interviewees in Los Angeles, twelve of twenty married domestic workers maintain one-parent-abroad transnational households. Only three married women maintain two-parent-abroad transnational households, which suggests that parents are hard-pressed to leave children behind without any direct parental supervision. Finally, five of six single women maintain adult-children-abroad transnational households.[4]

The two vignettes that follow place a microscope in the migrant family to interrogate its transformations, household dynamics, and the meanings and consequences of migration to family relations. Recognizing and examining the various ways and means by which migrants maintain their families illustrate the social process of transnational household formation. Hence, analyzing migrant households reveals the structures that mold and influence the family life of migrants and the resources that families in turn utilize to perform essential tasks in household maintenance.

Vicky Diaz: An Example of a One-Parent-Abroad Transnational Family

In 1988, Vicky Diaz, a thirty-four-year-old mother of five children between the ages of ten and two years old, left the Philippines for Taiwan. Lured by the financial rewards of employment outside the Philippines, Vicky Diaz had not been content with her salary as a public school teacher in the Philippines, nor had she been comfortable with the insecurities of running a travel agency in Manila. Although made more lucrative by the greater demand for employment outside the Philippines in the preceding ten years, the business of travel agencies had not been as profitable in the late 1980s. And so Vicky decided to move to Taiwan, because there the wages of a domestic worker would give her a more secure income.

In Taiwan, Vicky worked as a housekeeper and a factory worker but mostly as a janitor, for which she earned a salary of approximately one thousand dollars a month. Vicky, who speaks English very well, also subsidized her earnings by teaching English part-time at nights:

> In Taiwan, darling, what I mopped everyday would be five floors. If you put them all together, it would be around five miles. I surely learned how to use the floor polisher and mop the whole day. I would have to clean thirty bathrooms and thirty toilets, that much. I was able to work part-time in the evenings. At night, I got my chance to teach. I taught English grammar. I made good money doing that because

per head it is ten dollars an hour. And I had five students who would pay me and so that is fifty dollars an hour. That is how I made good money. Every other day, I would teach them English. That was my additional income.

Although satisfied with her earnings in Taiwan, Vicky found that the situation of illegal workers like herself became more tenuous with the greater enforcement of restrictive polices against migrants in the early 1990s. She decided to leave Taiwan and return to the Philippines in 1992.

Yet, her return to the Philippines after five years in Taiwan turned out to be just a "stopover" on her way to the United States:

> From Taiwan, I only stayed in the Philippines for three months. I used this time to fix my papers to come here. After Taiwan, my real target was the United States. It was because I knew that America is the land of promises and the land of opportunities. I had several friends who went to America and never went back to the Philippines. I figured it was because life was wonderful in the United States. . . . So, why not give myself the same opportunity?

Although geographically distanced from her children for at least five years, Vicky did not seem at all concerned about or interested in spending "quality" time with them. The prolonged distance from her family seemed to have fostered feelings of emotional distance in Vicky. Only a few months after her return to the Philippines, Vicky used her savings from Taiwan to pay a travel agency 160,000 pesos (approximately eight thousand dollars) for the use of another woman's passport to enter the United States. As Vicky herself states, "You know, in the Philippines, nothing is impossible if you have the money."

Considering her middle-class status after running a travel agency in the Philippines and her ability to raise such a huge sum of money for her trip to the United States, one can easily wonder why Vicky risked such a prolonged separation from her family. Over a span of nine years, Vicky spent only three months with her husband and children in the Philippines. Clearly an absentee mother for most of her children's adolescence, Vicky explained that it was for her family's benefit that she came in the United States:

> They were saddened by my departure. Even until now my children are trying to convince me to go home. . . . The children were not angry when I left because they were still very young when I left them. My husband could not get angry either because he knew that was the only way I could seriously help him raise our children, so that our children could be sent to school.

When assessing the effects of separation to her family, Vicky downplayed the emotional strains engendered by separation by highlighting its material rewards.

Neither her marriage nor her relations with her children were of great concern to her. Clearly, her family's desire for her to return to the Philippines was not given much consideration. Instead, Vicky insisted that her family needed her higher earnings outside the Philippines. Although aware of her children's persistent requests for her return to the Philippines, Vicky was not convinced that her family could sustain its middle-class status without her earnings outside the country.

In the United States, Vicky initially worked as a domestic worker, primarily caring for a two-year-old boy for a wealthy family in Beverly Hills. As the mother "would just be sitting around, smoking and making a mess," Vicky cleaned, cooked, and cared for the boy for four hundred dollars a week, clearly a sharp contrast to the forty dollars she pays her own family's live-in domestic worker in the Philippines. Vicky did not like being a housekeeper for two main reasons: the physically demanding load and the excruciating loneliness, heightened by the contradiction of caring for someone else's children while not caring for her own.

> Even though it paid well, you are sinking in the amount of your work. Even while you are ironing the clothes, they can still call you to the kitchen to wash the plates. It was also very depressing. The only thing you can do is give all your love to the child. In my absence from my children, the most I could do with my situation is give all my love to that child.

Not completely indifferent about the separation her family has endured for almost ten years, Vicky did entertain feelings of regret over missing the formative years of her children's adolescence:

> What saddens me the most about my situation is that during the formative years of their childhood, I was not there for them. That is the time when children really need their mother, and I was not there for them.

Yet for Vicky, the economic rewards of separation softened its emotional costs:

> In my one year in the US, I was able to invest on a jitney. I wanted to do that so that no matter what happens with me, my husband does not have a hard time financially. . . . *Of course, I have neglected them and the least I could do to make up for this is to make their lives a little bit easier. I could ease their lives for them materially.* That's how I console myself. . . . Besides the jitney, there's the washing machine and TV. In the Philippines, it is hard to get to buy these things, right? At least they are not desolate and are at least provided for well.

To overcome the emotional gaps in her family, Vicky relied on "commodifying her love" and compensated for her absence with material goods. Yet while Vicky claimed that she works outside the Philippines so that her family would not "starve," it is actually more accurate to say that Vicky worked in the United States to sustain a comfortable middle-class life for her family in the Philippines.

Vicky hoped that her family would eventually reunite in the United States, because she was convinced that there are few opportunities available for her family in the Philippines. Yet without legal documents, she was unable to sponsor the migration of her family. Obtaining legal status continues to be the biggest challenge for Vicky and has been the main obstacle blocking the reunification of her family. Yet, while Vicky hopes for the relocation of her entire family to the United States, her children ironically prefer to witness the reunification of their family much sooner and would rather have Vicky return to the Philippines.

Maria Batung: An Example of a Children-Abroad Transnational Household in Los Angeles

A single domestic worker in Los Angeles, Maria Batung has been working for a Filipino family for more than twelve years and supports her family in the Philippines with her earnings in the United States.

In the Philippines, Maria also worked as a domestic worker—a nanny—because without a college degree or appropriate networks she did not have access to other types of employment in Manila. Maria had been attending college prior to entering domestic work, but she had to give up her aspirations for a college degree because her parents, whose sole income had been her father's sporadic earnings as a carpenter, could not afford to send her or any of her five brothers and sisters to school.

In Manila, she usually worked for foreigners, mostly diplomats and businessmen. In 1980, ten years after she started working as a domestic helper, Maria accepted the offer of a former employer to move to London with them. Although she could have continued working for the English family, Maria decided, after four years in London, to take up the offer of another former employer, a Filipino family, but this time for a job in the United States. These employers were migrating to the United States to establish an import-export rattan furniture business in Southern California and, by investing capital in the United States, qualified to bring a small number of employees with them, including their former domestic worker, Maria. They covered all of her travel expenses and the costs of obtaining legal papers to work in the United States. With their sponsorship, Maria was able to obtain a green card to stay in the United States permanently.

Maria has been very satisfied with her work, earning far more than she ever did in London (one hundred fifty dollars per month), always having a manageable workload, and not having to deal with demanding or strict employers.

I earn enough so that I could help my family in the Philippines. I get more than a thousand dollars a month, and everything is free. They pay for my Social Security, and they handled my papers. They pay for my ticket home every year. When I go, they also give me vacation pay for two months. That is why I don't have a problem here. Everything is free and they also cover my insurance. . . . It is okay. Anytime I want to leave I can. . . . That is why I lasted long with this family. If that were not the case, I would have probably returned to the Philippines a long time ago.

Of all the employment benefits she receives, the one Maria appreciates the most is her annual vacation—a two-month paid vacation and a round-trip ticket to the Philippines—for it affords her time to spend with her father. Very satisfied with her job, Maria plans to work for them until she is old herself.

Without personal expenses to cover, Maria invests all of her earnings in her family in the Philippines. She has sent numerous relatives to college, wanting to ensure that no one else in her family has to abandon his or her studies and settle for domestic work as she was forced to do almost thirty years ago. When asked whether she had sent her relatives money, she replied,

I send my father money and my nieces and nephews I equally sent to school. For every single sibling of mine, I sent one of their children to school. So there is no jealousy. The rest they could send to school on their own, but each one of them I sent at least one of their children to school. It was equal so there were no bad feelings. . . .

So, I am very happy. Although I was not able to finish school, these are the ones that I was able to ensure finished their education. It is hard when you don't finish. I told them that they would have a hard time if they did not have a degree and that it was necessary that they finish school. Thank God they were able to finish school.

Because Maria sends most of her earnings to the Philippines, she has not been able to accumulate any savings after many years of domestic work, a fact not of concern for Maria. With her legal status in the United States, she is secure that she will qualify to receive government aid such as Social Security once she retires.

Maria's earnings not only cover the college education of younger relatives but also assist her family with day-to-day living expenses.

The last time I sent money it was for five hundred dollars. That is the lowest. It is mostly a thousand or six hundred or seven hundred dollars. So I have no savings. My bank is with all those that I sent to school. I also had a house built in the Philippines where my father lives right now. I had that house remodeled and everything. My father was telling me that maybe when I get older I would regret what I did because they would no longer recognize me. But I told him that they can do what they want to do, but I am happy that I was able to help them.

The generosity of Maria is voluntary, and for it her most satisfying rewards have been the love of her family and their appreciation for her tremendous financial support. While very appreciative of the money and material goods Maria provides them, Maria's relatives also hope that she will soon return and settle down in the Philippines so that they may have the opportunity to transform their relationship to one that is more intimate than the monthly remittances she sends them. A single adult migrant in a transnational family, Maria Batung works in Los Angeles to sustain her family in the Philippines.

Conclusion

The formation of transnational families is a creative response to and an adaptive strategy against the economic challenges and legal barriers faced by migrant workers. It has been adapted as a household form by members of numerous migrant groups in the United States, including those from the Philippines. By structurally reconstituting their family form from a nuclear to a transnational household, Filipino migrants, like other migrants, increase the material benefits afforded by their wages; maintain a family despite the legal restrictions constraining the migration of dependents; and, in many cases, reconstitute the traditional gender roles in the family. However, the formation of transnational households does more than reveal the creativity, agency, and resistance of migrants facing structural barriers in society. To some extent, it unavoidably causes emotional distance and strains among members of transnational families.

The challenge for members of transnational families is to confront and negotiate the emotional costs imposed by geographic distance. They do so in various ways. Like the Latina transnational mothers interviewed by Hondagneu-Sotelo and Avila (1997) in Los Angeles, Filipina transnational mothers and daughters rationalize distance by taking advantage of the communication technology in this age of late capitalism. They increase their familiarity with members of their families located thousands of miles away by using the telephone frequently and by writing letters at least once a week.

The familiarity allowed by the rationalization of distance is, however, limited and cannot replace fully the intimacy of daily interactions. Mothers such as Vicky Diaz and daughters such as Maria Batung are aware of this fact, but they reason that the financial gains afforded by the maintenance of transnational families is worth its emotional costs. Thus, adult children such as Maria generally do not see an end to their separation from their families in the near future as they plan to maximize their earnings and work until they are no longer able-bodied. Similarly, mothers such as Vicky Diaz extend the duration of separation in their families so as to maximize the financial gains of migration. Lured by the greater income available in the United States, most of them plan to stay indefinitely. In the process, they have to put emotional tensions in their families aside for the sake of financial security.

The priority given to material rewards in the family results in the temporal extension of transnational households. Parents in Los Angeles do wish for their children to somehow join them in the United States so as to take advantage of the greater opportunities in this country (especially education, as is recognized universally). Yet, in Los Angeles, many transnational mothers, like Vicky, are undocumented. If not undocumented, they have been caught in the legal bind of obtaining their legal status only after their children reach adult age, when children are no longer eligible for immediate family reunification. Hence, family reunification for US migrants may be possible only with their return to the Philippines. This may explain why the dependents of migrants such as Vicky and Maria strongly prefer to see their families reunify via return migration.

The emotional difficulties wrought in the maintenance of transnational households remain a continuous challenge for migrants and the relatives they have left behind in the Philippines. Interestingly, members of transnational households have varying opinions regarding this problem. Migrants tend to see the material gains of transnational households as being worth their emotional costs. This reasoning enables them to prolong the geographic separation of the family. In contrast, family members in the Philippines consider the material gains not worth the emotional costs. As a result, they prefer to see the immediate reunification of their families in the Philippines. This cross-national difference in opinion shows that, just like other family forms, the reproduction of the transnational household entails varying and sometimes conflicting experiences, concerns, and priorities for different members of the family.

NOTES

This chapter draws on my study of Filipina domestic workers in Rome and Los Angeles in the mid-1990s (Parreñas 1998a). I would like to thank Evelyn Nakano Glenn, Arlie Hochschild, Michael Omi, and Raka Ray for their helpful comments and suggestions. I would also like to thank Charlotte Chiu, Angela Gallegos, Mimi Motoyoshi, and Jennifer Lee for their support through the completion of this chapter.

1   See Basch, Schiller, and Blanc (1994); Chavez (1992); Curry (1988); Hondagneu-Sotelo (1994); Laguerre (1994); Massey et al. (1987); Paz-Cruz (1987).

2   In 1934, the Tydings-McDuffie Act limited the migration of Filipinos into the United States to an annual quota of fifty (Takaki 1989).

3   See the recent anthology by Perea (1997).

4   Only one single woman does not send remittances to her family in the Philippines regularly, because her parents and all of her siblings also live in Los Angeles. She therefore falls under the category of single householder.

REFERENCES

Agbayani-Siewart, Pauline, and Linda Revilla. 1995. "Filipino Americans." Pp. 134–168 in Pyong Gap Min, ed., *Asian Americans: Contemporary Trends and Issues*. Thousand Oaks, CA: Sage.

Almirol, Edwin. 1982. "Rights and Obligations in Filipino American Families." *Journal of Comparative Family Studies* 3 (3): 291–306.

Basch, Linda, Nina Glick Schiller, and Cristina Szanton Blanc. 1994. *Nations Unbound: Transnational Projects, Postcolonial Predicaments, and Deterritorialized Nation States*. Langhorne, PA: Gordon and Breach.

Chavez, Leo. 1992. *Shadowed Lives: Undocumented Immigrants in American Society*. Fort Worth, TX: Harcourt Brace.

———. 1997. "Immigration Reform and Nativism: The Nationalist Response to the Transnationalist Challenge." Pp. 61–77 in Juan F. Perea, ed., *Immigrants Out! The New Nativism and the Anti-Immigrant Impulse in the United States*. New York: New York University Press.

Curry, Julia. 1988. "Labor Migration and Familial Responsibilities: Experiences of Mexican Women." Pp. 47–63 in Margarita Melville, ed., *Mexicanas at Work in the United States*. Houston, TX: Mexican American Studies Program, University of Houston.

Espiritu, Yen Le. 1995. *Filipino American Lives*. Philadelphia: Temple University Press.

———. 1997. *Asian American Women and Men*. Thousand Oaks, CA: Sage.

Feagin, Joe. 1997. "Old Poison in New Bottles: The Deep Roots of Modern Nativism." Pp. 13–43 in Juan F. Perea, ed., *Immigrants Out! The New Nativism and the Anti-Immigrant Impulse in the United States*. New York: New York University Press.

Glenn, Evelyn Nakano. 1983. "Split Household, Small Producer and Dual Wage Earner: An Analysis of Chinese-American Family Strategies." *Journal of Marriage and the Family* 45: 35–46.

Hondagneu-Sotelo, Pierrette. 1994. *Gendered Transitions: Mexican Experiences of Migration*. Berkeley: University of California Press.

Hondagneu-Sotelo, Pierrette, and Ernistine Avila. 1997. "'I'm Here, but I'm There': The Meanings of Latina Transnational Motherhood." *Gender and Society* 11 (5): 548–571.

Laguerre, Michel. 1994. "Headquarters and Subsidiaries: Haitian Immigrant Family Households in New York City." Pp. 47–61 in Ronald Taylor, ed., *Minority Families in the United States*. Englewood Cliffs, NJ: Prentice Hall.

Martin, Philip. 1995. "Proposition 187 in California." *International Migration Review* 29 (1): 255–263.

Massey, Douglas, et al. 1987. *Return to Aztlan: The Social Process of International Migration from Western Mexico*. Berkeley: University of California Press.

Medina, Belinda T. G. 1991. *The Filipino Family: A Text with Selected Readings*. Quezon City: University of the Philippines Press.

Ong, Aihwa. 1996. "Cultural Citizenship as Subject-Making: Immigrants Negotiate Racial and Cultural Boundaries in the United States." *Contemporary Anthropology* 37 (5): 737–762.

Ong, Paul, and Tania Azores. 1994a. "Asian Immigrants in Los Angeles: Diversity and Divisions." Pp. 100–129 in Paul Ong et al., eds., *The New Asian Immigration in Los Angeles and Global Restructuring*. Philadelphia: Temple University Press.

———. 1994b. "The Migration and Incorporation of Filipino Nurses." Pp. 164–195 in Paul Ong et al., eds., *The New Asian Immigration in Los Angeles and Global Restructuring*. Philadelphia: Temple University Press.

Parreñas, Rhacel Salazar. 1998a. "The Global Servants: (Im)migrant Filipina Domestic Workers in Rome and Los Angeles." Doctoral dissertation, University of California, Berkeley.

———. 1998b. "'White Trash' Meets the 'Little Brown Monkeys': The Taxi Dance Hall as a Site of Interracial and Gender Alliances between White Working Class Women and Filipino Immigrant Men in the 1920s and 30s." *Amerasia Journal* 24 (2): 115–134.

Paz-Cruz, Victoria. 1987. *Seasonal Orphans and Solo Parents: The Impacts of Overseas Migration*. Quezon City: Scalabrini Migration Center.

Perea, Juan, ed. 1997. *Immigrants Out! The New Nativism and the Anti-Immigrant Impulse in the United States*. New York: New York University Press.

Peterson, Jean Treloggen. 1993. "Generalized Extended Family Exchange: A Case from the Philippines." *Journal of Marriage and the Family* 55: 570–584.

Portes, Alejandro, and Rubén Rumbaut. 1996. *Immigrant America: A Portrait*. 2nd ed. Berkeley: University of California Press.

Sassen, Saskia. 1988. *The Mobility of Labor and Capital: A Study in International Investment and Labor*. New York: Cambridge University Press.

———. 1994. *Cities in a World Economy*. Thousand Oaks, CA: Pine Forge Press.

Tadiar, Neferti Xina. 1997. "Domestic Bodies of the Philippines." *Sojourn* 12 (2): 153–191.

Takaki, Ronald. 1989. *Strangers in a Different Shore*. Boston: Little, Brown.

Yamanaka, Keiko, and Kent McClelland. 1994. "Earning the Model-Minority Image: Diverse Strategies of Economic Adaptation by Asian American Women." *Ethnic and Racial Studies* 17 (1): 79–114.

6

The Reorganization of Hmong American Families in Response to Poverty

YANG SAO XIONG

This chapter analyzes how Hmong former refugees and their children have employed a number of collective strategies in order to adapt to new social policies and economic circumstances in the United States.[1] Specifically, since the 1980s, Hmong families, largely in response to negative economic policies and chronic poverty, have actively engaged in secondary internal migration, formed new communities, and restructured families and households. These collective strategies, which Hmong families continued to develop throughout the 1990s and 2000s in response to cyclical events or public policies, have contributed to the reduction of the ethnic group's overall poverty.

In the sections that follow, I begin by describing Hmong's migration to the United States. Next, I illustrate some of the most daunting challenges that Hmong families encountered in their new contexts of reception. I pay particular attention to how the US policies of dispersing Southeast Asian refugees during the late 1970s and cutting public assistance to them in the early 1980s significantly impacted Hmong American families' networks of social support and their ability to form stable coethnic communities. Then I examine the changes in the size of Hmong American households and families since the 1990s. Finally, I consider the continuing significance of poverty in Hmong American communities and families.

Migration to the United States

Like other Southeast Asian refugees, Laotian Hmong refugees' migration to the United States was the direct result of the failed US foreign policy and military intervention in Southeast Asia. Between 1955 and 1975, the US government and its military were involved in various conventional and unconventional wars in Cambodia, Laos, and Vietnam, to try to contain the spread of communism in Southeastern Asia in particular and the Asian continent more generally. During the mid-1960s, about thirty thousand Hmong of northern Laos were recruited or drafted into the US Central Intelligence Agency's Secret Army, even as another segment of the Laotian Hmong population joined or were drafted into the Pathet Lao Army (Warner 1995; McCoy 2002).

Prolonged experiences with war, displacement, and dislocation distinguish the experiences of Southeast Asian refugees from those of most other post-1965 immigrants to the United States (Rumbaut 2000). By the time the civil war in Laos officially ended in 1973, an estimated two hundred thousand Laotian civilians and soldiers on both sides of the war had lost their lives (Stuart-Fox 1997, 144). Hundreds of thousands more were wounded and many among them became permanently disabled. Some estimates suggest that thirty thousand, or 10 percent of the Laotian Hmong population, which numbered about three hundred thousand before the war, perished during the Laotian war (N. Vang 2011, 10). As a direct result of the fifteen-year war in Laos, tens of thousands of Hmong became orphans, were adopted or raised as foster children, became widows or single parents, or became separated or otherwise were left without direct family support. To survive, Hmong have had to constantly re-create families—through remarrying, giving birth, adopting, fostering, and so on—and rebuild communities—through living together, supporting one another, marrying within the ethnic group, and so forth.

During their mass exodus from Laos, countless numbers of Laotian Hmong died while fleeing on foot or swimming across the Mekong River that divides Laos and Thailand. Many adults and children died from diseases, illnesses, malnutrition, and other unknown conditions while in the refugee camps in Thailand (Munger 1987; Conquergood 1988). Tens of thousands of stateless Hmong refugees lingered for years or decades in the United Nation–supported refugee camps of Thailand. Many among them either returned or were involuntarily repatriated to Laos (Chantawanit 1992). Some were eventually resettled in Western countries such as Australia, Canada, France, and the United States (Long 1993).

Between 1975 and 1990, the United States resettled a total of 213,519 Laotian refugees. Of these, 92,700 or 43 percent were Laotian highlanders, primarily Hmong (Rumbaut 2001, 316). According to Sucheng Chan (1994, 49), in December of 1975 "Congress admitted 3,466 Hmong under parole [and in] May 1976, another eleven thousand Laotians [including Hmong] were granted entry under parole."[2] Between 1976 and the mid-1990s, an average of 6,000 Laotian Hmong refugees arrived in the United States annually (Dunnigan et al. 1996, 191). By the early 1980s, moderate concentrations of Hmong (1,000 or more persons) were emerging in cities such as Denver, Des Moines, Portland, Seattle, and Providence. Larger concentrations of Hmong (3,000 or more) were developing in Minneapolis, Chicago, San Diego, Santa Ana, and Stockton (Bliatout 1982, 7). By 1990, Hmong former refugees and their US-born children numbered at least 94,400 (Pfeifer and Lee 2004).

In spite of their experiences with a half century of war and international migrations, the social structure of Hmong society and its basic function of organizing kinship relationships have remained largely unchanged. However, the appearance of this social structure, which is composed of three major segments or levels, clans made up of lineages, lineages made up of families, and families made up of persons (Dunnigan 1982; Lemoine 2008),[3] has taken on a more urban character. Whereas in the past, a typical Laotian Hmong village usually consisted of four to ten families, this small village arrangement changed significantly during the Laotian civil war when massive numbers of Laotian Hmong became internally displaced. As families from various regions of the country sought shelter together, large Hmong concentrations began to emerge in certain places such as Long Cheng, which was a military headquarter of the US Secret Army in Laos. These concentrations became even more prevalent when Hmong became refugees in Thailand. For instance, the Thailand-based camp of Ban Vinai, during its peak, served as a refuge to about fifty thousand Hmong refugees (Tapp and Lee 2010, 102). This pattern of concentrated residency, especially in central cities, would continue after Hmong refugees resettled in the United States.

Social and Economic Challenges upon Resettlement

During the late 1970s and early 1980s, the US policy of resettlement entailed scattering Southeast Asian refugee families across multiple cities and states (Miyares 1998, 26). This was done in order, primarily, to prevent overwhelming pressure on individual states' and localities' social services, and secondarily to rapidly assimilate refugees into America (Zaharlick and Brainard 1987). As a result of how this policy was implemented, Southeast Asian refugees, including Hmong refugees, were resettled in cities as far apart as San Diego, Portland, Des Moines, and Philadelphia. Some of the cities in which Laotian refugees initially settled had no or very small preexisting Asian communities, let alone Southeast Asian communities (Miyares 1998, 26). In spite of this, in October 1975, when seven families of Thai Dam (a Laotian group) arrived in Des Moines, Iowa, they were greeted by one of Governor Ray's aides with, "We are happy to have you in Iowa."[4] But, as we shall return to, Iowa's generally positive reception of Southeast Asian refugees was the exception rather than the norm across the United States.

Furthermore, the policy of dispersing refugees produced unintended, far-reaching consequences for Hmong families. As mentioned above, long before the first group of Hmong refugees had ever set foot on US soil, Hmong refugees of the Laotian war have been struggling with broken families and fragmented communities. The policy of dispersal greatly exacerbated this social problem. During the early 1980s and before formation of sizable Hmong communities in the 1990s, it was common for Hmong refugee families to be sponsored by non-Hmong families, some of whom lived in remote places of the United States. Indeed, many two-person and nuclear Hmong families were separated from members of their extended families and/or lineages when they were resettled. This separation added immense trauma to the already highly traumatic experience of arriving as strangers to a strange land. For, besides the family, the social relationships based on shared lineage have traditionally been Hmong persons' primary source of economic and social-cultural support. The fright and despair of being placed with a non-Asian sponsor is vividly described by a Hmong former refugee, sixty-one, who recounts what happened to his elderly aunt and uncle when they were sponsored by a white couple in 1980, apparently to live and work on the outskirts of Washington:

> Uncle and aunt Soua Lue [pseudonym] were sponsored by an American couple in 1980. When they arrived to a farm in a small town [in or near Spokane] in Washington, the American sponsors gave them cartons of milk, some fruits and cans of vegetables, and told them to eat those whenever they were hungry. My uncle and aunt spoke no word of English at all and they did not know how to drink or eat those things. They were so scared because they thought they had been left there [on the farm] to die. Days later, the [white] sponsors came back to find that they have not eaten any of the things. Worried that they were going to starve to death, the sponsors eventually brought a Lao person to the farm. When the Lao man got there, he asked if my uncle spoke Lao. The first thing my uncle did was cry his heart out; my uncle explained the whole "nightmare" and pleaded for the Lao person to help save them. The Lao man assured them not to be afraid. Under the circumstances, the sponsors gave up on the idea of having them live on the farm and wanted to help them find a Hmong community. . . . When asked, my aunt and uncle told them that they had nobody's telephone number. But, fortunately, the Lao person knew about the Hmong community in Portland. The sponsors eventually were able to make contact with [name of Hmong lineage leader] who now lives in Fresno and drove my uncle and aunt to Portland. When they eventually arrived to Portland and the home of [name of Hmong relative], the first thing both my aunt and uncle did when they saw him was cry their hearts out.[5]

Unfortunately, after resettling in Portland, the aunt became ill. After she and her husband relocated to Northern California, she succumbed to her illness. Her relatives, including my interviewee, attributed the cause of her chronic illness to the extremely frightening experience that she and her husband experienced upon arrival. Her husband passed away some years later.

Indeed, since the 1980s, numerous studies have documented Hmong refugees' posttraumatic stress disorders and various other mental and physical health medical conditions (Tobin and Friedman 1983; Westermeyer, Vang, and Neider 1983; Westermeyer, Neider, and Vang 1984; Westermeyer 1986, 1988; Hurie, Mast, and Davis 1992). One of the most troubling conditions that afflicted some Hmong refugees was a fatal condition known as sudden unexpected nocturnal death syndrome, or SUNDS (Bliatout 1982; Munger 1987; Adler 1994). The dramatic changes in Hmong's diet (from a low-meat, low-salt and -sugar diet to a high-meat, high-salt and -sugar diet) and lifestyle (from active to sedentary; from cool to humid weather to extreme cold or heat; from being almost exclusively pedestrians to being vehicle drivers) after their arrival in the United States have probably contributed to a host of other chronic diseases and health risk conditions within Hmong communities.

Given Hmong former refugees' lack of access to formal education in their former homeland, their prolonged intense experiences with war and displacement, and their extended stays in the refugee camps, it is not surprising that most Hmong refugee families faced many social and economic problems upon arrival. The lack of significant financial capital, the inability to communicate in English, the lack of transferable job skills and education credentials, and the lack of coethnic support were among the most significant challenges that Hmong refugees faced upon arrival (Xiong 2013). Especially for Hmong adults who have never had any formal training in the Hmong Romanized Popular Alphabets or another foreign language prior to immigrating to the United States, learning English was an extremely difficult if not impossible task.

Although most Hmong women and men were skilled in farming and crop harvesting, most of the skills that they brought with them became socially devalued in the new host society. Devalued, these skills became nontransferable in America's competitive, bifurcated labor markets. Lacking both socially recognized human and cultural capital, many Hmong adults were unable to obtain decent paying jobs (Cohn 1984; Downing et al. 1984). Second, Hmong refugees who arrived in the early 1980s confronted a bifurcated US labor market that was also experiencing a significant economic recession (Fass 1991). Under this context, the problems of unemployment and underemployment were common. For these reasons, but especially because of the high costs of living in most places, most Hmong refugee families have had to apply for and rely on some form of public assistance to meet their basic needs of food, clothing, shelter, and transportation.

During the 1980s and 1990s, Hmong became one of the most economically disadvantaged ethnic groups in American society. Table 6.1 presents the average poverty rate (the percentage of families or persons who are below poverty) among fifteen racial/ethnic categories based on the US censuses of 1990 and 2000. Several major Asian and Hispanic subcategories are displayed for comparison. Whether one compares Hmong's poverty rate (35 percent) to the overall US poverty rate (9.2 percent) or to the rates of other racial/ethnic categories, it is clear that the Hmong's position at the bottom of the poverty scale did not change between 1989 and 1999. Puerto Rican and Dominican families also experienced relatively high levels of poverty, but not as high as that of Hmong.

TABLE 6.1. Poverty Rate of Select Racial/Ethnic Categories, 1989–1999

	1989	1999
Filipino alone (persons)	6.4	6.3
White alone, non-Hispanic (families)	7.7	5.5
Asian alone (families)	11.0	9.7
Cuban alone (families)	11.4	11.0
Chinese alone (persons)	14.0	13.5
Hispanic or Latino alone (families)	22.3	20.0
Mexican alone (families)	23.4	20.7
Vietnamese alone (persons)	25.7	16.0
Black alone (families)	26.3	21.6
American Indian/Alaska Native alone (families)	27.0	21.8
Puerto Rican alone (families)	29.6	23.4
Dominican alone (families)	33.4	27.6
Laotian alone (persons)	34.7	18.5
Cambodian alone (persons)	42.6	29.3
Hmong alone (families)	62.0	34.8
Hmong alone (persons)	63.6	37.8
US average (families)	10.0	9.2

Source: US Census Bureau (1993, 2002).

To summarize, Hmong refugees faced significant social, health and economic problems in the years and decades immediately following their arrival in the United States. However, as I have pointed out elsewhere, Hmong's chronic poverty is not due to Hmong's cultural deficiency; rather, Hmong's poverty resulted from and is maintained by specific public policies and practices of social closure within America's social institutions (Xiong 2013). Next, we turn attention to the economic policies that have powerfully impacted Hmong families' economic conditions and shaped the development of their ethnic communities.

Hmong American Families' Adaptive Responses

Economic Policies and Secondary Migration

Initially, the federal government, through its Department of Health, Education, and Welfare, reimbursed state agencies and voluntary resettlement agencies (Volags) for providing welfare, medical, and social services to

Southeast Asian refugees (US Congress 1979). However, beginning in the early 1980s, the federal government left this fiscal responsibility more and more to the states. In May 1982, several years before other significant waves of Southeast Asian refugees arrived, the Reagan administration cut off cash and medical assistance to refugees. The government had previously promised that aid would last for thirty-six months after arrival. However, in 1982, this was shortened to eighteen months (Downing et al. 1984). To make matters worse, states such as Washington and Oregon, which previously relied on federal aid to support Southeast Asian refugees, chose not to allot any special funds to continue support to refugees after their federal aid programs were cut.[6] These conditions made the already highly disadvantaged Southeast Asian families even more vulnerable. Southeast Asian refugees, most of whom lacked the English skills and formal credentials to find gainful employment, were left with difficult choices: to stay or to move elsewhere.

In response to chronic poverty, thousands of Southeast Asian families, including Hmong, engaged in secondary migration on their own accord or as part of a government-sponsored program. For instance, many Southeast Asians took part in the Planned Secondary Resettlement program, sponsored by the US Department of Health and Human Services to encourage Southeast Asian refugees to relocate outside of their initial states. Most were trying to escape destitution by looking for jobs elsewhere (Fass 1985; Desbarats 1998). Having few state options, some Southeast Asian refugees migrated to states such as California, Illinois, Louisiana, Minnesota, and North Carolina (Nguyen and Haines 1997).[7] Many Hmong families decided to move to California, Minnesota, and Wisconsin because of the prospective job opportunities and availability of public assistance programs, including Aid to Families with Dependent Children (AFDC), food stamps, and Medicaid.

Although eligible Southeast Asian refugees were provided with public services such as cash aid and medical assistance, they were not provided with other concrete ways to obtain meaningful employment. Specifically, US federal policies, by not providing job training to refugees as part the resettlement process, exacerbated refugees' problems of unemployment and underemployment. As Fass (1985, 558) points out,

> [Federally funded] social service grants [for Southeast Asian refugees] did not support vocational training, and, more generally, services provided under the Comprehensive Employment and Training Act (CETA) were not made widely available to them. . . . The end result was that individuals and institutions with experience in finding work for seriously disadvantaged people were not made part of the resettlement effort.

Moreover, in some states such as California, welfare regulations were set up in such a way that there were major disincentives for the families already on public assistance to work. As Cohn (1984, 35) points out,

> The Hmong in Orange County are acutely aware of the double bind they are placed in by the present assistance structure: If they want to start work gradually and build up experience and skills to obtain better jobs and wages so that their families will no longer have to depend on public assistance and if they work over 100 hours per month, they must often live on less money than welfare payments, often not even enough to meet rent and basic expenses. In addition, without Medical those working at minimum wages risk not having sufficient health care for their children, something very few parents are willing to do.

In short, federal welfare policies have produced consequences that, in retrospect, were probably unintended given the prior intentions of the federal government to disperse refugees and their supposed impact on states' social services. The secondary migrations that these federal welfare policies generated led to the greater concentration of refugees in particular states. At the same time, state welfare policies that created disincentives to work reinforced federal welfare policies that cut off benefits and perpetuated the problem of poverty in Hmong American communities. The Hmong ethnic communities that have emerged during the past thirty years are by-products of this process. We discuss this next.

The Formation of Ethnic Communities

Through successive episodes of secondary migration, Hmong families have managed to form vibrant communities in particular regions of the United States. As shown in Table 6.2, during 1990, 2000, and 2010, the US decennial census enumerated 94,493, 169,428, and 247,596 Hmong, respectively. Three states—California, Minnesota, and Wisconsin—were home to about 89 percent of all Hmong Americans in 1990. By 2000, the Hmong population of these states composed 83 percent and, by 2010, 80 percent of all Hmong Americans.

Although the Hmong populations in these states continue to grow substantially every decade, their rate of growth is much less than those of other states such as North Carolina and Florida. For instance, between 1990 and 2000, North Carolina's Hmong population grew by 1,200 percent; South Carolina's Hmong population also grew by 1,200 percent; and Florida's Hmong population grew by 1,870 percent (not shown). In contrast, the Hmong population in the three most populist states saw significant, but far lower rates of increase: California's population increased by about 30 percent, Minnesota's by 140 percent, and Wisconsin's by 100 percent.

TABLE 6.2. Population of Hmong Alone by Select US States, 1990–2010

State	1990	2000	2010
California	49,343	65,095	86,989
Minnesota	17,764	41,800	63,619
Wisconsin	16,980	33,791	47,127
Michigan	2,304	5,385	5,580
Colorado	1,207	3,000	3,611
Rhode Island	1,185	1,001	909
Washington	853	1,294	2,186
Oregon	595	2,101	2,722
North Carolina	544	7,093	10,433
Kansas	543	1,004	1,645
Georgia	386	1,468	3,460
Massachusetts	134	1,127	992
All other states	2,601	5,271	18,323
United States	94,439	169,428	247,596

Source: US Census Bureau (1993, 2002, 2012).

Whether in California, Minnesota, or Wisconsin, the Hmong population makes up less than one percent of each state's total population. However, the three states differ significantly in terms of the relative Hmong population: specifically, Hmong as a proportion of the state's Asian American population. Whereas California's Hmong make up a mere 1.5 percent of its Asian American population, Minnesota's Hmong make up 26 percent of its Asian American population. In Wisconsin, Hmong make up an even higher percentage of the Asian American population: 35 percent. In both Minnesota and Wisconsin, Hmong are the largest Asian subgroup.[8] In contrast, Hmong Californians are dwarfed by several major Asian subgroups in that state. In Minnesota, Asians form the third largest minority group (3.6 percent), behind Hispanics (4 percent) and African Americans (4.3 percent). Similarly, in Wisconsin, Asians (2.1 percent) form the second largest group behind Hispanics (4.9 percent) and African Americans (5.9 percent). However, in California, Asians (12.4 percent) form the second largest group, behind only Hispanics who constitute 36 percent of the state's population.

Within each state, Hmong are more concentrated in some cities than in others. In California, Hmong are dispersed across nearly all of the Central Valley—a flat, agriculture-rich region that includes eighteen counties, stretching from Kern County in the south to Shasta County in the north (Umbach 1997).[9] According to the latest US census 2010 data, almost three-fourths of all Hmong Californians live in just three metropolitan statistical areas (MSA) within the Central Valley: the Fresno MSA (30,648), the Sacramento-Arden-Arcade-Roseville MSA (25,794), and the Merced MSA (6,920). In Minnesota, about 40,100 Hmong, or 80 percent of the ethnic group, live in the Saint Paul-Minneapolis MSA. They are much more concentrated in Saint Paul than in Minneapolis, however. Saint Paul alone is home to 28,591 Hmong, making them the largest Asian subgroup (68 percent) in the city. Finally, within the state of Wisconsin, about half of all Hmong persons live in four MSAs: the Milwaukee-Racine consolidated MSA (8,078 Hmong), the Appleton-Oshkosh-Neenah MSA (4,741), and the Wausau MSA (4,453). Although suburbanization has occurred in recent decades, the majority of the Hmong in these urban areas remain concentrated in the inner cities.

Changes in Hmong American Families and Households

Hmong adults have historically valued large extended family households over small nuclear families and nonfamily households. In this respect, they are not too different from peoples who live in the various underdeveloped countries of the world, where infant mortality is high, modern medical care is scarce or nonexistent, and the main means of self-subsistence is family-based farming, fishing, hunting, and animal husbandry. Various accounts that use the US standards as the yardsticks have pointed out that the Hmong refugees have large families and that they make up one of the youngest populations in the United States (Rumbaut and Weeks 1986; Yang 2001).

However, in the past two decades, one of the most striking changes in Hmong American society has been the change in the size of the Hmong family and the composition of the Hmong household.[10] Table 6.3 shows that between 1990 and 2010, Hmong's average family size dropped from 6.57 persons to 5.53 persons—a 16 percent decrease over twenty years (or 0.8 percent decrease per year). This change is remarkably rapid when compared to the US trend. For instance, between 1990 and 2010, the average US family size declined only very slightly, from 3.17 to 3.14 persons, representing less than a one percent decrease over twenty years.

TABLE 6.3. Average Household and Family Size by US General and US Hmong Populations

	1990	2000	2010
Average US household size	2.63	2.59	2.58
Average US family size	3.14	3.14	3.14
Average Hmong household size	6.37	6.27	5.22
Average Hmong family size	6.57	6.50	5.53

Source: US Census Bureau (1993, 2002, 2012).

The dramatic shrinkage in Hmong's family and household size can be interpreted as an adaptive response to a number of economic and noneconomic, structural, and personal factors. First, the decline in family size may be directly related to Hmong couples' personal decisions about fertility and the "ideal" size of a family in response to perceived economic constraints or opportunities. Such decisions probably would take account of the fact that the high costs of living in most semiurban to urban areas often exacerbate the poverty of relatively large and young families. Moreover, the enormous expenses of child care and education for children and young adults could discourage couples from having more children than they can afford. At the same time, given the lack of decent-paying jobs, it is increasingly necessary for both married women and men to work full-time in order to earn enough income to support their families. Working couples who are interested in raising their socioeconomic status may postpone having children or may have children further apart in order to avoid being overburdened with caring for multiple young children.

Second, the decline in the average family size probably represents Hmong adults' relatively rapid adoption of the contemporary dominant American value, which emphasizes small nuclear families over large extended families and prefers later marriages over earlier marriages. Whereas in Laos and Thailand Hmong households frequently consisted of persons of several generations (from grandparents to grandchildren) and several nuclear families (sons, daughters-in-law, and children), today such arrangement is less prevalent. For one thing, affordable rental units for large families or households are scarce and local regulations and/or landlords often place restrictions on the number of people who can live together in a rental unit. To comply with such regulations, members of the same household usually have to move out and form separate households when they get married or when the household becomes too crowded. However, this kind of separation, which sometimes separates grandparents from grandchildren, carries its own set of social and economic consequences. For example, nuclear families that move away or out of the city or state are left without grandparents to supervise or provide supplemental care for grandchildren. Instead, families have to seek out expensive child care arrangements. Furthermore, grandchildren have to grow up without the traditional storytellers and speakers or teachers of the heritage language.

Although early-age marriage occasionally occurs, today most Hmong parents discourage early-age marriage and encourage older-age marriage for both women and men. Postponing marriage has, in turn, enabled young Hmong adults to invest in human capital that they otherwise might not have the opportunity to invest later in life. For instance, many young Hmong adults who have graduated from high school go on to obtain college and graduate or professional degrees. Obtaining formal credentials increases their prospects of securing decent employment. Once decent employment is obtained and maintained, a person can help his or her family rise above the poverty level.

Third, the sharp decline in Hmong's average family size may be due to institutionalized work practices that directly or indirectly impact Hmong women's fertility choices. For instance, as more and more Hmong women work in competitive professional occupations, their work obligations may implicitly demand that they postpone having children in order to avoid losing job experiences or wages (Budig and England 2001). In summary, although the average sizes of Hmong families and households are still more than double those of the US population, they have declined dramatically over the past twenty years. This decline probably reflects Hmong's responses to real and perceived economic constraints and opportunities.

Cyclical Events, Recurring Responses, and the Continuing Significance of Poverty

In the mid-1990s, the political contexts of the reception changed dramatically for all immigrants as the US government made greater efforts to restrict legal and illegal immigration. In 1996, the US Congress passed the Personal Responsibility and Work Opportunity Reconciliation Act (PRWORA)[11] and the Illegal Immigration Reform and Immigrant Responsibility Act.[12] The PRWORA, among other things, replaced the AFDC public assistance program with a downgraded program called Temporary Aid to Needy Families (TANF) and required participation in work or work-related activities as a condition of receiving aid. PRWORA also caps aid recipients' eligibility to five years over their lifetime (Truong 2007). Beyond trying to control (or manage the impression of being in control of) the national border, PRWORA represents the welfare state's strategy of creating new subject categories and assigning differential consequences to these subject categories. In one category are those people whom the government deems deserving of public assistance; in another category are those whom it deems undeserving.

Prior to the PRWORA, most legal immigrants, including legal permanent residents, were eligible for food stamps. However, under the 1996 PRWORA, legal immigrants who were noncitizens became ineligible to receive food stamps and Supplemental Security Income (SSI) (Parrott, Kennedy, and Scott 1998; US Department of Agriculture 2003; Schmidt 2004). According to the US government, only certain groups deserve public assistance: those who or whose families have previously contributed documented labor or documented service. Specifically, only US citizens and three categories of noncitizens could be exempt from cuts to public assistance: (1) recent refugees and asylees within their first seven years in the United States, (2) immigrants who can document having worked forty quarters (about ten years) in the United States, and (3) immigrants who served in the US armed forces (Hwang 2002, 95–96). Consequently, in 1997, at least 935,000 low-income legal immigrants lost their federal food stamps as a result of the PRWORA. This figure represents 52 percent of the 1.8 million legal immigrants who received food stamps in 1995 (Cook 1998, 219).

In the aftermath of PRWORA, thousands of Hmong families engaged in yet another wave of internal migration. Like the secondary migrations of the early 1980s, the migrations of the mid-1990s and early 2000s were facilitated by Hmong's extensive social networks of lineage-based and clan-based ties. Between 1996 and 2000, thousands of Hmong individuals and families moved from California and Minnesota to states such as North Carolina, Oklahoma, Arkansas, Georgia, and Wisconsin. For some the move was temporary, but for many it became permanent. The latter category included people who were able to find stable employment and viable coethnic communities.

Most of the Hmong families who moved to Arkansas, Kansas, and Oklahoma did so because they wanted to lease or purchase property and farmland in order to start self-employed businesses in the poultry farming industry.[13] In these states, many Hmong adults and their working-age children worked in raising livestock, including chickens and cattle. Although there have been some stories of business success, the financial hardships, including bankruptcy during the US recession of the late 2000s, that many Hmong business men and women encountered in this new industry have only begun to be documented (C. Y. Vang 2010, 65–67). Anecdotal evidence collected through personal communications with Hmong individuals in these poultry farming states suggests that institutional racism and practices of social closure in the poultry industry may be among the main factors precluding opportunities for fair economic competition.[14] Beyond financial hardships, however, the impact that poultry farming could have on Hmong farmers' physical health and well-being remains an urgent but understudied topic.

In states such as North Carolina, Hmong adults worked in the garment industry. However, many workers worked for hourly wages rather than salaries. As a result of Hmong's in-migrations, states such as North Carolina saw an extraordinary increase in their Hmong populations between 1990 and 2000. For instance, whereas in 1990 there were only 540 Hmong in North Carolina, by 2000 the US census enumerated about 7,100 Hmong living in North Carolina.

Data from the five-year American Community Survey (2005–2010) indicate that the proportion of Hmong families in poverty declined in the past decade to 25.2 percent. This represents a significant decrease from 62 percent in 1989 and 35 percent in 1999. However, the aggregate figure hides more than it reveals about the continuing significance of poverty within Hmong communities and families. As shown in Table 6.4, whereas 21.3 percent of married-couple Hmong families were in poverty, 45.2 percent of female-headed Hmong families were in poverty. This is especially troubling considering that female-headed families represent about 19 percent of Hmong Americans' 40,254 families (not shown). Moreover, in general, families with minors tended to experience even greater poverty than families without minors.

TABLE 6.4. Proportion in Poverty by US and Hmong Family Type, 2005–2010

	Percentage (US General)	Percentage (Hmong Americans)
All families	10.1	25.2
With related children under 18 years	15.7	27.8
Married couple families	4.9	21.3
With related children under 18 years	7.0	23.0
Female householder, no husband present	28.9	42.0
With related children under 18 years	37.4	45.2

Source: US Census Bureau (2014).

When compared to the US general population, it is clear that Hmong Americans still have quite a way to go before they reach economic parity. Specifically, Hmong Americans' poverty is still over two times that of all Americans (10.1 percent). Nevertheless, there is reason to expect that Hmong families' average poverty rate will continue to decline as Hmong of the second and third generations continue to graduate from colleges and obtain meaningful employment.

Conclusion

The federal and state cuts to Southeast Asian refugees' public aid in the 1980s created serious financial problems for refugees, perpetuating their vulnerability and compelling them to engage in difficult interstate migrations. Internal migration has contributed to both the greater concentration of Hmong in particular states and the ever greater geographical dispersion of the US-based Hmong population. The average sizes of Hmong's families and households have declined significantly over the course of the past two decades. Such a decline reflects Hmong's adaptive response to poverty and the public policies that maintain it. Despite remarkable decreases in Hmong's poverty rate between 1989 and 2009, poverty continues to be one of the most significant challenges facing Hmong American communities. Given Hmong Americans' concentrations in the inner cities of major US cities, future research should examine how poverty and/or relative social mobility has impacted Hmong Americans' ability to move from inner cities into suburbs. The research should also try to investigate how the Hmong second generation is faring socioeconomically relative to the first generation and other major racial categories and ethnic groups in the United States.

NOTES

1 This chapter draws from various data including personal interviews, news accounts, and US census data.

2 The parole refers to the US attorney general's parole program that allowed refugees to be admitted to the United States beyond the 17,400 ceiling set on the annual "normal flow" permitted to be admitted. See Warren Brown, "Refugee Plan Would Hurt Laos Tribe, Hill Critics Say," *Washington Post*, March 24, 1979.

3 Marriage is the primary source of family formation within Hmong society and patrilocal residence is the norm. Most marriages between Hmong persons continue to follow the practice of clan exogamy—a practice in which persons of the same clan name are prohibited from intermarrying but persons of different clan names are permitted to intermarry. Although interethnic and, in the contexts of the United States, interracial marriages occasionally occur and help to maintain social relationships in Hmong society, it is endogamy that has largely been responsible for maintaining the interdependence between members of different clan groups within Hmong society.

4 "43 Indochinese Refugee Resettle in Corn Country," *Lawrence Journal-World*, October 27, 1975.

5 L. Xiong, personal communication, Fresno, CA, May 15, 2009.

6 "Recession Driving Thousands of Indochinese Out of Oregon," *Eugene Register-Guard*, April 15, 1982; Jay Matthews, "Federal Aid Reductions Spur Refugees to Flee Pacific Northwest," *Washington Post*, June 8, 1982.

7 May Lee, "Indochinese Urged to Go East for New Homes, Jobs," *Los Angeles Times*, December 8, 1986.

8 Within Minnesota, the largest Asian subgroups are Hmong, followed by Asian Indians (32,979) and Vietnamese (21,445). In Wisconsin, the largest Asian subgroups are Hmong, followed by Asian Indians (19,362) and Chinese (16,492). In California, the largest Asian subgroups are Chinese (1,164,102), followed by Filipinos (1,131,966) and Vietnamese (535,683). Source: US Census Bureau (2014).

9 The 2010 US census shows that 91 percent of Hmong Californians (86,989) live in the eighteen counties of the Central Valley (Butte, Colusa, Fresno, Glenn, Kern, Kings, Madera, Merced, Placer, Sacramento, San Joaquin, Shasta, Stanislaus, Sutter, Tehama, Tulare, Yolo, and Yuba Counties).

10 The US census defines a "household" as all of the persons who live in a housing unit such as a house, an apartment, or a single room. It defends a "family" as a group of two or more persons who are related by birth, marriage, or adoption and are living together.

11 Personal Responsibility and Work Opportunity Reconciliation Act of 1996, Pub. L. No. 104–193, August 22, 1996 (110 Stat. 2105). This act has come to be known as the Welfare Reform Act, a euphemism compared to the full name, which emphasizes individual responsibility and asserts the myth of equal work opportunity.

12 It was not a coincidence that these federal laws share similar titles. The Illegal Immigration Reform and Immigrant Responsibility Act of 1996 (Pub. L. No. 104–208, Division C, September 30, 1996 [110 Stat. 3009]), like many immigration laws before it, placed the blame on individual migrants rather than US corporations (for greed and exploitation) or its governments (for maintaining corporations and all sorts of inequities).

13 Chao Xiong, "Hmong Are Moving Again, This Time to Poultry Farms," *Wall Street Journal*, January 26, 2004.

14 See also Howard Witt, "Hmong Poultry Farmers Cry Foul, Sue," *Chicago Tribune*, May 15, 2006.

REFERENCES

Adler, Shelley Ruth. 1994. "Ethnomedical Pathogenesis and Hmong Immigrants' Sudden Nocturnal Deaths." *Culture, Medicine, and Psychiatry* 18 (1): 23–59.

Bliatout, Bruce. 1982. *Hmong Sudden Unexpected Nocturnal Death Syndrome: A Cultural Study*. Portland, OR: Sparkle.

Budig, Michelle J., and Paula England. 2001. "The Wage Penalty for Motherhood." *American Sociological Review* 66: 204–225.

Chan, Sucheng. 1994. *Hmong Means Free: Life in Laos and America*. Philadelphia: Temple University Press.

Chantawanit, Suphang. 1992. *The Lao Returnees in the Voluntary Repatriation Programme from Thailand*. Bangkok: Indochinese Refugee Information Center, Institute of Asian Studies, Chulalongkorn University.

Cohn, Mary. 1984. *The Hmong Resettlement Study: Site Report, Orange County, California*. Washington, DC: US Department of Health and Human Services, Social Security Administration, Office of Refugee Resettlement.

Conquergood, Dwight. 1988. "Health Theatre in a Hmong Refugee Camp: Performance, Communication, and Culture." *Drama Review* 32 (3): 174–208.

Cook, John T. 1998. "The Food Stamp Program and Low-Income Legal Immigrants." *Nutrition Reviews* 56 (7): 218–221.

Desbarats, Jacqueline. 1998. "The History and Immigration of Asian Americans." Pp. 184–201 in F. Ng, ed., *The History and Immigration of Asian Americans*. New York: Garland.

Downing, Bruce T., Douglas P. Olney, Sarah R. Mason, and Glenn L. Hendricks. 1984. "The Hmong Resettlement Study." Minneapolis: University of Minnesota, Southeast Asian Refugee Studies Project Center for Urban and Regional Affairs.

Dunnigan, Timothy. 1982. "Segmentary Kinship in an Urban Society: The Hmong of St. Paul-Minneapolis." *Anthropological Quarterly* 55 (3): 126–134.

Dunnigan, Timothy, Douglas P. Olney, Miles A. McNall, and Marline A. Spring. 1996. "Hmong." Pp. 191–212 in D. W. Haines, ed., *Refugees in America in the 1990s*. Westport, CT: Greenwood.

Fass, Simon M. 1985. "Through a Glass Darkly: Cause and Effect in Refugee Resettlement Policies." *Journal of Policy Analysis and Management* 4 (3): 554–572.

———. 1991. "The Hmong in Wisconsin: On the Road to Self-Sufficiency." Milwaukee: Wisconsin Policy Research Institute.

Hurie, Marjorie B., Eric E. Mast, and Jeffrey P. Davis. 1992. "Horizontal Transmission of Hepatitis B Virus Infection to United States-Born Children of Hmong Refugees." *Pediatrics* 89 (2): 269–273.

Hwang, Victor. 2002. "The Hmong Campaign for Justice: A Practitioner's Perspective." *Asian Law Journal* 9: 83–115.

Lemoine, Jacques. 2008. "To Tell the Truth." *Hmong Studies Journal* 9: 1.

Long, Lynellyn D. 1993. *Ban Vinai, the Refugee Camp*. New York: Columbia University Press.

McCoy, Alfred W. 2002. "America's Secret War in Laos, 1955–75." Pp. 283–313 in M. B. Young and R. Buzzanco, eds., *A Companion to the Vietnam War*. Malden, MA: Blackwell.

Miyares, Ines M. 1998. *The Hmong Refugee Experience in the United States: Crossing the River*. New York: Garland.

Munger, Ronald G. 1987. "Sudden Death in Sleep of Laotian-Hmong Refugees in Thailand: A Case-Control Study." *American Journal of Public Health* 77 (9): 1187–1190.

Nguyen, Manh Hung, and David Haines. 1997. "Vietnamese." Pp. 34–56 in D. W. Haines, ed., *Case Studies in Diversity: Refugees in America in the 1990s*. Westport, CT: Greenwood.

Parrott, Thomas M., Lenna D. Kennedy, and Charles G. Scott. 1998. "Noncitizens and the Supplemental Security Income Program." *Social Security Bulletin* 61 (4): 3–31.

Pfeifer, Mark Edward, and Serge Lee. 2004. "Hmong Population, Demographic, Socioeconomic, and Educational Trends in the 2000 Census." Pp. 3–11 in Hmong National Development and Hmong Cultural Center, ed., *Hmong 2000 Census Publication: Data & Analysis.* Washington, DC: Hmong National Development.

Rumbaut, Rubén G. 2000. "Vietnamese, Laotian, and Cambodian Americans." Pp. 175–206 in M. Zhou and J. V. Gatewood, eds., *Contemporary Asian America: A Multidisciplinary Reader.* New York: New York University Press.

———. 2001. "Vietnamese, Laotian, and Cambodian Americans." Pp. 308–346 in M. M. Suárez-Orozco, C. Suárez-Orozco, and D. Qin-Hilliard, eds., *Interdisciplinary Perspectives on the New Immigration.* New York: Routledge.

Rumbaut, Rubén G., and John R. Weeks. 1986. "Fertility and Adaptation: Indochinese Refugees in the United States." *International Migration Review* 20 (2): 428–466.

Schmidt, Lucie. 2004. "Effects of Welfare Reform on the Supplemental Security Income (SSI) Program." Ann Arbor: University of Michigan, Gerald R. Ford School of Public Policy.

Stuart-Fox, Martin. 1997. *A History of Laos.* Cambridge: Cambridge University Press.

Tapp, Nicholas, and Gary Yia Lee. 2010. *The Hmong of Australia: Culture and Diaspora.* Canberra: ANU Press.

Tobin, Joseph J., and Joan Friedman. 1983. "Spirits, Shamans, and Nightmare Death: Survivor Stress in a Hmong Refugee." *American Journal of Orthopsychiatry* 53 (3): 439–48.

Truong, Michael. 2007. "Welfare Reform and Liberal Governance: Disciplining Cambodian-American Bodies." *International Journal of Social Welfare* 16: 258–268.

Umbach, Kenneth W. 1997. "A Statistical Tour of California's Great Central Valley." Sacramento: California Research Bureau.

US Census Bureau. 1993. *1990 Census of Population: Asians and Pacific Islanders in the United States* (1990 CP-3-5). Washington, DC: Government Printing Office. https://www.census.gov/prod/cen1990/cp3/cp-3-5.pdf.

———. 2002. *The Asian Population, 2000* (2000 Census Briefs). https://www.census.gov/prod/2002pubs/c2kbr01-16.pdf.

———. 2012. *The Asian Population: 2010* (2010 Census Briefs). Washington, DC: US Department of Commerce, Economics and Statistics Administration.

———. 2014. *American Community Survey* (Public Use Microdata Samples) (2005–2010 Weighted Samples). Washington, DC: US Department of Commerce, American Community Survey Office. http://factfinder2.census.gov/faces/nav/jsf/pages/searchresults.xhtml?refresh=t&keepList=t (accessed November–December 2014).

US Congress. 1979. "Statement of J. Kenneth Fasick, Director, International Division, US General Accounting Office on Indochina Refugee Assistance Programs, Committee on the Judiciary, Subcommittee on Immigration, Refugees, and International Law." Washington, DC: Government Printing Office.

US Department of Agriculture. 2003. "Non-Citizen Requirements in the Food Stamp Program." Washington, DC: US Department of Agriculture, Food and Nutrition Service, and Food Stamp Program.

Vang, Chia Youyee. 2010. *Hmong America: Reconstructing Community in Diaspora.* Urbana: University of Illinois Press.

Vang, Nengher. 2011. "Political Transmigrants: Rethinking Hmong Political Activism in America." *Hmong Studies Journal* 12: 1–46.

Warner, Roger. 1995. *Back Fire: The CIA's Secret War in Laos and Its Link to the War in Vietnam.* New York: Simon & Schuster.

Westermeyer, Joseph. 1986. "Two Self-Rating Scales for Depression in Hmong Refugees: Assessment in Clinical and Nonclinical Samples." *Journal of Psychiatric Research* 20 (2): 103–113.

———. 1988. "DSM-III Psychiatric Disorders among Hmong Refugees in the United States: A Point Prevalence Study." *American Journal of Psychiatry* 145 (2): 197–202.

Westermeyer, Joseph, John Neider, and Tou Fu Vang. 1984. "Acculturation and Mental Health: A Study of Hmong Refugees at 1.5 and 3.5 Years Postmigration." *Social Science & Medicine* 18 (1): 87–93.

Westermeyer, Joseph, Tou Fu Vang, and John Neider. 1983. "Migration and Mental Health among Hmong Refugees. Association of Pre- and Postmigration Factors with Self-Rating Scales." *Journal of Nervous and Mental Disease* 171 (2) :92–96.

Xiong, Yang Sao. 2013. "An Analysis of Poverty in Hmong American Communities." Pp. 66–105 in M. E. Pfeifer, M. Chiu, and K. Yang, eds., *Diversity in Diaspora: Hmong Americans in the Twenty-First Century*. Honolulu: University of Hawai'i Press.

Yang, Kou. 2001. "Research Note: The Hmong in America: Twenty-Five Years after the U.S. Secret War in Laos." *Journal of Asian American Studies* 4 (2): 165–174.

Zaharlick, Ann Marie, and Jean Brainard. 1987. "Demographic Characteristics, Ethnicity and the Resettlement of Southeast Asian Refugees in the United States." *Urban Anthropology* 16: 327–373.

7

Enclaves, Ethnoburbs, and New Patterns of Settlement among Asian Immigrants

WEI LI, EMILY SKOP, AND WAN YU

Since the late 1960s, the combination of global economic restructuring, changing geopolitical contexts, and shifting American immigration policies has set in motion significant flows of Asian immigrants and refugees to the United States. Even as refugee admissions wax and wane, family-sponsored immigration continues to grow, and record numbers of highly skilled, professional immigrants and wealthy investors have also joined the flow. At the same time, patterns of Asian immigrant settlement have changed. Traditional central city enclaves such as "Chinatown," "Little Tokyo," or "Manilatown" no longer absorb the majority of newcomers from various countries of origin and with diverse socioeconomic backgrounds. Instead, many Asian immigrants (especially upper- and middle-class newcomers) tend to avoid central city enclaves since they have the financial resources to settle directly in suburbs that offer decent housing, high-performing schools, and superior living conditions and public amenities. As a result, more and more suburban neighborhoods in the nation are becoming increasingly multiracial, multiethnic, multilingual, multicultural, and multinational.

This chapter discusses the issues surrounding the changing settlement patterns among Asian American groups in the United States. It first provides a brief demographic overview of contemporary Asian America, followed by a description of shifting geographic distributions of the Asian American population at the state and metropolitan levels. The chapter then focuses on different settlement types among Asian American groups within metropolitan areas, from traditional central city enclaves to multiethnic suburbs (known as "ethnoburbs") and demonstrates the similarities and differences between these settlement types. The chapter concludes with a discussion of the implications of divergent settlement forms for the economic, cultural, and political incorporation of contemporary Asian Americans as well as how these patterns reinforce transnational processes in a globalizing world.

Demographic Overview of Asian Americans

Since the mid-nineteenth century, Asian Americans have been present in the United States, traditionally working as laborers in agriculture, fishing, mining, manufacturing, and construction, and as service workers and petty business owners. Historically, their numbers and growth rates have been low, primarily because of exclusionary national immigration and naturalization laws (like the 1882 Chinese Exclusion Act, the 1917 Asiatic Barred Zone, and the 1923 *US v. Bhagat Singh Thind* Supreme Court case) and restrictive state legislation on marriage, landholding, and voting (including antimiscegenation laws and anti-alien land laws). These discriminatory regulations, along with other prohibitive social practices, resulted in declining Asian immigration, extreme sex ratio imbalances, limited occupation choices, and forced spatial segregation in isolated communities. Imbalanced natural growth rates among different Asian American groups and the lack of significant and self-sustaining communities of Asian Americans existed well into the twentieth century.

In the 1960s the situation began to change. Since then, the number of Asian Americans has dramatically increased, primarily because of shifting US immigration policies, rapid economic development in Asia, as well as sometimes unstable geopolitical situations in home countries, like in Vietnam during and after the Vietnam War. Thus, the local, lived experiences of Asian Americans in the United States are set within the shifting landscape of globalization.

Because international economic restructuring promotes the flows of capital, information, services, and people across national borders, there has been a growing demand for a highly skilled workforce and capital investors to engage in an advanced economy. When such needs cannot be fulfilled domestically, the United States, along with other developed countries, looks overseas as an alternative source of labor and investors. Many immigrants from Asia are well prepared for, and fit into, the employment needs of the globalizing US economy: this fact is partially the result of the economic takeoff of the four Asian Little Dragons (Hong Kong, Singapore, South Korea, and Taiwan) beginning in the 1960s, followed by mainland China, India, and some ASEAN countries (e.g. Indonesia, Malaysia, and Thailand) in more recent decades. As these economies have become increasingly incorporated into the global economy, a highly educated and highly skilled middle- and upper-class population, some with entrepreneur experiences, has emerged. Many of these individuals are primed to immigrate to the United States because they have high levels of education, professional training, entrepreneur skills, and/or financial resources needed in the burgeoning knowledge-based economy.

Another important phenomenon is a large number of Asian migrants adjusting their legal status from temporary migrants to immigrants. A majority (53.6 percent) of lawful permanent residents (LPRs) in 2013, for instance, are status adjusters rather than newly arrived immigrants to the United States. Increasingly Asian international students are among these temporary migrants who eventually become highly skilled permanent residents. They often begin their journeys by becoming H-1B visa holders upon graduation before eventually going on to becoming LPRs. China and India top the list of source countries for Asian international students, and Asian students represented 63.8 percent of the 819,644 international students in the United States in academic year 2013.[1]

At the same time, a large number of lower skilled and less educated individuals, lured by family sponsorship and American job opportunities, have joined the migrant flow from Asia. In fact, family reunification is the most important avenue through which many individuals qualify for admission to become LPRs in the United States. Family reunification is particularly important for immigrants from places like the Philippines, Vietnam, and China. Moreover, the end of Vietnam War in 1975 yielded large refugee flows from Southeast Asia. Many Vietnamese, Cambodian, Laotian, and Hmong refugees arrived penniless and mentally distressed after surviving war and trauma when their lives were constantly threatened. But as refugees, they were able to access a variety of social service programs, which distinguishes their experiences from those of other types of newcomers to the United States, though that status no longer affords as many special rights as it once did.

The unprecedented growth of the Asian population in the United States since the 1960s could not have taken place without the key role of the state in initiating flows. The first of many US immigration policies to prompt this growth was the 1965 Immigration and Nationality Act, which opened the door to new flows of immigration from all parts of the world, including Asia, since the national-origin quota system was abolished and a preference system with an annual "per country ceiling" was introduced based on two general categories of admission: family-sponsored and employment-based. More recently, the 1980 Refugee Act facilitated the migration and settlement of many Southeast Asian refugees in the United States. Then, the Immigration and Nationality Act of 1990 prompted the growth of highly skilled immigration from Asia, especially from India and China, to the United States. The 1990 legislation tripled the ceiling on employment-based visas and created the H-1B nonimmigrant visa program to allow for the admission of temporary workers employed in "specialty occupations" that require highly specialized knowledge and at least a bachelor's degree or its equivalent. At the same time, that legislation allowed H-1B visa holders to bring their immediate families with them under the H-4 visa program (though these visa holders are not permitted to work until May 2015 as the result of an Obama administrative directive) and also made H-1B visa holders eligible to adjust their legal status to permanent residents during their six-year maximum visa period. In addition, other immigration legislation created L-1 visas (which allow companies operating both in the United States and abroad to transfer certain classes of employees from their foreign operations to US operations for up to seven years) and EB-5 visas (for investor immigrants who bring one million dollars, or half that amount if investing in distressed areas, and create at least ten full-time jobs).

The result of all of these shifting immigration policies is the rapid and continued growth of the Asian immigrant population in the United States. Indeed,
current immigration data reveal that Asia is the leading contributor of both
employment-based immigrants and H-1B temporary workers. Thus, even
though Asian Americans remain a relatively small part of the total population—
currently less than 5 percent—they are among the fastest growing minority
groups in the United States today. According to the US census, from 1990 to
2010, the Asian American population more than doubled, with an increase rate
of 112 percent, from 6.9 million in 1990 to 14.7 million in 2010. In comparison,
the total US population grew by 24.2 percent, from 248.7 million in 1990 to 309
million in 2010.[2]

Contemporary Asian America is not only growing but also more diverse than
it has ever been. As Figure 7.1 illustrates, the Asian population in 2014 includes
an increasing percentage of first-generation immigrants as well as a steadily
growing proportion of second-generation US-born natives, with a much smaller
share in the third generation or later. At the same time, among all subgroups,
the Chinese remain the largest subgroup with a total of 3.1 million in 2010, a 91
percent increase from 1990. Other Asian American subgroups include the rapidly increasing Asian Indian population, which reached 2.8 million in 2010 (a
249 percent increase from 1990), and the fast-growing Vietnamese population,
which grew to more than 1.5 million in 2010 (a 152 percent increase from 1990).
Other subgroups include the more moderately growing Filipino (2.5 million with
a 81.7 percent increase from 1990) and Korean (1.4 million with a 78.2 percent
increase during the same period) populations, as well as the slowly declining
Japanese population, which numbered 847,562 in 1990 and 763,325 in 2010 (with
a 9.9 percent rate of decline). The majority of this increase in contemporary
Asian America stems from immigration, mirrored by the growing foreign-born
percentage among all Asian subgroups. Yet, clearly, a natural increase has begun
to stimulate the growth of a burgeoning, US-born Asian American population,
while the process of aging has also slowed the growth of the US-born Japanese
population in particular.

Geographic Distribution of Asian Americans

The geographic distribution of Asian Americans in the United States has always
been uneven, but fairly stable, with the same ten states appearing on the list
year in and year out. California, New York, and Hawaii, as historical destination
states, have traditionally had the largest numbers of Asian Americans. These
three states remained as the top three concentrations for the Asian population
until 1990, when new patterns began to emerge. Most importantly, Hawaii was
surpassed by Texas and moved to the fourth position in 2000, and was passed
by Texas, New Jersey, and Illinois in 2010, thus dropping to the sixth position

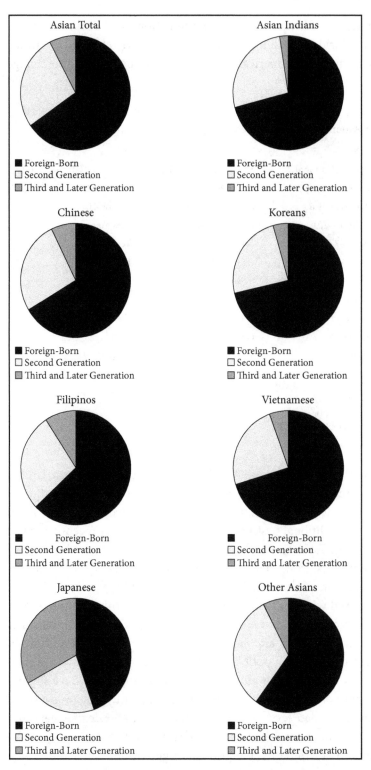

Figure 7.1. Detailed Asian Groups by Foreign-Born, Second Generation, and Third and Later Generations. *Source:* US Census Bureau (2014).

among the top ten states for Asian American population. At the same time, Illinois, Washington, Florida, Virginia, and Massachusetts have remained on the list of top ten states for the Asian American population since 1990, with little change between years.

TABLE 7.1. Asian Americans in the United States and Top Ten States, 1990–2010

	1990—% National Total	2000—% National Total	2010—% National Total
National total	6,908,638	10,242,998	14,674,252
1	California—39.6	California—36.1	California—33.1
2	New York—10.0	New York—10.2	New York—9.7
3	Hawaii—7.6	Texas—5.5	Texas—6.6
4	Texas—4.5	Hawaii—4.9	New Jersey—4.9
5	Illinois 4.1	New Jersey—4.7	Illinois—4.0
6	New Jersey 3.9	Illinois—4.1	Hawaii—3.6
7	Washington—2.8	Washington—3.1	Washington—3.3
8	Virginia 2.3	Florida 2.6	Florida—3.1
9	Florida—2.2	Virginia—2.5	Virginia—3.0
10	Massachusetts—2.1	Massachusetts—2.3	Massachusetts—2.4
% top ten total	79.00	76.20	73.66

Note: "Asian Americans" indicates Asian race alone.
Source: US Census Bureau (1990, 2000, 2010).

These top ten states still dominate Asian Americans' presence in the United States, with approximately three-quarters of the national total. However there is a slight trend toward de-concentration, largely due to the emergence and rapid increase of some untraditional destination states, especially for recently arrived migrants. As shown in Table 7.1, the share of top ten states combined has slightly decreased in recent years, from 79 percent in 1990 to 74 percent in 2010. California shows the most marked decline among these states; only 33 percent of Asian Americans, compared with nearly 40 percent in 1990, call this traditional destination home in 2010. Moreover, two other traditional major destination states for Asian Americans, New York and Hawaii, both experienced slight declines in their share of the total US Asian population. Meanwhile, new "immigrant gateway" states, such as Texas, Washington, Virginia, and Florida, all have slightly increased their share of the total US Asian population, which suggests a trend toward dispersion at the state level, though nowhere near to the degree that other nonmajority ethnic groups are deconcentrating in the United States.

Obviously, the most dramatic changes in the geographic distributions of Asian Americans have occurred among states that historically have had very limited numbers of Asian Americans. These new destination states include

Nevada and Georgia; both states ranked highest in terms of the overall growth of Asian Americans; Nevada experienced a 455 percent increase from 1990 to 2010, and Georgia's Asian American population grew by 326 percent between 1990 and 2010. By 2010, the number of Asian Americans in Georgia reached 314,467, which means that this state is now ranked thirteenth in terms of its Asian American population, whereas in 1990 it ranked sixteenth. North Carolina's Asian population grew 318 percent from 1990 to 2010. Arizona, Delaware, New Hampshire, Texas, and Florida also experienced at least 200 percent growth between 1990 and 2010. These numbers, of course, indicate that these states started with very small Asian population bases in 1990, but have since seen those absolute populations expand significantly in the past twenty years.

TABLE 7.2. Metropolitan Areas with Largest Asian American Populations, 2010

Rank 2010	2000	1990	Metro Area	Asian Population 2010	Share of Metro Area Population (%)
1	1	1	Los Angeles-Long Beach-Santa Ana, CA	1,884,669	14.7
2	2	2	New York-Northern New Jersey-Long Island, NY-NJ-PA	1,878,261	9.9
3	3	3	San Francisco-Oakland-Fremont, CA	1,005,823	23.2
4	4	5	San Jose-Sunnyvale-Santa Clara, CA	571,967	31.1
5	6	6	Chicago-Naperville-Joliet, IL-IN-WI	532,801	5.6
6	7	7	Washington-Arlington-Alexandria, DC-VA-MD-WV	517,458	9.3
7	5	4	Honolulu, HI	418,410	43.9
8	8	9	Seattle-Tacoma-Bellevue, WA	392,961	11.4
9	10	10	Houston-Baytown-Sugarland, TX	389,007	6.5
10	12	15	Dallas-Fort Worth-Arlington, TX	341,503	5.4

Source: Calculations based on Frey's (2006) analysis of US census data; US Census Bureau (1990, 2000, 2010).

Asian Americans are largely urban-bound, and this population continues to cluster in traditional immigrant gateways, which have built upon a rich history of immigration from Asia (and elsewhere), and which have been continually reshaped as a result. In fact, the ten metropolitan areas with the largest Asian populations remain mostly same in 2010 as in 1990, with two exceptions.

Dallas jumped from twelfth place in 2000 to tenth place in 2010 and San Diego dropped from eighth place in 1990 to eleventh place in 2010, as Table 7.2 illustrates. Los Angeles, New York, and San Francisco continue to be the highest ranking metropolitan areas. Silicon Valley now ranks as the fourth largest Asian American population concentration and has become increasingly important as a destination since 1990, indicating the role of high-tech in shifting settlement patterns. Meanwhile, Honolulu, which used to have one of the largest Asian American populations, continues to sustain population losses, especially in the 2000s. This trend is primarily because (1) fewer and fewer Asian Americans are moving to this metropolitan area and (2) the Asian Americans already living there are rapidly aging, so a natural decrease is more important than a natural increase in the decline of the population.

Still, Honolulu continues to have the highest percentage of Asian Americans (43.9 percent) as a proportion of the total population in the United States. Silicon Valley is next, with Asian Americans making up 31.1 percent of the total resident population of that metropolitan area, followed by San Francisco, where 23.2 percent of residents are Asian American. Other metropolitan areas with significant Asian American shares of the total population include Los Angeles and Seattle, where 14.7 percent and 11.4 percent of the total population is Asian American, respectively. Importantly, the larger overall presence of Asian Americans in these metropolitan areas gives some indication of the influence of this group as a whole on these cities' urban, social, and economic geographies.

TABLE 7.3. Metropolitan Areas with Asian American Population at Least One Percent of National Total

Rank	Metropolitan Area	Asian Population	Percentage of National Total
1	Los Angeles-Long Beach-Santa Ana, CA	1,884,669	13.3
2	New York-Northern New Jersey-Long Island, NY-NJ-PA	1,878,261	13.2
3	San Francisco-Oakland-Fremont, CA	1,005,823	7.1
4	San Jose-Sunnyvale-Santa Clara, CA	571,967	4.0
5	Chicago-Joliet-Naperville, IL-IN-WI	532,801	3.8
6	Washington-Arlington-Alexandria, DC-VA-MD-WV	517,458	3.6
7	Honolulu, HI	418,410	2.9
8	Seattle-Tacoma-Bellevue, WA	392,961	2.8
9	Houston-Sugar Land-Baytown, TX	389,007	2.7
10	Dallas-Fort Worth-Arlington, TX	341,503	2.4
11	San Diego-Carlsbad-San Marcos, CA	336,091	2.4

TABLE 7.3. (*cont.*)

Rank	Metropolitan Area	Asian Population	Percentage of National Total
12	Philadelphia-Camden-Wilmington, PA-NJ-DE-MD	295,766	2.1
13	Boston-Cambridge-Quincy, MA-NH	294,503	2.1
14	Riverside-San Bernardino-Ontario, CA	259,071	1.8
15	Sacramento-Arden-Arcade-Roseville, CA	255,995	1.8
16	Atlanta-Sandy Springs-Marietta, GA	254,307	1.8
17	Minneapolis-Saint Paul-Bloomington, MN-WI	188,018	1.3
18	Las Vegas-Paradise, NV	168,831	1.2
19	Detroit-Warren-Livonia, MI	141,316	1.0
20	Phoenix-Mesa-Glendale, AZ	138,717	1.0

Source: US Census Bureau (2010).

Interestingly, among the twenty metropolitan areas whose Asian population is above one percent of the national Asian total, the traditional immigrant gateways of Los Angeles and New York remain chief centers for Asian Americans settlement, as Table 7.3 illustrates. They each composes 13.3 percent and 13.2 percent of the total Asian population nationally, much higher than the third highest on the list, San Francisco (7.1 percent). The rest on the list illustrates a pattern of hierarchal order in terms of overall Asian American population share: the first group includes San Jose, Chicago, and Washington, which compose 3 percent to 4 percent of the national total; the second group generally includes many of the new immigrant gateways, counting for 2 percent to 3 percent of the national total; the third group includes those metropolitan areas with rapidly changing dynamics, representing between 1 percent to 2 percent of the total US Asian American population.

Of course, the geographic distributions of Asian Americans vary by subgroup. The traditional immigrant gateway states and metropolitan areas account for the lion's share of most individual Asian American groups. Even so, in the past two decades, nearly three-quarters of all US states (thirty-eight) witnessed a 100 percent or more increase in their Chinese population, topped by Nevada (318 percent) and North Carolina (265 percent). More drastically, forty-two states witnessed at least a 100 percent increase in their Vietnamese population growth, led by Georgia (480 percent). Twenty-six states saw their Filipino population more than double, led by Nevada (with an impressive 716 percent growth rate). The growth rates of Asian Indians are likewise remarkable during the same period, with many of the highest growth states known for their high-tech economic development, including Washington (645 percent), Georgia (590 percent), and Arizona (537 percent). On the other hand, while the population of Japanese grew significantly in Nevada (170 percent growth rate), about half the states in the United States experienced an absolute decrease of this group.

In terms of metropolitan-level distributions, the New York metropolitan area has the largest number of Chinese and Asian Indians, and the second largest share of Koreans. The greatest percentages of Koreans, Filipinos, and Vietnamese live in the Los Angeles metropolitan area, which also has the second highest concentration for Chinese and Japanese. Honolulu has the most Japanese and the fifth most Filipinos. Washington, D.C., is the third most important center of Asian Indian and Korean settlement, while Chicago acts as the second most important concentration for Asian Indians and San Diego becomes the third most for Filipinos. Finally, Houston and Dallas, both locations that are not typically thought of as Asian American population centers, are home to more than 6.8 percent of the nation's Vietnamese. So, there is considerable regional variation among Asian American subgroups. Though there are clearly some significant concentrations of each group in specific states and particular metropolitan areas, the overall trend over the past two decades is toward slight deconcentration, and the expansion of the Asian American population to new destinations.

Changing Asian American Settlement Forms

Metropolitan areas in the United States have traditionally been magnets for Asian Americans and recent Asian immigrants, but in the modern metropolis, more complex residential geographies materialize. This is primarily because metropolitan areas have undergone major restructuring since the earliest immigrants arrived in US cities. Indeed, the central city has lost its former preeminence as the staging ground for the integration of immigrant newcomers. This shift away from the central city has taken place as economic activity has moved to exurbia, diverse housing types and housing quality have appeared throughout metropolitan areas, and automobiles have transformed the urban landscape. The changing geography of immigrant settlement is also directly related to a shifting global political and social context, and the diversifying socioeconomic and ethnic origins of immigrants as a result of amended US immigration policy.

Urban ecology describes the process of immigrant spatial succession and assimilation, and its role in the development of the metropolis. The enduring Chicago School model suggests that, upon entry, new arrivals settle in central city ethnic enclaves to save transportation costs, locate near employment opportunities, access the cheapest housing, and gain support from coethnic networks. They also settle in these areas because more powerful residents in other parts of the city rarely welcome others, especially migrants from non-European countries. When the immigrants (and/or their children) move up the economic ladder, there are more opportunities to move away from ethnic-specific, central city enclaves to suburbs, where they can potentially become spatially dispersed among, and racially mixed with, the majority white community. Inherent in the model is the idea that the residential location of immigrants (and subsequent generations) reflects (and affects) the degree of sociocultural and economic incorporation of that ethnic group.

This scenario traditionally fits many Asian immigrants' settlement patterns. For instance, San Francisco's Chinatown (known among Chinese immigrants as "the first big city") has been a historical gateway for Chinese immigrants since the nineteenth century. The 1882 Chinese Exclusion Act further solidified this process, as large numbers of Chinese Americans, immigrants as well as US-born, sought refuge and sanctuary in the central city ethnic enclave. Filipinos, also hoping to take advantage of coethnic social networks and to avoid discrimination and violence settled in "Manilatown," adjacent to San Francisco's Chinatown. Other Chinese enclaves existed in Sacramento (known among Chinese immigrants as "the second city") and Stockton (known among Chinese immigrants as "the third city"). Similarly, the Japanese established "Japan Town" in San Francisco and "Little Tokyo" in Los Angeles. During the late nineteenth and early twentieth centuries, Chinatowns and other Asian central city enclaves were established across the country in many major metropolitan areas, almost exclusively in inner-city neighborhoods where low rents and run-down conditions predominated.

Some better-off Asian Americans moved out of Asian American-specific enclaves once they achieved socioeconomic success, but others were stuck in these central city neighborhoods regardless of their socioeconomic status as the result of restrictive covenants or discriminatory practices by realtors, lenders, or neighbors in other communities. In fact, large-scale suburbanization of Asian Americans did not begin until World War II. At that point, more mainstream jobs finally opened up to Asian Americans, racial discrimination in the housing market became outlawed, and the American urban landscape became a predominantly suburban landscape. Even then, however, the suburbanization trend included mostly well-to-do Asian Americans. This process became known as the "uptown versus downtown" phenomenon: assimilated immigrants or US-born Asian Americans with the economic means moved to suburbs and left the elderly, recently arrived, and poorer immigrants behind in downtown Chinatowns or other Asian central city enclaves.

Today, some central city Asian enclaves have survived and endured, as Figure 7.2 illustrates. Indeed, some of these communities continue to serve as immigrant gateways, especially the Chinatowns of New York City and San Francisco, as well as the smaller ethnic enclaves in other major cities like Chicago and Los Angeles. New immigrants land in these traditional ethnic neighborhoods with job opportunities and housing options, kinship ties, and/or social support networks, regardless of their immigration status and English proficiency or lack thereof.

Whether these central city enclaves will persist is a topic that is constantly subject to debate. While Chinatowns may remain significant areas of concentration,

Figure 7.2. Chinatown in San Francisco. *Source:* Photo by Wei Li.

given the fact that immigration from China continues at unprecedented rates and the fact that this subgroup is already the largest and longest-established of all Asian American subgroups, other predominant Asian American subgroups, like Japanese, Asian Indians, and Filipinos, face different situations. The Japanese do not have large new immigrant inflows to sustain central city enclaves, while Asian Indians and Filipinos do not have long-lasting ethnic enclaves in most cities to which to turn. Moreover, contemporary globalization trends include a variety of divergent and competing processes that make these central city enclaves a nexus for change. Foreign investment, in the form of financial inflows crossing the Pacific Ocean, as well as the emergence of gentrification in most major downtowns mean that these sites are ripe for urban restructuring. The situation becomes even more complex as these ethnic enclaves become increasingly heterogeneous due to the influx of a variety of newcomers from a multiplicity of sending communities, with heterogeneous legal, demographic, and socioeconomic profiles ranging from undocumented migrants to prominent politicians, from poor immigrants to wealthy second- and later-generation Americans who made their fortunes either in the United States or overseas.

So, the traditional notion of spatial assimilation that the Chicago School characterizes no longer encompasses the spectrum of sociospatial experiences of Asian Americans. While some Asian Americans disproportionately stay in centralized ethnic enclaves, most newcomers are more diverse in their residential behavior. The changing social geography of cities combined with the recent influx of heterogeneous immigrants, as well as the fact that second-generation (and later) offspring are reaching adulthood, results in both dispersed and concentrated forms.

Perhaps the most intriguing pattern exhibited by Asian Americans is their rapid rate of suburbanization in the United States. Indeed, empirical studies have documented the remarkable suburban-bound trend of contemporary Asian Americans. Data from the 2010 census indicate that, in 267 out of 365 metropolitan areas in the United States, Asian Americans are more likely to reside in the suburbs than in the principal cities. Specifically, according to the 2006 to 2010 American Community Survey (ACS), a majority of Asian American groups live in suburbia—nearly 60 percent of Asian Indians, and about 50 percent of Filipinos, Koreans, and Vietnamese. Yet just 42 percent of Chinese live in the suburbs currently, which could mark an important shift for this particular population, the reasons for which are just beginning to be explored.[3]

These results illustrate that newly arrived immigrants do not consider the often crowded and run-down neighborhoods in central cities as their ideal places to live. Most tend to have the financial resources to afford the newer houses, nicer neighborhoods, and better schools that suburbs typically offer. But poorer Asian Americans are also making their way to the suburbs; many are locating in predominantly renter-occupied and/or older inner-ring housing in less affluent suburbs. Consequently, increasing numbers of Asian Americans settle directly in the suburbs without ever having experienced living in a central city ethnic enclave.

Many Asian Americans live in scattered suburbs across metropolitan areas in what are known as dispersed, "heterolocal" communities. In these suburban communities, recent immigrants arrive in a metropolitan area and quickly adopt a dispersed pattern of residential location, all the while managing to maintain and re-create a cohesive community through a variety of means, at a variety of scales, from the local to the transnational. At the same time, immigrants in these suburban communities remain largely invisible because there are few significant, conspicuous concentrations in any particular neighborhoods. The sprinkling of job opportunities near major employers (particularly among highly skilled immigrants working in knowledge-based industries) and the location of well-ranked school districts are oftentimes the only clues to more dense clusters in particular suburban neighborhoods. Though some immigrant institutions and businesses also tend to be located near knowledge-based companies, they are not spatially concentrated either. The newcomers typically occupy what have been habitually thought of as "white" suburban neighborhoods, schools, workplaces, strip malls, movie theaters, and parks. Consequently, the quintessential ethnic enclave (e.g.,

"Little India" or "Manilatown") does not develop. As a result of living, working, and socializing in the spaces and places associated with "whiteness," the immigrants reinforce their invisible status within the larger sociopolitical community, though many newcomers preserve their ethnic identities through social and religious gatherings. Interestingly, the inconspicuousness of these "heterolocal" cultural landscapes means that immigrants and natives alike interact within both public and private spaces of the community. The scattered patterns of Asian Americans in particular suburban communities are quite common, as in the case of the "saffron suburbs" in metropolitan Phoenix or the "melting pot suburbs" of the Dallas-Fort Worth and Washington, D.C., metropolitan areas.

With the mushrooming of the Asian American population, particularly in the past decade, it is likely that previously dispersed groups will become increasingly more concentrated in the suburbs. In some places, chain migration has already begun to play an important role in the further agglomeration of Asian Americans. In some cases, Asian American realtors, along with overseas developers who are promoting particular neighborhoods, also direct customers to certain communities. Thus, sizeable concentrations emerge where once there were just a few families. Research on the Chinese in San Gabriel Valley in Los Angeles demonstrates this process. When the Asian American population reached a critical mass here in the mid-1990s, and as immigrants became increasingly heterogeneous, suburban residential concentrations materialized. In time, a wider range of ethnic-specific businesses and professional services proliferated, including travel agencies and language schools, realtors, ethnic supermarkets, and immigration, financial, and legal services. A more complete ethnic institutional structure emerged, as did a more collective political voice. The outcome was an "ethnoburb" (i.e., a multiethnic suburb), where visible, nonwhite ethnic clusters of residential areas and business districts materialize in the suburbs, and where both established and newer immigrants increasingly seek political representation. Unlike traditionally segregated ethnic enclaves, ethnoburbs are open communities where daily interactions occur among multiethnic and multilingual neighbors.

The San Gabriel Valley case is not unique. Filipinos have created their own ethnoburb in Daly City, California, as a result of suburbanization and immigration; and Vietnamese congregate in suburban Orange County, California, as a result of refugee secondary migration. Koreans have become increasingly concentrated both residentially and commercially in places like Bergen County, in northern New Jersey. Similarly, Asian Indians have a large presence in Edison, New Jersey, which, along with the surrounding communities of Middlesex County, is commonly known throughout the state and the New York metropolitan area as a main center of Asian American cultural diversity. Moreover, comparable dynamics at the global, national, and local levels have made the transformation of predominately white suburbs to multiethnic suburbs possible in other large metropolitan areas across the Pacific Rim.

In some cases, Asian Americans have established suburban enclaves in places where a particular group has a large concentration in a smaller geographic area. For instance, Vietnamese Americans, including first-generation refugees and their offspring, have lived in the easternmost suburbs of New Orleans since the late 1970s, making the area probably the densest Vietnamese settlement in the nation. In an area known as Village de l'Est, Vietnamese Americans represented 41.7 percent of total population in 2000. Despite falling victim to Hurricane Katrina in 2005, many returned and rebuilt their houses and businesses a few months later. Then, a community redevelopment plan carved by local Vietnamese Americans and architects from Vietnam envisioned this neighborhood becoming a future "Asian Quarter" of New Orleans, a parallel to the famous French Quarter in downtown. Indeed, by 2010, Vietnamese Americans reached 47.4 percent of the total population in that area of the city, an increase from 41.7 percent in 2000.

Most suburban communities are multiethnic communities; newcomers establish a significant concentration within particular neighborhoods, but do not necessarily compose a majority of the population. The ever-increasing heterogeneity within the immigrant community (stemming from a diversity of primary languages, provincialisms, religious affiliations, class statuses, and family types) results in more complex community structures. With continued growth of the knowledge economy and flexible US immigration policy, spatially clustered and socioeconomically heterogeneous multiethnic communities are likely to continually develop and increase. Unfortunately, this pattern could potentially lead to inter- and intragroup tensions. With increasing concentration and a large influx of immigrants with various backgrounds in the suburbs, there is an imperative need to examine the dynamics under which these communities evolve. The worry is that tensions among newcomers and longtime residents of various backgrounds may arise due to rapid changes of local demographic composition, residential and business landscapes, and community and political dynamics.

Suburban Communities: Implications for Economic, Cultural, and Political Incorporation

Immigrants are often perceived as those who arrive poor and uneducated, who achieve the American Dream after many years of hard work as manual laborers or through the success of their US-born children. In contrast, many Asian immigrants arrive armed with academic degrees, proficiency in English, professional training, and/or financial resources. As a result, most have some advantages and the means to integrate into US society at a much faster pace.[4] Many Asian Americans also possess the capabilities and know-how to rapidly transform local residential, business, and community landscapes in the suburbs that they call home.

The new suburban Asian American communities have important implications in terms of Asian American cultural, economic, and political incorporation. Many Asian Americans have integrated into various aspects of the local fabric by owning/operating businesses, presenting their cultural heritage, and participating in both grassroots and electoral politics. As more immigrants become American citizens, some also actively participate in local economic, cultural, and political affairs.

Cupertino, California, known as the "high-tech heart of Silicon Valley" and home of Apple, offers a rich case of transformation from a predominantly non-Hispanic white American suburb to a multiethnic community. Cupertino's residential landscapes have been altered with the influx of Asian Americans. Commercial infrastructures display prominent Asian signatures and multicultural activities abound in community centers. Many Asian Americans have become an integrated part in daily life and some participate in community affairs and electoral politics. But the transformation has not been without controversies, and sometimes has involved racially connoted incidents. Both Cupertino's city government and its residents are aware of these potential forces dividing their community and have carried out both top-town and bottom-up initiatives to address such concerns. They are committed to becoming a "model multicultural community in the twenty-first century." How this process happens in other rapidly changing suburban communities remains to be seen, though there is evidence that the metamorphosis of traditionally "white" suburban neighborhoods prompts a variety of reactions, including collectivity, cooperation, and/or conflict.

As many Asian Americans settle in the suburbs, suburban Asian American businesses oftentimes flourish, including those serving mainstream market's increasing taste for Asian food, fashion, or other culture, as well as those primarily serving coethnics. The latter is especially true in ethnoburbs. Moreover, contemporary Asian American businesses range from traditional mom-and-pop retail stores, gift shops, and restaurants to professional services, such as health, finance, insurance, real estate, and high-tech firms. At the same time, many of these businesses are no longer solely family-owned and -operated: often firms take on paid employees. Given that central city Asian American enclaves occupy smaller geographic areas with limited capability for further spatial expansion, the suburban Asian American ethnic economy will become an increasingly important and integrated part of the general US economy. As this process unfolds, and to ensure the overall success of Asian American-owned businesses, many hope that new immigrants will be provided more opportunities to not only learn about American business practices and government regulations, but also receive small business loans, in order to assist in their economic incorporation.

At the same time, with the increasing and rapid exchange of immigrants from all parts of Asia to the United States, the influence of Asian arts and culture has great consequences in this new setting. Asian immigrants and US-born natives blend both contemporary and traditional elements of Asian culture with American culture to create a hybridized Asian American culture, which includes literature, music, and the visual arts. In celebration of this transnational culture, Asian American festivals proliferate in both central city enclaves as well as in suburban settings. These festivals are popular in both traditional Asian American immigrant gateways such as New York City and San Francisco and in smaller Asian American communities such as in Phoenix, Arizona, or Austin, Texas. Chinese Lunar New Year celebrations, the Japanese American Masturi Festival, the Vietnamese Tet, and more pan-Asian festivals aim at incorporating both tradition and contemporary cultural traditions as well as educating other Americans about their cultures. Asian-language schools are also flourishing, often with the hopes of providing US-born Asian Americans with new cultural encounters and language skills beyond those experienced as a consequence of growing up in the United States. Concomitantly, Asian-language media, including print and audiovisual, have rapidly expanded across the country. These activities and institutions not only serve to preserve Asian American culture, but also facilitate the overall integration process. Asian languages and cultures have increasingly become evident in Mandarin, Cantonese, Korean, and other Asian language immersion programs in public schools and in the "Asian-inspired fashion" of the design world.

While cultural activities and festivals contribute to the appreciation and mutual understanding of different groups in various communities, political participation, in both grassroots and electoral politics, is more complicated. Still it is a key step for the overall incorporation of Asian Americans. Many new immigrants, due to their lack of understanding of American politics and/or their noncitizen status, stay away from overt forms of political activism. They often use their participation in community organizations as a way to become involved in local politics. For instance, many immigrant parents become involved in local school activities and some run for offices of local school boards. Others, through business organizations, trade unions, and professional organizations, actively participate in community organizing and volunteering in local events.

Some argue that this kind of local participation likely serves as an initial step for further political integration and activism. Still, it is important to note, especially for many Asian immigrants, particularly those of voting age, that it will take time to acquire English proficiency, to become naturalized, to register to vote, to get used to the American political system, and, for those interested in serving as political candidates, to build up their political resumes.

Among those areas with a strong Asian American presence, especially among later-generation Asian Americans, participating in grassroots and/or electoral politics is more common, as well as more imperative. Oftentimes, participation is a direct response to outlandish cries from some longtime US-born residents that immigrants are either "unassimilated" or "taking over our city." Thus, in ethnoburbs, where there are more educated and middle-class Asian American residents and voters, the potential political impacts on local, state, and eventually national political scenes are increasingly becoming more apparent and more important. Many actively participate in the political process as fund-raisers, campaigners, and/or volunteers. Meanwhile, increasing numbers of Asian Americans are being elected or appointed to local, regional, or national political positions. The newly elected 114th Congress, for instance, includes three new members and nine incumbent Asian American or Pacific Islander members, some of whom are immigrants themselves.

Summary

By outlining the changing demographics and geographic distributions of Asian Americans, along with the differences among various contemporary community forms within metropolitan areas, from traditional central city enclaves to multiethnic suburbs (known as ethnoburbs), this chapter begins the process of understanding the varied characteristics, outlooks, and concerns of Asian American communities in the United States. This kind of analysis is critical in creating a successful future, since Asian Americans are rapidly transforming what were previously known as the citadels of non-Hispanic white America to increasingly multiracial, multiethnic, multicultural, and multilingual communities.

NOTES

We are grateful for the invaluable research assistance of Yun Zhou at Arizona State University on an earlier version of this chapter. All possible errors that remain, however, are entirely ours. Inquiries can be sent to wei.li@asu.edu, eskop@uccs.edu, or wanyu@asu.edu.

1 See Institute of International Education, "Open Doors Data: International Students" (Chicago: Institute of International Education, 2013). These data include only what the US Census Bureau considers as source regions of Asian Americans, namely, East Asia, Southeast Asia, and South Asia; West Asia is excluded from this designation.

2 All 2000 and 2010 US census data used here include only Asian Americans who chose the "Asian alone" racial category.

3 The data should be viewed with caution. The American Community Survey is based on sample data, which means that the data are subject to sampling error, especially among minority populations.

4 This is not to say that there isn't any disparity in the integration experiences of Asian Americans, especially among the growing number of Asian Americans with less education and lower occupational status. Meanwhile, the "glass ceiling" effect is often encountered by higher status individuals. We in no way want to add to the myth of the "model minority" that already circles around this minority group by suggesting that all Asian Americans are successful.

REFERENCES

Asian American Justice Center and Asian American Legal Center. 2006. *A Community of Contrasts: Asian Americans and Pacific Islanders in the United States* Washington, DC: Asian American Justice Center.

Frazier, John W., and Eugene Tettey-Fio, eds. 2006. *Race, Ethnicity and Place in a Changing America*. Binghamton, NY: Global.

Frey, William H. 2006. *Diversity Spreads Out: Metropolitan Shifts in Hispanic, Asian, and Black Populations since 2000*. Living Cities Census Series. Washington, DC: Brookings Institute.

Li, Wei. 2009. *Ethnoburb: The New Ethnic Community in Urban America*. Honolulu: University of Hawaii Press.

Logan, John R., and Charles Zhang. 2010. "Global Neighborhoods: New Pathways to Diversity and Separation." *American Journal of Sociology* 115 (4): 1069–1109.

Skop, Emily. 2012. *The Immigration and Settlement of Asian Indians in Phoenix, Arizona 1965– 2011: Ethnic Pride vs. Racial Discrimination in the Suburbs*. New York: Edwin Mellen.

US Census Bureau. 1990. *US Census of Population and Housing* (Summary Tape File 1). http://www.census.gov/prod/www/decennial.html.

———. 2000. *US Census of Population and Housing* (Summary File 1 and Summary File 2). http://www.census.gov/prod/www/decennial.html.

———. 2010. *US Census of Population and Housing* (Summary File 1). http://www.census.gov/prod/www/decennial.html.

———. 2014. *Current Population Survey, 2013–2014* (IPUMS). https://cps.ipums.org/cps/.

Wilson, Jill H. 2014. *Immigrants Continue to Disperse, with Fastest Growth in Suburbs*. Washington, DC: Brookings Institute.

Yang, Philip. 2011. *Asian Immigration to the United States*. Cambridge: Polity.

Zelinsky, Wilbur, and Barrett A. Lee. 1998. "Heterolocalism: An Alternative Model of the Sociospatial Behaviour of Immigrant Ethnic Communities." *International Journal of Population Geography* 4: 1–18.

STUDY QUESTIONS

(1) How does global capitalism shape the family lives of women in the Philippines? How do the forces of globalization contribute to Filipina labor migration? How does Filipina labor migration affect migrants themselves and their loved ones left behind in the Philippines?

(2) What are the different emotional responses of the Filipinos who are part of transnational families? How do Filipina migrants rationalize their decision to leave their husbands and their children behind in the Philippines? What are their coping mechanisms for dealing with family separation?

(3) Describe some of the cultural, emotional, and occupational challenges that Hmong refugees faced upon their arrival in the United States. How were these challenges directly related to their experiences in Southeast Asia? What role did the American government play in shaping their migration patterns to the United States?

(4) How has migration to the United States reshaped the process of family formation for Hmong Americans? How are these transformations in family structure related to the unique economic and cultural challenges faced by Hmong communities in the United States?

(5) To which regions of the country have Asian immigrants historically settled and why? Why have Asian immigrants historically settled in urban locales? What advantages did they derive from these enclaves? When did Asian immigrants begin to settle in ethnoburbs? How do ethnoburbs differ from ethnic enclaves? What are some of the cultural, economic, and political implications of living in the suburbs?

(6) What global and local factors contribute to the development of Asian American ethnoburbs? What other key players and institutions are involved in the further development of Asian ethnoburbs? How do longtime residents of these areas respond to the continuing arrival of Asian immigrants and institutions?

(7) What are the advantages of having concentrated Asian suburbanization? Are there any disadvantages? To put it another way, how is the emergence of Asian ethnoburbs influencing the cultural, social, and political incorporation of Asian immigrants and their children in the United States?

SUGGESTED READINGS

Abraham, Margaret. 2002. "Addressing Domestic Violence and the South Asian Community in the United States." Pp. 191–202 in Linda Vo and Rick Bonus, eds., *Contemporary Asian American Communities: Intersections and Divergences*. Philadelphia: Temple University Press.

Bao, Jiemen. 2005. "Merit-Making Capitalism: Re-territorializing Thai Buddhism in Silicon Valley, California." *Journal of Asian American Studies* 8 (2): 115–142.

Cheng, Wendy. 2013. *The Changs Next Door to the Diazes: Remapping Race in Suburban America*. Minneapolis: University of Minneapolis Press.

Espiritu, Yen Le. 2003. *Home Bound: Filipino American Lives across Cultures, Communities, and Countries*. Berkeley: University of California Press.

Fong, Timothy. 1994. *The First Suburban Chinatown: The Remaking of Monterey Park, California*. Philadelphia: Temple University Press.

Gill, Dhara S., and Bennett Matthews. 1995. "Changes in the Breadwinner Role: Punjabi Families in Transition." *Journal of Comparative Family Studies* 26 (2): 255–264.

Glenn, Evelyn Nakano, and Rhacel Salazar Parreñas. 1996. "The Other Issei: Japanese Immigrant Women in the Pre–World War II Period." Pp. 124–140 in Silvia Pedraza and Rubén G.

Rumbaut, eds., *Origins and Destinies: Immigration, Race and Ethnicity in America*. Belmont, CA: Wadsworth.

Guevarra, Anna Romina. 2009. *Marketing Dreams, Manufacturing Heroes: The Transnational Labor Brokering of Filipino Workers*. New Brunswick, NJ: Rutgers University Press.

Kibria, Nazli. 1993. *Family Tightrope: The Changing Lives of Vietnamese Americans*. Princeton: Princeton University Press.

Li, Wei. 2009. *Ethnoburb: The New Ethnic Community in Urban America*. Honolulu: University of Hawaii Press.

Liu, Haiming. 2005. *The Transnational History of a Chinese Family: Immigrant Letters, Family Business, and Reverse Migration*. New Brunswick, NJ: Rutgers University Press.

Matsumoto, Valerie. 1993. *Farming the Homeplace: A Japanese American Community in California, 1919–1982*. Ithaca, NY: Cornell University Press.

Parreñas, Rhacel. 2008. *The Force of Domesticity: Filipina Migrants and Globalization*. New York: New York University Press.

Pyke, Karen. 2000. "'The Normal American Family' as an Interpretive Structure of Family Life among Grown Children of Korean and Vietnamese Immigrants." *Journal of Marriage and the Family* 62 (1): 240–255.

Smith-Hefner, Nancy J. 1998. *Khmer American: Identity and Moral Education in a Disaporic Community*. Berkeley: University of California Press.

Toji, Dean S., and Karen Umemoto. 2003. "The Paradox of Dispersal: Ethnic Continuity and Community Development among Japanese Americans in Little Tokyo." *AAPI Nexus* 1 (1): 21–46.

Vo, Linda, and Mary Y. Danico. 2004. "The Formation of Post-Suburban Communities: Koreatown and Little Saigon, Orange County." *International Journal of Sociology and Social Policy* 24 (7/8): 15–45.

Yoo, Grace, and Barbara Kim. 2014. *Caring across Generations: The Linked Lives of Korean American Families*. New York: New York University Press.

Zhao, Xiaojian. 2002. *Remaking Chinese America: Immigration, Family, and Community, 1940–1965*. New Brunswick, NJ: Rutgers University Press.

Zhou, Min, and Carl L. Bankston III. 1998. *Growing Up American: How Vietnamese Children Adapt to Life in the United States*. New York: Russell Sage Foundation.

Zhou, Min, and Susan S. Kim. 2006. "Community Forces, Social Capital, and Educational Achievement: The Case of Supplementary Education in the Chinese and Korean Immigrant Communities." *Harvard Educational Review* 76 (1): 1–29.

FILMS

Diaz, Ramona (producer/director). 2011. *The Learning* (90-minute documentary).

Flanary, Lisette Marie, and Evann Siebens (codirectors/coproducers). 2003. *American Aloha: Hula Beyond Hawai'i* (60-minute documentary).

Friedman, Daniel, and Sharon Grimberg (directors/producers). 1997. *Miss India Georgia* (56-minute documentary).

Ishizuka, Karen L. (producer). 1993. *Moving Memories* (31-minute documentary).

Koster, Henry (director). 1961. *Flower Drum Song* (132-minute comedy).

Krishnan, Indu (director). 1990. *Knowing Her Place* (40-minute documentary).

Mallozzi, Julie (director). 2004. *Monkey Dance* (65-minute documentary).

Mishran, Ahrin, and Nick Rothenberg (coproducers). 1994. *Bui Doi: Life Like Dust* (29-minute documentary).

Moyers, Bill (producer). 2003. *Becoming American: The Chinese Experience* (87-minute documentary).

Nakasako, Spencer (producer/director). 1998. *Kelly Loves Tony* (57-minute documentary).

Siegel, Taggart (producer/director), and Jim McSilver (producer). 2001. *The Split Horn: The Life of a Hmong Shaman in America* (56-minute documentary).

Uno, Michael T. (producer/director). 1988. *The Wash*. (94-minute drama).

Yasui, Lise (producer/director/writer). 1988. *A Family Gathering* (60- or 30-minute documentary).

PART IV

Struggling to Get Ahead

Economy and Work

8

Just Getting a Job Is Not Enough

How Indian Americans Navigate the Workplace

PAWAN DHINGRA

Popular conceptions of Indian Americans range from physicians and computer engineers to convenience store workers and small-town motel owners. Yet beyond media presentations, we know little about how Indian Americans, and ethnic minorities generally, actually experience work. This chapter places Indian Americans within their work context (and as such is limited to those who work for pay outside the domestic sphere). It explains the challenges workers face and how they respond to those challenges. Even US-born, highly educated Indian Americans must deal with hassles and barriers tied to race and culture, which shows that assimilation does not preclude a racialization. With that in mind, I argue that by understanding Indian Americans in the workplace, we can move past asking *if* race matters to asking *how* individuals and organizations interact within racialized environments to advance themselves (or not). While focused on Indian Americans, the framing and findings apply to Asian Americans more broadly.

History of Indian Americans

I start with a brief history of Indian Americans. In the late 1800s, immigrants from India moved to the Pacific Northwest. These men, mostly Punjabi Sikh and Muslims (from today India and Pakistan), worked in mills and the railroads. Anti-immigrant discrimination and violence pushed them down to California. They worked on farms and gradually started their own farms as well as other small businesses on occasion (Leonard 1992; McMahon 2001). While this contingent of Indians made up the largest settlement in the United States, others from India had entered and stayed in the East Coast, often engaged in trading (Bald 2007).

The "tide of turbans," as these men were known on the West Coast, aroused similar hostilities from white laborers as targeted against other Asian Americans. This hostility took many forms, including anti-immigration laws. The Immigration Act of 1917 stopped further immigration from India and other parts of Asia and the Middle East. As a result of this restriction, limited job opportunities, and an anti-Asian atmosphere, about half of the Indians living in California returned to India after this. It would take thirty years until immigration restrictions were loosened, with the Luce-Celler Act of 1946. This was a mostly symbolic gesture meant to appease foreign relations rather than change racist policy. It allowed in only one hundred immigrants from India per year, some of whom started in the motel industry.

Immigration laws changed time and again after 1946, but the largest change took place with the Immigration and Naturalization Act of 1965. This act removed the racist quotas on immigrants from Asia and other non-European areas, thereby allowing more immigrants to enter. For Asians, including Indians, the majority who entered for years following the act were professionals, due to the priority system within the legislation. Doctors, engineers, and university researchers were the largest contingent of Indians to enter.

Since then immigration has been quite diverse, but some trends are apparent. One trend is that this wave of post-1965 immigrants sponsored their relatives to immigrate, starting in the 1970s. Indian immigrants with more diverse occupational backgrounds arrived and settled in cities and rural areas. This included taxi drivers, motel owners, store employees, farmers, and more. Another trend is the influx of professionals in computer technology. They arrived in the 1980s and have continued to today as well, with another wave arriving in the 1990s due to fears around Y2K. They often arrived under a special visa system designed to buttress the US information technology (IT) industry. In fact, most Indian immigrants enter the United States on temporary worker visas (e.g., H-1 or L).[1] Missing within this picture of immigration laws and labor migration is that Indians also arrive as undocumented immigrants (making up the seventh highest ethnic group of undocumented persons in 2011).[2] Also, many arrive as spouses or parents of immigrants, who must then find a life for themselves in sometimes isolated conditions cut off from the public realm.

As we think about the experiences of this diverse population within the workplace, it is useful to divide them into three major occupational types common for immigrant populations and the general public: professionals, laborers, and small business owners (Portes and Rumbaut 2006). I refer to each type in turn.

Professionals

As noted above, Indian Americans are overrepresented as professionals and work in such fields as medicine, engineering, IT, finance, and more. For instance, one-tenth of doctors are Indian, making up the largest proportion of nonwhite physicians.[3] In Silicon Valley and other IT hubs, it is taken for granted that firms have Indian Americans working for them.[4] This highly professionalized workforce and concentration in the sciences is not due to any genetic disposition either toward these fields or for educational achievement but instead due to immigration laws of the 1950s and since, as mentioned above. Also, in the years following India's independence in 1947, the nation had been investing in math and sciences through the creation of education centers, councils, and universities (Chitnis 1993). Indian graduates found more job growth potential in the United States and so emigrated. Graduates arrive already having secured jobs, or they pursue graduate education here and then find a employment. Given the strong human capital of these immigrants, they rely somewhat but not extensively on ethnic networks to secure work (Poros 2010). Instead, their academic and work credentials and favorable institutional locations assist them. Professionals receive more attention when discussing problems at work and means of dealing with them.

Laborers

Like many Asian Americans, Indian Americans have a bipolar occupational distribution. Despite their predominant presence in professional jobs, many specialized in laborer positions. These include domestic servants, mechanics, farmers, taxi drivers, restaurant workers, convenience store and fast-food restaurant workers, and more. Like laborers generally, they may not receive health insurance through their work, may have to piece together part-time work, and may have substandard work conditions. Workers also may be undocumented immigrants, either having arrived without sufficient documents or working without the proper visa (Rangaswamy 2007).

Unlike professionals, whose networks through their schools or workplaces assist in finding work, laborers often rely on family and friends. Social capital takes the form of "informal exchanges of information, introductions, and vouching for a person's character" (Sanders, Nee, and Sernau 2002, 282). Oftentimes positions are not advertised, and without a connection one cannot learn about a job. Congregation within a few industries becomes more common as a result, since people know most about their own industries. Because they depend on word of mouth from their networks, immigrants often learn of jobs from coethnics and end up working alongside and/or for coethnics. In California, for instance, Punjabi men can be found as farm laborers, working for Punjabi landowning farmers.

This is not to suggest that laborers are not highly educated. Many in fact are. South Asians make up about 60 percent of taxi drivers in New York City, with about half of those being Indian. According to a study by Mitra (2008), 43 percent of Indian (Punjabi) taxi cab drivers in New York City have a college degree. But the drivers lack needed skills to translate that education into a professional career. For instance, they do not speak fluent English, their educational degrees are not recognized by US standards, they are educated in a field that has few job openings in the United States, and the like. So, once these men move to the

United States, they rely on word of mouth or kin networks to find jobs in what they know other Punjabis have chosen, such as taxi driving.

Small Business Owners

As for other Asian Americans, a segment of Indian Americans has made a mark in small business. Indian Americans are known as owning motels, gas stations, and fast-food restaurants (also IT startup companies, but these professionals are categorized with other professionals). About the same percentage of South Asian Americans owned businesses (11.5) as did whites (11.8) in 2007.[5]

Traditionally immigrants have started out as one of two types of small business owners: those within an ethnic enclave or middleman minorities (Zhou 2004). The former start businesses that primarily cater to coethnics, such as ethnic grocery stores, financial services in a native language, restaurants within the ethnic enclave, and the like. Middleman minority businesses serve people outside of one's ethnic group, most often the poor and/or minorities who are neglected by other business owners. These businesses are in segregated geographic areas. Indian American–owned businesses primarily serve people outside of the ethnic group, such as gas stations, motels, fast-food restaurants, and even Indian restaurants. Some notable Indian enclaves exist, such as in northern New Jersey, Queens (New York City), Chicago, and elsewhere. But these are comparably small compared to other ethnic enclaves, such as the Cuban area of Miami, the Chinese neighborhoods in New York City, San Francisco, and Los Angeles, and the like. Because Indian immigrants post-1965 often arrived with advanced English skills and professional opportunities, they could afford to live in middle-class residential areas over time. Immigrant laborers, including South Asian Americans, are the ones more often found within urban enclaves. Without large enclaves, the main option available to Indian Americans who lack very large resources has been starting as middleman minorities.

Because starting a business is not as straightforward a choice as choosing a professional or laborer occupation (which results from one's recognized education and skills primarily), scholars have spent considerable time analyzing the decision process. According to Yoon (1997), individuals start small businesses if they cannot secure suitable employment otherwise, if they have the money and expertise necessary, and if they can find appropriate business opportunities. Immigrants may not find suitable employment due to a variety of reasons. These include being in segregated markets without access to many opportunities, lacking the necessary skills (e.g., English fluency, ability to drive), discrimination in hiring practices, and more. This "disadvantage" in the workplace motivates individuals to turn to small business.

Turning motivation for small business into a practical plan depends on having sufficient money, skills, knowledge, and labor. Immigrant small business owners rely on coethnic relatives and friends for these resources. Indian Americans borrow money from one another, much like other immigrant groups have, and go into business together. Owners often like to hire coethnic laborers as well. Once an immigrant group becomes established within an industry, it develops professional associations designed to represent their ethnic group to outside parties, such as policymakers, vendors, and the like. For instance, Indian Americans have formed the Asian American Convenience Store Association, the Asian American Hotel Owners Association, and more.

To make serious inroads in an industry, there must be business opportunities available in the first place (Waldinger 1994). Immigrants typically enter into business niches that are experiencing a turnover in ownership and are relatively inexpensive and easy to run. This has been the case for Indians' entry into taxi driving, motels, and convenience stores. None of these are lucrative businesses, and they demand many hours of work to turn a profit. Immigrants with few other options seek these opportunities. As franchising has become more common within small business, large franchise corporations spur the growth of small businesses. Indian immigrants have taken advantage of this as well, creating new businesses rather than just taking over existing ones (Dhingra and Parker 2015).

Problems in the Workplace

Problems Impacting Professionals

Whether Indian Americans are impacted by discrimination in the workplace is a debated topic. For professionals, common measures of racial inequality are income inequality from whites and the glass ceiling. Indian Americans, like Asian Americans as a whole, have higher incomes than native-born whites, which would suggest that there is no income inequality. Yet, incomes are based on multiple factors, and the income statistic alone does not indicate much. One must take into account individuals' levels of education, years of experience, and other factors in order to gauge if they are paid a fair amount or not. For instance, if Indian Americans have the same incomes as whites but have higher levels of education, then an inequality would exist because they are not paid commensurate to their educational status (as found for Asian Americans generally; Hirschman and Wong 1984). Where one was educated also shapes the level of inequality. Degrees from overseas universities are not as well understood and recognized as those from US universities, which puts immigrants educated abroad at a disadvantage (Sakamoto, Goyette, and Kim 2009). Other objective factors impacting incomes include geography, occupational sector, and more.

Taking into account multiple variables that impact income, Asian immigrants receive lower wages than comparably educated whites (Zeng and Xie 2004). For Asian Americans raised and educated in the United States, incomes are practically equal to whites with comparable skills and abilities, although given that Asian Americans tend to live in regions with higher wages, they may still experience some discriminatory treatment (Sakamoto, Goyette, and Kim 2009). Other research finds that US-born Asian American men earn 8 percent less than white men, once taking into account geography, education, industry, and related factors (Kim and Sakamoto 2010). Asian American women—both US-born and immigrants—are less likely to be employed than equally qualified white women (Kim and Zhao 2014). Those that are employed have incomes on par with that of white women. Yet, the equal pay does not account for the fact that Asian American women can have more years of work experience than white women. So, in terms of both employment levels and income, Asian American women, including Indian women, experience a disadvantage, as do Asian American men (Stone, Purkayastha, and Berdahl 2006). On the other hand, others contend that US-raised Indian Americans, both men and women, for the most part have no income disparity with whites (Mar 2010). Clearer results are necessary.

Along with income inequality, the glass ceiling is another racialized issue, primarily for professionals. The glass ceiling refers to a limited level (i.e., a ceiling) that one can attain within professional careers, while seeing others equally or less qualified be promoted higher. Like those on income inequality, data on the glass ceiling effect are mixed. According to Kim (2010), immigrant and US-raised Indian Americans do not encounter a glass ceiling. But Fernandez (1998) argues that both immigrant and US-born Indian American men and women encounter a glass ceiling within Silicon Valley's IT sector (an industry and geography with a high concentration of Indians), even compared to immigrant whites.

Related to but distinct from a glass ceiling are employment structures that do not allow professionals the opportunity to advance in the first place. Indian immigrants make up the majority of H-1B visa holders in the United States, a large number of whom work in IT positions. Many of these jobs are on contract bases for companies that are hired by large firms for specialized IT work (Banerjee 2006). As contract workers, they can be let go at any moment. There are no promotions possible within the structure of the organization. The tenuous legal status of the visa holders, their specialized skills, and their lack of networks within the US labor market make them beholden to such organizations. The lack of unionization within the high-tech industry makes combatting these problems more difficult (Varma and Rogers 2004).

There are other challenges in the white-collar workplace not picked up on by statistical analyses of income levels and promotion rates. How employees feel about their workplaces is not necessarily revealed in their salaries or titles. In fact, employees may make what they consider to be unfair sacrifices in order to advance within their organization. Asian Americans, including Indian Americans, encounter cultural barriers from their coworkers. Even US-born and -raised Asian Americans, who have substantial cultural overlap with white peers, can feel removed from the culture of the workplace. Indian and other Asian Americans note differences in terms of family commitments, preferred topics of conversation, and styles of interacting (Dhingra 2007). For instance, in an interview a second-generation woman said about her white-collar corporate workplace,

> Sometimes it's uncomfortable because of some of the beliefs I have from being Indian American and the [different] way [coworkers] approach things. An example being, I go home so often [to New Orleans from Dallas]. I organized a surprise twenty-fifth anniversary party for my parents and took it very seriously. It was my parents, and the problem was that this was so important to me, and [my work] wouldn't let me take that Monday off after the weekend. And I had all my family members there. To them it was just another family get together that you don't want to go to. I was like, "No you don't understand, I like my family." They were like, "Yeah, that's great, but no." They don't understand what is important to me. I feel like I have to explain everything.

While cultural differences and racism can limit one's mobility, they do not have a uniform effect. Racism actually can assist Indian and other Asian Americans within the workplace. The model minority stereotype portrays Asian Americans as hardworking, quiet, technically skilled, and obedient. These are virtues that employers would like in employees. The racialization of Asian Americans can actually help them get hired (although not promoted). Even Asian Americans have these opinions of other Asian Americans. An Indian American woman managed a clothing store and relied on racial stereotypes in her hiring decisions. She recalled in an interview,

> You know, Asians work a little bit harder, I see my Vietnamese girl, and my Filipino girl, even my Hispanic girls, they work hard. I mean, my Vietnamese girl actually can, will work nine to nine, and she never gets tired. The reason I hire them is because they have the same ethics as me. Because I've been in other stores and I've seen, you know, laziness.

The notion of Asian Americans as hardworking is "the reason I hire them." While she does not explain whom she views as lazy in other stores, the racialization of Asian Americans as hardworking most often is invoked relative to the presumed "lazy" African Americans or Latinos. Asian Americans' benefit is these other groups' loss. All are treated in a racialized, biased way.

Problems Impacting Laborers

The amount of research on Indian American laborers has been much less than has been published on professionals, and so it is hard to elaborate on the problems laborers face in the workplace. To a large extent the problems are direct confrontations of racism and/or sexism tied to the lower status occupation. The obstacles are fundamentally different than those impacting professionals. Rather than worry about an unsupportive workplace, laborers have to fear for their safety and ability to earn a living. Taxi driving, for instance, is one of the most dangerous jobs in the country.[6] Driver have been attacked and even killed by anti-immigrant, anti-Muslim racists.[7] Police officers also perpetuate this racist treatment (Prashad 2000). As one driver said, "It's a disgusting job. . . . People curse you, don't pay you, call you a damned Paki and tell you to go back home."[8] In addition, city regulations create unrealistic expectations for drivers, who are seen as expendable "third-world" immigrants. For instance, drivers get tickets for minor offenses and can have their licenses suspended rather easily. Such brutality is on top of the class oppression they experience. Most drivers in New York City, for instance, start each day in debt, having to spend money on the lease of the taxi and gas, and work for much of the day just to recoup their expenses (Mathew 2008). They are classified as self-employed, and so are not provided health insurance, retirement savings, unemployment benefits, and the like.

Indian American women's laboring professions have not been studied sufficiently. Like immigrant women generally, they often work as domestic servants. According to a report on the South Asian American community in Washington, DC, a growing contingent of worker are domestic workers. The report states, "South Asian domestic workers can face a range of concerns related to exploitation in terms of wages, limitations due to immigration status, and a lack of knowledge and understanding of their rights."[9] In general, domestic servants are subject to harassment, lost wages, confinement, and emotionally abusive treatment (Ehrenreich and Hochschild 2002).

Working for coethnics does not mean one escapes exploitation, in the form of lower pay, longer hours, less safe work conditions, and the like. In fact, it could mean greater vulnerability to such subjugation, since small business jobs are typically not unionized (Kwong 1996). Owners also know the vulnerability of the worker and can take advantage of it. And, just like people hire certain individuals for certain jobs, as seen above, people do *not* hire other people for other jobs. For example, Indian American motel owners may not hire fellow Indian Americans to work the front desk of their motel, and instead work as cleaners, because they worry about racist customers denigrating the motel if they see an Indian there (Dhingra 2012). Gender segregation places women in lower paid service occupations, whether working in large companies or with one's own family. Within a small business women perform domestic and more menial tasks rather than the entrepreneurial side, of investing money and growing the business.

Earnings of laborers are often below the national average. As Kim and Zhao (2014, 645) write, "The net annual earnings of less-educated Asian Americans (i.e., high school graduates or dropouts) are lower than those of equally educated native-born white women, regardless of generation." Low incomes create physical and emotional burdens on the workers. As Rangaswamy (2007, 682) writes about laborers at Dunkin' Donuts,

> Two of the women employees interviewed expressed deep regret that they had moved to the United States at all. One was delegated to scrubbing floors, while another who was cleaning tables was miserable that she had had to leave her one-year-old baby back home in her mother's care when she came to the United States. She saw no hope of improvement in her situation in the near future as she estimated that the next few years' earnings would be eaten up in paying off a Rs. 6 lakhs debt to her contact in India.

Indian Americans, like other immigrants, work in labor positions because their skills, networks, residential location, gender, and stereotypes within popular discourse limit their job options. Yet, the effects of racialization, class inequality, and gender are not isolated to just extreme cases.

Problems Impacting Small Business Owners

Because Indian American small business owners tend to operate outside of the enclave, I focus here on problems that ensue when catering to non-coethnics. Because middleman minorities cater to disenfranchised populations who rightfully resent the lack of public investment in their neighborhoods, criticisms toward business owners develops. The tensions between owners and customers often is read racially, both by the customers and by the popular media (Abelmann and Lie 1995; Bonacich 1973). Racial hostilities between Asian American owners and black customers have been widely documented. Indian Americans have not encountered headline-grabbing episodes. Still, they encounter problems stemming in part from their racialization as foreigners. Tensions with minority customers occur, but for the most part Indian American business owners encounter racist treatment from locals regardless of racial background.

Indian Americans can be racialized as the obedient and technically proficient model minority or as the undesirable, third-world migrant. The former applies more to professionals, as seen above, and the latter applies more to lower-end small business owners and laborers. Customers could perceive small Indian-owned motels, for instance, as smelly or as poorly maintained, and so avoid them (Dhingra 2012). It was not uncommon for customers to avoid Indian-owned motels or criticize Indians when they are unhappy with their experience. As one owner said, "Price changes with season. Higher in summer. People say, last week was $35 and this week is $70? They get mad at Indians, [say] you guys are stealing our money." In fact, non-Indian owners have capitalized on the prejudice of customers. During the 1980s as Indians' presence in the industry grew,

"American-owned and operated" signs were put up outside motels to signify that the motels were not Indian-owned. These nativist signs became popular again following 9/11.

It is not only customers and owners who target Indian Americans. Owners complain of government authorities targeting them as well. Owners of lower budget motels can complain of pressures by police and city officials to close down their motels, since they are considered blights. At times owners complain of being racially targeted in this way (Jain 1989). Convenience store owners also have been targeted by the government. "Operation meth merchant" is the US Drug Enforcement Agency's name given to its 2005 crackdown on convenience stores in northwestern Georgia run by Indian Americans (mostly Patel). They were accused of selling common household items that, when mixed together, can help create methamphetamines (meth). While most stores in that area are white-owned, those targeted were run by Indian immigrants often with limited English skills.[10] Deportations resulted from this operation.

Gender division within small business reproduces and furthers domestic gender inequality. Wives often have less control than husbands over the entrepreneurial side of the business. That is, Indian American women rarely start their own businesses. Wives work alongside their husbands in running businesses, even as they do not get the credit they deserve (Assar 2000).

Navigating the Workplace

Indian Americans, like other Asian Americans, encounter a racialization, often gendered, and cultural differences across their various workplaces. Generally speaking, workers aim to be seen within their workplace as assets. Toward that end, they—like anyone else—downplay aspects of themselves that might mark them as deviant from others at work. At other times race and ethnicity could be an advantage. In any case, being seen as *too* ethnic or racial at work can create divisions from others. Employees have to strategize on their self-presentations.

Before elaborating on how employees navigate the workplace, it is useful to recognize that the workplace carries its own expectation for "proper behavior," and this varies across workplaces. Diversity seminars are common within large white-collar organizations, and these set the tone for how ethnicity and race can be talked about. Companies go about these seminars differently. Some tell employees to be careful not to harass others, which has the effect of silencing conversations on difference. As one employee said of his company's seminar,

> You go to training and they have a multicultural session, but that's just to cover their asses. They teach you to love one another, why can't we all get along. It's more along the lines of people of different backgrounds or beliefs, you don't want to offend anyone, and people may take things out of context given their various backgrounds.

Other companies see people's backgrounds as potential resources for greater profit. So people are encouraged to capitalize on their differences in ways that promote the company. The organization does not want to limit its profits and so does not want people to feel that their differences are not valued. Companies seek out ways to affirm that value. One employee attended a work seminar titled "Realizing Your Potential," designed for employees of color. The employee elaborated,

> Basically, it talks about, you know, here's how you become really respected and popular and here's how you manage your own career. But, you know, you sit in a room with other African Americans, Latin Americans, and Asian Americans primarily. We talked about whether or not we have ever experienced anything that we thought because of race or our culture that was excluding us from being successful in American business.

Seminars and workplaces differed in their approach to ethnicity and race. But this difference was only to a degree. Consistent across workplaces was workers' impression that ethnicity and race must be expressed, if at all, judiciously in ways that would not hurt them. At other times people strategically expressed difference in ways that were helpful, so as to "become really respected and popular," as one employee said.

Hiding One's Background

How did Indian Americans carry themselves at work? I concentrate here mostly on professionals. Environments with the first kind of diversity seminars, with an emphasis on avoiding references to differences, were commonplace for workers. Because whiteness is normative across the vast majority of workplaces, individuals had to conform to that. In effect this meant often hiding one's ethnic and racial differences. Individuals hid all types of ethnic culture, ranging from overt symbols to domestic ways of life. As an employee at a multinational food company said about speaking in a language other than English at work,

> I mean, you have to have some sense of professionalism when you're at work, and I think part of it is not to speak another language when you're in a English-speaking environment. I think it ends up creating conflict that you don't need to create. You end up segregating yourself with the Indians that you're associating with, and that there is some bond there that they have with you that you don't [with others], and so instead of just creating that sense of bias, I just don't prefer to do it. I'm not here as an Indian supposedly, I'm here as just an employee. I should act the way they want me to act and behave in a proper way.

His responsibility at work was to behave as "just an employee," which meant hiding symbols that drew attention to his ethnicity. Recognizing one's ethnicity would mean not behaving "in a proper way" and instead inciting "conflict" and "bias."

Culture consists of more than symbols. Asian Americans, including Indian Americans, can feel that family norms create deep divisions from the expectations of work. Traditionally speaking, Asian cultures prioritize sustained family commitments for youth and adults alike (e.g., living with one's parents as an adult is normal). This commitment is gendered, since family expectations on women differ from those on men. For instance, a female employee at a manufacturing firm wanted to take time off to be with her parents, who lived in a different state.

> Sometimes it's uncomfortable [at work] because of some of the beliefs I have from being Indian American and the way [coworkers] approach things. An example being, I go home so often. I organized a surprise twenty-fifth anniversary party for my parents and took it very seriously. It was my parents, and the problem was that this was so important to me, and they wouldn't let me take that Monday off after the weekend. And I had all my family members there. To them it was just another family get together that you don't want to go to. I was like, "No you don't understand, I like my family." They were like, "Yeah, that's great, but no." They don't understand what is important to me. I feel like I have to explain everything.

Her analysis of why her company did not give her time off is cultural rather than economic, that is, it was driven by a lack of appreciation for family rather than the economic needs of the organization. Her views depend on a stereotype of how her white colleagues view their families, which may be exaggerated. Still, her experiences have made her uncomfortable at work.

Alongside being seen as culturally deviant, workers worried about drawing attention to themselves as racialized foreigners. Because this stereotype is always assumed for Asian Americans, workers had to strive to deflect it even before it applied to them. For instance, a software engineer who grew up in the United States said about his workplace,

> They have the image of Indians in software as being immigrants, hardworking, not going to complain, and not being able to socialize. I speak English well and when I meet someone, they see that I can speak like them. I want them to know that I'm not like [the immigrants]. My way of thinking is very different from people straight from the motherland. The way you're raised is very different. The topics of conversation we choose.

The need to perform whiteness influenced how employees spoke, how they cared for their families, and whom they associated with at work.

As employees, whether professionals or laborers, it is expected that one would have to conform to the workplace culture. Small business owners presumably have control over their workplace culture and so be able to present their ethnicity freely. Such was not the case. Small business owners who catered to the general public, as typical for Indian Americans, also had to present a veneer of whiteness in order to avoid a racialization as untrustworthy foreigners. The effects of this racialization were tangible. Motel owners complained of customers driving off if they see an Indian behind the desk or of disagreements taking on a racial charge if the worker is Indian. As one owner said,

> I think you have to [have whites as desk clerks], and some of that kinda goes back to the glass ceiling as well. If you're running an upscale hotel with an Indian at the front desk, you know, unfortunately we still live in a society that uhh ... doesn't look upon us kindly at times.

Race is so powerful that even though one is a capitalist and sets the terms of the business, one cannot present oneself freely.

In addition to hiding their bodies, owners also presented a front stage of whiteness at their motels. This involved putting up Christmas trees, even though practically all owners were Hindu, and changing their names to Anglo names (e.g., Tom, Paul, Ann). Intentionally harder to spot for customers were Indian religious and cultural symbols in the lobby area, even for independently owned motels. In franchise small businesses, such as fast-food restaurants, the customer areas are mostly predetermined by the corporation. Indian American owners hire coethnics because such labor was readily available and trustworthy to them, cheaper, and/or more reliable in their opinion. But owners recognized the advantages that come with whiteness and pursued a non-Indian workforce when effective.

So, commonly Indian Americans presented themselves as assimilated when at work, and while at home had more freedom to display their ethnicity. This segregation of ethnicity to the private sphere fits standard assumptions of identity management (Alexander and Wiley 1981). Ethnic minorities try to fit into the dominant culture when in public and present their ethnic and racial interests when with their group members in leisure or domestic spheres. At other times, however, individuals navigated the workplace by making sure they were recognized as ethnically different, discussed next.

Expressing One's Background

Just as diversity seminars differed in their approach to discussing (or silencing) difference, so did workers. As explained above, employees often hid their differences from others as best they could, trying to assimilate. This suits the approach to diversity that it is best to not discuss it. Another worker strategy, suiting the latter kind of diversity seminar approach, was to express differences but in ways that suited the goals of the company. But, individuals do not simply perform their identities any way they like. Instead, they must recognize and conform to the cultural expectations of their workplaces. They must find ways to assert themselves while still being seen as "regular" employees.

An employee calculated when she would refer to her ethnicity and when she would not, dependent on its impact on her career. She would not discuss it

> unless it benefits you in some way. I mean if you're working at a firm and one of the partners is a man, and he's very much into his Indian culture, and he talks about it because you have something in common and that can open the door for you, yeah. But I certainly wouldn't do it for any other reason.

Employees navigated racialized stereotypes in addition to cultural notions, and sometimes they used race to their advantage. As one employee said,

> The high average educational background [of Indian Americans] is known. And I think that the overall industry I'm in, technology, Indians are seen as the forefront. You got a whole lot of talent out there: software developers, hardware, entrepreneurs. Indians go across the ranks. People attribute some competence without looking at the paper résumé. The managers and directors see that I will see it through, and I think being Indian may have something to do with that.

In effect, being Indian was a physical résumé builder that made the paper résumé less relevant. Playing up one's ethnic and racial background could assist one's career rather than detract from it.

Even those employees who felt more open to sharing their differences had to censure themselves at times. Fitting multicultural discourse, discussing superficial group differences, but not deeper cultural divisions, could be appropriate. As one employee said about her conversations with predominantly white coworkers in Dallas, a somewhat conservative Christian section of the country,

> People are always asking me questions. Like food, they are very interested in trying Indian food or interested in the whole, our dresses. Like, we are not going to bring up religion, obviously, unless you are really good friends with that person. It's more ethnicity, culture, where you're from and what you do.

As Indians and other ethnic groups find ways to express their racial and ethnic differences at work, they create a "lived hybridity" (Brettell and Nibbs 2009; Dhingra 2007). That is, they attended to seemingly incompatible aspects of their identities simultaneously, rather than segregating their identities commitments to separate spheres or times. In the process, they do not interfere with, and possibly even promote, their integration at work. So, it is not the case that some people chose to hide their background while others chose to share it. All individuals made a calculation regarding which parts of their background to share or keep hidden.

While professionals had some agency to navigate their workplaces, laborers had less flexible positions and had to respond to others' dictates regarding race and ethnicity. Taxi drivers often are asked from where they immigrated about their homeland. Given the power imbalance between the poor immigrant driver and the customer being driven, drivers comply with the questions. Yet, it is rarely the case that passengers bother to share where they are from, for they feel privileged to simply interview the driver as the one whose presence in the United States must be explained. The exchange of national backgrounds can be innocuous, even if annoying. Yet, discussions of religion can turn dangerous. Drivers are attacked so often in New York City, in part because they are suspected terrorists, that legislation has been introduced in the city to protect them as a special group.[11] For these reasons drivers are in the bind of not wanting to share too much of themselves, while still needing to share enough to satisfy the customer.

Beyond Ethnic Expressions

Laborers need more than sympathetic bosses or workplace cultures that allow them to express themselves. They need basic rights of fair wages, safe working conditions, decent treatment, and opportunities for growth. Unfortunately, many of the organizational mechanisms to provide this have not made their way into the industries in which Indian laborers often labor. Domestic workers, fast-food employees, staff within ethnic restaurants, housekeepers at small motels, and the like—all common occupations for Indian Americans—are mostly non-unionized. Unions can provide basic guarantees for workers, but unions have a poor history of reaching out to immigrants generally. While currently unions make a point of recruiting minorities and women, Asian Americans are underrepresented as organizers.[12]

A notable exception to this lack of organizing has been among the taxi drivers in New York City. Given the large number of South Asian American taxi drivers, this organizing is of great significance to Indian American work equality. The New York Taxi Workers Alliance (NYTWA) pushes for fairer city and state regulations, driver safety and respect, fair relationships with leasing companies, and the like. After more than a decade of effective independent organizing, the NYTWA joined the AFL-CIO in 2011. The executive director, Bharati Desai, explained,

> We've become the fifty-seventh national union under the AFL-CIO, the first non-traditional one in over sixty years, since the farm workers, and the first one ever

for independent contractors. We're really proud that we're kind of blazing the trail for non-contingent worker unionization in this country.

Another employment issue that deserves greater attention is the rights and experiences of visa holders. H-1 visa holders are allowed to work in United States based on their needed skills. A large number of H-1 visas granted in a given year are within the IT industry. India sends the largest number of such immigrants. The visa restricts the flexibility of the workers, such as the ease with which they can change jobs or get a green card. Treatment within the job can be unfair as well. Within the IT industry there is a divide between engineers with stable jobs and those who work on a contract basis, often hired by firms specializing in contract labor. According to Banerjee and Ridzi (2008, 103),

> Data collected from Indian immigrant IT workers on the H-1B visa indicates that job insecurity, economic exploitation, and a range of disciplining mechanisms that favor capital characterize the deployment of Indian immigrants in the technology-based professional sector of the service economy.

Given that they can be paid less than the peers educated in the United States, they are treated as threats to native workers. Resentment toward them is common.

Conclusion

An investigation into how ethnic minorities experience work elucidates not only the realities of the workplace but moreover how race, gender, ethnicity, culture, and class intersect and operate for ethnic minorities and the public sphere. Dominant theories of immigrant adaptation focus on whether race or other social categories are influential or not for ethnic minorities. Common measures are income levels, occupational titles, perceived incidents of racism, and the like. While of great significance, these measures allow for only a narrow understanding of how race operates and intersects with other social categories. Ethnic minorities experience race in multidimensional ways, sometimes overt and sometimes subtle. As seen in this chapter, even well-assimilated ethnic minorities recount obstacles in the multicultural, professional workplace. Such challenges pale in comparison to what laborers and the economically vulnerable face. Nor are small business owners spared from having to navigate racialized norms, despite ostensibly being in charge of their own workplaces. These individuals might be optimistic about their careers and might feel well compensated for their efforts. Yet, race and its intersections with other dimensions create an uncomfortable environment that they must consciously navigate.

Indian Americans per se are presumed to be a model minority. In fact, many have made real successes. But, even this group faces significant obstacles. The focus here is less on the problems per se and more on the everyday and collective actions that Indian Americans perform in order to overcome the obstacles. Some efforts are more successful than others, and effort alone is rarely sufficient. Changes to workplace cultures are in order. Some problems stem from federal legislation. Indian Americans will continue to grow as a population in the nation and be actively involved in all parts of the labor market. How they experience work will tell us about their lives and about how the United States treats immigrants more broadly.

NOTES

1 http://cadmus.eui.eu/bitstream/handle/1814/33531/INTERACT-RR-2014%20-%2032. pdf?sequence=1.
2 http://saalt.org/policy-change/immigrant-rights/ deferred-action-for-childhood-arrivals-daca/.
3 http://yaleglobal.yale.edu/content/indian-doctors-help-fill-us-health-care-needs.
4 http://www.theguardian.com/technology/2014/apr/11/powerful-indians-silicon-valley.
5 http://www.aasc.ucla.edu/aascpress/nexus9_1_2_full.pdf.
6 http://money.cnn.com/galleries/2010/news/1004/gallery.Most_dangerous_jobs/10.html.
7 http://cityroom.blogs.nytimes.com/2010/08/25/cabbie-attacked/.
8 http://www.nytimes.com/1998/05/15/nyregion/hailing-danger-a-special-report-behind-the-wheel-long-hours-and-hard-feelings.html?n=Top/Reference/TimesTopics/Subjects/T/Taxicabs.
9 http://saalt.electricembers.net/wp-content/uploads/2012/09/Washington-DeSi.pdf.
10 http://www.stopoperationmethmerchant.org/blog/2005/12/introducing-operation-meth-merchant.html (accessed November 24, 2009).
11 http://www.democracynow.org/2010/8/26/colleague_of_nyc_taxi_driver_stabbed; https://nytwa.org/campaigns/taxi-driver-protection-act/.
12 http://digitalcommons.ilr.cornell.edu/cgi/viewcontent.cgi?article=1832&context=articles.

REFERENCES

Abelmann, N., and J. Lie. 1995. *Blue Dreams: Korean Americans and the Los Angeles Riots*. Cambridge, MA: Harvard University Press.

Alexander, C., Jr., and M. Wiley. 1981. "Situated Activity and Identity Formation." Pp. 269–289 in M. Rosenburg and R. Turner, eds., *Social Psychology*. New Brunswick, NJ: Transaction.

Assar, Nandini. 2000. "Gender Hierarchy among Gujarati Immigrants: Linking Immigration Rules and Ethnic Norms." Doctoral dissertation, Virginia Polytechnic Institute and State University.

Bald, Vivek. 2007. "'Lost' in the City: Spaces and Stories of South Asian New York, 1917–1965." *South Asian Popular Culture* 5 (1): 59–76.

Banerjee, Payal. 2006. "Indian Information Technology Workers in the United States: The H-1B Visa, Flexible Production, and the Racialization of Labor." *Critical Sociology* 32 (2–3): 425–445.

Banerjee, Payal, and Frank Ridzi. 2008. "Indian IT Workers and Black TANF Clients in the New Economy: A Comparative Analysis of the Racialization of Immigration and Welfare Policies in the US." *Race, Gender & Class* 15 (1–2): 98–114.

Bonacich, Edna. 1973. "A Theory of Middleman Minorities." *American Sociological Review* 38 (5): 583–594.

Brettell, Caroline, and Faith Nibbs. 2009. "Lived Hybridity: Second-Generation Identity Construction through College Festival." *Identities: Global Studies in Culture and Power* 16 (6): 678–699.

Chitnis, S. 1993. "Gearing a Colonial System of Education to Take Independent India towards Development." *Higher Education* 26 (1): 21–41.

Dhingra, Pawan. 2007. *Managing Multicultural Lives: Asian American Professionals and the Challenge of Multiple Identities.* Palo Alto, CA: Stanford University Press.

———. 2012. *Life Behind the Lobby: Indian American Motel Owners and the American Dream.* Palo Alto, CA: Stanford University Press.

Dhingra, Pawan, and Jennifer Parker. 2015. "Franchising Ethnic Entrepreneurship: Immigrant Business Owners and an Alternative Economic Model." Pp. 231–252 in Jody Agius Vallejo, ed., *Research in the Sociology of Work: Immigration and Work,* vol. 27. Bingley: Emerald.

Ehrenreich, Barbara, and Arlie Russell Hochschild, eds. 2002. *Global Women.* New York: Henry Holt.

Ellis, Mark, and Richard Wright. 1999. "The Industrial Division of Labor Among Immigrants and Internal Migrants to the Los Angeles Economy." *International Migration Review* 33 (1): 26–54.

Fernandez, Marilyn. 1998. "Asian Indian Americans in the Bay Area and the Glass Ceiling." *Sociological Perspectives* 41: 119–149.

Hirschman, Charles, and Morrison G. Wong. 1984. "Socioeconomic Gains of Asian Americans, Blacks, and Hispanics: 1960–1976." *American Journal of Sociology* 90 (3): 584–607.

Jain, Usha. 1989. *The Gujaratis of San Francisco.* New York: AMS Press.

Kim, ChangHwan, and Arthur Sakamoto. 2010. "Have Asian American Men Achieved Labor Market Parity with White Men?" *American Sociological Review* 75 (6): 934–957.

Kim, ChangHwan, and Yang Zhao. 2014. "Are Asian American Women Advantaged? Labor Market Performance of College Educated Female Workers." *Social Forces* 93 (2): 623–652.

Kim, Marline. 2010. "Glass Ceiling." Pp. 107–110 in Edith Wen-Chu Chen and Grace J. Yoo, eds., *Encyclopedia of Asian American Issues Today.* Santa Barbara, CA: Greenwood.

Kwong, Peter. 1996. *The New Chinatown.* New York: Macmillan.

Leonard, K. 1992. *Making Ethnic Choices.* Philadelphia: Temple University Press.

Mar, Don. 2010. "Overview of Economic Issues." Pp. 91–98 in Edith Wen-Chu Chen and Grace J. Yoo, eds., *Encyclopedia of Asian American Issues Today..* Santa Barbara, CA: Greenwood.

Mathew, Biju. 2008. *Taxi! Cabs and Capitalism in New York City.* Ithaca, NY: Cornell University Press.

McMahon, Suzanne. 2001. *Echoes of Freedom: South Asian Pioneers in California, 1899–1965.* Berkeley: University of California, Berkeley.

Mitra, Diditi. 2008. "Punjabi American Taxi Drivers: The New White Working Class?" *Journal of Asian American Studies* 11 (3): 303–336.

Poros, Maritsa. 2010. *Modern Migrations: Gujarati Indian Networks in New York and London.* Palo Alto, CA: Stanford University Press.

Portes, Alejandro, and Rubin Rumbaut. 2006. *Immigrant America: A Portrait.* 3rd ed. Berkeley: University of California Press.

Prashad, Vijay. 2000. *The Karma of Brown Folk.* Minneapolis: University of Minnesota Press.

Rangaswamy, Padma. 2007. "South Asians in Dunkin' Donuts: Niche Development in the Franchise Industry." *Journal of Ethnic and Migration Studies* 33 (4): 671–686.

Sakamoto, Arthur, Kimberly Goyette, and ChangHwan Kim. 2009. "Socioeconomic Attainments of Asian Americans." *Annual Review of Sociology* 35: 255–276.

Sanders, Jimy, and Victor Nee. 1996. "Immigrant Self-Employment: The Family as Social Capital and the Value of Human Capital." *American Sociological Review* 61 (2): 231–249.

Sanders, Jimy, Victor Nee, and Scott Sernau. 2002. "Asian Immigrants' Reliance on Social Ties in a Multiethnic Labor Market." *Social Forces* 81: 281–314.

Stone, R. A. Torres, Bandana Purkayastha, and Terceira Ann Berdahl. 2006. "Beyond Asian American: Examining Conditions and Mechanisms of Earnings Inequality for Filipina and Asian Indian Women." *Sociological Perspectives* 49 (2): 261–281.

Varma, Roli, and Everett M. Rogers. 2004. "Indian Cyber Workers in US." *Economic and Political Weekly* 48 (12): 5645–5652.

Waldinger, Roger. 1994. "The Making of an Immigrant Niche." *International Migration Review* 28 (1): 3–30.

Yoon, In-Joon. 1997. *On My Own: Korean Businesses and Race Relations in America*. Chicago: University of Chicago Press.

Zeng, Zhen, and Yu Xie. 2004. "Asian Americans' Earnings Disadvantage Reexamined: The Role of Place of Education." *American Journal of Sociology* 109: 1075–1108.

Zhou, Min. 2004. "Revisiting Ethnic Entrepreneurship: Convergencies, Controversies, and Conceptual Advancements." *International Migration Review* 38 (3): 1040–1074.

9

Gender, Migration, and Work

Filipina Health Care Professionals to the United States

YEN LE ESPIRITU

The ferocity of US (neo)colonial exploitation, the mismanagement of the Philippines by the country's comprador elite, and the violence of globalized capitalism have flung Filipinos "to the ends of the earth" as contract workers, sojourners, expatriates, refugees, exiles, and immigrants (San Juan 1998, 190).[1] Although Filipinos could be found in more than 130 countries and territories by the early 1990s, with most earning a living as short-term contract workers, the vast majority of the Filipinos who migrated to the United States have resettled there as "permanent" immigrants (Tyner 1999). According to the 2000 US census, Filipinos numbered 1.8 million, composing the second largest immigrant group as well as the second largest Asian American group in the United States.[2] Filipino migration to the United States differs in many respects from that to other labor-importing states. The history of US colonialism in the Philippines, combined with a relatively liberal US immigration policy and the proximity to alternative "cheapened" labor supplies, particularly from Central America and the Caribbean, means that a larger proportion of Filipino immigrants in the United States than elsewhere find employment in higher status and higher skilled occupations (Tyner 1999).

Since 1960, women have dominated Philippine labor flows to the United States. In 2000, of the roughly 43,000 Filipinos who immigrated to the United States that year, 61 percent were women (US Immigration and Naturalization Service 2000). Unlike their counterparts in Europe, the Middle East, and East Asia, the majority of whom are contract domestic workers, Filipina immigrants in the United States are decidedly more concentrated within professional sectors, a phenomenon that can be largely accounted for by the migration of Filipina health care professionals, especially nurses (Tyner 1999). Since the 1970s, the Philippines has been the largest supplier of health care professionals to the United States, sending nearly 25,000 nurses to this country between 1966 and 1985 and another 10,000 between 1989 and 1991. In 1989, Filipino nurses composed close to 75 percent of the total US foreign nurses; in 2003, this figure had climbed to 85 percent (Advincula 2004; Ong and Azores 1994). In fact, many women (and increasingly men) in the Philippines studied nursing in the hope of securing employment abroad, and many of the nursing programs in the Philippines accordingly oriented themselves toward supplying the overseas markets (Ong and Azores 1994).[3]

There is a widespread assumption—in the scholarly literature as well as in the popular imagination—that immigrants, especially those from developing countries, come to the United States primarily for economic reasons such as obtaining a higher income and standard of living. These economic explanations are well documented in the "push-pull" approaches to the study of migration. The neoclassical economic theory casts the individual migrant as a calculating economic agent, weighing the benefits and costs of migrating from low-wage to high-wage economies (Thomas 1973; Borjas 1990); and the updated "new economics of labor migration" (Stark 1991) approach claims that migration decisions are made not just by individuals but by the whole family to maximize the household income and survival chances (Massey et al. 1993; Taylor 1999). But migrants do not act in a vacuum devoid of historical and political context. Linking US imperialism and migration to the United States, I argue that the overrepresentation of health professionals among contemporary Filipino immigrants is the result of intertwined influences of US (neo)colonialism in the Philippines, deliberate recruitment from US health institutions, transnationalism, and gender ideologies and practices in both the Philippines and the United States. As a much sought-after group among US immigrants, Filipina health care nurses can enter the United States as principal immigrants. A female-first migration, especially when the women are married, has enormous ramifications for both gender roles and family relations. Therefore, in the second half of the article, I examine how migration processes, labor recruitment practices, and employment conditions have reconfigured gender and family relations for Filipina health care professionals.

A Critical Transnational Perspective to Migration Studies

Transnational migration studies form a highly fragmented field; there continues to be much disagreement about the scope of the field and the outcome of the transnational processes under observation (Portes, Guarnizo, and Landolt 1999; Glick Schiller 1997). From an epistemological stance, I find transnationalism to be a valuable *conceptual* tool, one that disrupts the narrow emphasis on "modes of incorporation" characteristic of much of the field of US immigration studies and highlights instead the range and depth of migrants' lived experience in multinational social fields (Levitt 2001; Glick Schiller and Fouron 2001; Perez 2004). In this essay, I employ a critical transnational perspective to call attention to yet another way of thinking beyond the limits of the nation-state: one that stresses the global relations that set the context for immigration and immigrant life. That is, today's global world is not just some glorious hybrid, complex, mixity; it systematically divided and historically produced (Guarnizo and Smith 1999; Massey 1999).

In the United States, public discussions about immigration fundamentally center on people who cross borders. However, the media, elected officials, and the general public often represent border crossers to be desperate individuals migrating in search of the "land of opportunity." From the perspective of immigration restrictionists, immigrants unfairly "invade" the United States, drain its scarce resources, and threaten its cultural unity (Perea 1997). Besides fueling nativist hysteria, this anti-immigrant rhetoric makes invisible other important border crossers: US colonizers, the military, and corporations that invade and forcefully deplete the economic and cultural resources of less powerful countries (Lipsitz 1998, 54). Given these multiple forms of border crossing, a critical approach to immigration studies must begin with the unequal links between First and Third World nations forged by colonization, decolonization, and the globalization of late capitalism. A critical transnational perspective that stresses the global structures of inequality is critical for understanding Asian immigration and Asian American lives in the United States. Linking global economic development with global histories of colonialism, Edna Bonacich and Lucie Cheng (1984) argue that the pre–World War II immigration of Asians to the United States has to be understood within the context of the development of capitalism in Europe and the United States and the emergence of imperialism, especially in relation to Asia. From World War II onward, as the world economy has become much more globally integrated, Asia has been a site of US expansion. As a result, contemporary immigrants from the Philippines, South Vietnam, South Korea, Cambodia, and Laos come from countries that have been deeply disrupted by US colonialism, war, and neocolonial capitalism (Lowe 1996; Campomanes 1997).

In the case of the Philippines, the prior flow of population, armies, goods, capital, and culture—moving primarily from the United States to the Philippines—profoundly dislocated many Filipinos from their homes and subsequently spurred their migration to the United States and elsewhere. In 1902, in the aftermath of the Spanish-American War, the United States brutally took possession of the Philippines over native opposition and uprising, thereby extending its "Manifest Destiny" to Pacific Asia. US colonialism (1898–1946) stunted the Philippine national economy, imposed English as the lingua franca, installed a US-style educational system, and Americanized many Filipino values and aspirations (Espiritu 2003, chap. 2). Even long after the Philippines regained its independence in 1946, the United States continued to exert significant influence on the archipelago—through trade, foreign assistance, and military bases. Infected with US colonial culture and images of US abundance, and saddled by the grave economic and political conditions in the Philippines, many Filipinos migrated to the United States to claim for themselves the promises of the "land of opportunity" (Espiritu 2003, chap. 2).

US Colonialism, Labor Recruitment, and the Production of Filipina Nurse Migrants

Although many scholars have conceptualized the contemporary Filipina nurse migration to the United States as a post-1965 phenomenon,[4] Catherine Choy (2003) argues that we need to trace the origins of this international migrant labor force back to early twentieth-century US colonialism in the Philippines.[5] According to her, the introduction of nursing in the Philippines was part of a larger US colonial attempt to "civilize" and "sanitize" the medically defective Filipino bodies under the guise of benevolent rule. In a nuanced analysis of the role of colonial medicine in the formation of colonial hegemony, Warwick Anderson (1995) delineates the ways by which the language of American medical science in the Philippines fabricated and rationalized images of the bodies of the American colonizers and the Filipinos—and in so doing, biologized the social and historical context of US imperialism. The scientific papers produced by the colonial laboratory during the early 1900s racialized Filipino bodies as dangerous carriers of foreign antibodies and germs that threatened white bodies; and American bodies as vulnerable but resilient, capable of guarding against the invisible foreign parasites lodged in native bodies.[6] The fears of the "innately unhygienic" Filipinos led to and justified house-to-house sanitary inspections and the quarantining of the "sick" from the communities. As such, the American medial discourse, as a privileged site for producing the "truth" about the "tropics," served to consolidate racial hierarchies, naturalizing the power and legitimacy of American foreign bodies to appropriate, command, and contain the Philippines and its people.

Like previous American medical interventions, the introduction of nursing in the Philippines reinforced many of the racialist functions and beliefs of Western medicine—all in the name of a humane imperialism. The opening of the first government school of nursing school in the Philippines in 1907 was part of the larger US colonial project of transforming Filipino bodies into a strong and healthy people capable of self-rule. In other words, the racialist construction of the Philippines as always-already diseased justified the need for more American medical intervention in the form of nursing. Viewing the teaching of nursing to Filipinos as a "moral obligation," American nursing educators often derided their young Filipina charges for their perceived temporal backwardness, "primitive" health practices, and lack of "rudimentary knowledge" about sanitation (Choy 2003, 23–25). For their part, despite their initial rebuff of the idea of women nursing, Filipinas who attended American-founded nursing schools gradually learned American nursing work culture, gained English fluency, and came to associate the United States with glamour, opportunity, and upward mobility. Professional nursing provided them with newfound opportunities to interact with colonial government officials, to attend government functions, to enter a prestigious profession, to serve their country—and most of all, to travel (Choy 2003).

In the early twentieth century, as part of their effort to acculturate elite Filipinos and to augment their devotion to the United States, the US colonial government sent several hundred individuals, including those in nursing, to study in US colleges and universities. Highly selected, these *pensionados* often were the children of prominent Filipino families whose loyalty the colonial regime hoped to win (Lawcock 1975; Posadas and Guyotte 1990). As anticipated, these early exchange programs, which brought Filipinos to the United States for "advanced training," reconstructed a global, cultural, and intellectual hierarchy in which US institutions—educational, political, medical—were superior to those of the Philippines. As exchange visitors, Filipina nurses became Philippine cultural ambassadors in the United States, and US nursing ambassadors upon their return to the Philippines. The possibilities of going to America as exchange students and nurses dramatically increased nursing's popularity. Eventually, studying and working abroad in the United States became a de facto prerequisite for occupational mobility in the nursing profession in the Philippines.

During the post–World War II period, the establishment of the Exchange Visitor Program (EVP) in 1948, which allowed visitors to stay in the United States for two years for training, made the dream of going abroad to the United States a possibility not only for elite women, but for the majority of nurses in the Philippines. The prestige associated with study and work abroad propelled Filipino nurses to transform the EVP into an avenue for the first wave of mass migration of nurses to the United States, even despite troubling reports of exploitation by US hospitals, which largely regarded the exchange nurses as a "cheapened" workforce. By the late 1960s, 80 percent of exchange visitors in the United States were from the Philippines, with nurses composing the majority of the participants (Asperilla 1976). The long-established presence of an Americanized professional nursing training system in the Philippines coupled with the existence of a transnational community of Filipino nurses created by the EVP laid the professional, social, and cultural groundwork for a "feminized, highly-educated and exportable labor force" (Choy 2003, 13). Goaded by grave economic and political conditions in the Philippines, this available labor force took full advantage of the relaxation of US immigration rules and preference for health care professionals in 1965 to migrate en masse to the United States. Like other immigrants, Filipina migrant nurses have had to accept inequitable pay and work arrangements in exchange for the comparatively higher salaries and immigration opportunities available in the United States (Ong and Azores 1994).

The overrepresentation of health professionals among contemporary Filipino immigrants is also the result of deliberate and aggressive recruitment from US hospitals, nursing homes, and health organizations, seeking a "cheapened" workforce ostensibly in response to domestic shortages in trained nurses (Ong and Azores 1994; Chang 2000). Since the passage of the 1965 Immigration Act, US health organizations, in collaboration with Philippine travel agencies, have actively recruited Filipino nurses, especially former exchange nurses, to migrate to the United States for permanent employment in their institutions. Many hospitals and nursing homes have recruited workers via the H-1 nursing visa program, which enabled them to sponsor nurses from abroad on temporary work visas to fill permanent positions.[7] Recruitment advertisements, conspicuously placed in the major local newspapers and in the *Philippine Journal of Nursing*, promised potential migrants interest-free loans for travel expenses as well as such bonuses as continuing education, tuition assistance at US universities, a higher salary, health plans, pension plans, paid vacation, and sick leave (Ong and Azores 1994; Choy 2003, 99–101, 107). However, in their aggressive hunt for nurses, nurse recruiters have often misinformed recruited nurses about US licensing requirements, educational credentials, work conditions, and pay and benefits. Some recruiters demanded a "fee" averaging seven to nine thousand dollars from the recruitees ostensibly to pay for the recruiter's fee and to arrange the nurse's visa. Since few women could afford this fee, most agreed to have it deducted from their meager monthly wages, a condition that left many H-1 immigrants in "debt peonage for at least two years" (Chang 2000; also Choy 2003, 173; Ong and Azores 1994).

Gender and Migration: The Formation of a Gendered Labor Force

The field of gender and immigration research has moved from the "immigrant women only" approach that emphasizes sex differences in migration systems to one that examines how gender as a social system contextualizes migration processes for both women and men (Hondagneu-Sotelo 1999; Tyner 1999). In particular, this scholarship has interrogated the ways in which constructions of masculinities and femininities organize migration and migration outcomes (Hondagneu-Sotelo 1994). Although the concept of gender is invaluable for the understanding of migration experiences, women of color have argued that the gender process cannot be understood independently of class and race and other structures of oppression (Espiritu 1997; Glenn 2002). Accordingly, contemporary approaches to migration have increasingly questioned the premise of a universal, shared experience of womanhood and have developed theories and designed research that capture the multiple and mutually constitutive relations of race, class, nationality, and legal status (Pessar 1999).

Gender beliefs, often working in tandem with and through racial beliefs, affected the content and scope of US colonialist policies and practices in the Philippines. As feminist theorists have reminded us, the construction of "otherness" is achieved not only through racial but also through sexual and gendered modes of differentiation (Mohanty 1991; Stoler 1991; Yegenoglu 1998). Attentive to the mutually constitutive aspects of race and gender, historian Kristin Hoganson (1998) has shown how the racialization of Filipinos as biologically unfit for independence drew on ideas about gender. Through a careful reading of a range of official and cultural courses of the time, she convincingly demonstrates that the prominent stereotypes of the Filipinos—as uncivilized, savages, rapists, or children—all presented the Filipinos as lacking the *manly* character seen as necessary for self-government. She adds to this list the stereotype of the *feminized* Filipino: the depiction of the Philippines as woman, Filipino men as effeminate, and Filipino women as highly feminine and sexualized (Hoganson 1998, 137). The hyperfeminization of Filipino men and women misrepresented and distorted gender relations in the Philippines, pitting the two sexes against each other. They also bolstered the racialized conviction that Filipino men lacked the manly character for self-government and justified the need for US interventions to rectify the Philippine "unnatural" gender order (Espiritu 2003). The extensive US military presence in the Philippines (1898–1992) also produced stereotypes of Filipinas as desirable but dangerous "prostitutes" and/or submissive "mail-order" brides (Halualani 1995; Egan 1996). Many Filipino nationalists have charged that the "prostitution problem" in the Philippines stemmed from US and Philippine government policies that promoted a sex industry—brothels, bars, and massage parlors—for US servicemen stationed or on leave in the Philippines. During the Vietnam War, the Philippines was known as the "rest and recreation" center of Asia, housing approximately ten thousand US servicemen daily (Coronel and Rosca 1993; Warren 1993). In this context, *all* Filipinas were racialized as sexual commodities, usable and expendable. These established images often "travel" with Filipinas overseas and prescribe their racialization there. For example, Christine Chin (1998, 144–146) reports that many middle-class Malaysian employers regard their Filipina domestic workers as sexually promiscuous and thus in need of intense methods of surveillance and control.

US colonial nursing in the Philippines highlights the complex intersections of gender ideologies with those of race and class in shaping US colonial agendas and practices. US colonial training of Filipino nurses, recruited primarily from "respectable" families, involved the imposition of American's gendered (and also racialized and classed) assumptions about labor, which, as feminist scholar Louise Newman (1999, 34) points out, posited that "the more civilized the race, the more the men and women of that race had to differ from one another." Since American women colonialists linked differentiated gender roles with racial progress, they viewed the construction of a separate sphere of Filipino women nurses to be foundational to the uplift of the Filipino race. Thus the gendered notions of nursing as *women's* work—widely accepted in early twentieth-century white middle-class America—was an idea that American nursing educators "actively had to reproduce" in the Philippines (Choy 2003, 26). US colonial government deliberately separated and excluded Filipino men from the labor of nursing; it also attempted to legislate the creation of a female nursing labor force through a 1909 act that appropriated funds for women-only nursing classes (Choy 2003, 44). The construction of this gendered labor force—and gendered form of mobility—would lay the foundation for the significant women-dominated migrations of Filipino nurses beginning in the second half of the twentieth century.

The women-dominated migrations of Filipino nurses also reflect women's segmentation into nursing professions in the United States (Tyner 1999). The endemic and recurring shortage of nurses in the United States constitutes the primary underlying factor for the recruitment of Filipino nurses to the United States. Although fueled by the rapid growth in the demand for health care and changing character of US medical care, the shortage of nurses is also the result of sex-based discrimination in the profession (Ong and Azores 1994; Tyner 1999). Since nursing has consistently been women's work in the United States, wage levels in the field have been kept comparatively low. Even in a competitive market, where demand for nurses has consistently outstripped the supply of labor, wages for nurses have not risen to the levels needed to entice US-born women to enter the field (Ong and Azores 1994, 166). In response to this glaring wage disparity nurses in the United States have unionized and filed comparable-worth suits to demand higher pay (Blum 1991, 104–108; Hunter 1986, chap. 7). The lack of decent wages, poor working conditions, and a lack of professional prestige have induced many American nurses to leave the profession and others to shun these jobs (Ong and Azores 1994; Tyner 1999).

The US chronic labor shortage of nurses, most acute in inner-city and rural facilities, led to the active recruitment and continued preferential treatment of foreign-trained nurses in US immigration laws. In response, since the 1970s, the Philippine government has actively promoted the export of its nurses in exchange for their remittance dollars, which are critically needed to alleviate the nation's mounting external debt and trade deficits.[8] Once denigrated for abandoning the health needs of their own people for the mighty dollar, Filipino nurses working abroad became the Philippines' new national heroes whose earnings would help to revitalize the nation's economy (Choy 2003, 116). In a 1973 address to Filipino migrant nurses, Philippine Secretary of Health Clemente S. Gatmaitan proclaimed, "We are proud of you. Another benefit that accrues from your work is the precious dollar you earn and send back to your folks at home. In this manner, you help indirectly in the improvement of our economic conditions" (cited in Choy 2003, 117). Gatmaitan's declaration does not apply to nurses only, but reflects the Philippine nation-state's economic strategy since 1974: to "export" its workers worldwide in exchange for their remittances (Rafael 2000, 205–206).

Philippine government officials and recruitment agencies exploit gendered depictions of Filipinas to market the Filipino nurses. As expected, these officials and agencies extol the nurses' English-speaking skills and American professional training, both a legacy of US colonialism. However, in their aggressive promotion of the migration of nurses, they also praise Filipino nurses for their purported "tenderness" and natural knack for caregiving, thereby relying and perpetuating stereotypical depictions of the "Oriental women" as inherently feminine and servile. In a 2001 speech commemorating the 103rd founding anniversary of the Philippine Department of Foreign Affairs, Philippine Vice President and Foreign Affairs Secretary Teofisto T. Guingona, Jr. (2001) praised the Filipino migrant nurses' predisposition for the gendered work of nursing: "In Canada, in America, in Europe, and in other places Filipina nurses are in demand. Why? Because they do their job with a smile, with charm, with grace, with the real purpose of helping to ease the patients' pain, without looking at the clock, without minding the overtime, really trying to cure the patient and comforting him in his time of crisis. And that is why Filipino nurses are in demand." In addition to gendering the patient as male and the nurses as female, Guingona depicted Filipina nurses as cheerful about and even welcoming of their harsh working conditions such as long hours and hard physical labor. In the same way, Annabelle Reyes Borromeo (2004), founding president and CEO of STI-Universal Worker Inc., an international consulting firm based in the Philippines that specializes in training, educating, and preparing qualified nurses for careers abroad, imbued Filipina nurses with feminine virtues: "Our nurses need not necessarily be taught to care—they're natural at this—from the way we talk and touch, it's like second nature to us already and it's what they like about Filipino nurses."

Female-First Migration and Changing Gender Relations

Through the process of migration and settlement, patriarchal relations undergo continual negotiation as women and men rebuild their lives in the new country. An important task in the study of migration has been to examine this reconfiguration of gender relations. Central to the reconfiguration of gender hierarchies is the change in immigrant women's and men's relative positions of power and status in the country of settlement. Theoretically, migration may improve women's empowerment and social position if it leads to increased participation in wage employment, more control over earnings, and greater participation in family decision making (Pessar 1984). Alternatively, migration may leave gender asymmetries largely unchanged even though certain dimensions of gender inequalities are modified (Espiritu 1997).

As a result of the recurring shortage of nurses in the United States, Filipina health care workers are a much sought-after group among US immigrants, and thus can enter the United States as principal immigrants. This means that unmarried women can immigrate on their own accord and that married women can enter as the primary immigrants, with their husbands and children following as dependents. Drawing from in-depth interviews of Filipino Americans in San Diego, California, the rest of this essay explores the impact of the female-first migration of health care professionals on gender and family relations.[9] San Diego has long been a favorite site of settlement for Filipinos and is today the US destination with the third largest population of contemporary Filipino immigrants. In 2000, there were approximately 120,000 Filipinos in San Diego County. Although these immigrants represented only 4 percent of the country's general population, they constituted more than 50 percent of the Asian American population (Espiritu 2003, 17). A 1992 survey of approximately eight hundred Filipino high school students in San Diego found that close to a quarter of the respondents' mothers worked in the field of health care, about half of whom were registered nurses (Espiritu and Wolf 2001).

"We Were Young and We Wanted to See the World": Migration of Single Women

Rose Ocampo grew up in Cavite among four sisters and three brothers as the fourth of eight children. She decided to become a nurse because "it was a trend": "All my friends were going into nursing so I went ahead and went into nursing too." Rose came to the United States in 1961 under the auspices of the US EVP. She explained that she and a friend wanted to visit the United States "to see the country." "It wasn't for the money," she said quickly. "The stipend was only a hundred dollars a month and they worked you forty eight hours a week." What the two young women wanted was "a new environment, for adventure. We were young and we wanted to see the world." Rose was sent to a small town in Minnesota, where she befriended other EVP Filipino nurses who helped her to integrate into her new community. When her exchange visa expired at the end of two years, Rose wanted to extend her stay because "my friends and I still wanted to go around the world." Instead of returning to the Philippines, she exited the United States by going to Canada, where she worked for a year. However, just before she left for Canada, she befriended a Filipino American man who followed her to Canada. The two married a year later, which allowed Rose to officially immigrate to the United States.

Rose's experience illustrates the power of gender in shaping migration. First, it shows that gender-based transnational social networks circumscribe migration opportunities. Women nurses migrated to and settled in the United States with the help of other women. Through letters, phone calls, and return visits, Filipino nurses who had gone abroad created new expectations, goals, and desires among young Filipino women still in the Philippines. According to Luz Latus, her nursing friends' and colleagues' decisions to apply for US visas influenced her own decision to emigrate:

> After I graduated, I decided to come here. I though, "Well, it seems like everybody wants to go there." So I thought I'd try. Why not, you know? There is always a farewell party for so-and-so. She's leaving for the U.S., to do this and that. Well, somehow, a whole bunch of us, we decided, let's go ahead and apply. You know how when you were young, I mean … you know, you're really, just want to experience this. What is this thing they're talking about? America.

In the process of relocating and settling in the United States, Filipino health care migrants also create new transnational networks of support, helping each other to adjust to their new occupational, social, economic, and cultural settings (Choy 2003).

Second, Rose's experiences reveal that men and women often give different reasons for migrating. When asked about their motivations for migrating to the United States, the Filipino men in my study tended to give the following reasons: to better represent themselves as able economic providers and desirable sexual partners. In contrast, while Filipina nurses also mentioned economic motives, many more cited a desire to be liberated from gendered constraints: to see the world and experience untried ways of living (see also Parreñas 2001, 62–69). The EVP and the new occupational preference categories of the 1965 Immigration Act created opportunities for the Filipina women health professionals to enter the United States on their own accord. Indeed, the majority of the nurses whom I interviewed came to the United States initially as single women, a fact corroborated by other studies of Filipina nurses (Choy 2003). In the interviews, many of these nurses represented their decision to come to the United States as an effort to push gender roles, especially to unshackle themselves from family discipline that hindered their individual development. For example, Cecilia Bonus indicated that she applied to study in the United States because "my family was just so protective. I just kind of wanted to get away and be independent." Being away from home enabled many young women to free themselves temporarily from strict parental control on their activities and movements. In the United States, many traveled freely, socialized widely, lived in their own apartments, and stayed out late at night.

Perhaps most important, Filipina health care professionals reveled in their newfound freedom to befriend and date men. Carmen Reynila described how she and her fellow exchange nurses enjoyed company of Filipino sailors in town:[10]

> There used to be a lot of Filipino gatherings around. So you got to meet each other, and then the sailors, you know, they would come to our apartments, and then, you know, we would go out with them, but then always in a group [laughter]. Because I would say there is a safety in numbers [laughter].

Many Filipino women seize their newfound freedom to make more independent choices about marriage. Some elect to marry in the United States, partly to mute any possible objections from their parents. In an example, Rosie Roxas, who met her Filipino Navy husband while in San Diego, explained why she did not return to the Philippines to marry: "My parents would not have approved of him. Their background ... it would have been very difficult. ... They wanted me to marry a professional. ... He would not have passed." In her study of Filipino nurses, Choy (2003) reports that Philippine government health officials and nursing leaders used a rhetoric of spirituality and morality to create the new lifestyles of Filipino exchange nurses abroad. These critics charged that some Filipino exchange nurses had become morally corrupt and associated the nurses' new lifestyles in the United States with licentiousness. Choy accurately interprets these charges as efforts to persuade Filipino nurses to return to work in the Philippines. However, in light of the women's newfound independence, I believe these charges must also be viewed as retaliating moves to reassert patriarchal control over the bodies of these women.

Negotiating Changing Gender Roles: The Migration of Married Women

When the women are married, a female-first migration stream can have enormous ramifications for both family relations and domestic roles. In a reversal of historical patterns of migration, many married women health professionals enter the United States as primary immigrants, with their husbands and children following as dependents. Take Cecile Garcia's story, for example. Cecile had always dreamed of "America" and going abroad figured prominently in her decision to select a nursing career. In 1973, married with two young children, she left for the United States under the auspices of the EVP. Although both she and her mechanic husband shared a desire to move the family to the United States, it was her profession that allowed them to do so. As an exchange nurse, she came alone; her husband stayed behind to care for their two young daughters. Eighteen months later, when she had successfully adjusted her status from exchange visitor to permanent resident, she petitioned for her family to join her. But the temporary separation from the children had its costs:

> My daughter who was two when I left didn't even know me when I went back to get them. She would not come to me. I stayed there for three weeks when I picked them up ... still she would not come to me. I was very hurt by that. I was like a stranger ... and that really struck me. I don't want to not be known by my children.

These separations, even when temporary, can leave lifelong scars. At the age of twenty-one, Melanie Villa still harbored unresolved grief over her mother's decision to leave for the United States during her first two years of life: "Sometimes, I still think about it ... like the fact that I was never breast-fed like my sister, who was born here. . . . It doesn't seem fair, you know. . . . And I wonder if it had affected my relationship with my mother." These experiences of transnational motherhood, albeit temporary, continue a long historical legacy of people of color being incorporated into the United States through restrictive systems of labor that do not recognize the workers' family needs and rights (Dill 1988; Glenn 1986; Hondagneu-Sotelo and Avila 1997; Parreñas 2001).

A female-first migration stream also affects traditional gender roles. In many instances, men who immigrate as their wives' dependents experience downward occupational mobility in the United States, while their wives maintain their professional status. Pyong Gap Min (1998, 52) reports that among Korean immigrant families in New York, while Korean nurses hold stable jobs, many of their educated husbands are unemployed or underemployed. Gender role reversals—wives' increased economic role and husbands' reduced economic role—challenge men's sense of well-being and place undue stress on the family. For example, Elizabeth Mayor, a Filipina medical technologist, entered the United States in 1965 through the EVP, leaving behind her husband and two sons. One year later, Elizabeth changed her status to permanent resident and petitioned for her family. Elizabeth's husband, who had a degree in criminology, could not find work in the United States commensurate with his education and training. Elizabeth described their differential access to suitable employment:

> For me, since I had the training in Illinois, and had my license as a med tech, I was able to work in the medical profession in the laboratory. I had no problems find a job. But for him, it was difficult. He had to work odd jobs, anything that was available there. That was a minus for him. . . . My husband was more dependent on me because I had a stable job.

Her husband was "bitter" about this role reversal: "He had a big problem. His self-esteem was really low. When he first came, he worked as a janitor, then as a dishwasher. He was working all the time but in blue-collar jobs. It took a lot out of his self-esteem, as far as that goes." Because of this loss of status, Elizabeth's husband repeatedly expressed his desire to return to the Philippines—for the entire duration of their thirteen-year stay in Illinois. In 1989, Elizabeth's sister urged them to leave Chicago and join the family business in San Diego. Although Elizabeth had a "good job" in Chicago, she decided to accept her sister's invitation, in part because it included a job offer for her husband. At the time of our interview in 1994, Elizabeth reported that her husband's self-esteem has been restored: "My husband is happy now. That was the first steady job he'd held since he came to the United States." In contrast, Elizabeth had difficulty finding a stable job and instead worked part-time for a local company. But she expressed that she was content with her new life: "So it is just the opposite here. He has a steady job and now I work part-time. Which I like too. . . . As an

Oriental, my upbringing is . . . usually the husband is the bread earner back home. So that worked perfect for me. It's a lot better for him here than back East. So I am happy."

Elizabeth's account of her family experiences calls attention to the dissimilar structure of opportunities that many immigrant men and women encounter in contemporary United States (Hondagneu-Sotelo 1994; Espiritu 1997; Menjivar 1999). The dynamics of the US economy, in this case the shortage of medical personnel, place many women in a relatively favorable position with respect to access to paid work, whereas their male peers do not fare as well. At the same time, Elizabeth's experience challenges the relative resource models that predict that as women's earnings rise relative to their husbands', their authority and status in the family will correspondingly rise. Elizabeth's story suggests that the labor market advantage does not automatically or uniformly lead to more egalitarian relations in the family. Instead, perceived cultural ideals about gender and spousal relations that were held in the Philippines, some of which were imported through US colonialism, such as the belief that the men should be the primary economic provider and head of the household, continue to influence the outcomes of the changing balance of resources in the new country.

Working at Family Life

One of primary themes in gender and immigration research concerns the impact of immigrant women's employment on gender equality in the family. Like other case studies on gender relations among salaried professionals, my research on women health professionals indicates that women's employment has led to greater male involvement in household labor (Chen 1992; Min 1998; Pesquera 1993). However, this more equitable household division of labor is attributable not to women's earning power, but rather to women's demanding job schedules and the couple's recognition that at least two incomes are needed to "make it" in this country. Like other immigrants, the health care professionals' success requires the work of the whole family, with husbands and children at times having to assume tasks not usually expected of them.

A survey of Filipino nurses in Los Angeles County reveals that these women, to increase their incomes, tend to work double shifts or the higher paying evening shifts and night shifts (Ong and Azores 1994, 183–184).[11] Given the long hours and the graveyard shifts that typify a nurse's work schedule, many husbands have had to assume more child care and other household responsibilities in their wives' absences. Some nurses have elected to work the night shift, not only because of the higher pay, but also because they can leave the children with their husbands instead of with paid child care providers. According to Cecilia Bonus, "I work mostly at night. So my husband takes care of the kids. . . . He's pretty good at helping when I have to work. . . . He's pretty understanding as far as that goes." Maricela Rebay's mother took pride in the fact that she never left her children with babysitters:

> We never had babysitters. Oh, my mom is the toughest person in the world. She just managed. When she was in nursing, she would work at night. And my dad would take care of us when she was at work. So, like, in the morning, when she gets home, she makes breakfast for the kids, and then my dad drives us to school, and then she would go to sleep.

In her research on shift work and dual-earner spouses with children, Harriet Pressner (1988) finds that the husbands of night-shift workers do a significant part of child care; in most cases, the husbands supervise the often-rushed routines of getting their children up and off to school or to child care.

When wives and/or husbands are unable to manage around-the-clock care for their children, they sometimes rely on the eldest child to shoulder the responsibility. When Maria Galang turned fifteen, both of her parents worked the night shift, her mother as a nurse at the local hospital and her father as a janitor at the local mall. Maria was forced to take care of her younger sister during her parents' absence:

> Because mom and dad worked so much, I had to assume the role of mother hen. And it was a strain especially at that point when I hit high school. They figure that I was old enough now. I remember frequent nights when my sister would cry and she wanted mom. What could I do? While mom and dad provided that financial support, we needed emotional support as well which was often lacking.

This arrangement can take a toll on family relations: A child who has grown without the mother's presence may no longer respond to her authority (Hondagneu-Sotelo and Avila 1997, 562). As an example, for five years, Rose Dumlao "mothered" her younger brother while her navy father was away at sea and her nurse mother was working long hours at the hospital. As a result, Rose's brother channeled his affection and respect to Rose, his "other mother," instead of to his mother:

> I think the reason why my brother doesn't really respect my mom the way he should is because he never really saw my mom as the caretaker because she was never around. So even now, whenever my parents want my brother to do something, like if they have to talk to him, I have to be either in the room or I have to be the one that's talking to him because he's not going to listen to them. Because I spent more time with him.

Even when there are no younger siblings to care for, the parents' absence still pains their children. Gabriela Garcia, whose parents divorced when she was nine years old, recounted how she managed when her mother worked the graveyard shift:

> After my parents divorced, my mother was working two shifts. She would work basically from three in the afternoon till seven in the morning. She would be gone by the time I had come home from school. And then I was by myself. . . . So I slept by myself. I had to have the radio, the TV, and the light on because I was so scared sometimes.

Research on gender relations among salaried professionals indicates that gains in gender equality have been uneven. Even when there is greater male involvement in child care in these families, women continue to perform more of the household labor than their husband (Chen 1992; Min 1998; Pesquera 1993). Moreover, Pesquera (1993, 185) reports that, for the most part, the only way women have altered the distribution of household labor has been through conflict and confrontation, suggesting that ideologically most men continue to view housework as women's work. These findings remind us that professional women, like most other working women, have to juggle full-time work outside the home with the responsibilities of child care and housework. Cecilia Bonus, a nurse mother of three young children, confided that she felt overwhelmed by the never-ending chores: "Here you have to work so hard. You have to do every-thing. You have to wash the dishes, you have to do laundry, you have to clean the house, you have to take care of the kids. It's just endless." Although Cecilia's husband took care of the children when she worked the night shifts, she wished that he would do more:

> The husbands should help out more, I think . . . as far as the children go, and the housework. . . . That's one thing I like about Western culture. They have more liberty as a female and the rights that men have. It's not just a one-way thing where women have to do everything. Men should do things like chores at home, too, you know.

Cecilia, who came from a middle-class family in the Philippines, confided that she missed the "helpers" that she had in the Philippines. "Over there, you have maids to help you," she said. "You don't have to do the chores. You have one maid for each child. Life is so much easier there. Every little thing is offered to you, even a glass of water. I just wished I had a helper here." Like Cecilia, the majority of the women in my study longed for the "helpers" they once had or expected to have, had they stayed in the Philippines. In the United States, instead of enlisting their husbands' help with the housework, these women often chose to "solve" their "double-day syndrome" by hoping to displace it on less privileged women. As Parreñas (2001, 79) correctly observes, "As women transfer their reproductive labor to less and less privileged women, the traditional division of labor in the patriarchal nuclear household been significantly renegotiated in various countries in the world." At the same time, in the context of migration in which many Filipina nurses are working in higher paid jobs but leading lower status lives, the nurses' desire for "helpers" must also be understood as a longing for the social class status that many once had in the Philippines—one that entails the hiring of less privileged women to carry out reproductive chores.

Conclusion

Since 1960, women have dominated the Filipino immigrant population, the majority of whom are nurses. The development of this international mobile labor force is inextricably linked to the history of early twentieth-century US colonization of the Philippines, the preference for foreign-trained nurses by Philippine and US agencies, and the pervasive cultural Americanization of the Philippines, which exhorted Filipinos to regard US culture, politics, and way of life as the model par excellence for Philippine society. In other words, the development of the quintessential Filipina nursing care provider and the origins of Filipino nurse migration are not solely the results of contemporary global restructuring, the "liberalization" of US immigration rules, or individual economic desires, but rather are historical outcomes of early twentieth-century US colonial rule in the Philippines.

NOTES

Originally published in *Revue Europeenne des Migrations Internationales* 21: 55–75, 2005. Reprinted with permission of *REMI*.

1 International migration is so prevalent in the Philippines that in 1997, the Philippine secretary of foreign affairs called for "international migration" to be made a subject for elementary and high school students to prepare them for what he termed the "reality of immigration" (Okamura 1998, 5).

2 Filipinos composed the second largest immigrant group, behind Mexicans. According to the 2000 census, Chinese Americans, at more than 2.4 million, constituted the largest Asian American group in the United States. In California, Chinese Americans, who neared the 1 million mark, also pushed past Filipinos (918,678) to become the state's largest Asian group. Though the Filipino population rose by 31.5 percent nationwide and 25.6 percent statewide, it fell well short of predictions that the 2000 census would crown Filipinos as the largest Asian group in the nation and in California.

3 Beginning in the early 1960s, as the demand for nursing education exceeded the enrollment slots available in Philippine colleges and schools of nursing, Filipino businessmen and health educators opened new schools of nursing in the provinces as well as in urban areas. Between 1950 and 1970, the number of nursing schools in the Philippines increased from just 17 to 140 (Choy 2003).

4 The 1965 Immigration Act, which abolished the national origins quotas and permitted entry based primarily on family reunification or occupational characteristics, dramatically increased the number of Asian immigrants to the United States.

5 Catherine Choy's (2003) *Empire of Care* is the first and only study on the introduction of nursing in the Philippines during US colonial rule and on the impact of the US Exchange Visitor Program of the 1950s and 1960s on Filipino migration to the United States. Therefore, this section of my essay necessarily relies on Choy's pioneering research.

6 In his 1936 extraordinary popular autobiography, Victor Heiser, the commissioner of health in the Philippines, described Filipinos in the following terms: "grown-up children, dirty, unsanitary, diseased, ignorant, unscrupulous, superstitious, born actors, resigned to death, untrustworthy, cowards, a nation of invalids, incubators of leprosy, unhygienic" (cited in Anderson 1995, 100).

7 In 1970, a US immigration amendment introduced the H-1 temporary work visa program, which enables a hospital or nursing home to sponsor or bring a nurse with a professional license from abroad to work in the United States for two years. However, under this program applicants must pass the US nurses' licensing exam. If they pass, they can gain permanent residency after two years. If they fail the exam, they lose their temporary work visa status and face the threat of deportation (Chang 2000). The majority of foreign-trained nurses (between 75 and 90 percent) who took the exam failed (Ong and Azores 1994). In 1989, the Filipino Nurses Organization fought for passage of the Immigration Nursing Relief Act, which enabled H-1 visa nurses who were present in the United States on September 1, 1989, and had worked for three years as a registered nurse in the United States, to adjust their status to permanent resident (Ong and Azores 1994).

8 According to the Philippine Overseas Employment Administration, between 1989 and 1993, Filipino Americans remitted approximately $5 billion, averaging well over $1 billion each year (Okamura 1998, 126). By 1989, consumer goods sent via *balikbayan* (returnee or home-comer) boxes contributed 4.2 billion pesos (or $190 million) annually to the Philippine economy (Basch, Glick Schiller, and Szanton Blanc 1994, 257–258). These numbers are rising. In the first half of 1994, overseas Filipinos remitted almost $800 million through official bank transfers—a likely underestimate (Okamura 1998, 44, 126). In 2001, over seven million overseas Filipino workers sent over $6 billion in remittances to the Philippines (US Treasury Department 2003).

9 Over the course of eight years (1992–2000), I interviewed just over one hundred Filipinos in San Diego County. The majority of the interviewees were Filipino navy men, Filipino nurses, and their families.

10 During the ninety-four years of US military presence in the Philippines, US bases served as recruiting stations for the US Navy, Filipinos were the only foreign nationals who were allowed to enlist in the US armed forces; and the navy was the only military branch they could join. As a result, Filipino sailors have always formed a significant segment of the Filipino community in the United States, especially in San Diego, the home of the largest US naval base and the navy's primary West Coast training facility until 1998.

11 Data from the 1984 National Sample Survey of Registered Nurses indicate that Filipinas had the highest earnings among all groups, averaging almost five thousand dollars more annually than white nurses (Moses 1984). Ong and Azores (1994) report that Filipina nurses use various strategies to increase their earnings: working double shifts or in the higher-paying evening and night shifts, and in inner-city hospitals, which offer higher salaries than the national average. In other words, they earn more because they are more likely to work under the least desirable conditions.

REFERENCES

Advincula, Anthony D. 2004. "Filipino Nurses Get Gov't Support for NCLEX Initiative." *Filipino Express Online* 18 (4): 11–17.

Anderson, Warwick. 1995. "'Where Every Prospect Pleases and Only Man Is Vile': Laboratory Medicine as Colonial Discourse." Pp. 83–112 in Vicente Rafael, ed., *Discrepant Histories: Translocal Essays on Filipino Cultures.* Philadelphia: Temple University Press.

Asperilla, Purita Falgui. 1976. "Problems of Foreign Educated Nurses and Job Satisfaction of Filipino Nurses." Academy of Nursing of the Philippines Papers. July–September.

Basch, Linda, Nina Glick Schiller, and Cristina Szanton Blanc. 1994. *Nations Unbound: Transnational Projects, Postcolonial Predicaments, and Deterritorialized Nation-States.* Langhorn, PA: Gordon and Greach.

Blum, Linda. 1991. *Between Feminism and Labor: The Significance of the Comparable Worth Movement.* Berkeley: University of California Press.

Bonacich, Edna, and Lucie Cheng. 1984. "Introduction: A Theoretical Orientation to International Labor Migration." Pp. 1–56 in Lucie Cheng and Edna Bonacich, eds., *Labor Immigration under Capitalism: Asian Workers in the United States before World War II.* Berkeley: University of California Press.

Borjas, George. 1990. *Friends or Strangers: The Impact of Immigrants on the U.S. Economy.* New York: Basic Books.

Borromeo, Annabelle Reyes. 2004. "An IT-Enabled Healthcare." *Manila Times,* May 21.

Campomanes, Oscar. 1997. "New Formations of Asian American Studies and the Question of U.S. Imperialism." *Positions* 5 (2): 523–550.

Chang, Grace. 2000. "Importing Nurses: A Moneymaking Venture." *Dollars & Sense,* September.

Chen, Hsiang Shui. 1992. *Chinatown No More: Taiwan Immigrants in Contemporary New York.* Ithaca, NY: Cornell University Press.

Chin, Christine B. N. 1998. *In Service and Servitude: Foreign Female Domestic Workers and the Malaysian "Modernity" Project.* New York: Columbia University Press.

Choy, Catherine Ceniza. 2003. *Empire of Care: Nursing and Migration in Filipino American History.* Durham, NC: Duke University Press.

Coronel, Sheila, and Ninotchka Rosca. 1993. "For the Boys: Filipinas Expose Years of Sexual Slavery by the U.S. and Japan." *Ms.,* November/December.

Dill, Bonnie Thornton. 1988. "Our Mother's Grief: Racial-Ethnic Women and the Maintenance of Families. *Journal of Family History* 13: 415–431.

Egan, Timothy. 1996. "Mail-Order Marriage, Immigrant Dreams and Death." *New York Times,* May 26.

Espiritu, Yen Le. 1997. *Asian American Women and Men: Labor, Laws, and Love.* Thousand Oaks, CA: Sage.

———. 2003. *Home Bound: Filipino American Lives across Cultures, Communities, and Countries.* Berkeley: University of California Press.

Espiritu, Yen Le, and Diane L. Wolf. 2001. "The Paradox of Assimilation: Children of Filipino Immigrants in San Diego." Pp. 188–228 in Ruben Rumbaut and Alejandro Portes, eds., *Ethnicities: Children of Immigrants in America.* Berkeley: University of California Press.

Glenn, Evelyn Nakano. 1986. *Issei, Nisei, War Bride: Three Generations of Japanese American Women at Domestic Services.* Philadelphia: Temple University Press.

———. 2002. *Unequal Freedom: How Race and Gender Shaped American Citizenship and Labor.* Cambridge, MA: Harvard University Press.

Glick Schiller, Nina. 1997. "The Situation of Transnational Studies." *Identities* 4 (2): 155–166.

Glick Schiller, Nina, and Georges Eugene Fouron. 2001. *Georges Woke Up Laughing: Long-Distance Nationalism and the Search for Home.* Durham, NC: Duke University Press.

Guarnizo, Luis Eduardo, and Michael Peter Smith. 1998. "The Location of Transnationalism." Pp. 3–34 in Michael Peter Smith and Luis Eduardo Guarnizo, eds., *Transnationalism from Below.* New Brunswick, NJ: Transaction.

Guingona, Teofisto T., Jr. 2001. Speech at the 103rd founding anniversary of the Department of Foreign Affairs, Philippines, July 11.

Halualani, Rona Tamiko. 1995. "The Intersecting Hegemonic Discourses of an Asian Mail-Order Bride Catalog: Pilipina Oriental Butterfly' Dolls for Sale." *Women's Studies in Communication* 18 (1): 45–64.

Hoganson, Kristin L. 1998. *Fighting for American Manhood: How Gender Politics Provoked the Spanish-American and Philippine-American Wars*. New Haven, CT: Yale University Press.

Hondagneu-Sotelo, Pierette. 1994. *Gendered Transitions: Mexican Experiences of Immigration*. Berkeley: University of California Press.

———. 1999. "Introduction: Gender and Contemporary U.S. Immigration." *American Behavioral Scientist* 42 (4): 565–576.

Hondagneu-Sotelo, Pierette, and Ernestine Avila. 1997. "'I'm Here, but I'm Here': The Meanings of Latina Transnational Motherhood." *Gender & Society* 11 (5): 548–571.

Hunter, Frances. 1986. *Equal Pay for Comparable Worth*. New York: Praeger.

Lawcock, Larry Arden. 1975. "Filipino Students in the United States and the Philippine Independence Movement, 1900–1935." Doctoral dissertation, University of California, Berkeley.

Levitt, Peggy. 2001. *The Transnational Villagers*. Berkeley: University of California Press.

Lipsitz, George. 1998. *The Possessive Investment in Whiteness: How White People Profit from Identity Politics*. Philadelphia: Temple University Press.

Lowe, Lisa. 1996. *Immigrant Acts: On Asian American Cultural Politics*. Durham, NC: Duke University Press.

Massey, Doreen. 1999. "Imagining Globalization: Power-Geometries of Time-Space." Pp. 27–44 in Avtar Brah, Mary J. Hickman, and Mairtin Mac an Ghaill, eds., *Global Futures: Migration, Environment and Globalization*. New York: St. Martin's.

Massey, Douglas, Joaquin Arango, Graeme Hugo, Ali Kouaouchi, Adela Pellegrino, and J. Edward Taylor. 1993. "Theories of International Migration: A Review and Appraisal." *Population and Development Review* 19 (3): 431–466.

Menjivar, Cecilia. 1999. "The Intersection of Work and Gender: Central American Women and Employment in California." *American Behavioral Scientist* 42 (2): 601–627.

Min, Pyong Gap. 1998. *Changes and Conflicts: Korean Immigrant Families in New York*. Needham Heights, MA: Allyn & Bacon.

Mohanty, Chandra. 1991. "Cartographies of Struggle: Third World Women and the Politics of Feminism." Pp. 1–47 in Chandra Mohanty, Ann Russo, and Lourdes Torres, eds., *Third World Women and the Politics of Feminism*. Bloomington: Indiana University Press.

Moses, Evelyn B. 1984. "National Sample Survey of Registered Nurses, November 1984" [computer file]. Rockville, MD: Bureau of Health Professionals.

Newman, Louise Michele. 1999. *White Women's Rights: The Racial Origins of Feminism in the United States*. New York: Oxford University Press.

Okamura, Jonathan Y. 1998. *Imagining the Filipino American Diaspora: Transnational Relations, Identities, and Communities*. New York: Garland.

Ong, Paul, and Tania Azores. 1994. "The Migration of Incorporation of Filipino Nurses." Pp. 164–195 in Paul Ong, Edna Bonacich, and Lucie Cheng, eds., *The New Asian Immigration in Los Angeles and Global Restructuring*. Philadelphia: Temple University Press.

Parreñas, Rhaecel Salazar. 2001. *Servants of Globalization: Women, Migration, Domestic Work*. Stanford, CA: Stanford University Press.

Perea, Juan F., ed. 1997. *Immigrants Out! The New Nativism and the Anti-immigrant Impulse in the United States*. New York: New York University Press.

Perez, Gina M. 2004. *The New Northwest Side Story: Migration, Displacement, and Puerto Rican Families*. Berkeley: University of California Press.

Pesquera, Beatriz M. 1993. "'In the Beginning He Wouldn't Lift a Spoon': The Division of House-hold Labor." Pp. 181–195 in Adela de la Torre and Beatriz M. Pesquera, eds., *Building with Our Hands: New Dictions in Chicana Studies.* Berkeley: University of California Press.

Pessar, Patricia R. 1984. "The Linkage between the Household and Workplace in the Experience of Dominican Immigrant Women in the United States." *International Migration Review* 18 (4): 1188–1211.

———. 1999. "Engendering Migration Studies: The Case of New Immigrants in the United States." *American Behavioral Scientist* 42 (4): 577–600.

Portes, Alejandro, Luis E. Guarnizo, and Patricia Landolt. 1999. "The Study of Transnationalism: Pitfalls and Promises of an Emergent Research Field." *Ethnic and Racial Studies* 22 (2):217–237.

Posadas, Barbara M., and Roland L. Guyotte. 1990. "Unintentional Immigrants: Chicago's Filipino Foreign Students Become Settlers, 1900–1941." *Journal of American Ethnic History* 9: 26–48.

Pressner, Harriet. 1988. "Shift Work and Childcare among Young Dual-Earner American Parents." *Journal of Marriage and the Family* 50: 133–148.

Rafael, Vicente L. 2000. *White Love and Other Events in Filipino History.* Durham, NC: Duke University Press.

San Juan, E., Jr. 1998. *Beyond Postcolonial Theory.* New York: St. Martin's.

Stark, Oded. 1991. *The Migration of Labour.* Cambridge: Basil Blackwell.

Stoler, Ann Laura. 1991. "Carnal Knowledge and Imperial Power: Gender, Race, and Morality in Colonial Asia." Pp. 51–101 in Micaela di Leonardo, ed., *Gender at the Crossroads of Knowledge: Feminist Anthropology in the Postmodern Era.* Berkeley: University of California Press.

Taylor, Edward J. 1999. "The New Economics of Labor Migration and the Role of Remittances in the Migration Process." *International Migration* 37: 63–88.

Thomas, Brinley. 1973. *Migration and Economic Growth: A Study of Great Britain and the Atlantic Economy.* Cambridge: Cambridge University Press.

Tyner, James A. 1999. "The Global Context of Gendered Labor: Migration from the Philippines into the United States." *American Behavioral Scientist* 42 (4): 671–689.

US Immigration and Naturalization Service (INS). 2001. *2000 Statistics Yearbook.* Washington, DC: Government Printing Office.

US Treasury Department. 2003. "U.S.-Philippine Agrees to Improve Remittance Service." News release, May 20.

Warren, Jennifer. 1993. "Suits Asks Navy to Aid Children Left in Philippines." *Los Angeles Times,* March 5.

Yegenoglu, Meyda. 1998. *Colonial Fantasies towards a Feminist Reading of Orientalism.* Cambridge: Cambridge University Press.

Zolberg, Aristide. 1986. "International Factors in the Formation of Refugee Movements." *International Migration Review* 20: 151–169.

10

The Making and Transnationalization of an Ethnic Niche

Vietnamese Manicurists

SUSAN ECKSTEIN AND THANH-NGHI NGUYEN

Many ethnic groups cluster in distinct types of jobs, known as ethnic niches (Lieberson 1980; Light and Gold 2000; Waldinger 2001; Wilson 2003). Vietnamese involvement in nail care, the focus of this chapter, is illustrative of one such ethnic niche (Huynh 1996; Parmley 2002; Vo 2003; Doan 2004; Lazar 2005; Bui 2007). But sociological analyses of ethnic group employment in general, and of ethnic niches in particular, to date have inadequately documented and explained Vietnamese involvement in the development, expansion, transformation, and even transnationalization of the nail care niche.

After briefly reviewing extant literature on ethnic niche formation and dynamics relevant for understanding the Vietnamese niche, the chapter contains an elucidation, respectively, of the evolution of professional nail care work in the United States and Vietnamese involvement in it, conditions contributing to Vietnamese buildup and transformation of the niche, and, finally, Vietnamese expansion of the niche across country borders. The chapter concludes with propositions inductively extrapolated from the Vietnamese manicure experience about the evolution of immigrant labor market niching. The analysis draws primarily on published primary and secondary source material.[1] Information about the transnationalization of the US Vietnamese manicure niche to Vietnam comes from interviews with a few manicurists in Vietnam.

The Development of Ethnic Niches

To begin, how to define an ethnic niche? Waldinger and Bozorgmehr (1996, 33) and Waldinger and Der-Martirosian (2001, 237) use demographic criteria. According to them, niche formation rests on an ethnic group accounting for a greater percentage of persons employed in a line of work than their share of the overall labor force. Under such circumstances, the group is "overrepresented" in the form of employment. Specifically, Waldinger and collaborators define a niche as work employing minimally one thousand people, in which a group's share is at least 150 percent of its share of the total labor market.

In the United States historically, different immigrant groups have been associated with different labor market niches. Within a given macro context, the specific niches foreign-born have occupied has rested on (1) their offering goods and services previously unavailable, for which there is demand or for which they created demand; (2) their displacing native-born, when more skilled, disciplined, or willing to labor for less money at the work; and (3) their filling jobs native-born vacated upon accessing preferred jobs. Ethnic group association with particular niches may also rest on exclusionary practices of more powerful, established groups in the society at large who use their influence to monopolize jobs they prefer, while creating demand for other work that they have no interest in providing. No matter, the process by which immigrant groups have become associated with particular work has hinged on the interplay between assets and dynamics of the group on the one hand, and institutional conditions in particular times and places on the other hand.

The so-called new immigrants, who moved to the United States since the 1965 immigration reform went into effect (which opened legal immigration opportunities for peoples from developing countries, in eliminating national quotas) include Vietnamese. However, Vietnamese moved to the United States in large numbers only following the end to the Vietnamese War in 1975. In that they arrived as the United States shifted from an industrial to a service-based economy, if they clustered in distinctive segments of the labor market, they might be expected to do so both in new service sector jobs native-born, for whatever reason, did not fill and in remaining industrial jobs native-born abandoned when obtaining service sector work they preferred. Examples of service sector niches filled by new immigrants include Koreans in grocery businesses, Hispanics in domestic cleaning and home care, Asian Indians in motel management and information technology (IT), and Filipinos in nursing (Hondagneu-Sotelo 2001; Parreñas 2005; Min 2006; Brettell and Alstatt 2007). Many of the new immigrant labor market clusterings, with some important exceptions (e.g., Asian Indians in IT), involve jobs that pay poorly, that are physically demanding, that entail unhealthy work conditions, and that involve long, irregular, and undesirable hours of work, in essence, jobs the native-born, with better options, would rather not assume (Ong, Bonacich, and Cheng 1994).

Ethnic group niches may become so entrenched that they take hold nationwide, beyond the local labor market where first formed. Indeed, ethnic groups tend to occupy the same line of work across the United States (Waldinger 2001, 312). We will show that dynamics contributing to the "nationalization" of an ethnic niche may even contribute to its transnationalization. The original niche formation in one labor market may provide a building block on which the niche expands geographically, including across country borders.

In the United States, there is a labor market hierarchy with which immigrant and ethnic niches are associated (Waldinger 2001, 312). Overall, Asian immigrant groups fill the most economically desirable niches, Hispanics the least desirable. Studies report that among Asians, Vietnamese (along with Cambodians and Laotians), the least educated on average, are concentrated in the lowest paying, least prestigious jobs, although not in specific labor market niches (see, e.g., Rumbaut 1989; Gold 1992; Wilson 2003; Do 2006). While Vietnamese have been found to be "overrepresented" in manual labor jobs that have survived the macro industry to service economy restructuring, in 1990 in greater Los Angeles, where the largest concentration of Vietnamese live, ethnic labor market specialization reportedly was less among Vietnamese than among Asian Indians, and especially less than among Mexicans. Their rate was roughly the same as among Filipinos and Chinese, while greater than among Koreans and Cubans (Waldinger 2001, 260, 310–312).[2] And Vietnamese labor market concentration in Los Angeles declined slightly between 1980 and 1990.

Institutional conditions that contribute to immigrant group "niching" are partly state-based, linked to regulatory policies. Policies of possible consequence include job-related training and licensing requisites, and rights and benefits extended (or not) to immigrants, such as access to green cards (and, accordingly, access to public-sector jobs and to private-sector jobs involving employers who wish avoid fines for noncompliance with immigrant labor laws) and to refugee benefits that subsidize schooling, job and language training, and loans. Such policies do not necessarily predetermine the particular work immigrants do,[3] but they make specific lines of work more or less accessible (Waldinger 2008). The regulations result in illegal immigrants being pressed to do the least desirable and least regulated labor market work.

Nongovernmental institutional conditions may also affect labor market "niching." For example, bank lending practices may influence immigrant and ethnic entrepreneurial undertakings, enhancing opportunities for some groups while limiting them for others. Also, the languages in which private-sector training is offered affect the foreign-born likely to secure requisite skills for particular work.

Rath (2002) refers to the role that both features of immigrant group life and broader structures have on labor market sorting as mixed embeddedness. Within a broader institutional context, immigrant group skills, plus their social and financial assets, that is, their human, social, and economic capital, influence the work they do. In that job attainment in general and for immigrant groups in particular is heavily network-driven (Massey et al 1998), once some foreign-born establish a beachhead in a line of work, other group members tend to gravitate to it as well. They do so because they rely on friends and family to secure work and like jobs where they know others (Lieberson 1980, Waldinger 1994, 2001, Light and Gold 2000, 21; Card and DiNardo 2000).[4]

Women have been found to be especially reliant on personal ties for job attainment, with their networks tending to channel them to work where women cluster (Sassen 1995, 103). As a result, networks that result in inclusionary employment opportunities for one immigrant group, which may be gender-specific, prove exclusionary for others, an unintended consequence of in-group dynamics. Such inclusionary-exclusionary practices may occur anywhere in the labor market, in both high- and low-prestige jobs.

Network-based ethnic "niching" extends to the small business sector, and may involve persons self-employed. Immigrants have long been associated with small businesses and self-employment (Light 1972; Borjas 1986; Light and Sanchez 1987; Waldinger 1996, chap. 8 [254–299]; Bates 1998). This is particularly true of certain immigrant groups, such as Cubans, Koreans, and Chinese. Ivan Light, the first to analyze immigrant entrepreneurship systematically, pointed to how ethnic solidarity, now referred to as embeddedness, influences business involvement.[5] Drawing on human capital acquired in their homeland, and sometimes on financial resources with which they emigrated, entrepreneurial foreign-born may also benefit from family-based social capital that they develop where they resettle. Family social capital may involve unpaid and trusted labor from relatives, and financial resources that family members pool together (Portes and Zhou 1992; Sanders and Nee 1996). Immigrant entrepreneurs, in turn, may draw on cheap coethnic labor, especially when coethnics have few labor market options owing to their lack of proficiency in the language of the new country, labor market discrimination, or other constraints. The entrepreneurs may concomitantly generate business for coethnics (who, in turn, may hire coethnics). Coethnic business biases can provide bedrock for so-called enclave economies (Wilson and Portes 1980), involving communities with diverse, mutually sustaining coethnic businesses. The businesses benefit from the formation of markets for their goods and services among "their own."

Immigrant proclivity toward self-employment does not imply business success (Kim, Hurh, and Fernandez 1989; Yoon 1991). Indeed, immigrant groups differ in their business success. For example, among new immigrant Asian groups in the 1980s, sales and receipts for firms without paid employees were lower for Vietnamese than for Indians, Chinese, and Koreans (but higher than for Filipinos), and Vietnamese, on average, had the smallest businesses, with the fewest paid employees (Bonacich 1987, 448). Among Southeast Asian businesses, Vietnamese had the highest failure rate (Espiritu 1997, 79) and their businesses were the least profitable (with Indian businesses the most profitable [Bates 1993, 28]). By the turn of the century Vietnamese businesses still garnered the lowest average annual receipts of Asian American–owned businesses (Doan 2004, 33). The most successful immigrant businesses rarely cater exclusively to coethnics. Rather, they serve broader markets (as do, for example, Koreans dry cleaners and grocers).

The Development of the Nail Care Niche and Vietnamese Involvement in It: An Overview

Studies that highlight Vietnamese concentration in low-prestige, low-paying jobs in declining sectors of the economy, as well as those that note their lack of business success, ignore Vietnamese involvement in nail care work. Nail care is part of the beauty industry, a vibrant sector of the US economy. In the early 2000s beauty salons generated sixty billion dollars in sales and employed more than 1.6 million people.[6] Nail salons at the time accounted for approximately 10 percent of the revenue and 6 percent of employment in the sector (Nguyen 2010, Figures 3.1 and 3.5; *NAILS Magazine Big Book* 1997–2009).

Manicure work is a relatively new occupation, officially recognized only since the 1980s. The US Department of Labor first cited a nail care category, "fingernail former," as a job classification in the 1980s, and the US Bureau of Labor Statistics added "nail salons" to its business classifications for the first time in the latter 1990s.[7] Although a new line of work, it was one of the fastest growing by the early 2000s (USDL 2009).

Professional nail care initially was a secondary service that hair salons catering to well-to-do clientele offered (*American Salon's Green Book* 2005, 15). Self-standing nail salons began to proliferate only in the 1980s, with their number more than doubling between 1991 and 2008 (Figure 10.1) (but declining slightly between 2005 and 2008). By 2008 they accounted for 29 percent of all beauty sector shops (*NAILS Magazine Big Book* 2007–2008, 44). Meanwhile, nail salon share of all beauty sector revenue increased, while hair salon revenue decreased (although hair salons continued to account for most revenue in the sector) (Figure 10.2).

As nail salons proliferated, sales of nail products for home use, for self-manicures, diminished (*Consumer USA* 2008, 161–162). Many women had liked to have polished nails, but they had not considered professional nail care an affordable option. Indicative that the decline in self-manicures was associated with a turn to professional nail care, the number of women who reported salon manicures rose from one in four in 1997 to one in three just seven years later (*American Salon's Green Book* 2005, 37).

Vietnamese are closely associated with the growth of professional manicures. As of 2000, more Vietnamese were employed nationally in the US census category "hairdresser and other grooming services" than in any other occupation. In all, 13 percent of Vietnamese were so employed (Table 10.1). The next most common forms of Vietnamese employment, "clerical and administrative staff," "assembly line workers," and "industrial equipment operators," each involved 8 percent of employed Vietnamese.

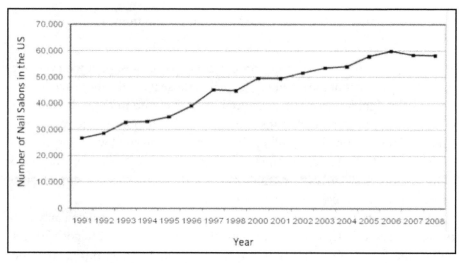

Figure 10.1. Number of Nail Salons in the United States, 1991–2008. *Source: NAILS Magazine Big Book* (1997–2009); tabulation by Nguyen.

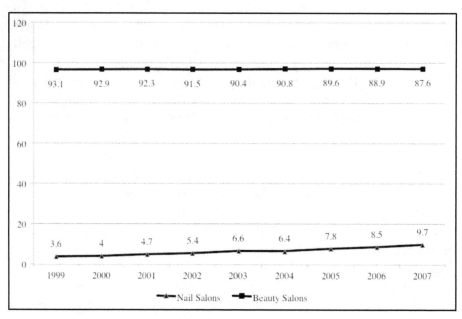

Figure 10.2. Nail and Beauty Salon Share of Total Revenue in the Beauty Sector, 1999–2007. *Source:* Adapted from USDL (1999–2007).

TABLE 10.1. Top Ten Countries of Origin of Foreign-Born Hairdresser and Grooming Service Workers in the United States in 2000

Country	Workers	Percentage of All Workers From That Country	Percentage of All Foreign-Born US Hairdresser/ Grooming Workers	Percentage of All US Hairdresser/ Grooming Workers
1. Vietnam	66,700	12.7	34.1	9.2
2. Mexico	20,100	0.4	10.3	2.8
3. North and South Korea	10,000	2.4	5.1	1.4
4. Dominican Republic	10,000	3.0	5.1	1.4
5. China	5,300	1.0	2.7	0.7
6. Philippines	4,400	0.5	2.2	0.6
7. Germany	4,300	0.9	2.2	0.6
8. Cuba	3,600	0.9	1.8	0.5
9. Italy	3,300	2.2	1.7	0.5
10. Colombia	3,100	1.1	1.6	0.4
Total foreign-born	195,700	n/a	100.0	27.0
Total US workers	724,815	n/a	n/a	100.0

Source: Adapted from Bloch, Carter, and Gebeloff (2009).

It is *immigrant* Vietnamese, in particular, who carved out the nail niche. Fewer than 1 percent of Vietnamese manicurists are US-born (Federman, Harrington, and Krynski 2006, 309; *NAILS Magazine* March 2007, 84). Meanwhile, Vietnamese, far more than other immigrants, work in the beauty sector. In 2000, for example, only 2 percent of Korean and 3 percent of Dominican immigrants worked in beauty sector jobs, the immigrant groups with the second and third largest percentages of persons so employed. Indeed, Vietnamese accounted for 34 percent of the foreign-born employed in the sector (Table 10.1).

Yet, Vietnamese work within the beauty sector is highly specialized, in manicuring. Since 2007 they have outnumbered all other ethnic and racial groups employed as professional manicurists (Table 10.2). In 2008, whites, by far the demographically largest group in the United States, accounted for 37 percent of manicurists, down from 50 percent six years earlier. During the same years Vietnamese, who composed less than 1 percent of the US population, rose to account for 43 percent of manicurists, up from 32 percent (USDC 2008; *NAILS Magazine Big Book* 2007–2008, 36). Vietnamese association with manicuring involved ethnic displacement, of whites in particular, but also their centrality to the growth in professional nail care employment.

TABLE 10.2. Percentage of Nail Technicians in the United States of Diverse
Ethnicities, 1999–2009

Ethnic Group	1999	2001	2002	2004	2005	2006	2007	2008	2009
Vietnamese	*	*	33	37	39	38	41	43	40
Caucasian	n/a	n/a	50	46	43	41	39	36	37
Hispanic	n/a	n/a	7	8	7	7	7	8	10
African American	n/a	n/a	4	6	8	8	10	10	10
Korean	*	*	6	*	2	2	2	2	2
Asian/other	27	39		3	1	4	1	1	1
Total	n/a	328,343	368,818	388,072	380,635	361,427	347,898	349,370	348,814

Note: *Grouped with Asian. n/a = data not available. The total number of nail technicians in each year is in the bottom row.
Source: NAILS Magazine Big Book (2001–2009); tabulations by Nguyen.

Manicurists include Vietnamese from diverse regions of Vietnam who arrived
in different years, as immigrants as well as refugees.[8] They also include Vietnamese of diverse ethnic backgrounds (including Chinese Vietnamese).[9] Thus,
although the pioneer manicurists were refugees, as detailed below, once nail care
became a job option, later arrivals, in greater numbers, became manicurists (see
Table 10.3).[10] The recent arrivals who pursue nail work sustain and reproduce the
ethnic base of the labor market niche that the first arrivals carved out.

TABLE 10.3. Vietnamese Manicurists by Year of Arrival (%), in 2007

Year of Arrival	Percentage
Before 1980	10.7
1980–1984	10.9
1985–1989	12.9
1990–1994	35.1
1995–1999	17.9
2000–present	12.5

Source: NAILS Magazine (March 2007, 84).

The experience in California reveals how closely Vietnamese are associated
with the growth in professional nail care. Federman, Harrrington, and Krynski
(2006) found that in 1987 ten times as many non-Vietnamese as Vietnamese
were registered manicurists in the state. The number of non-Vietnamese manicurists increased until 1990. Thereafter their numbers decreased, while the number of Vietnamese increased, to the point that by 1998 more Vietnamese than
non-Vietnamese were registered manicurists. Then, between 1998 and 2002 the

total number of manicurists doubled, while the number of Vietnamese manicurists increased tenfold.

Vietnamese involvement in and growing domination of manicuring seems not the result of their underpricing non-Vietnamese. Federman, Harrington, and Krynski (2006, 310) found in their California study that Vietnamese and non-Vietnamese, on average, earned similar wages. They also found that they worked, on average, similar hours per week.

Vietnamese domination of nail care work also cannot be demographically explained. While California is home to the largest concentration of Vietnamese, and it was in California, as detailed below, where Vietnamese initially became involved in professional nail care, they have also come to be associated with professional nail care work in states where few of them live.[11] They dominate nail work in Texas, the state with the second largest number of Vietnamese (Thịnh 2006; Tran 2008), as well as states such as Massachusetts.

Massachusetts serves as a window through which to observe the role Vietnamese have assumed in the development of the labor market niche where their small numbers would suggest they would be minimally, if at all, involved. Vietnamese account for only .7 percent of the state's population, and the state is home to 8 percent as many Vietnamese as California and 25 percent as many as Texas (USDC 2008; Nguyen 2010, Table 2.5). In Massachusetts Vietnamese are employed, along with other immigrant groups, in manufacturing assembly work (Allen and Turner 2007). However, as of 2007, 25 percent of Vietnamese in the state's labor force worked in nail care, more than in any other line of work. The nail industry developed in the state only as Vietnamese began to settle there.

The nail industry in Massachusetts is centered in Boston, where half of all Vietnamese in the state live. As is the case nationally, in Massachusetts in general and in Boston in particular Vietnamese cluster only in manicuring within the beauty sector. For example, about two-thirds of the over two hundred Vietnamese employed in the beauty service industry in Boston in 2008 worked as manicurists. In contrast, only 14 percent of them worked as cosmetologists and aestheticians, in beauty sector jobs that, overall, employ more people (Nguyen 2010, Table 2.10). Cosmetologists and aestheticians are licensed to provide manicure services, but also hair and skin care. Vietnamese cluster in the segment of the beauty industry that requires the least formal training. Over the years few of them have expanded their credentials to diversify the beauty work for which they are qualified, to pursue the more lucrative activity in the sector.

Meanwhile, in Massachusetts, as is the case nationally, Vietnamese dominate the nail niche as owners as well as employees. Most nail salons in the state are Vietnamese operated (Dickerson 1997; Murray 1997; Nguyen 2010). But Vietnamese almost exclusively own nail businesses, not beauty salons. In some cities in the greater Boston metropolitan area Vietnamese own the only manicure shops (Nguyen 2010, Tables 2.12–2.14). Even in cities such as Lowell, where

Cambodians account for 57 percent of the Asian population and Vietnamese only 9 percent, Vietnamese owned half the nail salons, a greater share than Cambodians.

The Vietnamese association with nail work is highly gendered, although somewhat less so than among non-Vietnamese manicurists. As of the early 2000s, nationally men accounted for only 4 percent of nail technicians (*NAILS Magazine* March 2007, 78). Among Vietnamese, men accounted for 28 percent. Yet, with one in five working-age Vietnamese women employed as manicurists (Nguyen 2010, 160; USDC 2008; *NAILS Magazine* March 2007, 78),[12] they are the primary force behind the growth of the nail niche.[13]

In sum, immigrant Vietnamese women were not the first to provide professional manicures, but they have been intricately associated with the expansion of professional nail care and its transformation into a specialized service within the beauty sector. Aggregate data on beauty sector employment conceal how Vietnamese developed the nail niche.

Origins of Vietnamese Involvement in Manicuring

How can we explain Vietnamese gravitation to manicuring, given that the line of work was unknown to the first post–Vietnam War arrivals before emigrating, and that the limited demand for professional nail care in the United States had been addressed by non-Vietnamese? And why did Vietnamese, not other new immigrants who needed work, come to dominate nail work? While discrimination, language barriers, and, for some, limited education constricted Vietnamese job options, how, for all intents and purposes, did they come to dominate the employment niche?

The initial Vietnamese involvement in manicuring is almost apocryphal. It reveals the role leadership may play, including by native-born. The actress Tippi Hedren (who starred in Alfred Hitchcock's *The Birds*), concerned with the plight of Vietnamese refugees housed in a tent city in California, sought to help the women "make it" in America (Hammond 2002). Allegedly impressed with the women's hand dexterity, in 1975 she brought her manicurist to teach them manicuring skills. She also persuaded a beauty school both to train the refugees, free of charge, and to help them find work.

One Vietnamese woman creatively built on her newly acquired manicure skills by opening the first Vietnamese American owned beauty salon, together with her husband (who had been a navy commander in South Vietnam before seeking refuge in the United States after the Vietnam War ended). They went on to open a beauty training school, the Advance Beauty College (ABC), in what became known as Little Saigon, the Vietnamese enclave in Orange County, California, and emergent hub of the Vietnamese community in the United States (Tran 2008).[14] The school offered training in a range of specialized beauty services, not limited to, but including, manicuring. Most important, ABC offered classes in Vietnamese, so that English proficiency was not a barrier to entry. The immigrant enclave, in turn, provided these entrepreneurial Vietnamese with a social and economic base for their school. And they hired employees their school had trained, all while their salon and training school served as models for other Vietnamese.

Faced with limited job options, Vietnamese women responded to these early initiatives. The training period was short, and they could acquire the training in their native language. Moreover, both the Vietnamese entrepreneurs who founded beauty schools and Vietnamese students who attended qualified, as refugees, for government assistance (Gold 1992, 159). The costs for their training and business undertakings, accordingly, were minimal.

Building on the job training and work opportunities, Vietnamese in Southern California developed a cluster of businesses that provided a bedrock for the ethnic niche. Southern California became home to a growing number of Vietnamese-owned beauty schools besides ABC that trained and helped certify Vietnamese for manicure work. Also, manufacturers and distributors of nail products established businesses in Southern California (Huynh 1996). Most important, the number of Vietnamese-owned nail shops that hired coethnics proliferated.

Under the circumstances, the number of Vietnamese who trained as nail technicians and who opened nail salons in Southern California surged. Many of the first Vietnamese manicurists initially held other jobs. They switched work, no doubt, because they considered manicuring preferable once learning of the possibility. However, by the late 1990s Vietnamese who entered the labor market for the first time tended to go directly into nail work (Doan 2004, 53). They considered manicuring an employment of choice, given their perceived labor market options.

Conditions Contributing to Vietnamese Buildup and Transformation of the Nail Care Niche

Economists presume that "invisible" market forces create demand for goods and services in response to a supply of cadre who provide them, and the converse, that demand induces people to address it. However, before Vietnamese became manicurists, both the supply and demand for professional nail care were limited and addressed by non-Vietnamese. Rather, Vietnamese involvement in nail care has rested on their *creating* broad-based demand for professional manicures, linked to their ability and readiness to obtain the work requisites and, most important, their development of a business model that generated employment opportunities for them, through their ethnic networks, as both owners and employees. They were able to fulfill regulatory requirements that might have stood in the way, owing to institutional changes that they helped bring about. Accordingly, Vietnamese development of, and association with, the nail niche is sociologically explicable, in ways elaborated below.

Vietnamese Broadening of Demand for Nail Care: Niche Stretching

More than responding to otherwise unsatisfied demand for professional nail care, Vietnamese fueled demand for it. They did so by "niche stretching," namely by broadening the customer base for professional nail care and "deepening," diversifying, the range of nail care offerings.

Until the early 1980s professional manicures had been a luxury service only wealthy women could afford. Upscale beauty salons, as noted, offered nail care as a secondary service to address their patrons' desire for manicures with "one-stop shopping." Under the circumstances, demand for professional manicure was minimal and class-specific, and addressed by non-Vietnamese.

Several changes reduced manicure operating costs, which could be passed on to consumers in lower fees for services. The lower charges made manicures affordable for the first time to women across socioeconomic classes. Vietnamese were intricately involved with some, though not all, of the changes. The first changes were technological. They allowed for greater work efficiency. Vietnamese played no role in the technological innovations, but they were quick to take advantage of them and popularized their usage. The most important technological change, in 1979, involved the development of an acrylic product for nails that offered multiple advantages over plastic nail tips, until then used in manicures (Kang 2010, 39). The new product strengthened nails, made them more flexible, and permitted application of longer tips. Also, the acrylic tips were cheaper than plastic tips.

Another technological innovation involved development of electric-powered nail files. An electric file allowed nail-shaping in half the time manual filing required. Vietnamese were quick to adopt this innovation as well, which further reduced their operating costs ("Nail File" 1997). Vietnamese also introduced use of wider and flatter brushes that allowed for faster application of polish.

Most important, Vietnamese were intricately associated with what might be called the "McNailing of America," a business innovation that transformed professional nail care into a mass service. The business innovation involved the establishment of stand-alone nail salons in the neighborhoods where people lived and worked that offered quick, assembly-line service on a walk-in, "no appointment necessary" basis, at half the price upscale beauty salons charged (Dang 1999). In making manicures both affordable and easy to obtain, Vietnamese created conditions that led women of diverse class, ethnic, and racial backgrounds to come to consider professional manicures de rigueur, important to their presentation of self—with nail "tastes" varying somewhat among the customer bases (e.g., coveted length of nails and nail polish design) (see Kang 2006).[15] Meanwhile, with nails needing ongoing care, demand for professional manicures became routinized among the broadened customer base.

Vietnamese nails-only shops revolutionized manicuring in much the same manner that McDonald's revolutionized inexpensive, fast food service. Like McDonald's, the nails-only shops appealed to busy Americans who wanted quick, dependable service, when convenient to their schedules, and who were content with the provisioning of the service in an impersonal manner.

Vietnamese were also intricately associated with an expansion of offerings that further fueled demand for professional nail care. In the latter 1990s they added inexpensive spa-style pedicures to their service menu (as opposed to regular pedicures, which they offered from the onset). While in performing pedicures they *defied* their homeland-acquired cultural disdain for handling people's feet (Nguyen 2010, 167), they did not allow their personal values to stand in the way of economic opportunity. And yet another technological innovation both stimulated new customer demand for pedicures, and helped Vietnamese overcome their cultural aversion to handling feet: the development of whirlpool pedicure spa chairs, known as pedicure thrones. The thrones enhanced clients' pedicure experience, and eased the work for nail technicians.

Reflecting the growing popularity of pedicures, the *American Salon's Green Book* (2005, 37) reported both that the percentage of women having salon pedicures more than doubled between 1997 and 2004, from 11 to 24, and that women had pedicures with growing frequency. Indicative of Vietnamese close association with the growing popularity of pedicures, a California-based manufacturer of pedicure thrones estimated, in 2006, that more than half of the company's sales went to Vietnamese-owned nail salons (Rust 2006). Women increasingly came to view pedicures, more expensive than hand manicures, also important to their dress code, especially in warm months when they wore sandals and open-toe shoes. As growing numbers of Americans viewed pedicures as essential, demand for nail care further increased.

Vietnamese further expanded demand for professional nail care by diversifying their manicure services to include nail art. Skilled manicurists perform fingernail artwork, involving intricate designs and such ornaments as beads and charms. Some manicurists even paint facsimiles of paintings by famous artists, such as by Van Gogh and Picasso (*NAILS Magazine* June 2007, 47–48). The nail art is especially popular among African Americans (Kang 2006, 11), a group upscale salons had not tapped.

Meanwhile, new nail enamels have become available, including those that glow in the dark, that are fragrant, and that, reportedly, respond to body heat and mood. Vietnamese manicurists have come to offer these nail options as well.

Some non-Vietnamese owners of upscale beauty salons that offered manicures as a secondary service fought the transformation of nail care into a less expensive, mass venture. They insinuated that the discount salons were unsanitary and unhealthy ("Nail File" 1997). Negative stereotyping of Asians fueled the controversy (Kang 2010, chap. 6). Their domination of the beauty industry notwithstanding, they failed in their campaign. They failed because growing numbers of Americans voted, in essence, with their hands and feet. When affordably priced and convenient to attain, they coveted professional nail care, and on an ongoing basis. As a result, upscale beauty salons that offered nail care found themselves at the sidelines of the "McNails" manicure revolution. Mounting consumer demand enabled Vietnamese, through their force of numbers, to win, quietly, the interethnic battle with multiservice high-end salons in the beauty service industry.

In sum, Vietnamese created new demand for professional nail care among diverse socioeconomic and racial groups. They did so by lowering the cost of manicures, by diversifying their offerings, and by bringing their services to locations where potential clientele lived and worked. They broadened the market for professional nail care by developing a new business model which, although small in scale, transformed nail care into an inexpensive mass product. In that the services for which they expanded demand were not distinctively Vietnamese, how did they come to dominate the newly created professional nail care niche?

Supply-Side Developments: Growth in the Pool of Workers and Entrepreneurs with the Requisites and Proclivity to Pursue Nail Niche Work

Vietnamese association with the nail niche rested concomitantly on supply-side developments, with the supply and demand forces separable analytically more than empirically. Not only did demand for nail care grow as the number of Vietnamese offering affordable, quick, convenient, and diverse nail services increased, but the number of trained nail technicians expanded in response to growing demand for commercial nail care. As in the case of demand, "invisible market forces" do not account for the growth in number of Vietnamese nail care providers. Institutional conditions, and social dynamics within the Vietnamese community, came to predispose Vietnamese immigrant women to work as manicurists, in ways that gave them an advantage over non-Vietnamese who might consider nail work preferable to their alternative labor market options. Rath (2002) refers to the combined importance of macro-structural forces and immigrant relations as mixed embeddedness.

Institutional Factors

The government, at the federal and state levels, regulates professional nail care. It requires licensing to do the work. States administer the licensing exams and establish their own standards as to the number of hours of training required and the language in which the exam may be taken. Government regulations also impact labor and work conditions.

Government regulations contribute to Vietnamese concentration in manicuring, the beauty sector with the most minimal qualifying requirements. Requisite hours of training vary by state (from zero in Connecticut to 750 in Alabama). The greater the number of hours, the greater the barrier to entry.[16] Whatever the number of hours, though, manicuring invariably requires fewer hours of training than other beauty sector work. Hairstylists, for example, often need more than three times as many hours of training as manicurists.[17]

Once an initial cluster of Vietnamese gravitated to manicuring, nongovernmental institutions, as well as government regulations, evolved that induced other Vietnamese to follow suit. Although professional manicurists must be licensed, states do not necessarily require that the formal training be in English. In allowing training in Vietnamese, Vietnamese with limited command of English can become manicurists. Indeed, most nail technicians are not proficient in English (Doan 2004, 42). Vietnamese have benefited from the opening of private vocational schools that offer training in Vietnamese. This occurred initially in California, where Vietnamese first became involved in nail care. However, schools offering training in Vietnamese subsequently opened in other states as well, as they saw a business opportunity. A survey in Massachusetts showed that even in a state where few Vietnamese live, Vietnamese mainly attended schools offering training in their native language (Doan 2004, 56).

Some state governments further facilitated Vietnamese entry into the profession by offering their licensing exam in Vietnamese, or by allowing exam takers to use Vietnamese translators. When California, in 1996, introduced a Vietnamese-language version of the licensing exam, the number of registered Vietnamese manicurists rose markedly (Federman, Harrington, and Krynski 2006, 303). The California experience illustrates both how state regulations shape barriers to entry to particular labor market work, and how governments may intervene to make a line of work accessible to immigrants for whom their limited command of English would otherwise exclude them. Not all states, however, offer the exam in Vietnamese. Massachusetts, for example, has not had a consistent language policy. In some years it has offered the exam in Vietnamese, in other years not.

The favorable institutional conditions, above all in California with the largest concentration of Vietnamese, help explain why Vietnamese pursued work as manicurists. But they do not explain why Vietnamese, far more than other immigrant groups, gravitated to manicuring. Vietnamese domination over Hispanics is especially noteworthy. Many more Hispanics than Vietnamese live in Southern California, where the Vietnamese nail niche first took hold, and in California, as well as in other states, training schools offer courses in Spanish and governments offer the licensing exam in Spanish, as well as in Vietnamese.

Accordingly, the institutional conditions may be necessary, but they are not sufficient to account for Vietnamese development and growing domination of the nail niche.

Vietnamese Development of Nail Niche Social Capital

Vietnamese domination over Hispanics is partly explicable at the entrepreneurial level, in ways that have contributed to Vietnamese employment bias. Vietnamese are nearly unique among immigrants in owning manicure salons (except in the New York metropolitan area, as noted, where Koreans own more salons), with their employment practices socially and culturally embedded in the Vietnamese community of which they form part. Because they typically employ coethnics, they provide work opportunities for Vietnamese, but not for Hispanics and other ethnic groups. In turn, owners' coethnic employment bias induces Vietnamese speakers who are not proficient in English to pursue careers as nail technicians, while not inducing other foreign-born to pursue such work. The salon owners can communicate with the non-English-speaking immigrants from their shared homeland.

But why do entrepreneurial Vietnamese specifically open nail salons? They do so partly because business entry barriers are low. They can fairly easily accumulate the requisite capital. If they work hard and save, they may be able to afford a salon after a few years. Moreover, in that many salons are family businesses, entrepreneurial Vietnamese can draw on requisite start-up capital that they pool from relatives (from distant as well as immediate kin) (Nguyen 2010, 159; Doan 2004, 53).[18] Since family members rarely charge interest, unlike banks, entrepreneurial Vietnamese can accordingly minimize their capital costs.[19]

Furthermore, because salons vary in worth, depending on size and location, entrepreneurial Vietnamese have a range of business acquisition options available to them. Consequently, there are opportunities for Vietnamese with different capital resources. Indicative of the variable cost of salon acquisitions, in 2008 the owner of a small manicuring shop in an upscale Boston suburb who wished to sell his business advertised it in a Vietnamese magazine for fifteen thousand dollars. In contrast, the listed selling price in the same magazine for another, larger salon in a different suburb was eighty-five thousand dollars (*Thăng Long* 2008, 81–82).

Family business ventures offer other advantages. To the extent that the salon owners rely on family members to help out, they also minimize their labor costs. And they can benefit from trust among kin, especially important in a business that often involves cash transactions.[20]

Low operating and acquisition costs, of course, should make ownership attractive to non-Vietnamese as well. Why, then, do mainly only Vietnamese become nail salon owners? Vietnamese, for one, have a comparative advantage in knowing the trade by the time they go into business for themselves. Typically, at the point of opening a salon they are experienced nail technicians. Since Vietnamese are more likely than other ethnic groups to work as nail technicians, they are better positioned to get the training in the trade on which the nail salon business rests. In general, employment in coethnic businesses tends to be associated with subsequent self-employment (Nee and Sanders 2001, 397).

Vietnamese salon owners, as well as Vietnamese rank and file, have informal as well as formal social networks to tap into that induce them to gravitate to nail care work, and that have the unintended effect of excluding non-Vietnamese while, possibly, driving down Vietnamese earnings owing to the ethnic competition their numbers generate (*as long as* the manicurists stay within a given consumer market). Ever since Vietnamese established themselves in the nail sector, salon owners have known fellow Vietnamese they can hire as employees and who can help them find employees. Many Vietnamese get their jobs through friends and family (Doan 2004, 44–45; Nguyen 2010). Moreover, Vietnamese salon owners can easily recruit workers through the Vietnamese training schools.

The Vietnamese media, in addition, provide both Vietnamese entrepreneurs and technicians in search of jobs access to work-relevant information unavailable to non–Vietnamese speakers. The de facto discriminatory practices associated with exclusion from the information circuit contribute to Vietnamese domination of the nail care niche, as both owners and employees.[21] According to a 2007 survey of Vietnamese salons, 70 percent of Vietnamese nail technicians prefer to read in Vietnamese (*NAILS Magazine* March 2007, 76). Vietnamese manicurists in search of work, as well as salons to purchase, know to consult Vietnamese newspapers and magazines. Approximately half of the 118 nail industry related advertisements listed in the November 4, 2008, issue of the Vietnamese Boston magazine *Thăng Long*, for example, noted employee job openings in nail salons, and slightly more than one-third specified salons for sale. A Vietnamese newspaper in Falls Church, Virginia, showed a roughly similar advertising breakdown (*Thương mãi miền Đông* 2008). In addition, Vietnamese salon owners have access to twenty-four-hour Vietnamese cable television channels in certain cities that carry advertisements for nail care supplies and salon services (Nguyen 2010, 175).

Vietnamese neighborhoods, however, cannot offer sufficient business and employment opportunities for qualified Vietnamese manicurists. Vietnamese have developed and expanded their nail niche involvement by targeting other neighborhoods, what Ram and Hillin (1994) call "breaking out." So extensive has their geographic dispersal been that Vietnamese have coined a phrase, *làm nail xuyên bang*, which, translated literally, means "doing nails across states." Indicative of their growing geographic spread, between 2000 and 2007 the number of nail technicians per thousand people declined in California while increasing in other states. Also indicative, in 2007 about 15 percent of Vietnamese manicurists in Massachusetts had been trained in some other state (Nguyen 2010, 172). As Vietnamese have dispersed across the United States, entrepreneurial Vietnamese have come to have coethnic labor to draw on nationwide and new locations where they can develop customer markets.

While most salons are mom-and-pop (and mainly mom!) undertakings, the most entrepreneurial Vietnamese have opened multiple stores, including nail chain franchises. Some of the franchises operate in multiple states. The largest nail chain is Regal Nails, located inside Walmart stores, started by Quy Charlie Ton in 1997. Ten years later his company operated 925 salons that employed 3,700 nail technicians (Roy 2007, 110). Because Quy Ton was biased toward hiring coethnics, Vietnamese immigrants own more than 99 percent of his franchises (Miller 2007; Doan 2004, 60). Accordingly, although Regal Nails, in its affiliation with Walmart, is associated with a business model that has eroded immigrant and other small business opportunities, Quy Ton has incorporated Vietnamese into the transformation of nail care provisioning that he has overseen. While transforming conditions of ownership, the franchises retain small business practices. Consequently, his chain is likely to have far less effect on employment than the Walmart stores in which his salons are situated. Ownership concentration differs in its impact in the retail service versus goods sector.

More likely to impact on Vietnamese involvement in the nail niche in the years to come is the immigration of new Vietnamese women. In that almost without exception only foreign-born Vietnamese work as manicurists, there is a generational life cycle to the labor market niche. Children of Vietnamese immigrants, as they get educated and fluent in English, gravitate to other jobs they consider preferable. Under the circumstances, the continuation of Vietnamese domination of the nail niche hinges on the arrival of new Vietnamese who take advantage of the institutional arrangements and social networks that earlier Vietnamese women immigrants put in place. Thus far, the immigrant stream, as detailed in Table 10.3, continues to fuel the labor market niche. However, should economic opportunities improve substantially in Vietnam, with the deepening of government economic reforms there, or should the US government reduce the number of Vietnamese to whom it grants immigration rights, the ethnic group's association with nail care would likely diminish.

With US-born Vietnamese gravitating to other types of work, once they acquire more human and cultural capital than their immigrant parents have, and possibly access also to more financial capital, immigrant Vietnamese social capital proves limited. Immigrant networks provide access to a narrow range of work, and they, in effect, fuel intraethnic competition. Consequently, when Vietnamese acquire other forms of capital, their ethnic ties diminish as a source of capital. Vietnamese ties function most as a source of capital when they lack English-speaking cultural capital and the human capital required for preferable jobs. In essence, Vietnamese social capital contains seeds of its own intergenerational demise.[22]

The Deepening of Vietnamese Vested Economic Interests in the Nail Niche

For the time being, though, Vietnamese diversification of business involvements in the nail economy further contributes to their association with the labor market niche. The businesses amplify the economic base of the nail niche and deepen Vietnamese economic interests in it. Some of the diversification has furthered the Vietnamese competitive edge in the niche.

For one, entrepreneurial Vietnamese have developed "backward linkages" in the nail sector. They have established companies that manufacture polish and acrylic systems, plus other products, Vietnamese salon owners buy (Doan 2004, 57). One such company is Odyssey Nail Systems, founded in 2000 by Trang Nguyen, an internationally acclaimed, award-winning nail specialist. His company manufactures a full range of nail care products (Bui 2007).

Misa Cosmetics is another Vietnamese American–owned company that produces nail care supplies. Brian Tran, the owner, together with family members, had owned a motorcycle seat manufacturing company in Vietnam. After immigrating to the United States in the early 1980s he found work in a Vietnamese nail salon. Building on his business experience in Vietnam and familiarity with the nail sector he acquired in the United States, he founded, in the 1990s, Misa Cosmetics (Rust 2006). Tran exemplifies how immigrants can leverage home country education and work experience to capitalize on opportunities where they move, in this case to capitalize on opportunities his fellow Vietnamese created in manicuring. But he did not come to the United States with specific nail care experience.

Quy Charlie Ton, who franchises Regal Nails salons, developed, in turn, forward linkages in the nail sector (Doan 2004; Roy 2007; Miller 2007). His initial involvement in the nail niche was as a manufacturer and supplier. His companies, Alfalfa Nail Supply and T4 Spa, manufacture nearly everything nail salons use, from emery boards to pedicure thrones. He innovatively built his mass network of manicure shops in Walmart stores to create a secure market for his manicure supply businesses. Until then he had experienced difficulty finding markets for his products.

Coethnic solidarity has helped create and sustain market opportunities for such Vietnamese manufacturers and distributors.[23] However, the Vietnamese-owned manicure-related manufacture businesses remain too small to explain the vibrancy of the ethnic niche. Previously described ethnic dynamics are more consequential. Such non-Vietnamese-owned companies as OPI and CND, for example, are key suppliers of nail polish for salons.

Transnationalization of the Vietnamese Nail Niche

Although the Vietnamese nail niche is a US-based invention, it is transnationalizing, and in two distinct ways. Vietnamese in the United States have inspired the development of similar nail care niches in other countries, and the US nail niche supply chain has shifted partly to Vietnam.[24]

Vietnamese Americans have exported their expertise to other countries, and Vietnamese immigrants in other countries have developed nail niches inspired by the US Vietnamese example. This is true, for example, in England (Bagwell 2006, 2008) and in the Czech Republic (Gissübelová 2007). The British example is telling.[25] By 2003 nail shops, known as nail bars, accounted for nearly half of all Vietnamese businesses in greater London. The first nail bar opened in 1997, but most opened only after the turn of the twenty-first century. The initial Vietnamese shop owners either learned the manicure trade from US family in the business or operated manicure businesses in the United States before spotting the market opportunity in England. And they tended to make occasional trips to the United States to keep up with nail care developments there. In this manner Vietnamese are beginning a trend of doing nails "across nations," in addition to doing nails "across states."

One entrepreneurial Vietnamese who had worked for suppliers in the United States before setting up his own business in Seattle later moved to London. He contributed to the proliferation of Vietnamese nail bars in London by marketing "start-up kits" and advising on licensing requirements. He claimed to have hundreds of Vietnamese clients who found him through word of mouth.

After the formation of the London niche, transnational networks became less important there. Vietnamese who subsequently became manicurists learned the trade in England, including from friends and family. Yet, incipient economically useful "reverse transnationalism" seems also to be at play in London, among British-born Vietnamese. Some second-generation Vietnamese women go to the United States, especially to California's "Little Saigon," to learn what they perceive to be superior nail techniques practiced there. Since they are bilingual as well, upon returning they offer assets to the nail bars run by the Vietnam-born (Barber 2011).[26] Meanwhile, as the London market has become saturated, enterprising Vietnamese have spread across England, in search of less competitive markets. Thus, in England, as in the United States, Vietnamese creatively mastered ways to both improve their manicure offerings and create new markets for their services by dispersing globally.

The entrepreneurial Vietnamese man who developed "start-up" kits proceeded to expand his market even beyond England. In this vein, he recruited Vietnamese in Paris, including relatives, to come to London to learn nail care work. Although the Vietnamese community in France is older and more established than that in England, Vietnamese manicuring, based on the US model of stand-alone nail shops offering quick, inexpensive manicures, apparently developed in France only after transnational networks, ultimately traceable to the US Vietnamese nail niche, took hold.

In turn, Vietnamese Americans have "Vietnamized" the niche they developed in the United States, in part by returning to their homeland and opening US-style nail salons and offering manicure services on a scale previously unknown there.[27] The names of many of the shops include the word "Nail," reflecting their diaspora origin (Lê 2005). Changes in communist Vietnamese government policies created the conditions that made this possible, in allowing home visits and return migration, and reforming the economy to allow private entrepreneurship.

As in the United States and England, in Vietnam professional manicuring has increasingly become available nationwide. The first Vietnamese salons opened in Saigon (officially known as Ho Chi Minh City), from where the core of the Vietnamese diaspora originated. More recently, though, salons have opened elsewhere in the country, especially in Hanoi (Nguyen 2010, 200).

In Vietnam, however, the nail niche is evolving in a more class-segmented manner, owing to the greater poverty in the country and associated disparities both in consumer purchasing power and possible capital accumulation for business investment. Unlike in the United States, where stand-alone manicures draw clientele from diverse social classes (except the well-to-do, who continue to patronize high-end beauty salons that offer manicures as a secondary service), manicurists in Vietnam, with different economic assets to invest in their businesses, appeal to customers of distinct socioeconomic classes. The stand-alone salons with the best facilities attract relatively well-off clientele. Poorer manicurists, who cannot afford the cost of a salon and who can afford only inferior equipment, work as mobile manicurists. They peddle their services in the neighborhoods where less well-off customers live and work (Nguyen 2010, 203–206).

Vietnam has also become a "backward link" of the nail niche in the United States, and, more recently, in other countries, such as England. This is true in both the labor and the materials supply chains. Some Vietnamese who seek to work abroad as manicurists now acquire their training in their home country, where it costs much less. And if trained in Vietnam, they can begin work almost immediately after emigrating. They often can count on family to hire them, even if they lack legal work permits and have not passed their licensing exam (Tran 2008, 1). In exchange for employment, the just-arrived immigrants offer cheap, loyal labor, which keeps salon owners' costs down and, in principle, their profit margins up. Accordingly, the nail niche has become transnationally embedded as well as transnationally sustained.

Vietnam, in addition, has become a source of nail industry supplies for overseas salons. Some Vietnamese Americans take advantage of homeland trips to purchase supplies, including nail files, clippers, and even salon chairs, for their US salons, at a fraction of the price US suppliers charge.

The transnationalization of the nail niche remains at an incipient stage. Yet, for the foreseeable future, it is likely to continue to expand "horizontally," through the formation of homologous salons around the world, modeled after those in the United States, and "vertically, backward," through the development of material and, especially, labor supply chains in Vietnam. The Vietnamization of the supply chain reduces the operating costs of businesses in the United States and other wealthy countries, which helps keep the price of Vietnamese nail care offerings low. In turn, Vietnamese-born, in targeting overseas manicure employment opportunities through their diaspora ties, provide labor that helps sustain the mainly first-generation immigrant-based niche. This is most true of women.

Conclusion

In sum, Vietnamese created an ethnic labor market niche in manicuring. While they were not the first to offer nail care services, they transformed and expanded the sector and became the main group of providers. They created a broad-based market for professional nail care independent of demand for other beauty services, and addressed the demand.

They generated multiclass, multiracial demand for a service that non-Vietnamese had previously provided only for the well-to-do. Vietnamese did so by introducing affordable, quick, and easily attainable nail care, and diversifying their offerings. While "stretching" and "deepening" the niche, they created a broadened social base for nail care, transformed nail care norms, and routinized demand for their services.

Concomitantly, growing numbers of Vietnamese immigrants acquired the training to do professional nail care. They could do so because the barriers to entry became surmountable to them, as their force of numbers contributed to the creation of institutional conditions facilitating their acquisition of necessary credentials, and because they developed a business model that transformed professional nail care into what can be called "McNails." In turn, ethnic-based networks enabled them to monopolize, increasingly, employment opportunities in the niche, as both entrepreneurs and rank-and-file employees.

The niche Vietnamese created constitutes a vibrant and increasingly important segment of the beauty industry, linked to the expanding service economy in the United States. However, they work in the least skilled, least revenue-generating segment of the beauty industry. Most typically, when Vietnamese entrepreneurs expand their business involvements they do so by opening additional salons of the same sort, not by diversifying their beauty care offerings to include those that are most profitable. Similarly, nail technicians do not invest in additional training to qualify for the better paying jobs in the beauty industry. Vietnamese, accordingly, are creating conditions that work against their own longer-term interests. They are fueling intraethnic competition that is likely to drive down their earnings, unless they increase demand for their services. For the immediate future, niche expansion rests on transnational developments. That expansion includes "Vietnamizing" the niche resource supply chain, in a manner that contains costs while sustaining the US-based niche.

The Vietnamese experience in manicuring suggests the following propositions about immigrant labor market niche creation, growth, maintenance, and transnationalization:

Niche creation: An immigrant group may carve out a sector of the labor market for themselves, as owners as well as employees, even when their command of the host country language and their formal education are limited, and even when they lack political and economic power. They can do so if they are innovative and quick to capitalize on relevant innovations by others, and if they create demand for their labor. Involvement in a niche may be mainly gender-specific. It is network-driven, and contingent on favorable institutional conditions that an immigrant group may help create.

Niche expansion: An immigrant group may expand the base of its niche through "niche stretching." It can do so by broadening the territorial, class, racial, and ethnic markets for its labor, as well as by diversifying its offerings, even within a narrow range.

Niche maintenance: An immigrant group may sustain a niche that offers less than ideal earnings and work conditions if ongoing homeland immigration provides labor to sustain the economic activity. New arrivals will gravitate to the niche when they consider the line of work attractive, relative to their preimmigration and perceived new country options, and when they rely on coethnic networks for work. As long as job-relevant networks are ethnically based, ethnically inclusive ties have the unintended effect of excluding others from the niche. Inclusionary and exclusionary practices transpire simultaneously and are mutually reinforcing.

Niche transnationalization: An immigrant-formed niche may transnationalize if members of a group apply in new countries expertise and resources they developed initially in one specific country. The transnationalization may involve the provisioning of goods or services in new countries that build on the skills, financial, and social capital developed in the original niche. It may also involve the development of "backward supply linkages," in countries where resources are cheaper, that lower operating costs and contribute to the immigrant group sustaining a competitive edge in the labor market where the niche initially formed. In principle, the niche might also transnationalize through the formation of "forward linkages," involving the development of new niche-based goods and services marketed across borders. To date, the Vietnamese, however, have not developed this mode of transnationalization. They did not even develop "forward linkages" in the beauty sector in the United States, where they established the manicure niche.

The generalizability of these propositions, of course, necessarily awaits in-depth analyses of immigrant involvement in other labor market niches.

NOTES

Originally published in *International Migration Review* 45 (3): 639–674, 2011. ©2011 *International Migration Review*, reprint by permission.

1 Thanh-nghi Nguyen conducted the research on Vietnamese manicurists for this article. Although this article draws primarily on statistical and secondary source data, in conjunction with her dissertation she interviewed thirty-two nail salon owners and technicians in the Boston area, using snowball sampling. Interviewees were asked questions about their biographical backgrounds, transnational ties, work histories, work conditions and their views toward the work conditions, how they became involved in nail work, relations with coethnic manicurists, work aspirations, and training and licensing experiences. In Vietnam a few manicurists were interviewed about how the manicure niche evolved there. For more detail about the interviews, see Nguyen (2010). These interviews helped in developing an understanding of Vietnamese involvement in the nail niche, even though they are not specifically cited in this article. Susan Eckstein wrote the article.

2 Waldinger found Vietnamese employment concentration, however, to be less than that of Cuban and West Indian immigrants.

3 Notable exceptions in the United States include immigrants who come on temporary job visas, for particular work, such as Indians in the high-tech sector and agricultural workers.

4 Although we are concerned with immigrant labor market niches, different native-born groups have also been associated with distinctive niches, sometimes with different niches over time (Waldinger 1996).

5 On the embeddedness of ethnic entrepreneurship, see also Zhou (2004).

6 "Salon City Reports on Professional Beauty Federation's Capitol Hill Event," http://www.ewire.com/display.cfm/Wire_ID/5342. By way of contrast, box office movie revenue totaled $9.8 billion in 2008. See "US Movie Market Summary for 2008," http://www.the-numbers.com/market/2008.php. Both online references were accessed in November 2009.

7 Based on Nguyen's tracing of Department of Labor and Bureau of Labor Statistics publications, beginning in 1960.

8 The number of Vietnamese-born in the United States rose from a mere 4,600 in 1960 to over a million shortly after the turn of the century (Cheng 1994; Portes and Rumbaut 2006; USDC 2008). The largest number moved to the United States immediately after the Vietnam War ended in 1975, as refugees (Nguyen 2010, table 2.3).

9 On Chinese-Vietnamese employment and entrepreneurship in Southern California, see Gold (1994).

10 On the social backgrounds of the different émigré waves, see Gold (1992, 57–61).

11 New York City (and nearby New Jersey) is the one area where Vietnamese are not the main ethnic group manicurists. Koreans are. And in New York Koreans have been upgrading their services to include massages and eyebrow and leg waxing, and to involve high-tech equipment (Lee 2006; Oh 2007; Kang 2010).

12 Willett (2005, 68) attributes the higher percentage of men among Vietnamese manicurists to the discrimination they receive in other sectors of the labor market.

13 Despite the patriarchal nature of the Vietnamese family, Vietnamese culture contains a strong tradition of female autonomy, independence, and entrepreneurship (Gold 1992, 55; Kibria 1993).

14 As of 2000 Orange County and San Jose, both in California, accounted for one-fifth of Vietnamese in the United States (Portes and Rumbaut 2006, 42).

15 For a discussion of how nail technicians have developed different customer relations in salons catering to different racial and class clientele, in principle to cater to different conditions of customer satisfaction, see Kang (2010).

16 In some states non-Vietnamese have pressed for an upgrading of requirements to limit ethnic competition (Kang 2010, 233).

17 Alabama Board of Cosmetology, "FAQs," http://www.aboc.state.al.us/FAQs.htm (accessed July 2010); Connecticut Department of Public Health, "Nail Technician and Esthetician Information," http://www.ct.gov/dph/cwp/view.asp?a=3121&q=389378 (accessed July 2010).

18 Vietnamese here draw on their high valuation of family. See Gold (1992, 55).

19 Vietnamese in general tend to limit themselves to businesses that they can undertake with their own and family resources. For example, an Orange Country study of Vietnamese businesses found that nearly two-thirds of owners relied either on their own or family savings (Gold 1992, 100).

20 On Vietnamese valuation of family, and trust in family, see Hitchcock and Wesner (2009).

21 On ethnic-based closure as an unintended consequence of ethno-linguistic dependence among other Asian immigrant groups, see Sanders, Nee, and Sernau (2002).

22 The objective quality of nail care work conditions (e.g., earnings, job security, health conditions) and Vietnamese perceptions of them are beyond the scope of this article. The fact that second-generation immigrants do not pursue manicuring, even though they could easily access the networks to make it possible, suggests Vietnamese valuation of manicuring changes with their job options.

23 In California coethnic solidarity has even come to involve "purchasing groups" that buy nail products in bulk at discount. In lowering their supply costs, Vietnamese members of purchasing groups created an economic advantage for themselves. Non-Vietnamese salon owners typically buy for themselves or for a few friends (Hammond 2002).

24 This mode of transnationalization differs from modes noted among other immigrant entrepreneurs. Other bases of transnational entrepreneurship include ownership of export and import businesses and businesses where ownership or investment is based in one country while production is located in another (Zhou 2004, 1054–1060).

25 The discussion of England draws on Bagwell (2008).

26 As in the United States, nail shops tend to be family businesses that rely heavily on trust and personal networks, including for advice, financing, and supplies (Bagwell 2006).

27 The discussion of the Vietnamization of the Vietnamese-American nail niche draws entirely on open-ended interviews with a select number of Vietnamese in Vietnam conducted in conjunction with Thanhnghi Nguyen's doctoral dissertation. See Nguyen (2010, chap. 6). A more detailed analysis of the Vietnamization of the US nail niche awaits future research.

REFERENCES

Allen, James P., and Eugene Turner. 2007. "New Patterns in Boston's Ethnic Quilt: A Geographic Perspective." *AAG (American Association of Geography) Newsletter*, November.

American Salon's Green Book. 2005. Cleveland, OH: Advanstar Communications.

Bagwell, Susan. 2006. "UK Vietnamese Businesses: Cultural Influences and Intracultural Differences." *Environment and Planning C: Government and Policy* 24 (10): 51–69.

———. 2008. "Transnational Family Networks and Ethnic Minority Business Development: The Case of Vietnamese Nail-Shops in the UK." *International Journal of Entrepreneurial Behavior and Research* 14 (6): 377–394.

Barber, Tamsin. 2011. "Negotiating Identity and Belonging among British Born Vietnamese in London." Doctoral dissertation, Roehampton University.

Bates, Timothy. 1993. "Determinants of Survival and Profitability among Asian Immigrant-Owned Small Businesses." Discussion paper CES 93-11, Center for Economics Studies, August 1993. http://www.ces.census.gov/docs/cache/paper_contents_100200.pdf (accessed April 2008).

———. 1998. "Exiting Self-Employment: An Analysis of Asian Immigrant-Owned Small Businesses." Discussion paper CES 98–13, Center for Economics Studies. http://www.ces.census.gov/docs/cache/paper_contents_101569.pdf (accessed April 2008).

Bloch, Matthew, Shan Carter, and Rob Gebeloff. 2009. "Immigration and Jobs: Where U.S. Workers Come From." *New York Times*, April 7. http://www.nytimes.com/interactive/2009/04/07/us/20090407-immigration-occupation.html (accessed April 2009).

Bonacich, Edna. 1987. "'Making It' in America: A Social Evaluation of the Ethics of Immigrant Entrepreneurship." *Sociological Perspectives* 30 (4): 446–466.

Borjas, George. 1986. "The Self-Employment Experiences of Immigrants." *Journal of Human Resources* 21 (4): 485–506.

Brettell, Caroline B., and Kristopher E. Alstatt. 2007. "The Agency of Immigrant Entrepreneurs: Biographies of the Self-Employed in Ethnic and Occupational Niches of the Urban Labor Market." *Journal of Anthropological Research* 63: 383–397.

Bui, Tara. 2007. "Vietnamese Dominate Nail Salon Business in the U.S." *Nguoi Viet*, April 7. http://news.newamericamedia.org/news/view_article.html?article_id=7e8aa26e7e87046f04f827375b36a6c1 (accessed April 2008).

Card, David, and John DiNardo. 2000. "Do Immigrant Inflows Lead to Native Outflows?" *American Economic Review* 90 (2): 360–367.

Cheng, Lucie. 1994. "Introduction." Pp. 3–35 in Paul Ong, Edna Bonacich, and Lucie Cheng, eds., *The New Asian Immigration in Los Angeles and Global Restructuring*. Philadelphia: Temple University Press.

Consumer USA. 2008. Chicago: Euromonitor International.

Dang, Janet. 1999. "A Hand for Vietnamese Americans: Discount Nail Salons Bring Success to Their Fingertips." *AsianWeek* 21 (14).

Dickerson, Debra. 1997. "Racial Fingernail Politics." *U.S. News & World Report*, April 14, 33–35. http://www.usnews.com/usnews/news/articles/970414/archive_006694.htm (accessed March 2009).

Do, Dzung. 2006. "Vietnamese Nail Businesses Prosper in Florida." Translated by Van Dang. *Nguoi Viet Online*, March 15. http://www.nguoi-viet.com/absolutenm/anmviewer.asp?a=42432 (accessed April 14, 2008).

Doan, Tam Minh Thi. 2004. "Tapping into Social Resources to Address Occupational Health: A Network Analysis of Vietnamese-Owned Nail Salons." Master's thesis, Massachusetts Institute of Technology.

Espiritu, Yen Le. 1997. *Asian American Women and Men: Labor, Laws, and Love*. Thousand Oaks, CA: Sage.

Federman, Maya N., David E. Harrington, and Kathy J. Krynski. 2006. "Vietnamese Manicurists: Are Immigrants Displacing Natives or Finding New Nails to Polish?" *Industrial and Labor Relations Review* 59 (2): 302–318.

Gissübelová, Jaroslava. 2007. "Le premier courrier de mars" [The first newsletter in March]. *Radio Prague*. http://www.radio.cz/fr/article/88902 (accessed November 2008).

Gold, Steven J. 1992. *Refugee Communities: A Comparative Field Study*. Newbury Park, CA: Sage.

———. 1994. "Chinese-Vietnamese Entrepreneurs in California." Pp. 196–226 in Paul Ong, Edna Bonacich, and Lucie Cheng, eds., *The New Asian Immigration in Los Angeles and Global Restructuring*. Philadelphia: Temple University Press.

Hammond, Jody. 2002. *A Hand Up: The Vietnamese Nail Salon Success Story*. Documentary film.

Hitchcock, Michael, and Simone Wesner. 2009. "Vietnamese Values, Networks and Family Businesses in London." *Asian Pacific Business Review* 15 (2): 265–282.

Hondagneu-Sotelo, Pierrette. 2001. *Doméstica: Immigrant Workers Cleaning and Caring in the Shadows of Affluence*. Berkeley: University of California Press.

Huynh, Craig Trinh-Phat. 1996. "Vietnamese-Owned Manicure Businesses in Los Angeles." Pp. 195–203 in Bill Ong Hing and Ronald Lee, eds., *The State of Asian Pacific America: Reframing the Immigration Debate—A Public Policy Report*. Los Angeles: LEAP Asian Pacific American Public Policy Institute and UCLA Asian American Studies Center.

Kang, Miliann. 2006. "Hooked on Nails: Competing Constructions of Beauty by Black and White Women." Paper presented at the annual meeting of the American Sociological Association, Montreal, August 16.

———. 2010. *The Managed Hand: Race, Gender, and the Body in Beauty Service Work*. Berkeley: University of California Press.

Kibria, Nazli. 1993. *Family Tightrope: The Changing Lives of Vietnamese Americans*. Princeton, NJ: Princeton University Press.

Kim, Kwang Chung, Won Moo Hurh, and Marilyn Fernandez. 1989. "Intra-Group Differences in Business Participation: Three Asian Immigrant Groups." *International Migration Review* 23 (1): 73–95.

Lazar, Kay. 2005. "Getting a Foothold in a Crowded Field." *Boston Globe*, May 26, Globe North sec., p. 1.

Lê, Mai Thi. 2005. "Vẽ tranh trên móng" [Drawing on the nails]. *Sài Gòn Giải Phóng*, June 17. http://www.sggp.org.vn/xahoi/nam2005/thang6/55516/ (accessed April 2009).

Lee, Eunju. 2006. *Gendered Processes: Korean Immigrant Small Business Ownership*. New York: LFB.

Lieberson, Stanley. 1980. *A Piece of the Pie: Blacks and White Immigrants since 1880*. Berkeley: University of California Press.

Light, Ivan. 1972. *Ethnic Enterprise in America: Business and Welfare among Chinese, Japanese, and Blacks*. Berkeley: University of California Press.

Light, Ivan, and Steven J. Gold. 2000. *Ethnic Economies*. San Diego, CA: Academic Press.

Light, Ivan, and Angel Sanchez. 1987. "Immigrant Entrepreneurs in 272 SMSAs." *Sociological Perspectives* 30 (4): 373–399.

Massey, Douglas S., Joaquin Arango, Graeme Hugo, Ali Kouaouchi, Adela Pellegrino, and J. Edward Taylor. 1998. *Worlds in Motion: Understanding International Migration at the End of the Millennium*. Oxford: Clarendon.

Miller, Kerry. 2007. "Greener Shades for Nail Salons." *Business Week*, March 5. http://www.businessweek.com/smallbiz/content/mar2007/sb20070305_568525.htm (accessed July 2009).

Min, Pyong Gap. 2006. "Korean Americans." Pp. 230–259 in Pyong Gap Min, ed., *Asian Americans: Contemporary Trends and Issues*. Thousand Oaks, CA: Pine Forge Press.

Murray, Anne Warren. 1997. "Shops Offer Fast, Inexpensive Service." *Patriot Ledger* (Quincy, MA), December 15, 20.

"Nail File: The Economic Meaning of Manicures." 1997. Gale Group. https://reason.com/archives/1997/10/01/the-nail-file (accessed October 5, 2015).

NAILS Magazine. 2007. March. http://www.nailsmag.com/magazine/2007/03.

NAILS Magazine Big Book. 1997–2009. Redondo Beach, CA: Bobit Business Media.

Nee, Victor, and Jimy Sanders. 2001. "Understanding the Diversity of Immigrant Incorporation: A Forms-of-Capital Model." *Ethnic and Racial Studies* 24 (3): 386–411.

Nguyen, Thanh-Nghi B. 2010. "Vietnamese Manicurists: The Making of an Ethnic Niche." Doctoral dissertation, Boston University.

Oh, Joong-Hwan. 2007. "Economic Incentive, Embeddedness, and Social Support: A Study of Korean-Owned Nail Salon Workers' Rotating Credit Associations." *International Migration Review* 41: 623–655.

Ong, Paul, Edna Bonacich, and Lucie Cheng. 1994. *The New Asian Immigration in Los Angeles and Global Restructuring*. Philadelphia: Temple University Press.

Parmley, Suzette. 2002. "Vietnamese Flocking to Nail-Salon Industry." *Billings Gazette*, June 16. http://www.billingsgazette.com/business/article_010c035a-231d-5c0b-81ed-7706a7fab017.html (accessed April 2008).

Parreñas, Rhacel Salazar. 2005. "The Gender Paradox in the Transnational Families of Filipino Migrant Women." *Asian and Pacific Migration Journal* 14 (3): 243–268.

Portes, Alejandro, and Ruben Rumbaut. 2006. *Immigrant America: A Portrait*. 3rd ed. Berkeley: University of California Press.

Portes, Alejandro, and Steven Shafer. 2007. "Revisiting the Enclave Hypothesis: Miami Twenty-Five Years Later." *Sociology of Entrepreneurship* 25: 157–190.

Portes, Alejandro, and Min Zhou. 1992. "Self-Employment and the Earnings of Immigrants." *American Sociological Review* 61: 219–230.

Postrel, Virginia. 1997. "The Nail File: The Economic Meaning of Manicures." *Reason* 29 (5): 4–7.

Ram, Monder, and Guy Hillin. 1994. "Achieving Break-Out: Developing Mainstream Ethnic Minority Business." *Small Business Enterprise and Development* 1 (2): 15–21.

Rath, Jan. 2002. "A Quintessential Immigrant Niche? The Non-case of Immigrants in the Dutch Construction Industry." *Entrepreneurship and Regional Development* 14: 355–372.

Roy, Sree. 2007. "Can These Emerging Salon Chains Become the 'Starbucks of Nails'?" *NAILS Magazine*, September, 108–116.

Rumbaut, Ruben. 1989. "Portraits, Patterns, and Predictors of the Refugee Adaptation Process: Results and Reflections from the IHARP Panel Study." Pp. 138–182 in David W. Haines, ed., *Refugees as Immigrants: Cambodians, Laotians, and Vietnamese in America*. Totowa, NJ: Rowman & Littlefield.

Rust, Jayna. 2006. "A Vietnamese American Dynasty." *NAILS Magazine*, March 2006. http://www.nailsmag.com/feature.aspx?fid=129&ft=1 (accessed April 2008).

Sanders, Jimy, and Victor Nee. 1996. "Immigrant Self-Employment: The Family's Social Capital and the Value of Human Capital." *American Sociological Review* 61 (2): 231–249.

Sanders, Jimy, Victor Nee, and Scott Sernau. 2002. "Networks Beyond the Ethnic Labor Market." *Social Forces* 81 (1): 281–314.

Sassen, Saskia. 1995. "Immigration and Local Labor Markets." Pp. 87–127 in Alejandro Portes, ed., *The Economic Sociology of Immigration: Essays on Networks, Ethnicity, and Entrepreneurship*. New York: Russell Sage Foundation.

Thăng Long. 2008. No. 707, November 4.

Thịnh, Quang. 2006. "Công việc nơi đất khách—Nghề phổ biến của người Việt ở Mỹ" [Work on the foreign land—the popular job of Vietnamese in the United States]. *VietnamNet*, March 4. http://nguoivienxu.vietnamnet.vn/nguoivietbonphuong/2006/03/547247/ (accessed July 2009).

Thương mại miền Đông. 2008. No. 806, September 5.

"Tiny Brushes, Huge Talents, Old Masters." 2007. *NAILS Magazine. Big Book 1997–2008*, June, 74–78.

"Top 25 Nail Competitors." 2008. *NAILS Magazine. Big Book 1997–2008*, August, 42.

Tran, My-Thuan. 2008. "Vietnamese Nail Down the U.S. Manicure Business." *Los Angeles Times*, May 5, 2008. http://articles.latimes.com/2008/may/05/local/me-nails5 (accessed April 2008).

US Department of Commerce (USDC), US Census Bureau. 2008. *American Community Survey 2008*. http://factfinder.census.gov/servlet/DatasetMainPageServlet?_program=ACS (accessed February 2009).

US Department of Homeland Security. 2009. *2009 Yearbook of Immigrant Statistics*. http://www.dhs.gov/files/statistics/immigration.shtm (accessed December 26, 2010).

US Department of Labor (USDL), US Bureau of Labor Statistics. 1999–2007. *Occupational Employment Statistics*. http://www.bls.gov/oes/oes_arch.htm (accessed April 2009).

———. 2009. "Barbers, Cosmetologists, and Other Personal Appearance Workers." In *Occupational Outlook Handbook 2008-2009*. http://www.bls.gov/oco/ocos169.htm (accessed February 2009).

Vo, Linda Trinh. 2003. "Managing Survival: Economic Realities for Vietnamese American Women." Pp. 237–252 in Shirley Hune and Gail M. Nomura, eds., *Asian/Pacific Islander American Women: A Historical Anthology*. New York: New York University Press.

Waldinger, Roger. 1994. "The Making of an Immigrant Niche." *International Migration Review* 28 (1): 3–30.

———. 1996. *Still the Promised City? African-Americans and New Immigrants in Postindustrial New York*. Cambridge, MA: Harvard University Press.

———. 2001. "The Immigrant Niche in Global City-Regions: Concept, Pattern, Controversy." Pp. 299–324 in Allen J. Scott, ed., *Global City-Regions: Trends, Theory, Policy*. New York: Oxford University Press.

———. 2008. "Between 'Here' and 'There': Immigrant Cross-Border Activities and Loyalties." *International Migration Review* 42 (1): 3–29.

Waldinger, Roger, and Mehdi Bozorgmehr. 1996. "The Making of a Multicultural Metropolis." Pp. 3–38 in Roger Waldinger and Mehdi Bozorgmehr, eds., *Ethnic Los Angeles*. New York: Russell Sage Foundation.

Waldinger, Roger, and Claudia Der-Martirosian. 2001. "The Immigrant Niche: Pervasive, Persistent, Diverse." Pp. 228–271 in Roger Waldinger, ed., *Strangers at the Gates: New Immigrants in Urban America*. Berkeley: University of California Press.

Willett, Julie A. 2005. "'Hands across the Table': A Short History of the Manicurist in the Twentieth Century." *Journal of Women's History* 17 (3): 59–80.

Wilson, Franklin D. 2003. "Ethnic Niching and Metropolitan Labor Markets." *Social Science Research* 32: 429–466.

Wilson, K., and Alejandro Portes. 1980. "Immigrant Enclaves: An Analysis of the Labor Market Experiences of Cubans in Miami." *American Journal of Sociology* 86: 295–319.

Yoon, In-Jin. 1991. "The Changing Significance of Ethnic and Class Resources in Immigrant Businesses: The Case of Korean Immigrant Businesses in Chicago." *International Migration Review* 25 (2): 303–332.

Zhou, Min. 2004. "Revisiting Ethnic Entrepreneurship: Convergencies, Controversies, and Conceptual Advancements." *International Migration Review* 38 (3): 1040–1074.

STUDY QUESTIONS

(1) Dhingra's chapter is concerned not with *if* Indian Americans experience race in the work-place, but rather *how* they experience race. What are the primary occupational sectors in which Indian Americans are working in today's society? How does that differ from the situation of their predecessors who migrated in the early twentieth century? How does the occupational sector in which Indians work affect how they experience race in US society?

(2) What strategies do Indian American workers employ to counteract their racialization in the workplace? In what ways do they assimilate to workplace culture? In what ways do they show their resistance to assimilation? What are the implications of these findings for other Asian American workers in the United States?

(3) Espiritu's chapter examines the phenomenon of Filipina immigrant nurses in the United States. How did nursing historically become a popular profession in the Philippines? What were the economic push and pull factors that contributed to the migration of Filipina nurses to the United States? What were their assimilation experiences in the United States? Compare and contrast the challenges faced by Filipina immigrant women to those of other immigrant workers in the United States.

(4) In what ways was the migration of Filipina nurses to the United States both a racialized and a gendered phenomenon? How did Filipina immigrant nurses renegotiate their ideologies about race and gender upon their arrival in the United States? How do these understandings compare to the experiences of Vietnamese manicurists?

(5) What is an ethnic niche? What constellation of factors needs to be in place for ethnic niches to develop? Based on the chapter by Eckstein and Nguyen, what are some factors that might explain why some immigrant groups been able to develop ethnic niches while others have not?

(6) How did Vietnamese immigrant women come to dominate the nail salon industry? What sets of institutional and cultural factors contributed to their ability to carve out a unique ethnic niche? What made nail work preferable to other types of occupations in the United States? How has Vietnamese entrepreneurship in the nail salon industry led to a transnational ethnic niche?

SUGGESTED READINGS

Chan, Sucheng. 2004. *Survivors: Cambodian Refugees in the United States*. Champaign: University of Illinois Press.

Chin, Margaret. 2005. *Sewing Women: Immigrants and the New York City Garment Industry*. New York: Columbia University Press.

de Castro, A. B., T. Rue, and D. T. Takeuchi. 2010. "Employment Frustration among Asian American Immigrants: Physical and Mental Health Consequences of Job Denial in the U.S. Labor Force." *Public Health Nursing* 27 (6): 492–503.

Donnelly, Nancy D. 1997. *Changing Lives of Refugee Hmong Women*. Seattle: University of Washington Press.

Faderman, Lillian, with Ghia Xiong. 1998. *I Begin My Life All Over: The Hmong and the American Immigrant Experience*. Boston: Beacon.

Glenn, Evelyn Nakano. 2004. *Unequal Freedom: How Race and Gender Shaped American Citizenship and Labor*. Cambridge, MA: Harvard University Press.

Kalita, S. Mitra. 2003. *Suburban Sahibs: Three Immigrant Families and Their Passage from India to America*. New Brunswick, NJ: Rutgers University Press.

Kang, Milliann. 2003. "The Managed Hand: The Commercialization of Bodies and Emotions in Korean Immigrant–Owned Nail Salons." *Gender and Society* 17: 820–839.

Kim, Chang Hwan, and Arthur Sakamoto. 2010. "Have Asian American Men Achieved Labor Market Parity with White Men?" *American Sociological Review* 75 (6): 934–957.

Leonard, Karen, and Chandra S. Tibrewal. 1993. "Asian Indians in Southern California: Occupations and Ethnicity." Pp. 141–162 in Ivan Light and Parminder Bhachu, eds., *Immigration and Entrepreneurship: Culture, Capital, and Ethnic Networks.* New Brunswick, NJ: Transaction.

Leong, Andrew. 1997. "The Asian Exclusion Act of 1996: Welfare Reform and Asian Pacific America." *Asian American Policy Review* 7: 88–101.

Leong, Frederick T. L., and Mark C. Johnson. 1994. "Mothers of Vietnamese Amerasians: Psychological Distress and High-Risk Factors." *Asian American and Pacific Islander Journal of Health* 2 (1): 31–48.

Min, Pyong Gap. 1996. *Caught in the Middle: Korean Merchants in America's Multiethnic Cities.* Berkeley: University of California Press.

Nagasawa, R., Z. Qian, and P. Wong. 2001. "Theory of Segmented Assimilation and the Adoption of Marijuana Use and Delinquent Behavior by Asian Pacific Youth." *Sociological Quarterly* 42 (3): 351–372.

Ong, Paul, and Tania Azores. 1994. "The Migration and Incorporation of Filipino Nurses." Pp. 164–198 in Paul Ong, Edna Bonacich, and Lucie Cheng, eds., *The New Asian Immigration in Los Angeles and Global Restructuring.* Philadelphia: Temple University Press.

Park, Kyeyoung. 1997. *The Korean American Dream: Immigrants and Small Business in New York City.* Ithaca, NY: Cornell University Press.

Park, Lisa Sun-Hee. 2005. *Consuming Citizenship: Children of Asian Immigrant Entrepreneurs.* Stanford, CA: Stanford University Press.

Park, Yungsuhn. 2005. "The Immigrant Workers Union: Challenges Facing Low-Wage Immigrant Workers in Los Angeles." *Asian Law Journal* 12: 67–81.

Parreñas, Rhacel S. 2001. *Servants of Globalization: Women, Migration, and Domestic Work.* Stanford, CA: Stanford University Press.

Sakamoto, Arthur, Kimberly A. Govette, and Chang Hwan Kim. 2009. "Socioeconomic Attainments of Asian Americans." *Annual Review of Sociology* 35: 255–276.

Wu, Diana Ting Liu. 1997. *Asian Pacific Americans in the Workplace.* Walnut Creek, CA: AltaMira.

Zhou, Min. 1992. *Chinatown: The Socioeconomic Potential of an Urban Enclave.* Philadelphia: Temple University Press.

Zhou, Min, and Myungduk Cho. 2010. "Noneconomic Effects of Ethnic Entrepreneurship: A Focused Look at the Chinese and Korean Enclave Economies in Los Angeles." *Thunderbird International Business Review* 52: 83–96.

FILMS

Aroy, Marissa (director), and Niall McKay (producer). 2012. *The Delano Manongs: Forgotten Heroes of the United Farmworkers* (28-minute documentary).

Boti, Marie (director). 1997. *Modern Heroes, Modern Slaves* (45-minute documentary).

Choy, Christine (director and producer). 2006. *Agent Yellow* (28-minute documentary).

Choy, Christine, and Elaine Kim (coproducers). 1993. *Sa-I-Gu: From Korean Women's Perspectives* (36-minute documentary).

Ding, Loni (producer/director). 1982. *Four Women* (30-minute documentary).

——(producer/director). 1982. *Frankly Speaking* (30-minute documentary).

Dunn, Geoffrey, and Mark Schwartz (codirectors). 1984. *Dollar a Day, Ten Cents a Dance* (29-minute documentary).

Nakasako, Spencer, and Sokly Ny (codirectors). 1995. *a.k.a. Don Bonus* (55-minute documentary).

Sakya, Sapana, Donald Young, and Kyung Yu (codirectors). 2003. *Searching for Asian America* (30-minute documentary).

Suzara, Grace, and Ted Unarce (producers). 2010. *Modern Day Slaves* (50-minute documentary).

Tajima-Peña, Renee (director). 2002. *Labor Women* (35-minute documentary).

Tang, Eric (director). 2001. *Eating Welfare* (57-minute documentary).

Tsumo, Keiko (director). 1990. *The Story of Vinh* (60-minute documentary).

Vinluan, Ermena (producer). 2010. *Tea & Justice: NYPD's 1st Asian Women Officers* (55-minute documentary).

Wang, Wayne (director). 1989. *Eat a Bowl of Tea* (103-minute drama).

Witness Production. 2000. *The Empire's New Clothes* (10-minute documentary).

Young, Donarld (director). 1994. *Chrysanthemums and Salt* (25-minute documentary).

PART V

Sexuality in Asian America

11

"Tomboys" and "Baklas"

Experiences of Lesbian and Gay Filipino Americans

KEVIN L. NADAL AND MELISSA J. H. CORPUS

The nature of identifying as LGBT (lesbian, gay, bisexual, and transgender) and as a person of color can present several intricacies. Although both groups (e.g., people of color and LGBT people) experience historical and present-day marginalization (e.g., stereotyping, oppression, stigmatization, and microaggressions) by their respective dominant groups, marrying the two identities can compel individuals to choose one identity over the other. Moreover, many communities of color have been overtly intolerant of LGBT persons, influencing LGBT people of color to seek membership in a general LGBT community rather than within their own racial or ethnic group. Some LGBT persons of color may want to identify as both their racial/ethnic and sexual identities, but struggle as they feel negative repercussions from both of their groups (Chung and Singh 2009; Chung and Szymanski 2006). Consequently, LGBT people of color may experience an array of psychological stressors including identity confusion, self-esteem issues, emotional trauma, suicidal ideation, and substance abuse problems (see Nadal 2010 for a review).

Although it is clear that LGBT persons of color are presented with unique experiences, a limited amount of research focusing on this population exists. Specifically, Asian Americans and Pacific Islanders (AAPIs) receive the least amount of attention in the realm of LGBT-focused research (Chan 1989; Nadal 2010). Meanwhile, research on AAPIs often centers specifically on East Asian Americans (e.g., Chinese, Japanese, and Korean) or lumps Asians as a homogenous group, leaving certain subgroups (e.g., Southeast Asians, Pacific Islanders) to be overlooked in the literature (Nadal 2004, 2011). This trend is prevalent with major studies on LGBT Asian Americans, in which the majority of the samples are East Asian Americans (see Chan 1989; Kimmel and Yi 2004), results are assumed to apply to all Asian Americans, or both. Thus, the purpose of this article is to disaggregate the research on LGBT AAPIs, by highlighting the experiences of one underresearched group—LGBT Filipino Americans.

Experiences of Filipino Americans

Filipino Americans are the second largest Asian American group in the United States and the second largest immigrant group in the country (Nadal 2011). Having a unique colonial history and cultural value system, Filipinos and Filipino Americans are one of the only ethnic groups that have been placed into several racial and ethnic categories (Nadal 2004, 2011). For example, the 2000 US census classifies Filipino Americans as Asian American (Barnes and Bennett 2002), although the US Department of Education has previously categorized them as Pacific Islanders (Horn 1995) or even as Hispanic (Trevino 1987). Moreover, California Senate Bill 1813, passed in 1988, requires California state personnel surveys or statistical tabulations to classify persons of Filipino ancestry as Filipino instead of Asian, Pacific Islander, or Hispanic (Espiritu 1992). Given this history, Filipinos have been misclassified in a number of arenas, resulting in limited or inaccurate research or scholarship about the group.

There are three primary cultural characteristics that decipher Filipino Americans from other Asian American groups and may be helpful in understanding LGBT experiences. First, due to the colonization of the Philippines by Spain and the United States, Filipinos often affiliate more with Latino values (which are based on similar colonial histories) and less with traditional East Asian values (which are based on Buddhist and Confucian teachings). In fact, one study found Filipino American college students to possess cultural values contrary to those of Chinese, Korean, and Japanese American college students (Kim et al. 2001). Moreover, the Philippines is the only Asian country where 90 percent of the population subscribes to Catholicism or Christianity (Nadal 2011), leading to unique experiences of religion and spirituality than other Asians. Furthermore, contrary to strictly patriarchic gender role construction in other Asian countries, Filipina women are encouraged to maintain their roles as caretakers, although also pursuing educational attainment and professional development (Maramba 2008). Thus, Filipino families are viewed as equally patriarchal and matriarchal, in that women also manage the household finances, discipline children, dictate the rules of the household, and are taught to be as assertive and independent as men (Nadal 2011). Finally, a third distinguishing characteristic between Filipinos and other Asian groups (particularly East Asians) is their phenotypic appearances. Filipinos' skin color can range from light brown to dark brown, and their hair texture can vary from straight to curly; accordingly, Filipinos are often mistaken for other racial/ ethnic groups such as Latinos and Pacific Islanders (Nadal 2011; Nadal et al. 2012). This differs from East Asian Americans, who are likely to always be perceived as Asian. Thus, it can be hypothesized that the experiences of LGBT Filipino Americans may differ from those of LGBT people of other Asian American ethnicities. For example, perhaps religion, gender roles, and experiences of racism may influence LGBT Filipino Americans differently than other LGBT AAPIs.

Previous Research on LGBT Filipinos

The small percentage of LGBT Filipino research that does exist focuses primarily on traditional Filipino concepts in the Philippines and tends not to expand on Filipino Americans in the United States. Moreover, these studies tend to be more sociological and anthropological in nature and do not examine sexuality using psychological methods. However, this literature does highlight how homosexuality and bisexuality may be conceptualized differently in the Philippines than in the United States. First, the term *bakla*, which is the common synonym for "gay," has also been defined in Tagalog dictionaries as "hermaphrodite" and often "conflates the categories of homosexuality, hermaphroditism, cross-dressing and effeminacy" (Manalansan 2003, 25). Second, contrary to the Western view where same-sex sexual acts are equated with being gay or lesbian, the Filipino culture does not stringently associate sexual behavior with sexual orientation; rather, sexuality is based on one's gendered behavior (i.e., whether one acts feminine or masculine) or sexual role (i.e., whether a man gives or receives anal sex; Manalansan 2003). Similarly, women with a more "masculine" appearance (e.g., clothing, hairstyle) are often referred to as "tomboys" rather than lesbian, although women who are "femme" may still be deemed heterosexual (Nadal 2011).

Most studies on the experiences of LGBT Filipinos focus primarily on gay men, some of whom may not even identify as gay (Tan 1995). For example, *parloristas* are seen as individuals who take on traditional female roles (e.g., working as a hair stylist in a beauty salon, dressing up as a drag queen, or serving as domestic help). Typically, parloristas are perceived as effeminate, flamboyant individuals who are often subjected to jokes and dehumanizing portrayals in the media. Second, call boys or male sex workers can engage in sex with both men and women. However, their sexual behavior is perceived as a consequence of the weak economic structure (i.e., underemployment) and social class landscape (i.e., high percentage of poverty) of the Philippines. Hence, it is perceived as a means to obtain monetary funds, not sexual enjoyment. Third, gay men perceived as "masculine" oftentimes are not open about their sexuality, which may be attributed to numerous factors including Catholicism, conservative family values, or the emphasis of *machismo* (i.e., Spanish term that emphasizes masculine behavior for men) in Filipino culture. In black and Latino communities, this is often referred to as being down-low; these men retain masculine-like behavior and physical appearances and reject a gay or bisexual identity despite their sexual activities with other men (Nadal 2010).

Literature involving the coming out process for gay men in the Philippines may highlight some cultural nuances regarding sexuality. One author has cited that Filipinos in the Philippines view coming out as unnecessary and somewhat excessive to accepting their sexuality (Manalansan 2003). A Filipino's gay sexuality is often understood, intuited, and not needed to be discussed by one's gay peers, friends, or family; in fact, "coming out" is often viewed as an unnecessary "American" trait that does not need to be declared (Manalansan 2003). Although Western cultures may perceive coming out as demonstrating self-acceptance and liberation (see Brady and Busse 1994), many Filipinos may feel it to be a superfluous and unnecessary process. However, there is a dearth of research to support that Filipino Americans in the United States feel similarly. Furthermore, although this literature involved the types of gay men and their coming out processes, there is little to no information about Filipina lesbians or Filipino transgender people. For example, a PsycINFO search on June 12, 2012, yielded only four articles using the keywords "Filipino" and "lesbian," and only one of those articles focused explicitly on Filipina lesbians (see Lipat et al. 1997); similarly using the keywords "Filipino" and "transgender" yielded only one article, which did focus entirely on Filipino transgender people (see Winter and Sass King 2008). Thus, it is unknown whether the previous research on gay Filipino men can be applied to lesbian or transgender Filipino Americans.

Although the previously mentioned cultural characteristics of LGBT Filipinos is essential to understanding identity development and its therapeutic implications, it can be hypothesized that LGBT Filipino Americans may not share the same experiences as their counterparts in the Philippines. In fact, LGBT Filipino Americans may interweave values and beliefs from both the Filipino culture and American culture, with each uniquely impacting the development of a Filipino American's sexual and gender identity. For example, the influence of the American culture may compel LGBT Filipino Americans to disclose their sexuality; asserting their liberty to disclose their sexual orientation may be seen as more optimal decision to make. Furthermore, perhaps Filipino Americans may subscribe to more fluid gender roles, in that they may feel they have more freedom to exercise either feminine or masculine roles or both.

Research Questions

The purpose of this research is to explore the experiences of lesbian, gay, and bisexual (LGB) Filipino Americans. We hypothesize that LGB Filipino Americans maintain unique experiences that differ from those of heterosexual Filipinos, non-Filipino LGB people, and LGB Filipinos in the Philippines. We focus on sexual orientation explicitly, as we believe that gender identity should be studied separately. Our research questions include the following:

1. How do LGB Filipino Americans feel about their intersections of their racial, ethnic, and sexual identities?
2. How do these identities impact the experiences of LGB Filipino Americans?

3. How do LGB Filipino Americans perceive their experiences to be similar or different to LGB Asian Americans, other LGB people of color, and LGB whites?

Method

The present study utilized a qualitative method to examine the experiences of lesbian, gay, and bisexual Filipino Americans. Four focus groups were conducted in New York and California, with one male and one female group for each region. Both men and women were included in order to capture the experiences of both groups and to notice similarities and differences based on gender. There were a total of twenty-four participants in the study altogether; fourteen participants were female and ten were male. One female participant identified as transgender male to female and partook in the female focus group. Because we did not want to exclude her from participating (which may be viewed as a microaggression), we invited her to stay. (We discuss this further in the limitations section.) All of the men identified as gay; twelve women identified as lesbian and two self-identified as "queer." The average age was thirty two years old for females ($SD = 5.7$) and twenty-eight for males ($SD = 5.3$). In all, nine participants were interviewed in California, fifteen in New York. Ten participants were second-generation Filipino American (born and raised in the United States), whereas fourteen were immigrants from the Philippines. The sample was also college educated, with the females averaging 17.2 years of education ($SD = 1.7$) and the males 16.6 years ($SD = 1.3$).

After receiving approval from the principal investigators' Institutional Review Boards, participants were recruited by email announcements that were sent through various Filipino American, Asian American, and LGBT listservs, which advertised for "Filipino Americans who identified as lesbian, gay, or bisexual." Interested participants contacted the principal investigators and were notified of a meeting time for the focus groups. Before beginning the session, all participants were informed that their responses would be confidential and secured; the focus groups lasted approximately an hour and a half. There were no incentives to participating. The principal investigators led the focus group of their same gender and asked a number of open-ended questions to elicit an open and honest dialogue about the participants' experiences. Sample questions included these:

1. How you feel about being both lesbian/gay/bisexual and Filipino American?
2. How have the intersections of both identities affected your daily life experiences?
3. What is it like to be a Filipino American in the larger LGBT community, and what is it like to be an LGBT person in the Filipino American community?

4. How might your experience differ from or be similar to heterosexual Filipino Americans? LGBT Asian Americans? LGBT black Americans? LGBT Hispanic/Latinos?

Four researchers participated in this study. The two principal investigators included one gay second-generation Filipino American male and one gay second-generation Filipina American female; the two other analysts included a gay second-generation Filipino American male and a gay Latino male. One of the principal investigators is a professor who has been trained extensively on qualitative research and has previously conducted and participated in several research projects utilizing the consensual qualitative research (CQR) method for both general and Filipino American populations. The other researchers were graduate students who had been trained in the CQR method as well. In order to analyze qualitative research neutrally, the researchers convened to discuss any potential biases, values, or assumptions that would be detrimental in the analysis of the data (Fassinger 2005; Hill, Thompson, and Williams 1997). For example, one bias was that we assumed participants would be able to openly discuss the nuances of being both Filipino and American; we also discussed how we presumed that there would be different perspectives based on gender. In admitting to our assumptions, we aimed to minimize the bias in our interviewing techniques and data analyses, as each researcher was given the task and responsibility of challenging himself or herself and the group in maintaining an impartial analysis.

The CQR methods (Hill et al. 2005; Hill, Thompson, and Williams 1997) were employed in analyzing the data. A three-person research analysis team reviewed all of the raw data independently and created domains based on general similarities in participants' answers. Next, these three analysts regrouped to share and consensually agree upon domains and to discuss core ideas. The team then independently created themes based on these core ideas. They then met again to agree upon the themes and examples that would best demonstrate the themes. A cross-analysis was conducted to ensure that the themes were present across all four focus groups. The analysts then submitted these domains and themes to an external auditor. The auditor, who is a self-identified gay Filipino American, independently reviewed the raw data and the team's collective analysis. Because the auditor worked separately, it was hoped that he would not be influenced by group dynamics (e.g., conformity, groupthink) and that he would be able to provide new insight about the group's analysis. The group reconvened one final time to incorporate the auditors' feedback, finalize themes, and choose the best sample quotes to demonstrate each theme.

The CQR method was used for many reasons. First, the method utilizes a "checks and balances" approach, in which all analysts must consensually agree on the data analysis, leading to an increased reliability and nonbiased investigation. Second, it has been effectively used with both LGBT people of color (e.g., Goode-Cross and Tager 2011) and Filipino Americans (e.g., Nadal et al. 2010). Finally, because the study was exploratory in nature without any specific hypotheses or existing models, the CQR method allowed the researchers to collect a broad range of data, which could then be systemically organized into domains and themes to capture the experiences of the population.

Results

The following sections delineate five domains that were gathered from the collective focus groups. These domains include (1) religious influence on sexual and gender identity, (2) family influence on gender and sexual identity, (3) experiences with race, (4) process of negotiating multiple identities, and (5) variant experiences between Filipino subgroups. Each domain also was also organized into several themes (see Table 11.1). Although traditional CQR approaches utilize "typical" and "variant" as descriptors to depict the quantity of responses for each theme, we chose not to label participants' responses as such, primarily due to our focus group methodology. For example, many times participants would share an opinion and all others in the group would silently smile and nod in agreement, which mostly likely would indicate shared

TABLE 11.1. Domains and Themes

Domain	Theme
1. Religious influence on sexual and gender identity	1. Religion as a major hindrance to coming out 2. Conflicting relationships with religious family members 3. Religious interventions 4. Guilt and shame
2. Family influence on gender and sexual identity	1. Denial and difficulty in family accepting lesbian, gay, or bisexual identity 2. Unspoken issues with sexual orientation 3. Filial piety 4. Gender role norms 5. Subtle messages about LGBTQ identity
3. Experiences with race	1. Differentiating in identifying as Asian and Filipino 2. Navigating through different communities 3. Stereotypes of exoticization 4. Race influencing gender roles
4. Process of negotiating multiple identities	1. Lack of support and knowledge from gay and ethnic 2. Prioritizing of reference groups 3. Conforming or stripping of race
5. Variant experiences between Filipino subgroups	1. Gender 2. Geography 3. Immigration status

experience. Thus, we measured consensus through our observations of group dynamics (e.g., head nods, facial expressions, verbal appraisals, body language, and laughter). However, with each domain, we noted when there were noticeable differences or a lack of shared experiences, particularly based on gender or immigration status.

Domain 1: Religious Influence on Sexual and Gender Identity

Religion emerged as a salient domain, particularly for male participants. As previously mentioned, Catholicism is culturally embedded in the Philippines, as majority of Filipino people are Catholics. Accordingly, there were several themes that materialized. The first theme, religion as a major hindrance to coming out, stemmed from the multiple narratives that suggested Catholicism impeded the assertion or expression of sexual identity. Many participants reported that their parents believe homosexuality is morally wrong according to their interpretation of the Catholic teachings. Participants (both immigrants and native-born) purported that the combination of being Filipino, gay, and Catholic were competing identities that could not be reconciled. One male stated,

> I grew up in a really Catholic home. We prayed four times a day, went to church at least two times a week. . . . And when I started to find out that I was gay or who I was, I pretended or tried to put the thoughts out of my mind. . . . I felt I couldn't be gay and Catholic at the same time.

Another group member expressed, "I think that religion really was a major hindrance, in me accepting myself earlier." These statements illuminate how participants attribute the challenges in their coming out process to the major role that Catholicism played in their upbringing.

The second theme, conflicting relationships with religious family members, was premised on the stories of family members who practiced Catholicism in a vigilant manner. Moreover, both male and female cohorts shared that their families would pray several times a day and attend church one to two times per week. This seems to contextualize the emotional reactions that they received from their parents. For example, one male participant shared, "We were talking about marriage. And then I said 'I don't think it's gonna happen . . . because I like guys.' They asked, 'Oh, can you explain that? What do you mean?' My mom was crying."

Numerous narratives also highlighted how participants' parents oftentimes considered being gay as aberrant or morally reprehensible. A male group member stated,

I grew up in a very religious household, my grandparents were very active in the church. I guess I didn't start questioning myself until I got here in America. It's my relatives and my mom who tells me that it's wrong to be gay.

The opposition to homosexuality was clearly based upon religious mores and caused conflict between the gay individuals and their families.

The religious overtones in Filipino households have prompted occasions of a third theme: religious interventions. Participants revealed disparate accounts of how religion was utilized (by either oneself or one's family) to dispel feelings of homosexuality. One male participant shared, "I didn't accept it. I thought it was weird and I don't know. . . . My first approach was to go to religion and became religious." Contrary to self-imposing Catholicism to shed feelings of same-sex attraction, other participants shared that family members tried to employ religious-based interventions. One male participant disclosed,

I started coming out to cousins, female cousins, not male cousins . . . but then about last year, all my cousins wanted to have a family intervention. It became religious in scope. I think that the hardest blocks to coming out was the religious aspect.

Similarly, a female participant shared that when she mentioned to her family that she was dating a woman, her mother frequently instructed her to read Bible verses from the book of Leviticus.

The final theme subsumed under religion, guilt and shame, is anchored in the participants' perception that religion has been a major function of their inability to uphold a healthy conception of being gay. Some focus group members contend that religion has adversely impacted their sexual identity development. "You feel guilty for feeling this. And I thought that when I was seventeen . . . and now [I'm] slowly getting over that . . . that you should be ashamed of this or that." In addition, there are others who shared being liberated after turning away from religion. One male participant proclaimed, "I don't have any shame or guilt . . . anymore. . . . That's because I made sure, I broke my faith with the Catholic faith."

Domain 2: Family Influence on Gender and Sexual Identity

In addition to religion as a central aspect of the Filipino culture, family plays an equally critical role. Family seemed to be considered central to participants' identities, underscoring that collectivism trumps individualism. A number of participants revealed how challenging it was for their parents to accept their sexual identity, particularly because they perceived their parents as being more conservative or less acculturated. The first theme, denial and difficulty in family accepting lesbian, gay, or bisexual identity, seemed paramount among all stories concerning family. Participants shared a few humorous, but emotionally evocative stories that alluded to their parents' denial of their sexual identity. One female participant jokingly shared,

> When I was in my twenties, I felt like I had to come out to my mother like several times before she realized I was gay. . . . And I would just be like "I really have something to tell you" in college and I'd tell her and she'd cry and the next day she would ask me. . . . And then I would just be like, "Mom I have to come out to you again!" and then after four or five years, I'm still coming out to my parents.

Another male participant shared,

> I always thought for the longest time that it was important for me to tell my parents, to come out, but it took me several tries to tell my mom. She just kind of hushed it. . . . [One time] my heart was pounding. . . . Here it is, here's the opportunity, and she said "My blood pressure is going up. We better go home, we can't talk anymore." So I knew then that the opportunity was shot down, and I felt there's no need to tell them. It's not that I didn't try, but they chose not to listen.

The second theme, unspoken issues with sexual orientation, was also pervasive throughout male and female focus groups. The majority of participants shared that they did not have the luxury of openly communicating about their sexual identity with their parents. There seemed to be a cultural nuance of silence among Filipinos; they do not create conflict among the family by talking about one's sexual orientation and the experiences that coincide (i.e., dating or reactions to discrimination). One male participant revealed,

> Being gay and Filipino in [the] Filipino community or in my family was really difficult because it put a huge block between me and my parents and our relationship. . . . It's the fear of who I was and the fact that I couldn't open myself up to them. That caused me to hold a lot of secrets from them. And that was our biggest problem.

Some participants assumed their families had suspicions of their sexualities, but chose to remain silent about it; for example, one male participant disclosed,

> If I go home, I don't mention anything. Even in the household, everything is not spoken. And if they do find out, because there are some cousins that know, they usually give me hints, I just ignore or let it pass. But I'm ready if everyone knows, or if *tsismis* [gossip] spreads really fast. I'm sure everyone knows but they don't say anything, out of respect.

Thus, participants' narratives revealed that parents have often silenced their children indirectly, through either denial or lack of acknowledgment. Participants appeared to mirror this behavior as well, masking their sexual identity when they were in the company of their family. Although silence has been argued as being a cultural value among Asian Americans in general (Chae and Chae 2010), silence and conflict avoidance may help LGBT Asian Americans in navigating their sexual identities with their cultural and ethnic identities (Chan 1989; Nadal 2010).

This third theme of filial piety resonates with the majority of the male and female participants. The fact that most participants are reticent about their lives concerning their sexual identity may stem from the cultural norm of *utang ng loob* (debt or reciprocity). Utang ng loob, or filial piety, in the Filipino culture connotes a sense of pleasing others (particularly one's parents) and putting others' needs before one's own (Nadal 2011). Moreover, coming out to one's family or other Filipinos may shame the family, which can result in jeopardizing one's connectedness to the family. One female participant shared,

> Filipinos are the last people I would tell that I was a lesbian and that's the way that it's come about because of not wanting to be separated from my family. It's sort of like . . . it's all about family ultimately. You want to be as close to your family as possible and I'm not saying that I didn't tell them, because I did, but I would never tell my grandparents.

A male participant articulated how he also puts his family first before his feelings:

> You can't come out because you'll shame the family. It's all about them. Well what about me? [laughter] Who cares what people say? That still happens now. That's what I'm talking about . . . walking on eggshells.

Thus, the data illuminate that many participants have sacrificed their need to self-express or to be heard because they do not want to shame their family or feel disconnected from them.

Gender role norms, the fourth theme, were evident among both the male and female cohorts. Although the type of messages they received from their family may have slightly differed between sexes, the stories shared similar meanings. Families imparted that gender roles are stringently defined within the Filipino culture. A male participant shared,

> I just kind of did my normal thing . . . hang out with girls. . . . I didn't think anything was wrong with it until an outsider would say something . . . like my grandparents would say "Why are you hanging out with the girls and not with the boys?"

In addition to the message that it was not proper to associate with the opposite sex, participants' narratives also illustrated that families often reprimanded them for gender-variant mannerisms or style of dress. Male group members frequently talked about how their parents corrected their body movement. One participant shared, "[Family members would say] 'Stop moving this way or stop sitting like that or don't cross your legs.' Womanly traits, or whatever. But I [was] always told not to act like that, but I didn't really care."

Male participants shared how they were encouraged to uphold the value of machismo, in which men are taught to be dominant and masculine. One male participant stated,

> I've gravitated toward the women, but my uncles always want me to be more manly. So the gender roles that were defined for me were . . . kind of blurry for me. Because the women were a lot nicer and I wanted to be like them . . . the guys in my family were always really guys, and they always wanted me to be like them. I never really liked being macho, I always thought it was dumb. I really struggle with that even today.

Women in the focus groups also seemed to struggle with the messages they received about gender. However, their stories were primarily associated with styles of physical appearance or dress. For example, one woman stated how her mother, even in adulthood, would constantly encourage her to wear skirts. Meanwhile, a different female participant shared,

> I go back [home] pretty regularly and decided to go back with my head shaved. And my grandfather could not like . . . he was really . . . he was . . . um my grandfather was never ever mean to me in my life and he could not he . . . he could not even look at me.

The last theme we identified, subtle messages about LGBTQ identity, illustrates the positive and negative messages they received about their sexual identity. A few men pointed out how gay men are often perceived as funny or "entertainers" by both loved ones and in the Philippine media. One male participant stated, "They want to laugh at us," while another male participant affirmed, "Maybe it's for entertainment purposes. Something funny, not threatening, nothing sexual." However, a few attendees (particularly females) shared that their parents eventually accepted their sexual identity in a subtle way. A female participant recounted,

> We have another best friend down in San Diego . . . it's us three and they refer to us as "brodders" [that is, brothers pronounced with a Filipino accent]. . . . We go to each other's family parties and our parents are like totally proud of who we

are. . . . They don't feel ashamed of us. . . . I think as time goes by, they accept it more.

One female participant stated,

> He'll say things like "Hey Magic, how are you doing?" And you know "Magic" is a slang word for butch in the Philippines . . . it's like he's calling me a queer slang name but doing it in an affectionate way.

Through these subtle terms of humor and endearment, participants are able to feel love from her parents. Although it may not be a direct communication about acceptance, participants reported that these types of messages were sufficient or positive.

Domain 3: Experiences with Race

Because of the uniqueness of Filipino culture, participants seemed to have various race-related experiences. The first theme, differentiating in identifying as Asian and Filipino, demonstrates how numerous group members identified more strongly with their ethnic identification as Filipino rather than their racial classification as Asian. A female participant articulated, "I don't feel like I can relate to other Asian American cultures as much as I can feel like I can relate to, like, the Mexican culture." Furthermore, another female participant recounted her experiences of feeling omitted from the discourse on race. She stated,

> We grew up in places where it's a dichotomy . . . black or white and they think separate [of] Asian, but when you grow older you think Filipinos aren't Asian-Asian: most people think of East Asians. . . . I don't know . . . I see a lot of Hispanic Latin influences.

This was also supported by a male participant who emphasized the vast within-group diversity among Asians. He remarked, "People lump Asian together for everything. And I talk about it with my friends from different parts of Asia. Every country is so different in how [sexuality] is handled." There was a notable consensus surrounding this issue; the majority of participants felt a lack of cultural commonalities with the Asian racial group. Therefore, it appeared that the majority of group members held an allegiance to their ethnic identity as Filipinos.

Despite the focus groups' consensus regarding their strong ethnic identification, they shared a diversity of experiences while navigating through different communities. This theme captured the fact that participants encounter a host of experiences that suggest fluidity between various racial communities. More-over, participants felt as if they could relate to other racial groups because their perception of the Filipino culture is eclectic, drawing from cultural values, tradi-tions, and beliefs of other racial communities. One male participant shared, "Fit me in the black community, no problem. Fit me in the Latino community, no problem. Fit me in [the] white [community], no problem. I feel we're, like, so universal out of all of gay men." Another female participant contends solidarity with other people of color:

> I think it's easier for me to bond with, I guess like, I have a lot of black friends and a lot of Latin friends but I guess when it comes to having white friends I definitely don't have that many.

Although participants asserted that they have positive experiences with other racial groups, there are several group members who revealed negative experi-ences as well. Most of their narratives touched on issues with a third theme, stereotypes of exoticization. Both male and female participants expressed being deemed exotic. One male participant affirmed, "There's this exoticiza-tion of Asian males or Filipino males . . . like we're going to be oversexual or kinky or fulfill some of your needs." However, another participant shared that exoticization applied to all people of color. "I think the similarities with Filipinos and APIs, Latinos, and African Americans . . . in terms of how we are marketed. We're all kind of exoticized." Microaggressions involving exoti-cization have been reported by Asian American women in general (Sue et al. 2009) and Filipino American women specifically (Nadal et al. 2012), but appar-ently are also encountered by gay Asian American (and gay Filipino American) men.

The fourth theme identified within this domain, race influencing gender roles, highlights the gender attributions in the LGBT community associated with the Asian race. The male participants seemed to contend with rigid gen-der roles imposed upon them, particularly the notion of being submissive. One male participant shared, "We're viewed as subordinate. We're viewed as we have no voice. We're viewed as bottoms mostly. And that's something we have to deal with when we go out to the mainstream." Another male participant asserted, "With the APIs and Filipinos, a lot of us aren't seen as male as the other . . . eth-nicities. We're not as male as the Latinos [or] Chicanos, we're not as masculine as the African Americans. We're more feminized." Although feeling demasculin-ized was reported by Filipino American men in a previous study (Nadal et al. 2012), the male participants in this study reported feeling angry, frustrated, and bitter because of the messages they have heard that Asians are undesirable in the LGBT community. This experience was not pervasively reported among the female participants.

Domain 4: Process of Negotiating Multiple Identities

The fourth domain, process of negotiating identities, underscores the complexity of belonging to multiple minority statuses. Lack of support and knowledge from gay and ethnic communities was abundantly apparent among all participants. One male participant asserted,

> It's kind of like living two lives for some reason. Like, if I'm out on my own, with my friends at work, anywhere else from my house or relatives, I'm free. As soon as I step into that realm of family, I feel like I'm walking on eggshells . . . because I feel like I'm not complete with myself, my being, my whole sexuality.

It is evident that some participants do not have the liberty to share this part of their lives with their family members. Other participants spoke about their experiences with white LGBT people. A female participant shared,

> I just felt really, like, isolated and tokenized and kind of not really fully comfortable ever because there wasn't really people that looked like me at all really. . . . And, like, you'd find a queer person but they'd be white so it was different.

As a consequence of having multiple minority statuses, it was evident that most participants had to pick and choose which reference group (i.e., race/ethnicity, sexual orientation, or gender) was most salient for them. A woman stated, "They're very separate issues to be Filipino American and a queer woman . . . I still struggle with even trying to integrate them." Certain contexts (e.g., school, workplace, or community) call for prioritizing because many participants often felt that one of their identities was not acknowledged or accepted.

The second theme, prioritizing of reference groups, encapsulates the experiences of the majority of focus group members. Some participants expressed frustration when needing to constantly shift identities. One female participant shared,

> I always felt like I had to choose one or the other like I'm queer in these spaces and I'm *pinay* [Filipina] in these spaces and so it was kind of hard in navigating that and finding spaces where I could be both and finding people that would understand me in both ways.

Participants also conceded feelings regarding a third theme, conforming or stripping of race to fit into the LGBTQ community. One male participant articulated,

> It just seems like we as Filipinos and people of color haven't been incorporated into this grand master scheme of what it means to be gay or queer. So when I first came out, I stripped myself of the color so that I could fit in.

In addition, another male participant stated, "The majority of us are trying to navigate what it does mean to be Filipino and gay, where is the intersect, that we can define our sexuality . . . our identity. . . . It feels like a constant fight." It appeared that most participants experienced struggles with integrating their multiple identities.

Domain 5: Variant Experiences between Filipino Subgroups

There were several different experiences that seemed to occur between different Filipino subgroups (e.g., gender, geography, immigration status). These distinctions were consensually agreed upon by the analysts. As mentioned earlier, there were three distinct differences based on gender: (1) the higher prevalence of religious influences for men, (2) the different types of family gender role expectations for men and women, and (3) the experiences of racially based gender roles for men. It seemed that many of the male participants were encouraged by their parents to be priests or get married, although the female participants were not encouraged to become nuns.

Second, it seemed that geography had an influence on one's experiences. Participants who lived in self-described "liberal environments" seemed to have an easier time in grappling with their identities. One female participant shared,

> I came out way after college . . . I went to high school in the Philippines and college [in Hawaii] . . . so being that close to home and that close to the culture, there was no way for me to come out. I needed to get out of that box.

When one perceives the environment to be conservative, one may have difficulty in fully accepting or disclosing one's LGBT identity, and vice versa.

Immigration status had an influence on one's experiences. Participants who immigrated discussed messages that they learned in the Philippines and how those might differ in the United States. One male participant revealed,

> What I observed is that back home, there are more rigid definitions of what it means to be gay and lesbian, versus in the United States, there's more flexibility. You have to fit into a caricature back home, versus here it's not unfathomable to be a guy and gay or femme and gay. And same thing with being lesbian, you can be perceived as being a woman and feminine and lesbian and you don't have to fit the stereotype that you're butch or tomboy if you're lesbian.

Another male participant added,

> When I was growing up in the Philippines, all I really knew about being gay was being really feminine, looking like a woman, acting like a woman, dressing like

one. I had an uncle who was "super gay." [laughter] He was basically a hairdresser, wore women's clothes, makeup, acted like a woman. . . . So in my mind, I always thought that was being gay.

The synonymous images of gay male and transgender match the aforementioned "bakla" and "tomboy" spectrums that conflate sexual orientation and gender. However, although Filipino Americans may still have cultural influences that teach them about their gay identity, they also learn Western, American ideals that impact their experiences as well.

Discussion

The primary purpose of this study was to understand the experiences of lesbian and gay Filipino Americans. First, it appears that through the intersection of race, ethnicity, gender, and sexual orientation, LGB Filipino Americans have a number of experiences that have not been fully described in the literature. Participants revealed their needs to hide themselves from their families; they described the racial stressors or lack of full acceptance in the LGB community; and they reported feelings of depression, anger, and frustration. The constant battle with conflicting messages may lead to psychological distress and other mental health issues, including internalized homophobia, depression, and low self-esteem. Second, contrary to the research that has been conducted on gay males in the Philippines, this study demonstrates that LGB Filipino Americans in the United States may have experiences that vary. Although rigid notions of "baklas" and "tomboys" are prevalent in the Philippines, LGB Filipino Americans learn to balance identities, deal with racism and stereotypes in the United States, maintain both Filipino and American cultural values, and navigate gender roles in ways than what has been previously described.

Results also indicate that religion, family, and gender role expectations all contribute to the psychological distress of LGB Filipino Americans. Participants, particularly males, described how Catholicism was a principal influence in their families' lives, which often led to the inability for their families to accept their sexual identities. Furthermore, cultural values and family dynamics also affected individuals' abilities to come out to their families and their opportunities to be honest about their romantic relationships with family members. Finally, culture seemed to play a huge role in gender role construction; although male participants were given strong messages about acceptable masculine behaviors, women were reinforced with lessons about dress and appearance.

Finally, the issue of race brought up unique types of racial discrimination for Filipino Americans that has not been addressed in previous literature. Previous studies have found that, in general, Filipino Americans are likely to experience higher incidents of racial discrimination than East Asian Americans (Alvarez,

Juang, and Liang 2006), and that they may experience similar types of racial discrimination as black or Latino populations (Nadal et al. 2012). However, our participants, particularly males, reported they are grouped into a larger Asian category and are stereotyped to be exotic and passive. This experience speaks to the notion of dual identities and yields two major implications. First, having an LGB identity impacts racial identity (and vice versa). Second, experiences of oppression are felt most by the conflict between identities, in that participants reported feeling discrimination within both communities. For instance, racism was felt most by whites in the LGB community, although homophobia was felt most by individuals' heterosexual families and Filipino American communities. So although these LGB Filipino Americans may experience similar types of racism as their heterosexual counterparts, it appeared to not be their most pervasive form of discrimination.

Further research may investigate how multiple identities impact experiences with racism, sexism, homophobia, and other forms of discrimination. Furthermore, both qualitative and quantitative research may examine how discrimination may influence other variables for LGB Filipino Americans, such as mental health, self-efficacy, and physical health. Finally, studies that focus on bisexual, transgender, or gender nonconforming Filipino Americans can be essential in capturing the full experience of the LGBT Filipino American community, and studies that focus on other LGBT Asian American ethnic groups (e.g., Vietnamese, Asian Indians) can reveal the spectrum of LGBT experiences in the Asian American community.

Implications for Asian American Psychology

There are several implications for Asian American psychology. First, it is important to recognize that much like other LGB individuals, LGB Filipino Americans do need extensive outreach, education, and support to demonstrate acceptance of their LGB identities. As evidenced through this study, one can recognize the influence of race and ethnicity on sexual identity, calling for the need for psychologists to be more culturally competent with this population. Given the cultural mistrust that Filipino Americans experience in psychotherapy (David 2010), as well as the dissatisfaction with psychotherapy that is experienced by LGB clients in general (Liddle 1996) and LGB people of color (Avery, Hellman, and Sudderth 2001), clinicians must be aware of the myriad of factors that may impede LGBT Filipino Americans' ability to seek support (e.g., family shame or religious guilt). Participants who felt the most supported were those who belonged to communities or organizations that celebrated both their ethnic and sexual identities. Accordingly, psychologists must provide spaces, resources, and funding for such environments. More specifically, because many participants described feelings of depression, anxiety, and low self-esteem as a result of balancing their multiple identities, it is necessary for clinicians to provide opportunities for clients to dispute irrational beliefs, particularly those involving internalized homophobia and internalized racism.

This study demonstrates the importance of looking at intersectional identities, particularly in the field of Asian American psychology. Participants shared that they often have to choose one identity or the other, often feeling like an outsider by other Filipinos and other LGBT persons. Dominant group members must recognize their privileges and biases toward marginalized groups. For heterosexual Asian Americans, it is necessary to acknowledge the heterosexism that occurs in the community, whereas LGBT white persons must be conscious of the racism that affects LGBT people of color. In doing so, one can attempt to give voice and empowerment to dual minority groups like LGBT Filipino Americans.

Limitations

Although the results provide insight in understanding the experiences and psychological processes of LGB Filipino Americans, it is necessary to identify the limitations of the current study. First, we recognize that the sample represents only a small portion of the LGBT Filipino American population, in that it was small ($N = 24$) and included only one transgender participant. Although the transgender participant shared similar sentiments as the others regarding cultural conflicts, family pressures, and discrimination, she did not have the opportunity to describe her experiences related to gender identity; thus, the findings did not capture the transgender Filipino American experience. Furthermore, because the sample consisted mostly of educated adults in their late twenties and early thirties, who were from more liberal geographic locations (i.e., New York and California), who had access to Filipino American listservs, and who were all "out" with their sexual identities, it may not be reflective of LGBT Filipino Americans, particularly youth discovering their identities. Another major limitation is the potential for researcher bias during data analyses. Although we tried to control for bias by discussing them at the beginning of the study, our own perceptions, assumptions, and experiences may have influenced the analyses when identifying particular domains and themes for each example. Finally, as in any focus group study, participants may have been influenced by group dynamics (e.g., social desirability, conformity, or groupthink). Future studies could utilize individual interviews in order to capture participants' lived experiences in more unbiased ways. Despite these limitations, results from the study offer many implications for the field of Asian American psychology and clinical practice that may be useful in conducting more research this population, as well as providing culturally competent services for LGBT Filipino Americans.

NOTE

Originally published in *Asian American Journal of Psychology* 4 (3): 166–175, 2013. ©2013 *Asian American Journal of Psychology*, reprint by permission.

REFERENCES

Alvarez, A. N., L. Juang, and C. T. H. Liang. 2006. "Asian Americans and Racism: When Bad Things Happen to 'Model Minorities.'" *Cultural Diversity and Ethnic Minority Psychology* 12: 477–492. doi:10.1037/1099-9809.12.3.477.

Avery, A. M., R. E. Hellman, and L. K. Sudderth. 2001. "Satisfaction with Mental Health Services among Sexual Minorities with Major Mental Illness." *American Journal of Public Health* 91: 990–991. doi:10.2105/AJPH.91.6.990.

Barnes, J. S., and C. E. Bennett. 2002. "The Asian Population, 2000. U.S. Census Brief." http://www.census.gov.

Brady, S., and W. J. Busse. 1994. "The Gay Identity Questionnaire: A Brief Measure of Homosexual Identity Formation." *Journal of Homosexuality* 26: 1–22. doi:10.1300/J082v26n04_01.

Chae, M. H., and S. Y. Chae. 2010. "Asian American Men and Fatherhood: An Ecological Systems Perspective." Pp. 109–126 in W. M. Liu, D. K. Iwamoto, and M. H. Chae, eds., *Culturally Responsive Counseling with Asian American Men*. New York: Routledge.

Chan, C. 1989. "Issues of Identity Development among Asian-American Lesbians and Gay Men." *Journal of Counseling and Development* 68: 16–20. doi:10.1002/j.1556-6676.1989.tb02485.x.

Chung, Y. B., and A. Singh. 2009. "Lesbian, Gay, Bisexual, and Transgender Asian Americans." Pp. 233–246 in N. Tewari and A. N. Alvarez, eds., *Asian American Psychology: Current Perspectives*. New York: Taylor & Francis.

Chung, Y. B., and D. M. Szymanski. 2006. "Racial and Sexual Identities of Asian American Gay Men." *Journal of LGBT Issues in Counseling* 1: 67–93. doi:10.1300/J462v01n02_05.

David, E. J. R. 2010. "Cultural Mistrust and Mental Health Help-Seeking Attitudes among Filipino Americans." *Asian American Journal of Psychology* 1: 57–66. doi:10.1037/a0018814.

Espiritu, Y. L. 1992. *Asian American Panethnicity: Bridging Institutions and Identities*. Philadelphia: Temple University Press.

Fassinger, R. E. 2005. "Paradigms, Praxis, Problems, and Promise: Grounded Theory in Counseling Psychology Research." *Journal of Counseling Psychology* 52: 156–166. doi:10.1037/0022-0167.52.2.156.

Goode-Cross, D. T., and D. Tager. 2011. "Negotiating Multiple Identities: How African-American Gay and Bisexual Men Persist at a Predominantly White Institution." *Journal of Homosexuality* 58: 1235–1254. doi:10.1080/00918369.2011.605736.

Hill, C. E., S. Knox, B. J. Thompson, E. N. Williams, S. A. Hess, and N. Ladany. 2005. "Consensual Qualitative Research: An Update." *Journal of Counseling Psychology* 52: 196–205. doi:10.1037/0022-0167.52.2.196.

Hill, C. E., B. J. Thompson, and E. N. Williams. 1997. "A Guide to Conducting Consensual Qualitative Research." *Counseling Psychologist* 25: 517–572. doi:10.1177/0011000097254001.

Horn, L. 1995. "Minority Undergraduate Population in Postsecondary Education." National Center for Education Statistics Report 95–166. Washington, DC: US Department of Education.

Kim, B. S. K., P. H. Yang, D. R. Atkinson, M. M. Wolfe, and S. Hong. 2001. "Cultural Value Similarities and Differences among Asian American Ethnic Groups." *Cultural Diversity and Ethnic Minority Psychology* 7: 343–361. doi:10.1037/1099-9809.7.4.343.

Kimmel, D. C., and H. Yi. 2004. "Characteristics of Gay, Lesbian, and Bisexual Asians, Asian Americans, and Immigrants from Asia to the USA." *Journal of Homosexuality* 47: 143–171. doi:10.1300/J082v47n02_09.

Liddle, B. J. 1996. "Therapist Sexual Orientation, Gender, and Counseling Practices as They Relate to Ratings of Helpfulness by Gay and Lesbian Clients." *Journal of Counseling Psychology* 43: 394–401. doi:10.1037/ 0022–0167.43.4.394.

Lipat, C. T., T. A. Ordona, C. Pamintuan Stewart, and M. A. Ubaldo. 1997. "Tomboy, Dyke, Lezzie, and Bi: Filipina Lesbian and Bisexual Women Speak Out." Pp. 230–246 in M. P. P. Root, ed., *Filipino Americans: Transformation and Identity*. Thousand Oaks, CA: Sage. doi:10.4135/9781452243177.n16.

Manalansan, M. F. 2003. *Global Divas: Filipino Gay Men in the Diaspora*. Durham, NC: Duke University Press.

Maramba, D. C. 2008. "Immigrant Families and the College Experience: Perspectives of Filipina Americans." *Journal of College Student Development* 49: 336–350. doi:10.1353/csd.0.0012.

Nadal, K. L. 2004. "Filipino American Identity Development Model." *Journal of Multicultural Counseling and Development* 32: 44–61.

———. 2010. "Sexual Orientation and Identity Development for Gay and Bisexual Asian American Men: Implications for Culturally Competent Counseling." Pp. 113–134 in W. Liu, D. Iwamoto, and M. Chae, eds., *Culturally Responsive Counseling with Asian American Men*. New York: Routledge.

———. 2011. *Filipino American Psychology: A Handbook of Theory, Research, and Clinical Practice*. New York: John Wiley. doi:10.1002/9781118094747.

Nadal, K. L., K. M. Escobar, G. Prado, E. J. R. David, and K. Haynes. 2012. "Racial microaggressions and the Filipino American Experience: Recommendations for Counseling and Development." *Journal of Multicultural Counseling and Development* 40: 156–173. doi:10.1002/j.2161–1912.2012.00015.x.

Nadal, K. L., S. T. Pituc, M. P. Johnston, and T. Esparrago. 2010. "Overcoming the Model Minority Myth: Experiences of Filipino American Graduate Students." *Journal of College Student Development* 51: 1–13.

Sue, D. W., J. M. Bucceri, A. I. Lin, K. L. Nadal, and G. C. Torino. 2009. "Racial Microaggressions and the Asian American Experience." *Asian American Journal of Psychology* 1: 88–101. doi:10.1037/1948–1985.S.1.88.

Tan, M. L. 1995. "From Bakla to Gay: Shifting Gender Identities and Sexual Behaviors in the Philippines." Pp. 85–96 in R. G. Parker and J. H. Gagnon, eds., *Conceiving Sexuality: Approaches to Sex Research in a Postmodern World*. New York: Routledge.

Trevino, F. M. 1987. "Standardized Terminology for Hispanic Populations." *American Journal of Public Health* 77: 69–72. doi:10.2105/AJPH.77.1.69.

Winter, S. R. S., and M. Sass King. 2008. "Transgendered Women of the Philippines." *International Journal of Transgenderism* 10: 79–90.

12

No Fats, Femmes, or Asians

The Utility of Critical Race Theory in Examining the Role of Gay Stock Stories in the Marginalization of Gay Asian Men

C. WINTER HAN

Several years ago, a prominent gay and lesbian organization released a poster as part of a national campaign to raise awareness of gay issues. Minimalist in design, the poster featured the innocent image of a toddler with text that was both foreboding and promising. "We'll be here," it told us, "when his parents kick him out." The subtext, of course, the one "we" are supposed to understand, was that in the event that the toddler's parents reject him because of his sexuality, "we" will be there to provide the support that he will need. The name of the organization that released this poster is not really important, as posters with similar messages continue to grace the lobbies of many gay organizations, adorn the walls of many gay businesses, and find their way into numerous gay publications. What is important is the message that they convey: gay men and women often live under the weight of the very real possibility that their sexual and emotional attractions to members of the same sex put them in the unenviable position of being rejected by their family and friends. Given this tangible threat, there is a critical need for the gay community to address that threat head-on. As such, the "we" in the poster is not the organization per se, but the collective "we" of the gay community, the collective "we" that should be, and must be, responsible for the welfare of all of "our" members. More important, this poster, and all those like it, is part of the larger stock stories told within the gay community.

The stock stories tell us that gays and lesbians, because they are members of an oppressed group, are incapable of oppressing others. As such, these stories paint a portrait of an inviting gay community where all people, regardless of color, are welcomed with open arms.

However, the counterstories told by gay men and women of color portray a gay community that is largely white and middle-class where people of color are relegated to the margins. From these stories, we learn that rather than a welcoming environment that might be expected based on what gay white people say, and perhaps even believe, gay people of color often confront racism and racial hierarchies that mirror the mainstream. As such, these counterstories "cast doubt on the validity of accepted premise or myths, especially ones held by the majority"

(Delgado and Stefancic 2001, 144). While the majority of gay white men and women may believe that the gay community is accepting of racial minorities and that gay is not simply "white," counterstories told by gay men and women of color challenge these beliefs by exposing the racism that is still prevalent in the gay community.

In this essay, I use the critical race theory perspective to highlight narratives written by gay white men and by gay men of Asian decent living in Western countries in order to challenge the welcoming image of the larger gay community that is dominated by white men and women. I do this by (1) examining the gay stock stories about race, (2) examining the stock stories specifically about gay Asian men, (3) examining the counterstories told by gay Asian men, (4) examining the responses to the gay Asian counterstories by gay white men, and (5) examining the influence that the stock stories have on gay Asian men's well-being. Doing so, I not only expose the subtle forms of racism that exist within the larger gay community toward gay Asian men and, by extension, all people of color, but also show that such subtle acts of racism can lead to dire negative consequences for nonwhite gay men.

A Critical Race Theory Primer

Developed in the mid-1970s, critical race theory (CRT) was a response to what many legal scholars of color believed was a failure of critical legal studies (CLS) to address the issues of race and racism. Despite the goal of CLS to address the fallacy of an American meritocracy, many legal scholars of color believed that CLS failed to address how race and racial oppression were embedded into the larger social structure.

Rather than view racism as isolated or rare incidents, proponents of CRT believed that racism was, and continues to be, a "fact of daily life in American society" (Taylor 1998, 122). Certainly, isolated incidents of gross racism catch our attention, get played out in the media, and lead us to question the racial order. Yet from a CRT perspective, the everyday experiences of racism faced by men and women of color go largely ignored.

So ingrained is the racial social order and so immune are we from seeing it in its everyday apparition that only acts of gross indignities, such as the 1998 murder of James Byrd in Jasper, Texas, by three white men who dragged him for over three miles behind a pickup truck, reach the collective consciousness of the nation. When such events enter the public consciousness, they are often dismissed as the acts of racist lunatics. However, from a CRT perspective, these "shocking" incidents are simply a part of the everyday experiences, albeit taken to their extreme fringes, of people of color. In fact, given the invisibility of racism in the white imagination, the same incidents are often interpreted differently by white and black America. For example, while the 1991 beating of Rodney King by

four Los Angeles police officers was viewed by most white Americans as an isolated incident perpetrated by rogue police officers on a "drug-addicted criminal,"
it was seen by the majority of black Americans as representative of police abuse
that occurs on a daily basis in black communities.

Rather than seeing racism as a collection of isolated acts by individual perpetrators that are the result of individual bigotry and prejudice, early pioneers
of CRT believed that there was a need to view racism as ingrained in the social
structure of American life that influences the daily lives of men and women of
color (Bell 1992; Delgado 1989). As such, one of the primary goals of CRT is to
examine the everyday lives of men and women of color to show precisely how
ingrained race and racism are to our everyday experiences.

Given this tendency to examine the everyday experiences of men and women
of color, one of the central tenets of CRT is to examine the counterstories told
by men and women of color (Matsuda 1995). A means of exposing the deeply
ingrained racism in American society, "counter stories allow for the challenging of privileged discourse, the discourse of the majority, therefore, serving as a
means for giving voice to marginalized groups" (DeCuir and Dixson 2004, 27).
The idea is that the majority creates a reality through stock stories. Through these
stock stories, the majority attempts to create a color-blind society where racism
and bigotry are largely eradicated (Bonilla-Silva 2001). In addition, people of
color tell a counterstory. In these counterstories, incidents of racism, both small
and large, that occur on a daily basis are constantly exposed. As such, the alternative perspective can be seen in counterstories that are told by marginalized
groups. Rather than simply anecdotal accounts of minority experiences, counterstories organize minority experiences into "temporally meaningful episodes" that
organize the everyday experiences of people of color, thereby giving meaning to
their collective experiences (Richardson 1990, 118). By doing so, counterstories
expose the continuing influence of race and racism on their daily lives.

Critical Race Theory and Sociology

As Aguirre (2000, 322) points out, storytelling is often suspect in sociology, given
scholars' collective tendency to define our "relationship to persons, objects, and
events as empirical statements about social phenomena." However, as he also
eloquently notes, storytelling has always been present in sociological research,
whether it be through case histories, personal interviews, content analysis, historical texts, or ethnographic fieldwork. More difficult to overcome than our
suspicions about storytelling may be our tendency to rely on empirical research
that utilizes random sampling methods and tests hypothesis in order to make
statements about society.

Yet, from a CRT perspective, there is less concern for sampling because race
and racism are believed to permeate every aspect of our lives. Because race

and racism do permeate every aspect of our lives, counterstories can be found anywhere. Rather than being used to test hypothesis, counterstories can help "us begin to see life through the eyes of the outsider" (Delgado 1990, 109). By bringing personal experiences to the forefront, "CRT stories instruct sociologists about the minority's social reality, especially such issues as oppression and victimization, that is often ignored in traditional sociological research" (Aguirre 2000, 322). As such, the goals of CRT are twofold. First is to expose the stock stories and the hidden assumptions that they contain about race and racism. In addition, we must also examine the counterstories told by marginalized groups and bring them to the forefront.

As Agger (1991, 127) noted about critical theory, poststructuralism, and postmodernism, utilizing CRT in sociology will require us to "rethink the prevailing definition of what counts as sociology." At the same time, much of what he wrote about those three perspectives can also be noted about CRT, specifically that we "stand to gain an enriched perspective on the literary and substantive practice" of our own discipline.

This chapter uses stories from a variety of sources selected for the representativeness of the type of stories that are told in different arenas. For the first section examining the gay stock stories about race and racial inclusion, I use the June 2006 "Pride" issue of the *Advocate*, the "national gay and lesbian newsmagazine," to examine the stock stories told within the gay media and, by extension, the gay community. I chose this particular special issue for two reasons. First, the *Advocate* is the largest and most respected gay publication in the country. As such, its influence is national rather than local, which is common for the vast majority of publications targeting a gay audience. More important, I chose the special "Pride" issue precisely because it is an annual attempt by the publication to answer the question, "what is gay?" So rather than including features about gay celebrities (or straight celebrities with a large gay following) or report on specific issues affecting the gay community, the special "Pride" issue attempts to paint a textual and visual image of what they believe is the gay community.

I then examine the stock stories specifically about gay Asian men. To do so, I chose a special issue of *Frontiers Newsmagazine* from 2001 because it is the only mainstream "gay" magazine that I was able to find that featured a special issue on gay and lesbian Asian Pacific Islander Americans. While there has been, and continues to be, specialty gay publications that feature gay Asian and Pacific Islanders, these magazines are either pornographic magazines where gay Asian men are the "products" meant for gay white male consumption or magazines that are published by gay Asian men or women.

Next, I examine the counterstories told by gay Asian men. For this section, I used stories told by gay Asian men from a variety of sources, most noticeably the website *Bathhouse Diaries*. I specifically chose *Bathhouse Diaries* because it included postings by gay white men who responded to the writings by gay

Asians. As such, I was able to expose the blatant forms of racism found in the responses of gay white men toward accusations of racism within the gay community and how those responses further marginalize gay Asian men.

Finally, I explore gay Asian men's stories that address their experiences within the larger gay community to show how the marginalization of gay Asian men can have dire negative consequences on their emotional and physical well-being.

In examining the stories, I was guided by tenets of critical discourse analysis (CDA). As an analytical perspective, CDA is interested in exposing the power embedded in text and images by the discursive choices that are made by the writer. Proponents of CDA understand that there is an unequal access to the various modes of discursive productions and view discursive tactics as a method of social domination (Van Leeuwen 1993). As such, discursive practices maintain a reality based on dominant group expectations of what that reality should be. "Doing" CDA involves (1) examining how text is framed, that is, how the text is presented, what particular "angle" the author is taking, including the general "mood" of the text; (2) what information is foreground, that is, what concepts are given textual prominence while others are in the background; (3) what presuppositions and/or insinuations the narrator makes; (4) which subjects are topicalized, that is, who is the subject and who is the object; (5) what is omitted; and (6) how visual aids are used to support the narrator's arguments (Huckin 1995). By allowing us to examine narratives in their original context, CDA provides us with the opportunity to explore where stock stories and counterstories get told, how they are constructed, and for the purpose they serve in constructing the everyday experiences of marginalized groups. Given the above, CDA provides a well-suited analytical tool for examining stock stories and counterstories from a CRT perspective.

The Gay Stock Story about Race

Told both textually and visually, the promotion of the gay stock story is blatantly evident in the June 2006 "Pride" issue of the *Advocate*. In the "giant 2006 Pride special issue," faces of color are generously sprinkled throughout the entire publication, including the cover, which features eight gays and lesbians from throughout the United States, three of whom are people of color.

Early in the issue, we are bombarded with images and text that suggest a racially integrated gay community. The first feature story, about "the original and largest LGBT [lesbian, gay, bisexual, and transgender] youth prom," features a photo of Harvey Tennessee, a black gay youth who "gracefully moved through the crowd as friends reached out to touch him" (Henderson 2006, 27). Rather than being shunned and isolated due to his race, he is a celebrity within gay circles. On the next page we are introduced to Rod McCullom, a black gay blogger. On this page we also see that a photo of an Asian woman is used to accompany the "strange stat" column that informs us that 51 percent of people who use only cell phones believe that same-sex marriage should be legal, compared to only 37 percent who also use a landline. A few pages in we find a "first-person" reflection by HIV-positive photographer Luna Luis Ortiz, as told to Cator Sparks. The irony here is that while three black men are prominently featured through photographs, there is no mention of their race in the text. Ironically, even the reflection by Ortiz, written by Sparks, about living with HIV fails to address the fact that gay men of color are astronomically more likely to contract HIV than gay white men (CDC 2004). In textually ignoring the race of the subject, while making it visually explicit, the *Advocate* practices an extreme version of color blindness that attempts to erase race while simultaneously spotlighting it.

The feature story, "Future Gay Leaders '06," introduces us to seven young gay activists who are "already making a difference and are set to take over the fight for equality in the future" (Kennedy 2006, 74). In a salute to multicultural America, four of the seven future gay leaders are nonwhite, including one transgender Asian woman, two black men, and a lesbian woman who is half Puerto Rican. Not surprisingly, given the racial integration theme of the magazine's special issue, the race of the two black men and the Latina woman is not mentioned. Although the race of the transgender Asian woman is noted, it is only in reference to her role as the Asian Pacific Islander media manager for the Gay and Lesbian Alliance Against Defamation and to label her as a "prominent transgender Asian activist" (Kennedy 2006, 75). By simply ignoring race, the magazine promotes a vision of the gay community where "race" is a nonissue.

The textual narrative for the "Future Gay Leaders '06" article also contributes to the myth of the welcoming gay community. In telling the story of Jason Haas, the author describes the "near-constant anti-gay harassment" Haas endured in school and how "he called up the New England legal rights organization Gay and Lesbian Advocates and Defenders," who helped him successfully sue the school (Kennedy 2006, 76). Celia La Luz's salvation came in the form of "an understanding therapist who referred her to San Francisco's Lavender Youth Recreation and Information Center," who helped her find her voice after years of harassment at school, which led her "to the point of wanting to stop speaking" (Kennedy 2006, 78). Likewise, Antonio Locus was also victimized by cruel peers until he was "recruited by GLSEN [Gay, Lesbian and Straight Education Network] when he contacted the organization while writing a story on gay-straight alliances for his school's newspaper" (Kennedy 2006, 80). Taken together, these stock stories portray youths, both white and of color, who are tormented because of their sexuality but are welcomed and "rescued" by organizations in the gay community that embrace them without regard to their race or ethnicity.

Not surprising considering the focus on multiculturalism in the gay stock story, there are seven men and one woman of color among the fifteen people portrayed for the cover story, "What's 'Gay' Now?" Among the fifteen profiled, eight answered the question, "Is the gay community welcoming to people of color?" One white lesbian woman answered,

> I think the gay community has problems with people who are bisexual or straight. (Lam and Broverman 2006, 82)

A white bisexual transgendered woman answered,

> Any great political movement is a constant chipping away at the monolithic stereotype. We still have a ways to go, but we're starting to see there's such diversity. "Gay" now conjures up a multitude of images. (Lam and Broverman 2006, 88)

Finally, a white gay/butch-trans person answered,

> It seems, unfortunately, that we're still very segregated in terms of [racial] representation. (Lam and Broverman 2006, 96)

Despite the last answer, the gay community, as portrayed by the white respondents, is a welcoming place for gays and lesbians of color. In the first answer, the respondent refuses to even address the question of racial tolerance, instead focusing on the "problems with people who are bisexual or straight." In this way the issue of racial tolerance and by extension of racial prejudice is simply ignored. The second respondent couches her statement by arguing that "any great political movement" is fraught with stereotypes that need to be addressed. Again, while she attempts to dismiss the notion of racial prejudice in the gay community, she simultaneously absolves gay white men and women of responsibility by deflecting blame away from gay whites to the "great political movement" and what she claims is the nature of such movements.

It is important to note here that the magazine did provide an opportunity for gay men and women of color to provide answers to the same questions asked of white respondents. Not surprisingly, the responses made by the people of color reflect a different reality about race. Although one bisexual black woman indicated that racial discrimination was not a problem in the gay and lesbian community, the men had a different view. According to one Latino man,

> People of color have demanded a place at the table and the [gay] community has responded in kind. It's not about being welcomed to the table; it's about crashing the party. (Lam and Broverman 2006, 89)

A gay black man answered,

I think there's still a bit of [racial prejudice] in the gay community. I don't know if you call it racist or not. Your color takes precedence over your sexuality. (Lam and Broverman 2006, 90)

A second gay black man answered,

The gay community is welcoming to people of color from a distance. It's not like, "No, don't come here," but [rather] "I won't date you. I won't give you more than one show on my network." The gay community has always represented "white." (Lam and Broverman 2006, 92)

Finally, another gay black man answered,

In dating, people can be as racist as they want. If a white guy wants a black guy, he doesn't want me. He doesn't know I have two Ivy League degrees and that I manage $3 billion in client relationships. (Lam and Broverman 2006, 96)

Taken together, the counterstories told by the gay men of color featured in this magazine expose the subtle forms of racism found in the gay community. Most noticeable seems to be that gay men of color are not considered desirable by gay men. In the final answer, the reference to the "$3 billion in client relationships" can be seen as an attempt to confront the stereotypes about black men that the author is assumed to face in his everyday life. Also, as the final respondent noted, being accepted often means tokenization for gays and lesbians of color. While gay television stations might provide one show with nonwhite characters, they are often relegated to that one show rather than representative on the entire scheduling lineup.

The highlighting of men and women of color in the "giant 2006 Pride special" is ironic given that an average issue of the *Advocate* is virtually absent of nonwhite faces (Han, forthcoming). Yet despite the invisibility of nonwhite images in gay publications on an everyday basis, when asked by the magazine to respond to the statement "is gay White?," only 8 percent of the readers responded "yes," while 84 percent responded "no." Similarly, in virtually any survey of gay white people, the overwhelming majority believe that the gay community is welcoming to people of color. In fact, while the special "Pride" issue includes the results of an *Advocate* poll of 3,225 *Advocate* readers that include questions about gender, age, sexuality, geographic location, friendship circles, sexual practices, and a number of other personal information that will highlight "who we are," there is no attempt to inquire about the readers' race or ethnicity, making race a nonissue. Clearly, the majority of gay white America has unquestioningly accepted the stock stories of a multicultural gay community that embraces all sexual minorities regardless of race.

Stock Stories about Gay Asian Men

In addition to the stock stories told about race as described above, there are also stock stories about members of specific racial categories. Although narratives about gay Asian men are limited in mainstream gay publications (Han, forthcoming), the few available stock stories attempt to portray the gay community as being open to, and accepting of, gay Asian men. To make this point, I turn to a special issue of *Frontiers Newsmagazine* published in 2001. This specific issue was unique in that it featured an Asian man on the cover with the tagline, "Asian Pacific Islanders make their mark on queer culture." For anyone who has picked up a gay publication, it should be blatantly obvious that people of color, particularly Asian people, rarely, if ever, make it on to the cover of a gay publication. In the feature story titled "Queer Asian and Pacific Islanders: Crossing Borders, Creating Home," author Ankita Kelly proposes to chronicle "how far the queer Asian and Pacific islander community has come" (Kelly 2001, 12). Despite several quotes from gay Asian and Pacific Islanders regarding the difficulty of coming out to family and confronting homophobia within ethnic communities, the only mention of difficulties in the gay community is attributed to the "task of relating to and within a predominantly white mainstream LGBT community" (Kelly 2001, 14). In the same article, the author attempts to explain homophobia among Chinese Americans by noting that "the Chinese community does not understand gay issues" (Kelly 2001, 14). By minimizing racism within the gay community and maximizing homophobia in ethnic communities, these stock stories absolve gay white men and women from any real responsibility of addressing white privilege or racial injustice within gay spaces.

However, the real power of stock stories comes from their ability to move racial minorities away from the center of discussion to the periphery where they can more easily be ignored. As such, the stock stories told in the gay press work to position gay Asian men outside of the larger gay community. For example, the February 2005 issue of *OUT* magazine ran a column titled, "How to Gab in Gaysian," which was introduced in this way:

> Sometimes members of a group pepper their conversations with sexual euphemisms, saucy slang terms, and just flat-out un-PC parlance. Since there isn't an official English-Gaysian dictionary, *OUT* offers you a small menu of words you might want to know in order to verbal-vogue it *like a queer Asian*. (Lee 2005, 28, emphasis added)

The column works to relegate gay Asian men to the margins of the gay community in several ways. First, by providing an English/Gaysian "dictionary," the column presupposes that the reader is white. In addition, it is the gay white reader who is provided with a "service" to decipher the language of a "foreign" group. As such, gay Asian men are not expected to be readers of this "gay" magazine.

Counterstories by Gay Asian Men

Moving away from the stock stories told generally about racial acceptance in the gay community and specifically about gay Asian men, I now turn to counterstories told by gay Asian men. The counterstories told by gay Asian men portray the subtle racism they confront on a daily basis. Take this story for example:

> I want to tell you a little bit about myself. Even though I am in my thirties, I still look a decade younger. Anytime I meet someone new, the first question they ask is, "What are you taking in college?" or "Do you go to school?" I have this youthful, boyish face. . . . I have a nice short haircut, dimples on both cheeks, and an okay body (nobody's perfect). One person has described me as having a certain down-home, apple-pie stoic sweetness about myself. But when I go to the baths I usually go home empty handed. Ninety-nine percent of the time, I do not even have an encounter with anyone at the baths. Why would I have this problem? After describing myself, I must have tons of guys chasing after me. Because it is generally agreed, but unspoken in the gay community, that Asian men are completely undesirable by gay men of any color, including their own. (*Bathhouse Diaries* 2005)

Another gay Asian man writes,

> The pain of being a gay Asian, however, is not just the pain of direct discrimination but the pain of being negated again and again by a culture that doesn't acknowledge my presence. I remember when I came out, I didn't even know I was "Asian." I thought I was like everyone else—just gay. . . . Alienated from our own sexuality, the only way we become sexualized is through the predatory consumption of a rice queen [white men who prefer Asian men as sexual partners]. With little presence in the Western erotic imagination, we find we have even less power when it comes to our presence on the sexual menu, except as "boy toys" for white men. . . . While white men cruised looking for their prey, most Asians stood back, lined up against the wall like beauty pageant queens waiting to be chose. . . . With all the attention focused on white guys, I instinctively knew that as a gay Asian, I rarely had the power to choose and would always be the one chosen. (Cho 1998, 2–3)

Often gay Asian men are explicitly told that they are not wanted. As one gay Asian men notes,

> Over the years, I have experienced three typical responses on the gay scene. First, there is overt belligerence: the drunk queens who shout in my face, "Go back to

your own country"; the tag line at the end of gay personal classifieds—"No Fats, Femmes, or Asians"; the guys who hissed at me in the back room, "I'm not into Asians." (Ayres 1999, 89)

The above quotes demonstrate the everyday experience of gay Asian men. Rather than the expected welcoming atmosphere presented in the gay stock stories, the counterstories told by gay Asian men expose the everyday forms of racism within the larger gay community. First, gay Asian men know themselves to be outside of the gay mainstream. Within the gay imagination, gay Asian men are both invisible and undesirable. In addition, the second narrative highlights the power difference between gay white men and gay Asian men. Marked as being undesirable, gay Asian men do not possess the power to choose sexual partners but instead must wait to be chosen.

The White Response

In the white imagination, these subtle forms of racism found in gay Asian men's stock stories are easily dismissed. According to one gay white man who wrote into the *Bathhouse Diaries* after reading the stories by a gay Asian man,

> IT'S NOT MY FAULT!!!!!!!!!! I did not enslave you, I did not reject you, and I didn't make you gay or tell you to desire white guys. Apparently someone in your family's past decided they lived in the worst country on earth and begged to come here for a better life. If you hate white guys so much look elsewhere for your fulfillment, and if you dislike my country so much, leave! Since I happen to have been born here, I don't have YOUR convenience of blaming other people for my troubles. GET OVER YOURSELF! (*Bathhouse Diaries* 2005, emphasis original)

Yet being more blatant, another gay white man writes,

> While white men have masculine underwear parties where guys take off their shirts and expose rippling stomach muscles, Asian gay men have "Miss Asia" beauty pageants with Asian men dressing in drag, badly miming the words of Whitney Houston (their lips don't even match the words because they can't even speak English properly). ... With Asians, almost all of them do drag or walk like a faggot, are skinny, limp wrist and will basically suck off any old fat white man that they come across because that is all they are able to get looking the foul way they do. ... Even most Asians are repulsed by their own kind and chase white men because even they find themselves disgusting. ... If Asian gay men want to be accepted, try acting like a man. ... *It has nothing to do with race, it's to do with Asian gay men being sissy, limp wrist with a hairstyle that looks like the head of a circumcised penis and little round circular steel rimmed glasses.* (*Bathhouse Diaries* 2005, emphasis added)

As noted earlier, the stock stories told by the dominant group work to absolve members of the dominant group from their responsibility in creating and maintaining the racial hierarchy. In the first narrative, the gay white man denies his responsibility in the maintenance of white privilege. Much like the way whites deny the historical legacy of slavery by arguing that they were not slave owners, the first author insists that "it's not [his] fault." In addition, the author's narrative "places" the gay Asian man "in his place." Despite the fact that there is no indication in the original narrative written by the gay Asian man regarding immigrant status or place of birth, the white narrator assumes that the Asian author must be an immigrant and therefore "foreign." In fact, he writes, "If you dislike *my* country so much, leave!" In this narrative, it is clear the gay white man defines membership in a country along race. Because he is white, he can claim membership while the Asian man is denied membership. As Burley (2005, 118) notes, this "universalization of whiteness where being human and being American is equated with being white" may be the result of an inability to see racial privilege in a world they believe is color-blind. Because he cannot see his own racial privilege, he places the blame of discrimination on the gay Asian man, whom he claims must "hate white guys and dislike [his] country." Clearly, he is using the charge of "reverse racism" that has now become so popular among whites afraid of seeing their own racial privilege.

In the second narrative, the author writes that "it has nothing to do with race," despite his racist comments that gay Asians "can't even speak English properly." According to the response, it isn't racism that leads to gay Asians being marginalized, but rather their own actions. As such, gay white men are not to be blamed for discriminating against gay Asian men, who would be well accepted if they would only "try acting like a man." More important, the blame of racial discrimination is thrust upon gay Asian men themselves when the second author notes that "even most Asians are repulsed by their own kind."

These white responses to gay Asian counterstories trivialize the racism experienced by gay Asian men along two dimensions. First, any negative experiences of gay Asian men are believed to be the result of their own doing. As such, gay Asian men are believed to be able to avoid these experiences if they simply change their own behavior. More important, it is believed that as "foreigners" they should be grateful for the treatment that they receive in the gay community given that it is still better than anything they could expect from their "own" countries or from own ethnic communities without regard to what their "own" country might actually be. Much like the narratives that highlight homophobia in ethnic communities and minimize racism in the gay community, the "foreignization" of gay Asian men allows gay white men to avoid responsibility by making the erroneous argument that any treatment in the gay community is better than any alternative.

The Effects of Subtle Racism

Despite the white response, gay Asian men's counterstories about their personal experiences make it harder to ignore the end results of such subtle forms of racism. According to one gay Asian man,

> The journey of finding self-worth naturally began at the gym, that factory where white Gods are cloned, and where my shamefully slim Oriental frame could be transformed into a more desirable western body. (Chuang 1999, 33)

Speaking of the feminization of male Asian bodies, one gay Asian man writes,

> Essentially, the "masculine" body is aggressive, in control, and powerful while the "feminine" body is passive, relinquishing control, and powerless. Most images of gay Asian men that I've seen ... are "feminine" in nature compared to representations of the Caucasian body in the mainstream gay media, which are aggressively masculine. (Ayres 1999, 94)

More important, the same writer observes what these subtle forms of racism can do to gay Asian men. For example,

> [Gay Asian men] are competing for the attention of the limited number of Caucasian men who desire Asian men. Intellectually I know that this inability to feel attracted to other Asian men is a form of internalized racism. I know that at some basic psychic level I am unable to come to terms with my own body. ... I don't think people consciously choose their desires. But the very fact of this separation of desire into racial categories indicates a kind of institutional racism. (Ayres 1999, 92)

The above quotes highlight the negative consequences that whiteness has for gay Asian men. The primacy of white masculinity within the gay community not only leads gay Asian men to lose power over their sexual choices, waiting to be chosen instead, but also leads to internalized self-hatred. The more devastating consequence is that gay Asian men, rather than seeing each other as allies in the fight against this "institutional racism," come to see each other as competitors.

The final result may be even more devastating. In fact, several scholars have hypothesized that the racism within the gay community may be actively contributing to the increasing rates of HIV/AIDS among gay men of color (Choi et al. 1999; Diaz 1998; Nemoto et al. 2003; Stokes and Peterson 1998). According to one gay Asian man,

> Before, being so young and naïve, I didn't have a care for myself. I wanted to please this other person and was willing to give up what I believe. It is about low

self-esteem. There is no one for gay Asian males to look up to. When you have low self-esteem, you don't want to lose them, you don't want to get them angry and you just want to please them. Low self-esteem means not believing in yourself, and not knowing what you are capable of achieving. (Choi et al. 1999, 49)

Likewise,

Being gay, sometimes it is very superficial in the sense that many things are based on physicality. Physical beauty, the standard is the model, and all the models are white. Then you think that you are less than that. (Choi et al. 1999, 50)

Rather than a nuisance, the subtle forms of racism practiced within the larger gay community have a negative consequence for gay Asian men. Pushed to the margins, they experience lower self-esteem and attempt to alleviate it by engaging in unsafe sex with white partners whom they don't want to "anger" for fear of losing them. As such, the stock stories told by gay white men not only maintain racial hierarchies but also have seriously detrimental consequences for gay Asian men.

Conclusion

Much has been written about the need to examine the intersectionality of various marginalized identities. For example, Kimberlé Crenshaw (1995) calls for examining the intersection of race and sex by examining the experiences of black women. In her work, she argues that rather than experiencing oppression along separate axis, the experiences of women of color are the result of the interplay between racism and sexism that are multiplicative rather than additive. Citing Crenshaw, Parker and Lynn (2002, 12) note that such "intersectional analysis forces us to see the relationship between sexism and racism as symbiotic" rather than as essentialized identities that are "frozen fixed frames."

Certainly, there is a great need within sociology and other social sciences to examine the intersectionality of marginalized identities. However, despite the call for examining the "intersectionality" of race and other marginalized identities, little has been done in terms of examining how marginalized groups stigmatize other groups and the role that the "possessive investment in whiteness" has played in how groups take on characteristics of the dominant group in order to oppress other marginalized groups (Lipsitz 1998). That is, little is written about the intersectionality of a marginalized identity with a dominant identity. In the above examples, I've shown how gay white men use their dominant racial status to relegate gay Asian men to the margins of the gay community. Ironically, because gay white men make an "investment in whiteness," they erase much of the male privilege that gay Asian men may have by relegating them to the feminine position (Han 2006).

In this chapter, I examined the stock stories told about race and racial inclusion in the gay community, stock stories told about gay Asian men, the counter-stories that gay Asian men tell about their experiences in the gay community, and the responses made by white men about the gay Asian men's stock stories. Doing so, I showed how the subtle forms of racism, perpetuated by the gay stock stories, have a negative effect on the lives of gay Asian men.

To date, CRT scholars have largely examined how the stock stories told by the dominant group oppresses and victimized subaltern populations. However, my study shows how marginalized groups can also use the stock stories to marginalize other subaltern groups. The oppression experiences by gay Asian men, and I suspect other gay men of color, have to do not only with their experiences of being both sexual and racial minorities but also because they are both sexual and racial minorities. They do not experience homophobia in the same way that gay white men do, and they do not experience racism in the same way straight men of color do. For example, heterosexual Asian men may be able to leverage their male privilege, but gay Asian men may not be able to do the same given the feminization of gay Asian men within the larger gay community. In addition, gay white men may be able to leverage their racial privilege, but gay Asian men may not be able to do the same given their racial status. On the one hand, gay Asian men experience racism and homophobia from the dominant society as gay men of color. At the same time, they experience racism from their sexual communities because they are men of color and homophobia from their ethnic communities because they are gay men, two sets of experiences not felt by either gay white men or straight men of color. If we truly are going to examine all intersecting arenas of oppression, we need to move away from simply examining how the dominant groups use stock stories to oppress subaltern groups and examine how subaltern groups also use stock stories to oppress other marginalized groups.

As I have demonstrated, CRT provides an excellent framework for examining racial oppression from the dominant group and can also be used to examine the experiences of those who are doubly marginalized along multiple dimensions and how marginalized groups can also utilize the dominant stock stories to further marginalize others. Certainly, this short chapter has not addressed many aspects of CRT and its full utility for sociologists. At the same time, if one of the goals of sociology is to work toward social justice and "give voice" to those who are often neglected, we need to begin examining the narratives actually created by the very voices we claim to want to "give voice" to as they try to make sense of the world around them. At the same time, we also need to begin acknowledging that the intersection of identities involves not only multiply oppressed identities but also dominant identities. Doing so will allow us to examine the full spectrum of intergroup relations rather than relying on the simple dichotomy of dominant and submissive groups.

NOTE

Originally published in *Contemporary Justice Review* 11 (1): 11–22, 2008. ©2008 *Contemporary Justice Review*, reprint by permission.

REFERENCES

Agger, Ben. 1991. "Critical Theory, Poststructuralism, Postmodernism: Their Sociological Relevance." *Annual Review of Sociology* 17: 105–131.

Aguirre, Adalberto. 2000. "Academic Storytelling: A Critical Race Theory Story of Affirmative Action." *Sociological Perspectives* 43 (2): 319–339.

Anonymous. 2000. "Racism or Preference (at the Baths?)." *Bathhouse Diaries*. www.bathhouse-blues.com/racism.html (accessed February 10, 2005).

Ayres, Tony. 1999. "China Doll: The Experience of Being a Gay Chinese Australian." *Journal of Homosexuality* 36 (3/4): 87–97.

Bell, Derick. 1992. *Faces at the Bottom of the Well: The Permanence of Racism*. New York: Basic Books.

Bonilla-Silva, Eduardo. 2001. *White Supremacy and Racism in the Post–Civil Rights Era*. Boulder, CO: Lynne Rienner.

Burley, David. 2005. "White Racial Reasoning: Rational Racism in the Perception of White Males." *Humanity and Society* 29 (2): 116–125.

Centers for Disease Control and Prevention (CDC). 2004. "HIV/AIDS Surveillance Report, 2004." Vol. 16. Atlanta: US Department of Health and Human Services, CDC. http://www.cdc.gov/hiv/topics/surveillance/resources/reports/2004report.

Cho, Song. 1998. *Rice: Explorations into Gay Asian Culture and Politics*. Toronto: Queer Press.

Choi, Kyung-Hee, Eugene Kumekawa, Quant Dang, Susan M. Kegeles, Robert B. Hays, and Ronald Stall. 1999. "Risk and Protective Factors Affecting Sexual Behavior among Young Asian and Pacific Islander Men Who Have Sex with Men: Implications for HIV Prevention." *Journal of Sex Education* 24 (1/2): 47–55.

Chuang, Kent. 1999. "Using Chopsticks to Eat Steak." *Journal of Homosexuality* 36 (3/4): 29–41.

Crenshaw, Kimberlé. 1995. "Race, Reform and Retrenchment: Transformation and Anti Discrimination Law." *Harvard Law Review* 101 (7): 1331–1387.

DeCuir, Jessica, and Adrienne Dixson. 2004. "'So When It Comes Out, They Aren't That Surprised That It Is There': Using Critical Race Theory as a Tool of Analysis of Race and Racism in Education." *Educational Researcher* 33 (6): 26–31.

Delgado, Richard. 1989. "Storytelling for Oppositionists and Others: A Plea for Narrative." *Michigan Law Review* 87 (7): 2411–2441.

———. 1990. "When a Story Is Just a Story: Does Voice Really Matter?" *Virginia Law Review* 76 (1): 95–111.

Delgado, Richard, and Jean Stefancic. 2001. *Critical Race Theory: An Introduction*. New York: New York University Press.

Diaz, Rafael. 1998. *Latino Gay Men and HIV: Culture, Sexuality, and Risk Behavior*. New York: Routledge.

Han, Chong-suk. 2006. "Geisha of a Different Kind: Gay Asian Men and the Gendering of Sexual Identity." *Sexuality and Culture* 10 (3): 3–28.

———. Forthcoming. "Sexy Like a Girl and Horny Like a Boy: Contemporary Gay Western Narratives about Gay Asian Men." *Critical Sociology*.

Henderson, William. 2006. "A Prom for All." *Advocate*, June, 27.

Huckin, Thomas. 1995. "Critical Discourse Analysis." In Tom Miller, ed., *Functional Approaches to Written Text*. Paris: USIS. http://exchanges.state.gov/education/engteaching/pubs/BR/functionalsec3_6.htm (accessed June 2002).

Kelly, Ankita Sadaf. 2001. "Queer Asian and Pacific Islanders: Crossing Borders, Creating Home." *Frontiers Newsmagazine* 19 (24): 12–16.

Kennedy, Sean. 2006. "Future Gay Leaders '06." *Advocate*, June, 74–80.

Lam, Steven, and Neal Broverman. 2006. "What's 'Gay' Now?" *Advocate*, June, 82–96.

Lee, Daniel. 2005. "How to Gab in Gaysian." *OUT*, February, 28.

Lipsitz, George. 1998. *The Possessive Investment in Whiteness: How White People Benefit from Identity Politics*. Philadelphia: Temple University Press.

Matsuda, Mari. 1995. "Looking to the Bottom: Critical Legal Studies and Reparations." Pp. 63–79 in Kimberlé Crenshaw, Neil Gotanda, Garry Peller, and Kendall Thomas, eds., *Critical Race Theory: The Key Writings That Formed the Movement*. New York: New Press.

Nemoto, Tooru, Don Operario, Toho Soma, Daniel Bao, Alberto Vajrabukka, and Vincent Crisostomo. 2003. "HIV Risk and Prevention among Asian/Pacific Islander Men Who Have Sex with Men: Listen to Our Stories." *AIDS Education and Prevention* 15 (suppl. A): 7–20.

Parker, Laurence, and Marvin Lynn. 2002. "What's Race Got to Do with It? Critical Race Theory's Conflicts with and Connections to Qualitative Research Methodology and Epistemology." *Qualitative Inquiry* 8 (1): 7–22.

Richardson, Laurel. 1990. "Narrative and Sociology." *Journal of Contemporary Ethnography* 19 (1): 116–135.

Stokes, Joseph, and John Peterson. 1998. "Homophobia, Self-Esteem and Risk for HIV among African American Men Who Have Sex with Men." *AIDS Education and Prevention* 10 (3): 278–292.

Taylor, Edward. 1998. "A Primer on Critical Race Theory." *Journal of Blacks in Higher Education* 19: 122–124.

Van Leeuwen, Theo. 1993. "Genre and Field in Critical Discourse Analysis: A Synopsis." *Discourse and Society* 4 (2): 193–223.

STUDY QUESTIONS

(1) What are some of the cultural distinctions that Nadal notes between Filipino Americans and East Asian Americans (e.g., Chinese, Japanese, and Korean)? How have these cultural differences affected the way that gay and lesbian Filipinos deal with their sexuality in the context of their families and communities? What are the implications of these differences for how teachers, psychologists, and other authority figures address the specific needs of gay and lesbian Filipinos?

(2) How do gay and lesbian Filipinos negotiate both their ethnic and sexual identity? How does being gay or lesbian affect their experiences within their families and ethnic communities? In turn, how does being Filipino affect their ability to find support within mainstream LGBT organizations and social spaces?

(3) Han's chapter highlights the racial schisms that exist in the larger LGBT community. In what ways have LGBT publications addressed the interests of queer people of color? In what ways have they failed to do so? Within publications like the *Advocate* and *Frontiers*, how do the narratives of white LGBT individuals differ from those of racial minorities? Do you believe that race is an issue within the larger LGBT community?

(4) What is critical race theory (CRT)? How has a CRT framework allowed Han to uncover the "counterstories" of Asian American gay men? In ways is a CRT framework useful for better understanding the intersectionality of ethnic, gender, and sexual identities?

(5) In your opinion, how have your courses in Asian American studies addressed issues of sexuality? How have LGBT Asian Americans been represented in your classes, readings, and even conversations related to Asian American issues? What strategies can you think of that can improve the representation of LGBT Asian Americans in the larger field of Asian American studies? How might these strategies vary depending on whether someone is LGBT or a straight ally?

SUGGESTED READINGS

Cheung, King-Kok. 1998. "Of Men and Men: Reconstructing Chinese American Masculinity." Pp. 173–199 in Sandra Stanley, ed., *Other Sisterhoods: Literary Theory and U.S. Women of Color.* Urbana: University of Illinois Press.

Chou, Rosalind. 2012. *Asian American Sexual Politics: The Construction of Race, Gender, and Sexuality.* Lanham, MD: Rowman & Littlefield.

Cruz-Malavé, Arnaldo, and Matin Manalansan, eds. 2002. *Queer Globalizations.* New York: York University Press.

Eng, David, and Alice Hom, eds. 1998. *Q&A: Queer in Asian America.* Philadelphia: Temple University Press.

Espiritu, Yen Le. 2001. "'We Don't Sleep Around Like White Girls Do': Family, Culture, and Gender in Filipina American Lives." *Signs* 26 (2): 415–440.

Fung, Richard. 1998. "Looking for My Penis: The Eroticized Asian in Gay Porn." Pp. 115–134 in David Eng and Alice Hom, eds., *Q&A: Queer in Asian America.* Philadelphia: Temple University Press.

Fuss, Diana. 1991. "Inside/Out." Pp. 1–10 in Diana Fuss, ed., *Inside/Out.* New York: Routledge.

Green, Donald, Dara Strolovitch, Janelle Wong, and Robert Bailey. 2001. "Measuring Gay Population Density and the Incidence of Anti-gay Hate Crime." *Social Science Quarterly* 82 (2): 281–297.

Hahm, H., and C. Adkins. 2009. "A Model of Asian and Pacific Islander Sexual Minority Acculturation." *Journal of LGBT Youth* 6 (2–3): 155–173.

Jew, Victor. 2003. "'Chinese Demons': The Violent Articulation of Chinese Otherness and Interracial Sexuality in the U.S. Midwest, 1885–1889." *Journal of Social History* 37 (2): 389–410.

Kim, Daniel. 1998. "The Strange Love of Frank Chin." Pp. 270–303 in David Eng and Alice Hom, eds., *Q&A: Queer in Asian America.* Philadelphia: Temple University Press.

Kimmel, D. C., and H. Yi. 2004. "Characteristics of Gay, Lesbian, and Bisexual Asians, Asian Americans, and Immigrants from Asia to the USA." *Journal of Homosexuality* 47 (2): 143–172.

Lana, Mobydeen. 2004. "Something Old, Something New, Something Borrowed, Something Mail Ordered?" *Wayne Law Review* 49: 939–974.

Leong, Russell, ed. 1996. *Asian American Sexualities: Dimensions of the Gay and Lesbian Experience.* New York: Routledge.

Maira, Sunaina Marr. 2001. "B-Boys and Bass Girls: Sex, Style, and Mobility in Indian American Youth Culture." *Souls* 3 (3): 65–86.

Manalansan, Martin. 2003. *Global Divas: Filipino Gay Men in the Diaspora.* Durham, NC: Duke University Press.

Ocampo, Anthony C. 2014. "The Gay Second Generation: Sexual Identity and the Family Relations of Filipino and Latino Gay Men." *Journal of Ethnic and Migration Studies* 40 (1): 155–73.

Ordona, Trinity. 2003. "Asian Lesbians in San Francisco: Struggles to Create a Safe Space, 1970s–1980s." Pp. 319–334 in Shirley Hune and Gail M. Nomura, eds., *Asian/Pacific Islander American Women: A Historical Anthology.* New York: New York University Press.

Pyke, Karen, and Denise L. Johnson. 2003. "Asian American Women and Racialized Feminists: 'Doing' Gender across Cultural Worlds." *Gender & Society* 17 (1): 33–53.

Shimizu, Celine P. 2012. *Straitjacket Sexualities: Unbinding Asian American Manhoods in the Movies.* Stanford, CA: Stanford University Press.

Sueyoshi, Amy, and Russell Leong, eds. 2006. "Asian Americans in the Marriage Equality Debate." Special issue, *Amerasia Journal* 32 (1).

Ting, Jennifer P. 1998. "The Power of Sexuality." *Journal of Asian American Studies* 1 (1): 65–82.

Tong, Yuying. 2013. "Acculturation, Gender Disparity, and the Sexual Behavior of Asian American Youth." *Journal of Sex Research* 50 (6): 560–573.

Wat, Eric C. 2002. *The Making of a Gay Community: An Oral History of Pre-AIDS Los Angeles.* Lanham, MD: Rowman & Littlefield.

Wilson, Patrick A., and Hirokazu Yoshikawa. 2004. "Experiences of and Responses to Social Discrimination among Asian and Pacific Islander Gay Men: Their Relationship to HIV Risk." *AIDS Education and Prevention* 16 (1): 68–83.

FILMS

Bautista, Pablo (producer). 1992. *Fated to Be Queer* (25-minute documentary).

Choy, Christine (producer/director). 1994. *Out in Silence: AIDS in the Pacific American Community* (37-minute documentary).

Fung, Richard (producer/director). 1984. *Orientations* (52-minute documentary).

——(producer/director). 1995. *Dirty Laundry* (30-minute documentary).

Ganatra, Nisha (producer/director). 1997. *Junky Punky Girlz* (12-minute experimental).

Hima, B. (director). 1996. *Coming Out/Coming Home: Asian & Pacific Islander Family Stories* (44-minute documentary).

Hong, Yunah (producer/director). 2011. *Anna May Wong: In Her Own Words* (56-minute documentary).

Lee, Ang (producer/director). 1993. *The Wedding Banquet* (106-minute drama).

Lee, Grace (producer/director). 2005. *The Grace Lee Project* (68-minute documentary).

Lee, Quentin (producer/director). 1995. *Flow* (80-minute experimental).

——(director). 2012. *White Frog* (93-minute film).

Lum, Debbie (director). 2012. *Seeking Asian Female* (84-minute film).

Okazaki, Steven (producer/director). 1994. *American Sons* (28-minute documentary).

Park, Regina (director). 2007. *Neverperfect* (65-minute documentary).

PART VI

Race and Asian American Identity

13

Are Asians Black?

The Asian American Civil Rights Agenda and the Contemporary Significance of the Paradigm

JANINE YOUNG KIM

The phrase "civil rights movement" evokes the powerful words and images of the mass movement by Black Americans in the United States during the 1950s and 1960s. In recent years, however, Asian Americans have increasingly laid claim to a place in the history of the struggle for civil rights. Just as Derrick A. Bell harkens back to *Dred Scott v. Sandford* as the first of the "leading cases" in civil rights (Bell 1980), Hyung-Chan Kim's anthology of Asian American civil rights cases and essays recalls cases such as *Yick Wo v. Hopkins* as proof of Asian Americans' long-standing participation in the development of civil rights law in the United States (Kim 1992).

When tensions within American multicultural, multiracial society exploded in Los Angeles in 1992, not only history but immediate reality itself seemed to insist on the inclusion of Asian Americans within the larger discourse on civil rights. Because what began as an arguably Black (Rodney King)–White (LAPD officers) conflict transformed into multiracial strife involving not only Black and White Americans but also Latinos and Asian Americans, the riots brought into sharp relief the complex racial interrelationships within Los Angeles. As a result, two race scholars announced that the riots "marked the beginning of a new period of U.S. racial politics," one that must "decisively break with the bipolar model of race" (Omi and Winant 1994, 154–155).[1] Since then, the black/white paradigm has been a subject of increasing academic debate; the controversy has likely entered the popular consciousness as well, due to the highly publicized conflict between Angela Oh and John Hope Franklin within President Clinton's race relations commission.[2]

Although existing legal scholarship on the paradigm generally assumes the paradigm to be a biracial model of racism that focuses exclusively on the relationship between Black and White Americans, an explicit definition is rare and difficult to find (Calmore 1997; Chang 1994; Omi and Winant 1994; Perea 1997; Ramirez 1995; Tamayo 1995). The dearth of legal scholarship that endeavors to outline the contours of the black/white paradigm is problematic not only because the inadequacy of the paradigm is an often unexplored and unchallenged assumption, but also because the assumption may be incorrect or misleading.

This essay focuses on the (uneasy) relationship between the black/white paradigm and the Asian American civil rights agenda. My primary project is to intervene in the seemingly unproblematic discussion of the black/white paradigm in order to caution that current race discourse oversimplifies the paradigm and fails to articulate the full cost of its abandonment. One reason for my argument is that a paradigm once so powerful should not, as a principle, be discarded without serious analysis. A second, more compelling, reason is that the black/white paradigm retains contemporary significance despite demographic changes in American society. It is, therefore, imperative that race scholars understand the paradigm's enduring resonance and potential before concluding that it nevertheless ought to be abandoned. It is my belief, however, that the paradigm is important to the Asian American civil rights agenda today and that to eliminate it from race discourse would mean losing an important tool for living in and understanding our evolving, racially stratified society.

The second part of this essay very briefly summarizes some scholarship on the black/white paradigm and questions the boundaries and assumptions embedded within the scholarship. The third part clarifies my own assumptions about race and race relationships—namely that they are constructed and therefore unstable—and identifies six dimensions of the black/white paradigm. These six dimensions, through which I attempt to (re)define the black/white paradigm, are elaborated in the fourth part. The final part is devoted to addressing the objection that the black/white paradigm is inapplicable to the Asian American civil rights agenda by analyzing immigrants' rights and affirmative action through the lens of the paradigm as I envision it.

"Black/White": Scholarship on the Paradigm

Condemnation of the black/white paradigm is usually premised on the argument that the nation is no longer Black and White but multiracial, such that the paradigm has become obsolete. This critique of the black/white paradigm suggests that many scholars reduce the black/white paradigm to serve a purely descriptive function; the paradigm was acceptable in 1960 when 96 percent of the minority population was Black, but now that Black Americans constitute only 50 percent of the people of color, the paradigm can no longer stand (Ramirez 1995).

While the descriptive function is a significant aspect of the black/white paradigm, it is not the paradigm's only, nor its most important, function. Thus, a rejection of the paradigm based solely on its apparent failure to reflect racial demographics underestimates its sophistication and fails to explain its longevity. Recent race scholarship by Asian American and Latino/a scholars has relied on this oversimplified, descriptive version of the black/white paradigm (Chang 1994; Omi and Winant 1994; Perea 1997). The works of Robert Chang, a leading American race theorist, and Juan Perea, a Latino scholar who has grappled directly with the "dominant and pervasive character" of the black/white paradigm, are particularly thoughtful. Still, neither Chang nor Perea takes the discussion of the paradigm much further than Michael Omi and Howard Winant's seminal work on the racial formation theory and their 1994 critique of the black/white bipolar model (Omi and Winant 1994). This section summarizes the scholars' representations of the black/white paradigm and questions some of their assumptions and prescriptions.

Omi and Winant and the Los Angeles Riot

Michael Omi and Howard Winant's project on racial formation in the United States is to explore the construction of race (Omi and Winant 1994). They argue that race is not essential, but social and political; the concept of race can be transformed through political struggle and sociohistorical processes generally. They call this continual process of constructing and reconstructing race "racial formation" (55). The theory of racial formation embraces the notion that race is not merely a classificatory system based on the distinctions among human bodies at any given moment, but also contains traces of past struggle over, and present understanding of, social and political relationships.

In the epilogue to the second edition of *Racial Formation in the United States*, written after the 1992 Los Angeles riots, Omi and Winant (1994) seem to address the prevalence of the black/white paradigm.[3] They reject the project of dichotomizing race and identify five problems in the black/white conception. First, they argue that the complex nature of race relations must be analyzed in light of changing dynamics within and among racial groups. Second, they suggest that biracial theories ignore issues specific to non-Black, non-White racial groups. Third, in a related point, they argue that biracial theories also ignore the different consequences of policies such as affirmative action or welfare to different racial groups. Fourth, they assert that the black/white model overlooks "particularities of contemporary racial politics" such as nativism (154). Finally, they posit that the model marginalizes or eliminates other—non-Black, non-White—voices in race discourse.

These critiques provide important insights, but Omi and Winant (1994) clearly indicate that their critiques are aimed at biracial theorizing because the privileging of the Black-White relationship ignores "widespread and multiracial discontent" (153). There is, however, a difference between a focus on the Black-White relationship and the black/white paradigm, and Omi and Winant's discussion does not clarify to which they object.

Juan Perea and Race Paradigms

Juan Perea's "The Binary Paradigm of Race: The 'Normal Science' of American Racial Thought" (1997) can be seen as an extension of the discussion Omi and Winant began in *Racial Formation in the United States.* Perea attempts to prove the existence of the black/white paradigm by applying Thomas Kuhn's study of paradigms to race discourse (Kuhn 1970). Perea finds that even as paradigms help us to frame knowledge, they also exclude and distort by defining and thus limiting relevance. Accordingly, he defines the black/white paradigm as "the conception that race in America consists, either exclusively or primarily, of only two constituent racial groups, the Black and the White" (Perea 1997, 1219). Perea then documents the ways in which the black/white binary paradigm has excluded the experiences and struggles of Latinos and other non-Black, non-White groups by examining textbooks and history books that purport to deal with the race problem in general but focus primarily on the struggles of the African American population.

Perea focuses largely on the effect of the black/white paradigm on scholarship and "normal research" on race (Perea 1997, 1219). I emphatically agree with Perea that the absence or marginalization in scholarship of other racialized groups such as Latinos, Asian Americans, and Native Americans is harmful not only to these groups, but to the richness of race discourse in general. But I disagree with his suggestion that the black/white paradigm has an unimportant role in forming or understanding the racial identities and positions of non-White, non-Black groups and individuals because, as I attempt to demonstrate in the fourth part, the black/white paradigm is more sophisticated than Perea's narrow, race-specific definition of it.

Moreover, the ultimate purpose of Perea's discussion remains somewhat confusing. He states that he opposes the use of paradigms and instead advocates the development of an inclusive and particularized understanding of race. Although he denies that his "new understanding" of race is another paradigm, it is not clear how or why it manages not to be one (1254).[4]

Robert Chang and a Theory of Asian American Legal Scholarship

Within Asian American legal academia, Robert Chang has been one of the most vocal scholars in denouncing the paradigm as "inadequate" to address the concerns of the Asian American community. His article, "Toward an Asian American Legal Scholarship: Critical Race Theory, Post-structuralism, and Narrative Space," suggests themes and theories of Asian American legal scholarship, offering a generalized perspective on the direction that the scholarship should take (Chang 1994). One of the most noteworthy sections in his article is Chang's critique of the current racial paradigm, which he identifies as the black/white paradigm. Chang claims to analyze the paradigm on two levels. First, on the level of lived reality, he observes that the color of the American population has become variegated in the past four decades. He calls this conflict between the black/white paradigm and demographic transformations a "problem of coverage" (1266). Second, Chang argues (in a maneuver that conflates the black/white paradigm with the civil rights movement) that the theory and philosophy of the traditional civil rights movement—that is, its focus on individual rights—is antithetical to many Asian philosophies of no-self.[5]

Unfortunately, Chang's short critique (about six paragraphs) of the current racial paradigm begs more questions about the author's assumptions than it answers. For example, he does not explain why the black/white paradigm should be identified with traditional civil rights work, and he fails to defend his assertion that traditional civil rights is indeed centrally concerned with individual rights as opposed to group rights or equal protection.[6] Moreover, he glosses over the unverified and essentializing notion that Asian Americans share a no-self worldview that is theoretically opposed to individual rights.

Although Chang writes about Asian American civil rights on two levels, his main critique of the traditional civil rights movement and the contemporary dominance of the black/white paradigm is devoted to the problem of coverage. He forcefully argues that the black/white paradigm "misunderstands" the racial situation in the United States because race hierarchy has "more than just a top and a bottom" (Chang 1994, 1267). By framing the argument in this way, Chang implies that Asian Americans fall somewhere in the middle of the race hierarchy. On the other hand, such an understanding tends to confuse his own position on the "model minority myth," which he claims is a "complimentary façade . . . [that] works a dual harm by (1) denying the existence of present-day discrimination against Asian Americans and the present-day effects of past discrimination, and (2) legitimizing the oppression of other racial minorities and poor whites" (20). If indeed the "model minority" is a façade and race hierarchy is not bipolar, where or how are Asian Americans situated in the racial landscape? Although he denies the black/white paradigm a place in Asian American legal scholarship, Chang does not offer an answer to this question.

"Black/White": The Meaning and Impact of the Paradigm

THE JUDGE: But now, why do you refer to you people as blacks? Why not brown people? I mean you people are more brown than black.
BIKO: In the same way as I think white people are more pink than white.[7]

A shared assumption among Omi, Winant, Perea, and Chang is that the black/white paradigm is a race-specific, descriptive model of race in the United States. The new conventional wisdom seems to be that (at least) "yellow," "brown," and "red" need to be included in order for race discourse to be inclusive and effective toward the eradication of discrimination. In other words, these critics of the black/white paradigm emphatically declare that yellow, brown, and red are neither black nor white.

One problem with this view of the black/white paradigm is that it considers only one of the paradigm's many dimensions. As Gary Okihiro (1994) has noted (in the context of speaking about Asian Americans), the simple question of whether yellow is black or white or neither encompasses many other more complex questions: questions of American identity, Asian American identity, third-world identity, the relationships among people of color, and the nature of American racial formation. I would add that the question of black or white is also explicitly a question of the accumulation and concatenation of social and cultural symbols and meanings about race, at any given moment, recognizing that such symbols and meanings continually change. This view reflects the "constructedness" of racialized individuals and groups in society.

Race scholars in the United States have explored extensively the social and legal construction of race. Omi and Winant's racial formation theory is one prominent example of an antiessentialist perspective on the "social nature of race" (Omi and Winant 1994, 4). Ian Haney Lopez (1996) has taken the racial formations theory further and examined the legal construction of race by analyzing citizenship and naturalization cases that attempted to define "white" with confusing and contradictory results, especially as whiteness related to Asians and Latinos. With this project, Haney Lopez destabilizes whiteness by exploring some of the biological and anthropological alternatives that American law and society considered in its attempt to circumscribe racial privilege. He writes that "race is highly contingent, specific to times, places, and situations. ... [H]owever powerful and however deeply a part of our society race may be, races are still only human inventions" (Haney Lopez 1996, xiii–xiv). Hence, to recognize the "constructedness" of race is also to understand that "black" and "white" may signify more than our immediate understanding of specific racial categories. Haney Lopez's examination of the racial prerequisite cases of the late nineteenth and first half of the twentieth centuries reveals that "white" stands not simply for members of the White race, but for a set of concepts and privileges associated with that race. Accordingly, "black" is defined by the denial of those same privileges (Haney Lopez 1996).[8]

Thus, the black/white paradigm is rife with complexities that reach beyond the races for which the words "black" and "white" stand. There are at least six significant dimensions to the paradigm: (1) descriptive, (2) theoretical, (3) political, (4) historical, (5) linguistic/poetic, and (6) subversive. The descriptive dimension is the most limiting because of its association with specific races, although, as I argue in the fourth part, there is more even to the descriptive dimension than critics of the paradigm acknowledge. But it is the theoretical dimension of the black/white paradigm that reveals the paradigm's full scope as well as its possibilities. Recognition of these various dimensions is important for the American civil rights agenda and legal scholarship because they reveal where and how Asian Americans are situated within American racial structure and suggest openings for collective, counterhegemonic discourse.

Although the six dimensions are presented more or less discretely below, they are, in fact, interdependent aspects of the paradigm. Each must be fleshed out and examined before rejection of the paradigm can be justified. On the other hand, such an investigation may lead to a revitalization of the paradigm for the Asian American civil rights agenda.

The Six Dimensions of the Black/White Paradigm

The Descriptive Dimension

There are two ways in which the black/white paradigm could occupy a descriptive role in race discourse. The first and more facile would be to view the black/white paradigm as descriptive of the relationship between two specific races: "black" signifying African Americans and possibly West Indians, and "white" signifying European Americans. This descriptive definition is of central importance in Chang's and Perea's articles, as well as in Omi and Winant's book. If the black/white paradigm's sole purpose is to reflect racial demographics, it would be truly false and underinclusive, rendering invisible Asians, Latinos, Native Americans, and other groups in race discourse. In that case, the paradigm would indeed suffer from a problem of "coverage" by failing to understand and incorporate the experiences of other groups that also contend with racism and discrimination. Another harmful effect of a race-specific paradigm would be its ratification of the notion that only the relationship between Blacks and Whites matters. This is the starting point for Perea's critique of the black/white paradigm as expressed in textbooks and history books that do not document the struggle of Asian Americans, Latinos, or Native Americans while purporting to write about race and civil rights history in general. In this way, both Chang and Perea are attempting to discuss what they perceive to be certain groups' fundamentally existential crisis in race discourse in the United States.

This definition is, however, too limited and superficial. A more complex aspect of the descriptive dimension of the paradigm is its reflection of racial stratification and conceptualization in the United States (Calmore 1995).[9] This more complex descriptive dimension is implicit in both Chang's and Perea's discussions of the black/white paradigm's persistence in race discourse. Racial conceptualization and stratification in the United States are dominated by the notion that "black" and "white" are positioned at opposite extremes that denote race oppression and privilege.

The black/white structure may exist in the form that it does because of the priority in time of racial discrimination against Blacks or because of the sheer virulence of racism targeting Blacks, thereby rendering the Black American experience most salient. Regardless of how the paradigm came about, it is undeniably one of the chief mechanisms by which individuals and groups become racialized, and even self-identify, on both legal and social/cultural planes. One example of how Asian Americans have been racialized according to the black/white paradigm can be found in *People v. Hall*,[10] a case that nullified a Chinese witness's testimony under a law that prohibited Blacks, Mulattos, and Indians from testifying in trials involving White defendants. In that decision, the court determined that "Black" included all non-White. An event of self-identification within the black/white paradigm occurred in *Hudgins v. Wright*,[11] a case that illustrates how slavery laws constructed to be almost synonymous with "enslavement" in 1806, prompting three Native American women to declare themselves not black (Davis 1996a, 703). Finally, Haney Lopez's analysis of the racial prerequisite cases demonstrates that both dynamics can occur simultaneously through legal and social pressures (Haney Lopez 1996). "White" in the late nineteenth and early twentieth centuries meant citizenship, and individuals of Asian ancestry attempted to define themselves as "white" in order to naturalize and acquire the rights attendant to citizenship.[12] But because Blacks were also granted citizenship by the US government, the prerequisite cases reveal that Asians attempting to define themselves as "white" may have wanted more than citizenship: by casting themselves as "white" rather than "black," they rejected the negative attributes and stereotypes associated with blackness.

Racialization by association with blackness and whiteness endures. Frank Wu has been most eloquent in discussing the ways in which Asian Americans have interacted with the paradigm. In an article on affirmative action, Wu writes that "[r]acial groups are conceived of as white, black, honorary whites, or constructive blacks" (Wu 1995, 249). Wu's choice of the words "honorary" and "constructive" expresses the poles of privilege and oppression. Asian Americans have stood on unstable ground between "black" and "white," falling under the honorary white category in anti–affirmative action arguments, but considered constructive blacks for the purposes of school segregation or antimiscegenation laws (249–250). To say that Asian Americans have been perceived as honorary whites or constructive blacks is, however, slightly misleading in that it tends to convey a notion of race specificity. It is important to keep in mind that although the status of honorary white does affect identity, recognition, and appellation, its more insidious function is co-optation. For example, within the economy of affirmative action policy, "whiteness" encompasses victimization through "reverse racism" and race-based disadvantage in certain educational or occupational opportunities. Insofar as a conservative like Newt Gingrich treats Asian Americans as honorary whites,[13] he refers to common experience under affirmative action, not racial similarity.

In exploring the descriptive dimension of the black/white paradigm, I do not mean to ascribe a naturalness to the current race hierarchy. It is true that the black/white paradigm has played a leading role in shaping race discourse and ideology in the United States, and as such, it is not merely descriptive of a thing already in existence. As Davis (1996b, 615) remarked, "[T]he black-white paradigm is an intriguing piece of white supremacy." The black/white paradigm is derived from a racism that has created this particular hierarchy and method of race conceptualization. To that extent, the black/white paradigm not only posits that the Black American race experience is the paradigmatic race experience in the United States, but describes the manifestations and systematic organization of racism as well.

The Theoretical Dimension

Breaking down the notion that the "black" and the "white" of the black/white paradigm are race-specific clears space for a refreshed understanding about racial stratification in the United States and the role of the paradigm. It should be clear from the discussion so far that the paradigm is not simply race-specific. To be nonwhite is to be the other, and that other is constructed as black, regardless of where a particular individual or group comes from or what it looks like.[14] The theoretical dimension of the black/white binary paradigm is perhaps most significant because of its clarity on the issue of domination and subordination. In the binary system, Whites "fashioned themselves as the superior opposite to those constructed as others" (Haney Lopez 1996, 167). Those "others" have included various White races, but the fluidity or ambiguity of their positions within the black/white paradigm has sometimes served to cloud the bases upon which dominance and subordinance are conditioned.

The othered status of Asians was plainer in the nineteenth century and first half of the twentieth. It was manifested in race-based exclusion laws, naturalization laws, and miscegenation laws. Asians' racially subordinated status was also socially and culturally evident: it has been said that the status that the White American preferred Asians to occupy was one of "biped domestic animals in the white man's service" (Haney Lopez 1996, 167). The association between Asian and black was also more explicit in the nineteenth century: there has been important scholarship on the "negotiation" of the Chinese and the attribution to the Chinese of characteristics formerly ascribed to Blacks, Black slaves in particular (Haney Lopez 1996; Okihiro 1994).

In the latter half of the twentieth century, the subordinated status of Asian Americans has become obfuscated. The most obvious example of this obfuscation at work is the model minority myth, which has been embraced not only by White Americans in order to allege reverse discrimination, but to some degree by Asian Americans content to claim their superiority over Blacks and Latinos

(Wu 1995).[15] Placing Asian Americans in the middle, however, does not necessarily mean that they are beyond or outside of the black/white paradigm. Asian Americans are now defined by their proximity to White conservative values and economic success as much as they were formerly compared to Blacks. The process of racialization and correlated valuation of individuals and groups occurs regardless of whether Asian Americans actually possess White or Black traits, whatever such traits may be. Okihiro (1994, 34) expresses this instability (and arbitrariness) in the following way:

> Asian Americans have served the master class, whether as "blacks" in the past or as "near-whites" in the present or as "marginal men" in both the past and the present. Yellow is emphatically neither white nor black; but insofar as Asians and Africans share a subordinate position to the master class, yellow is a shade of black, and black, a shade of yellow.

In light of the indeterminacy of "black" and "white," it is unclear what it means to go beyond the black/white paradigm. For Perea, going beyond the black/white paradigm would mean the rejection of any type of race paradigm in favor of "the development of particularized understanding of the histories of each and every racial groups" (Perea 1997, 1256). But we have seen through the scholarship of Haney Lopez, Davis, and Okihiro that close examination of these groups' histories magnifies the ways in which the black/white paradigm organizes groups' social, legal, and racial identities and relationships in the United States. Although critics of the paradigm may condemn this method of organization, it is important to account for the fact that the paradigm may be a part of many people's understanding and experiences.

The Political Dimension

The black/white paradigm offers a robust, unequivocal understanding of the relationship between race-based domination and subordination. Its political dimension is closely related to its theoretical one in that a claim to blackness by Asian Americans can lead to coalition-building among people of color against white supremacy.

The notion of a coalition against white supremacy is forcefully articulated by Charles Lawrence, although, curiously, he rejects the black/white paradigm as "dysfunctional in a multiracial society" because it is "not first about the eradication of white supremacy" (Lawrence 1995, 819, 826). Lawrence writes of the need for a theory that seeks societal transformation, a theory that "sees [racism's] injury as done to the collective, as suffered by us all" (825). He unfortunately fails to explain why the black/white paradigm does not capture the spirit of the nonwhite collective "whom white supremacy ... relegates to varying degrees of inferiority" (826).

Chris Iijima, on the other hand, identifies the potential of the black/white paradigm to accomplish the goals articulated by Lawrence. According to Iijima, "deconstructing the old black/white paradigm carries with it new dangers. ... The original paradigm, while constructing and reaffirming white dominance, also permitted a useful counterfocus on the effect and operation of white supremacy" (Iijima 1997, 69). In other words, to recognize the operation of white supremacy, we are forced to rely on the black/white paradigm. Iijima illustrates this proposition by analyzing the racialization of Blacks and Koreans during the 1992 Los Angeles riots:

It is significant to note that in the construction of the conflict, nativist arguments that Koreans were foreigners and less American positioned African Americans as "white" relative to Asians. On the other hand, Korean Americans were also placed within the entrepreneurial American Dream and positioned as white. This kind of positioning becomes coherent only if the assumptions of the old paradigm and the placement of whiteness within it are accepted as the operating framework (70).[16]

Iijima makes a subtle point here about the black/white paradigm. He argues that even as the paradigm forces us to speak about race experiences according to its vocabulary and not one of our own choosing, it also permits us to understand (and potentially counter) the deployment of white supremacy and privilege.

Iijima (1997) adds another important insight about the critique of the black/white paradigm. He argues that the current focus on "categories of difference" may have overtaken the "search for political commonality" among those raced as non-White (55). For Iijima, the black/white paradigm helps forge political identities for people of color and allows a "reverse discourse" organized around antisubordination and antisupremacist ideology (74).

The establishment of a strong antisubordination principle is especially important for Asian Americans because they are positioned in the "model minority" middle and could contribute knowingly or unwittingly to the further oppression of African Americans. This buffer position renders Asian Americans especially vulnerable to political manipulation or, even worse, can cause a blindness or amnesia among Asian Americans about discrimination they themselves face. To advocate a coalition among those people of color raced as "black" is not to declare that there are no interethnic conflicts or that the experiences of racism for Blacks, Asians, Latinos, and Native Americans are identical (Calmore 1995).[17] Political alignment and acknowledgment of differences are not mutually exclusive; non-White people of color should "negotiate their common agendas,"[18] one of which must undoubtedly be a broad goal of antisubordination (Calmore 1995, 1233, 1263).

The Historical Dimension

To be sure, the antisubordination principle does not by itself justify the black/white paradigm; that principle could probably be expressed in many different ways. Reliance on the antisubordination principle to legitimate the paradigm would be defeated by arguments offered by Chang and Perea; those scholars may object to the very words "black" and "white" on the grounds that they are indicative of specific races to the exclusion of others. Even if "black" and "white" are not race-specific, they may be so construed by people who write or read books on race, or by people who propose or make civil rights legislation. This result could be harmful to non-Black people of color because they may indeed end up marginalized from race discourse and remedies. The next three dimensions of the black/white paradigm that will be discussed—historical, poetic/linguistic, and subversive—will illustrate why the risk we take in preserving the black/white paradigm may be justified.

The historical dimension of the paradigm first and most fundamentally refers to the Black-White struggle since the birth of this nation. The history of the kidnapping, enslavement, and subhuman treatment of Africans by White European Americans is simply the most vivid and terrifying example of white supremacy in American history. The black/white paradigm also serves as a constant reminder of the continued racial oppression of African Americans in the legal, political, and social arenas: mob violence culminating in lynchings, Jim Crow laws, and ghettoization, to name a few of the strategies of subjugation. At the same time that the paradigm evokes this most notorious period in American history, it also recalls the civil rights movement of the 1950s and 1960s and the battle to revolutionize the race hierarchy and power structure of the United States. It brings to mind the inspirational stories of Black activists like Martin Luther King, Thurgood Marshall, and Rosa Parks. In this way, the black/white paradigm not only highlights the long-standing racist ideology of the nation, but also suggests tactical opposition to that ideology.

Exploring the changing nature and content of the black/white paradigm also offers insights into supremacist ideology as applied to non-Black races. As I have argued above, the paradigm now describes more than the Black and White races; it has developed to articulate a hierarchical vision of racial groups that includes Latinos, Asian Americans, and Native Americans. From this perspective, the black/white paradigm infuses a sense of continuity and to the civil rights work of non-Black people of color by revealing the ways in which these groups' histories intersect with the history of Black Americans. One example of historical intersection is the importation of Chinese laborers to replace slave labor during the Reconstruction Era. The Chinese were described as "more obedient and industrious than the negro, [able to] work as well without as with an overseer, and at the same time are more cleanly in their habits and persons than the freedmen" (cited in Wu 1995, 231). This "praise" of Chinese laborers is revealing in that it (1) places the Chinese in an intermediate position between Blacks and Whites, (2) denigrates Blacks further, and (3) subordinates the Chinese as the new "obedient" slave labor force in the place of Blacks (Wu 1995, 229). This example, cited by Wu as the origin of the model minority, demonstrates not only that Asian American history cannot be divorced from the black/white paradigm, but also that the legacy of the paradigm remains a vibrant part of contemporary Asian American experience. Another clear moment of historical intersection is the Los Angeles riots, where the histories of at least three non-White racial groups intersected explosively.[19]

These historical examples affirm Neil Gotanda's observation that "[e]ven as the possibilities of racial stratification and the embedded ideological constructions of Orientalism are examined, awareness of the continuation of that basic axis of power and privilege [between Whites and African Americans] must continue" (Gotanda 1996, 246). Any analysis of racial oppression in the United States, including that of Asian Americans, has as its starting point the enslavement and continued subjugation of African Americans. From *Hudgins* in 1806 to the Los Angeles riots in 1992,[20] White privilege and domination over non-Black people of color have been defined and organized within the context of the Black/ White relationship. This relationship, as well as subsequent formations, has been expressed specifically through the black/white paradigm.

A failure to acknowledge the significance of the relationship and the origin of the Black/White paradigm has repercussions for Asian American legal scholarship on race.[21] When the acknowledgment is no more than a concession to recorded facts, Asian American civil rights history itself flounders. Harold Koh (1992), for example, has noted the absence of a sense of "movement" and continuity in the Asian American civil rights struggle. Koh's comment supports Perea's argument because the absence of Asian American civil rights history in casebooks and the law school classroom contributes to a "scattered" impression of that history. But this may also be in part due to a failure to recognize the historical intersections among Blacks, Asian Americans, Latinos, and other non-White people of color, leading to a decontextualized and scattered understanding of non–African American civil rights activism.

The Linguistic/Poetic Dimension

Another notable aspect of the black/white paradigm is the vitality of its vocabulary in race discourse. The exchange between the Judge and Steve Biko, as transcribed in Donald Woods's *Biko* (and quoted in the epigraph to the third part), illustrates the hermeneutics of the words "black" and "white" (Woods 1978).

In attempting to understand the way in which Biko uses the word "black," the Judge suggests that "black" is an inaccurate description of the physical appearance of Africans.[22] Biko's reply demonstrates that, in fact, the words "black" and "white" are pregnant with negative and positive meanings, respectively.[23] Biko asserts that his embrace of the word "black" is aimed at the black man so that the word may be "elevate[d] ... to a position where we can look upon ourselves positively; because even if we [Blacks] choose to be called 'brown,' there will still be reference to 'blacks' in an inferior sense in literature and in speeches by white racists in our society" (Woods 1978, 165–166).

Biko's response reveals three crucial insights. The first is that "black" and "white" have developed in opposition to each other in our language. This is not limited to political or racist language; as Biko observed, it exists in literary language. Examples abound: One of the more obvious would be Joseph Conrad's *Heart of Darkness*, where "black" stands for the sinister and unknowable (Conrad 1899/1991). Setting aside whatever political views Conrad might have had, his novella could be interpreted as the story of a man whose descent into madness (and finally death) is caused by his liminal racial position in the jungles of the Congo. In this sense, the pairing of "black" and "white" is almost poetic; its apparent simplicity is, in fact, so expressive of difference and opposition that it approaches the visual.

The second insight is that the black/white paradigm is not one that we can escape through our own will. This indicates not only that we are raced but also that we are raced in specific terms, whether those terms be "black" and "white" or "Black" and "White." This has particular applicability to Asian Americans demanding a third category (perhaps "yellow") that would capture their sense of difference from the black and the white. As Steve Biko observed, we can call ourselves "brown" or "yellow" until we are blue in the face, but it is unlikely that those terms will be adopted or will displace the vocabulary of the black/white paradigm successfully (cited in Wu 1996, 205).

Moreover, it is naive to assume that we can fully control the content of the words that we choose. This leads to Biko's third insight: rather than attempting to create a parallel racial vocabulary, it may be more effective to undermine the content of the words white racism has chosen. This is a tactic that not only contains the element of surprise, but also explodes the assumptions embedded in the current, dominant vocabulary of race. Such explosions happen when Asians in England call themselves "black" (Chang 1996). They also happen when Asians, Whites, and multiracials in South Africa call themselves "black" (Lawrence 1995). This tactic may also explain why the term "African American" is fading out of discourse: it includes West Indians and Muslim Blacks who do not fit neatly under the category of "African American" but share similar experiences and feelings of solidarity.

The Subversive Dimension

The discussion on the linguistic dimension of the black/white paradigm hints at the rich possibility of subversion. Subversion is, in my view, the only way that racialization will progress beyond the black/white paradigm to a discourse that will be not only more inclusive, but also more rational. Each of the different dimensions I have discussed in this essay contains this element of subversion.

The descriptive dimension of the paradigm serves as the foundation for the process of subversion. Scholars such as Omi, Winant, Haney Lopez, and Wu have eloquently argued that race is a social and legal construction, and that race groups in the United States have been defined in relation to blackness and whiteness. This process has been most evident for Asian Americans, whose racial status has shifted from basically "black" to almost "white" over time. The black/white paradigm determines social status and denies free self-definition; this aspect of the paradigm is the most insidious because it creates a self-perpetuating race hierarchy in which the goal is to maintain the status quo for those situated at the top. Understanding the black/white paradigm in this way means that Asian Americans can begin to grapple with both how racial identity is constructed and how it can be reconstructed. Such a step requires a critical analysis of the black/white paradigm as a mechanism that situates various racial groups within a structure that restricts access to privileges such as citizenship, education, and employment.

Recognition of the black/white paradigm as an iteration of race hierarchy brings into focus the overarching strategy of domination over all those categorized as "others." But even as the paradigm oppresses, it betrays a small opening for political counteraction in the form of Iijima's "reverse discourse" and through the paradigm's inherent caricature of race relations within its descriptive dimension (Iijima 1997). This also leads to the possibility of coalition among people of color who share the antisubordination agenda. Moreover, the paradigm contextualizes the civil rights agenda, reminding us not only of historical race oppression but also of historical resistance against oppression, especially salient to those who share a sense of intersecting civil rights histories.

In at least one sense, Asian Americans possess greater opportunities to subvert race hierarchy and become agents of change than other people of color. Because Asian Americans have been situated as the model minority, they enjoy greater opportunities in education and occupation. Yet the model minority status is problematic, especially as it contributes to the maintenance of racist polarity. In the same way that racial categories become destabilized when Asians call themselves black, a rejection of the model minority status destabilizes racial relationships. This means first that Asian Americans who have achieved financial or political success through the black/white paradigm (and its own unofficial affirmative action) also have the means to effect change by using their position. Second, Asians can subvert race hierarchy by refusing to adopt the politically conservative views that are imputed to the model minority. Both of these decisions require a deep understanding of the paradigm.

The Asian American Civil Rights Agenda: Identifying the Differences

Banishing the black/white paradigm from legal scholarship disconnects it from Asian American civil rights activism. On the other hand, confrontation with, as well as redeployment of, the paradigm by legal scholars has the potential to contribute to activism and further the civil rights agenda. Existing scholarship challenges this notion and argues that the black/white paradigm does not fit the Asian American experience or that community's goals.[24] First, they argue that the discrimination experienced by Asian Americans follows not a color axis but a "foreigner axis." That is, whereas Blacks deal with second-class citizenship, a status repugnant to principles of American democracy, Asian Americans are viewed as outsiders to whom access is rightly denied (Ancheta 1998; Park 1996). The assumption is that because Blacks are assumed to be American citizens, the demand for equal rights, opportunities, and privileges appears more legitimate than when immigrants demand those same things. Second, they argue that some of the most pressing civil rights issues concerning Asian Americans either do not concern Black Americans or affect them differently (Ancheta 1998; Omi and Winant 1994). The logical conclusion to this statement is that a race paradigm that fits the Black civil rights agenda may not necessarily fit the Asian American agenda.

Racism or Nativism?

Angelo Ancheta's uses the term "foreigner axis" to explain subordination based on "racial" origin (Ancheta 1998, 64). Therefore, Asian Americans, Latinos, and Arab Americans are categorized as foreigners and immigrants, regardless of actual citizenship status or place of birth. Ancheta calls this mechanism "outsider racialization" (Ancheta 1998, 64). Outsider racialization closely resembles "nativism," a distinctive type of racism aimed at groups like Asian Americans, Latinos, and Arab Americans. Nativistic arguments about Asian Americans or Latinos are prevalent in political discourse—the controversy over Asian American contributions to the Democratic National Committee in 1996, Proposition 187 in California, the English-only movement, and the myth of the Japanese takeover—exemplify the power of nativistic sentiments in the American social and political consciousness. Nativism has, as Chang notes, a certain allure because it tends to express racism and oppression in seemingly race-neutral terms such as "immigrants" and "foreigners" (Chang 1994).

Although nativism is one of the most salient aspects of Asian American experience, Ancheta's argument that Asian Americans are not affected by the color axis seems overstated since nativistic arguments are aimed at those who are classified as non-White.[25] This is why I believe that the term "outsider racialization" is superior to "nativism": it successfully conveys that race and national origin have been combined for discriminatory purposes. Thus, it is curious that Ancheta denies the effect of the color axis in favor of the foreigner axis alone. The assumption of nativist racists is that the United States is a White nation and that anyone who is not (or does not look) White is a foreigner (Brimelow 1995). As Pat Chew has observed, "Like African Americans, Asian Americans' skin color and other facial features physically distinguish them. . . . As Justice Sutherland noted in *United States v. Bhagat Singh* 'it cannot be doubted that the children born in this country of Hindu parents would retain indefinitely the clear evidence of their ancestry'" (Chew 1994, 34). Thus, nativism properly can be seen as a refined derivative of discrimination based on the color axis.[26]

Notwithstanding the significance of the color axis, the question remains whether outsider racialization "fits" within the black/white paradigm. The role of outsider racialization within the paradigm can be more clearly discerned by examining the way "reverse nativism" is used to discriminate against Black Americans. There is evidence that Blacks who have accents, and are thereby identified as immigrants or foreigners, are treated with less overt discrimination than Blacks who do not have accents. Malcolm Gladwell (1996) argues that the success of West Indians in New York, whom he compares to Korean and Chinese immigrants, is "one last, vicious twist" in the discrimination against Black Americans. He explains,

> Their advantage depends on their remaining outsiders. . . . There is already some evidence that the considerable economic and social advantages that West Indians hold over American blacks begin to dissipate by the second generation, when the island accent has faded, and those in positions of power who draw distinctions between good blacks and bad blacks begin to lump West Indians with everyone else.
>
> . . .
>
> In the new racism, as in the old, somebody always has to be the nigger. (79, 81)

While reinforcing the idea that "black" within the paradigm is not specific, reverse nativism sheds light on the interaction between outsider racialization and the black/white paradigm. Comparing the way in which outsider racialization is articulated against Black Americans in New York and against Korean Americans in Los Angeles, it becomes clear that it is deployed opportunistically between poles of blackness and whiteness. The treatment of Black Americans in New York also suggests that the history of White-on-Black oppression, as well as the accumulation of its signs, may inform the treatment of immigrant groups. It is also plausible to conclude from this example that the treatment of immigrants, in turn, informs the treatment of Black Americans.

Thus, to the extent that racial foreignness contains attributes of whiteness or of blackness, the paradigm captures the subordinated status not only of actual foreigners, but more aptly of permanent residents and citizens who happen to be people of color. This is the mode of analysis employed by Iijima in his analysis of the Los Angeles riots, and it can also be usefully employed to examine Proposition 187 in California (Iijima 1997; Haney Lopez 1996). Nonetheless, outsider racialization perhaps does not achieve a perfect "fit" with the black/white paradigm because despite theoretical consistency, the application of the paradigm to the foreigner axis aspect of outsider racialization in the Asian American context remains somewhat counterintuitive.

Items on the Asian American Civil Rights Agenda

The Asian American civil rights agenda encompasses issues such as immigration, welfare, affirmative action, education, and suffrage. Although some of these issues (education, suffrage) coincide with those of the traditional civil rights movement, others (affirmative action, immigration) present newer challenges to civil rights activists.

1. AFFIRMATIVE ACTION AND THE MODEL MINORITY MYTH

Asian Americans play a strange and contorted role in the affirmative action debate. Those who would eliminate affirmative action use the Asian American population to exemplify how affirmative action disadvantages non-Whites as well as Whites. This is especially true for affirmative action in higher education, where some Asian Americans have been told—and have come to believe—that the program hurts Asian American students' chances of attending certain universities. Newt Gingrich's warning that "Asian Americans are facing a very real danger of being discriminated against" has been heeded by many Asian Americans, as evidenced in their voting pattern on this issue (cited in Wu 1996, 225).

Asian American scholars have expressed concerns about the deployment of Asian Americans as the "example that defeats affirmative action" (Chang 1996; Wu 1995, 225). Frank Wu vigorously attacks the notion that banning action would actually help Asian Americans:

> The real risk to Asian Americans is that they will be squeezed out to provide proportionate representation to whites, not due to the marginal impact of setting aside a few spaces for African Americans. The linkage of Asian Americans and affirmative action . . . is an intentional maneuver by conservative politicians to provide a response to charges of racism. (Wu 1996, 226)[27]

The discussion of action is most often bundled with the myth of the "model minority," which has been used to describe Asians in American society. Somewhat reminiscent of Edna Bonacich's groundbreaking sociological theory of the middleman minority (Bonacich 1973), the model minority myth works to divide the interests of subordinated racial groups. At the same time, it debilitates Asian Americans as individuals (Asians are brainy but lack personality) and as a political entity (Asians are successful and therefore not discriminated against).

The model minority myth can be fruitfully analyzed within the framework of the paradigm. As I have argued above, situating Asian Americans as a buffer between black and white positions Asian Americans not outside of the black/white paradigm, but rather in a vulnerable place where they can be manipulated to serve the interests of the dominant group. This is most likely what occurred in California when a large percentage of Asian Americans voted to eliminate affirmative action programs in the controversial Civil Rights Initiative of 1996. The myth also ultimately leads to further subordination of Asian Americans, especially by thwarting political mobilization, not only within the Asian American population, but also across racial lines. The paradigm can be used to help deconstruct the myth and clarify the subordinated position of Asian Americans in the race hierarchy. Only then can Asian Americans make informed political decisions and meaningfully pursue a civil rights agenda.

2. IMMIGRATION

The question of immigration is an especially volatile issue within the Asian American community. Although Gabriel Chin has argued that the immigration amendments of 1965 equalized immigration opportunities for Asians as compared with immigrants from the Western Hemisphere, the resulting visible increase in the number of immigrants in the United States has precipitated a backlash from White Americans who seek to preserve Anglo American "culture" (Chin 1996). Demographic anxiety has increased in the face of a growing number of people of color. According to a poll reported in the *New York Times*, White Americans believe that the population of Blacks, Asians, and Latinos in the United States is over twice as large (50.1 percent) as it actually is (24.4 percent).[28]

Demographic anxiety among White Americans can be relieved in two possible ways: the first is to restrict immigration of people of color, and the second is to oppress those people of color who are already in the country (Ancheta 1998). Although both reactions stem from racism, they are distinct phenomena. Therefore, when Asian Americans speak of "immigration," a distinction must be made between *immigration* rights and *immigrants'* rights.[29] The treatment of immigrants presents some serious civil rights issues because under the equal protection doctrine, the recent laws that affect immigrants may violate the Constitution (Fiss 1999).[30] One example of such laws is the welfare reform law of 1996, which denies many forms of federal assistance to legal immigrants and their children.[31] Another example is Proposition 187, a measure that denies public education and all nonemergency medical care to undocumented aliens.

Proposition 187 provides fertile ground for analysis using the black/white paradigm. An initiative that was quite obviously directed against illegal immigrants from Mexico, Proposition 187 preyed upon nativist sentiments. Thus, much of the rhetoric of Proposition 187 focused on the idea that illegal immigrants were foreigners taking American jobs and benefits, entitlements belonging to legal residents only. According to John Park (1996, 177–178),

> Among people of color, the resentment toward undocumented immigrants was especially acute. Kevin Ross, an Inglewood deputy district attorney and political action chairman of the NAACP chapter of Los Angeles, noted that "[f]ifty percent of African American youth are unemployed. When the assertion is made that illegal immigrants do the jobs others wouldn't do in the first place, the black community is offended."

This reaction was not limited to African Americans; many Asian Americans and Latinos voted in support of Proposition 187.[32] The strategy behind Proposition 187 successfully positioned legal residents as "white" relative to illegal immigrants because legal residents possessed the rights to work, to go to school, and to receive medical care.

Proposition 187 should also be understood as a case of outsider racialization against more than just the illegal immigrant community in California, although that community is certainly the law's primary target. The "xenophobic climate" created by Proposition 187 also affects entire Latino and Asian American communities because of its tendency for inclusiveness. As many civil rights workers and scholars have already noted, one major problem with Proposition 187 is its "unintended" effects on all people of color who look or sound foreign (Cervantes, Khoka, and Murray 1995; Park 1996).

But extremist propaganda in support of the proposition also makes it clear that the issue was not limited to illegal immigration but intertwined with race and white supremacy:

> Two days before the November 1994 elections . . . flyers were distributed . . . depicting an image of a machine gun firing bullets at a dark skinned man. The flyer reads: "How's this for a new slogan for the U.S. Border Patrol? 'If it ain't white WASTE IT!' Remember, it's stop the Mudslide . . . or drown! 187 Yes! We need a real border. First we get the spics, then the gooks, and at last we get the niggers. They're all going home." (Cervantes, Khoka, and Murray 1995, 6)

There can hardly be a clearer representation of the active dichotomy that informs race discourse today.

Conclusion

The increasing visibility of people of color and the much-discussed demographic predictions for the next have led to increased debate about race, law, and resources in the United States. And it is probably safe to conclude that the call for a more complex theory of race relations—one that better incorporates various people of color—has been heeded by the mainstream. This is most lately exemplified by President Clinton's race initiative.

This essay, however, has sought to demonstrate that the paradigm is a complex theory of race relations and should be recognized as such. An understanding of the paradigm's six dimensions (and there may be more) reveals its capacity both to contextualize race discourse and to express a clear antisubordination agenda. Moreover, the paradigm's persistence in race relations and discourse attests to its continuing relevance and growing complexity. Asian American scholars must resist the temptation to oversimplify or underestimate the paradigm's ability to perpetuate and refine itself by erasing histories, manipulating racial status, and dividing political alliances. Indeed, an alternative theory cannot emerge unless people of color dismantle the current organization and vocabulary of race, which have been articulated through the paradigm.

NOTES

Reprinted by permission of *The Yale Law Journal* Company and William S. Hein Company from *The Yale Law Journal*, Vol. 108 (1999): 2385–2412.

1 Omi and Winant (1994, 153) also note that the riots "served to focus media attention on generally neglected subjects—Koreans, Central Americans, who were both victims and victimizers."

2 When Angela Oh argued that the commission should look "beyond" the black/white paradigm, John Hope Franklin is reported to have resisted that suggestion by replying that "[t]his country cut its eyeteeth on racism in the black-white sphere." In this essay, I use the lowercase form of "black" and "white" where the terms are used theoretically, politically, and figuratively.

3 It should be noted that Omi and Winant (1994) do not actually employ the word "paradigm" but alternately use terms such as "model," "conception," "vision," and "theory."

4 Perea's thesis is weak for another reason. Although the early sections of his article seemed to lead to a final, radical demand that the history and experience of groups such as Asian Americans, Latinos, and Native Americans be included in race/civil rights scholarship, Perea ends by merely objecting to the inference that scholarship on the black/white relationship addresses American racism in its totality.

5 For other Asian American legal scholars who take a similar two-tiered approach to the black/white paradigm, see Tamayo (1995) and Wu (1995).

6 Omi and Winant (1994, p. 70), on the other hand, have suggested that the focus on individual rights and remedies, as well as color-blind racial policy, is a deliberate neoconservative strategy of the 1970s and 1980s.

7 Woods (1978, 165).

8 This conception of "black" and "white" can also be found in Adrienne Davis's analysis of *Hudgins v. Wrights*, 11 Va. (1 Hen. & M.) 134 (1806). In *Hudgins*, three enslaved women

sought to be declared free by claiming Native American status. According to Davis (1996a), at the core of the racialized slave system existed White anxiety about being mistakenly enslaved; hence the development of a strong association, and legal presumption, between slavery and blackness, freedom and whiteness.

9 Calmore (1995) identified this as the matrix of domination and system of oppression that lies within the black/white paradigm.

10 *People v. Hall*, 4 Cal. 399 (1854).

11 *Hudgins v. Wright*, 11 Va. (1 Hen. & M) 134 (1806).

12 Haney Lopez (1996, 79–92) discusses *Ozawa v. United States*, 260 US 178 (1927), in which Takao Ozawa, a man of Japanese origin, claimed the right to naturalize based on his assimilated lifestyle and "white" skin color, and *United States v. Thind*, 261 US 204, in which Bhagat Singh Thind, a man of Indian origin, claimed the right to naturalize based on his "scientific" classification as "Caucasian."

13 Gingrich has asserted that Asian Americans are facing a very real danger of being discriminated against because they are becoming too numerous at prestigious universities that have affirmative action (see Wu 1995, 225).

14 It bears repeating that the category "White" is also constructed and that many of those individuals now classified as White were not White less than a century ago (Jacobson 1998).

15 It would be naive to assert that Asian Americans are not tempted by the advantages of assimilation. Haney Lopez (1996, 63–64) has observed, "I do believe ... that dominant America will attempt to situate Asians, Pacific Islanders and Latinos squarely within its efforts to determine who will be 'white' in the twenty-first century. ... It is a call to follow the European immigrant example of groups who, with each generation, have moved into a twilight ethnicity and paid the price of linguistic extinction and cultural loss for the privilege of white racial status." Wu (1996) has characterized the rise of Asian Americans as "a rise toward whiteness."

16 See Haney Lopez (1996, 166), where he explained that during the Los Angeles riots, Asians-as-victims-of-Black-violence came to stand in for Whites in the racial semiotics of Los Angeles, but Asians-as-victims-of-crime were Black for the purposes of police protection in the same semiotics.

17 We ought to heed Calmore's warning that it is analytically and strategically wrong to exaggerate the degree of commonality among people of color (1995).

18 This phrase is used in Calmore 1995.

19 Comparing the histories of Asian Americans and Black Americans is yet another way of understanding the methods of discrimination directed at Asian Americans. Exploring the paradoxes of being Asian American, Pat Chew (1994) describes how Asian Americans "have been victims of lynching, race riots, and slavery," methods of subjugation that are widely known to have been used to oppress Blacks.

20 11 Va. (1 Hen. M.) 134 (1806).

21 Calmore (1995) states that most advocates of moving beyond the paradigm would reject the importance of understanding Black-White racism. Because there are a few scholars who acknowledge the need for understanding the relationship (Valdes 1998, 1087), cautioning against the failure to appreciate the "singular facts and histories that the Black experience of slavery and subordination in this country," and because scholarship that focuses on the paradigm is so limited, I am not yet in agreement with Calmore's view.

22 See Woods (1978, 165).

23 Steve Biko refers to the meaning of the word in "black magic," "black market," and "black sheep of the family" (Woods 1978, 164).

24 Ancheta (1998) argues that the axis of the subordination of Asian Americans is not white versus black; Chang (1998) notes that the black/white paradigm treats Asian Americans as interlopers in race discourse; Tamayo (1995) observed that the paradigm is inadequate.

25 This was not always the case. Nativistic sentiment was rampant in the early 1900s when immigration from Eastern and Southern Europe increased. The debate on restricting the immigration influx vacillated between biological arguments based on the racial inferiority of the new immigrants and social arguments based on their ethnic inferiority (see Feagin 1997).

26 Haney Lopez's analysis of the prerequisite cases also reveals how the foreigner axis works not to the exclusion of the color axis, but rather in conjunction with it (see Haney Lopez 1996, 79–109). Haney Lopez's *White by Law* "provides the crucial link between the analysis of race relations through a black-white paradigm and the treatment of Asian Americans under a citizen-foreigner paradigm" (Wu 1995, 206).

27 Gladwell (1996, 79) notes, "The success of West Indians is not proof that discrimination against American blacks does not exist. Rather, it is the means by which discrimination against American blacks is given one last, vicious twist: I am not so shallow as to despise you for the color of your skin, because I have found people of your color that I like. Now I can despise you for who you are."

28 See Priscilla Labovitz, "Immigration—Just the Facts," *New York Times*, March 25, 1996, A15.

29 The historical bias against Asians in immigration law is by now infamous. Immigration rights complicate the race issue in the United States because a powerful argument for state sovereignty can be made in defense of restricting immigration. The issue of open or fair immigration, while important, is beyond the scope of my essay.

30 Fiss (1999) argues that laws imposing social disabilities on immigrants create social "pariahs" and violate the Equal Protection Clause.

31 See Personal Responsibility and Work Opportunity Reconciliation Act of 1996, Pub. L. No. 104–193, 110 Stat. 2105; see also Statement by President of the United States, 1996 USCCAN 2891 (Aug. 22, 1996) ("I am deeply disappointed that this legislation would deny Federal assistance to legal immigrants and their children, and give States the option of doing the same"); Patrick J. Immigrants to Be Warned of Benefit Cuts, L.A. Feb. 1, 1997 (reporting on the removal of hundreds of thousands of legal immigrants from the Supplemental Security Income rolls).

32 According to Park (1996), 22 percent Latinos and almost half of all Asian Americans and African American voters in California voted in favor of Proposition 187.

REFERENCES

Ancheta, Angelo N. 1998. *Race, Rights, and the Asian American Experience*. New Brunswick, NJ: Rutgers University Press.

Bell, Derrick A., ed. 1980. *Civil Rights: Leading Cases*. Boston: Little, Brown.

Bonacich, Edna. 1973. "A Theory of Middleman Minorities." *American Sociological Review* 38: 583–594.

Brimelow, Peter. 1995. *Alien Nation: Common Sense about America's Immigration Disaster*. New York: Random House.

Calmore, John O. 1995. "Racialized Space and the Culture of Segregation: 'Hewing a Stone of Hope from a Mountain of Despair.'" *University of Pennsylvania Law Review* 143: 1233–1263.

———. 1997. "Our Private Obsession, Our Public Sin: Exploring Michael Omi's 'Messy' Real World of Race." *Law Journal* 15 (25): 56–57.

Cervantes, Nancy, Sasha Khoka, and Bobbie Murray. 1995. "Hate Unleashed: Los Angeles in the Aftermath of Proposition 187." *Chicano-Latino Law Review* 17 (1): 1–21.

Chang, Robert S. 1994. "Toward an Asian American Legal Scholarship: Critical Race Theory, Post-structuralism, and Narrative Space." *Asian American Law Journal* 1 (1): 1241–1323.

———. 1996. "The End of Innocence or Politics the Fall of the Essential Subject." *American University Law Review* 45: 687–691.

———. 1998. "Dreaming in Black and White: Racial-Sexual Policing in *The Birth of a Nation, The Cheat*, and *Who Killed Vincent Chin?*" *Asian Law Journal* 5: 41–42.

Chew, Pat K. 1994. "Asian Americans: The 'Reticent' Minority and Their Paradoxes." *William and Mary Law Review* 36: 1–94.

Chin, Gabriel J. 1996. "The Civil Rights Revolution Comes to Immigration Law: A New Look at the Immigration and Nationality Act of 1965." *N.C. Law Review* 273: 300–303.

Conrad, Joseph. 1899/1991. *Heart of Darkness*. New York: Doubleday.

Davis, Adrienne. 1996a. "Identity Notes Part One: Playing in the Light." *American University Law Review* 45: 695–709.

———. 1996b. "Race, Law and Justice: The Rehnquist Court and the American Dilemma." *American University Law Review* 45: 567–615.

Feagin, Joe. 1997. "Old Poison in New Bottles: The Deep Roots of Modem Nativism." Pp. 13–43 in Juan F. Perea, ed., *Immigrants Out! The New Nativism and the Anti-immigrant Impulse in the United States*. New York: New York University Press.

Fiss, Owen M. 1999. "The Immigrant as Pariah." Pp. 3–21 in Owen M. Fiss, ed., *A Community of Equals: The Constitutional Protection of New Americans*. Boston: Beacon.

Gladwell, Malcolm. 1996. "Black Like Them." *New Yorker*, April 19–May 6, 74–81.

Gordon, Avery F., and Christopher Newfield, eds. 1996. *Mapping Multiculturalism*. Minneapolis: University of Minnesota Press.

Gotanda, Neil. 1996. "Multiculturalism and Racial Stratification." Pp. 238–246 in Avery F. Gordon and Christopher Newfield, eds., *Mapping Multiculturalism*. Minneapolis: University of Minnesota Press.

Grant, Madison. 1924. "The Racial Transformation of America." *North American Review* 2 (9): 350–352.

Haney Lopez, Ian F. 1996. *White by Law: The Legal Construction of Race*. New York: New York University Press.

Iijima, Chris K. 1997. "The Era of We-Construction: Reclaiming the Politics of Asian Pacific American Identity and Reflections on the Critique of the Paradigm." *Columbia Human Rights Law Review* 29: 47–90.

Jacobson, Matthew Frye. 1998. *Whiteness of a Different Color: European Immigrants and the Alchemy of Race*. Cambridge, MA: Harvard University Press.

Kim, Hyung-Chan. 1992. *Asian Americans and the Supreme Court: A Documentary History*. Santa Barbara, CA: Greenwood.

Koh, Harold Hongju. 1992. "Foreword." Pp. ix–x in Hyung-Chan Kim, *Asian Americans and the Supreme Court: A Documentary History*. Santa Barbara, CA: Greenwood.

Kuhn, Thomas. 1970. *The Structure of Scientific Revolutions*. 2nd ed. Chicago: University of Chicago Press.

Lawrence, Charles R. 1995. "Foreword: Race, Multiculturalism, and the Jurisprudence of Transformation." *Stanford Law Review* 47: 819–826.

Okihiro, Gary. 1994. *Margins and Mainstreams: Asians in American History and Culture*. Seattle: University of Washington Press.

Omi, Michael, and Howard Winant. 1994. *Racial Formation in the United States: From the 1960s to the 1990s*. New York: Routledge.

Park, John S. W. Park. 1996. "Race Discourse and Proposition 187." *Michigan Journal of Race and Law* 2 (1): 175–204.

Perea, Juan F. 1997. "The Binary Paradigm of Race: The 'Normal Science' of American Racial Thought." *California Law Review* 85: 1213–1258.

Ramirez, Deborah. 1995. "Multicultural Empowerment: It's Not Just Black and White." *Stanford Law Review* 47: 957–959.

Tamayo, William R. 1995. "When the 'Coloreds' Are Neither Black nor Citizens: The United States Civil Rights Movement and Global Migration." *Asian Law Journal* 2 (1): 1–32.

Valdes, Francisco. 1998. "Foreword: Under Consciousness, Community, and Theory." *California Law Review* 85: 1087–1104.

Woods, Donald. 1978. *Biko*. New York: Henry Holt.

Wu, Frank H. 1995. "Neither Black nor White: Asian Americans and Affirmative Action." *B.C. Third World Law Journal* 15: 225–284.

———. 1996. "From Black to White and Back Again." *Asian Law Journal* 3: 185–212.

14

Are Second-Generation Filipinos "Becoming" Asian American or Latino?

Historical Colonialism, Culture, and Panethnicity

ANTHONY C. OCAMPO

During his 2011 visit to the Philippines, Pulitzer Prize–winning Latino author Junot Díaz had this to say to a local reporter:

> You should come to the Dominican Republic because from what I've seen so far, Filipinos would have no problem over there. You wouldn't even notice you'd left. . . . We have certain strong similarities. Our countries have been colonized by both the Spanish and [American]. I feel the similarities very strongly. (quoted in Matilla 2011)

Having grown up around Filipinos in New Jersey, Díaz is alluding to the history of Spanish and American colonialism shared by the Philippines and many Latin American societies. Díaz implicitly blurs the boundaries between Filipinos and Latinos by drawing from what Cornell and Hartmann (1998) term a "symbolic repertoire"—the stories, histories, and cultural markers that bond different groups together. These historical and cultural connections between Filipinos and Latinos are echoed by scholars, historians, and journalists (Guevarra 2012; Morrow 2007; Pisares 2006). However, within the US context, Filipinos are classified as Asian rather than Hispanic. Filipinos were also involved in the establishment of the Asian American movement and continue to participate in pan-Asian organizations today (Espiritu 1992).

The links of Filipinos with both Latinos and Asians introduce an interesting question: How do second-generation Filipinos understand and negotiate their panethnic identity, given their connections to two of the largest panethnic groups in the United States? In everyday life, race involves the complex negotiation of factors beyond institutional designations, including outsiders' perceptions, cultural knowledge, and ways of behaving (Jackson 2001). Racial categorizations constantly evolve, and groups may develop a panethnic consciousness that transgresses official designations. To address my question, I use multiple data sources that elucidate Filipino panethnic identity patterns. First, I draw from in-depth interviews and surveys of fifty second-generation Filipino adults from Los Angeles, a multiethnic city and the primary destination of Filipino immigrants. Second, I analyze two large-scale surveys of the immigrant second generation—the Immigrant and Intergenerational Mobility in Metropolitan Los Angeles (IIMMLA) and Children of Immigrants Longitudinal Study (CILS)—which provide a baseline of panethnic identity patterns of Filipinos and other Asians.

Though it was not the original intent of the study to examine how colonialism affects panethnicity, the majority of interview respondents themselves brought up both Spanish and US colonialism in the Philippines when discussing identity. Previous research highlights colonialism as an important historical backdrop for understanding assimilation (Portes and Rumbaut 2001). As Massey and colleagues (1993) have argued, colonialism matters because it creates cultural links between members of the sending and receiving countries. However, past studies mainly consider how colonialism links immigrant groups to *mainstream* members of the host country.[1] As such, this study focuses on the way colonialism shapes how immigrant groups relate with *minority* members of society. In addition, this study also examines how colonialism might affect assimilation outcomes specifically among *children of immigrants* in a multiethnic society. Although children of immigrants may not have been socialized within the colonized society, colonialism has an enduring imprint on the culture passed on to them by their parents, which in turn affects identity (Kasinitz et al. 2008). Filipinos draw on their colonially influenced culture when negotiating boundaries between themselves and other groups.

Classical assimilation models once posited that immigrants and their children would assimilate into a white middle-class mainstream (Gordon 1964), but contemporary frameworks have shown them now being incorporated into diverse segments of US society (Portes and Zhou 1993). Ongoing Latino and Asian migration is dramatically changing the US racial landscape, which in turn is reshaping immigrant assimilation processes. For example, in Los Angeles, among the top destinations for Latino and Asian immigrants, nearly half of the residents are of Latino descent, and non-Hispanic whites constitute a mere 28 percent of the population (US Census Bureau 2010). Children of immigrants living in such multiethnic contexts might find more incentive in identifying with their minority peers, rather than align themselves with groups associated with the white mainstream.

Understanding panethnic identity through a cultural lens, Filipinos cited US colonialism as a reason to demarcate themselves from Asians while alluding to the cultural legacies of Spanish colonialism to blur boundaries with Latinos. While existing scholarship has explained panethnicity as a function of shared class status or political interests (Espiritu 1992), I find that the cultural legacies of Spanish and US colonialism play a defining role for Filipinos' panethnic identity development. These findings challenge studies that suggest that children of immigrants prefer identities associated with upward mobility (in this case, Asian over Latino) and highlight the mechanisms that facilitate panethnic consciousness *across* class lines, a phenomenon less discussed in previous research. This study also considers how identity is shaped by the negotiation of cultural aspects associated with both the premigration society and the multiethnic landscape of contemporary US society.

Theories of Assimilation and Panethnicity

Identity has long been considered a mechanism of immigrant group assimilation. Early scholars asserted that immigrants and their children identify as unhyphenated Americans to fully assimilate into US society (Gordon 1964; Park 1950). However, contemporary reformulations of assimilation suggest that children of immigrants are incorporated into different segments of society due to a constellation of structural, economic, and cultural factors, a perspective known as segmented assimilation (Portes and Zhou 1993). Notably, this framework posits that connections to *ethnic* identity allow children of immigrants to acquire social and economic resources that facilitate upward mobility (Zhou and Bankston 1998). However, studies in this tradition say relatively less about the mechanisms shaping *racial* or *panethnic* identification. Some have critiqued these studies for overemphasizing the negative aspects associated with ascribing to racial identities that are externally imposed (Neckerman, Carter, and Lee 1999).

Theories of panethnicity have highlighted the social, economic, and political advantages of identifying with one's racial group (Espiritu 1992). Recent studies discuss the viability of panethnic identification, highlighting how children of immigrants seamlessly switch between ethnic and panethnic labels depending on the situation (Kasinitz et al. 2008), rather than viewing them as mutually exclusive options. However, intragroup dynamics and racialized constructions in mass media often prompt individuals to develop culturally based notions of panethnicity (Dhingra 2007). When these individuals feel they do not fit the "rules" for panethnic membership, they in turn express ambivalence or resistance to being lumped into these racial categories (Kibria 1998).

Colonialism and Assimilation

Some scholars have argued that assimilation, identity, and panethnicity models are implicitly US-centric and overlook the transnational nature of these processes (Espiritu 2004). Recent studies show that assimilation and identity formation of immigrant groups are influenced by US economic or military presence in the home country (Espiritu 2003; Kim 2008), transnational media (Roth 2009), and migratory flows between sending and host societies (Jiménez 2010). Focusing on colonialism can highlight how historical and contemporary relations between sending and receiving nations interact with immigrant experiences in the US context to shape assimilation.

The effect of colonialism on immigration and assimilation patterns is multilayered. Colonial regimes exploit the natural resources and labor of the colonized society, and the resulting economic underdevelopment of the latter creates the impetus for members of its society to migrate in the first place. Second, colonial relationships influence policies that facilitate the socioeconomic selectivity of individuals who migrate even in the postcolonial period (Choy 2003). Third, the institutional and cultural influences of colonial regimes "prepare" members of the colonized society to migrate. Potential migrants in these societies possess cultural and institutional familiarity with the colonizing nation long before crossing international borders. This familiarity in turn facilitates the decision to migrate and ability to assimilate into mainstream jobs, neighborhoods, and organizations (Portes and Rumbaut 2001). Such findings should not at all suggest that colonialism should be framed in any positive light. Scholars show that colonialism breeds feelings of racial inferiority among immigrant groups even after the colonial period has ended, which in turn can lead to detachment from one's coethnic community (David and Okazaki 2006).

While studies have examined how colonialism affects the immigrant generation, few address how it distinctly influences second-generation outcomes. As Jiménez (2010) argues, immigration scholars should be more precise about colonialism's effects across generation, rather than assume that it permanently relegates immigrants with colonial histories to second-class status. Without discounting the exploitative history of colonialism, Waters (1999) notes that European colonialism has served as a basis of panethnic consciousness among second-generation West Indians from different societies—though Waters's study is among the few that considers how colonialism creates connections with other minority populations. Building on this research, this study shows how Filipino children of immigrants negotiate their colonial history when navigating panethnic boundaries with other ethnic groups. Warikoo (2011) provides a template of how this might occur. Her research shows that second-generation Indo-Caribbeans inherit South Asian cultural practices from their immigrant parents' society, but the degree to which these practices shape their identity depends on the value that Indian culture carries within their racial context.

Filipino Migration to the United States

The Philippines became part of the Spanish Empire during the early sixteenth century, the period when Spain established Nueva España in modern-day Mexico. Considered an extension of their empire in Latin America, Spain established the Acapulco-Manila galleon trade, which facilitated extensive cultural exchange between Filipinos and Mexicans for three centuries (Guevarra 2012).

The Spanish period ended in 1899 but left enduring imprints on modern-day Philippine society. Spanish language has had a strong influence on Tagalog, which along with English is the current lingua franca of Philippine society (see Table 14.1). Filipinos were also given Spanish surnames (e.g., Torres, Rodríguez, Santos) during the colonial period. And similar to Spain's Latin American colonies, the Philippines remains a predominantly Catholic society, one of only two throughout Asia.[2] Over 80 percent of Filipinos living in the Philippines and abroad are Catholic (Rodríguez 2006).

TABLE 14.1. Everyday Words in English, Spanish, and Tagalog

English		Spanish	Tagalog
Household			
	Table	mesa	mesa
	Living room	sala	sala
	Chair	silla	silya
Kinship			
	Uncle	tío	tito
	Aunt	tía	tita
Clothing			
	Pants	pantalones	pantalon
	Jacket	chaqueta	dyaket
	Shoes	zapatos	sapatos
Food-related			
	Fork	tenedor	tinidor
	Spoon	cuchara	kutsara
	Snack	merienda	meryenda
Days			
	Monday	Lunes	Lunes
	Tuesday	Martes	Martes
	Wednesday	Miércoles	Miyerkoles

Despite Filipino revolutionary efforts in 1899, the Philippines was acquired by the United States following the Spanish-American War. Under the guise of "benevolent assimilation," the Americans used cultural imperialism to subjugate the native population, establishing US-style schools and English as the medium of instruction and national language (Choy 2003). Colonial policies granted Filipinos the status of US nationals, a legal status created by the American government specifically to facilitate large-scale migration of mostly male laborers to low-wage agricultural and factory work. Despite their ability to migrate, Filipino workers encountered violent resistance from white nativists, who eventually helped lobby Congress to pass the 1934 Tydings-McDuffie Act,[3] which granted the Philippines independence and effectively halted Filipino migration (Baldoz 2011).

Ironically, the legacies of the American colonial period set the stage for a highly selective group of Filipinos to migrate when the Hart-Celler Act reopened US borders to nonwhite immigrants in 1965. US-modeled schools socialized Filipinos to American ways of life and provided widespread access to higher education. Filipinos had access to health care training institutions, initially established to aid US military stationed in the Philippines (Choy 2003). After US colonialism, the Philippine economy remained underdeveloped, and unemployment was rampant, creating a surplus pool of highly educated, English-speaking Filipino workers. During the 1970s, the Philippine government implemented aggressive labor emigration policies, transforming the country into a labor brokerage state (Rodriguez 2010). Millions within the surplus labor pool were primed to fill shortages in US professional sectors, particularly in the health care industry.

These legacies explain why Filipinos are more linguistically and residentially assimilated than their Asian counterparts. Over two-thirds of Filipino migrants speak English "very well," in contrast to fewer than a third of other Asian migrants (Portes and Rumbaut 2006). In addition, there are no culturally homogenous ethnic enclaves for Filipinos that compare to Chinatown, Koreatown, or Little Saigon, as they generally reside in racially integrated neighborhoods (Vergara 2008). These factors also explain why higher proportions of Filipinos enter mainstream, English-speaking occupations versus ethnic economies. Filipinos are actively recruited by US employers into health care, teaching, and other professional sectors (Ong and Azores 1994). However, the language barriers and residential concentration more common among Chinese, Korean, and Vietnamese mean that these groups can remain in occupational sectors that are ethnically insular (Zhou 2009).

Like their parents, Filipino children of immigrants are distinct from their second-generation Asian peers. Among second-generation Asians, Filipinos by far have the highest rates of being monolingual English speakers (Zhou and Xiong 2005). Interestingly, while Filipino migrants generally have more mainstream occupational pathways than other Asian migrants, their children fare less well in educational outcomes than their Asian peers. While most second-generation Filipinos pursue higher education, they are less likely than their Chinese, Korean, and Vietnamese counterparts to attend four-year universities, more likely to opt for less prestigious institutions, and less likely to graduate with a four-year degree (Teranishi et al. 2004; Zhou and Xiong 2005). Moreover, research by Teranishi (2002) shows that Filipinos are treated like remedial students while their East

Asian counterparts are automatically perceived as more high achieving—all part of what Espiritu and Wolf (2001) have termed a "paradox of assimilation."

Espiritu (1992) argues that the cultural differences rooted in colonialism also explain why Filipinos of different generations have had challenges developing panethnic consciousness with other Asians. She suggests that the history of Spanish colonialism presents the possibility for Filipinos to build panethnic alliances with Latinos, or in the least can be utilized as political leverage within pan-Asian organizations (Espiritu 1992, 172). While Asian cultures and experiences are indeed heterogeneous, there are cultural distinctions unique to Filipinos historically rooted in their dual colonial past.[4] This article explores how the cultural residuals of this past influence how Filipinos negotiate panethnic boundaries between themselves and other ethnic groups.

Methodology

In-Depth Interviews

This study draws from in-depth interviews with fifty second-generation Filipinos from two middle-class, multiethnic neighborhoods in Los Angeles: Eagle Rock and Carson. Unlike other Asian immigrants in Los Angeles, there are no ethnically homogenous Filipino neighborhoods in the region comparable to Chinatown, Koreatown, and Little Saigon. Filipinos live in multiethnic neighborhoods and are often the primary Asian-origin group in the area (US Census Bureau 2010). Eagle Rock and Carson are two such neighborhoods that are also well-known Filipino settlements (Gorman 2007; Ibanez and Ibanez 2009). There are Filipino restaurants, community centers, and immigrant service centers, though they do not dominate the neighborhood landscape in the same fashion as other Asian "ethnoburbs" (Zhou 2009).

Eagle Rock and Carson are majority-minority neighborhoods that are also middle-class—the median household income in both Eagle Rock and Carson is about sixty-seven thousand dollars, well above the national average (US Census Bureau 2010). In both neighborhoods, 20 percent of residents are Filipino and over 35 percent are Mexican. However, in Eagle Rock, the remaining population is white, whereas in Carson, it is mostly African American with a small, but visible number of Samoans (about 3 percent). Lacy (2008) suggests that comparing neighborhoods with distinct racial contexts yields insights into the heterogeneous identity trajectories of middle-class minorities. While neighborhood racial context is not the central focus of this article, I do examine how it may mitigate the relationship between colonialism and identity.

The interviews were conducted between March 2009 and January 2010, and each lasted approximately ninety minutes. Half of the respondents were recruited through messages distributed on an online networking website. One-fourth of respondents were recruited through contacts established during casual interactions in coffee shops, churches, parks, and shopping centers in the neighborhoods. The remaining were referred by those already interviewed. Respondents in the study each had Philippine-born migrant parents, were born in the United States (or had migrated by age five), and were between twenty-one and thirty years old at the time of the interview.

Several interview questions addressed panethnic identity. I asked respondents (1) "What would you consider to be your racial identity?" (2) "Which ethnic and racial groups do you feel you and other Filipinos are most similar to?" and (3) "Have you ever identified as Asian American?" I also asked why Filipinos might or might not identify with certain panethnic labels or groups. The interview included topics that previous studies have linked to identify formation, such as neighborhood experiences, school experiences, and interactions with family and friends. I noted moments when respondents discussed panethnic identity both explicitly (e.g., "I am Asian American") and implicitly (e.g., "We [Filipinos and another group] are the same").

While this article discusses colonialism, this was not a theme originally included in the interview protocol, nor was it a topic that I introduced during the conversation. However, the majority of respondents brought up the theme of colonialism on their own accord when discussing Filipino identity. When they did, I probed further into the way they used this frame when negotiating panethnic boundaries. I also paid attention to whether the association between colonialism and identity was mitigated by other factors, such as neighborhood context, socioeconomic status, or interracial encounters.

Following each interview, respondents were asked to fill out a brief demographic survey with questions about their level of education, socioeconomic status, and ethnic and racial identity choices. Respondents first answered the open-ended question, "How do you self-identify?" For a subsequent question, "What is your racial background?" respondents were asked to indicate whether they identified as white, African American, Latino, Asian, or Pacific Islander.

Immigrant and Intergenerational Mobility in Metropolitan Los Angeles (IIMMLA)

The IIMMLA is a cross-sectional survey of second-generation adults in the greater Los Angeles area conducted in 2004. Researchers targeted adult children of immigrants of Latino or Asian origin.[5] Participants were surveyed during a thirty-five-minute telephone interview and asked questions related to their incorporation and mobility, including national origin, socioeconomic status, educational background, occupation, and cultural involvements. In this article, I draw only from surveys of the 1,617 respondents of four primary Asian groups included—Filipino, Chinese, Vietnamese, and Korean—also the four largest

Asian ethnicities in Los Angeles (US Census Bureau 2010). To examine pan-ethnic identity, I focus on their responses to this question: "For classification purposes, we'd like to know what your racial background is. Are you White, Black or African American, Asian, Pacific Islander, American Indian, Alaskan native, or member of another race, or a combination of these?"

Children of Immigrants Longitudinal Study (CILS)

The CILS is a longitudinal survey of second-generation immigrants from San Diego, California, and Fort Lauderdale/Miami, Florida. Three waves of the survey were conducted in 1992, 1995, and 2001–2003, when respondents' average age was about fourteen, seventeen, and mid-twenties, respectively. The CILS shares similar objectives to the IIMMLA in that it aims to elucidate the mechanisms underlying second-generation assimilation and acculturation. Key variables include language, educational achievement, socioeconomic status, and ethnic and racial identification. I draw only from the San Diego subsample because the number of Filipino-origin respondents in Miami is negligible. My analysis is limited to the four primary Asian descent subgroups included in the survey— Filipino, Vietnamese, Laotian, and other Southeast Asian (mainly Hmong and Cambodian). Because the second wave of the study (1995) was the only one that asked respondents to both self-identify and choose from a discrete set of racial categories,[6] my analysis is based on the 921 Asian-origin respondents surveyed during this wave. To examine panethnic identity, I focus on their responses to this question: "Which of the races listed do you consider yourself to be—White, Black, Asian, Multiracial, Other?"

Although the interviews are not from respondents of the IIMMLA and CILS, the surveys provide a baseline comparison of panethnic identity patterns among second-generation Filipinos and Asians, which complement the qualitative findings. In addition, both are based in Southern California, where Filipinos negotiate ethnic boundaries vis-à-vis the large numbers of Latinos and Asians in the region. While surveys may not address respondents' reasons for selecting panethnic labels or may not show implicit forms of panethnic consciousness, they illustrate how Asian panethnicity resonates differently among Asian-origin groups.

Cultural Marginalization within Asian America

A.O.: Do you ever identify as Asian American?
RONALD: Not really. It's like denying what I am. It's like denying that I'm Filipino, like not really acknowledging my culture.

Despite its political origins, Asian panethnicity has evolved to take on cultural meanings, as Ronald's remarks indicate. When presented with the question,

"What groups are Filipinos most similar to?" respondents interpreted this to mean, "Whose culture is most similar to that of Filipinos?" Filipinos were generally reticent about identifying as Asian, and this had to do with cultural factors. Few felt cultural connections between themselves and other Asians, and the ones they noted were superficial at best, such as food or geography. As one respondent noted, "Filipinos' diet is very Asian, like rice, fish, and stuff a normal American wouldn't eat." Beyond this, most associated Asian American identity with East Asian cultural stereotypes, which they felt did not fit Filipinos. As Kevin asserted, "The face of Asian Americans is an East Asian face, literally. Not a Filipino one."

Respondents referred to the Americanization of Filipino culture as a reason to demarcate themselves from other Asians. Some felt different from other Asians because the latter had a "real history and therefore, had a real culture." Jenn noted that, in contrast to other Asians, Filipino culture was associated with hybridity because of the colonial influences throughout Philippine history:

> We're not really Asian. I feel like on a cultural level, we don't relate. The Chinese have this long history that's very established, and it's written. We've been colonized like how many times? Where's the identity in that? Are we Spanish, Muslim, Chinese, and now, are we American? Because if you go to Manila, it's practically like Los Angeles. It's so Americanized.

Echoing Jenn's remarks, others felt that this colonial history was antithetical to being Asian American because "real" Asian culture is "untouched by Western influences."

Others framed the postcolonial American influence as an advantage that made Filipinos "less foreign" than other Asians. Franky noted, "When whites see other Asian groups, they seem them as being 'fobbier' [more 'fresh off the boat']. But then they see Filipinos and we're more assimilated to American culture." Eddie pointed to the Americanized aspects of Philippine media: "A lot of the popular culture and styles and music are based on [America]. When you watch Filipino variety shows, what do you see? They're playing Usher, Lady Gaga, and American pop and hip hop." Implicit in such comments is the assumption that Asian culture is inherently foreign, while Filipino culture is more Westernized, and thus, *not* Asian. By contrasting up-to-date trends in Philippine culture with a "fobbier" Asian culture, these remarks also imply that Asian identity is "uncool," which may further explain Filipinos' aversion to pan-Asian identity.

Respondents also said that the English proficiency of Filipinos in the United States—an outgrowth of American colonialism—distinguished them from Asians. Lynette recalled an uncomfortable moment in an Asian American studies course in college when her class had a discussion about the typical Asian American experience:

I felt like there was a difference between those who were Chinese, Korean, and those who were Filipino. It just *felt* different. I think because a lot of the "Asian American experiences" that we read about in our class talked about language. The other Asians would talk about their parents only being able to speak Mandarin or Vietnamese and having to be the mediator between two cultures—*that* was the Asian American experience. But I felt that wasn't the case for me. I was like, "You know, my parents speak English just fine."

Ironically, while Asian American studies was created to foster a shared sense of panethnic identity among different Asian ethnicities, Lynette's experience served the opposite function—it highlighted differences between Filipinos' experiences and those of East Asians, who many felt dominate mainstream Asian American narratives.

Several noted the cultural construction of Asian panethnicity on a global level. They recounted times when others referred to Filipinos as the "wetback Asians," or the "Mexicans" or "blacks" of Asia. Raymond said, "[Filipinos] do the manual labor all over the world." Kevin, in turn, argued that when people think of Asians, they automatically refer to China, Japan, and Korea, or as he noted, "the three countries that have power." While Raymond and Kevin grew up middle-class and have professional parents, their remarks show how their sense of pan-Asian identity is influenced by the international community of Filipino laborers. Their comments illustrate that panethnicity is not entirely a US-based construction, but rather, at least in part, a transnational ideological construction (Espiritu 2004; Roth 2009).

The lack of other Asian ethnicities in their childhood neighborhoods also explains why Filipinos expressed weak panethnic ties. Proximity facilitates opportunities for people to identify commonalities across ethnic lines and develop a panethnic consciousness.

In Eagle Rock and Carson, Filipinos had minimal opportunity to interact with other Asians. Most did not interact with Asians until their college years. As Jacob noted, "College was the first time I really was around a bunch of Asians!" Grace described her first days at UC Irvine (where non-Filipino Asians are 40 percent of the student body) as a "culture shock" because "everyone is super Asian." Such characterizations imply how both felt that Filipinos were not part of the pan-Asian collective.

Colonial Panethnicity: Filipino and Latino Cultural Connections

Even though respondents used colonialism to distance Filipinos from other Asians, they used the colonialism frame to blur boundaries with Latinos. While no respondent identified as Latino outright, many more closely associated Filipinos with Mexicans and other Latinos because of the shared history of Spanish colonialism, including some who checked "Asian" on the postinterview survey.

As Lia noted the "Latinizing" effect of this history on Filipino culture, noting that Filipinos "have more similarities with Latin culture than other Asians."

Some felt Filipinos "must have Spanish blood" because both coethnics and Latinos commonly mistook them as Mexican due to their phenotype (e.g., they "looked Mexican") or Spanish surname. Nearly half of respondents recalled being spoken to in Spanish by Latinos, and some were even mistaken as Latino by other Filipinos. In her first days working as a nurse, Adriana recalled that her Filipina coworkers spoke Tagalog to each other yet conversed with her in English. When Adriana replied in Tagalog, one coworker expressed her surprise: "I didn't know you were Filipina. I thought you were Hispanic!"

Respondents bonded with Latinos based on three main cultural similarities—language, surnames, and Catholicism. Jon, a hotel manager, recalled being mistaken as Latino by the Mexican immigrants he worked with:

> When they see me in the hall, they speak to me in Spanish. Then I tell them, "No hablo español," and they're like, "Why don't you speak Spanish?" and then I tell them I'm Filipino. And then they insist, "Well, some Filipinos speak Spanish. You have Spanish last names, right?"

Respondents recalled efforts by Filipino and Latino immigrants to communicate with each other when interacting in the neighborhood, given the heavy overlap in everyday words in Spanish and Tagalog (see Table 14.1). When I asked him whether he saw Filipinos and Latinos interact much, Jayson answered, "All the time! My mom, for example, whenever she goes to the market, she [and the Latino workers] will be like, 'Hola, amigo. Hola, amiga.' Because of the similarities in our language, you can communicate in [each other's] native tongue." While language bridged Filipinos with Latinos, it created further rifts with Asians. Ronald said interacting with other Asian immigrants was relatively more difficult "because there's virtually no overlap between Tagalog and say, Chinese or Vietnamese."

Catholicism was another colonial legacy that Filipinos used to liken themselves with Latinos. Diana said Filipinos were "definitely" more similar to Latinos because her "parents have *santos* and the Virgin Mary all around the house, and that's just like Latinos. I'd go to my Guatemalan friend's house, and you'd see the same thing. There's a lot of religion intermingled with her culture and my culture." Many Filipino and Latino ethnic practices also had a religious component. Alma noted how religion was embedded in rites of passages for Filipina and Mexican young women (debuts and *quinceañeras*, respectively). She added, "When you hear Filipino and Latino, you think Catholic automatically. I don't think religion when I think of Asians. Or if I do, maybe I think of Buddha, but not Jesus or Mary." Though Catholicism might not have prompted outsiders to racialize respondents as Latino, it nonetheless affected how Filipinos racially positioned themselves vis-à-vis Latinos and other Asians.

This cultural closeness became evident in situations where other Filipinos were not even present. Alex attended a private college with many East Asians and Latinos, but few Filipinos. Coming from Eagle Rock, he initially felt disconnected from his Asian classmates, yet noted a sense of closeness with his Latino peers, who also invoked the colonial frame. At a party sponsored by one of the Latino organizations, Alex recounted,

> I never felt out of place at the party, even though it was all Latinos. Funny enough. My one friend who was half-Mexican, but looked more white and was from like a bougie [rich], all-white town got flack for being there. They kept calling him "white boy." But with me, a bunch of the guys would come up to me and be like, "Oh what? You're Filipino? It's practically the same thing [as Latino]. We all got punked by Spain anyway, right?" Most of my friends in college ended up being Latino because they were the next closest thing to Filipinos.

Alex's experience shows that the negotiation of panethnic boundaries is not determined solely by national origin—otherwise, his "white-looking" friend should have felt more at home at the predominantly Latino event. Alex's comfort stemmed from his experiences growing up with Latinos, which allowed him to fit in more than someone who was "biologically" Mexican. Alex also noted that Latino events were "more fun" and "cooler" than those sponsored by other Asians, whom he and other Filipinos stereotyped as studious and bookish.

This idea that Filipinos and Latinos were "the same thing" was echoed in conversations about interracial dating. While having dated Mexican women in the past, Nelson expressed a newfound anxiety about dating a Vietnamese woman:

NELSON: I'm kind of nervous about the girl I'm dating. She's Vietnamese, so this is the first time I'm dating someone from a different culture.
A.O.: Didn't you say that you dated a bunch of Mexican girls before?
NELSON, LAUGHING: Ha, that doesn't count. Mexicans are the same as Filipinos!

For Nelson, cultural differences between Filipinos and Latinos are less salient than those with Asians. Such comments illustrate how the cultural boundaries of racial categories subconsciously influence Filipinos' sense of "we-ness" with Asians and Latinos.

Respondents' identification with Latinos is interesting given that Filipinos, on the aggregate level, have a higher socioeconomic status than Latinos. At the same time, Eagle Rock and Carson have a large minority middle class, including middle-class Mexican Americans. The narratives suggest that there was more class convergence between Filipinos and Mexicans in these neighborhoods than statistical data might indicate. While nearly every respondent identified as middle-class, most noted having close connections with relatives who were working-class (both in the United States and abroad) or recalled having been working-class earlier in life. As such, class differences did not necessarily disrupt the connections they felt with Latinos who lived in the less affluent parts of Eagle Rock or Carson. However, Filipino-Latino connections did weaken when negative media stereotypes of Latinos were discussed. Franky said that while he felt close with Latinos in terms of religion and culture, he did not relate to the "stereotypical cholo [gangster] looking ones." In addition, Filipino-Latino connections seemed to break down in the school context. Those attending public high schools said that while teachers viewed Filipinos as high-achieving students,[7] "Latinos weren't seen as honors students by school officials." These findings suggest that Filipinos' connection with Latinos might decline if the association potentially compromised their middle-class standing or mobility.

Filipino Panethnic Identity Patterns

Respondents filled out a brief survey that asked an open-ended question about identity and then they chose a racial identity from a set of discrete options. I had the opportunity to observe respondents as they answered these questions. For the open-ended question, every respondent wrote "Filipino" without hesitation. However, when asked to select their racial background, many vacillated between the given options. Half inquired whether they could write in "Filipino" as their race. Table 14.2 shows that respondents were split between choosing "Asian" and "Pacific Islander." There was also a clear relationship between panethnic identification and neighborhood.

TABLE 14.2. Panethnic Identification of Respondents ($N = 50$)

	Neighborhood		
	Eagle Rock	Carson	All
Asian	20%	84%	52%
	(5)	(21)	(26)
Pacific Islander	80%	16	48%
	(20)	(4)	(24)
Total	100%	100%	100%
	(25)	(25)	(50)

Given the racial ambivalence of Filipinos in both neighborhoods, what explains this difference? The interviews suggest that choosing "Pacific Islander" was a function of not wanting to choose "Asian." Eagle Rock respondents selected Pacific Islander, but had few concrete notions of what this identity meant. When prompted about why he felt Filipinos were "more Pacific Islander than Asian," Vince said, "I don't know. Probably because the Philippines are islands in the Pacific?" Others displayed the same lack of investment, noting merely that it was "better than choosing Asian." Carson respondents had more concrete ideas of Pacific Islander identity because of their interactions with Samoans. Bryan said, "Pacific Islander is for the Samoans. And there's no Asians in Carson besides Filipinos, so I guess we can fill that in." Such responses illustrate that Carson Filipinos did not necessarily express strong attachments to Asian identity, even if they chose it on the form. These findings show that Filipinos' identity options depend largely on the availability and meaning of categories within their local context.

TABLE 14.3. Panethnic Identification by Ethnicity, Second-Generation Asians ($N = 1,617$)

	Filipino	Chinese	Vietnamese	Korean
Asian	47%	96%	98%	98%
	(189)	(395)	(393)	(393)
Pacific Islander	45%	1%	1%	1%
	(182)	(5)	(4)	(2)
Other	8%	3%	1%	2%
	(31)	(13)	(4)	(6)
Total	100%	100%	100%	100%
	(402)	(413)	(401)	(401)

Source: Rumbaut et al. (2004).

TABLE 14.4. Panethnic Identification by Ethnicity, Second-Generation Asians ($N = 921$)

	Filipino	Vietnamese	Laotian	Southeast Asian
Asian	63%	91%	93%	89%
	(351)	(172)	(98)	(59)
National origin	22%	5%	4%	2%
	(121)	(9)	(4)	(1)
Other	15%	4%	3%	9%
	(89)	(8)	(3)	(6)
Total	100%	100%	100%	100%
	(561)	(189)	(105)	(66)

Source: Portes and Rumbaut (2001–2003).

Filipino identity patterns on the IIMMLA and CILS parallel those from my interview respondents (see Tables 14.3 and 14.4). Fewer than one half (47 percent) and two-thirds (63 percent) of Filipino IIMMLA and CILS respondents, respectively, identified as Asian, in contrast to about 90 percent of other Asians. These findings are interesting given that Asian is stereotyped as a middle-class or upwardly mobile identity (Zhou 2009). One might expect Southeast Asians, the most socioeconomically disadvantaged subgroup, would be least inclined to identify as Asian, given that studies show panethnicity to be a function of class commonality (Carter 2005). Ultimately, these findings complement the interview data by illustrating that Filipinos' panethnic ambivalence occurs across different contexts (Los Angeles and San Diego) and ages (adults and teenagers).[8]

Conclusion

Despite linguistic, socioeconomic, and cultural differences, ethnic groups develop panethnic consciousness by organizing for political interests, emphasizing cultural commonalities, or highlighting shared racial experiences. Filipinos have done all these things with both Asians and Latinos, and thus can justifiably be categorized as either. Ultimately, they are officially Asian, according to the US Census Bureau. At the same time, individuals do not always ascribe to the panethnic labels imposed on them, and the unique colonial history of the Philippines has prompted Filipinos to be vocally ambivalent about their racial designation. In Espiritu's seminal book *Asian American Panethnicity* (1992, 107), one Filipino despondently asserted that Filipinos were Asian because of a "geographical accident." Espiritu notes the possibility of Filipinos joining Latino panethnic coalitions, but ultimately acknowledges that both the pan-Asian and pan-Latino options present significant challenges.

If these historical and cultural connections mean that Filipinos are "kind of Asian and kind of Latino," as one respondent put it, how did the young adults in this study negotiate panethnic identity? The term "Asian American" was born as a politicized identity, yet it was not a lack of political engagement that prompted their ambivalence. Rather, the cultural legacies of Spanish and US colonialism in the Philippines played a more significant role in how respondents negotiated panethnic boundaries. It is worth noting that despite the cultural links between US and Philippine societies, no respondent identified as an unhyphenated American, signaling the continued significance of race in America society.

As the narratives revealed, the cultural hybridity resulting from Spanish and US colonialism was a central part of Filipino ethnic identity. Whether talking about culture, language, or religion, respondents would embed them within colonial contexts. This culturally based understanding of ethnicity extended to their negotiation of panethnicity. US colonialism created a rift between Filipinos and other Asians. Their experiences of feeling more Americanized, having English-speaking households, and being less bicultural than other Asians prompted their feelings of disconnection. This social distancing was further amplified by their internalization of the Asian forever foreigner stereotype and lack of interaction with other Asians in their neighborhoods. Moreover, the surveys reflected the lukewarm resonance of Asian panethnicity for Filipinos, relative to other Asian ethnicities.

In turn, Spanish colonialism bonded them with Latinos, a sentiment that at times was mutual, as the opening quote from Junot Díaz illustrates. In their everyday lives, reminders of Spanish colonialism are present in their parents' language, surnames, and religion. The presence of Latinos in their neighborhood further "replenished" the Spanish aspects of Filipino ethnic culture (Jiménez 2010), making the Filipino-Latino link especially salient. These findings challenge previous studies suggest that Filipinos should align themselves with Asians, a group stereotyped as upwardly mobile. Within the context of a middle-class neighborhood, colonial commonalities prompt Filipinos to blur boundaries with Latinos (minus situations where it compromised their social standing).

Are Filipino Americans a unique case? Certainly, the extensive colonial history in the Philippines distinguishes them from other Asians. Nonetheless, colonialism also represents an extreme case of cultural shifts in premigration societies that persist today, due to US militarism, foreign policy, transnational media, and migration-related cultural exchanges (Kim 2008). Cultural shifts in the premigration society shape the identity toolkit that children of immigrants use to relate with groups in a multiethnic society (Warikoo 2011). However, the use of this toolkit is also contingent on the value of "symbolic repertoires" that children of immigrants possess. In a Latinized city like Los Angeles, there is symbolic value to aligning oneself with Latinos rather than Asians, particularly for young adults who at the time may be more concerned with social standing than economic mobility. Though a study of second-generation experiences in Los Angeles may not be generalizable across the country, the choice of research site elucidates important social phenomena bound to take place in other parts of the country affected by migration: negotiation of race beyond the black-white binary, the emergence of new panethnic categories, and the interaction of historical legacies with new racial contexts. Ultimately, the Filipino case highlights the ever-evolving process of panethnic identity construction—a process that is not US-centric in nature, but one shaped heavily by the interaction of historical legacies with the changing racial landscape of American society.

NOTES

Originally published in *Ethnic and Racial Studies* 37 (3): 425–445, 2014. ©2014 reprint by permission of Taylor & Francis. I am grateful to Min Zhou, Roger Waldinger, Wendy Roth, Jennifer Jones, Kerry Ann Rockquemore, and anonymous reviewers for their feedback throughout various stages of this chapter.

1   Studies of European migration have more thoroughly detailed how colonialism affects assimilation among postcolonial migrants. Studies of the Indian migration in the British colonial era show how colonial policies facilitated the movement of Indian professionals to East Africa during the early twentieth century. British-Indian colonial relations allowed Indians in East Africa to then migrate to the United Kingdom when African societies later gained independence. While their colonial status allowed them entry into Britain, it also became a marker of their second-class citizenship in their new host society (Dhingra 2012).

2   East Timor, a former Portuguese colony of one million people (1 percent the size of the Philippines), is the only other Catholic society in Asia.

3   Filipino migrants of the early twentieth century encountered hostility and violence from white nativists hoping to halt Filipino migration. However, it was not until 1934 that nativists coalesced with midwestern agribusiness players, who were worried about competition with Philippine agricultural products. These constituencies lobbied Congress to pass the Tydings-McDuffie Act in 1934 and grant the Philippines independence following a ten-year transition period succeeding its passage (Baldoz 2011, chap. 5).

4   Philippines is not the only Asian country with a colonial past. While countries like Korea experienced colonialism, they are qualitatively different in many respects. First, the Philippines was colonized longer than most other Asian countries. Second, the legacies of both Spanish and US colonialism are more deeply embedded within the mainstream culture of contemporary Philippine society. The closest parallel is British colonialism in India, which lasted nearly as long as in the Philippines. This partly explains why, besides Filipinos, there are challenges to including Indians within the pan-Asian collective (Kibria 1998).

5   Second-generation studies generally include both 1.5- and second-generation individuals.

6   Respondents were asked the open-ended question, "How do you identify, that is what do you call yourself?" before asked about panethnic identity.

7   Teranishi (2002) revealed that Filipinos were treated as remedial students while Chinese were dubbed model minorities. In this study, Filipinos were the only Asians present in the school, leading teachers to designate them model minorities, relative to the other groups present.

8   When surveyed, IIMMLA respondents were adults, while CILS respondents were teenagers.

REFERENCES

Baldoz, Rick. 2011. *The Third Asiatic Invasion: Migration and Empire in Filipino America, 1898–1946*. New York: New York University Press.

Carter, Prudence. 2005. *Keepin' It Real: School Success in Black and White*. New York: Oxford University Press.

Choy, Catherine. 2003. *Empire of Care: Nursing and Migration in Filipino American History*. Durham, NC: Duke University Press.

Cornell, Stephen, and Douglas Hartmann. 1998. *Ethnicity and Race: Making Identities in a Changing World*. Thousand Oaks, CA: Pine Forge Press.

David, E. J. R., and Sumie Okazaki. 2006. "The Colonial Mentality Scale for Filipino Americans." *Journal of Counseling Psychology* 53 (2): 241–252.

Dhingra, Pawan. 2007. *Managing Multicultural Lives*. Stanford, CA: Stanford University Press.

———. 2012. *Life behind the Lobby*. Stanford, CA: Stanford University Press.

Espiritu, Yen Le. 1992. *Asian American Panethnicity: Bridging Institutions and Identities*. Philadelphia: Temple University Press.

———. 2003. *Home Bound: Filipino American Lives across Cultures, Communities, and Countries*. Berkeley: University of California Press.

———. 2004. "Asian American Panethnicity." Pp. 217–236 in N. Foner and G. Frederickson, eds., *Not Just Black and White*. New York: Russell Sage Foundation.

Espiritu, Yen Le, and Diane Wolf. 2001. "The Paradox of Assimilation: Children of Filipino Immigrants in San Diego." Pp. 157–186 in A. Portes and R. Rumbaut, eds., *Ethnicities*. Berkeley: University of California Press.

Gordon, Milton. 1964. *Assimilation in American Life: The Role of Race, Religion, and National Origins*. New York: Oxford University Press.

Gorman, Anna. 2007. "Mall Anchors Thriving Filipino Community." *Los Angeles Times*, August 22. http://articles.latimes.com/2007/aug/22/local/me-filipino22 (accessed January 5, 2010).

Guevarra, Rudy. 2012. *Becoming Mexipino: Multiethnic Communities and Identities in San Diego*. New Brunswick, NJ: Rutgers University Press.

Ibanez, Florante, and Roselyn Ibanez. 2009. *Filipinos in Carson and the South Bay*. Mt. Pleasant, SC: Arcadia Press.

Jackson, John. 2001. *Harlemworld: Doing Race and Class in Contemporary Black America*. Chicago: University of Chicago Press.

Jiménez, Tomás. 2010. *Replenished Ethnicity: Mexican Americans, Immigration, and Identity*. Berkeley: University of California Press.

Kasinitz, Philip, et al. 2008. *Inheriting the City*. New York: Russell Sage Foundation.

Kibria, Nazli. 1998. "The Contested Meanings of 'Asian American': Racial Dilemmas in the Contemporary U.S." *Ethnic and Racial Studies* 21: 939–958.

Kim, Nadia. 2008. *Imperial Citizens: Koreans and Race from Seoul to L.A.* Stanford, CA: Stanford University Press.

Lacy, Karyn. 2008. *Blue-Chip Black: Race, Class, and Status in the New Black Middle Class*. Berkeley: University of California Press.

Louie, Vivian. 2004. *Compelled to Excel*. Stanford, CA: Stanford University Press.

Massey, Douglas, Joaquin Arango, Graeme Hugo, Ali Kouaouchi, Adela Pellegrino, and J. Edward Taylor. 1993. "Theories of International Migration." *Population and Development Review* 19 (3): 431–466.

Matilla, Dexter. 2011. "Pulitzer Prize–Winning Novelist Junot Díaz." *Philippine Daily Inquirer*, December 26. http://lifestyle.inquirer.net/28907/pulitzer-prize-winning-novelist-junot-diaz (accessed January 15, 2012).

Morrow, Paul. 2007. "Mexico Is Just Not a Town in Pampanga." *Pilipino Express*, October 1. http://www.pilipino-express.com/history-a-culture/in-other-words/225-mexico-is-not-just-a-town-in-pampanga.html (accessed June 12, 2012).

Neckerman, Kathryn, Prudence Carter, and Jennifer Lee. 1999. "Segmented Assimilation and Minority Cultures of Mobility." *Ethnic and Racial Studies* 22: 945–965.

Omi, Michael, and Howard Winant. 1994. *Racial Formation in the United States: From the 1960s to the 1990s*. New York: Routledge.

Ong, Paul, and Tania Azores. 1994. "The Migration and Incorporation of Filipino Nurses." Pp. 164–195 in P. Ong, E. Bonacich, and L. Cheng, eds., *The New Asian Immigration in Los Angeles and Global Restructuring*. Philadelphia: Temple University Press.

Park, Robert. 1950. *Race and Culture*. Glencoe, IL: Free Press.

Pisares, Elizabeth. 2006. "Do You (Mis)recognize Me?" Pp. 172–198 in A. Tiongson, E. Gutierrez, and R. Gutierrez, eds., *Positively No Filipinos Allowed: Building Communities and Discourse*. Philadelphia: Temple University Press.

Portes, Alejandro, and Rubén Rumbaut. 2001. *Legacies: The Story of the Immigrant Second Generation*. Berkeley: University of California Press.

———. 1991–2006. *Children of Immigrants Longitudinal Study (CILS)*. Ann Arbor, MI: Inter-university Consortium for Political and Social Research.

———. 2006. *Immigrant America*. Berkeley: University of California Press.

Portes, Alejandro, and Min Zhou. 1993. "The New Second Generation: Segmented Assimilation and Its Variants." *Annals of the American Academy of Political and Social Science* 530: 74–96.

Rodríguez, Evelyn. 2006. "Primerang Bituin: Philippine-Mexico Relations at the Dawn of the Pacific Rim Century." *Asia Pacific Perspectives* 6 (1): 4–12.

Rodriguez, Robyn. 2010. *Migrants for Export: How the Philippine State Brokers Labor to the World*. Minneapolis: University of Minnesota Press.

Roth, Wendy. 2009. "Latino before the World: The Transnational Extension of Panethnicity." *Ethnic and Racial Studies* 32 (6): 927–947.

Rumbaut, R., F. Bean, L. Chavez, J. Lee, S. Brown, L. DeSipio, and M. Zhou. 2004. *Immigrant and Intergenerational Mobility in Metropolitan Los Angeles (IIMMLA)*. Ann Arbor, MI: Interuniversity Consortium for Political and Social Research.

Teranishi, Robert. 2002. "Asian Pacific Americans and Critical Race Theory: An Examination of School Racial Climate." *Equity and Excellence in Education* 35: 144–154.

Teranishi, Robert, Miguel Ceja, Anthony Lising Antonio, Walter Recharde Allen, and Patricia M. McDonough. 2004. "The College-Choice Process for Asian Americans: Ethnicity and Social Class in Context." *Review of Higher Education* 27: 527–551.

US Census Bureau. 2010. *Statistical Abstract of the United States*. Washington, DC: US Census Bureau.

Vergara, Benito, Jr. 2008. *Pinoy Capital: The Filipino Nation in Daly City*. Philadelphia: Temple University Press.

Warikoo, Natasha. 2011. *Balancing Acts*. Berkeley: University of California Press.

Waters, Mary. 1999. *Black Identities: West Indian Immigrant Dreams and American Realities*. New York: Russell Sage Foundation.

Zhou, Min. 2004. "Are Asian Americans Becoming White?" *Context* 3 (1): 29–37.

———. 2009. *Contemporary Chinese America: Immigration, Ethnicity, and Community Transformation*. Philadelphia: Temple University Press.

Zhou, Min, and Carl Bankston. 1998. *Growing Up American: How Vietnamese Children Adapt to Life in the United States*. New York: Russell Sage Foundation.

Zhou, Min, and Yang Xiong. 2005. "The Multifaceted American Experience of the Children of Asian Immigrants: Lessons for Segmented Assimilation." *Ethnic and Racial Studies* 28 (6): 1119–1152.

15

Are Asian Americans Becoming White?

MIN ZHOU

I never asked to be white. I am not literally white. That is, I do not have white skin or white ancestors. I have yellow skin and yellow ancestors, hundreds of generations of them. But like so many other Asian Americans of the second generation, I find myself now the bearer of a strange new status: white, by acclamation. Thus it is that I have been described as an "honorary white," by other whites, and as a "banana" by other Asians ... to the extent that I have moved away from the periphery and toward the center of American life, I have become white inside.
—Eric Liu, *The Accidental Asian*

"Are Asian Americans becoming white?" For many public officials the answer must be yes, because they classify Asian-origin Americans with European-origin Americans for equal opportunity programs; neither are underrepresented groups, as blacks, Latinos, and Native Americans are. But this answer is premature and based on false premises. Although Asian Americans as a group have attained career and financial success equated with being white, and although many have moved near to or even married whites, they still remain culturally distinct and suspect in a white society.

At issue is how to define Asian American and white. The term "Asian American" was coined by the late historian and activist Yuji Ichioka during the ethnic consciousness movements of the late 1960s. To adopt this identity is to reject the Western-imposed label of "Oriental." Today, "Asian American" is an umbrella category that includes both US citizens and immigrants whose ancestors came from Asia east of Pakistan. Although the term is widely used in public discussions, most Asian-origin Americans are ambivalent about this label, reflecting the difficulty of being American and still keeping some ethnic identity: is one, for example, Asian American or Japanese American?

Similarly, "white" is an arbitrary label having more to do with privilege than biology. In the United States, groups initially considered nonwhite such as Irish and Jews have attained "white" membership by acquiring status and wealth. It is hardly surprising, then, that nonwhites would aspire to becoming "white" as a mark of and a tool for material success. However, becoming white can mean distancing oneself from "people of color" or selling out one's ethnicity. Panethnic identities—Asian American, African American, Hispanic American—are one way the politically vocal in any group try to stem defections; these collective identities may restrain aspirations for individual mobility.

Varieties of Asian Americans

Privately, few Americans of Asian ancestry would spontaneously identify themselves as Asian, and fewer still as Asian American. They instead link their identities to specific countries of origin, such as Chinese, Japanese, Korean, Filipino, Indian, Vietnamese, and so on. In a study of Vietnamese youth in San Diego, for example, I found that 53 percent identified themselves as Vietnamese, 32 percent as Vietnamese American, and only 14 percent as Asian American, and that nearly 60 percent of these youth considered their chosen identity as very important to them.

Some Americans of Asian ancestry have family histories in the United States longer than many Americans of Eastern or Southern European origin. However, they became numerous only after 1970, rising from 1.4 million to 11.9 million, or 4 percent of the total US population, in 2000. Before 1970, the Asian-origin population was largely made up of Japanese, Chinese, and Filipinos. In 2000, Americans of Chinese and Filipino ancestries were the largest subgroups (at 2.8 million and 2.4 million, respectively), followed by Indians, Koreans, Vietnamese, and Japanese (at more than one million). Some twenty other national-origin groups, such as Cambodians, Pakistanis, Lao, Thai, Indonesians, and Bangladeshis, were officially counted in government statistics only after 1980, and together amounted to more than two million residents in 2000.

The sevenfold growth of the Asian-origin population in the span of thirty-odd years is primarily due to the accelerated immigration subsequent to the Hart-Celler Act of 1965, which ended the national origins quota system, and the historic resettlement of Southeast Asian refugees after the Vietnam War. Currently, of the Asian-origin population about 60 percent are foreign-born (the first generation), another 28 percent are US-born of foreign-born parents (the second generation), and just 12 percent are born to US-born parents (the third generation and beyond). The only exception to this pattern is Japanese Americans, who have a fourth generation and many US-born elderly.

Unlike earlier immigrants from Asia or Europe, who were mostly low-skilled laborers looking for work, contemporary immigrants from Asia have more varied backgrounds and come for many reasons, such as to join their families, to invest their money in the US economy, to fulfill the demand for highly skilled labor, or to escape war, political, or religious persecution and economic hardship. For example, Chinese, Taiwanese, Indian, and Filipino Americans tend to be over-represented among scientists, engineers, physicians, and other skilled professionals, but less educated, low-skilled workers are more common among Vietnamese,

Cambodian, Laotian, and Hmong Americans, most of whom entered the United States as refugees. While middle-class immigrants are able to start their American lives with high-paying professional careers and comfortable suburban living, low-skilled immigrants and refugees often have to endure low-paying menial jobs and live in inner-city ghettos.

Asian Americans tend to settle in large metropolitan areas and concentrate in the West. California is home to 35 percent of all Asian Americans. But recently, other states such as Texas, Minnesota, and Wisconsin, which historically received few Asian immigrants, have become destinations for Asian American settlement. Traditional ethnic enclaves such as Chinatown, Little Tokyo, Manilatown, Koreatown, Little Phnom Penh, and Thaitown persist or have emerged in gateway cities, helping new arrivals to cope with cultural and language difficulties in their initial stage of resettlement. However, affluent and highly skilled immigrants tend to bypass inner-city enclaves and settle in suburbs upon arrival, belying the stereotype of the "unacculturated" immigrant. Today, more than half of the Asian-origin population is spreading out in suburbs surrounding traditional gateway cities, as well as in new urban centers of Asian settlement across the country.

Differences in national origins, timing of immigration, affluence, and settlement patterns profoundly affect the formation of a panethnic identity. Recent arrivals are less likely than those born or raised in the United States to identify as Asian American. They are also so busy settling in that they have little time to think about being Asian or Asian American, or, for that matter, white. Their diverse origins evoke drastic differences in languages and dialects, religions, foodways, and customs. Many nationalities also brought to America their histories of conflict (such as the Japanese colonization of Korea and Taiwan, Japanese attacks on China, and the Chinese invasion of Vietnam). Immigrants who are predominantly middle-class professionals such as the Taiwanese and Indians, or predominantly small business owners such as the Koreans, share few of the same concerns and priorities as those who are predominantly uneducated, low-skilled refugees, such as Cambodians and Hmong. Finally, Asian-origin people living in San Francisco or Los Angeles among many other Asians and self-conscious Asian Americans develop sharper ethnic sensitivity than those living in, say, Latin-dominant Miami or white-dominant Minneapolis. A politician might get away with calling Asians "Oriental" in Miami but get into big trouble in San Francisco. All of these differences can create obstacles to fostering a cohesive pan-Asian solidarity. As Yen Le Espiritu shows in her research, pan-Asianism is primarily a political ideology of US-born, American-educated, and middle-class Asians rather than of Asian immigrants, who are conscious of their national origins and overburdened with their daily struggles for survival.

Underneath the Model Minority: "White" or "Other"

The celebrated "model minority" image of Asian Americans appeared in the mid-1960s, at the peak of the civil rights movement and the ethnic consciousness movements, but *before* the rising waves of immigration and refugee influx from Asia. Two articles in 1966—"Success Story, Japanese-American Style," by William Petersen in the *New York Times Magazine*, and "Success of One Minority Group in U.S.," by the *U.S. News & World Report* staff, marked a significant departure from how Asian immigrants and their descendants had been traditionally depicted in the media. Both articles extolled Japanese and Chinese Americans for their persistence in overcoming extreme hardships and discrimination to achieve success, unmatched even by US-born whites, with "their own almost totally unaided effort" and "no help from anyone else." The press attributed their winning wealth and respect in American society to hard work, family solidarity, discipline, delayed gratification, nonconfrontation, and eschewing welfare.

One consequence of the model minority stereotype is to buttress the myth that the United States is devoid of racism and accords equal opportunity to all, and that those who lag behind do so because of their own poor choices and inferior culture. Celebrating this model minority can help thwart other racial minorities' demands for social justice by pitting minority groups against each other. It can also pit Asian Americans against whites. On the surface, Asian Americans seem to be on their way to becoming white, just like the offspring of earlier European immigrants. But the model minority image implicitly casts Asian Americans as different from whites. By placing Asian Americans above whites, the model minority image also sets them apart from other Americans, white or nonwhite, in the public mind.

Let me point to two less obvious effects. The model minority stereotype holds Asian Americans to higher standards, distinguishing them from average Americans. "What's wrong with being a model minority?," asked a black student in a class I taught on race. "I'd rather be in the model minority than in the downtrodden minority that nobody respects." Whether people are in a model minority or a downtrodden minority, they are judged by standards *different* from average Americans. Also the model minority stereotype places particular expectations on members of the group so labeled, channeling them to specific avenues of success, such as science and engineering, which in turn unintentionally reinforces barriers for Asian Americans in pursuing careers outside these designated fields. Falling into this trap, a Chinese immigrant father might be upset if his son told him that he had decided to change his major from engineering to English. Disregarding his son's passion and talent for creative writing, the father would rationalize his concern, "You have a 90 percent chance of getting a decent job with an engineering degree, but what chance would you have of earning income as a writer?" This rationale reflects more than simple parental concern over career choices typical of middle-class families; it constitutes the self-fulfilling prophecy of a stereotype.

In the end, the celebration of Asian Americans as a model minority is based on the judgment that many Asian Americans perform at levels above the American average, which sets them apart not only from other minorities but also from whites. The truth of the matter is that the larger than average size of the middle and upper-middle classes in some Asian-origin groups, such as the Chinese, Indian, and Korean, paves a much smoother path for the immigrants and their offspring to regain their middle-class status in the new homeland. The financial resources that immigrants brought with them to this country also help build viable ethnic economies and institutions, such as private after-school programs, for the less fortunate group members to move ahead in society at a much faster pace than they would if they did not have access to these ethnic resources.

"It's Not So Much Being White as Being American"

Most Asian Americans seem to accept that "white" is mainstream, average, and normal, and look to whites as their frame of reference for attaining higher social position. Similarly, researchers often use non-Hispanic whites as the standard against which other groups are compared, even though there is great diversity among whites, too. Like most other immigrants to the United States, many Asian immigrants tend to believe in the American Dream and measure their achievements materially. As a Chinese immigrant said to me in an interview, "I hope to accomplish nothing but three things: to own a home, to be my own boss, and to send my children to the Ivy League." Those with sufficient education, job skills, and money manage to move into white middle-class suburban neighborhoods immediately upon arrival, while others work intensively to accumulate enough savings to move their families up and out of inner-city ethnic enclaves. Consequently, many children of Asian ancestry have lived their entire childhood in white communities, made friends with mostly white peers, and grown up speaking only English. In fact, Asian Americans are the most acculturated non-European group in the United States. By the second generation, most have lost fluency in their parents' native languages. David Lopez finds that in Los Angeles, more than three-quarters of second-generation Asian Americans, (as opposed to about one-quarter of second-generation Mexicans) speak only English at home. Asian Americans also intermarry extensively with whites and with members of other minority groups. Jennifer Lee and Frank Bean find that more than one-quarter of married Asian Americans have a partner of a different racial background, and 87 percent of intermarried Asians marry whites; they also find that 12 percent of all Asian Americans claim a multiracial background, compared to 2 percent of whites and 4 percent of blacks.

Even though US-born or US-raised Asian Americans are relatively acculturated and often intermarry with whites, they may be more ambivalent about becoming white than their immigrant parents. Many only cynically agree that "white" is synonymous with "American." A Vietnamese high school student in New Orleans told me in an interview, "An American is white. You often hear people say, hey, so-and-so is dating an 'American.' You know she's dating a white boy. If he were black, then people would say he's black." But while they recognize whites as a frame of reference, some reject the idea of becoming white themselves—"It's not so much being white as being American," commented a Korean American student in my class on the new second generation. This aversion to becoming white is particularly common among the well-educated and privileged second-generation colleges student who have taken ethnic studies courses, or among Asian American community activists. However, most of the second generation continues to strive for the privileged status associated with whiteness, just like their parents. For example, most US-born or US-raised Chinese American youth end up studying engineering, medicine, and law at college, believing that these areas of study would guarantee well-paying jobs and middle-class living and enhance social contact with whites.

Second-generation Asian Americans are also more conscious of the disadvantages associated being nonwhite than their parents are, who as immigrants tend to be optimistic about overcoming the disadvantages. As a Chinese American woman points out from her own experience, "The truth is, no matter how American you think you are or try to be, if you have almond-shaped eyes, straight black hair, and a yellow complexion, you are a foreigner by default. ... You can certainly be as good as or even better than whites, but you will never become accepted as white." This remark echoes a common-felt frustration among second-generation Asian Americans who detest being treated as immigrants or foreigners. Their experience suggests that whitening has more to do with the beliefs of white America, than with the actual situation of Asian Americans. Speaking perfect English, effortlessly adopting mainstream cultural values, and even intermarrying members of the dominant group may help reduce this "otherness" at the individual level, but have little effect on the group as a whole. New stereotypes can emerge and unwhiten Asian Americans anytime and anywhere, no matter how "successful" and "assimilated" they have become. For example, Congressman David Wu was once invited by the Asian American employees of the US Department of Energy to give a speech in celebration of the Asian American Heritage Month. Yet he and his Asian American staff were not allowed into the department building, even after presenting their congressional IDs, and were repeatedly asked about their citizenship and country of origin. They were told that this was standard procedure for the Department of Energy and that a congressional ID was not a reliable document. A congressman of Italian descent was allowed to enter the same building the next day with his congressional ID, no questions were asked.

The stereotype of the "honorary white" or model minority goes hand in hand with that of the "forever foreigner." Today, globalization and US-Asia relations, combined with continually high rates of immigration, affect how Asian Americans are perceived in American society. Most of the historical stereotypes, such as the "yellow peril" and "Fu Manchu," have found their way into contemporary American life, as revealed in such highly publicized incidents as the murder of Vincent Chin, a Chinese American mistaken for Japanese and beaten to death by disgruntled white autoworkers in the 1980s; the trial of Wen Ho Lee, a nuclear scientist suspected of spying for the Chinese government in the mid-1990s; the 1996 presidential campaign finance scandal, which implicated Asian Americans in funneling foreign contributions to the Clinton campaign; and most recently, in 2001, the Abercrombie & Fitch T-shirts that depicted Asian cartoon characters in stereotypically negative ways—slanted eyes, thick glasses, and heavy Asian accents. Ironically, the ambivalent, conditional nature of white acceptance of Asian Americans prompts them to organize panethnically to fight back—which consequently heightens their racial distinctiveness. So becoming white or not is beside the point. The bottom line is: Americans of Asian ancestry still have to constantly prove they are truly loyal American.

NOTE

Originally published in *Contexts* 3 (1): 29–37, 2004. ©2004 The Asian Sociological Association, reprint by permission of the University of California Press.

STUDY QUESTIONS

(1) Kim argues that a discussion of civil rights in the United States naturally invokes a discussion of race as a relationship between whites and blacks. What—according to Kim—are some of the limitations of this model? Why does she urge us to retain it as a mode of analysis? Based upon Kim's analysis, how would you answer the question, "Are Asians Black?" How else might one describe the identities of Asian Americans? In what ways do the experiences of Asian Americans complicate our understanding of civil liberties in the twenty-first century?

(2) Why do scholars argue that the black/white racial paradigm is becoming obsolete? What are the historical and demographic factors that have contributed to these critiques of the black/white racial paradigm? In what ways are the six dimensions of the black/white paradigm applicable to Asian Americans' racial experience in the United States?

(3) Kim identifies affirmative action and immigration as two of the most important Asian American civil rights issues of our day. How is the black/white racial paradigm related to these two major issues? Are there other Asian American civil rights issues that Kim did not address? How might the black/white paradigm shape our understanding of these other issues?

(4) What different cultural and social behaviors do Filipino Americans associate with race? How do Filipino Americans' individual conceptualizations of race help explain why they identify with both Asian Americans and Latinos? What role does the demographic composition of Los Angeles play in shaping the panethnic identification of Filipino Americans?

(5) Under what conditions do Filipino Americans identify with other Asian Americans? Might the findings of Ocampo's research differ if this study had been conducted in a different city, such as San Francisco or New York? What about if it had been conducted in a "new destination," such as a city in the American South? Under what conditions do Filipino Americans identify with Mexican Americans and other Latinos? How does class shape this process?

(6) According to Zhou, why would Asian Americans, by some measures, be considered white? How is whiteness being defined in this context? What events in the 1960s and 1970s prompted some to see Asian Americans as "white"? In what ways is this characterization both inaccurate and problematic?

(7) Why have some Asian Americans felt that they are perceived as "forever foreigners"? In what ways are the "honorary white" and "forever foreigner" stereotypes congruent with each other? How have global events within Asia contributed to the reification of these stereotypes within the United States?

(8) Zhou notes that many Americans of Asian ancestry are ambivalent about the term "Asian American," preferring instead to identify themselves (typically) by their parents' country of origin. Why do you think they identify themselves in this manner? What effects do class background, education, and immigrant status have on this phenomenon? Under what circumstances do members of Asian-origin groups (Korean American, Filipino American, etc.) embrace a pan–Asian American identity? Under what circumstances do Asian Americans build coalitions with other ethnic and racial groups (including whites)?

(9) In discussing the implications of the model minority hypothesis, Zhou writes, "The model minority image implicitly casts Asian Americans as different from whites. By placing Asian Americans above whites, the model minority image also sets them apart from other Americans, white or nonwhite, in the public mind." Explain what she means and cite evidence from the article to support/refute this idea. When Zhou asks, "Are Asian Americans Becoming White?" what exactly is she suggesting and why? What criteria does American society use to assess whiteness and judge Asian Americans and members of racial minority groups? Based upon your reading of Kim's article, how might Kim respond to this question? How does Asian America look if the privileges of whiteness are projected upon Asian Americans?

SUGGESTED READINGS

Bonus, Rick. 2000. *Locating Filipino Americans: Ethnicity and the Cultural Politics of Space*. Philadelphia: Temple University Press.

Carnes, Tony, and Fenggang Yang, eds. 2004. *Asian American Religions: The Making and Remaking of Borders and Boundaries*. New York: New York University Press.

Dhingra, Pawan H. 2003. "Being American between Black and White: Second-Generation Asian American Professionals' Racial Identities." *Journal of Asian American Studies* 6 (2): 117–147.

Espiritu, Yen Le. 1993. *Asian American Panethnicity: Bridging Institutions and Identities*. Philadelphia: Temple University Press.

Jeung, Russell. 2005. *Faithful Generations: Race and New Asian American Churches*. New Brunswick, NJ: Rutgers University Press.

Kibria, Nazli. 2002. *Becoming Asian American: Second Generation Chinese and Korean American Identities*. Baltimore: Johns Hopkins University Press.

Kim, Rebecca Y. 2006. *God's New Whiz Kids? Second-Generation Korean American Evangelicals on Campus*. New York: New York University Press.

Kurien, P. 2001. "Constructing 'Indianness' in Southern California: The Role of Hindu and Muslim Indian Immigrants." Pp. 289–312 in Marta Lopez-Garza and David R. Diaz, eds., *Asian and Latino Immigrants in a Restructuring Economy*. Stanford, CA: Stanford University Press.

Lee, Jennifer, and Min Zhou. 2015. *The Asian American Achievement Paradox*. New York: Russell Sage Foundation.

Lien, Pei-te, M. Margaret Conway, and Janelle Wong. 2003. "The Contours and Sources of Ethnic Identity Choices among Asian Americans." *Social Science Quarterly* 84 (2): 461–481.

Liu, Eric. 1998. *The Accidental Asian: Notes of a Native Speaker*. New York: Vintage.

Louie, Andrea. 2004. *Chineseness across Borders: Renegotiating Chinese Identities in China and the United States*. Durham, NC: Duke University Press.

Ocampo, Anthony C. 2015. *The Latinos of Asia: How Filipinos Break the Rules of Race*. Stanford, CA: Stanford University Press.

Okamoto, Dina. 2014. *Redefining Race: Asian American Panethnicity and Shifting Ethnic Boundaries*. New York: Russell Sage Foundation Press.

Park, Kyeyoung. 1999. "'I Really Do Feel I'm 1.5!' The Construction of Self and Community by Young Korean Americans." *Amerasia Journal* 25 (1): 139–164.

Shah, Soniah, ed. 1997. *Dragon Ladies: Asian American Feminists Breathe Fire*. Boston: South End.

Shankar, L. D., and P. R. Balgopal. 2001. "South Asian Immigrants before 1950: The Formation of Ethnic, Symbolic, and Group Identity." *Amerasia Journal* 27 (1): 55–84.

Takahashi, J. 1998. *Nisei/Sansei: Shifting Japanese American Identities and Politics*. Philadelphia: Temple University Press.

Takezawa, Y. 1991. "Children of Inmates: The Effects of the Redress Movement among Third Generation Japanese Americans." *Qualitative Sociology* 14 (1): 39–56.

Tamura, Eileen. 1994. *Americanization, Acculturation, and Ethnic Identity: The Nisei Generation in Hawaii*. Urbana: University of Illinois Press.

Thangaraj, Stanley. 2015. *Desi Hoop Dreams: Pickup Basketball and the Making of Asian American Masculinity*. New York: New York University Press.

Tsai, J. L., Y. Ying, and P. A. Lee. 2000. "The Meaning of 'Being Chinese' and 'Being American': Variation among Chinese American Young Adults." *Journal of Cross-Cultural Psychology* 31 (3): 302–332.

Wong, K. Scott, and Sucheng Chan, eds. 1998. *Claiming America: Constructing Chinese American Identities during the Exclusion Era*. Philadelphia: Temple University Press.

Wu, Ellen D. 2013. *The Color of Success: Asian Americans and the Origins of the Model Minority.* Princeton: Princeton University Press.

Yang, Fenggang. 1999. *Chinese Christians in America: Conversion, Assimilation, and Adhesive Identities.* University Park: Pennsylvania State University Press.

Zhou, Min, and Jennifer Lee. 2004. "The Making of Culture, Identity, and Ethnicity among Asian American Youth." Pp. 1–30 in Jennifer Lee and Min Zhou, eds., *Asian American Youth: Culture, Identity, and Ethnicity.* New York: Routledge.

Zhou, Min, and Yang Sao Xiong. 2005. "The Multifaceted American Experiences of the Children of Asian Immigrants: Lessons for Segmented Assimilation." *Ethnic and Racial Studies* 28 (6): 1119–1152.

FILMS

Chien, Windy (producer/director). 1992. *Assimilation/A Simulation* (14-minute experimental).

Grimberg, Sharon, and Daniel Friedman (producers/directors). 1997. *Miss India Georgia* (56-minute documentary).

Jayaswal, Leena, and Indira Somani (producers/directors). 2008. *Crossing Lines* (32-minute documentary).

Nakamura, Robert A. (director). 1995. *Something Strong Within* (40-minute documentary).

Ning, Stephen C. (director). *Freckled Rice* (48-minute documentary).

Riggs, Marlon (director). 1974. *Ethnic Notions* (56-minute documentary).

Soe, Valerie (director). 1986. *All Orientals Look Alike* (1.5-minute experimental).

———(director). 1990. *Black Sheep* (6-minute documentary).

Vu, Trac Minh (producer/director). 1997. *Letters to Thien* (57-minute documentary).

Wang, Wayne (director). 1988. *Dim Sum Take Out* (12-minute drama).

PART VII

Intermarriages and Multiracial Ethnicity

16

Are We "Postracial"?

Intermarriage, Multiracial Identification, and Changing Color Lines

JENNIFER LEE AND FRANK D. BEAN

The 2000 US census was the first to allow Americans to select "one or more races" to mark their racial identification, reflecting the view that race is no longer conceived of as an exclusive and bounded category. In 2000, 6.8 million people, or 2.4 percent of the US population, that is, one in every forty Americans, identified as multiracial. By 2050, demographers project that this ratio could soar to one in five, and by 2100, to one in three Americans (Farley 2002). The growing multiracial population has led some pundits to speculate that the United States is becoming "postracial," meaning that racial boundaries are declining in significance for all Americans. Asian Americans are at the vanguard. In 2000, 12.4 percent of Asian Americans claimed a multiracial background, and by 2050, the percentage could soar to 35 percent (Smith and Edmonston 1997). The growth of the Asian multiracial population is a result of the growing trends in intermarriage among Asians. Today, about one in four married Asians is intermarried, the majority of whom marry whites, and among third- and higher-generation Asians, intermarriage accounts for more than two out of every five marriages.

Along with the rise in intermarriage has been the growth of contemporary immigrants from Latin America and Asia. Immigrants and their children currently total more than 72 million Americans, and account for 23 percent of the US population. The increase in immigration from non-European countries since 1965 has converted the United States from a largely black-white society to one composed of a kaleidoscope of racial/ethnic groups (Alba and Nee 2003; Bean and Stevens 2003; Waldinger and Lee 2001). Rising trends in immigration and intermarriage and the landmark change in the way in which the US census measures racial identification reflect a weakening of racial boundaries, but do these trends suggest that we are becoming "postracial"? Combining data from the US census and Current Population Surveys, we examine the patterns of intermarriage, multiracial identification, and immigration to explain what they reveal about the changing nature of the Asian American category, America's changing color lines, and the prospect of a "postracial" America.

The Rise of Intermarriage in the United States

Interracial marriage is on the rise, and accounts for one in twelve marriages in the United States. Among recent marriages, the ratio narrows to one in seven (Frey 2014). Intermarriage has risen dramatically since the 1967 Supreme Court ruling of *Loving v. Commonwealth of Virginia* that overturned state laws prohibiting interracial marriage and sex. Within a thirty-year period alone between 1960 and 1990, the rate of intermarriage between whites and nonwhites increased tenfold from 150,000 in 1960 to 1.6 million in 1990 (Jacoby 2001; Waters 1999). Today, more than one-quarter of all Asians and Latinos marry someone of a different racial background, mostly whites. Intermarriage rates are even higher among younger, native-born Asians and Latinos, and are likely to increase in future generations.

The change in intermarriage rates is salient because social scientists conceive of intermarriage between whites and nonwhites as a measure of decreasing social distance between groups and changing racial boundaries (Davis 1941; Gilbertson, Fitzpatrick, and Yang 1996; Gordon 1964; Kalmijn 1993, 1998; Lee and Fernandez 1998; Lieberson and Waters 1988; Merton 1941). Hence, differences in the intermarriage rates among groups provide a measure of which racial boundaries are fading most rapidly and which continue to endure.

TABLE 16.1. Rates of Exogamy among Marriages Containing at Least One Member of the Racial/Ethnic Group

	White Rate (%)	N	Black Rate (%)	N	Asian Rate (%)	N	Latino Rate (%)	N	Other Rate (%)	N
Total marriages	100.0	155,534	100.0	11,593	100.0	7,313	100.0	28,993	100.0	2,342
Same race	94.2	143,596	89.8	10,190	72.8	5,152	71.6	20,180	25.8	761
Intermarried	5.8	11,938	10.2	1,403	27.2	2,161	28.4	8,813	74.2	1,581
White	—	—	69.1	848	86.8	1,788	90.0	7,949	88.4	1,353
Black	11.0	848	—	—	4.8	85	5.3	432	3.2	38
Asian	20.7	1,788	7.2	85	—	—	3.0	265	1.3	23
Hispanic	55.2	7,949	20.7	432	7.6	265	—	—	7.2	167
Other	13.1	1,353	3.0	38	0.8	23	1.7	167	—	—

Source: Combined US March Current Population Surveys (US Census Bureau 1995–2001).

As Table 16.1 shows, more than one-quarter of all married Asians and Latinos have a partner of different racial background, at 27.2 and 28.4 percent, respectively.[1] Even more striking is that intermarriage increases among the US-born; two out of every five marriages are interracial (Lee and Bean 2010). Among the young US-born, the ratio is even higher; two-thirds of young native-born Asians and two-fifths of young native-born Latinos marry someone of a different race, the majority of whom marry whites (Qian 1997). The rates of intermarriage among Asians and Latinos are even more striking when we compare them to the intermarriage rates of blacks; only 10 percent of married blacks have a spouse of a different race.

Not only is intermarriage more common among Asians and Latinos than among blacks, the rate at which Asians intermarry with whites is also much higher. As Table 16.1 shows, of intermarried Asians, 86.8 percent marry whites, 7.6 percent marry Hispanics, and 4.8 percent marry blacks. Among intermarried Latinos, 90.0 percent marry whites, 5.3 percent marry blacks, and 3.0 percent marry Asians. Intermarried blacks are also more likely to marry whites, at 69.1 percent, but this figure is far lower than those of intermarried Asians and Latinos. Hence, both Asians and Latinos are considerably more likely to marry whites as are blacks.

America's Multiracial Movement

The rise in interracial marriage has resulted in a growing multiracial population that became highly visible when, for the first time in the US history, the 2000 census allowed Americans to mark "one or more races" to indicate their racial identification. Spawned by a small but highly influential multiracial movement, the change in the way the US census measures racial identification reveals how racial boundaries are changing in the United States (DaCosta 2007; Farley 2002; Hirschman, Alba, and Farley 2000; Waters 2000; Williams 2006).

The multiracial movement was composed most prominently of advocates from groups such as the Association for Multiethnic Americans (AMEA) and Project RACE (Reclassify All Children Equally). These groups criticized the standards of the Office of Management and Budget's (OMB) Statistical Policy Directive Number 15, which asks individuals to mark their "race" on the census. Advocates argued that forced monoracial identification was an affront to them and/or their children. Not only was this practice inaccurate because it denied the existence of interracial marriage and multiracial Americans, but they also argued that forcing children to choose only one racial category could produce psychological damage. Furthermore, advocates from AMEA and Project RACE argued that this practice was discriminatory.

A year later in 1994, the OMB declared that racial categories in Statistical Directive 15 were of decreasing value and considered an alternate strategy—to provide Americans the option to identify with as many racial categories as respondents wished. Hence, the racial options on the 2000 census included "White," "Black," "Asian," "Native Hawaiian or Other Pacific Islander," "American Indian and Alaska Native," and "Other." While "Latino" or "Hispanic" was not a racial category on the 2000 census, OMB's directive mandated two distinct questions regarding a person's racial/ethnic background: one about race and a second about whether a person is "Spanish/Hispanic/Latino." Since someone who self-designates as "Spanish/Hispanic/Latino" can be of any race, the census asked both questions in order to identify the Latino population in the United States.

While advocates of the multiracial movement had pushed for a separate "multiracial" category and were not entirely satisfied with this option, they conceded that the option to mark "one or more" was an improvement over forced monoracial identification. On October 30, 1997, the US Census Bureau announced its final decision that all Americans would have the option to identify with two or more races, starting with the 2000 census and extending to all federal data systems by 2003.

America's Multiracial Population

In 2000, 2.4 percent of the US population identified itself as multiracial, and these figures could rise to 21 percent by 2050, with as many as 35 percent of Asians and 45 percent of Hispanics claiming a multiracial background (Smith and Edmonston 1997). The multiracial population is young, and twice as likely as other groups to be under the age of eighteen, signaling that this group is likely to continue to grow in the future (Lee and Bean 2010). Of those who marked more than one race on the 2000 census, 93 percent reported exactly two races, 6 percent reported three races, and only 1 percent reported four or more races.

Those who identified with more than one race, however, are not evenly distributed across all racial groups. As Table 16.2 illustrates, the groups with a high percentage of multiracial reporting are Native Hawaiian or Other Pacific Islander (45 percent), American Indian and Alaska Native (36 percent), Other (16 percent), and Asian (12 percent). The groups with the lowest proportion of persons who claim a multiracial background are whites and blacks. However, because whites account for 77 percent of the total US population, most individuals who report a multiracial identity also mark white. More specifically, while 5.1 million whites claim a multiracial background, this accounts for only 2.3 percent of the total white population. Like whites, the proportion of blacks who claim a multiracial background is also quite small, accounting for only 4.2 percent of the total black population in 2000. Hence, today's newest immigrant groups—Asians and Latinos—are more likely to claim a multiracial identification than both whites and blacks.

TABLE 16.2. Multiracial Identification by Census Racial Categories

	Racial Identification (Millions)[a]	Multiracial Identification (Millions)[b]	Percentage Multiracial
White	216.5	5.1	2.3
Black	36.2	1.5	4.2
Asian	11.7	1.4	12.4
Other	18.4	3.0	16.4
American Indian and Alaska Native	3.9	1.4	36.4
Native Hawaiian or Other Pacific Islander	0.7	0.3	44.8

Source: US Census Bureau (2000).
a. Racial/ethnic group totals do not sum to the total US population because multiracial persons are counted here in more than one group.
b. Multiracial persons are counted for each race category mentioned.

If we examine the rates of black-white, Asian-white, and Latino-white multiracial combinations as a percentage of the total black, Asian, and Latino populations, we find these figures equal 1.9, 7.0, and 4.6 percent, respectively. That is, among Asians, the Asian-white multiracial combination is about *three and a half times* more likely, and among Latinos, the Latino-white combination *more than two and a half times* more likely as the black-white combination among blacks. That black-white multiracials are less likely to identify multiracially compared to their Asian-white and Latino-white counterparts is vexing considering that the US Census Bureau estimates that, given the history of racial mixing, at least three-quarters of the black population in the United States is ancestrally multiracial (Spencer 1997). In other words, while at least 75 percent of black Americans have some white ancestry and thus could claim a multiracial identity on this basis, just over 4 percent choose to do so.

The tendency of black Americans not to report a multiracial identification is a result of the legacy of slavery, including lasting discrimination and the legal and de facto invocation of the "one-drop rule" of hypodescent, by which anyone with any trace of black ancestry was defined as black (DaCosta 2007; Gullickson and Morning 2011; Hollinger 2008; Nobles 2000; Roth 2005). The one-drop rule was once used to justify slavery, later used to support Jim Crow segregation, and also employed to deny any multiracial black-white children the rights to the property of their white fathers (Davis 1991; Lee and Bean 2010). In no other country and for no other racial/ethnic group has the one-drop rule applied, resulting in the historical constraining of identity options for multiracial blacks in the United States.

The one-drop rule has not been similarly imposed on Asians, Latinos, or American Indians, resulting in more racial options for these groups. For example, research shows that about 50 percent of American Indian/white and Asian/white intermarried couples report a white racial identity for their children (Eschbach 1995; Saenz et al. 1995; Xie and Goyette 1997). In a study of multiracial Hispanic students, the authors find that only 44 percent choose a Hispanic identity (Stephan and Stephan 1989). Hence, unlike the traditional "one-drop rule" that has historically imposed a black racial identity on black Americans, multiracial Asians, Latinos, and American Indians appear to have much more leeway to choose among different racial options, including multiracial and white identities. That multiracial blacks have been historically denied similar options continues to constrain their racial identification, even today (Lee and Bean 2007).

In addition, because a significant proportion of Latinos and Asians in the United States are either immigrants or the children of immigrants, their understanding of race, racial boundaries, and the black-white color divide is shaped by a different set of circumstances than those of black Americans. Most important, what sets Latinos and Asians apart from African Americans is that the experiences of the former groups are not rooted in a historical legacy of slavery with its systematic and persistent patterns of legal and institutional exclusion, discrimination, and inequality by which the tenacious black-white divide was born and cemented. The unique history and experience of black Americans in this country makes the black-white divide qualitatively and quantitatively different from the Latino-white or Asian-white divides. For these reasons, racial/ethnic boundaries are more fluid for America's newest immigrants than for native-born blacks, providing multiracial Asians and Latinos more racial options than their multiracial black counterparts.

It is also critical to remember that race is a social and cultural construct, rather than a fixed category that is rooted in biology or genetics. A legion of social scientists have documented the processes by which racial categories have undergone change throughout our nation's history (Gans 1999; Gerstle 1999; Omi and Winant 1994; Waters 1990, 1999). For example, when Irish, Italians, and Jews first arrived in the United States in the nineteenth century, they were considered racially distinct from and inferior to Anglo-Americans. However, they successfully achieved whiteness by attaining economic mobility, and by deliberately and forcefully distinguishing themselves from African Americans (Alba 1985, 1990; Brodkin 1998; Foner 2000; Ignatiev 1995; Roediger 1991). Today, few would contest the claim that Irish, Italians, and Jews are white.

Race and racial boundaries have also changed for other groups, including Asians. For example, the Chinese in Mississippi changed their racial status from almost black to almost white. Loewen (1988) details how the Mississippi Chinese achieved near white status by attaining economic parity with whites, emulating their cultural and social practices, setting up parallel institutions with whites, and distancing themselves from African Americans and the Chinese who married them. The change in racial classification among ethnic groups from nonwhite to almost white illustrates that race is a social category that has expanded over time to incorporate earlier European immigrant groups, and may be stretching again to incorporate some of America's contemporary immigrants (Gerstle 1999).

Some social scientists have posited that Asians may be the next in line to become white with multiracial Asians at the head of the queue. Whether this hypothesis is correct will depend on a number of factors, including their rate of intermarriage, multiracial identification, continued immigration from Asia, the selectivity of immigration from Asia, and Asian American economic and political incorporation. Considering that 40 percent of third-generation Asians intermarry today, and that the children of these unions have the option to iden-tify as "white," Asians may indeed be following the path of their earlier European predecessors. Moreover, that the median household income for Asian Americans not only exceeds the national average but also exceeds that that of white house-holds also bodes in favor of this hypothesis. However, continued immigration from Asia and the persistent racial stereotypes of Asian Americans as "forever foreign" and the "model minority" signal that the whiteness hypothesis is far from inevitable (Lee and Zhou 2014, 2015). Hence, whether Asians—or at least some Asian ethnic groups—are the next in line to become white still remains to be seen.

The Geography of the Multiracial Identities

Like the patterns of immigration, patterns of multiracial identification vary across the country. Forty percent of all those who report a multiracial identi-fication reside in the West, a region of the United States that has demonstrated substantially more tolerance for racial/ethnic diversity than other parts of the country (Baldassare 2000; Godfrey 1988). As Table 16.3 indicates, California leads as the state with the largest number of multiracial Americans, and is the only state with a multiracial population that exceeds one million. The multiracial population accounts for 4.7 percent of California's population, or one in every twenty-one Californians (about twice the national average). Like America's mul-tiracial population, California's multiracial population is young: 7.3 percent of Californians under the age of eighteen are identified as multiracial. This popula-tion is growing rapidly, and to help put the growth into perspective, it is worth noting that the number of multiracial children born each year in California already exceeds the number of black and Asian children born in the state (Lee and Bean 2010).

Like California, other states with large Asian and Latino immigrant popula-tions and evince larger multiracial populations. Nearly two-thirds of multiracial Americans (64 percent) reside in just ten states—California, New York, Texas, Florida, Hawaii, Illinois, New Jersey, Washington, Michigan, and Ohio—all of which have relatively high immigrant populations. In essence, America's "new diversity states" (as reflected in the percentage of the population that is *not* non-Hispanic white or non-Hispanic black) boast much larger multiracial populations than states that are less racially diverse (Lee and Bean 2010).

TABLE 16.3. Most and Least Multiracial States

Rank	State	Number of Multiracial Persons	Multiracial Population (Percentage*)
1	Hawaii	259,343	21.4
2	Alaska	34,146	5.4
3	California	1,607,646	4.7
4	Oklahoma	155,985	4.5
5	Nevada	76,428	3.8
6	New Mexico	66,327	3.6
7	Washington	213,519	3.6
8	New York	590,182	3.1
9	Oregon	104,745	3.1
10	Arizona	146,526	2.9
42	Tennessee	63,109	1.1
43	Iowa	31,778	1.1
44	Louisiana	48,265	1.1
45	New Hampshire	13,214	1.1
46	Kentucky	42,443	1.1
47	South Carolina	39,950	1.0
48	Alabama	44,179	1.0
49	Maine	12,647	1.0
50	West Virginia	15,788	0.9
51	Mississippi	20,021	0.7

Source: US Census Bureau (2000). *Percentage *not* non-Hispanic white or non-Hispanic black.

On the opposite end of the diversity spectrum are states like West Virginia and Maine that have small racial minority populations, and thereby exhibit very low levels of multiracial reporting. States like Mississippi, Alabama, South Carolina, and Louisiana, however, have relatively large black populations yet evince low levels of multiracial reporting nevertheless. In these southern states, the traditional dividing line between blacks and whites and the historically constraining "one-drop rule" of hypodescent constrain multiracial identification, leading Americans to be more likely to identify monoracially as either white or black rather than adopt a multiracial identity (Davis 1991; Farley 2002; Nobles 2000).

Hence, while national patterns in interracial marriage and multiracial identification signal a loosening of racial boundaries, particularly for Asians and Latinos, these shifts are occurring more rapidly in certain parts of the United States. Parts of the country that have lower levels of immigration and consequently less racial/ethnic diversity expose the tenacity of the black-white divide that has historically demarcated race relations. Hence, while some parts of the United States, like the West, may reveal the fading of racial boundaries, especially between blacks and nonblacks, other areas such as the South prove that the traditional black-white color line continues to endure.

The New Color Line in the Twenty-First Century

The US Census Bureau's decision to allow Americans to "mark one or more races" to identify themselves is a sweeping change in the way the US government collects data on race. This landmark change gave official status and recognition to Americans who wish to claim a multiracial identification—an acknowledgment that speaks volumes about how far the country has come since the days when the "one-drop rule" enjoyed legal legitimacy. This change appears to signal that old racial divides are fading, and we may be approaching a "postracial" America.

At first glance, these patterns offer an optimistic portrait, especially considering that interracial marriage was illegal in sixteen states as recently as 1967. Upon closer examination, however, we find that patterns of intermarriage and multiracial identification are equally distributed across all racial/ethnic groups. Not only are Latinos and Asians more likely to intermarry than blacks, but they are also more likely to report a multiracial identification. In other words, of the three groups, blacks are the least likely to intermarry and the least likely to claim a multiracial identification. The different rates of Asian, Latino, and black intermarriage and multiracial reporting suggest that while racial boundaries may be fading, they are not eroding at the same pace for all groups, revealing that some racial boundaries are more enduring than others.

What is crucial here is how we interpret the intermarriage and multiracial identification findings for Asians and Latinos. If we consider Asians and Latinos as racialized minorities and thus closer to blacks than whites along some scale of social disadvantage, the high levels of multiracial identification in these groups suggest that racial prejudice and boundaries might be fading for all nonwhite groups. In other words, if these groups are similarly disadvantaged because of their racial status, then this suggests the optimistic conclusion that race relations might be improving for all nonwhite groups. If, on the other hand, we consider Asians and Latinos as new immigrant groups whose disadvantage derives from their immigrant status (rather than their racial status), then their high levels of intermarriage and multiracial reporting signal that their experience may be different from that of blacks. Furthermore, it suggests that the trends and patterns for Asians and Latinos do not necessarily mean that similar improvements can be expected among blacks.

This distinction is critical since it helps us to differentiate whether America's color lines are shifting for all racial/ethnic minority groups, or whether they are fading mostly in the cases of nonblack immigrant groups. Based on the patterns of intermarriage and multiracial identification, the color line appears less rigid for Asians and Latinos than blacks. In their cases, Asians and Latinos have high rates of intermarriage and multiracial reporting because they do not share the legacy of black in the United States. While the color line is shifting for blacks, this shift is occurring more slowly, revealing that Asians and Latinos closer to whites than they are to blacks at this point in time. As a result, we may be witnessing the emergence of a black/nonblack divide that continues to leave black Americans at a position of extreme disadvantage, pointing to a pattern of "black exceptionalism" (Lee and Bean 2007, 2010). While much of America's racial history to date has revolved around who was white and who was not, the next phase of race relations may revolve around who is black and who is not.

The emergence of a black/nonblack divide in a context where diversity is increasing and racial/ethnic boundaries are diminishing represents both good and bad news for twenty-first-century America. That a white/nonwhite color line does not seem to be emerging is the good news. But that newer nonwhite immigrant groups appear to be jumping ahead of African Americans in a hierarchy divided by race is unquestionably bad news. Based on immigration, intermarriage, and multiracial identification, it appears that Asians and Latinos are closer to whites than to blacks at this point in time, and consequently, they may be participants in a new color line that continues to separate blacks from other groups. Hence, America's new color line may consist of a racial/ethnic divide that places many blacks in disadvantaged positions relatively similar to those perpetuated by the traditional black-white divide, pointing to a persistent pattern of "black exceptionalism" in the United States.

Conclusion

Since the legalization of interracial marriage in 1967, intermarriage between whites and nonwhites has increased tenfold, and the increase has gone hand in hand with a growing multiracial population in the United States. The 2000 US census officially recognized America's multiracial population by providing the option to "mark one or more" races to identify themselves and members of their households. Coinciding with rising intermarriage and a growing multiracial population was a new immigrant stream from Latin America and Asia that began in 1965 with the passage of the Immigration and Nationality Act. As a result of these changes, the United States is more racially/ethnically diverse than at any point in our history.

While the black-white color no longer captures America's demographic realities, the question remains what color line will take its place, or whether color lines will disappear altogether thereby forecasting a "postracial" future.

The trends in intermarriage and patterns of multiracial identification reveal that the color line is shifting more readily to accommodate newer immigrant groups such as Latinos and Asians than it is for blacks. While the color line is shifting for blacks, this shift is occurring much more slowly, pointing to a stubborn pattern of "black exceptionalism." Where do Asians and Latinos currently fit along this divide? At this time, the changing pace of the shifting color lines for these groups points to the emergence of a black/nonblack divide that places Asians and Latinos closer to whites than to blacks. This is most evident in "new diversity" states and metropolitan areas with high concentrations of immigrants, high levels of racial/ethnic diversity, and high levels of multiracial reporting. While a "postracial" future may be ideal, we are far from there, even for Asian Americans for whom patterns of integration do not mean full inclusion.

NOTES

This chapter is based on material from Jennifer Lee and Frank D. Bean's *The Diversity Paradox: Immigration and the Color Line in 21st Century America* (New York: Russell Sage Foundation). Funding for this research was generously provided by the Russell Sage Foundation.

1   For present purposes, we refer to Latinos as if they were an official "racial" group, although government data allow persons indicating that they are Latino to report themselves as belonging to any racial group.

REFERENCES

Alba, Richard D. 1985. *Italian Americans: Into the Twilight of Ethnicity.* Englewood Cliffs, NJ: Prentice Hall.

———. 1990. *Ethnic Identity: The Transformation of White America.* New Haven, CT: Yale University Press.

Alba, Richard, and Victor Nee. 2003. *Remaking the American Mainstream: Assimilation and Contemporary Immigration.* Cambridge, MA: Harvard University Press.

Baldassare, Mark. 2000. *California in the New Millennium: The Changing Social and Political Landscape.* Berkeley: University of California Press.

Bean, Frank D., and Gillian Stevens. 2003. *America's Newcomers and the Dynamics of Diversity.* New York: Russell Sage Foundation.

Brodkin, Karen. 1998. *How Jews Became White Folks and What That Says about Race in America.* New Brunswick, NJ: Rutgers University Press.

DaCosta, Kimberly McClain. 2007. *Making Multiracials: State, Family, and Market in the Redrawing of the Color Line.* Stanford, CA: Stanford University Press.

Davis, F. James. 1991. *Who Is Black?* University Park: Pennsylvania State University Press.

Davis, Kingsley. 1941. "Intermarriage in Caste Societies." *American Anthropologist* 43: 376–395.

Eschbach, Karl. 1995. "The Enduring and Vanishing American Indian: American Indian Population Growth and Intermarriage in 1980." *Ethnic and Racial Studies* 18 (1): 89–108.

Farley, Reynolds. 2002. "Racial Identities in 2000: The Response to the Multiple-Race Response Option." Pp. 33–61 in Joel Perlmann and Mary C. Waters, eds., *The New Race Question: How the Census Counts Multiracial Individuals.* New York: Russell Sage Foundation.

Foner, Nancy. 2000. *From Ellis Island to JFK: New York's Two Great Waves of Immigration*. New Haven, CT: Yale University Press.

Frey, William H. 2014. *Diversity Explosion: How New Racial Demographics Are Remaking America*. Washington, DC: Brookings Institution.

Gans, Herbert J. 1999. "The Possibility of a New Racial Hierarchy in the Twenty-First Century United States." Pp. 371–390 in Michèle Lamont, ed., *The Cultural Territories of Race*. Chicago: University of Chicago Press.

Gerstle, Gary. 1999. "Liberty, Coercion, and the Making of Americans." Pp. 275–293 in Charles Hirschman, Philip Kasinitz, and Josh DeWind, eds., *The Handbook of International Migration*. New York: Russell Sage Foundation.

Gilbertson, Greta, Joseph F. Fitzpatrick, and Lijun Yang. 1996. "Hispanic Intermarriage in New York City: New Evidence from 1991." *International Migration Review* 30 (2): 445–459.

Godfrey, Brian J. 1988. *Neighborhoods in Transition: The Making of San Francisco's Ethnic and Nonconformist Communities*. Berkeley: University of California Press.

Gordon, Milton. 1964. *Assimilation in American Life*. New York: Oxford University Press.

Gullickson, Aaron, and Ann Morning. 2011. "Choosing Race: Multiracial Ancestry and Identification." *Social Science Research* 40 (2): 498–512.

Hirschman, Charles, Richard Alba, and Reynolds Farley. 2000. "The Meaning and Measurement of Race in the U.S. Census: Glimpses into the Future." *Demography* 37: 381–393.

Hollinger, David A. 2008. "Obama, the Instability of Color Lines, and the Promise of a Postethnic Future." *Callaloo* 31 (4): 1033–1037.

Ignatiev, Noel. 1995. *How the Irish Became White*. New York: Routledge.

Jacoby, Tamar. 2001. "An End to Counting Race?" *Commentary* 111 (6): 37–40.

Kalmijn, Matthijs. 1993. "Patterns in Black/White Intermarriage." *Social Forces* 72 (1): 119–146.

———. 1998. "Intermarriage and Homogamy—Causes, Patterns, Trends." *Annual Review of Sociology* 23: 395–421.

Lee, Jennifer, and Frank D. Bean. 2007. "Reinventing the Color Line: Immigration and America's New Racial/Ethnic Divide." *Social Forces* 86 (2): 561–586.

———. 2010. *The Diversity Paradox: Immigration and the Color Line in 21st Century America*. New York: Russell Sage Foundation.

Lee, Jennifer, and Min Zhou. 2014. "From Unassimilable to Exceptional: The Rise of Asian Americans and 'Stereotype Promise.'" *New Diversities* 16 (1): 7–22.

———. 2015. *The Asian American Achievement Paradox*. New York: Russell Sage Foundation.

Lee, Sharon M., and Marilyn Fernandez. 1998. "Patterns in Asian American Racial/Ethnic Intermarriage: A Comparison of 1980 and 1990 Census Data." *Sociological Perspectives* 41 (2): 323–342.

Lieberson, Stanley, and Mary C. Waters. 1988. *From Many Strands: Ethnic and Racial Groups in Contemporary America*. New York: Russell Sage Foundation.

Loewen, James. 1988. *The Mississippi Chinese: Between Black and White*. Prospect Heights, IL: Waveland.

Merton, Robert K. 1941. "Intermarriage and the Social Structure: Fact and Theory." *Psychiatry* 4: 361–374.

Nobles, Melissa. 2000. *Shades of Citizenship: Race and the Census in Modern Politics*. Stanford, CA: Stanford University Press.

Omi, Michael, and Howard Winant. 1994. *Racial Formation in the United States: From the 1960s to the 1980s*. New York: Routledge.

Qian, Zhenchao. 1997. "Breaking the Racial Barriers: Variations in Interracial Marriage between 1980 and 1990." *Demography* 34 (2): 263–276.

Roediger, David. 1991. *The Wages of Whiteness*. New York: Verso.

Roth, Wendy D. 2005. "The End of the One-Drop Rule? Labeling of Multiracial Children in Black Intermarriages." *Sociological Forum* 20 (1): 35–67.

Saenz, Rogelio, Sean-Shong Hwang, Benigno E. Aguirre, and Robert N. Anderson. 1995. "Persistence and Change in Asian Identity among Children of Intermarried Couples." *Sociological Perspectives* 38 (2): 175–194.

Smith, James P., and Barry Edmonston. 1997. *The New Americans*. Washington, DC: National Academy Press.

Spencer, Jon Michael. 1997. *The New Colored People: The Mixed-Race Movement in America*. New York: New York University Press.

Stephan, Cookie White, and Walter G. Stephan. 1989. "After Intermarriage: Ethnic Identity among Mixed-Heritage Japanese-Americans and Hispanics." *Journal of Marriage and Family* 51: 507–519.

US Census Bureau. 1995–2001. *Current Population Survey*. Washington, DC: US Census Bureau.

———. 2000. *Statistical Portrait of the United States*. Washington, DC: US Census Bureau.

Waldinger, Roger, and Jennifer Lee. 2001. "New Immigrants in Urban America." Pp. 30–79 in Roger Waldinger, ed., *Strangers at the Gates: New Immigrants in Urban America*. Berkeley: University of California Press.

Waters, Mary C. 1990. *Ethnic Options: Choosing Identities in America*. Berkeley: University of California Press.

———. 1999. *Black Identities: West Indian Immigrant Dreams and American Realities*. Cambridge, MA: Harvard University Press.

———. 2000. "Immigration, Intermarriage, and the Challenges of Measuring Racial/Ethnic Identities." *American Journal of Public Health* 90: 1735–1737.

Williams, Kim M. 2006. *Mark One or More: Civil Rights in Multiracial America*. Ann Arbor: University of Michigan Press.

Xie, Yu, and Kimberly Goyette. 1997. "The Racial Identification of Biracial Children with One Asian Parent: Evidence from the 1990 Census." *Social Forces* 76 (2): 547–570.

17

Mapping Multiple Histories of Korean American Transnational Adoption

KIM PARK NELSON

The practice of Korean transnational adoption has a history of more than fifty years that includes multiple overlapping layers. One history is specific to the aftermath of the Korean War and subsequent US-South Korean geopolitical relations. Another is the history of racialization of Korean adoptees as Asian Americans, and as a part of an ongoing history of American transracial adoption. Yet another is the history of US immigration policy which, for Korean adoptees, has swung to extremes. And finally, there is also the history of Korean adoptee communities themselves. All these rich histories that directly or indirectly affect Korean adoption and the sociopolitical history of changing attitudes about transracial and transnational adoption have particular significance in telling the story of Korean adoption in America. These histories include the policies, laws, social, cultural, and political events that have made transnational adoption more and more commonplace since the first Korean transnational adoption in the 1950s. This essay addresses these multiple, interwoven histories of Korean American adoption.

Geopolitical Histories: Adoption and the Aftermath of the Korean War

The first generation of Korean adoptees consisted mainly of war orphans sent to the United States in the immediate aftermath of the Korean War, and constitutes only a tiny fraction of the current overall population of Korean adoptees (less than 4 percent of the current Korean American adoptee population was adopted before 1962).[1] Despite their small numbers, these adoptees have become iconic in Americans' understandings of Korean adoption and the transracial adoptee experience. The broadly understood narrative of a child orphaned by war and rescued through adoption into a benevolent American family has its roots in this generation. The cultural role of the Korean American adoptee was largely established during the 1950s and 1960s as a result of media attention given to this small group of Korean immigrants who arrived in the United States when almost all other Asian nationals were barred from legal American immigration by a strict policy of Asian exclusion that had been in effect in some form since

1882.[2] So, even the trope of the Korean adoptee as "exceptional" (in terms of cultural assimilation, psychological adjustment, and social accomplishments) among American peoples of color and among immigrants began with this small group of adoptees—who are now the elders of Korean adoptee communities in the United States and throughout the world.

In examining this first generation of Korean American adoptees, it is essential to consider the effects of the Korean War on Korean society and on US-Korean relations. The transnational adoption program that began between the United States and South Korea in 1953 was a direct response to the consequences of American actions in Korea, including the deployment of troops to the Korean peninsula and the limited occupation of South Korea by American troops that has continued to present day. War orphans, the first adoptees, were configured as "refugees" from war and as unfortunates who carried the stigma of mixed-race parentage (many were the offspring of Korean mothers and American GI fathers), a socially unacceptable situation in Korea in the postwar period (or even today). Like the war itself, the practice of transnational adoption was in large part a product of American intervention; it was (and in many cases still is) widely believed that it would be far better for these children to be placed in the United States than to remain in Korea, a nation that was imagined as war-torn, culturally backward, and impoverished in the American consciousness.

Ramsay Liem characterizes the Korean War as the "first 'hot' war of the Cold War . . . [the United States'] first encounter on the Asian mainland; it was also the first failure to achieve victory [for the United States]."[3] In many ways, since the Korean War was the first shooting war of the Cold War, it also represented the first test of America's political and ideological will against communism in Asia, which had particular strategic interest for America, as cohabitants of the Soviet hemisphere. He also notes that the war separated (and continues to separate) as many as ten million Koreans across the DMZ.[4] Liem attempts to link the partition of Korea to emigration from the northern part of Korea through oral histories of Korean Americans in the United States,[5] and finds that the trauma of civil war for Korean Americans is very much a part of the memories of first- and second-generation Korean American immigrants.[6] However, the Korean War also served as the germinal event that has led to the permanent separation of tens of thousands of Korean children from their biological parents through adoption abroad, a reality that has received far less attention from studies of the Korean diaspora.[7]

Though the existence of some of the first Korean adoptees, biracial children of American paternity, was a direct result of the presence of the American military in Korea, transnational adoption out of Korea to the United States was sustained by the popularity of the practice among the American public, whether motivated by sympathy, a sense of obligation, national pride, or convenience. Policies governing the relationship between the United States and South Korea have been hotly debated in both nations (though probably more so in Korea), while both the occupation of South Korea by American military personnel and the emigration of Korean children for transnational adoption have continued uninterrupted since the Korean War.

Korean adoption might have remained a social phenomenon of the immediate postwar period as it had been in some European nations after World War II, had it not been for the media sensation that surrounded the adoption of eight Korean children by Bertha and Harry Holt in 1955. As a result of this coverage, the Holts received a flood of correspondence from prospective parents interested in adopting from Korea, and the Holts helped many of these people achieve that goal. The Holts went on to establish the Holt Adoption Agency, which initially devoted all its efforts to adoption from Korea. Because the Holt Agency saw itself as fulfilling an evangelical mission, it did not base its placement decisions on standard child welfare criteria—but did require that adoptive parents be Christians.[8] These practices, and the fact that the Holts' operations did not utilize the services of professional social workers, exposed the agency to strong criticism from social work and child welfare organizations.[9] This early facilitation by the Holts, whose own attempts to adopt children domestically had been rejected by American adoption agencies, played a huge role in making transnational adoption a viable option for Americans at a time when American adoption criteria barred single persons, those who already had children or could have children, and older adults from becoming adoptive parents. While this was an important step in dismantling the discriminatory policies based on age and economic class that had been used against many prospective parents by the American adoption system, it also created a separate set of standards for the adoption of foreign children—standards that were notably more lenient than those applied to the adoption of American-born children. This divide, opened by the Holts seeking to "rescue" as many Korean children as possible by exploiting the lack of standards around the then-uncommon occurrence of transnational adoption, has never been closed. Even though the Holts and the agency they founded initially restricted their efforts to facilitating the adoption of war orphans and biracial children, eventually American demand for Korean children outstripped this supply, and later the Holt Adoption Agency began placing children who were neither biracial nor war-orphaned, and still does so today.

The initial framing of Korean adoption as both a humanitarian project and an evangelical mission has left an indelible mark on Korean and other transnational adoptions. Although it has been decades since South Korea has needed international humanitarian aid, Korean adoptees are still understood as recipients of charitable, often Christian, acts. Through their position as both a marginalized and a privileged group of Korean immigrants, adoptees have been used as examples both of the best and the worst outcomes of imperial practice—either as beneficiaries of a benevolent imperialism (saved from the barbarities of their birth country through relocation to superior societies) or as victims of involuntary relocation and cultural commodification (as cultural assets to be acquired by richer, more powerful nations). In this sociopolitical context, transnational adoption can be seen as an imperialist process, born of military, cultural, and economic domination and through which individuals (usually white) from rich and powerful nations adopt individuals (usually not white) from poor nations that are under the political influence of the adopting country. The positions of adoptees in adoptive nations are complicated and often contradictory, in light of their roles as immigrants, citizens, and racialized others.

While transnational adoption started out as a solution for children in crisis, it has become a national custom: it is estimated that more than two hundred thousand Korean children have now been transnationally adopted worldwide.[10] One reason is because American parents are both able and willing to pay for adoptable children. The South Korean government has been, for the most part, extremely compliant in meeting this demand. In many accounts, the lack of a comprehensive social welfare system in South Korea is directly linked to that nation's export of babies and children by the thousand. This is despite South Korea's rising GNP, which is the highest of any "sending" country in the transnational adoption network of exchange.

Korean transnational adoption was the first sustained intercountry adoption program in history (all previous intercountry adoption programs were temporary, in response to national disasters or emergencies); the current permanent practice of transnational adoption, whereby prospective adoptive parents in the United States or another receiving country can expect to have a choice of countries from which to adopt children, can be traced to Korean adoption. Indeed, most countries that have sought to develop transnational adoption programs have used the South Korean model on some level, since South Korea has the longest-running, most predictable, and most stable overseas adoption program in the world.

The fact that transnational adoption has sustained itself for more than fifty years is also attributable to changing racial preferences and beliefs among the American adopting public, and to social changes in what constitutes an acceptable American family. In addition, transnational adoption is encouraged by current immigration policies that privilege transnational adoptees over any other type of immigrant. However, the current migration of thousands of children a year for the purposes of transnational adoption can all be traced to the first wave of Korean adoptees who arrived in the United States shortly after the Korean War into an American cultural environment of racial assimilation, social conformity, and Cold War sentimentalism about Asia and its children.[11]

Racial Histories of Korean American Adoption and the Beginnings of American Transracial Adoption

Sustained large-scale transracial adoption, including transnational adoptions, which were almost always also transracial placements (until Russia and the former Eastern Bloc nations began to open transnational adoption programs in the 1990s),[12] began in the 1950s and continues today. The first recorded Korean transnational adoption took place in 1953,[13] just five years after the first American domestic transracial adoption of an African American child to a white family.[14] In 1958, just five years after Korean transnational adoption began, the Indian Adoption Project began as a national program with the goal of placing American Indian children in white American homes.[15] Clearly, American domestic transracial adoption as a formal practice barely predates the start of Korean transnational adoption. As a result, the histories of transnational and domestic adoptions are closely interconnected.

Roughly 15,000 transnational adoptions occurred between 1953 and 1962. Greater numbers of these placements took place in the United States starting in the late 1960s and early 1970s, with 37,469 transnational adoptions from 1965 to 1976.[16] In-country adoption statistics are largely unavailable since 1977, when the US government stopped collecting this information. It is known that 831 black children were adopted into white families in 1975.[17]

The increase in transracial and transnational adoptions during the 1960s and 1970s has been attributed to a number of factors. The set of circumstances most cited is the decrease in the number of adoptable white infants during this period due to the greater availability of family planning,[18] combined with the growing number of prospective parents as the baby boom generation reached the age of parenthood, creating high demand for adoptable children. The civil rights movement may have also contributed to the increased popularity of transracial adoption, as efforts to desegregate American society encouraged whites to become more comfortable with the idea of sharing their lives with people of other races. Economic class issues, too, have always been part of adoption history; children born to working-class parents are more often given up for adoption.[19] During the 1960s and 1970s, class divisions were strongly correlated with racial categories, as the middle class was made up primarily of educated whites and the working class included more African Americans. At the same time, as the number of adoptable children was decreasing, adoption agencies were becoming more selective in their placements. Stricter screening criteria for adoptive parents included standards for income and age, and a requirement that couples be infertile. These criteria (particularly minimum income requirements) may have restricted access to adoptable African American children by African Americans wanting to adopt and indirectly encouraged transracial adoption of nonwhites by whites.[20] However, some researchers have also suggested that African Americans were and are less interested in adoption than white Americans: "Evidence seems to suggest that the plight of adoptable black children does not rank high on the list of black adults' social priorities, even when they seem to be aware of the problem's severity,"[21] reinforcing racial divides in the American adoption industry. In 1994, the North American Council on Adoptable Children found that relatively few black adoptive families could be found for in-race adoption, though this may be due to the fact that many agencies did not have African Americans on staff and because prospective adoptive parents were poorly recruited in black communities.[22]

Despite the similarities and shared histories of transracial and transnational adoptions, transracial adoption of American children has faced significant criticism, especially in the case of African American and Native American adoptions, while transnational adoption has gone largely unquestioned. Opposition to the practice of transracial domestic adoption crystallized in the early 1970s and led to implementation of within-race adoption preferences at many adoption agencies by 1975. Two events during the 1970s signaled a broad shift in attitudes toward transracial adoption.

At its conference in 1971, the National Association of Black Social Workers (NABSW) repudiated transracial adoption, predicting that transracial adoptees would have poor psychological adjustment and racial identity, and be unable to cope with episodes of racism and discrimination without the guidance of a parent of the same color; subsequently, the organization led efforts to end out-of-race adoption of African American children under a stated goal of protecting children and preventing "cultural genocide." The same year, a meeting of American Indian leaders issued a statement that also identified transracial adoption as "cultural genocide."[23]

In 1978, the federal government enacted the Indian Child Welfare Act (ICWA), prohibiting the transracial placement of American Indian children outside the Indian tribe of their birth without the consent of the tribe in question. This legislation was possible because of the relationship American Indians had with the US federal government; since Indian nations have limited rights of sovereignty with respect to the US government, they can be granted protections and rights as nations that are not available to other groups of American people of color. ICWA also represented an acknowledgment of many decades of governmental abuses of American Indian families, including forced removal of children by placement in white-run boarding schools (1878–1930s) or by adoption into white families (1958–1967).

As domestic transracial adoptions declined throughout the 1970s in response to these two events and the social forces surrounding them,[24] many social workers began to question the appropriateness of transracial placements. Organized opposition to transracial adoption in the 1970s, drawing attention to past racism in adoption policies and the potential for future abuse, focused on African American and American Indian populations—minorities that had high visibility in the civil rights movements of the period. In contrast, Asian Americans and Asians living in the United States were much less visible because their populations were relatively small and tended to be concentrated in a few geographic areas. These factors contributed to a popular perception (which continues today) that Asians and Asian Americans did not suffer from racial discrimination and other forms of racism. While the plight of injustices faced by African Americans had been widely publicized by the 1970s, those affecting Asian Americans were not. In addition, tacit beliefs in a racial hierarchy that placed Asian closest to white as the "model minority" contributed to the perception that Asian Americans were not suffering from racism.[25] In light of the emphasis on historical injustices that informed the anti-transracial-adoption position taken by the NABSW and the proponents of ICWA, the perceived absence of racial discrimination against Asian Americans made the transracial adoption of Asians into white homes appear "safe," and did not evoke the same race-based cultural conflicts that dominated debates on domestic transracial adoption. Not only did the Asian American community not respond negatively to these adoptions (then or now), adoptive parents could believe that their Asian adopted children could expect a life without negative exposure to racism. While an increase in the number of adoptions from other communities or countries was probably not one of the goals of NABSW or the proponents of ICWA, this was certainly a major outcome of these milestones in American adoption history. This demand for adoptable children among the American adoptive public would not be easily suppressed, but would drive a relentless search for other sources of children.

During the 1980s, restrictions on transracial adoptions were challenged in court by white adoptive parents, as well as by the American Civil Liberties Union. Courts were unanimous in ruling that race could not be the chief consideration in adoption, but many states maintained laws limiting transracial adoption.[26] In the 1990s, such state laws were largely superseded by new federal legislation regulating the role of race in adoption. The Multiethnic Placement Act (MEPA) of 1994,[27] amended by the Interethnic Placement Act of 1996,[28] and the Adoption and Safe Families Act of 1997 mandated that transracial adoptions be handled the same way as all other adoptions, and forbade the consideration of race as a factor in determining the suitability of an adoptive placement.[29] MEPA and subsequent adoption-related legislation all but ensured that transracial adoptions would continue, probably with greater frequency than ever before. Though a major rationale behind these acts was to get children into permanent homes as quickly as possible, in 1998, children of color constituted 60 percent of all children in out-of-home care.[30] At the present time, many prospective parents do not undertake domestic adoptions because the children available do not match parents' demands; most prospective adoptive parents seek to adopt healthy infants, while two-thirds of American children in foster care are over age five, and many have health problems or disabilities.[31]

Because American laws generally understand parents to be biologically related to their children, they tend to favor birth parents and generally privilege sanguinary relationships over other types of kinship in establishing custody rights, leaving domestic adoption subject to potential legal challenges. In addition to the NABSW's formal renewal of its position opposing transracial adoption in 1991, a small number of highly publicized court cases resulting in children of color being returned to birth mothers highlighted the possibility that adoptive parents could be forced to give up their children. Public discussions leading up to the passage of MEPA portrayed domestic transracial adoption as controversial, potentially reversible, fraught with emotional risk, and possibly unethical. By the end of the 1990s, these controversies and the new federal legislation had raised public awareness of the potential pitfalls and complications of domestic transracial adoption.

A Transition to Transnational Transracial Adoption

The practice of formalized adoption in the United States began to show growing pains as adoptive families struggled for acceptance as "normal" American families and legal dramas that pitted biological parents against adoptive parents started to become public. Since American family law has historically privileged parents over other family members in custody disputes, the legal foundation for birth parents' rights to maintain guardianship of their children had been established before legal adoption became commonplace; until recently, this legal corpus was frequently interpreted as favoring biological parents in custody disputes involving adoption. The anxiety created by the prospect of birth families exercising legitimate legal claims to adopted or about-to-be-adopted children in the United States was, and continues to be, a barrier for many prospective parents considering domestic adoption. In contrast, biological parents of foreign children in transnational adoption are largely understood to have no legal rights or claims to the children they relinquish. The scant evidence currently available on transnational adoptions disputed by birth families is largely anecdotal, because these cases are rarely covered by the press, and have generally not resulted in the return of children to birth parents. Instead, it appears that adoption agencies in sending countries often resolve these problems on their own, perhaps taking advantage of the low social and economic positions of birth parents, especially birth mothers. In the free-market economics of transnational adoption today, the socioeconomic status of birth mothers who are induced by economic or social pressures to give up their children for adoption works in favor of adoptive parents and the adoption agencies they support.

Since the 1980s,[32] the American child welfare system has aggressively used child removal (state removal of children from the custody of their parents, often leading to involuntary termination of parental rights) as a supposedly child-centered remedy for a host of ills, including child neglect or abuse, substance abuse in the home, and the incarceration of parents. Unfortunately, these policies have been unevenly applied to the public, resulting in children from poor, black, and brown homes entering the child welfare system in disproportionately high numbers. While this result has undoubtedly made more children in the American child welfare system available for adoption, ironically, it also made this population of potentially adoptable children less appealing to prospective parents because the children are understood to have been damaged by abuse or neglect, by being brought up in harmful environments, or by being born of "bad stock"—recalling persistent prejudices against adopted children as "bad seeds."[33]

Because large-scale transnational adoption began in the United States around the same time as domestic transracial adoption, and because, as a practice, it had not faced the same kinds of attacks as domestic transracial adoption, the fact that prospective adoptive parents began to prefer transnational adoption from Korea—which was for many years the only large-scale sending country in the transnational adoption industry—is not surprising. By the 1970s, South Korea was the only country with a long and established history of overseas adoption and offered an easy alternative for American adoptive parents.

Indeed, in the 1970s and 1980s, the number of adoptions from Korea began to rise,[34] while the numbers of domestic transracial adoptions leveled or dropped off. In 1986, the peak year for Korean transnational adoption, 6,138 Korean children were adopted in the United States,[35] while in the following year only 1,411 African American transracial domestic adoptions took place.[36] By the 1980s, multiculturalism had begun to gain popularity and the realization of the "rainbow family" including one or more transracially and/or transnationally adopted children came to be seen as a way to put multicultural ideals into practice. However, like with the so-called weak multiculturalism that became so popular in the 1980s,[37] there were still some critical structural issues in positioning these families as multicultural ideals. Historically (and currently), Korean and other transracial adoption has largely been a white act—that is, the overwhelming majority of children are adopted into homes where both parents and all members of the extended biological family are white. Similar to the embrace of weak multiculturalism among white Americans, these multiracial adoptive families did little to empower communities of color or correct the effects of past racism. Instead, these families imported and placed adoptees as people of color in largely white social contexts, where the experiences of the child's birth culture could only be vaguely imagined by the adoptive family based on flawed or distorted cues gleaned from popular culture, and assimilation was tacitly or explicitly expected. In the case of Korean adoption, most families did not travel to Korea to obtain their children; most Korean adoptive parents had never even been to Korea at all, and many knew few or no Korean Americans to act as resources for teaching adopted children about Korean culture.

As new legal frameworks and new social attitudes altered the landscape of domestic adoption in America, the number of US transnational adoptions almost doubled between 1989 and 1998, when 15,744 transnational adoptions were recorded.[38] In 1989, South Korea was the only country with a sizable foreign adoption program sending adoptable children to the United States; by 1998, China, Russia, Guatemala, Columbia, India, the Philippines, Vietnam, Romania, and Cambodia had also developed transnational adoption programs to the United States.[39] Although South Korea was for decades the most prolific sending country, it has been surpassed by other countries as its own participation in transnational adoption has declined. From fewer than 100 adoptive placements to the United States in 1990, adoption from China grew to more than 5,000 children annually by the mid-2000s.[40] The total number of transnational adoptions has also increased dramatically: the average number of children from overseas adopted each year in the 1970s was less than 5,000; by the 1980s, that number had grown to almost 8,000; and in the 1990s it averaged more than 10,000 per year. In 2006, 20,679 children were adopted from overseas, the largest numbers from mainland China (5,453), Guatemala (4,728), Russia (2,310), Ethiopia (1,255), and South Korea (939).[41] Although detailed statistical records are unavailable, the number of domestic transracial adoptions is believed to be stable, with African American adoption to white homes estimated to represent 1.2 percent of all adoptions in the United States.[42]

A Social History of Korean American Transnational Adoption

The emergence (and general acceptance) of racially mixed adoptive families since the 1950s is indicative of—and supported by—profound transformations within American society during this period. A progressive liberalization of social attitudes toward race, including the formulation of multiculturalism as a popular ideology, has been complemented by the growth of economic liberalism, including the growth of global markets supporting transracial and transnational consumerism. These two forms of liberalism have worked together to make adoption, particularly adoption from outside the United States, appealing to prospective parents looking for nonbiological options to family building.

The ideals of modern social liberalism regarding race achieved wide public acceptance as a result of civil rights movements that began in the 1950s, with empowerment movements affirming the legal and social equality of different groups of people of color. These ideals were subsequently used to support "colorblind" understandings of family formation—commonly rendered in transracial adoption as disregard for racial and genetic differences between white parents and nonwhite children, focusing instead on the relational bonds forged within the parent-child relationship.

The principles of economic liberalism, notably the encouragement of open access to global free markets for goods and labor, has likewise helped to transform transnational adoption from a small-scale humanitarian intervention to a global industry in which international enterprises compete for resources and market share. Configuring consumer choice as a key right of the individual, economic liberalism (especially during and after the 1970s) has not only encouraged the international transfer of children, but also encouraged adoptive parents to approach the adoption process as an act of consumption in which adoption fees are exchanged for the custody of a suitable child.[43] On a transnational scale, this process, sometimes referred to as "globalization," confers a kind of global citizenship through participation in a global marketplace.

The latter half of the twentieth century was also characterized by rapid advances in reproductive technologies, both scientific and sociopolitical: medical advances such as in vitro fertilization were accompanied by social innovations such as formalized and legally regulated adoption between races, classes, and countries.[44] They continued to become more popular through the 1970s and 1980s, and became commonplace by the 1990s on through the present. However, social critiques and legal obstacles to domestic transracial adoption have limited the number of domestic transracial placements since the 1970s. Domestic transracial placements have not increased, but have stalled since the 1970s, while (first) Korean and (then) other transnational adoption placements have become much more common. Why is this? Opponents of transnational adoption in American communities of color successfully lobbied against the growing incidence of these placements starting in the 1970s. Critiques of transracial adoption by NABSW and in ICWA federal legislation provided both social and legal (in the case of ICWA) pressure to curtail or end American transracial adoptive placements. Even though most transracial domestic adoptions are still legal, prospective adoptive parents seem reluctant to complete them. In contrast, very little public criticism has been voiced about international transracial adoption. Instead, according to adoption advocates Rita Simon and Howard Alstein, parents see the practice as "achiev[ing] instant sainthood."[45] Simon and Alstein note that "[i]n adopting foreign children, the parents feel that they are cooperating in their children's efforts to burn their bridges. The children have no option but to adapt to the new world. There is no going back."[46]

Immigration Histories, from Least to Most Wanted Immigrants

Although many Korean adoptees do not see themselves as immigrants, they do share many characteristics with the members of immigrant populations, not the least of which is the phenomenon of return migration to the land of their birth. Politically, they are born in countries that are under the imperialist influence of richer, more politically powerful nations. As children born to Korean citizens, they are born with legal membership in Korea (though their social membership there may be less certain).[47] They move to nations that have diplomatic (and historically imperial, in the case of the United States) relations with South Korea. They are perceived to have better economic and social opportunities as a result of this move. The primary difference between Korean adoptees and other immigrants is the relative political ease with which adoptees can make their migratory transition: their immigration aided, sponsored, and advocated for by (usually) white adoptive parents, citizens of some of the richest and most powerful nations in the world.

In spite of these similarities, the fact that Korean American adoptees are included in nonimmigrant adoptive families generally prevents them from developing identities as immigrants. Adoptive parents are not generally members of politically or socially marginalized groups; as agents of adoptee immigration, adoptive parents are treated very differently by federal and state agencies than nonadoptee immigrants (who are often neither white nor middle-class, and are obviously not citizens).While adoptive parents have to go through lengthy legal procedures as part of the adoption process, these procedures are different from those for other immigrants. As a result, adoptive families can avoid contact with immigrants (and, by extension, any possibility that their children will be legally or socially associated with immigrants) during their dealings with immigration authorities. In short, Korean adoptees, from the moment of their adoption, are considered by their adoptive parents—and by the US government—as children of American nationals rather than as members of an immigrant population.

This policy stands in stark contrast to historic and current policies governing immigration by most other Asians. Of particular note is Chinese exclusion, a set of policies through which Chinese people became the first and only group to be prohibited from immigration to the United States solely on the basis of national origin.[48] The criminalization of immigration to the United States began with Chinese exclusion, and the current state of anti-immigration legislation and immigrant suspicion has deep roots in this history.[49] Not surprisingly, many of the strategies used by Chinese migrants to undercut immigration law are still in use today by new groups of scrutinized immigrants. The United States continues its assault on illegal immigration, currently focusing on Latinos and those of Middle Eastern descent as suspects, one group as illegal immigrants, one as terrorists, using tactics that continue to undermine the civil liberties and human rights of its targets.[50]

Historically, immigration policy has greatly influenced the ways in which different immigrant groups are racialized in American society. Chinese exclusion is one example; since 1965, exclusion has given way to a liberalized (though formally deracialized) system of immigrant admission under which federal laws restrict access by most immigrants, but make exceptions for "special" admission of certain professionals and privilege family unification, through which adoptees are able to easily enter the United States as children of American citizens. Asian immigrants have been subject to racializing and class hierarchical placement through unequal access to legal and cultural citizenship. If exclusion and other anti-immigrant policies are on one end of the immigration spectrum, transnational adoption is on the other, offering ease of access for America's most desired immigrants—child adoptees.

Adoptees from Korea have entered the United States with preferential immigration status since the 1950s, when they were initially admitted as refugees. In 1961, the first piece of federal immigration legislation was passed that specifically included provisions for transnationally adopted children, and since then, they have been admitted to the American immigration queue separately from other immigrants. Since the passage of the Child Citizenship Act in 2000, transnationally adopted children of US citizens have even had access to automatic citizenship, without the legal necessity of a naturalization process. Although the act was passed before the events of September 11, 2001, this extreme liberalization in immigration and citizenship policy has never been questioned, despite the fact that it privileges certain nonwhite foreign nationals at a time when most similar immigrants are regarded with deep suspicion by immigration authorities and the public, emphasizing the almost total disregard for the status of the adoptee migrant as an immigrant. As transnational adoption has become a common family building strategy in the United States, understanding adoptees as deracialized members of American families—not as racialized threats in the form of alien immigrants—has become a matter of supporting American families, and is never criticized as leniency in immigration and naturalization law.

The dominant paradigm within federal structures of naturalization is assimilationist: a high degree of assimilation must be demonstrated through language proficiency, cultural competency, and long-term residence before citizenship can be considered. As a response to this framework of a nationalized political system, many researchers theorize that citizenship allows some access to political agency, desirable to immigrants who are minorities in both their naturalization and racial status.[51]

Transnational adoptees are assumed to be easily assimilated because they arrive in the United States as young children and are raised by members of dominant sociocultural groups. Because of these perceived advantages, adoptees are placed at the apex of the immigration hierarchy. Raised in the United States, they can be expected to have a native's command of English and to be as well-versed in American culture and society as any other person raised in the United States. They do not carry the family memories of immigration, as most adoptees are adopted too young to remember their own immigration journeys, and they are not accompanied by members of their birth families who might preserve their immigration stories. The only attributes of dominant culture transnational adoptees generally lack are the phenotypical attributes of whiteness. Because of the acceptance of racial minorities as Americans, the lack of whiteness certainly is problematic for many adoptees to navigate, but is not necessarily synonymous with the lack of Americanness. The high acculturation or preassimilation of adoptees through rearing in American homes warrants the easiest naturalization process of any group of immigrants in the United States.[52] Indeed, the formation of transnationally adopted children into US citizens seems to be justified through their American parentage and cultural upbringing as "native" Americans.

Immigrants are generally acknowledged as having family in the nation of emigration, from whom they may be separated by citizenship. Thus, for other immigrants, familial ties to a "homeland" or ancestral land are recognized. This condition is more complicated in the case of transnational adoption, because adoptees are physically and legally separated from family in their countries of birth. In many cases, they are also encouraged to sever emotional ties (or are prevented from having these ties in the first place) to birth nation and family. In exchange, they are granted entry into American families and inserted into American genealogies. Through the easy access to citizenship that transnational adoptees enjoy, the adoptive family nation supersedes previous categories of national membership; family and nation are unified, as family units serve as the building blocks of a nation.

For most transnational adoptees today, American citizenship can be taken for granted. The privileged immigration status that adoptees and their families enjoy eases adoptees' political transition into citizenship by virtually guaranteeing their instant naturalization.

Before February 27, 2001, parents had to submit several forms in order to apply for naturalization on behalf of their transracial adoptee children, following a procedure specific to transnational adoptees, with no exam or residence requirement for minor children, and with the proviso that at least one parent had to be a citizen of the United States. Even though this process made naturalization considerably easier for adoptive parents than for nonadoptee immigrants, laws concerning the naturalization of transnational adoptees were subsequently changed to make the naturalization process even simpler. Under the Child Citizenship Act of 2000,[53] transnational adoptees under the age of eighteen living in the legal and physical custody of a citizen parent automatically receive citizenship when their adoptions are legally finalized.[54]

One of the reasons this legislation was enacted is because many parents were not aware that their transnationally adopted children were not already automatically receiving citizenship.[55] As a result, transnational adoptees who were never naturalized were subject to deportation (like other noncitizens) if they were ever convicted of a felony. The consequences of deportation in these cases were especially extreme because most transnational adoptees have no cultural ties to their birth countries. This legislation is not without gaps; parents who have not physically contacted their adopted children before adoption (as is true in many cases where parents do not travel to the birth country to pick up their adopted children) are not considered to have a finalized adoption, and must readopt their children in their home states before citizenship will be granted.[56] In the American assimilationist immigration and naturalization system, the inclusion of transnational adoptees is now a mere formality. Unlike most other groups of immigrants who seek permanent entry into the United States, for transnational adoptees, the gates are wide open.

Korean Adoptee Community Histories

As the adult Korean adoptee population has grown, more and more adoptees have entered public discourses on adoption. Their positions as artists, writers, organizers, activists, and scholars, in conjunction with their identities as Korean adoptees, have given rise to the "public adoptee"—sometimes lauded as an adoption expert, sometimes denigrated for a supposed lack of objectivity or for a perspective perceived as self-centered.

The members of this loosely connected but growing community of Korean American adoptees often consider their Koreanness, as well as their adoption experience, to be the basis for creative or scholarly work, as well as for community building with other Korean adoptees. While this group constitutes a small minority of all Korean American adoptees, it is probably the most publicly visible segment of the Korean adoptee population; these are the adoptees who write about their adoption experiences, produce art that comments on what it means to have lived as adoptees, hold social and educational events, provide support programming for adult adoptees, disseminate information about adoption and adoptees to other adoptees, conduct research and write scholarly articles and books, and attend and organize Korean adoption conferences. This small but visible group of public adoptees has the power to mobilize larger groups of interested adoptees, adoptive families, and others.

While many of these public adoptees do not attempt to advance political agendas of the kind typically associated with "activism," they may be considered activists nonetheless because of their focus on Korean adoptee identity and experience, which occupies a minority position within both white American and Asian American social structures. Most of these adoptee activists see the act of claiming their Korean adoptee identity as liberatory, in that it is taken in defiance of the assimilationist ideals of color blindness and whiteness within their white families and communities; many adoptees describe a diminishing relationship to family during and after the expansion of their Korean adoptee identities.

Among the most visible adoptee groups are Also Known As (New York), Asian Adult Adoptees of Washington, AKConnection (Minnesota), and the Global Overseas Adoptees' Link (GOAL) (Seoul). Despite these groups' visibility within adoptee communities, political activism focused on controversial issues such as adoption procedures is, by and large, conspicuously absent from their activities. Exceptions include explicitly activist groups such as ASK (Adoptee

Solidarity Korea) and TRACK (Truth and Reconciliation for the Adoption Community in Korea) in Seoul, but most of the member groups represented in the International Korean Adoptee Associations (IKAA)—the largest international Korean adoptee umbrella organization—have a decidedly neutral political position. While organizations of adult Korean adoptees might at first glance appear to be ideally situated to support political activism on issues of race and racism, the opposite is generally true; the apolitical stance taken by many leaders within their organizations serves to support adoptees who are recognized as a socially and politically diverse group. Most of the leaders of these groups, while acknowledging their own political beliefs and desires, believe strongly that an apolitical position around adoption—and, to some degree, around race—is important in order to maintain a welcoming atmosphere for all Korean adoptees. This also means that many of the adult Korean adoptee groups emphasize programming focused on socializing and networking among adoptees, allowing the organizations to serve as safe "gateways" to the adoptee community for adoptees who have had limited exposure to other adoptees. Unfortunately, organizations that focus on social activities often fail to retain older members who want more intellectually or politically meaningful programming.

In the late 1990s, conferences for Korean adoptees and their families were organized for the first time in the United States. Two annual adoptee conferences began during this period. In 1998, the Korean American Adoptee/Adoptive Family Network (KAAN) held its first conference for Korean adoptees and their families to discuss adoption issues and develop the adoption community. The conference continues to take place every July, usually in the United States, though the 2007 conference took place in Seoul.

In 1999, the International Gathering of Adult Korean Adoptees (referred to informally within adoptee communities as "The Gathering") convened for the first time. Originally sponsored by Holt, the first American adoption agency to facilitate Korean adoptions, the conference is now sponsored and organized by the International Korean Adoptee Associations and its member organizations. Nearly four hundred Korean adoptees attended the first Gathering, and the conference has since convened again in Norway and twice more in Korea (in 2004 and 2007). The assemblage of adult transracial adoptees at national and international conferences signifies the formation of identity as adoptees within this population. It is also indicative of the large number of Korean adoptees who have come of age and who are seeking adoptee community.

For most Korean adoptees who participate in these types of networking activities, the "community" is limited to other adoptees, and to some degree, to their partners and children. Parents are accepted as part of *adoption* communities, but are generally not included in *adoptee* communities. The difference here is significant and manifests itself personally and politically for adoptee leaders as they engage in adoptee community building—and for some parents who don't grasp the difference. For example, the 2004 attempt to organize a gathering of Korean adoptees in Seoul over the summer of 2004 resulted in a request from KAAN, the only American national organization for families of Korean adoptees, to participate in conference organizing. Because of KAAN's status as an adoptive-parent-run organization, this request was denied, despite KAAN's stated mission of supporting Korean adoptees; organizers of the Gathering were adamant that an experience that supported interests and needs of adoptees could not also cater to adoptive parents, though an adherence to this principle may have damaged organizational and personal relationships. In the end, parents were allowed to register for the conference (though few did) but were barred from attending most sessions, which were designated as "adoptee-only." The inclusion or exclusion of adoptive parents in other adoptee-organized events, such as lectures, readings, or discussions, is a topic of explicit discussion and decision making within Korean adoptee groups. While some adoptee-run groups include parents in community-building efforts, they are also careful to program events for adoptees only.

The Emergence of Adoptee Artists and Academics

A cohort of Korean adoptee artists has recently begun to emerge and, through the public display and consumption of their work, has brought early attention to the experience of Korean American adoptees. While these artists' works hardly represent the experience of all adoptees, they do resonate with many and have changed the terms of American public discourse around transnational Asian adoption. While the general public still broadly understands Korean and other Asian adoptees as child foundlings who are lucky to have the opportunity to become American, artists such as memoirists Jane Jeong Trenka and Katy Robinson, filmmakers Deann Borshay Liem, Nathan Adolfson, Tammy Chu, and Jennifer Ardnt Johns, poets Jennifer Kwon Dobbs, Lee Herrick, and Sun Yung Shin, and visual artists Kate Hers, Mihee-Nathalie Lemoine, and Jane Jin Kaisen have begun to perforate these tranquil images with much more complicated realities.[57] Like artists the world over who are motivated by the need to express themselves and represent their experiences, these artists have been among the first to challenge dominant white narratives of transnational adoption as an emotionally seamless act of child salvation; instead, they wrestle with the grittier realities of identity crisis, displacement, birth family loss, and American racism. They have done so despite resistance to these stories in many adoption communities, created to support adoptive parents. Their efforts have paved the way toward a more unified adoptee identity, as early orators of complicated and often painful adoption experiences that have now been retold over and over in adoptee networking groups and to adoption researchers.

Behavioral scientists have conducted research on transracial adoptees since the 1970s, but in the past ten years transnational and transracial adoption studies have become a burgeoning field (probably related to the heightened visibility of transnational and transracial adoptees as more and more become adults). As has been the case in many new fields, most adoptees and other academics studying Korean adoption are still junior scholars developing new ideas and research within more traditional fields the same time period has been notable for the emergence of the adoptee academic.

At once observers and participants, these "insider" researchers in the field of adoption studies produce work that echoes the activist battle cry for inclusion: "Nothing About Us Without Us!" The evolving position of these adoptee academics calls to mind historical upheavals in many academic disciplines touched off by the entry into the academic mainstream of scholars from ethnic and cultural groups that had been traditional subjects of academic inquiry; among other effects, these upheavals led to the creation of new disciplines such as ethnic studies and women's/gender/sexuality studies that began as fields by, about, and for these same groups. Community-based and adoptee-centered methodologies lead to significant differences in both research questions and outcomes. In these community-based research efforts, there is more emphasis on the social, psychological, political, and cultural consequences of Korean adoption than ever before. Instead of the traditional reliance on parental perspectives and the interpretation of adoption as only a family-building strategy, there is now greater interest in and research on the life experiences of individual adoptees. This new emphasis in Korean adoption studies opens the door to new areas of sociocultural inquiry: the effects of raising nonwhite persons in white families; the meaning of whiteness and the role of race in family, society, and politics; and the complex and multilayered identities of transnationally adopted persons. In addition, this community-based research is linked to social justice movements and to anti-imperialist and anticolonial ideologies through its critiques of the racism, geopolitical imbalances, class discrimination, and sexism against women in the global East and South (who are deemed to be less worthy of parental rights in comparison with white women in the global North and West) that are inherent in the current configuration of adoption from Korea (and from many other countries). Finally, the role of Korean adoption studies research has now been peeled away from the interests of the adoption industry, because an adoptee focus is (and sometimes must be) independent of the adoption process and the pursuit of "best practices" for adoption procedures.

For those adoptees who choose to participate in public discourse about adoption, whether as artists, activists, organizers, or academics, the role of the public adoptee carries many potential liabilities and benefits. Personal stakes can be high, and for many the separation of work and personal life becomes a foregone luxury, or at least a hard-fought accomplishment. The benefits, however, can also be high, as Korean and other transracial and/or transnational adoptees finally articulate their experiences and ideas about the overlapping and intersecting categories of race, class, gender, family, policy, and nation that make transnational adoption such a rich and productive site of inquiry.

Making Adoptees Korean Again: Korean American Adoptees in Seoul

If American orphan visas and the Child Citizenship Act of 2000 make Korean adoptees American, the South Korean F-4 visa can make them Korean again—at least for as long as they choose to stay in South Korea. This special visa for overseas Koreans, created in 1999 by the Act on the Immigration and Legal Status of Overseas Koreans and partially in response to appeals for permanent legal residency by Korean adoptees living in South Korea, is available exclusively to "overseas Koreans"—those with verifiable past citizenship in South Korea and their descendents.[58] The F-4 is the least restrictive of any South Korean residence visa, granting all the rights of native Koreans (except voting), including unlimited entry and exit privileges, the right to own property and businesses, and the right to reside in South Korea without a work-related sponsor. The F-4 has a two-year term, but may be renewed indefinitely. It is as close to South Korean citizenship as any foreign national can get.

The F-4 has attracted controversy because it is available only to overseas Koreans who were born as or are descended from South Korean citizens, mainly diasporic migrants who reside in Western nations; the visa is not available to the descendants of those who left Korea before the establishment of the South Korean state in 1948, including 5.65 million other ethnic Koreans, many living in China, Russia, and Japan.[59] For this reason, the act has been attacked as discriminatory against the ethnic Koreans in these locations, especially the Korean-Chinese. In addition, there has been critical reaction to the promotion of unity among ethnic Koreans over other those of other ethnicities that live and work in Korea.[60]

Since Korean adoption did not formally begin until 1953, all Korean adoptees are eligible for the F-4 visa, though the application process can be onerous. In order to obtain an F-4, an adoptee must provide documentation of onetime Korean citizenship, as well as documentation of the loss of that citizenship. Proving current citizenship is seldom a hardship, but to obtain proof of Korean ancestry, adoptees must obtain their Korean family registry, or *hojeok*, which lists the entire known patrilineal family; because these records are generally accurate and complete genealogies, they are the basis on which claims of citizenship can be made. Adoptees who have no information on birth family must obtain an orphan hojeok, which contains only themselves, from their Korean adoption agency in order to fulfill the requirement for proof of past Korean citizenship.

Many adoptees who have located their Korean birth families determine that an orphan hojeok is still logistically preferable. Many were never entered into family hojeoks, or were removed after adoption. Even if the adoptee's name appears in his or her birth family hojeok, the information may conflict with documentation from the adoptee's other records, because important personal details like birth dates, parental identities, and family circumstances are often changed by adoption agencies in the adoption process; the orphan hojeok can be made to be a better match to the adoptee's American identity papers, removing the possibility of conflicts of information within the visa application materials. In addition, since an adoptee's legal identity is completely changed through the adoption process, the adoptee with access to birth family records may have no way to legally prove that he or she is the person as listed on his or her birth family hojeok.[61]

For adoptees who seek the F-4 visa, the irony in claiming legal orphan status in order to reconnect with Korea, Korean people, and possibly Korean birth family, is enormous. Unlike other overseas Koreans, who must show a familial connection to other Koreans to obtain an F-4, adoptees usually must present documentary evidence that they share no biological relationship with any other Korean citizen—in the Korean context, they are not related to anyone. Only by acknowledging the total loss of their identities can overseas adoptees regain their status as Koreans.

While the F-4 visa provides a readily accessible legal toehold for adoptees to live and work in South Korea among Korean people, it is far from clear that adoptees truly "become Korean" simply because the South Korean government removes legal barriers to their return migration. Instead, many of the adoptees who live in Korea find little acceptance in Korean society, and are deeply folded into adoptee communities, where they can connect with others who have similar experiences as themselves. Most Korean adoptee ethnic return migrants plan to stay in Korea for periods ranging from one to five years and do not consider a permanent move to Korea to be a viable option.

Conclusion

Today, South Korea is no longer the country that sends the most adoptees to the United States or to Western nations. International attention during the Seoul Olympics in 1988 exposed a deep sense of national shame about continuing to send unwanted children away. Since the 1990s, South Korea's economic growth—it is now the world's sixteenth largest economy—has also contributed to a decrease in the number of adoptees the nation is willing to send out of the country, and it appears likely that South Korean transnational adoption will end completely in the near future. China, Russia, and Guatemala are now among the top adoptee-sending countries, each passing thousands of children to the United States every year. As South Korea bows out as a sending country, poorer countries are induced to step in and respond to the American demand for adoptable children. Looking further into the future, a number of other nations including

Mexico, Bolivia, Columbia, Peru, and Ethiopia appear to make up the next set of major sending countries. Meanwhile, American domestic transracial adoption continues at a stable rate of about twelve hundred children annually.

Transracial adoption affects Asian American, African American, American Indian, and Latina/o communities in America, as well as white American communities into which most of these adoptees are placed. While Korean adoptees are not the only transracial adoptees, they are currently the largest group of adult transracial adoptees, and are the only group of transracial adoptees in America who have self-organized into networking and political advocacy groups based solely on their shared identities as adoptees. Thus, Korean adoptees are in a position to advocate for other transracial adoptees, as well as for generations to come. In twenty years, Chinese American adoptees will likely constitute the largest population of adult transracial adoptees; in forty years, it might be Ethiopian American adoptees. The struggles of these future generations of transracial adoptees will almost certainly be influenced by the leadership and political activity of current Korean adoptee organizations today. Research on today's adult Korean adoptees lays the foundation for future comparative explorations of the issues affecting current and future transracial adoptee populations.

NOTES

Originally published in the Working Paper Series of the U.S.-Korea Institute at KAIS. ©2008 by the U.S.-Korea Institute, reprinted by permission.

1 From demographic sources compiled by Tobias Hübinette (1948–1978), from Richard H. Weil, "International Adoption: The Quiet Migration," *International Migration Review* 18, no. 2 (1984): 276–293.

2 The Chinese Exclusion Act, passed May 6, 1882, was the first piece of anti-immigration legislation enacted in the United States, and the only one in American history that excluded a specified nationality.

3 Ramsay Liem, "History, Trauma, and Identity: The Legacy of the Korean War for Korean Americans," *Amerasian Journal* 29 (2003–2004): 114.

4 Ibid.

5 Ibid., 115.

6 Ibid., 126.

7 This may be at least in part due to the fact that most Korean Americans do not have much contact with Korean American adoptees, and generally do not consider adoptees as part of their diasporic communities.

8 Jae Ran Kim, "Scattered Seeds: The Christian Influence on Korean Adoption," in *Outsiders Within*, ed. Jane Jeong Trenka, Julia Chinyere Oparah, and Sun Yung Shin (New York: South End Press, 2006), 151–64.

9 Ellen Herman, "Bertha and Harry Holt" (Adoption History Project, Department of History, University of Oregon, November 28, 2008), http://pages.uoregon.edu/adoption/people/holt. htm.

10 Over half were adopted in the United States and Canada, and, according to Tobias Hübinette, most of the rest went to European countries and Australia. See Hübinette, "Comforting an Orphaned Nation: Representations of International Adoption and Adopted Koreans in Korean Popular Culture" (doctoral diss., Stockholm University, 2006).

11 For a thorough examination of the phenomenon of sentimentalism in the context of the Cold War in Asia, see Christina Klein, *Cold War Orientalism Asia in the Middlebrow Imagination, 1945–1961* (Berkeley: University of California Press, 2003).

12 Peter Selman, "Intercountry Adoption in the Twenty-First Century: An Examination of the Rise and Fall of Countries of Origin," in *Proceedings of the First Korean Adoption Studies Research Symposium*, ed. Kim Park Nelson, Eleana Kim, and Lene Myoung Peterson (Seoul: International Korean Adoptee Associations, 2007), 55–75.

13 Eleana Kim, personal communication, 2006.

14 Ellen Herman, "Transracial Adoptions" (Adoption History Project, Department of History, University of Oregon, November 21, 2008), http://pages.uoregon.edu/adoption/topics/transracialadoption.htm.

15 Ibid.

16 Rita James Simon and Howard Altstein, *Adoption across Borders: Serving the Children in Transracial and Intercountry Adoptions* (Lanham, MD: Rowman & Littlefield, 2000), 2.

17 Ibid., 5.

18 Constance Pohl and Kathy Harris, *Transracial Adoption: Children and Parents Speak* (New York: Franklin Watts, 1992), 29.

19 Elaine Tyler May, *Barren in the Promised Land: Childless Americans and the Pursuit of Happiness* (Cambridge, MA: Harvard University Press, 1995), 142.

20 Pohl and Harris, *Transracial Adoption*, 30.

21 Rita James Simon and Howard Altstein, *Transracial Adoption* (New York: John Wiley, 1977), 34.

22 Ruth G. McRoy, "Attachment and Racial Identity Issues: Implications for Child Placement Decision Making," *Journal of Multicultural Social Work* 3 (1994): 59–74, 70.

23 Charles E. Jones and John F. Else, "Racial and Cultural Issues in Adoption," *Child Welfare United States* 58, no. 6 (1979): 374.

24 Ibid.

25 A number of scholarly works explore the insidious nature of the model minority myth for Asian Americans; one of the most useful is Mia Tuan, *Forever Foreigners or Honorary Whites? The Asian Ethnic Experience Today* (New Brunswick, NJ: Rutgers University Press, 1998).

26 Pohl and Harris, *Transracial Adoption*, 33.

27 Multiethnic Placement Act of 1994, Pub. L. No. 103–382 (October 20, 1994).

28 Removal of Barriers to Interethnic Adoption Provisions, sec. 1808 of Small Business Job Protection Act of 1996, Pub. L. No. 104–188 (August 20, 1996).

29 Adoption and Safe Families Act of 1997, Pub. L. No. 105–89, titles IV-B and IV-E, secs. 403(b), 453, and 1130(a) of the Social Security Act.

30 Ruth G. McRoy and Helen Grape, "Skin Color in Transracial and Inracial Adoptive Placements: Implications for Special Needs Adoptions," *Child Welfare* 78, no. 5 (1999): 674.

31 Kim Clark and Nancy Shute, "The Adoption Maze," *U.S. News & World Report* March 4, 2001, 60–66.

32 Dorothy Roberts, *Shattered Bonds: The Color of Child Welfare* (New York: Basic Civitas Books, 2002).

33 Laura Briggs and Ana Teresa Ortiz, "The Culture of Poverty, Crack Babies, and Welfare Cheats: The Making of the 'Healthy White Baby Crisis,'" *Social Text* 21, no. 3 (2003): 39–57.

34 Weil, "International Adoption"; and Francisco Pilotti, "Intercountry Adoption: Trends, Issues, and Policy Implications for the 1990s," *Childhood* 1 (1993): 165–177.

35 Pilotti, "Intercountry Adoption."

36 Simon and Altstein, *Adoption across Borders*, 5.

37 For a discussion of "weak multiculturalism," which attempted to celebrate difference without acknowledging America's racist national histories and polices, see Daniel I. O'Neill, "Multicultural Liberals and the Rushdie Affair: A Critique of Kymlicka, Taylor, and Walzer," *Review of Politics* 61, no. 2 (Spring 1999): 219.

38 Ibid.

39 "Immigrant Visas Issued to Orphans Coming to the U.S." (US Department of State, March 13, 2007), http://www.passportsusa.com/family/adoption/stats/stats_451.html.

40 Nam Soon Huh and William J. Reid, "Intercountry, Transracial Adoption and Ethnic Identity: A Korean Example," *International Social Work* 43, no. 1 (2000): 75.

41 "Immigrant Visas Issued."

42 Simon and Altstein, *Adoption across Borders*, 4.

43 Kim Park Nelson, "Shopping for Children in the International Marketplace," in Trenka, Oparah, and Shin, *Outsiders Within*, 89–104.

44 Here both medical and social "advances" that enable parenting for infertile couples or individuals are understood as technologies, including both medical procedures and social changes. Through these technologies, cultural expectations of parenting in Western countries have transformed into rights, in that many adults now understand parenting to be an option even if they are unable or unwilling to conceive without medical or legal procedures.

45 Rita J. Simon and Howard Altstein, *Transracial Adoption: A Follow-Up* (Lexington, MA: Lexington Books, 1981), 106.

46 Ibid., 105.

47 South Korean nationality law stipulated South Korean citizenship for children born to South Korean fathers until 1997. After 1997, children with a South Korean father or mother were considered South Korean. From the formation of the South Korean state in 1948 until 1997, children with South Korean mothers and foreign fathers were not considered South Korean nationals.

48 Erika Lee, *At America's Gates: Chinese Immigration during the Exclusion Era, 1882–1943* (Chapel Hill: University of North Carolina Press, 2003), 19–20.

49 Ibid., 6.

50 Ibid., 253.

51 See Bill Ong Hing, "Beyond the Rhetoric of Assimilation and Cultural Pluralism: Addressing the Tension of Separatism and Conflict in an Immigration-Driven Multiracial Society," *California Law Review* 81, no. 4 (1993): 910; and Noah Pickus, "To Make Natural: Creating Citizens for the Twenty-First Century," in *Immigration and Citizenship in the Twenty-First Century*, ed. Noah Pickus (Lanham, MD: Rowman & Littlefield, 1998), 125.

52 I use the term "pre-assimilation" to denote the general lack of choice in engaging in assimilative processes for most transnational and transracial adoptees; while assimilation is certainly a survival mechanism for adoptees of color in the America, I argue that it is not generally chosen, but (perhaps inadvertently, but still powerfully and predominantly) assigned by the white families and communities of many adoptees.

53 Child Citizenship Act of 2000, Pub. L. No. 106–395 (October 30, 2000).

54 "Fact Sheet: Child Citizenship Act of 2000" (US Department of State, 2000), http://www. uscis.gov/archive/archive-news/child-citizenship-act-2000-fact-sheet.

55 Ken Maguire, "Law Makes Foreign Adoptees Citizens" (Holt International, February 26, 2001), http://www.holtinternational.org/infoupdates/pdfs/aparticle.pdf.

56 Patricia M. Urban, "International Adoption: U.S. Proof of Citizenship. What You Need to Know about Adoption" (April 30, 2003), http://www.adopting.org/adoptions/international-adoption-us-proof-of-citizenship.html.

57 Anthropologist Eleana Kim has written about the phenomenon of Korean adoptee artists in scholarly journals and in her dissertation; see "Our Adoptee, Our Alien: Transnational Adoptees as Specters of Foreignness and Family in South Korea," *Anthropological Quarterly* 80, no. 2 (2007): 497–531; and "Remembering Loss: The Cultural Politics of Overseas Adoption from South Korea" (doctoral diss., New York University, 2007).

58 In-Jin Yoon, "A Comparison of South and North Korean Policy for Overseas Koreans" (paper, International Conference on the Korean Diaspora and Strategies of Global Korean Network, Seoul, October 11, 2002).

59 Jeanyoung Lee, "Korea's Policy for Ethnic Koreans Overseas," *Korea Focus* 11, no. 4 (2003): 108–132.

60 Jaeho Jeon, "Changes in the Korean Identity in the Globalization Era," *Quarterly New Asia* 12, no. 1 (2005).

61 Jane Jeong Trenka, "Adoption Is a Feminist Issue: Towards an Imaginative Feminism" (paper, Korean Association for Feminist Studies in English Literature, Seoul, June 9, 2007).

STUDY QUESTIONS

(1) Lee and Bean's article adds another level of complexity to our understanding of the Asian American population, calling attention to the increasing number of Asians who claim a multiracial background. In what ways has the new immigration contributed to the increasingly racially and ethnically diverse populations in many parts of our country? Why do Asians and Latinos in the United States evince higher rates of multiracial identification than blacks? In what parts of the United States do we find higher rates of multiracial identification, and why?

(2) What are the intermarriage patterns of Asian Americans and other immigrant groups? How do these intermarriage patterns compare with those of African Americans? Why do sociologists see intermarriage as an important measure of assimilation? What are the implications of these differences in intermarriage rates of Asian Americans versus other minorities in the United States?

(3) According to Lee and Bean, what is the black/nonblack divide? How is this racial paradigm distinct from the historical black/white binary? How do Asian Americans fit within the racial framework proposed by Lee and Bean? In your opinion, is the black/nonblack divide applicable to all parts of the country?

(4) How are the state relations between the United States and Korea related to the rise of Korean transnational adoption in America? What political and legal factors within the United States contributed to the popularity of Korean transnational adoption?

(5) In what ways are Korean adoptees similar to other types of immigrants? In what ways are they different? In particular, how does adoption at a young age influence the identity development and assimilation process for Korean adoptees? Given their high levels of acculturation, what strategies have they used to deal with their racial experiences (e.g., in their art, activism, academics, organizations)?

SUGGESTED READINGS

Brunsma, David L., ed. 2006. *Mixed Messages: Multiracial Identities in the "Color-Blind" Era.* Boulder, CO: Lynne Reinner.

Chen, J., and D. T. Takeuchi. 2011. "Intermarriage, Ethnic Identity, and Perceived Social Standing among Asian Women in the United States." *Journal of Marriage and Family* 73 (4): 876–889.

Chong, Kelly H. 2013. "Relevance of Race: Children and the Shifting Engagement with Racial/Ethnic Identity among Second-Generation Interracially Married Asian Americans." *Journal of Asian American Studies* 16 (2): 189–221.

Choy, Catherine Ceniza. 2013. *Global Families: A History of Asian International Adoption in America.* New York: New York University Press.

Coronado, Marc, Rudy P. Guevarra, Jeffrey A. S. Moniz, and Laura Furian Szanto, eds. 2005. *Crossing Lines: Race and Mixed Race across the Geohistorical Divide.* Walnut Creek, CA: AltaMira.

Daniel, G. Reginald. 1992. "Passers and Pluralists: Subverting the Racial Divide." Pp. 91–107 in Maria P. P. Root, ed., *Racially Mixed People in America.* Thousand Oaks, CA: Sage.

Feliciano, Cynthia, Belinda Robnett, and Golnaz Komaie. 2009. "Gendered Racial Exclusion among White Internet Daters." *Social Science Research* 38 (1): 39–54 .

Guevarra, Rudy. 2012. *Becoming Mexipino: Multiethnic Identities and Communities in San Diego.* New Brunswick, NJ: Rutgers University Press.

Kibria, Nazli. 2002. *Becoming Asian American: Second Generation Chinese and Korean American Identities.* Baltimore: Johns Hopkins University Press.

Kitano, Harry H., Diane C. Fujino, and Jane Takahashi Sato. 1998. "Interracial Marriages: Where Are the Asian Americans and Where Are They Going?" Pp. 233–260 in Lee C. Lee and Nolan W. S. Zane, eds., *Handbook of Asian American Psychology*. Thousand Oaks, CA: Sage.

Labov, T., and J. Jacobs. 1986. "Intermarriage in Hawaii, 1950–1983." *Journal of Marriage and the Family* 48: 79–88.

Lee, S. M., and K. Yamanaka. 1990. "Patterns of Asian American Intermarriages and Marital Assimilation." *Journal of Comparative Family Studies* 21: 287–305.

Louie, Andrea. 2015. *How Chinese Are You? Adopted Chinese Youth and Their Families Negotiate Identity and Culture*. New York: New York University Press.

Min, Pyong Gap, and Chigon Kim. 2009. "Patterns of Intermarriages and Cross-Generational In-Marriages among Native-Born Asian Americans." *International Migration Review* 43 (3): 447–470.

Qian, Z., S. L. Blair, and S. D. Ruf. 2001. "Asian American Interracial and Interethnic Marriages: Differences by Education and Nativity." *International Migration Review* 35 (134): 557–586.

Shiao, Jiannbin Lee, and Mia H. Tuan. 2008. "Korean Adoptees and the Social Context of Ethnic Exploration." *American Journal of Sociology* 113 (4): 1023–1066.

Spickard, Paul R. 1989. *Mixed Blood: Intermarriage and Ethnic Identity in Twentieth-Century America*. Madison: University of Wisconsin Press.

Spickard, Paul R., and Rowena Fong. 1995. "Pacific Islander Americans and Multiethnicity: A Vision of America's Future." *Social Forces* 73 (4): 1365–1383.

Stephan, C. W., and W. G. Stephan. 1989. "After Intermarriage: Ethnic Identity among Mixed Heritage Japanese Americans and Hispanics." *Journal of Marriage and the Family* 51: 507–519.

Sung, Betty Lee. 1990. *Chinese American Intermarriage*. Staten Island, NY: Center for Migration Studies.

Thai, H. 1999. "'Splitting Things in Half Is So White!' Conception of Family Life and Friendship and the Formation of Ethnic Identity among Second Generation Vietnamese Americans." *Amerasia Journal* 25 (1): 53–88.

Weisman, Jan. 2001. "The Tiger and His Stripes: Thai and American Reactions to Tiger Wood's (Multi-) 'Racial Self.'" Pp. 231–244 in Teresa Williams-Leon and Cynthia L. Nakashima, eds., *The Sum of Our Parts: Mixed Heritage Asian Americans*. Philadelphia: Temple University Press.

Williams-Leon, Teresa, and Cynthia L. Nakashima, eds. 2001. *The Sum of Our Parts: Mixed Heritage Asian Americans*. Philadelphia: Temple University Press.

FILMS

Adolfson, Nathan (producer director). 1998. *Passing Through* (37-minute documentary).

C-SPAN. 2009. *Experiences of Operation Babylift Adoptees* (89-minute documentary).

Gow, William, and Sharon Lee (directors). 2003. *More to the Chinese Side* (17-minute documentary).

Gradner, Janet, and Thai Quoc Pham. 2001. *Precious Cargo: Vietnamese Adoptees Discover Their Past* (57-minute documentary).

Fulbeck, Kip (producer/director). 1990. *Banana Split* (32-minute experimental).

——(director). 2003. *Lilo & Me* (10-minute documentary).

Hart, Jayasri Majumdar (director). 1998. *Roots in the Sand* (57-minute documentary).

Hosly, David (director). 2004. *A Beautiful Blend* (27-minute documentary).

Hwang, Jason (producer/director). 1982. *Afterbirth* (34-minute documentary).

Lee, Hosup (producer/director). 2004. *And Thereafter: A Korean "War Bride" in an Alien Land* (56-minute documentary).

Liem, Deann (director/writer). 2010. *In the Matter of Cha Jung Hee* (62-minute film).

Nair, Mira (director). 1991. *Mississippi Masala* (118-minute drama).

Soe, Valerie (producer/director). 1992. *Mixed Blood* (20-minute documentary).

Sperandeo, Midori (producer). 2001. *Hapa* (26-minute documentary).

Yonemoto, Bruce, and Norman Yonemoto (producers/directors). 1982. *Green Card: An American Romance* (80-minute drama).

PART VIII

Confronting Adversity

Racism, Stereotyping, and Exclusion

18

A Letter to My Sister and a Twenty-Five-Year Anniversary

LISA PARK

It's been almost 6 years since your suicide. Now when I think about you (and I think about you often), I feel you are somehow with me. My dreams of us together are as vivid and life-composing as any conscious, waking moment. Some like to think that our waking lives are more real, because we believe we can determine them through the choices we make, and that our dreams are merely their epiphenomenal reflections or, worse, expressions of unfulfilled desires. Your presence is more than a memory or a wish. My dreams are ghostly impressions of our collective past, as well as a *spontaneous living* of experiences I know we never shared before you died, like the dream I had of you and I walking arm in arm. I remembered it as if it was a lost memory, even though I know it never "really happened." I am sometimes grateful for this, because your phantom presence helps me to continue remembering, which I know is important even though it almost rips me apart. No matter how hard I try to subdue, through forgetting, the pain that came with the destruction of our lives, I must bear witness to the crimes committed against you (and against us) that led to your suicide. Conscious memories require constant attention, or else history will erase what happened, and you will disappear as if you had never existed at all. Isn't this why you haunt me to this day, to inscribe what you had learned from living under siege?

I remember the first time, when I found you after you had cut your wrists with a kitchen knife, and later when our father, using his deft surgical skills, sewed you back up in his office. For a while after you had cut your wrists, you undertook to "better" your life and attitude, even though it inevitably meant reinserting yourself into the old vise of conformity. One of the ways you tried to affirm your "new" resolve was to change your physical appearance through plastic surgery, for which our parents willingly put up the money in an effort to keep you happy. They were at their wits' end trying to appease you, but their efforts to pacify you pushed you further into self-hatred. (The annihilation of uniqueness and self-worth is indeed the pacifying aim.) Your obsession with plastic surgery exposed the myth of the whole beauty industry, which portrays plastic surgery as a beautifying, renewing experience, "something special you do just for you." It began with your eyes and nose, and you continued to go back for more. You tried to box yourself into a pre-conditioned, Euroamerican ideal and literally excised the parts that would not fit. But plastic surgery is irreversible and so were the twenty-one years of assimilation. You told the doctors in the psychiatric ward, where they placed you just after your second suicide attempt, the reason you took all those pills (which your psychiatrist had given you) was because the plastic surgeons had "ruined" your face. Did you come to a realization (under the advice of your doctors) that you were obsessed with changing your looks, which could only dishearten you further because it medically legitimated your neurosis? Or did you think that the surgery botched up your corporeal plan, which you realized you would have had to live with for the rest of your life? The plastic surgeon referred you to a psychiatrist to help you "work out" your obsession. Help is a four-letter word. You decided death was your only alternative to being stuck with an inescapable body. As soon as you were released from the hospital, you committed yourself to finding a way to kill yourself. Now, on top of what you considered a mistake of a body, you wanted to avoid being thrown into a mental institution, where you were sure you were headed as a consequence of being found out by the psychiatrists.

The first time was different in many ways. First of all, no professional psychologists or mental health experts knew about it. Everyone in our family kept your suicide attempt secret and normalized it as if it had never happened. Secondly, I know you did not want to die, but to get our attention. I remember coming home and discovering you in bed with your wrists bandaged and the bathtub full of blood and water. You thrust your limp arms into the air and cried, pleading for my help. I was devastated, broken-hearted, sickened, and bizarrely nervous all the while about what our parents would do if they had to be interrupted at work! I looked to our brothers for direction, but they acted as if there was no big emergency. I convinced myself that you were not dying, that your slashed wrists were not much worse than a cut finger. When our parents finally discovered you, they became hysterical and burst into wails of anguish—I was so taken aback by their rare show of sympathy that I began crying myself, throwing my body onto yours, because only then did I feel safe enough to reach out to you. Once our mother wondered aloud why I had not told them right away about your suicide attempt. I did not explain myself to her, but it was because all the violence in our lives, both physical and emotional, made your suicide attempt seem normal, everyday. It was not that I was unaware of what a crisis looked like, but that I was used to having to assimilate them into quotidian experience. I was more worried about controlling the "disruption" than what was actually happening to you. That was the extent of our spiritual and emotional isolation. Do you see how our culture of pain worked? I knew there was an emergency, I was ready to do something! But then I felt I was supposed to walk away, like all the other times when one of us was in distress. Silence was disciplined into us. How did we get to be so utterly ruined? How did we get to the point where we turned our backs on each other?

I feel comfortable placing blame on everyone, and some more than others. We have taken in the values that ultimately hurt and divide us, while some benefit from the suffering of "others." We were too stupid (not innocently, but the result of engineered ignorance) to see it happening to us. Even when it was clear, oftentimes all I could bear was to take care of myself, for my own survival. Most of all, I blame dominant institutions and mainstream society, because of the impossible alternatives they set up for us. They set up what is "good," what is "normal"—everything else is secondary, the "other." And they are very clever about it—they fix it so that the suicide looks like an individual problem, not a social or political matter. Labels of "mental illness" and "madness" are ways of silencing difference and shifting blame from the social to the individual. The social stigma of "dysfunctionality" kept our family secret and prevented us from seeking assistance from those who could offer it. For a long time, I felt we were atypically and inherently flawed, as individuals and as a family, but later learned from other Asian women that our experiences were neither unusual nor indicative of an intrinsic, Asian cultural pathology. However, regardless of any real possibility for collectivity, we had few means for support outside the family. We distrusted social workers and counselors, who had little insight into what we were experiencing.

The Asian "model minority" is *not* doing well. Do you see what a lie it is and how it is used to reinforce the American Dream and punish those of us who don't "succeed," or who succeed "too much"? It is making me mad knowing the truth of this culture, which is so obvious and yet so strategically dissimulated into the everyday that it becomes invisible, and nothing is left but the violence that results from its disappearance. How do you point out the horror of something that is so fundamentally banal and routine that it ceases to appear traumatic? And when you do point out the lie that is the truth, you feel (and usually are) alone in seeing this and wanting to root it out. It's enough to make you paranoid, because it is such a thorough conspiracy—how can you reform something that is so structural, so absolutely essential to the constitution of this society? Therapy and social work are out of the question, because the point is not to heal or to cope—no token of change can rectify our injury. Why would you want to place yourself into the hands of an institution that seeks to resocialize you into the environment that made a mess of you in the first place? Our inclusion into the American process turned out to be our worst form of oppression. Most people are proud to call themselves Americans, but why would you want to become a productive, well-adjusted citizen when the primary requisite of Americanness is racism? Isn't our madness often the only evidence we have at all to show for this civilizing terror?

I remember when you got arrested for stealing a car in order to escape the nearly all-white university you were attending. A white woman social worker ordered by the courts came to check up on you at home, where you were remanded for probation. Even though you had locked yourself in your bedroom, the social worker tried to break down the door when you refused to see her, despite all of our protests. I was desperate for you to break out of our circle of torment, but I knew my familial and social duty was to defuse the awkwardness and shame of divulging our "personal" problems. As far as our family was concerned, the state was the last place we would look for help, and according to standards of social acceptability, there was no such thing as a family problem that could not be solved within the family. So I put on a calm, diplomatic façade for the social worker, who had finally given up on making you understand that she was only there to help and decided to interview me instead about our family situation, which her limited thinking deduced to be the problem. I assured her she was wasting her time and that everything was fine. That was enough to satisfy the social worker, and she never came back.

It is a very insidious process that starts when we are young. One of my first memories of the "weeding out" was when we visited our father's place of work. When we were introduced to his co-workers, one of them looked at me and said to our father, "Oh, this one has big eyes." Pretty/normal=big eyes, white. And I at least had relatively "big" eyes. So, did I pass? Can my brothers and sister come, too? Racial passing was impossible for us, even though we were continually pitted against each other according to their racial fantasies.

Another memory: we were on a school bus; our brother broke an implicit rule and occupied one of the rear seats, which one white boy decided he wanted. I burned with rage and humiliation, not knowing what to do, as I watched the white boy repeatedly bang our brother's head against the bus window. (Our brother remembers it a different way, but for a long time I could only recall the young thug's taunting laughter.) Although I pleaded with the bus driver to intervene, which he did only too slowly, I felt helpless. I was afraid to call attention to myself and my already awkward difference. This was only the beginning of our conditioning by their divide-and-conquer strategy.

We became pathetic victims of whiteness. We permed our hair and could afford to buy trendy clothes. Money, at least, gave us some material status. But we knew we could never become "popular," in other words, accepted. It had something to do with our "almond-shaped" eyes, but we never called it racism. You once asked, "What's wrong with trying to be white?" You said your way of dealing with racism was not to let them know it bothered you. But they don't *want* it to bother us. If it did, they would have a revolution on their hands. The "just-convince-them-they-should-be-like-us" tactic. It is so important for the American racial hierarchy to keep us consuming its ideals so that we attack ourselves instead of the racial neuroses it manufactures.

I feel disgusted and angry and so, so sorry when I think of how I participated in the self-hatred that helped to kill you. I did not like to be reminded of my own "Orientalness," and I could not be satisfied with our failure to fit into the white

American mold. Our parents were accomplices and victims, too. I remember when our mother once criticized you for cutting off your long, straight, black hair (in your effort to appear less "exotic"). Insulting you, she said, "You have such a round, flat face." She always told us, "You not American. Why you try to be American?" Our father could not understand our dilemma, either: "Your only job is study—Be number one—Do what your father tell you and you never go wrong." When he was challenged, which was usually by you, the one-who-paved-the-way-for-the-rest-of-us, he became a frustrated madman and abuser. We interpreted this as a failure in communication, a clash of cultural values, but the conflict ran deeper than a matter of individual understanding or cultural sensitivity. We did not believe in the possibility of surviving as an Oriental in an American society. Oriental/American. Our only choices. This is what we call a serious identity crisis.

I know people thought they could pick on you because you wore pink Laura Ashley dresses and glasses. Racists think "Oriental" girls never fight back. You told me some white girl, backed by her white thug friends, was threatening to beat the shit out of you. But you were more than this Laura Ashley reflection. The white girl was in for a big shock the day you put on your fighting gear and confronted her in the girls' restroom. You had to "toughen up" just to survive. (What does that entail, what price did you pay?) Our schizophrenia was a conditioned disease. You always and never had a grip on who you were.

You could draw a picture of a tiger springing to attack, frontal view, at the age of nine, and it would be good enough to pass for a *National Geographic* illustration. You were the fastest runner in elementary school and broke the school record for the fifty-yard dash. You made the junior high school track team, but our mother forbade you to run because she thought it would make your legs big and ugly. When our mother told your track coach, you were so embarrassed and humiliated that you never tried to run again. You stopped drawing, too, because you were being groomed by our father to become a doctor. You used to sell your drawings for 25 cents each to other classmates in elementary school, but soon learned you had no time for art (or "fooling around," as our father would say) because you had to study hard. You broke down one day after having received a B on an exam, because you were afraid it would ruin your straight-A record. Our father told me you had asked your white, male professor to reconsider the grade, but he told you he never gave *foreign* students A's! The real irony was that you were always a capable student, and more importantly, an insightful, critical thinker.

I had a desperate feeling something very bad was going to happen. So I wrote a letter to you a week before your second suicide attempt, warning you about my premonition, but the letter never got to you. I wrote that I wanted you to take care of yourself and that, like you, I was barely getting by. (You once wrote a good-bye note to me before you ran away—or was it meant to be read after your death?—that read, "I still don't know how you do it.") I wrote that I would be there for you and to have FAITH, because no one else was going to do it for us. But mostly, I expressed a deep sense of urgency. I sensed that if you did not do something about the crisis you were living, I was sure you would explode.

We spoke on the phone two nights before you took the pills. I was worried and impatient with you, because I wanted you to reassure me that you would not do anything self-destructive, so you told me you were not feeling suicidal. You even said you thought you were "probably the most fucked-up person on this planet," but you felt "good" about how you were going to handle it. I got off the phone feeling relieved, for the moment. Handle it? Was it supposed to be a hint (but I couldn't get it)? Our mother told me you cried, "Mommy, I'm sorry," which she believed signaled your regret for the "mistakes" you had made. "If you can't do anything good for society, you might as well kill yourself." Still, she told me your death took an important part of her, a connection she felt most strongly with you because you had her face. The same face she insulted and helped you to "reconstruct." Our father laughed when you told him the reason you wanted the plastic surgery was because you did not want to look like our mother.

In some ways, your death has shocked this family out of denial. For the first time, our parents owned up to the abuse they inflicted, as well as the suffering they endured from their own social alienation. Imagine how hard it was to maintain their dignity, having to work three times as hard as their white colleagues, who turned up their noses at broken English, and their own kids thinking they were stupid. Our brothers began to rely on me for support they used to get from you. You once told me what our lives would be like if you died. I realize now all the things you told me are true. But without these traumatic changes, I never would have appreciated your wisdom. I wonder if your vision was part of a plan. Did you know what you had to do?

I think you left because you could not live in the world that you knew. It hurts (so much) to imagine your pain and loneliness, . . . but I also know of your courage. You told me you were not afraid to die. *How much you must have known to feel so comfortable with death.* You weren't just a victim. However compromised, your suicide was also a form of resistance, a refusal to carry on under such brutal conditions.

I still have some of your old belongings, including some postsurgery photos that were hidden in a box. I didn't recognize you in the pictures at first. *My* sister is the girl I joked around with, shared a bed with and respected, who cut my hair, let me tag along, took some beatings for me, tolerated my impatience, envied me (too much) and was sometimes proud of me, saved animals with me, spoke Korean more fluently than the rest of us, was the dependable one, the pride of our father, the closest to our mother, the one with the "good heart," the confidant of our grandmother, the toughest one, who could beat us up and occasionally did, our younger brother's favorite sister, the only one who could really talk to our older brother, the one to have my teachers first, and the smart one. My perceptions of you. You said later, "I always feel obligated." Mired in my own world view, I refused to believe you had it so hard. Your suicide was finally something that belonged to *you*.

I pieced together the events of your suicide through stories told by our family. You pawned a TV set and bought a .38 Magnum. Put blank cartridges into where the bullets should be and sat in bed with the gun hidden underneath the covers. Our mother had spent the day tailing your car around the city, following you from one pawn shop to the next, begging the dealers not to sell you a gun. Eventually she found you at home safely in bed, and reassured you that everything was going to be fine. You asked her if you would have to go back there, to the psychiatric place. Our mother tried to comfort you and then left to get you a glass of orange juice, but she had walked no further than the bathroom down the hall when she heard an explosion. You were declared "dead" a few hours later.

So, why am I writing to you, dearest sister? It would be nice to extract an ultimate meaning from all this, to acquire some comfort from analysis, but I am still confronted with the abyssal magnitude of my soullessness. (That is what it feels like, the utter uprootedness of living in this lobotomizing culture.) I cannot hope to achieve a level of wholeness, because my soullessness refuses to be quiescent under this civilizing regime. I am writing to let you know that I still remember, and I will live to tell it regardless of my state of ruin, which means I think it is possible to militate against violence and loss without buying into civility and unity. I am not even calling for anarchy; I cannot allow myself that luxury because we already live in a (nation-)state of organized chaos. Your presence haunts and compels me to recount your death. Maybe my story will be useful in some way—to galvanize a historical or political consciousness—who knows? Maybe through remembering I will even find a patchwork place for myself to take root, just as we do in my dreams.

A Twenty-Five-Year Anniversary

It's been twenty-five years since you've been gone. And, still, the pain of remembrance has not left me. Before I sat down to write this letter, which I have been putting off for so long, I reread my letter to you. I can never get through it without crying. A quarter of a lifetime has passed and so many things, both wonderful and terrible, have happened, yet it is astonishing how the past can recur as if nothing has changed, and I'm the same soulless individual from all those years ago.

The memories come like raw flashes and literally arrest me; my everyday consciousness stops, and I am reliving the past as if it is happening now. I feel as if my body reverts to a primordial state until the moment I am released and returned to mundane experience. Thankfully, I still have our dreams; I am so grateful for them because they allow us a parallel life together, like the times when you come to visit your nephews, my children. Those dreams come to me out of the blue, as if you are dropping in to check on us. Those dreams help me to believe in your phantom presence, somehow just on the other side and intersecting with mine during my nonwaking moments.

Dearest Sister! So much has happened since you've been gone. You have a niece and three nephews. We lost another niece, our aunt, and our grandmother. One of your nephews survived a life-threatening illness. Our mother fought cancer. Our brother is fighting depression. Aging, illness, death, and rebirth are more obvious features of life now. Life keeps going. Is this what it means to move on?

Two things are certain: There is no such thing as progress. There is no such thing as closure. At least not the way we were brought up to believe. As in the American Dream, things always get better, we always improve, and society always advances. Why did we just accept that? What guarantees this? The myth of progress breeds complacency and a destructive belief in a natural social order. Some people say racism is diminishing and that "race relations" are improving, because . . . just because. They can never follow their own rationalization to its end, but they are able to accept the racial teleology with blind faith. It allows them to become ignorant to all the ways in which things are not getting better, and actually getting worse. They are blind to the fact that there is nothing natural about the social order. Racism is not natural. And "racial progress" is not guaranteed. The myth provides the perfect logic for reproducing stupid social sheep, which never question, and certainly never act to change, the state of things. In reality, the "natural" state of things includes the blind acceptance of the pathology of everyday racism and sexism, as well as their casualties.

And what about the body in pain? What does the myth of progress do to those? The teleological endpoint is closure, as in pulling yourself up by your bootstraps, enduring, achieving wholeness, and becoming better and wiser for your suffering. Like a phoenix rising from the ashes or a Christian attaining redemption from one's suffering. If you cannot find closure, you are "crazy" or "ill." You are a failure. And since pain makes people feel uncomfortable, you are forced to compartmentalize that aspect of yourself. Hence, the recurring flashes of pain. Unresolved, they manifest in other ways.

Like the time Mom got breast cancer. In traditional Asian medicine, the breast is where you hold negative energy, like trauma, anger, and sadness. Even in Western medicine, some forms of breast cancer are believed to be caused by stress. I don't think I fully empathized with her pain of losing you, or truly understood her strength, until I became a mother myself, especially after I came close to losing your nephew, my own child. That kind of pain is unspeakable. It is the most primitive, world-ripping state. I listen to her recalling, in her small voice, what it was like mothering her young children, reliving and regretting but understanding the lessons which she tries to pass on to me. I told a friend that I thought our mother's cancer was rooted in the trauma of your suicide. The friend asked, "Wasn't that a long time ago?" To me, she might as well have said, "That was the past. Hasn't she moved on yet?" In studies of trauma, such as the effects of internment on Japanese Americans, evidence of psychological damage is shown to be long-term, even transgenerationally affecting those who never directly experienced being displaced and incarcerated themselves. In this case, the model of transgenerational trauma must be revised, because it is not just passed down from the old to the new; it can also damage across generations in reverse.

I conveyed before that our parents were shocked out of denial, but it was a small victory. For our father, there was a big gap between understanding what happened to you and changing how he acted in the world. He still could not cope when things seemed to be beyond his control, which meant he still could not choose how to react, except to choose rigidity, frustration, and anger, his usual way of being. In some ways, he has softened, but not without an irreversible cost. Your death has aged him, and now he is defeated, sad, and full of regret.

Our brothers, who momentarily turned to me instead of you for help, are no closer to closure. Our younger brother, who looked up to you more like a parent than a sister, is more like a lost soul than a being in this world. Like you, he is smart, creative, and sensitive, but he has been floating from place to place, job to job, and crisis to crisis. He is reclusive and lonely. He received a diagnosis of depression, which described him like a marionette. He has a way of expressing flat affect, as if he is just moving through the motions of life but not fully experiencing it. Our older brother, the one that only you could really talk to, never got a chance to share with you the pain of losing your niece, his daughter. Now, he has another child, but, on our mother's insistence, he is raising her in Vietnam. Now, our mother understands that the model minority is not doing well, and she rejects the myth that this country is a safe place to bring up children. The American Dream promises that each generation will be more successful than the preceding ones, but we are proof that assimilation is making us worse.

Our grandmother, who was like a mother to us and raised us from birth, always told me how much she missed you. During every visit I made with her, without fail, she would reminisce out loud about you, so I wondered if it was because I reminded her of you and hoped she would take comfort in that. She must have questioned how she, who had experienced wars, colonial occupations, poverty, and hunger, could have outlived by decades a granddaughter, who lived in the richest and most powerful country in the world.

As for me, I have responded to our loss by learning, writing, and sharing as much as I can about suicide. Now, more people are studying and talking about Asian American suicide, depression, and mental illness, thanks mostly to Asian Americans who are bringing attention to the issues that are important to our communities. We know now that certain age and gender groups have the highest risk for suicide, including elderly Asian American women, and young girls! What is causing suicide to become the leading cause of death for young Asian American girls? More researchers are studying the impact of the model minority myth as an important psychological stressor for Asian Americans. They are talking more about the influences of subtle racism and sexism, or "microaggressions," on the terror of everyday life. I discovered from my own research that the difference between dying and surviving suicide is not anything unique about the stories of suffering themselves, but often the presence or absence of support. It can take the form of a friend, a teacher, a counselor, a spiritual guide, a family member, or even a personal diary, which help us to survive.

I am doing everything I can to honor your life and your death, but the only way I can do it is by separating the "personal" from the "work." Do you know why I chose to use a pseudonym? It is not about shame; it is not about stigma. Some people think Asian Americans are shame-based communities, slaves to our cultural values and controlled by the threat of social stigma and of "losing face." This is not the case for us. It is because of the difficulty of speaking. I can never get through sharing our story without breaking down emotionally. At every conference, forum, or workshop, it happens. Even in social situations. I could be at a party at a friend's house, enjoying myself and just being in the moment, and then someone would ask me about you. There is violence in it. The moment ruptures, and the past is forced upon me, again. Our parents are devastated; they have lost their child. Yet sometimes people ask them about my work. I want them to have some peace, so I keep the work separate. I will tell your story, but this is my lone commitment to you.

You said that you wanted to write about your life, so I have made it my life's work. To bear witness, remember, and voice our experiences, in the hope of reaching just one Asian American teenager or girl who might be reading this letter. The progress of history tends toward erasure. In situations of suffering, the mind-body tends to turn away and to deny. We as a society are uncomfortable facing ugly things or feelings, but the effect is to divide and conquer us. We silence and isolate ourselves and each other around violence and suffering, which prevents supportive networks from forming. I think this is why the repressed always returns, why you continue to haunt my dreams. The recurrence of the past is instructive; moving on does not mean leaving the past behind.

What is healing for us if there is no closure? Everything that I have been taught about healing is founded on ideas of normalcy, wholeness, transcendence, progress, and hope. We learned that those are ideas, not our family's realities. Healing is not a linear process, and it is not guaranteed. At the same time, we reject the dualistic thinking that if we are not Healed, then we must be Victims— ill, utterly destroyed, abject, or stagnant. Because there is movement. My dreams and flashbacks are forms of movement, of process. And everyday life goes on.

Living fills the spaces and you take up less of my conscious memory. Maybe healing is the accumulation of life experiences and the feelings and slivers of wisdom that come from their interactions, and the process of integrating how they sometimes fit together and sometimes don't.

Looking back twenty-five years later, I see one thing clearly: You were just a kid, barely a young woman. Believe me, that understanding is fraught with so many different meanings and feelings, I do not take it lightly. But I hope you can see: Just as you had joys and highs besides your struggles and suffering when you were alive, you would have had many more years of life-composing experiences. They would have included many more joys, as well as tragedies, and they would have affected you. I can't predict how, but each life-composing moment would have been another moment of agency. After your final act of agency, your refusal to carry on, there are no more potential moments left.

I wish you had not refused.

Because I still miss you.

I still miss you.

19

"Racial Profiling" in the War on Terror

Cultural Citizenship and South Asian Muslim Youth in the United States

SUNAINA MAIRA

Since the attacks of September 11, 2001 and the War on Terror waged by the United States at home and abroad, questions of citizenship and racialization have taken on new, urgent meanings for South Asian immigrant youth. Many South Asian Americans, Arab Americans, and Muslim Americans, or individuals who appeared "Muslim," have been targeted for surveillance, detention, and deportation by the state. In the public sphere as well, South Asian, Muslim, and Arab Americans have been the objects of intensified scrutiny and suspicion and, in some cases, have experienced physical assaults and racial profiling as part of the renewed anti-Muslim backlash and demonization of Arabs in the United States.[1] There has been a shift in US race politics after 9/11 where the fault lines are no longer just between those racialized as white Americans/people of color or black/white Americans, but between those categorized as Muslim/non-Muslim, American/"foreign," or citizen/noncitizen. This chapter examines the experiences of South Asian Muslim youth in the United States, who emigrated from Bangladesh, India, and Pakistan, in the context of this shifting racial formation and intensified exclusion of Arab and Muslim Americans from national belonging.

The War on Terror

Within six weeks of September 11, 2001, Congress hastily passed the USA PATRIOT Act, which conveniently stands for Uniting and Strengthening America by Providing Appropriate Tools Required to Intercept and Obstruct Terrorism Act. The new laws to prosecute the War on Terror by eroding civil liberties were pushed through under considerable pressure from Attorney General John Ashcroft who threatened critics of the act "that those who scare peace-loving people with phantoms of lost liberties . . . only aid terrorists."[2] Not so conveniently for Muslim, Arab, and South Asian Americans, the PATRIOT Act gave the government sweeping new powers of investigation and surveillance targeting their communities.[3] It did this by creating an ambiguously defined category of "domestic terrorism," by granting the government enhanced surveillance powers, and by taking away due process rights from noncitizens who could be placed in mandatory (and in actuality, indefinite and secret) detention and deported because of participation in broadly defined "terrorist activity" (often for minor immigration violations and also in secret.[4] The act's provisions violated basic constitutional rights of due process and free speech and, in effect, sacrificed the liberties of specific minority groups in exchange for a presumed sense of "safety" of the larger majority. Before 9/11, about 80 percent of the American public thought it was wrong for law enforcement to use "racial profiling," a phrase popularly used to refer to the disproportionate targeting of African American drivers by police for the offense of "driving while black; after the shock of the 9/11 attacks, 60 percent favored racial profiling, "at least as long as it was directed at Arabs and Muslims."[5]

It is important to note that discrimination against and suspicion of Arab Americans and Muslim Americans existed in the United States well before 9/11.[6] However, South Asian Americans, particularly Sikh and Muslim males, suddenly found themselves scrutinized as potential "enemy" threats. Surveillance of Arab American communities has always been linked to US foreign policies in the Middle East, and is closely tied to US support of the Israeli occupation of Palestine and military interventions in the region. Arab Americans, and others, who have protested these policies have been monitored at various moments since the 1967 Israeli-Arab war, from the FBI's surveillance of the General Union of Palestinian Students in the 1980s, to the attempted deportation of the pro-Palestinian activists known as the "L.A. 8," to the nationwide monitoring and interviews of Arab American individuals and organizations before and during the first Gulf War.[7] Racial profiling must be understood not just as a scrutiny of certain groups because of presumed differences of "racial" or ethnic identity, or just in terms of cultural and social exclusion, but as an everyday practice that is linked to state policies. Racial profiling after 9/11, in particular, highlights the ways in which particular immigrant communities are positioned in relation to the nation-state, domestically and globally.

The shift in racialization of South Asian Americans after 9/11 is significant because South Asians in this country have had a different relationship than Arab Americans to the policies of the national security state. They have generally not been viewed as potentially working against the state's interests, at least not since the early twentieth century, when Indian nationalists in the United States who were engaged in transnational activism against British colonialism were subjected to state surveillance.[8] But South Asian immigrants, regardless of their political orientation or class status, have always been positioned within the United States in ways reflecting the state's economic and political interests. The primary influx of immigrants from South Asia came to the United States after the Immigration Act of 1965 as part of an effort by the United States to shore up its scientific and military technology expertise during the Cold War.

These graduate students, scientists, and professionals generally did not engage in challenges to their adopted home state's policies. Despite economically strategic lobbying for minority status in the 1970s to avail of civil rights benefits, the first wave of South Asians has for the most part tried hard to live up to the mythic "model minority" image.[9]

The second wave of South Asian immigrants, however, that began coming to the United States in the 1980s through family reunification provisions of the 1965 act were less affluent than their predecessors, were more likely to come from small towns or even villages, and have had a very different exposure to US race politics and the welfare state than those who reside in middle- and upper-middle-class, predominantly white suburbs. These more recent immigrants generally live in urban areas, often in multiethnic communities, and work in service-sector jobs or in small businesses. The civil rights crisis after 9/11 not only affected South Asian, Arab, and Muslim African Americans differently due to their varied histories of arrival and residence in the United States, and the different relationships of the United States with their home nation-states, but it also affected various South Asian American communities unevenly, based on their class status and previous understandings of US racism.

The crisis of civil rights of South Asian Americans after 9/11 is the most virulent example of large-scale scapegoating of South Asians in the United States since the anti-Indian riots on the West Coast in the early twentieth century.[10] As part of the domestic "War on Terror," at least twelve hundred Muslim immigrant men were rounded up and detained within seven weeks in the immediate aftermath of 9/11, none of them with any criminal charges, and some in high-security prisons.[11] Nearly 40 percent of the detainees were thought to be Pakistani nationals, though virtually none of the detainees were identified publicly and the locations where they were held remained secret.[12] These men began to "disappear" into the vast American prison-industrial complex, "a vast system of immigration prisons that had been detaining 150,000 people annually since the mid-1990s and now hold more than 200,000 people each year."[13] Many Muslim families who experienced the "disappearances" of their husbands, brothers, and sons ended up leaving the country after indefinite separations and loss of the means of family support.[14] There were mass deportations of Pakistani nationals on chartered planes, some leaving in the middle of the night from New York State, that went unreported in the mainstream media.[15]

In June 2002, the National Security Entry-Exit Registration System (also known as "Special Registration") was established, requiring all male nationals over sixteen years from twenty-four Muslim-majority countries including Pakistan and Bangladesh, as well as North Korea, to submit to photographing and fingerprinting at federal immigration facilities.[16] Over eighty thousand men complied with the Special Registration program even though information about the process was badly disseminated. Many of these men, however, never came out; 2,870 were detained and 13,799 were put into deportation proceedings.[17] After news broke of mass arrests of Iranians complying with Special Registration in Southern California in December 2002, many undocumented immigrants and those with pending immigration applications tried to flee to Canada. By March 12, 2003, the Canadian immigration service reported 2,111 refugee claims by Pakistanis since January 1.[18] More than 15,000 undocumented Pakistanis had reportedly left the country for Canada, Europe, and Pakistan by June 2003, according to the Pakistani Embassy in Washington.[19]

The profiling of Muslim and Arab immigrants affects the composition of communities and the nature of relationships within them, particularly in areas with large concentrations of these populations which have seen an exodus of immigrants, such as Brooklyn's Little Pakistan on Coney Island Avenue.[20] Perhaps more alarming, "an unknowable number of immigrants have burrowed deeper underground," creating an even more precarious world of individuals who cannot fully admit they exist, who cannot safely live their lives openly for fear of deportation and so live in the shadows, if not under siege.[21] The "war on terrorism" has been waged primarily against immigrants, heightening the distinction between citizens and noncitizens and making citizenship a crucible for the post-9/11 crackdown.[22] In fact, the War on Terror is an extension of the "war on immigrants," waged since the late 1980s and continuing with the anti-immigrant Proposition 187 passed in California in 1994 and the heightened policing of US borders.[23] The Anti-Terrorism and Effective Death Penalty Act and the Illegal Immigration Reform and Immigrant Responsibility Act of 1996, both passed under the Clinton administration, laid the groundwork for the PATRIOT Act by stripping civil rights from noncitizens in the name of national security. The war on civil liberties did not begin after 9/11 but was accelerated after the Twin Towers tragedy.[24]

The heightened fear and anxiety of those targeted as suspects in the domestic War on Terror in the first year after 9/11 seems to have largely diminished in the public sphere, and within South Asian American communities, seems to be borne ever more by Muslim and Sikh Americans to the exclusion of those who feel they are not "targets" of the War on Terror. My own work on issues of immigrant rights with South Asian Americans in Massachusetts revealed that there was, understandably, a heightened sense of fear and vulnerability in Muslim immigrant communities, particularly among working-class immigrants who cannot as easily afford legal counsel to help them if they are harassed or detained. This fear about surveillance, detention, and deportation persists in Muslim American communities around the nation, for Muslims and Arabs continue to be associated with "terrorist" threats to the nation as the "War on Terror" continues to be used by the Bush administration to rally the nation.

South Asian Muslim Immigrant Youth in Wellford

The "war at home" in the aftermath of 9/11 raises questions about what the racial profiling and anti-Muslim backlash mean for South Asian and Muslim immigrant youth coming of age in the United States at a moment when their belonging in the nation is suspect. How do US immigration and "homeland security" policies targeting Muslim immigrants affect the understandings of race, nationalism, and citizenship of South Asian Muslim immigrant youth? This essay is based on an ethnographic study that I began in fall 2001, focused on working-class Indian, Pakistani, and Bangladeshi immigrant students in a public high school in a town in Massachusetts that I call Wellford. As part of my research, I also interviewed immigrant parents, school staff, community and religious leaders, city officials, and community activists. I argue here that young Muslim immigrants' understandings of citizenship shed light on the ways in which belonging in the United States is defined in relation to transnationalism and globalization, multiculturalism, and polyculturalism, and increasingly overtly, to the links between domestic and foreign policy that underlie US imperial power.

Wellford is an interesting site for this research, for while media attention and community discussions of racial profiling were primarily focused on South Asians in the New York/New Jersey area, there were hundreds of incidents around the country in places where South Asians have not been as visible in the public sphere or as organized, including incidents in New England. It is also interesting to focus on communities such as Wellford, that are known to be politically liberal, to understand what kinds of responses such a setting allows and does not allow, particularly for youth. The Wellford public high school has an extremely diverse student body reflecting the city's changing population, with students from Latin America, the Caribbean, Africa, and Asia. Students from India, Pakistan, Bangladesh, and Afghanistan constituted the largest Muslim population in the school, followed by youth from Ethiopia, Somalia, and Morocco. At the time I did my research, there were about sixty students of South Asian origin, including a few Nepali and Tibetan youth, who were almost evenly split between immigrant students and second-generation youth.

The South Asian immigrant student population in Wellford is predominantly working- to lower-middle-class, recently arrived (within five to seven years), and with minimal to moderate fluency in English. These youth generally seemed to socialize predominantly with other South Asian immigrant youth and with other immigrant students in the bilingual education program. The majority of the Indian immigrant youth were from Muslim families, mostly from small towns or villages in Gujarat in western India. Several of the South Asian students were actually related to one another as their families had sponsored relatives as part of an ongoing chain migration. Whole families had migrated from the same village in Gujarat, re-creating their extended family networks in the same apartment building in Wellford. The parents of these youth generally worked in low-income jobs in the service sector, and they themselves worked after school, up to thirty hours a week, in fast-food restaurants, gas stations, and retail stores and as security guards.

The families of these South Asian (Sunni) Muslim youth are not very involved in local Muslim organizations or mosques that draw a diverse Arab, North African, Asian, and African American population. They tend to socialize mainly with people from their own ethnic community; but they do not seem to affiliate with the Indian American or Pakistani American community organizations in the area either, which tend to involve mainly middle- to upper-middle-class, suburban families.[25] Thus the responses of these immigrant youth are rooted in the specificities of their urban, working-class experience, an experience that is often completely unknown to their more privileged South Asian American counterparts in the area.

Cultural Citizenship

I found that in nearly all my conversations with South Asian immigrant youth, as well as their parents, the discussion would inevitably turn to citizenship, for this was an issue that had profoundly shaped their lives and driven their experiences of migration. There is very little research on youth and citizenship and much work on young people's understandings of politics has a rather narrow definition of what constitutes the "political," tied to electoral politics, which is not useful when studying youth who are generally not involved in formal politics. More recent work challenges these assumptions and pays attention to young people's own understandings of politics in different realms of their everyday life.[26]

Young people may not be interested in voting, but they express their relationship to the state in different ways and develop particular understandings of their role as "citizens." Citizenship has traditionally been thought of in political, economic, and civic terms, but increasingly analyses focus on the notion of cultural citizenship, or cultural belonging in the nation, which is a useful concept when considering the relationship of youth to the nation-state. This notion is very relevant to immigrant communities as multiethnic societies are forced to confront questions of difference that undergird social inequity. It has become increasingly clear that the rights and obligations of civic citizenship are mediated by race, ethnicity, gender, and sexuality, as well as religion, as apparent in the post-9/11 backlash.[27] Cultural citizenship, according to Lok Siu, is the "behaviors, discourses, and practices that give meaning to citizenship as lived experience" in the context of "webs of power relations" and the daily "practices of inclusion and exclusion."[28] Cultural citizenship is an important notion to examine after 9/11 because legal citizenship is clearly no longer enough to guarantee protection under the law with the state's War on Terror, as is clear from the profiling, surveillance, and detention of Muslim Americans who are US citizens.

The concept of cultural citizenship has been developed by Latino studies scholars such as Renato Rosaldo, William Flores, and Rina Benmayor, who are interested in social movements for immigrant and civil rights. Their use of cultural citizenship analyzes "how cultural phenomena—from practices that organize the daily life of individuals, families, and the community, to linguistic and artistic expression—cross the political realm and contribute to the process of affirming and building an emerging Latino identity and political and social consciousness."[29] It has also been developed by cultural theorists such as Aihwa Ong, who are concerned with citizenship as a process by which the state regulates and disciplines citizens. Ong defines cultural citizenship as "a dual process of self-making and being-made within webs of power linked to the nation-state and civil society."[30] Some scholars, such as Toby Miller, are somewhat skeptical about the possibility for using citizenship as the collective basis for political transformation for it is increasingly individualized and privatized in neoliberal capitalist states, such as the United States, where being a citizen is more akin to being a consumer of services or social goods offered by the state. My work, in a sense, bridges these two approaches: I am interested in the critical possibilities of cultural citizenship for galvanizing struggles for civil and immigrant rights as suggested by the work of Latino studies scholars. At the same time, I view citizenship as a limited basis for social transformation, given that it is tied to the state and is often based on a model of consumer citizenship.[31]

In my research, I found that there are three major ways in which South Asian immigrant youth understand and practice cultural citizenship: *flexible citizenship*, *multicultural or polycultural citizenship*, and *dissenting citizenship*. These terms are drawn from the ways in which the young immigrants in my study expressed and practiced cultural citizenship. It is also important to note that legal citizenship remains very important, especially given that the War on Terror has used citizenship as a major weapon in its crackdown on undocumented immigrants and noncitizens and that less affluent immigrants were generally the ones most severely affected. Cultural citizenship always has to be considered in relation to questions of formal documentation and economic citizenship, as my research shows.[32]

The forms of citizenship that emerged from this study—flexible, multicultural and polycultural, and dissenting—are responses that these immigrant youth expressed simultaneously. They are not exclusive of one another, nor do they exist in some kind of hierarchy of political or social development. I view these modes of citizenship not as static categories in a typology but as processes that are dynamic across different spheres: social, economic, and political. These citizenship practices are performed by adults as well, but it is clear that young people have to negotiate particular concerns due to their positioning in the family and social structure, and their participation in education. While immigrant youth have to deal with the migration choices of their parents and the demands of being both students and workers, it is clear that their lives are deeply shaped by the state and economic policies that drive their parents to cross national borders. Young people, too, grapple with the meaning of the state's role in their lives and with the implications of war, violence, and racism for an ethics of belonging.

Flexible Citizenship

"Flexible citizenship" describes the experience of migrants who use transnational links to provide political or material resources not available to them within a single nation-state,[33] as has been argued for affluent Chinese migrants by Aihwa Ong.[34] It is different from traditional notions of dual citizenship, which imply an actual legal status as citizen of two nation-states, for it leaves open questions of national loyalty or strategic uses of citizenship status. The Muslim immigrant youth in my study display modes of flexible citizenship, for they understand citizenship in relation to the United States as well as one or more nations in South Asia. For them, national affiliations (such as "Indian" or "Bangladeshi") as well as linguistic-regional identities such as Gujarati or Pathan were very important, and they viewed all these identifications as compatible with national belonging in the United States. They came to the United States sponsored by relatives who are permanent residents or citizens, in some cases fathers who migrated alone many years earlier, so they had grown up in transnational families spanning two continents. Transnational marriages and social ties are common in their families. However, their experiences of flexible citizenship were often more difficult than the elite Asian immigrant families studied by Ong and others. At least two boys had been separated from their fathers for about fifteen years; Faisal said his father had left Pakistan for the United States right after he was born, and in effect missed his son's childhood while he was working in the United States to support him and his family till they could be reunited. By the time Faisal came to the United States, however, his older brother was too old to enroll in high school and had to struggle to get a GED and find a job with limited English skills, so this flexible citizenship had its costs for these working- and lower-middle-class migrant families.

Most of these young immigrants desired and had applied for US citizenship, because of what they perceived as its civic and also economic benefits: a few stated that they wanted to be able to vote, and several said that they wanted to be able to travel freely between the United States and South Asia, to be mobile in work and family life. About half of these South Asian Muslim immigrant youth have green cards already; the remaining are a mix of citizens and undocumented immigrants. After 9/11, of course, citizenship has become less a matter of choice for immigrants, particularly Muslims and South Asian/Arab Americans, than a hoped-for shield against the abuses of civil rights. In fact, a few youth I spoke to were surprised that I myself had not obtained citizenship yet in the fall of 2001, and were in some cases concerned that I seemed to have taken so long to obtain this vital document!

Citizenship for these immigrant youth is part of a carefully planned, long-term, family-based strategy of migration in response to economic pressures on those living in, or at the edge of, the middle class in South Asia. Some of these youth in Wellford imagine their lives spanning national borders and speak of returning to South Asia, at least temporarily, once they have become US citizens and perhaps when their parents have retired there. For example, Ismail, who worked as a computer assistant after school, wanted to set up a transnational hi-tech business so that he could live part-time in Gujarat and part-time in Boston while supporting his parents. He saw this as a strategy for nonresident Indians (or NRIs, a term used by the Indian government) to fulfill their obligations to the home nation-state, using the benefits of US citizenship. It seems to me that these young immigrants' notions of flexible citizenship are based on at least two linked processes of "self-making and being-made" as citizens in relation to multiple nation-states.[35] First, their identification with India or Pakistan is based largely on transnational popular culture, on Bollywood films, South Asian television serials, and Hindi music that they access through video, DVDs, satellite TV, and the Internet. In the interest of space, I cannot delve into an analysis of transnational popular culture here, but it is clearly an important arena for the expression of transnational cultural citizenship by immigrant youth.[36]

Second, flexible citizenship is intertwined with labor and education, areas that are interrelated for working-class, immigrant youth. These youth have come to the United States with their families, in some sense, as migrant workers. They work in low-wage, part-time jobs in retail and fast-food restaurants and struggle in school to get credentials for class mobility. These service-sector jobs are generally occupied by young people of diverse ethnic backgrounds in the United States.[37] However, unlike nonimmigrants who provide this flexible labor, immigrant youth can perform economic citizenship, which is based on individual productivity in the capitalist state, and they may aspire to the American Dream but they cannot win cultural citizenship because they are nonwhite and immigrant, and currently because they are identified as Muslim, so they are excluded from full national belonging. Their participation in US public culture, in fact, is largely through work; their relations outside the school and community are mainly with other immigrant or young workers and with employers. For example, Walid, a Pakistani immigrant boy, lamented that he could never go out into the city with his friends because they all worked on different schedules and it was almost impossible for them to have a night off together, given that he worked night shifts at his weekend job as a security guard.

Compared to more affluent South Asian immigrants, these working-class youth are more ambiguously positioned in relation to what Ong calls the US neoliberal ideology that emphasizes "freedom, progress, and individualism."[38] They see the limits of this model of the self-reliant consumer-citizen—and of the "American Dream"—in their own lives, and that of their families. Soman, who worked in his family's Bengali restaurant after school and who often waited on more affluent South Asian immigrant students from the prestigious university down the street, said, "Here, you live in a golden cage, but it's still a cage . . . my life is so limited. I go to school, come to work, study, go to sleep." Soman's comment about being imprisoned by the "golden cage" of the American Dream is profound because in a single image it points to the glittering appeal of American capitalism and the confining imprisonment of belief in this illusion. It also suggests that young immigrants and their families may acknowledge the self-delusion, but continue to participate in it because at least, for immigrant youth, there is little alternative now that they are in the United States.

The idea of productive citizenship is tied to the need for a low-wage, undocumented/noncitizen labor pool by employers who wish to depress wages and keep labor compliant. Citizenship requirements discipline workers and keep immigrants vulnerable to exploitation and fear of dissent, as is very evident after 9/11 with the ongoing arrests and deportations of immigrant workers for visa violations.[39] There continues to be fear among noncitizens who have transnational ties, political or familial, that are increasingly suspect when the "threat" to national security is attributed to specific foreign nations.

Yet, in the face of such regulations of citizenship and national boundaries, it became apparent to me that these young Muslim immigrants thought about citizenship in ways that were themselves flexible, shifting, and contextual. In some cases, it seems that religious identity actually prompts youth to think of themselves as belonging to the United States or at least identifying with its concerns, if not identifying as "American." Ismail said to me in the fall of 2001, "Islam teaches [us that] what country you live in, you should support them. . . . See, if I live in America, I have to support America, I cannot go to India." This of course is the same boy who said that he ultimately wanted to return to India and support its development. But these statements are not as contradictory as they first appear; Ismail is able to frame his relationship to Islam in a way that will help him think through questions of loyalty at a moment in the United States when Muslims are being framed as noncitizens *because* of a particular construction of Islam. Ismail instead uses Islam to counter this exclusion of Muslims from the nation-state, both officially and unofficially, and to develop a flexible definition of citizenship. Flexible citizenship is clearly an economic/family strategy for these youth but also part of a cultural strategy that allows them to manage diverse national affiliations.

Multicultural/Polycultural Citizenship

Not surprisingly, some of these immigrant youth talked about ideas of cultural difference and relationships with others in terms of multicultural citizenship, since multiculturalism is such a pervasive discourse of cultural belonging in the United States, particularly in the arena of education. Multicultural citizenship, in Will Kymlicka's perspective, is based on the idea of minority cultural rights, or the rights of minority groups within multiethnic nations to express their cultural identity.[40] The high school, implicitly and explicitly, promoted this notion of multicultural citizenship through visual symbols and support for ethnic-based student activities. Outside the high school's main office was a display case with changing exhibits which often focused on the theme of cultural diversity, among other issues, acknowledging the different ethnic groups in the school through artistic and cultural products, often tied to ethnic heritage month celebrations.

For South Asian immigrant students, multicultural citizenship was expressed through everyday understandings of pluralism embedded in the social fabric of their relationships. Most of them emphasized that they had friendships crossing ethnic and racial boundaries as Walid did in commenting on his black, Egyptian, Moroccan, and Gujarati Indian friends. In their daily lives, these youth did, in fact, hang out with Latino, Caribbean, African American, and Asian students, and especially with Muslim African youth from Somalia, Ethiopia, or Egypt, potentially forming a pan-Islamic identity. Yet it was also apparent that students in the school, as in most American high schools and even colleges, tended to cluster by ethnic group in the cafeteria and on the playground. Ismail commented that his friendships with non–South Asian students were sometimes questioned by "desi" (South Asian) youth, but he defended this by arguing for a more expansive conception of community:

> I hang out with different kids but even I heard it from a lot of desis who say, "Why you go with them?" They don't like it, but I say if you want to live in a different world, you have to exist with them. . . . Sometimes you have to go outside [your group] and say, yeah, alright, we are friends too, we are not going to discriminate [against] you, because . . . we don't look like you . . . your relationship is gonna be bigger, right. But if you're gonna live in the desi community, you're only going to know desi people, not the other people.

Ismail traced the value he places on multiculturalist coexistence to a notion of India as a multiethnic nation. He said, "India is a really good place to live in . . . because they've got a lot of religions, different languages, different people." But this was before the massacre of Muslim Indians during the Gujarat riots in spring 2002 shook the belief in the reality and depth of Indian secularism for many Indians, especially Muslims, even though the Indian Muslim youth I spoke to continued to cling to their belief in Indian pluralism after the riots.

Coexisting with this idea of multicultural inclusion were moments of tension among different groups of youth in the school, as there are in any school or community. After September 11, some of the South Asian immigrant youth, particularly the Muslim boys, felt targeted by other high school youth. Accusations of "you're a terrorist" or "you're a bin Laden" entered into fights among boys who flung these new racial epithets at one another as part of a national discourse about Muslims and Arabs as the "enemy threat" that was intensified after 9/11. The South Asian Muslim boys, and girls, felt this acutely: did this mean *they* were the enemy, and how could they live as such?

One of the anti-Muslim incidents in Wellford after 9/11 occurred in the school, when an African American girl accused two Pakistani boys, Amir and Walid, of "killing people" and reportedly called them "Muslim niggers." The girl was eventually suspended but Amir was, in fact, a friend of the girl's brother and said he tried to intervene to soften her punishment. Both boys emphatically refused to portray the incident as a black/South Asian or black/Muslim conflict; they insisted that this was the case of a lone individual who Walid half-jokingly said must have been "drunk" or "high." Amir, in fact, said that he thought African Americans were less likely to have an uncritically nationalist response to the events of 9/11 than white Americans, even though he was hesitant to extend this generalization to their responses to the military campaign in Afghanistan.

For Walid and Amir, 9/11 prompted a heightened self-consciousness about racialization that seemed, if anything, to reinforce the black-white racial polarization. Walid felt that African Americans were not as shattered by the attacks on the United States because, in his view, black Americans feel alienated from the nation-state due to the legacy of slavery. While this racialized difference after 9/11 is more complex than Walid suggests, what is important is that he *believes* that African Americans share his experience of marginalization within the nation. But Walid does not completely dismiss the renewed nationalism of Americans after 9/11, saying, "The first thing is they're born here in the USA, so that's their country. . . . We are immigrants. . . . If something happens in back home, like, and someone else did something, we're gonna be angry too, right?" Yet it is also apparent that 9/11 seems to have drawn him into an understanding of citizenship that is based on racialized fissures in claims to national identity and affiliation with other youth of color.

For Walid and others, the response of African Americans seems more significant than Latinos or even Arab Americans because on the one hand they are the largest group of students of color in the school, and on the other hand, they stand for a particular manifestation of contested US citizenship to these youth, even if not all are actually US-born. The responses of these Pakistani boys seems to suggest to me a potentially *polycultural citizenship*, based not on the reification of cultural difference that multiculturalism implies, but on a complex set of political affiliations and social boundary-crossings. Robin Kelley's notion of polyculturalism suggests that "we were multi-ethnic and polycultural from the get-go." A polycultural approach to difference suggests that cultures are inevitably already hybridized, and that there are no discrete, "pure" cultures.[41] Polycultural citizenship is embedded in the messiness and nuances of relationships of different groups with one other and with the state, and is based on a political, not just cultural resonance, based on particular historical and material conjunctures.

Polycultural citizenship is not an idealization, however, of the complexities of race politics. I do not want to suggest that polyculturalism exists in the absence of antiblack racism in this community, or that racialized antagonisms and suspicion in the school are not imbibed at all by immigrant youth; in getting to know these youth over a period of time, I have found that these tensions do indeed exist. Rather, there is room in my notion of polycultural citizenship to acknowledge the resentment and competition bred by daily struggles for turf or resources. These young immigrants simultaneously invoke a multiculturalist discourse of pluralist coexistence and a polyculturalist notion of boundary-crossing and affiliation, embedded in political experience but also in popular culture practices shared with youth of color. These young people are not involved in formal political organizations or in traditionally defined activism, but their deepened understanding of racism is based on a political, not just cultural, resonance with other youth of color in the school based on their shared experiences after 9/11.

Muslim immigrant youth sense a connection with other youth of color and with African Muslim youth in the city, even as they struggle with the challenges that Muslim identity has posed to liberal multiculturalism. Multiculturalist responses to the assault on the civil liberties of Muslim and Arab Americans have tended to consider racial profiling within a racialized framework of minority victimhood. "Muslim Americans," or the trio of "Arab, Muslim, and South Asian Americans," are constructed as just another, culturally (and religiously) distinct ethnic category whose problems can be contained within a discourse of domestic racism. The assumption is that "racial profiling" can be addressed simply by "cross-cultural understanding" or interreligious "dialogue" that leads to inclusion within the multicultural nation. However, the War on Terror has highlighted the limitations of multicultural citizenship as a response to state policies targeting Muslim and Arab Americans after 9/11, for these were based not just on racial or religious, but political, profiling. "Muslim" identity has been ethnicized since 9/11 but it is not an ethnic or racial category at all, even within the ambiguous construction of race in the United States, although Muslims have certainly experienced an intensified racialization as a demonized "other." But it is important to keep in mind that "racial profiling" and Islamophobia after 9/11 are at root tied to imperial policies that drive the global War on Terror, particularly US interests in dominating the Middle East. However, liberal multiculturalism suppresses a critique of the state and evades discussions of political injustice through a discourse of cultural difference.

After 9/11, it also became apparent that minority groups who had traditionally borne the brunt of racial profiling were not completely resistant to the anti-Arab and anti-Muslim suspicion and paranoia of the "war on terrorism." There are many reasons for the failure of interracial alliances between these groups, historically and politically, that could be clarified in a longer discussion. Such a discussion would have to include the resistance of some South Asians to affiliate with marginalized groups of color in their desire to achieve model minority status and the hyper-nationalism that emerged in the United States after 9/11 and that absorbed even marginalized groups. The US empire uses difference and consumption, in its domestic subordination of marginalized groups, to divide struggles against racism at home from movements for justice and against imperialism abroad.

Dissenting Citizenship

Muslim Americans and Arab Americans are defined, particularly after 9/11 but also at other moments, such as the Iran hostage crisis and the Gulf War, as political scapegoats and *therefore* cultural aliens.[42] Their presumed cultural difference is highlighted as part of a political and cultural doctrine that defines American interests and national identity in opposition to a "foreign enemy" and an "enemy within." Syed Khan, an Indian immigrant who was on the Board of Religious Directors of the Islamic Center of Sharon, was the founder of Muslim Community Support Services, an organization that held forums on issues of civil rights and cultural citizenship for Muslim Americans after 9/11. Khan commented in the fall of 2002 on the White House's early public embrace and then neglect of Muslim American leaders after 9/11: "Initially leaders including Bush had spoken up [against racial profiling], but afterwards, when it wasn't as critical, outreach to Muslim Americans has stopped completely. Now, it's bashing time." Other South Asian Muslims I spoke to were quick to point to the outpouring of support offered by neighbors and friends after 9/11. The two perspectives are, of course, both true. Individual acts of solidarity have coexisted with acts of discrimination, private and state-sponsored, on a mass scale.[43] The two processes often work together in racial profiling through contradictions of official rhetoric, which emphasized multicultural inclusion, and state policy, which continued to target Muslim and Arab Americans through surveillance, detention, deportation, and programs such as Special Registration.

Khan worried, as others in the community did, that Muslim Americans were not speaking up enough against the prospect of social and political, if not physical, internment, given the specter of the mass internment of Japanese Americans as "enemy" threats during World War II that loomed in historical memory when the mass detentions of Muslim and Arab Americans took place after 9/11. However, my research demonstrated that some Muslim immigrant youth were willing to voice political views, even publicly, that most South Asian middle-class community leaders were afraid of expressing. The Muslim immigrant youth I spoke to had an analysis of 9/11 and the US war in Afghanistan that drew on a notion of international human rights and resisted the nationalization of the Twin Towers tragedy. Amir said to me in December 2001,

> You have to look at it in two ways. It's not right that ordinary people over there [in Afghanistan], like you and me, just doing their work, get killed. They don't have anything to do with . . . the attacks in New York, but they're getting killed. And also the people in New York who got killed, that's not right either.

Aliyah, a Gujarati American girl who could very easily pass for Latina, chose to write the words "INDIA + MUSLIM" on her bag after 9/11. For her, this was a gesture of defiance responding to the casting of Muslims as potentially disloyal citizens; she said, "Just because one Muslim did it in New York, you can't involve everybody in there, you know what I'm sayin.'" Issues of innocence, culpability, justice, and collective punishment were foremost in the minds of the South Asian Muslim students when discussing this topic, even for new immigrants such as Zeenat. She thought that the bombing of Afghanistan in response to the attacks of 9/11 was "wrong" because the United States was attacking people who were not involved in the terrorist attacks and, echoing Ayesha's remark, said, "After September 11, they [Americans] hate the Muslims. . . . I think they want the government to hate the Muslims, like, all Muslims are same."

After the anti-Muslim incident in the high school, the International Student Center organized a student assembly featuring two Arab American speakers who criticized the war on terrorism and the attack on civil liberties. Amir, Walid, and a Gujarati Muslim girl, Samiyah, delivered eloquent speeches condemning racism to an auditorium filled with their peers. Amir said that when he was threatened by some young men in Boston, "I could have done the same thing, but I don't think it's the right thing to do." Amir is a muscular young man and his call for nonviolent response was a powerful one at that assembly, one that could also be taken to be a larger political statement about the US response to the attacks. Samiyah stood up in her salwar kameez and said, "We have to respect each other if we want to change society. You have to stand up for your rights." Muslim immigrant youth were being publicly drawn into race politics and civil rights debates in the local community, although it is not clear yet what the impact of this politicization will be over time. But a year later on the anniversary of September 11, when the International Student Center organized another student assembly, Samiyah's younger sister and another Gujarati Muslim girl, Mumtaz, voluntarily made similar speeches that were reported in the local press. Mumtaz spoke of her sadness at the events of 9/11, and also said "that it's not right to go after Pakistan and Afghanistan and all Muslims who had nothing to do with it."

Even though these working-class youth do not have the support of, or time to participate in, community or political organizations, they have become spokespersons in the public sphere willing to voice a dissenting view. Other Muslim American youth have been forced to play the role of educators as well, giving speeches at their schools and in community forums about Islam, though a coordinator of a Muslim youth group at the Central Square mosque says that it is a role not without pressure or fatigue for young Muslim Americans. Understandably some of them are also hesitant to speak publicly about political issues given that even legal citizens are worried about expressing political critique or dissent in the era of the PATRIOT Act. Repression works on two levels to silence dissent, as Corey Robin points out: on a state level, and also on the level of civil society, where individuals internalize repression and censor themselves.[44] Robin argues that "fear does the work—or enhances the work—of repression," noting that the effects of "Fear, American Style" are most evident today in immigrant, Middle Eastern, and South Asian communities, as well as in the workplace where "suppression of dissent" is evident since 9/11.[45]

In the face of such repression, I have found these Muslim immigrant youth to be engaged in a practice of dissenting citizenship based on a critique of state policies, both privately and publicly. Their expression of dissenting citizenship means they stand apart from the dominant perspective in the nation at some moments, even as they stand together with others outside the borders of the nation who are affected by US foreign policy. Jamila, a Bangladeshi girl, said of the war in Afghanistan, "I felt bad for those poor people there. Because America didn't have no proof that they actually did it, but they were killing all those innocent people who had nothing to do with it." Amir and other youth emphasized the importance of political justice and respect for international human rights, denouncing both the terrorist attacks and militarized state aggression as a means of retribution. Dissenting citizenship captures some of the ambivalence toward the United States that these youth experience, for America is simultaneously a place invested with their parents' desire for economic advancement and security and their own hopes to belong in a new home, and also the site of alienation, discrimination, and anxiety about belonging.

The perspective of Muslim immigrant youth is very much rooted in their identities *as* Muslims, for they are targeted as Muslims by the state, and it also sheds light on the links between US policies at home and abroad. These young immigrants are subjects of both the wars on terror *and* the war on immigration. The dissenting views of Muslim immigrant youth implicitly critique US imperial power through their linking of warfare *within* the state to international war. It is this link between the domestic and imperial that makes their perspective an important mode of dissent because the imperial project of the new Cold

War works by obscuring the links between domestic and foreign policies. The United States has had a long history, since its wars in Cuba, Puerto Rico, and the Philippines in 1898, of "imperialism without colonies" or of "informal empire" and of neocolonial occupation, as in Iraq.[46] The conceptualization of US empire is a project that has drawn renewed attention now that the term "empire" has come out of the closet, in the academy and mass media. Despite the different forms that US empire has taken in exercising direct or indirect control, such as through proxy wars or client states (such as Israel, Jordan, and now Afghanistan), the dominance of US military, economic, and political power, the three major aspects of imperial power, is still paramount.[47] The war at home and the war abroad, the two fronts of empire, actually work in tandem with each other at the expense of ordinary people everywhere.

Conclusion

It is important to remember that there are important continuities before and after 9/11 that are often not acknowledged enough in discussing the War on Terror. My use of "post-9/11" is not meant to signify a radical historical or political rupture in US politics, but rather a moment of renewed contestation over ongoing issues of citizenship and transnationalism, religion and nationalism, civil rights and immigrant rights. This state of emergency, the crisis of civil rights and warfare, is in fact not exceptional in the United States,[48] for the post-9/11 moment builds on measures and forms of power already in place. This is a state of everyday life in empire. The research here is an attempt to craft an ethnography of the new empire in order to understand the everyday struggles of those, such as immigrants and youth, whose lives have been transformed by this ongoing crisis and who have found subtle and complex ways to express their dissent.

NOTES

Originally published as "Youth Culture, Citizenship and Globalization: South Asian Muslim Youth in the United States after September 11," *Comparative Studies of South Asia, Africa and the Middle East* 24 (1): 219–231, 2004. ©2004 *Comparative Studies of South Asia, Africa and the Middle East*. All rights reserved. Used by permission of the publisher. The research on which this essay is based was funded by the Russell Sage Foundation and supported by my research assistants, Palav Babaria and Sarah Khan. Thanks to Louise Cainkar for her editorial feedback on an earlier version of this article.

1   There were seven hundred reported hate crimes against South Asian Americans, Arab Americans, and Muslim Americans, including four homicides (two involving South Asian American victims), in the three weeks following September 11 (Jeff Coen, "Hate Crimes Reports Reach Record Level," *Chicago Tribune*, October 9, 2001). At least two hundred hate crimes were reported against Sikh Americans alone (Jane Lampan, "Under Attack, Sikhs Defend Their Religious Liberties," *Christian Science Monitor*, October 31, 2001). The Council on American-Islamic Relations reported that it had documented 960 incidents of racial profiling in the five weeks after 9/11, with hate crimes declining and incidents of

airport profiling and workplace discrimination on the increase ("Hate Crime Reports Down, Civil Rights Complaints Up," Associated Press, October 25, 2001).

2 Nancy Chang, *Silencing Political Dissent: How Post-September 11 Anti-terrorism Measures Threaten Our Civil Liberties* (New York: Seven Stories/Open Media, 2002), 94.

3 Ibid., 29–32.

4 Ibid.

5 David Cole and James Dempsey, *Terrorism and the Constitution: Sacrificing Civil Liberties in the Name of National Security* (New York: New Press, 2002), 168.

6 Council on American-Islamic Relations (CAIR), *The Status of Muslim Civil Rights in the United States: Patterns of Discrimination* (Washington, DC: CAIR Research Center, 1998); Jack G. Shaheen, "Hollywood's Reel Arabs and Muslims," in *Muslims and Islamization in North America: Problems and Prospects,* ed. Ambreen Haque (Beltsville, MD: Amana, 1999), 179–202.

7 Cole and Dempsey, *Terrorism,* 35–48; Louise Cainkar, "No Longer Invisible: Arab and Muslim Exclusion After September 11," *Middle East Report* 224 (fall 2002), http://www.merip.org/mer/mer224/224_cainkar.html; Jordan Green, "Silencing Dissent," *ColorLines* 6, no. 2 (2003): 17–20.

8 Joan Jensen, *Passage from India: Asian Indian Immigrants in North America* (New Haven, CT: Yale University Press, 1988).

9 Vijay Prashad, *The Karma of Brown Folk* (Minneapolis: University of Minnesota Press, 2000).

10 Jensen, *Passage from India.*

11 L. Cainkar and S. Maira, "Targeting Arab/Muslim/South Asian Americans: Criminalization and Cultural Citizenship," *Amerasia Journal* 31, no. 3 (2006): 1–27.

12 Stephen J. Schulhofer, *The Enemy Within: Intelligence Gathering, Law Enforcement, and Civil Liberties in the Wake of September 11* (New York: Century Foundation Press, 2002), 11.

13 Tram Nguyen, *We Are All Suspects Now: Untold Stories from Immigrant Communities after 9/11* (Boston: Beacon, 2005), 7.

14 Chang, *Silencing Political Dissent,* 69–87.

15 Oliver Ryan, "Empty Shops, Empty Promises for Coney Island Pakistanis," *ColorLines* 6, no. 2 (2003): 14–16, see 16.

16 The re-registration component of the program was officially ended by the Department of Homeland Security in December 2003, after protests by immigrant/civil rights and grassroots community organizations, while other aspects of the program remained in place, and the detentions and deportations put in place by the program continue.

17 Nguyen, *We Are All Suspects Now,* xviii.

18 Ryan, "Empty Shops," 16.

19 Rachel L. Swarns, "More Than 13,000 May Face Deportation," *New York Times,* June 7, 2003.

20 Ryan, "Empty Shops."

21 Swarns, "More Than 13,000."

22 David Cole, *Double Standards and Constitutional Freedoms in the War on Terrorism* (New York: New Press, 2003), 21.

23 Bill O. Hing, "No Place for Angels: In Reaction to Kevin Johnson," *University of Illinois Law Review* 2 (2000): 559–601; Bill O. Hing, "The Dark Side of Operation Gatekeeper," *UC Davis Journal of International Law & Policy* 7, no. 2 (2001): 123–167.

24 Kathleen Moore, "A Closer Look at Anti-terrorism Law: American Arab Anti-discrimination Committee v. Reno and the Construction of Aliens' Rights," in *Arabs in America: Building a New Future,* ed. Michael Suleiman (Philadelphia: Temple University Press, 1999), 84–99, see 95. From 1996 to 2000, the government sought to use secret

evidence to detain and deport two dozen immigrants, almost all of them Muslims, but ultimately the government evidence was thrown out and the accused were released (Cole and Dempsey, *Terrorism*, 127).

25 The 2000 census reported 2,720 Indian immigrants (2.7 percent of the population), 125 Pakistanis, and 120 Bangladeshis in Wellford, a city that is 68.1 percent White American, 11.9 percent African American, 11.9 percent Asian American, and 7.4 percent Latino (US Census Bureau, *Statistical Abstract of the United States* [Washington, DC: US Census Bureau, 2000]). This, of course, does not include undocumented immigrants. The "native" population is 74.1 percent and foreign-born is 25.9 percent; 17.7 percent are not citizens and 31.2 percent speak a language other than English.

26 Kum-Kum Bhavnani, *Talking Politics: A Psychological Framing for Views from Youth in Britain* (Wellford: Wellford University Press, 1991); David Buckingham, *The Making of Citizens: Young People, News, and Politics* (London: Routledge, 2000).

27 Lauren Berlant, *The Queen of America Goes to Washington City: Essays on Sex and Citizenship* (Durham, NC: Duke University Press, 1997); Kathleen Coll, "Problemas y necesidades: Latina Vernaculars of Citizenship and Coalition-Building in Chinatown, San Francisco" (paper, Racial (Trans)Formations: Latinos and Asians Remaking the United States, New York, March 2002); Toby Miller, *The Well-Tempered Subject: Citizenship, Culture, and the Postmodern Subject* (Baltimore: Johns Hopkins University Press, 1993); Renato Rosaldo, "Cultural Citizenship, Inequality, and Multiculturalism," in *Latino Cultural Citizenship: Claiming Identity, Space, and Rights*, ed. William. F. Flores and Rina Benmayor (Boston: Beacon, 1997), 27–38.

28 Lok Siu, "Diasporic Cultural Citizenship: Chineseness and Belonging in Central America and Panama," *Social Text* 19, no. 4 (2001): 7–28, see 9.

29 Flores and Benmayor, *Latino Cultural Citizenship*, 6.

30 Aihwa Ong, "Cultural Citizenship as Subject-Making," *Current Anthropology* 37, no. 5 (December 1996): 738.

31 Gill Jones and Claire Wallace, *Youth, Family, and Citizenship* (Buckingham: Open University Press, 1992).

32 T. H. Marshall, *Citizenship and Social Class* (Wellford: Wellford University Press, 1950).

33 Linda Basch, Nina Glick Schiller, and Cristina Szanton Blanc, eds., *Nations Unbound: Transnational Projects, Postcolonial Predicaments, and Deterritorialized Nation-States* (Amsterdam: Gordon and Breach, 1994).

34 Aihwa Ong, *Flexible Citizenship: The Cultural Logics of Transnationality* (Durham, NC: Duke University Press, 1999).

35 Ong, "Cultural Citizenship," 737; Ong, *Flexible Citizenship*.

36 Sunaima Maira, *Missing: Youth, Citizenship, and Empire after 9/11* (Durham, NC: Duke University Press, 2009).

37 Katherine S. Newman, *No Shame in My Game: The Working Poor in the Inner City* (New York: Knopf, 1999); Stuart Tannock, *Youth at Work: The Unionized Fast-Food and Grocery Workplace* (Philadelphia: Temple University Press, 2001).

38 Ong, "Cultural Citizenship," 739.

39 Manu Vimalassery, "Passports and Pink Slips," *SAMAR (South Asian Magazine for Action and Reflection)* 15 (2002): 7–8, 20; see Ong, "Cultural Citizenship," for a fuller discussion.

40 Will Kymlicka, *Multicultural Citizenship: A Liberal Theory of Minority Rights* (Oxford: Oxford University Press, 1995).

41 Robin D. Kelley, *Yo' Mama's Disfunktional! Fighting the Culture Wars in Urban America* (Boston: Beacon, 1997).

42 Cole and Dempsey, *Terrorism*; Fereydoun Safizadeh, "Children of the Revolution: Transnational Identity among Young Iranians in Northern California," in *A World Between: Poems, Short Stories, and Essays by Iranian-Americans*, ed. Persis Karim and Mohammad M. Khorrami (New York: George Braziller, 1999), 255–276.

43 Bill O. Hing, "Vigilante Racism: The De-Americanization of Immigrant America," *Michigan Journal of Race and Law* 7, no. 2 (2002): 441–456; Vijay Prashad, "The Green Menace: McCarthyism after 9/11," *Subcontinental: A Journal of South Asian American Political Identity* 1, no. 1 (2003): 65–75; Corey Robin, "Fear, American Style: Civil Liberty after 9/11," in *Implicating Empire: Globalization and Resistance in the 21st Century World Order*, ed. Stanley Aronowitz and Heather Gautney (New York: Basic Books, 2003), 47–64.

44 Robin, "Fear," 47–64.

45 Ibid., 48, 53.

46 Amy Kaplan, "Where Is Guantánamo?," in "Legal Borderlands: Law and the Construction of American Borders," ed. Mary Dudziak and Leti Volpp, special issue, *American Quarterly* 57, no. 3 (2005): 831–858; Harry Magdoff, *Imperialism without Colonies* (New York: Monthly Review Press, 2003); Ediberto Román, "Membership Denied: An Outsider's Story of Subordination and Subjugation under U.S. Colonialism," in *Moral Imperialism: A Critical Anthology*, ed. Berta Esperanza Hernández-Truyol (New York: New York University Press, 2002), 269–284.

47 Alain Joxe, *Empire of Disorder* (Los Angeles: Semiotext(e), 2002).

48 Keya Ganguly, *States of Exception: Everyday Life and Postcolonial Identity* (Minneapolis: University of Minnesota Press, 2001).

20

Racial Microaggressions and the Asian American Experience

DERALD WING SUE, JENNIFER BUCCERI, ANNIE I. LIN, KEVIN L. NADAL, AND GINA C. TORINO

It is well documented that racism has been a constant, continuing, and embedded part of American history and society (Jones 1997; Smedley and Smedley 2005). Many Americans still cling to the belief, however, that the civil rights movement eliminated racism in our nation and created equality between whites and people of color (Thompson and Neville 1999). Although the civil rights movement had a significant impact on changing racial attitudes and overt prejudicial behaviors, racism is far from eradicated and continues to plague the nation (President's Initiative on Race 1998; Sue 2003). Instead of overt expressions of white racial superiority, research supports the contention that racism has evolved into more subtle, ambiguous, and unintentional manifestations in American social, political, and economic life (Sue 2003; Dovidio et al. 2002). The "old-fashioned" type where racial hatred was overt, direct, and often intentional has increasingly morphed into a contemporary form that is subtle, indirect, and often disguised. Studies on the existence of implicit stereotyping suggest that the new form of racism is most likely to be evident in well-intentioned white Americans who are unaware they hold beliefs and attitudes that are detrimental to people of color (Banaji 2001; Banaji, Hardin, and Rothman 1993; DeVos and Banaji 2005). The "new" manifestation of racism has been likened to carbon monoxide, invisible, but potentially lethal (Sue and Sue 2003; Tinsley-Jones 2003). Some researchers prefer to use the term "racial microaggression" to describe this form of racism which occurs in the daily lives of people of color. They are so common and innocuous that they are often overlooked and unacknowledged (Solorzano, Ceja, and Yosso 2000). Sue et al. (2007, 271) define microaggressions as "brief and commonplace daily verbal, behavioral and environmental indignities, whether intentional or unintentional, that communicate hostile, derogatory or negative racial slights and insults that potentially have harmful or unpleasant psychological impact on the target person or group." Simply stated, microaggressions are brief, everyday exchanges that send denigrating messages to people of color because they belong to a racial minority group. These exchanges are so pervasive and automatic in daily interactions that they are often dismissed and glossed over as being innocuous. What constitutes racial microaggressions, how they impact people of color, and the strategies used to deal with them have not been well conceptualized or researched (Sue et al. 2007).

Although it is generally accepted that African Americans and Latino/Hispanic Americans experience both overt and covert forms of prejudice and discrimination, Asian Americans are frequently viewed as a model minority who have made it in this society and experience little in the form of racism (Wong and Halgin 2006). Despite the long documented history of racism toward Asian Americans, there has been a lack of attention paid to prejudice and discrimination directed against them (Sue and Sue 2003). One reason may be that many white Americans tend to dichotomize racial issues in black and white terms (Liang, Li, and Kim 2004). As a result, the psychological needs of Asian Americans arising from racism are often overshadowed by the experiences of whites and blacks, and research findings for these racial groups are often assumed to speak to the experiences of Asian Americans as well.

Despite the belief that Asian Americans have somehow "made it" in our society and are "immune" to racism, widespread prejudice and discrimination continue to take a toll on their standard of living, self-esteem, and psychological well being (Wong and Halgin 2006). Indeed, the study of Asians in America is the study of widespread prejudice and discrimination leveled at this group. Denied the rights of citizenship, forbidden to own land, and incarcerated in internment camps, this group has been the target of large-scale governmental actions to deny them basic civil and human rights (Sue and Sue 2003).

Research reveals that overt racial discrimination is identified as one of the potential social risk factors of mental illness, is related to physical and psychological well-being, and contributes to stress, depression, and anger in its victims (Chakraborty and McKenzie 2002; Kim 2002). For example, in a survey of studies examining racism, mental health researchers found that higher levels of discrimination were associated with lower levels of happiness, life satisfaction, self-esteem, and mastery or control (Williams, Neighbors, and Jackson 2003). However, many of the existing studies examining the relationship between racist events and mental health typically have not included the experiences of Asian Americans (Liang, Li, and Kim 2004). As a result, these findings may not accurately describe the Asian American experience of racism and high levels of discrimination.

An interesting and valuable means of studying the manifestation and impact of racism upon Asian Americans is through the concept of racial microaggressions. Microaggressions have been described as subtle, stunning, often automatic exchanges that are "put-downs" (Pierce et al. 1978, 66). People of color experience them as subtle insults directed toward them, often automatically and unconsciously (Solorzano, Ceja, and Yosso 2000). Social psychologists have outlined the many ways contemporary racism can be expressed resulting in harm and disadvantage to the target person or group (Jones 1997; Dovidio et al. 2002).

Some examples of racial microaggressions include (1) teachers who ignore students of color, (2) taxi drivers who fail to pick up passengers of color, or (3) airport security personnel screening passengers of color with greater frequency and care. Because microaggressions often occur outside the level of conscious awareness, well-intentioned individuals can engage in these biased acts without guilt or knowledge of their discriminatory actions (Sue 2003). Despite the intentions of the perpetrator, these acts of discrimination can significantly harm the victims (Delucchi and Do 1996; Sue 2003). Racial microaggressions can also take form as verbal statements such as, "You speak such good English," "But you speak without an accent," and "So where are you really from?" (Solorzano, Ceja, and Yosso 2000). Asian Americans and Latino/Hispanic Americans indicate that they perceive these statements as invalidating and insulting because they reflect a worldview that racial/ethnic minorities are aliens in their own country (DeVos and Banaji 2005; Sue and Sue 2003). Unfortunately, through selective perception, many whites are unlikely to hear the inadvertent racial slights that are made in their presence (Lawrence 1987). As a result, white individuals may unconsciously perpetuate Eurocentric attitudes of white supremacy and in effect cause individuals of color to feel invalidated or inferior.

Ever since the civil rights movement, critical race theory has provided a means for challenging Eurocentric epistemologies and dominant ideologies such as beliefs in objectivity and meritocracy that has masked the operation of racism, especially as they relate to groups like Asian Americans (Matsuda et al. 1993; Sleeter and Bernal 2004). Although the field has not referred to them as microaggressions, Asian American studies has used counterstorytelling, media/film analyses, and narrative critiques to elucidate the Asian American experience of both overt and covert forms of racism (Hu-DeHart 1995; Hyun 2005; Nakanishi 1995). Although the ethnic and Asian American studies literature lends support to the existence of racial microaggressions, there is a paucity of psychological studies on their effects for all racial groups (Delgado and Stefancic 1992; Johnson 1988; Lawrence 1987). A review of that literature reveals only one study on African Americans that focuses specifically on microaggressions (Solorzano, Ceja, and Yosso 2000). The investigators reported that microaggressions resulted in a negative racial climate for blacks, and often fostered emotions of self-doubt, frustration, and isolation on the part of the victims (Solorzano, Ceja, and Yosso 2000). They concluded that the cumulative effects of racial microaggressions can be quite devastating. Sue (2003) believes that "this contemporary form of racism is many times over more problematic, damaging, and injurious to persons of color than overt racist acts" (48). It has been noted that the collective effects of racial microaggressions may theoretically result in "diminished mortality, augmented morbidity and flattened confidence" (Pierce 1995, 281). Without documentation and analysis to help better understand microaggressions, the threats that they pose and the assaults they justify can easily be ignored or downplayed (Solorzano, Ceja, and Yosso 2000).

Sue et al. (2007) have proposed a taxonomy of racial microaggressions that classifies them under three forms: microassault, microinsult, and microinvalidation. Microassaults are defined as explicit racial derogations that are verbal (e.g., racial epithets), nonverbal (behavioral discrimination), or environmental (offensive visual displays) attacks meant to hurt the person of color. It is generally deliberate and conscious. Calling someone a "Chink" or "Jap," white parents discouraging a son or daughter from dating Asian Americans, or displaying Asian caricatures of exaggerated slanted eyes and large buck teeth are examples. Microassaults are most similar to old fashioned forms of racism in that they are deliberate and conscious acts by the aggressor (Dovidio and Gaertner 2000).

The two other forms (microinsults and microinvalidations), however, tend to operate unconsciously, are unintentional, and generally outside the level of conscious awareness. They are seemingly consistent with the research literature on the power of implicit racist attitudes and beliefs (Banaji 2001; DeVos and Banaji 2005). These microaggressions are not consciously intended by the perpetrator, but from the perspective of the recipient, they represent a negative experience. A microinsult is a behavioral action or verbal remark that conveys rudeness, insensitivity, or demeans a person's racial identity or heritage. A white manager who states to a prospective applicant of color that "the most qualified person should get the job" may be perceived as implying that people of color are not qualified. Microinvalidations are actions that exclude, negate or nullify the psychological thoughts, feelings or experiential reality of a person of color. When an Asian American is complimented for speaking good English or when blacks are warned not to be so oversensitive, the underlying messages may be that Asians are perpetual foreigners in their own country and that the experiential reality of racism for African Americans is not real.

Because Sue et al. (2007) were more concerned with the unintentional and automatic expressions of microaggressions, they chose to concentrate on the latter two rather than microassaults. They created a taxonomy of microaggressions and proposed categories of each with their own distinct themes: (1) microinsult (*ascription of intelligence*—assigning high or low intelligence to a racial group; *second-class citizenship*—treated as a lesser being or group; *pathologizing values/ communications*—notion that values and/or communication styles of people of color are abnormal; and *assumption of criminal status*—presumed to be a criminal, dangerous, or deviant based on race) and (2) microinvalidation (*alien in own land*—assumption that racial minority citizens are foreigners; *color blindness*— denial or pretense that one does not see color; *myth of meritocracy*—success in life is due to individual effort and not race; and *denial of individual racism*— denial that personal racism or one's role in its perpetuation). A ninth category, environmental invalidation, was identified, but it appears to be more of a mechanism for delivering microaggressions (verbal, behavioral, and environmental) instead of a freestanding and distinct expression.

Although there is considerable conceptual and anecdotal support for the researchers' taxonomy and classification scheme (American Counseling Association 1999; Banaji 2001; Dovidio et al. 2002), its recent formulation has not been adequately researched. Studies examining the deleterious effects of "old-fashioned" or overt forms of racism are plentiful, but few have examined the more covert forms as manifested in microaggressions. Furthermore, the above taxonomy was derived from considering microaggressions across several racial/ethnic minority groups (African Americans, Asian Americans, and Latino/Hispanic Americans), and there is an underlying assumption that they apply equally to all groups of color. Although many social scientists have suggested that racism and stereotyping operate under similar principles for all marginalized groups (Biernat 2003; Jones 1997), some have hypothesized that there may be qualitative differences of how racism is expressed against Asian Americans as opposed to African Americans or Latino/Hispanic Americans (Liang, Li, and Kim 2004; Yoo and Lee 2005). Understanding the manifestations of racism is critical to designing effective interventions to counter the negative effects of racial oppression (Thompson and Neville 1999), especially as it affects Asian Americans (Noh et al. 1999). The current study was conducted in order to qualitatively explore the experience of racial microaggressions among Asian Americans and to identify typical microaggressive themes. By exploring the types of microaggressions Asian Americans experience, messages being conveyed, reactions to these experiences, and how individuals deal with the effects of these encounters, we hope to increase understanding of the dynamics of subtle racism directed at Asian Americans.

Method

The present study utilized a qualitative method to identify microaggressions directed at Asian Americans, explored the various forms they take, studied their impact upon recipients, and determined the means used to cope with their impact. Focus groups were used as a method to capture the richness of the participants' experiences by allowing the social group interactions to facilitate the development of meaning (Krueger 1998). Focus groups have been found to be an effective means of obtaining in-depth information about a relatively unexplored concept (Seal, Bogart, and Ehrhardt 1998; Krueger 1994) and used successfully to explore racial perceptions on a number of topics (Saint-Germain, Bassford, and Montano 1993; Solorzano, Ceja, and Yosso 2000; Thompson, Bazile, and Akbar 2004). In this case, we were interested in understanding social interactions and events related to experiences of subtle racism directed toward Asian Americans by describing, comparing, contrasting, cataloguing, and classifying microaggressions.

Participants

The ideal number for effective focus group analysis ranges from four to twelve people (Seal, Bogart, and Ehrhardt 1998). Participants were selected based on purposive criterion with the aim of choosing a sample that typifies the phenomenon under investigation (Patton 1990). All participants in the two focus groups had to self identify with being Asian American, were born and raised in the United States, and agree that racism and discrimination against people of color (particularly Asian Americans) exist in the United States. These three criteria were essential to ensure that the phenomena under investigation would be present in the discussions. A total of ten self-identified Asian Americans participated in the study: one male and nine female. The one male participant was Vietnamese American. Among the female participants were four Chinese Americans, two Filipino Americans, one Korean American, one Japanese/German American, and one Asian Indian/European American. Eight were students, two were working professionals, and all were in their mid-twenties, with only one in her early forties. Two focus groups of five were formed from the volunteers.

Researchers

The researchers for the study consisted of five doctoral and five master's students in counseling psychology taking a graduate research seminar in racism and antiracism taught by the senior author at a private eastern university. Because qualitative research places the role of the researcher as the central means of data collection, identification of personal values, assumptions, and biases is required at the initial onset of the study (Fassinger 2005). This allows us to account for potential biases and assures that the contributions to the research setting, methodology, analysis, and interpretation can be useful rather than detrimental (Krueger 1998; Polkinghorne 2005). All students taking the course did so voluntarily because of their strong interest in the topic of racism. The team consisted of three African Americans, three Asian Americans (including the senior author), two Latinos, and three white Americans. The instructor (senior author) has over thirty years of research related to topics of diversity, multiculturalism, racism, and antiracism. As this was a two-year seminar, considerable time was spent in the study of racism directed toward Asian Americans, which allowed for the informed formulation of the study. It is also clear that team members bring certain biases to the study. Team members believe, for example, that subtle racism exists, that it occurs against Asian Americans, that it possesses detrimental psychological consequences, and that it may be ethnic-group-specific. Furthermore, all were members of a research seminar, which might have inadvertently influenced their work on the project (pleasing the instructor). As a result, every effort was made to ensure objectivity, but it is acknowledged that these biases may shape the way data were collected, viewed, and interpreted.

Measure

Two formal means of collecting data were used: (1) a brief demographic questionnaire aimed at obtaining basic information related to Asian ethnicity, gender, age, occupation, and education, and (2) a semistructured interview protocol. The protocol was developed from a review of the literature on microaggressions (Pierce et al. 1978; Solorzano, Ceja, and Yosso 2000; Sue 2003), implicit and explicit stereotyping (Banaji 2001; Banaji, Hardin, and Rothman 1993), aversive racism (Dovidio et al. 2002; Jones 1997), and Asian American experiences of racism (Kim 2002; Liang, Li, and Kim 2004; Wong and Halgin 2006). As we wanted to allow the participants considerable freedom in responding to the questions and prompts, all questions were open-ended, and generally aimed at eliciting real-life examples that they experienced. In general, the eight questions were intended to generate a variety of microaggressive examples, explore the impact they had on participants, construe meaning from the interaction, and outline how participants responded. Transition and ending questions were also developed to aid in moving from one topic to another and to bring closure to the focus group activity. A copy of the interview protocol is presented in the appendix.

Procedures

Participants were solicited throughout the local university community (campus and neighborhood) through posted flyers, word of mouth, classroom invitations, and a website asking for volunteers. Asian American participants who volunteered were placed in one of two focus groups. No financial compensation was offered. Each focus group lasted for two hours and was conducted by a two-person team: the facilitator and observer. Both the facilitator and observer were Asian Americans and part of the research team. As the topic dealt with subtle racism against Asian Americans, it was believed that facilitators of the same race would minimize any hesitancy or reluctance to disclose negative sentiment about interactions with those outside of their own group. The role of the facilitator was to lead the discussion, while the observer noted nonverbal behaviors and group dynamics (Krueger 1998). Prior to the interview, both researchers went through a brief behavioral rehearsal related to moderating the focus group discussion, and anticipating and overcoming possible resistances to the flow of the discussion. Immediately after the interview and after the focus group was dismissed, a debriefing session was held between the two researchers related to their own reactions, observations about the group, major themes that arose, climate in the room, and discussion of problematic issues. The focus group discussions took place in an enclosed private room at the eastern private university where the study was based. All participants were asked to sign a consent form that included permission to audiotape the entire session. The debriefing between the two researchers was also audiotaped. The tapes were transcribed verbatim making sure that the identities of participants were removed. Tapes were destroyed after transcription. The transcript was subsequently checked for accuracy by the two facilitators before it was presented to the team for qualitative analysis.

A four-person research team, which included the facilitator and observer, went over the entire transcript to record responses or situations illustrating microaggressions generated in the focus groups and the content of responses from the group participants were analyzed qualitatively. The team task was to look at what types of microaggressions Asian Americans experience, the messages that are being conveyed via these microaggressions, and the type of reactions (i.e., behavioral, cognitive, and/or affective) Asian Americans have in response to these microaggressions. In keeping with focus group analysis (Seal, Bogart, and Ehrhardt 1998; Krueger 1998; Miles and Huberman 1994), each member of the research team individually identified topic areas or domains used to conceptually organize the overwhelming amount of data generated from the group discussion. The narratives and descriptions from the group participants were analyzed qualitatively along the following domains: (1) identifying microaggressions from the perspective of the participant, (2) producing illustrative critical incidents, (3) analyzing the unintentional/intentional themes, (4) categorizing their impact, and (5) describing typical responses to microaggressions.

The preliminary analysis was then presented to the senior author and other seminar members who acted as auditors in reviewing and providing feedback to the team in order to reach consensus that approximate the "truth." The procedure used in the consensual process was similar to the one described in consensual qualitative research (CQR; Hill, Thompson, and Williams 1997; Hill et al. 2005), although the unit of study was a focus group rather than an individual. Because of member interactions in the two groups, using CQR to analyze general, typical, or variant themes independently among individuals was compromised. Rather, transcripts were analyzed according to the degree of uniform consensus reached by each group during a discussion of the microaggressive episode. As qualitative research is ultimately about the study of experience or experiences, using a modified CQR procedure to arrive at consensus was considered an appropriate methodology (Polkinghorne 2005). Once consensus was reached in the large group, the team members were asked to individually extract core ideas from the domains. Core ideas are defined as a summary or abstract derived from the domains that integrate the data in a holistic fashion linked to the context of the phenomenon under study. Once accomplished, the members of the team presented their individual analysis to one another, reached consensus about their contributions in a group meeting, and presented it to the auditors. The roles of the auditors, as prescribed in CQR, were threefold: (1) compare and contrast the work of the independent team members, (2) minimize the effects of groupthink by encouraging divergent perspectives, and (3) help finalize the themes in a group working session. The results of both focus groups were then combined.

Results

The following section provides examples of the themes gleaned from the combined focus group transcripts. In addition, the messages conveyed by each microaggression to the recipient and the intent of the aggressor are explicated to reach a deeper understanding of their meanings. Eight microaggressive themes were identified. There were, however, several microaggressive incidents that could not be classified under any of these themes and/or did not receive group consensus to develop an additional category. Thus, we used the category "undeveloped incidents/responses" to include these incidents.

Theme 1: Alien in Own Land

This theme emerges from both focus groups and can be described as a microaggression that embodies the assumption that all Asian Americans are foreigners or foreign-born. An example of this theme was universally voiced by Asian Americans of all ethnicities and manifested in questions or remarks like "Where are you from?" "Where were you born?" or "You speak good English." The participants were often torn between whether the comments were well-intentioned expressions of interest in them or perceptions that they were foreigners and did not belong in America. Furthermore, the meaning construed by recipients is that they were different, were less than others, and could not possibly be "real" Americans. That this phenomenon has empirical reality was a finding that white Americans, on an implicit level, equated "white" and "American" with one another while Asian and African Americans were less likely associated with the term "American" (DeVos and Banaji 2005).

On the whole, the participants did not see the questions or "compliments" as benign and curious, but disturbing and uncomfortable. One Chinese American participant shared that while she was working in a restaurant, a white customer came in and attempted to converse with her in Japanese. She interpreted the behavior as the person perceiving her as a foreigner and not fluent in English. Worse yet, the person could not distinguish between Chinese and Japanese Americans. The focus group members did not perceive the intent of the questions to be overtly malevolent. They believed the person might have been attempting to establish a relationship with the Chinese American and might have wanted to indicate that he was not like other white Americans and could speak an Asian language.

Theme 2: Ascription of Intelligence

This theme also emerges from both focus groups. It is described as a microaggression that occurs when a degree of intelligence is assigned to an Asian American based on his or her race. Many of the participants described teachers and fellow students making statements such as "You are really good at math," "You people always do well in school," or "If I see lots of Asian students in my class, I know it's going to be a hard class." The message conveyed is that all Asians are bright and smart, especially in math and science. Interestingly, the work on stereotype threat suggests that this belief is shared by many whites, and that it may actually depress academic performance among them when in the presence of Asian Americans (Steele 1997; Steele and Aronson 1995).

The participants believed that the conscious intent of these statements was to compliment Asian Americans, since being good at math was perceived by aggressors as a positive quality. However, the impact of assuming Asian Americans are good at math can be harmful. Participants describe feeling pressured to conform to a stereotype that they did not endorse, particularly if they were not good at math or did not enjoy it. In essence, they expressed feelings of being trapped. One Korean woman, for example, described her coworkers bringing every math question for her to solve. Not only did it seem to operate from a stereotype, but it added pressure to help them, and resulted in a heavier workload for the woman. She also expressed discomfort at another major side effect: Asian Americans were viewed as intelligent while other people of color were perceived as less intelligent. It created tensions between her and other black and Latino coworkers.

Theme 3: Denial of Racial Reality

Participants of all Asian ethnic backgrounds shared that many microaggressions invalidate their experiences of discrimination. In one case, a Vietnamese American male was told that "Asians are the new whites." The participant in the study indicated that the remark dismissed his experiences of racism, indicated that Asians experience no discrimination, and suggested that inequities do not exist for Asians and that they have made it in society. In other words, the Vietnamese male felt that the perpetrator saw Asians as a model minority, similar to whites, and experience minimal socioeconomic or educational disadvantages. While the intent of the aggressor may be to compliment the Asian American individual by saying that Asians are more successful than other people of color, the negating message is that Asians do not experience racism—denying their experiential reality of bias and discrimination.

Theme 4: Exoticization of Asian American Women

A fourth theme found in both focus groups is exoticization of Asian American women who are relegated to an exotic category. One Chinese American women stated, "White men believe that Asian women are great girlfriends, wait hand and foot on men, and don't back-talk or give them shit. Asian women have beautiful skin and are just sexy and have silky hair." One Korean American woman indicated that she is frequently approached by white men who are very forthcoming with their "Asian fetishes" of subservience and pleasing them sexually. Nearly all members of the focus groups interpreted these microaggressions as indicating that Asian women are only needed for the physical needs of white men and nothing more. Again, participants felt that the intent of the aggressor in these situations may be to praise Asian women for their ability to take care of a man's every need. One participant was quite vocal in stating that the continual subjugation of Asian American women to roles of sexual objects, domestic servants, and exotic images of Geishas, ultimately "equates our identities to that of passive companions to White men." Many of the participants also suggested that the exotic image of Asian American women also serves as an unconscious backlash to feminist values and that it potentially creates antagonism with white women as well.

Theme 5: Invalidation of Interethnic Differences

This theme is most closely associated with the statement "All Asians look alike." One Filipino American woman stated, "I am always asked, 'are you Chinese?'" Another example of this is conveyed by a Chinese American who stated that new acquaintances oftentimes make statements like, "Oh, my ex-girlfriend was Chinese, or my neighbor was Japanese." These microaggressions tend to minimize or deny differences that may exist between interethnic groups or the existence of other Asian American groups. Participants believed the microaggression suggests that all Asian Americans are alike and that differences between groups do not exist and/or do not matter. The intent of the aggressor in this situation is to express that they are familiar with Asians, but instead the message received is that the aggressor assumes that all Asians are Chinese or Japanese. Moreover, it is assumed by the aggressor that most Asians are familiar with each other, regardless of their Asian ethnic background.

Theme 6: Pathologizing Cultural Values/Communication Styles

Another microaggression theme involves the perception of cultural values and communication styles other than that of the white majority as being less desirable or indicators of deficits. One Chinese American woman expressed exasperation at how class participation (usually verbal) is valued strongly in academic settings and that grades are often based upon it. Because of Asian cultural values that emphasize the value of silence, less verbal Asians are often perceived as lacking in interest, disengaged, or inattentive by the teacher. Many of the participants felt disadvantaged, for example, when verbal participation in class was graded. They felt forced to conform to Western norms and values ("talking more") when such behavior violated their cultural upbringing. Although the Asian participants could see that educators might be attempting to enforce an objective grading standard, they unintentionally negated traditional Asian cultural values and penalized their Asian American students. Another example was relayed by a Vietnamese American male who described being derided and teased by friends for using chopsticks as a utensil. He stated that the message was quite clear; eating with forks, knives, and spoons is the right/correct way to eat and "the American way."

Theme 7: Second-Class Citizenship

Being treated as a lesser being or second-class citizen was another common experience. A number of Asian Americans relayed similar stories of whites being given preferential treatment as consumers over Asian American customers. A typical story involved a Korean American female who told of dining with white friends. Although she frequently ordered the wine, her friends were usually asked to taste and approve the wine selection. She would often feel snubbed because whites were believed to be more knowledgeable about wine, and their opinions were more important. Another Asian American woman described how her eight family members were taken to a table in the back of the restaurant, even though there were available tables elsewhere. She interpreted the action to mean that they were lesser customers and did not deserve a table in the front of the restaurant. The message, they believed, was that Asian Americans are not deserving of good service and are lesser than their white counterparts.

Theme 8: Invisibility

This theme is used to label incidents that involve the experience of being overlooked without the conscious intention of the aggressor. Experiences with the theme of invisibility are commonplace among Asian American individuals of all ethnic groups, who shared that they were often left out whenever issues of race were discussed or acknowledged. One Chinese American female stated, "Like even most race dialogues are like very black and white . . . like sometimes I feel like there's a lot of talk about black and white, and there's a huge Asian population here and where do we fit into that?" Another example involved an Asian American appointed to a committee and having someone suggest that they needed "to appoint a person of color" to the group as well. The messages being conveyed were that Asians are not an ethnic minority group, they experience little or no discrimination, and their racial concerns are unimportant. In addition, the Asian participants felt trapped in that when issues of race were discussed, they were considered like whites, but were never fully accepted by their white peers.

Theme 9: Undeveloped Incidents/Responses

There were a number of stories told by participants that could not be categorized easily. The eight themes identified above seemed universally endorsed by the informants. Some of the incidents, however, were mentioned by one or two individuals in the group, and it was difficult to determine the degree of consensus. It is believed that with more time and probing, it might have been possible to more clearly identify a particular theme. For example, one Chinese American woman described an experience she had while she was driving her mother's car, with her Chinese name and last name on the license plate. She recalled being pulled over despite the fact that she was in the middle of a pack of three cars that were all going relatively the same speed. The stereotype operating here was that Asians are poor drivers, and therefore she was singled out. Another example of the stereotype theme occurred when a gay Vietnamese male shared that an online dating site posted a statement that read, "No Asians, real men only." The message being conveyed in this situation was that Asian men do not fit the masculine qualities of whites and therefore are not deemed as "real" men.

Discussion

The primary purpose of this study was to identify the types and dynamics of racial microaggressions experienced by Asian Americans. Although the eight racial microaggression themes seemed to be universally endorsed by Asian Americans in both focus groups, caution must be exercised in generalizing these findings to all Asian American groups. Our study consisted of only ten participants, did not include all Asian ethnicities, and was not gender-balanced. There was only one male participant, for example, which may make these themes gender-specific. Although such an argument can be made, especially with respect to the exoticization of Asian women, sufficient anecdotal and scholarly literature suggests that the other seven are commonly mentioned by Asian Americans of both genders (Yoo and Lee 2005; Wong and Halgin 2006). Nevertheless, future studies might explore how gender may potentially interact with race and influence the types of microaggressions likely to be experienced by both women and men.

It could also be argued that the "second-class citizenship" theme arose from our interview questions that used the phrase and may have artificially created the category. Although we were cognizant of this potential problem, we also defined the category as "inferior treatment of Asian Americans in preference to others over them." Thus, we believe that the commonalities of these microaggressive incidents are more important than the categorical name as the theme "inferior/ lesser treatment" could have been used instead. In addition, a reanalysis of our transcripts revealed that an overwhelming number of microaggressive incidents classified under this theme arose from the previous six questions, prior to using the term "second-class citizen."

Our study provides strong support that microaggressions are not minimally harmful and possess detrimental consequences for the recipients. Most participants described strong and lasting negative reactions to the constant racial microaggressions they experienced from well-intentioned friends, neighbors, teachers, coworkers, and colleagues. They described feelings of belittlement, anger, rage, frustration, and alienation and of constantly being invalidated. Common comments from the groups were they felt trapped, invisible, and unrecognized. Although we wanted to more clearly identify how the Asian American participants behaviorally responded to what they perceived as a racial microaggression, the strategies they used to deal with it, and the impact it had on them, the focus group members spent the majority of time (1) describing microaggressive events, (2) interpreting what the message meant to them, and (3) talking about the intent of the perpetrator.

Interestingly, most of the participants acknowledged that the majority of those who engaged in microaggressions did so unintentionally, and the perpetrators often perceived their own remarks or actions in a positive light (interest in the Asian American person: "Where were you born?"). Nevertheless, most of the Asian American participants were clear that the remarks reflected a biased worldview that tended to communicate something negative and disrespectful about their group. In general, it appears that most of the Asian American participants experienced psychological conflict and distress because of several dilemmas they faced.

First, they remarked that it was often difficult to determine whether a microaggression occurred. Were they being oversensitive or misreading the remarks or questions? They described spending considerable cognitive energy trying to discern the motives of the person and/or dealing with inner turmoil and agitation caused by the event. A few stated that it was often easier to deal with a clearly overt act of bias than microaggressions that often created a "guessing game."

Second, most of the racial microaggressions that occurred came from peers, neighbors, friends, or authority figures. It disturbed them that personal or respected acquaintances could make such insensitive or hurtful remarks. What bothered them most, however, was their occasional tendency to "make excuses" for friends by rationalizing away their biases and by denying their own racial reality. Although we did not specifically explore the differential impact of microaggressions from acquaintances versus strangers, it appears that some of the participants felt that microaggressive behaviors were easier to handle and less problematic when they came from strangers.

Third, many expressed severe conflict about whether to respond to microaggressions given that most were unintentional and outside the level of awareness of the perpetrator. Pointing out a microaggression to a friend, for example, generally resulted in denial, defensiveness, and a negative outcome for the relationship. A few shared that they simply were at a loss for how to respond, or that the incident occurred so quickly the chance for resolution had long passed. They described being angered and upset without any recourse other than to "stew on it." Some indicated being especially angry at themselves when they finally thought of what they could have said or done ("Damn it, that's what I should have said"). Again, we did not explore this aspect of the participants' inner turmoil: blaming themselves for not having a comeback and having to deal with the agitation for a prolonged period of time. We can only conclude that the emotional turmoil could be long-lasting and take a psychological toll on the recipient.

Last, deciding to respond also had major consequences. Some of the informants stated that responding with anger, striking back, or confronting the person generally did no good. It only served to make the victim appear "paranoid" or suggest that the responder had some major personal problem. Unfortunately, our study did not explore the adaptive strategies used effectively by Asian American participants. In a future study it will be important to explore more deeply the psychological impact microaggressions had on the recipients, how they handled the situation, what outcome resulted, and what they would have done differently upon reflection.

Our study also points out that microaggressions often play a role in denying the racial reality of Asian Americans and strongly perpetuate the "model minority" myth. As mentioned previously, there is a strong belief that they are somehow immune to the effects of racism (Liang, Li, and Kim 2004; Wong and Halgin 2006). Testimony from Asian Americans indicates that racial microaggressions are very hurtful and distressing to them. Besides the individual pain suffered by Asians in America, the belief that they fare better than other minority groups in achieving success in education and employment has major social implications. First, when the model minority myth is endorsed, it can become a justifiable reason to ignore the problem of discrimination against Asian Americans and can be used as a convenient rationale to neglect them in research and intervention programs (Miller 1992; Wong and Halgin 2006). Second, it is often used by some to reaffirm the belief in a democratic society in which any group can be successful if they work hard enough or possess the right values. The result is to minimize racism or societal oppression as important forces in how minority groups thrive in America (Sue and Sue 2003). Third, the model minority myth can foster hard feelings and interethnic conflicts between Asian Americans and other groups of color. This was constantly mentioned in the themes above. Thus, it is important for social scientists and the general public to possess a realistic picture of Asian Americans and to understand the many overt and covert manifestations of racism directed at them.

Our study also potentially adds meaning to the original taxonomy of microaggressions proposed by Sue et al. (2007). Four of eight themes were similar and/or overlapping: alien in own land, ascription of intelligence, pathologizing cultural values/communication styles, and second-class citizen. The four other themes, color blindness, criminality/assumption of criminal status, denial of individual racism, and myth of meritocracy, did not arise from our focus groups. It is important to note that the current study also identified four themes not originally proposed in the Sue et al. (2007) taxonomy: denial of racial reality, exoticization of Asian American women, invalidation of interethnic differences, and invisibility.

One major explanation is the strong possibility that different racial groups may be more likely to experience certain classes of microaggressions than others. Asian Americans, for example, may be more likely than African Americans to experience microaggressions with themes that revolve around "alien in own land," "invisibility," and "invalidation of interethnic differences." This statement is not meant to suggest that blacks may not also be victim to these racial microaggression themes, but they may be more prone than Asian Americans to experience racial microaggressions around other themes, like "assumption of criminal status" and "color blindness." Furthermore, the form that microaggressions take in a similar category may be quite different between two racial groups. The "ascription of intelligence" theme for Asian Americans (intelligent and good in math and science) is contrasted to that of African Americans (intellectually inferior). In addition, a closer analysis of twelve themes derived from both studies (collapsing the four common ones) reveals the possibility of further coalition into a higher order category. For example, the "denial of racial reality" theme is very similar in its effects to "color blindness." It is clear that further research regarding the taxonomy of microaggressions and their culture-specific manifestations would be valuable in clarifying these issues.

Although the qualitative method used in this study was rich and informative, it would be helpful to begin developing survey scales or instruments that allow for and supplement the qualitative findings on Asian American racial microaggressions. Fortunately, there has been an increasing number of studies addressing the issue of perceived discrimination against Asian Americans (Noh et al. 1999; Barry and Grillo 2003), quantification of coping strategies (Yoo and Lee 2005), and the development of inventories to measure race-related stress among Asian Americans (Liang, Li, and Kim 2004). Indeed, the latter researchers have developed the Asian American Racism-Related Stress Inventory (AARRSI), a twenty-nine-item Likert-type scale consisting of three subscales: general racism, sociohistorical, and perpetual foreigner. Although reliability and validity appear good, it is the specific items that seem very consistent with our qualitative findings. For example, the AARRSI contains items such as "At a restaurant you notice that a White couple who came in after you is served first," "You are asked where you are really from," and "Someone you do not know asks you to help him/her fix his/her computer."

The experiential reality of Asian Americans has continued to indicate the existence of racial microaggressions, but their ambiguous and subtle nature makes them difficult to identify and quantify (Sue et al. 2007). Sue (2003) has often stated that the task in the study of subtle and implicit racism is "to make the invisible, visible." Using the categories developed in this study and combining them with the conceptual items of the AARRSI may prove fruitful as a guide to developing items that allow for their measurement and ultimate unmasking of Asian American microaggressions.

Appendix: Interview Protocol

Script for Asian American Facilitator

Hi, my name is "facilitator." Thank you for coming here today to participate in this focus group. The purpose of this group is to gain a better understanding of day-to-day discrimination and experiences of subtle racism. I am sure that you are familiar with overt forms of discrimination such as racial slurs or hate crimes. However, today we are interested in hearing about your experiences of subtle acts of being discriminated against because of your race. These experiences may have occurred in any setting or at anytime in your life. We will be asking you some questions that we encourage you to answer to the best of your ability and we recognize that many of you will have unique experiences of being subtly discriminated against. There are no wrong answers.

At this time, I'd like to introduce "observer," who will be a nonparticipating member of our group today. He/she is here to record our conversation so that I can be involved in the group without having to take too many notes. Okay, so, I am going to give everyone a form now which basically states that your participation in this group is entirely voluntary and that you may decline to participate and leave the group at any time. Please read this sheet carefully before signing it. It discusses potential risks to you as members of this group as well as the use of audiotaping during this session. I'd like to give everyone the opportunity to ask any questions they may have before we begin the group. *Question/Answer.* ...

Statement of Confidentiality

We will be audiotaping this session in an effort to maintain the integrity of your dialogue. However, your identities will not be revealed to anyone, and only the researchers will have access to this tape. This discussion is to be considered confidential, and we would hope that you will all respect each other rights to privacy by not repeating any portion of this discussion outside of this session.

Opening Question

At this time we would like for each of you to say your first name, your occupation, and why you are interested in participating in this study.

General Question

Asian Americans often have experiences in which they are subtly, invalidated, discriminated against, and made to feel uncomfortable because of their race. In thinking about your daily experiences, could you describe a situation in which you witnessed or were personally subtly discriminated against because of your race?

Interview Questions

- What are some subtle ways that people treat you differently because of your race?
- Describe a situation in which you felt uncomfortable, insulted, or disrespected by a comment that had racial overtones.
- Think of some of the stereotypes that exist about your racial group. How have others subtly expressed their stereotypical beliefs about you?
- In what ways have others made you feel "put down" because of your cultural values or communication style?
- In what ways have people subtly expressed that "the White way is the right way"?
- In what subtle ways have others expressed that they think you're a second-class citizen or inferior to them?
- How have people suggested that you do not belong here because of your race?
- What have people done or said to invalidate your experiences of being discriminated against?

Transition Questions

- What are some of the ways that you dealt with these experiences?
- What do you think the overall impact of your experiences has been on your lives?

Ending Questions

So today you shared several experiences of subtle discrimination. Some of you said. . . .
There were several themes that were consistent across many of your experiences. These
   themes include. . . .
Does that sound correct? If not, what themes might you add?

482 | SUE, BUCCERI, LIN, NADAL, AND TORINO

NOTE

Originally published in *Cultural Diversity and Ethnic Minority Psychology* 13 (1): 72–81, 2007. ©2007, reprint by permission.

REFERENCES

American Counseling Association. 1999. *Racism: Healing Its Effects.* Alexandria, VA: American Counseling Association.

Banaji, M. R. 2001. "Implicit Attitudes Can Be Measured." Pp. 117–150 in H. L. Roediger, III, J. S. Nairne, I. Neath, and A. Surprenant, eds., *The Nature of Remembering: Essays in Honor of Robert G. Crowder.* Washington, DC: American Psychological Association.

Banaji, M. R., C. Hardin, and A. J. Rothman. 1993. "Implicit Stereotyping in Person Judgment." *Journal of Personality and Social Psychology* 65: 272–281.

Barry, D. T., and C. M. Grillo. 2003. "Cultural, Self-Esteem, and Demographic Correlates of Perception of Personal and Group Discrimination among East Asian Immigrants." *American Journal of Orthopsychiatry* 73: 223–229.

Biernat, M. 2003. "Toward a Broader View of Social Stereotyping." *American Psychologist* 58: 1019–1027.

Chakraborty, A., and K. McKenzie. 2002. "Does Racial Discrimination Cause Mental Illness?" *British Journal of Psychiatry* 180: 475–477.

Delgado, R., and J. Stefancic. 1992. "Images of the Outsider in American Law and Culture: Can Free Expression Remedy Systemic Social Ills?" *Cornell Law Review* 77: 1258–1297.

Delucchi, M., and H. D. Do. 1996. "The Model Minority Myth and Perceptions of Asian-Americans as Victims of Racial Harassment." *College Student Journal* 30: 411–414.

DeVos, T., and M. R. Banaji. 2005. "American = White?" *Journal of Personality and Social Psychology* 88: 447–466.

Dovidio, J. F., and S. L. Gaertner. 2000. "Aversive Racism and Selection Decisions: 1989 and 1999." *Psychological Science* 11: 315–319.

Dovidio, J. F., S. L. Gaertner, K. Kawakami, and G. Hodson. 2002. "Why Can't We All Just Get Along? Interpersonal Biases and Interracial Distrust." *Cultural Diversity and Ethnicity Minority Psychology* 8: 88–102.

Fassinger, R. E. 2005. "Paradigms, Praxis, Problems, and Promise: Grounded Theory in Counseling Psychology Research." *Journal of Counseling Psychology* 52: 156–166.

Hill, C. E., B. J. Thompson, S. A. Hess, S. Knox, E. N. Williams, and N. Ladany. 2005. "Consensual Qualitative Research: An Update." *Journal of Counseling Psychology* 52: 196–205.

Hill, C. E., B. J. Thompson, and E. N. Williams. 1997. "A Guide to Conducting Consensual Qualitative Research." *Counseling Psychologist* 25: 517–572.

Hu-DeHart, E. 1995. "Ethnic Studies in U.S. Higher Education: History, Development, and Goals." Pp. 696–707 in J. A. Banks and C. A. M. Banks, eds., *Handbook of Research on Multicultural Education.* New York: Macmillan.

Hyun, J. 2005. *Breaking the Bamboo Ceiling.* New York: HarperCollins.

Johnson, S. 1988. "Unconscious Racism and the Criminal Law." *Cornell Law Review* 73: 1016–1037.

Jones, J. M. 1997. *Prejudice and Racism.* 2nd ed. Washington, DC: McGraw-Hill.

Kim, J. G. S. 2002. "Racial Perceptions and Psychological Well Being in Asian and Hispanic Americans." *Dissertation Abstracts International* 63 (2-B): 1033B.

Krueger, R. A. 1994. *Focus Groups: A Practical Guide for Applied Research.* 2nd ed. Thousand Oaks, CA: Sage.

———. 1998. *Analyzing and Reporting Focus Group Results.* Thousand Oaks, CA: Sage.

Lawrence, C. 1987. "The Id, the Ego, and Equal Protection: Reckoning with Unconscious Racism." *Stanford Law Review* 39: 317–388.

Liang, C. T. H., L. C. Li, and B. S. K. Kim. 2004. "The Asian American Racism-Related Stress Inventory: Development, Factor Analysis, Reliability, and Validity." *Journal of Counseling Psychology* 51: 103–114.

Matsuda, M., C. Lawrence, R. Delgado, and K. Crenshaw, eds. 1993. *Words That Wound: Critical Race Theory, Assaultive Speech, and the First Amendment.* Boulder, CO: Westview.

Miles, M. B., and A. M. Huberman. 1994. *Qualitative Data Analysis: An Expanded Sourcebook.* 2nd ed. Thousand Oaks, CA: Sage.

Miller, S. K. 1992. "Asian Americans Bump Against Glass Ceilings." *Science* 258: 1224–1226.

Nakanishi, D. T. 1995. "Asian Pacific Americans and Colleges and Universities." Pp. 683–695 in J. A. Banks and C. A. M. Banks, eds., *Handbook of Research on Multicultural Education.* New York: Macmillan.

Noh, S., M. Beiser, V. Kaspar, F. Hou, and J. Rummens. 1990. "Perceived Racial Discrimination, Depression and Coping: A Study of Southeast Asian Refugees in Canada." *Journal of Health and Social Behavior* 40: 193–207.

Patton, M. Q. 1990. *Qualitative Evaluation and Research Methods.* Thousand Oaks, CA: Sage.

Pierce, C. 1995. "Stress Analogs of Racism and Sexism: Terrorism, Torture, and Disaster." Pp. 277–293 in C. Willie, P. Rieker, B. Kramer, and B. Brown, eds., *Mental Heath, Racism, and Sexism.* Pittsburgh: University of Pittsburgh Press.

Pierce, C., J. Carew, D. Pierce-Gonzalez, and D. Willis. 1978. "An Experiment in Racism: TV Commercials." Pp. 62–88 in C. Pierce, ed., *Television and Education.* Beverly Hills, CA: Sage.

Polkinghorne, D. E. 2005. "Language and Meaning: Data Collection in Qualitative Research." *Journal of Counseling Psychology* 52: 137–145.

President's Initiative on Race. 1998. *One America in the Twenty-First Century.* Washington, DC: Government Printing Office.

Saint-Germain, M. A., T. L. Bassford, and G. Montano. 1993. "Surveys and Focus Groups in Health Research with Older Hispanic Women." *Qualitative Health Research* 3: 341–367.

Seal, D. W., L. M. Bogart, and A. A. Ehrhardt. 1998. "Small Group Dynamics: The Utility of Focus Group Discussions as a Research Method." *Group Dynamics: Theory, Research, and Practice* 2: 253–266.

Sleeter, C. E., and D. D. Bernal. 2004. "Critical Pedagogy, Critical Race Theory, and Antiracist Education." In J. A. Banks and C. A. M. Banks, eds., *Handbook of Research on Multicultural Education.* San Francisco: Jossey-Bass.

Smedley, A., and B. D. Smedley. 2005. "Race as Biology Is Fiction, Racism as a Social Problem Is Real." *American Psychologist* 60: 16–26.

Solorzano, D., M. Ceja, and T. Yosso. 2000. "Critical Race Theory, Racial Microaggressions, and Campus Racial Climate: The Experiences of African American College Students." *Journal of Negro Education* 69: 60–73.

Steele, C. M. 1997. "A Threat in the Air: How Stereotypes Shape Intellectual Identity and Performance." *American Psychologist* 52: 613–629.

Steele, C. M., and J. Aronson. 1995. "Stereotype Threat and the Intellectual Test Performance of African Americans." *Journal of Personality and social Psychology* 69: 797–811.

Sue, D. W. 2003. *Overcoming Our Racism: The Journey to Liberation.* San Francisco:: Jossey-Bass.

Sue, D. W., C. M. Capodilupo, G. C. Torino, J. M. Bucceri, A. M. B. Holder, M. E. Esquilin, et al. 2007. "Racial Microaggressions in Everyday Life: Implications for Counseling." *American Psychologist* 62 (4): 271–286.

Sue, D. W., and D. Sue. 2003. *Counseling the Culturally Diverse: Theory and Practice.* New York: John Wiley.

Thompson, C. E., and H. A. Neville. 1999. "Racism, Mental Health, and Mental Health Practice." *Counseling Psychologist* 27: 155–223.

Thompson, V. L. S., A. Bazile, and M. Akbar. 2004. "African Americans' Perceptions of Psychotherapy and Psychotherapists." *Professional Psychology: Research and Practice* 35: 19–26.

Tinsley-Jones, H. 2003. "Racism: Calling a Spade a Spade." *Psychotherapy: Theory, Research, Practice, Training* 40: 179–186.

Williams, D. R., H. W. Neighbors, and J. S. Jackson. 2003. "Racial/Ethnic Discrimination and Health: Findings from Community Studies." *American Journal of Public Health* 93: 200–208.

Wong, F., and R. Halgin. 2006. "The 'Model Minority,' Bane or Blessing for Asian Americans?" *Journal of Multicultural Counseling and Development* 34: 38–49.

Yoo, H. C., and R. M. Lee. 2005. "Ethnic Identity and Approach-Type Coping as Moderators of the Racial Discrimination/Well-Being Relation in Asian Americans." *Journal of Counseling Psychology* 52: 497–506.

STUDY QUESTIONS

(1) Lisa Park candidly reflects on the events leading up to her sister's tragic suicide. How did the experience of "otherness" influence Park's sister's sense of worth? What was the relationship between race and beauty in her sister's bout with mental illness? What effect did the model minority stereotype have on the mental health of Park and her sister?

(2) Silence is a major theme in Lisa Park's recounting of her sister's suicide. What factors influenced the Park family to be silent about the "personal" problems that Lisa's sister was experiencing? What effect did this silence have on Lisa and her sister? In what contexts did Lisa and her sister remain silent in the face of racism? What role did her sister's suicide have in the family silence?

(3) Park illustrates, through a letter to her sister, how the model minority myth is a destructive force in the Asian American community today. She poses a dismal view of mental health and its relationship to the community, even asking, at one point, "Why would you want to place yourself into the hands of an institution that seeks to resocialize you into the environment that made a mess of you in the first place?" What are the social forces in the larger society and within the community that pushed her sister toward multiple suicide attempts? What obstacles prevented her sister and her family from seeking mental health counseling? To what extent do her sister's tragic experiences mirror the experiences of young people growing up in the Asian American community? What lessons can we draw from this tragedy?

(4) How did the September 11 terrorist attacks on the United States shift the racial paradigms of everyday Americans, specifically in the way they viewed South Asian Americans, Arab Americans, and Muslim Americans? What was the relationship between religion and racial formation in the aftermath of the attacks? How did the 9/11 attacks influence public opinion about racial profiling and deportation?

(5) How do Maira and other scholars define "cultural citizenship"? How does cultural citizenship relate to immigration? What were the three distinct ways in which South Asian immigrant youth understood and practiced cultural citizenship? Describe some concrete examples that illustrate these three distinct forms of cultural citizenship.

(6) According to psychologist Derald Wing Sue and his colleagues, what are racial microaggressions? How do racial microaggressions differ from "old-fashioned" forms of racism? What do racial microaggressions look like? Can "positive" stereotyping serve as a type of racial microaggression? Why or why not?

(7) What were the eight distinct ways that Sue and his colleagues found that Asian Americans experienced racial microaggressions? What effects did these racial microaggressions have on Asian Americans' social interactions in school, work, and their personal lives? Are there any other racial microaggressions that were not included in Sue's study?

SUGGESTED READINGS

Ancheta, Angelo N. 1998. *Race, Rights, and the Asian American Experience*. New Brunswick, NJ: Rutgers University Press.

Bow, Leslie. 2010. *Partly Colored: Asian Americans and Racial Anomaly in the Segregated South*. New York: New York University Press.

Das Gupta, M. 2004. "A View of Post-9/11 Justice from below." *Peace Review* 16 (2): 141–148.

Dhingra, Pawan, and Robyn Rodriguez. 2014. *Asian America: Sociological and Interdisciplinary Perspectives*. Cambridge: Polity.

Du, Phuoc Long, and Laura Ricard. 1996. *The Dream Shattered: Vietnamese Gangs in America*. Boston: Northeastern University Press.

Gee, Gilbert C., Michael S. Spencer, Juan Chen, and David Takeuchi. 2007. "A Nationwide Study of Discrimination and Chronic Health Conditions among Asian Americans." *American Journal of Public Health* 97 (7): 1275–1282.

Green, Donald, Dara Strolovitch, and Janelle Wong. 1998. "Defended Neighborhoods, Integration, and Racially Motivated Hate Crime." *American Journal of Sociology* 104 (2): 372–403.

Hamamoto, Darrell Y. 1994. *Monitored Peril: Asian Americans and the Politics of TV Representation.* Minneapolis: University of Minnesota Press.

Hyun, Jane. 2006. *Breaking the Bamboo Ceiling: Career Strategies for Asian Americans.* New York: HarperCollins.

Kurashige, S. 2000. "Beyond Random Acts of Hatred: Analyzing Urban Patterns of Anti-Asian Violence." *Amerasia Journal* 26 (1): 208–231.

Lien, Pei-te. 1997. *The Political Participation of Asian Americans: Voting Behavior in Southern California.* New York: Garland.

McClain, Charles J. 1996. *In Search of Equality: The Chinese Struggle Against Discrimination in Nineteenth-Century America.* Berkeley: University of California Press.

Ngai, Mae. 1998. "Legacies of Exclusion: Illegal Chinese Immigration during the Cold War Years." *Journal of American Ethnic History* 18: 3–35.

———. 2002. "From Colonial Subject to Undesirable Alien: Filipino Migration, Exclusion, and Repatriation, 1920–1940." Pp. 111–126 in Josephine Lee, Imogene Lim, and Yuko Matsukawa, eds., *Re/collecting Early Asian America: Readings in Cultural History.* Philadelphia: Temple University Press.

Onishi, Yuichiro. 2014. *Transpacific Antiracism: Afro-Asian Solidarity in 20th Century Black America, Japan, and Okinawa.* New York: New York University Press.

Rana, Junaid Akram. 2006. *Forced Return: US Deportations to Pakistan after 9/11.* Madison, WI: American Institute of Pakistan Studies.

Salyer, Lucy E. 1995. *Law Harsh as Tigers: Chinese Immigrants and the Shaping of Modern Immigration Law.* Chapel Hill: University of North Carolina Press.

Sethi, Rita C. 1994. "Smells Like Racism: A Plan for Mobilizing Against Anti-Asian Bias." Pp. 235–250 in Karin Guillar-San Juan, ed., *The State of Asian America: Activism and Resistance in the 1990s.* Boston: South End.

Shih, Johanna. 2006. "Circumventing Discrimination: Gender and Ethnic Strategies in Silicon Valley." *Gender & Society* 20 (2): 177–206.

Shimabukuro, Sadamu. 2001. *Born in Seattle: The Campaign for Japanese American Redress.* Seattle: University of Washington Press.

Takagi, Dana Y. 1993. *Retreat from Race: Asian-American Admissions Policies and Racial Politics.* New Brunswick, NJ: Rutgers University Press.

Watanabe, M. E. 1995. "Asian American Investigators Decry Glass Ceiling in Academic Administration." *Scientist* 9 (11): 1.

Woo, Deborah. 2000. *Glass Ceilings and Asian Americans: The New Face of Workplace Barriers.* Walnut Creek, CA: AltaMira.

Xiong, Yang Sao, and Min Zhou. 2005. "Selective Testing and Tracking for Minority Students in California." Pp. 145–171 in Daniel J. B. Mitchell, ed., *California Policy Options.* Los Angeles: UCLA Lewis Center.

FILMS

Breyer, Richard, and David Coryell (producers). 2003. *North of 49* (43-minute documentary).

Cardillo, Lauren (producer/writer). 2004. *Casting Calls* (47-minute documentary).

Cho, Margaret (writer), and Lorene Machado (producer). 2004. *Cho Revolution* (85-minute stand-up comedy performance).

Cho, Michael (producer/director). 1996. *Another America* (56-minute documentary).

Choy, Christine (director). 2009. *Long Story Short* (53-minute documentary).

Choy, Christine, and Renee Tajima (producers/directors). 1988. *Who Killed Vincent Chin?* (87–minute documentary).

Deep Focus Productions. 2008. *Hollywood Chinese: The Chinese in American Feature Films* (89-minute documentary).

Ina, Satsuki Ina (producer). 1999. *Children of the Camps* (57-minute documentary).

Krauss, Kenneth, and Mariam Jobrani (producers). 2002. *With Us or Against Us: Afghans in America* (27-minute documentary).

Nakasako, Spencer, and Vincent DiGirolamo (coproducers/codirectors). 1982. *Monterey's Boat People* (29-minute documentary).

Okazaki, Steven (producer/director). 1990. *Days of Waiting* (28-minute documentary).

Omori, Emiko, and Chizuko Omori (coproducers). 1999. *Rabbit in the Moon* (85-minute documentary).

Park, Regina (director). 2007. *Never Perfect* (64-minute documentary).

Siegel, Taggart (director). 1988. *Blue Collar and Buddha* (57-minute documentary).

Soe, Valerie (producer/director). 1986. *All Orientals Look the Same* (1.5-minute experimental).

Takagi, J. T., and Hye Jung Park (producers/directors/writers). 1996. *The Women Outside* (53-minute documentary).

Vu, Trac Minh (producer/director). 1997. *Letters to Thien* (57-minute documentary).

Yeager, Tami (producer/director). 2007. *A Dream in Doubt* (57-minute documentary).

PART IX

Behind the Model Minority

21

Jeremy Lin's Model Minority Problem

MAXWELL LEUNG

By the time the New York Knicks and Los Angeles Lakers faced off in New York in February 2012, breakout star Jeremy Lin had led the Knicks to a phenomenal three-game winning streak. Less than four minutes into the first quarter, the Knicks were leading 7 to 4, and Lin threw a perfect half-court pass to Tyson Chandler for an easy two-point slam. As fans in Madison Square Garden cheered the offensive attack, Lin mouthed the words "Come on!" The Knicks pressed their defensive attack, and a player from the Lakers dropped the ball.

The crowd sensed another quick score. Lin scooped up the ball and drove in for an easy layup. The Lakers called a time out and the fans erupted into a frenzy. Less than five minutes in, the Knicks had an uncontested ten-point run. Lin already had nine points and two assists.

That night, a thousand miles away at Grinnell College in Iowa, I joined students from the Asian and Asian American Alliance to cheer on Jeremy Lin. Although we were unaware of it at the time, the game against the Lakers was one of the high points of what came to be known as "Linsanity"—the global cultural phenomenon that accompanied Lin's meteoric rise from an unknown player to an international star.

The excitement began with Lin's first game as a Knick in February 2012 and ended with the announcement of a season-ending knee injury only a month later. Since that time, Lin left the Knicks to join the Houston Rockets and later the Lakers and has struggled as a player. The national adulation that surrounded his breakout performance has largely faded.

The story of how Jeremy Lin became an NBA star is one of denied opportunities, enduring racism, and barrier breaking in professional sports. Although his star has dimmed, Lin's story is worth our attention.

The Model Minority—Again

Jeremy Lin's success in the face of daunting obstacles both challenges the prevailing racial narrative of basketball and reinforces it, offering Asian Americans the chance to see themselves as something other than doctors, engineers, or accountants, while also affirming the belief that they are high achievers. In effect, Linsanity affirmed the myth of Asian Americans as the "model minority."

Through hard work and perseverance, Asian Americans supposedly show how any minority can overcome institutionalized inequality. At the same time, Lin's achievements alone could do little to undo understandings of Asian men, exemplified by the docile honor student, that are at odds with male achievement in sports.

The model minority trope is taken for granted in US media. In June 2012 the Pew Research Center released a report titled "The Rise of Asian Americans," and it was big news. The report *should* have given Asian Americans—who compose nearly 6 percent of the national population—a reason to celebrate. Sampling more than thirty-five hundred people from six of the largest Asian ethnic groups (Chinese, Filipino, Indian, Vietnamese, Korean, and Japanese Americans), Pew's report portrayed Asian Americans as an immigrant group that has successfully broken many social, political, and economic barriers. On the whole, Pew found, Asian Americans are highly educated, possess an admirable work ethic, and earn higher-than-average incomes.

The report goes on to describe Asian Americans' strong family ties and high levels of happiness:

> Most Asian Americans feel good about their lives in the U.S. They see themselves as having achieved economic prosperity on the strength of hard work, a character trait they say is much more prevalent among Asian Americans than among the rest of the U.S. population. Most say they are better off than their parents were at a comparable age. And among the foreign born, very few say that if they had to do it all over again, they would stay in their home country rather than emigrate to the U.S.

Scholars, Asian American organizations, and advocacy groups—from the Japanese American Citizens League to the National Council of Asian Pacific Americans—criticized the report as "one-dimensional," "exclusionary," and full of "overgeneralizations" that portrayed Asian Americans as the torchbearers of American exceptionalism. California Congresswoman Judy Chu, who chairs the Congressional Asian Pacific American Caucus, stated, "I would strongly caution against using the data [in the report] to validate the 'model minority' myth." As she pointed out, "Our community is one of stark contrasts, with significant disparities within and between various subgroups."

For example, another recent report, this time from the Asian American Center for Advancing Justice, showed that while Asian Americans are successful in terms of educational achievement compared to whites, specific ethnic groups (such as Hmong, Cambodian, Laotian, and Vietnamese Americans) have high school graduation rates as low as 61 percent and even lower rates of college graduation—numbers comparable to those of Latinos and African Americans. The Pew Report had lumped all these groups together as "Asian American," ignoring some of the most distressed communities and the economic, health, and other challenges they face.

When research and portraits of Asian Americans are consistently framed this way, Asian Americans are almost always seen as superior to other minority groups in terms of educational achievement, economic stability, and social acceptance. Supposed exemplary Asian cultural values—hard work, perseverance, strong family traditions, a reverence for education, self-reliance, even self-sacrifice—are portrayed as unique among ethnic groups. As this story goes, even when Asian Americans face cultural and linguistic barriers, institutional racism, and other dramatically unequal treatment, they will not only overcome the obstacles, but do so without protest or complaint.

Popular culture has long portrayed Asian American men as geniuses, overachievers, computer geeks, or nerds. They're shy and docile, humble and passive. If Asian American women are presented as exotic and hypersexualized, men are rendered effete, weak, and physically and sexually inferior. Examples range from the insufferable Long Duk Dong in the 1984 film *Sixteen Candles* to William Hung, famous for his cringe-worthy rendition of "She Bangs" on *American Idol* in 2008. The character Raj on the hugely popular sitcom *The Big Bang Theory* is the most recent example of an image of a socially dysfunctional Asian American man. Such representations leave Asian Americans to struggle against broad stereotypes that are as inaccurate as they are negative—especially in a culture that prizes traditional masculinity.

Jeremy Lin's breakout success gave Asian American men a striking respite from these oppressive images. Lin is tall, strong, aggressive, and physically gifted. Far from shy or quiet, he's a powerful player in a physically demanding sport, displaying style and swagger on a huge media stage. The Linsanity phenomenon marked more than just the international embrace of a spectacular new Asian American sports star—it posed a challenge to emasculating stereotypes.

At the same time, Lin could be the poster child for the Pew Report. He was smart and driven, but overlooked by college recruiters and NBA draft scouts, and he bounced from team to team. His hard work and focus—model behavior—paid off in the form of a phenomenal ascent to the upper echelons of a multibillion-dollar sport.

Invisible Man?

The myth of the model minority is central to understanding the story of Jeremy Lin's encounter with discrimination and his subsequent success as a professional basketball player. Likely because he did not fit expectations about what an elite basketball player looks like, Lin was a talented player but flew under the radar. The fact that many college coaches and recruiters later admitted that they'd failed to recognize Lin's talents suggests they couldn't see "past" his Asian features.

As Lin himself said in an interview with ESPN in 2012, "I was very disappointed, discouraged. I'm undrafted, I'm out of Harvard. 'Asian American.' That was kind of the perception everyone had of me and that was kind of the perception I had of myself. And when everyone thinks that, then it's hard to break that."

Yet Asians and Asian Americans who play basketball are not a wholly new phenomenon. There have been Asian players in the NBA—most notably Yao Ming of the Houston Rockets and Wataru Misaka, the first Japanese American to play professional basketball with the New York Knicks in 1947. There have also been standout Asian American college players such as Raymond Townsend, part-Filipino, who played for UCLA in the 1970s; Corey Gaines, part-Japanese, who played for Loyola Marymount University in the 1980s, and Rex Walters, part-Japanese, who played for Kansas in the early 1990s.

As Lin's remarks on ESPN and in a more recent television interview suggest, he *is* the first professional basketball player to deliberately and comfortably claim his Asian American heritage and be acknowledged as such by his fans. He has directly confronted the experience of social invisibility he experienced on his way up. And yet Lin's success as a Knick is still couched in the default language of the model minority: he worked very hard to get to the top. He's got intelligence—not just talent. If African American point guards are the norm in basketball, then Jeremy Lin is an anomaly whose existence demands an explanation.

In his second career appearance, against the Houston Rockets, Lin had an impressive showing, even though his Knicks trailed throughout the game and eventually lost. Late in the third quarter, one of the television sports show hosts commented about Lin's overall performance: "He's a hustler; he runs the show. Very intelligent player. Does the fact that he went to Harvard help that? Absolutely!"

But what *does* Lin's intelligence or Harvard degree have to do with his basketball skills? One could say that all professional athletes need intelligence to perform exceptionally. One might also observe that playing point guard requires especially intelligent play—a successful player in this role must read defenses, make plays, and provide assists. But in relation to race, "intelligence" is a loaded word.

According to sociologist Douglas Hartmann, "because of sport's *de facto* association with bodies and the mind/body dualisms ... African American athletic excellence serves to reinforce racial stereotypes by grounding them in essentialized, biological terms." He continues, "Athletic prowess is believed to be inversely associated with intellectual and/or moral excellence." Reporting and commentary about black basketball players, for example, often refer not to their formal education, but to an "urban experience" of playing basketball in the streets.

In contrast, Lin's "intelligence" on the court was tied explicitly to his Ivy League education, even though Lin began playing the game at his local YMCA and on neighborhood playgrounds in Palo Alto, California. It's the model minority discourse at work: educational achievements are primary, and the physical experience of playing ball is less central.

In the Lin narrative, basketball is a meritocracy based on skill, and those who rise to the top earn their rewards. This reaffirms the classic American story that those "who work hard and possess the right stuff will always prevail"—and *deserve* to, according to sociologist of sport Susan Birrell. Conversely, those who try and fail? They didn't work hard enough.

Trying to Flip the Script

Despite the Asian American basketball players who came before Jeremy Lin, his stunning performance on the national stage confirmed something Asian Americans know, but had rarely witnessed: we can jump, drive, and shoot the ball. According to sociologist Oliver Wang, Linsanity made Asian Americans playing professional basketball "a national concept." Lin's triumph resonated with Asian Americans and many others, and it led some to believe Lin could present a real challenge to longstanding stereotypes.

Not only do Asian Americans hope that Lin is the real deal, a truly talented basketball player of NBA caliber, we also want to see the devotion he has generated translate into real changes in perceptions of Asian Americans. For us, it is hard to overestimate the pure euphoria of seeing this man lead on the court, outmaneuver defenders, and make clutch plays—all with confidence, bravado, and off-court dignity.

This year, the documentary *Linsanity*, directed by Evan Jackson Leong, premiered at the Sundance Film Festival and opened San Francisco's Center for Asian American Media's annual film festival. Audiences cheered, rising to offer a standing ovation. An inspirational basketball story told through Jeremy Lin's eyes, the film documents his rise to stardom.

Although Linsanity lasted just three glorious weeks, Lin still offers a powerful new image of Asian American male sport prowess that both challenges and reaffirms the model minority myth. His success offers a critical commentary on how we understand the contradictory and often frustrating place of Asian Americans in American culture.

In March 2013, *Wall Street Journal* columnist Jeff Yang, discussing the Leong documentary, told eager readers, "Keep your eyes peeled, sports fans. Linsanity may well end up having a sequel." Although Jeremy Lin has faded from basketball stardom, his story, by reaffirming some stereotypes while calling others into question, gives us a way to understand Asian Americans' complicated relationship to American cultural values.

NOTE

Originally published in *Contexts* 12 (3): 52–56, 2013. ©2013 *Contexts*, reprint by permission.

RECOMMENDED RESOURCES

Carrington, Ben. 2010. *Race, Sport and Politics: The Sporting Black Diaspora*. Thousand Oaks, CA: Sage. Using postcolonial theory, cultural studies, and poststructuralist theory, Carrington's work interrogates how race and racial difference is made through the spectacle of sport.

Chou, Rosalind S., and Joe R. Feagin. 2008. *The Myth of the Model Minority: Asian Americans Facing Racism*. Boulder, CO: Paradigm. Chou and Feagin's study of subjects from different nationalities and geographic locales reveals the extent, reach, and penetration of the model minority stereotype.

Fong, Timothy. 2008. *The Contemporary Asian American Experience*. New York: Prentice Hall. Fong's work surveys key contemporary issues impacting Asian Americans and includes a special section on sports.

Hartmann, Douglas. 2000. "Rethinking the Relationships between Sport and Race in American Culture: Golden Ghettos and Contested Terrain." *Sociology of Sport Journal* 17: 229–253. Hartmann's work is a key article that helps problematize the racial spectacle of sport as a hegemonic formation while at the same time acknowledges the potential for racial resistance and change.

Yep, Kathleen S. 2008. *Outside the Paint: When Basketball Ruled at the Chinese Playground*. Philadelphia: Temple University Press. Yep's scholarship is a historical book on the development of Chinese American men's and women's basketball leagues in San Francisco Chinatown from the 1930s to the 1940s.

22

Continuing Significance of the Model Minority Myth

The Second Generation

LISA SUN-HEE PARK

Immigrant life is understood as consisting of constant doubt and justification of one's presence in a foreign land (Yoon 1997). Interviews with the children of immigrants indicate that this insecurity does not end with the immigrant generation. For the second generation, their life consists of constant doubt and justification of their reasons for being in, not a foreign land, but their *own* land. As part of a larger study of second-generation Asian Americans, I interviewed eighty-eight Chinese and Korean American children of immigrants. One of the more remarkable patterns garnered from these interviews with high school and college-age young adults was how strikingly similar all of their responses were in describing their family's migration experience. Regardless of whether they were Chinese American or Korean American, middle-class, working-class, or upper-middle-class, lived in Chicago, Illinois, or Santa Clara, California, every respondent told essentially the same story of migration. In addition, their varying age at migration, gender, and birth order did not have any impact on the basic foundation of their narratives of why and how they arrived in the United States. I was puzzled as to how this could happen. How could the differences in race, class, and region—not to mention the history, culture, and global relationship of China and Korea as two entirely separate countries—not influence these children's retelling of such a seminal familial event?

The respondents shared two basic characteristics in their immigration narrative. First, the children knew very little about the actual experience of their parents' decision to emigrate and their experiences upon arrival. Second, the limited knowledge and memories the children do possess are strikingly similar to one another. This article builds upon a more cursory analysis of second-generation migration narratives provided in an earlier work (Park 2005) by further investigating what is absent and what little is present in these children's stories. I approach these immigration stories as a significant source in understanding second-generation Asian Americans' sense of why they are here and, consequently, how they "fit" into this country.

It is ironic that second-generation Asian Americans—who supposedly embody the stereotypical measures of a "model minority," including hardworking, college educated, law abiding, and so on—feel compelled to constantly justify their presence in the United States, a "nation of immigrants." Few researchers acknowledge this sense of doubt since most continue to believe in the model minority myth. This myth portrays Asian Americans as exemplary models for other minorities based (usually) upon measures of income, education, and public benefit utilization rates (Cheng and Yang 2000; Osajima 2000). However, a number of studies have critiqued these assumptions. For instance, in her study of Indian American youth culture, Maira (2002) concludes that the presumed Asian American "model minority" has little relevance for the substantial numbers of working- and lower-middle-class people in their community. Maira's study points to the growing economic bifurcation of incoming Asian immigrants and their children. Cheng and Yang (2000) also critique this powerful image in their careful study of the vast differences, including class, education, and income, within Asian America.

On its face, the model minority myth is a seemingly positive image that seduces both liberal and conservative political inclinations. The moral "pull yourself up by your bootstraps" lessons regarding individual responsibility and upward economic mobility derived from this imagery continue to hold favor in the current movement to dismantle the social welfare state. The model minority myth wholly endorses the American Dream of meritocracy and democracy with the notion that anyone regardless of race, class, or gender has an equal opportunity to work hard and consequently is justly rewarded for their labor though economic upward mobility. Intrinsic to this myth is the fact that a model minority is a minority nonetheless; racial minorities can pull their bootstraps only so far—tokens notwithstanding.

For example, favorite tokens include Jerry Yang, cofounder of Yahoo, and news anchor Connie Chung, both of whom are mistakenly regarded as normative representatives of Asians in America. By definition and practice, racial minorities do not enjoy the same rights and social status as the majority in the United States. For instance, Delgado (1997) argues that at its founding, the US Constitution explicitly reserved citizenship for white men of property. This initial intent has had a profound legacy in today's racial politics. The notion of a model minority implies not full citizenship rights but, rather, a secondary citizenship reserved for particular minorities who "behave" appropriately and stay in their designated secondary space without complaint. This secondary space is a socially marginal one in which Asian Americans, despite their legal citizenship, continue to hold a foreigner status. Kim (2000) argues that the model minority construction socially defines Asian Americans as an inferior "other." This process of racial "othering" is essential in upholding racial power, or the systemic self-reproduction of the racial status quo. In this way, the model minority myth actually reinforces established racial inequalities and places second-generation Asian Americans within a precarious defensive dilemma in which they must constantly prove their worth as "real" Americans.

Drawing from interviews with children of immigrants, I argue that the model minority myth plays an ongoing role not only in perpetuating the marginal status of Asian Americans, but also in limiting the avenues for progressive social change among the second generation. Not coincidentally, this myth regarding Asian Americans as "well-behaved" and justly rewarded minorities first came about in 1966, during the height of the civil rights movement. In her study of Chinese American children, Vivian Louie (2004, xvii) points out that the myth was "an effective way of disciplining such claims of inequality without ever naming the dominant group's vested interest in the existing paradigm of race relations." Similar to Aihwa Ong's (1987) definition of capitalist discipline, the model minority myth promotes the "enforced and induced compliance" of the second generation with specific political, social, and economic objectives. Ong (1987, 5) defines *discipline* as the "effects of the exercise of power on the subjugated, and the enforced and induced compliance with the political, social, and economic objectives, considered rational and functional for capital production." The model minority myth functions as a political mechanism of control that alters one's sense of reality to justify the unequal social order. What Ong makes clear is that this disciplinary function is at work during times of "noncrisis"; in fact, the power of this disciplinary measure is its stealth nature, whereby unequal institutionalized power relations are surreptitiously encased in a seemingly complimentary or positive façade.

The immigrant narratives by Korean and Chinese American children of immigrants illustrate an underlying, consistent effort to reassert their presence as legitimate within a contested political context that is, at best, ambivalent toward the growing numbers of racially ethnic immigrants. Not surprisingly, these stories follow a distinctly American narrative construction and function to normalize their presence in the United States. As a form of American mythology, the idea of the model minority can be traced back to American Puritanism, which promoted a sense of independence and self-reliance through individual achievement and understood success and failure as a moral distinction (Weiss 1969). Similar to the rags-to-riches stories of the nineteenth century, the model minority myth associates virtue with success and sin with failure. Inevitably, there are disciplinary side effects inherent in this effort. For Asian Americans, deviation from the model minority ideology not only implies a moral shortcoming due to their own individual failure, but also separates them from the American norm, thereby reinforcing their foreigner status.

These migration narrative constructions have a generic or formulaic quality. The stories could describe almost any immigrant group in almost any historical period. It is, in fact, a retelling of the familiar American myth of "national origins," in which the nation is born with the migration of poor peasants who come to the "land of opportunity" with nothing but their determination and hard work and subsequently "melt into the pot." According to Espiritu (2003), the history of conquest and annexation conveniently disappears in this story. It is a truly patriotic drama of rescue and escape from tyranny, whether of poverty or politics. What is not familiar to everyone is that these narratives represent a double-edge sword for Asian Americans. According to this narrative, the role of the good Asian American is that of the perpetual foreigner/victim who must be rescued, welcomed, and domesticated again and again. This scenario is in line with Espiritu's notion of differential inclusion "whereby a group of people is deemed integral to the nation's economy, culture, identity, and power—but integral only or precisely because of their designated subordinate standing" (Espiritu 2003, 47). The role of the perpetual foreigner who "makes it" on his or her own in the land of opportunity requires constant and persistent maintenance.

The logic is paradoxical by design. Asian Americans, as a marginal racial minority, are compelled to adapt their history to fit into an Orientalist drama that requires that they play the foreigner/outsider repeatedly, all in an effort to establish their legitimate membership/insider role within the state. In essence, Asian Americans must be foreign to fit into the United States. At the same time, if they do not adhere to the model minority, they are marginalized/punished as foreign as well. It appears that whether or not one follows the doctrine of the model minority, Asian Americans play the role of the foreigner.

In light of the experiences of racialized inclusion, such as legal subordination, economic exploitation, and cultural degradation, the promise of full, unquestioned social citizenship that motivates the maintenance of the model minority myth is powerful. In the following section, I analyze these narratives in more detail, placing what little information the respondents do provide within current political and economic contexts. I conclude with a discussion of what is missing or absent in these stories and of the implications for social justice.

The American Narrative

In the end, the immigrant narrative, as articulated by the second generation, is more about themselves than of their immigrant parents. The stories represent a particular understanding of why they are here and, subsequently, who they are. There are two basic elements that exist in each rendition of this story: (1) the parents came to the United States for better opportunities and/or education for their children; and (2) once here, the parents experienced significant hardships, which they overcame to a certain extent. These similarities exist regardless of the immigrant's country of origin, time of migration, or access to social and cultural capital. The hardships generally include little or no money, limited English-language proficiency, physically demanding labor, and social isolation. What are missing from these remarkably familiar stories are actual histories of their home country, which include issues such as colonialism, imperialism, and occupation. Their remarkably consistent memories inevitably begin at the moment of their entry into the United States and subsequently follow a familiar narrative trajectory. In line with an implicit "don't ask, don't tell" policy of family interaction, the children know not to ask about certain potentially traumatic events—and migration is one such topic. Joe, a nineteen-year-old Korean American, explained, "We don't talk about our migration experience. We all understand that we rather prefer here than Korea." There is a sense of filial piety or parental respect implied in Joe's remark. To talk about migration has the potential to raise painful events and perhaps even question the parents' decision to emigrate. This is dangerous familial terrain given the tenuous circumstances that immigrant parents may experience. The intense push for economic and social stability by immigrant parents is a direct reaction to the daily insecurities and stresses that plague new immigrants as they endure a marginal existence (Park 1997). To probe further could raise issues that disturb the American Dream and potentially create an uncomfortable situation in which the parents feel compelled to explicitly hide their experiences. Instead, immigrant parents divulge as little as possible and in strategic ways. The children, then, string together bits and pieces of their memories to create a familiar story of immigrant struggle.

Also characteristic of these immigration stories are the practical tones with which they are told. Children of immigrants are careful not to sensationalize their immigration narratives. They try to avoid falling into the easy trap of exoticization. The point of these stories is to illustrate their legitimate place within society, not to heighten their outsider status or foreignness. Mike, a Chinese American college student, illustrates this point:

> It was hard on my dad. All he did was go to school and go to work. He told me that sometimes he was so tired at work at the assembly job that he would just sneak away and sleep under a desk. So I know it was pretty tough, unless he was lying about it. They don't talk about it much.

Mike could have made his point in a variety of ways. Certainly, the imagery of a man so exhausted from his daily labor that he contorts his body into the square frame of a desk for a brief reprieve can be dramatic. Instead, Mike tells the story with an even tone, as if he were reading a grocery list. His tone renders sneaking away and sleeping under a desk a normal strategy to combat sleep deprivation; but more important, that is not the point of his retelling. Rather, there is a clear lesson regarding necessary hard work contained in this narrative.

This is also evident in a story told by Sam, a Chinese American college student, of his father's first few years in the United States:

> My dad was homeless for a while in New York, living in Times Square for a while. He couldn't find a job, so he lived on the streets. I don't think it was too long. He usually uses it to teach us lessons. He doesn't really show any emotion when he talks about it. . . . That's about all they will say about it.

Again, there is a practical, almost casual tone in Sam's retelling: he didn't have a job, so of course he slept on the doorsteps of buildings in Times Square. There is no room for sentimentality in this story about immigrant hardships and upward mobility. Today, Sam's father, a college graduate, works as a "meat technician" at a local supermarket with health and dental insurance—a far cry from his initial migration experience, but a difficult job nonetheless. Sam takes to heart the lessons embedded in his father's story. He ruminated about his father's current job:

> My dad is kind of bitter. He doesn't show it, though. Working for that low pay for so long. He always wants us to do better. He says, "You have to work hard now and reap the benefits later. You have better opportunities than we did, don't let them go." Over and over again.

Although his father does not outwardly complain about his job as a butcher, Sam notices his father's tired, drawn face at the end of a twelve-hour workday. It is obvious to Sam that his father does not enjoy his job, which he has held for over fifteen years.

At nineteen years of age, Sam has worked at a number of jobs already: umpiring for coed softball, shelving books in the engineering library, processing photographs at a local one-hour photo shop, and volunteering as an assistant zookeeper at the city zoo. He is currently an engineering major, but his most rewarding experience thus far is working with animals:

> I was thinking I was probably going to get an engineering job to get financial experience and then explore other occupations to find something that appeals to me. Engineering is just there for the money, for a stable job. I wanted to be a zoologist, but my parents talked me into something more secure.

Sam makes clear that the point of a job is first and foremost financial security. He has learned to separate expectations of happiness from one's career. What little Sam knows about his father's migration has shaped his focus on future financial security. This is a reoccurring theme. For instance, Sarah, a twenty-year-old college student, said this about her parents' migration: "I'm assuming it was hard. They talk about it only in general, not in detail." She then described her parents' current job as contract painters: "They work 7 AM to 5 PM. No benefits. They don't enjoy what they do. It's hard work. They do it for a living, but if they had a choice, they would do something that was easier on them. I have no wish to follow in their footsteps." When asked about her parents' number one priority, Sarah replied, "financially making it." She added, "I've learned you are going to have to work hard to get what you want in life. Not everything is always going to be given to you." These lessons regarding financial security and one's career appear largely consistent across class levels for children of immigrants. For example, Annie, a twenty-year-old Korean American, grew up with a father who worked as an international banker and a mother who stayed at home. Annie took the frustrations of her mother to heart:

> My mom, being a housewife, growing up she always emphasized to my sister and me that she wanted us to work hard. She graduated from Seoul University with a degree in French, but she never really got a chance to use it because she didn't even know English. She always sort of regretted it. That is why she always told us to study hard. She said that it is important so that we don't end up like her, staying at home and wishing that we could have had a career.

Annie notes that she does not really know why her parents immigrated. Her only recollection was that of her older sister, five years her senior: "I know that it was, from what I understand, hard for my sister to be the one to learn English quickly and to translate and communicate for the family. . . . It was a challenge for her. In terms of my parents, I'm not really sure." Annie's sister was nine years old when they immigrated to Southern California.

Some children of immigrants interpret the silence or lack of detail as an ethnic characteristic. Dean, a Korean American college student, said,

> My mom keeps on telling me that she did it, like most Asian families, because their family always comes first. I think they did it for just the children, to get a better education and opportunities. . . . Money was always hard around the house. I don't think we ever got to a point of desperation, but there was never a constant flow of income. They don't talk about it too much. I kind of expect them to, but they don't. In American families, the parent will talk about the hard times, but not Koreans.

In this story, Koreans—and, by extension, Asians—are understood as stoic and humble, in contrast to "Americans." In addition, the boundary between childhood and adulthood is enforced by these silences. The children interpret the silence as a form of parental protection. At the same time, "Asianness," particularly as it is applied to parenting, can also be construed as restrictive or backward. Sarah's view is indicative of this seemingly contradictory interpretation. When asked about her parents' reaction to her future career plans to work for a large information technology firm, she replied,

> My parents are happy with my plans. Of course, they want me to do well, but I don't think I would call them typical Korean parents. They never pushed too hard. Basically, they said, "It's your future and whatever I say won't affect you. It's up to you." They want me to do certain things, but they don't force me.

In this case, a "typical Korean parent" is "pushy" and forces the children into decisions against their will. Evidently, Koreanness or Chineseness is applied for positive and negative purposes. They become important cultural explanations that are used for strategic purposes in immigration narratives. The use-value of these concepts derives from the fact that they can be applied for multiple purposes regardless of their contradictory logic. In the end, the children are careful to paint a sympathetic picture of their parents, whether they use a positive or negative interpretation of Korean or Chinese culture.

The flexibility evident in the children's use of cultural explanations extends to the methods used to assemble a coherent story. Since most of the children were very young during migration or were born in the United States, they rely primarily upon their parents for information. And, apparently, this information is heavily guarded. Li, a twenty-one-year-old Chinese American college student, explained that his parents rarely discussed what life was like immediately after migration: "When we went to New York, my dad visited his brother. They were talking about the old times when they still lived in Hong Kong. To the kids, they don't really talk about it." The children are left to their own devices to fill in this history through a patchwork of sources. They rely on indirect sources to accumulate bits and pieces of their family's history, including overheard "adult" conversations, family pictures, occasional stories from a grandparent, and sometimes school assignments. This was the case for Tim, a twenty-year-old Chinese American college student, who took an ethnic studies course: "I really never talked to my parents about it before. Reading and taking classes definitely got me thinking. I wouldn't even have wondered. I was born here. I figured that they just got to come here." He added,

> I've talked to them about their migration experience after coming to college and being an ethnic studies major; I was reading about these things. You can see your parents' experience through the books, like chronologically where they fit in. I'm pretty sure that everyone in my family who came over here from Taiwan was under that 1965 [immigration] act. Without it, they might not have been able to come over. All their friends did too. . . . The best part about college for me was taking that first Asian American studies class. That's when I switched majors. I was majoring in econ for a year and a half before that.

Given the parents' repeated emphasis on higher education, these students can hardly deny an interview request for a school assignment.

A Disciplinary Narrative

It becomes evident very early on that these young adults have absorbed or "adapted" to American culture quite readily. Their immigration stories, as brief as they are, hit all the right cues to construct the quintessential American tale of its national origins. The myth of the model minority is an essential element in this tale, and the Chinese and Korean American children of immigrants appear to fall in line with this stereotype. A critical analysis of this American narrative reveals what is evidently absent: the disciplinary nature of this narrative.

Writing on the importance of investigating social myths, Richard Slotkin (1973, 4) states, "A people unaware of its myths is likely to continue living by them, though the world around that people may change and demand changes in their psychology, their worldview, their ethics, and their institutions." In the case of the model minority myth, Asian Americans are tightly cast in a role with seemingly little chance for variation. One is either a "good" or "bad" immigrant/minority; there is no gray area in this mythology. A "good" immigrant or model minority is generally defined primarily in economic terms as one who is viewed as contributing greater benefits than costs to the larger mainstream society. In fact, the second generation becomes the primary evidence of their parents' successful or unsuccessful incorporation into the United States. The reality that a model minority designation does not imply full social citizenship or belonging, but is rather a secondary status afforded to those minorities who "behave" and stay in their designated social space, runs directly counter to the American Dream ideology.

The second-generation narratives of migration illustrate how little they actually know about their own family's migration. The bits and pieces of information are made to fit an existing story of the American Dream. There is seemingly little alternative to this powerful disciplinary narrative. The consequences of a "bad" immigrant/minority designation, in which one is viewed as a public burden, can be severe. Examples of the many possible dehumanizing depictions that function to discipline one's social behavior are the constant barrage of images representing the "illegal immigrant" and "welfare queens." Consequently, discourses that counter the Asian American success story are strongly discouraged. For instance, the logic of this disciplinary narrative assumes that hardships experienced by the first generation will dissipate with time. By the second generation, there is no discourse that allows for continued hardships or discrimination. Instead, narratives of "personal responsibility" supplant any discussion of structural or institutional responsibility. Clear examples of this continuing trend are the welfare reform legislation, formally titled the Personal Responsibility and Work Opportunity Reconciliation Act of 1996, and the immigration legislation passed in the same year, the Illegal Immigration Reform and Immigrant Responsibility Act. In line with Robert Park's (1950) traditional notion of assimilation, difficulties in economic or social incorporation of the first generation are understood as functional, or "natural," and temporary. This rationale obscures any questioning of a social structure that maintains a hierarchical system that differentially rewards its members based upon ascribed values and at the same time incessantly promotes a national discourse of meritocracy and equality. The second generation, then, is faced with a thorny situation within this model minority myth. Any difficulties they experience are made invisible or "personal."

Lack of knowledge of one's own history is maintained within a scenario in which children are taught not to ask questions. The practical tone with which the respondents tell their brief stories is an effort to divert an "Orientalizing" or exoticizing gaze, but it also functions to minimize attention to real, legitimate social conditions. Moreover, the consuming focus on financial stability, while understandable as an attempt to be a "good" son/daughter and "good" immigrant/minority, also has its consequences. The cycle of rescue and domestication that accompanies this American national origins narrative is not something to which these children aspire. They must always inhabit the foreigner role, which in this case is depicted by the model minority myth. In fact, the exoticizing effect of this narrative directly counters the goal of the second generation to legitimately or unquestionably belong to American society. I would argue that the model minority myth, and its accompanying disciplinary silence, is a central barrier for Asian Americans seeking to establish their social belonging. This new generation, it appears, requires a new set of questions to scrutinize their individual behavior and, more important, the rationale of larger social institutions and legislation that dictate their behavior in the first place. Clearly, there are significant consequences in the continued treatment of the second generation as foreign and marginal. Asian Americans remain largely invisible in many, if not most, public policy discussions regarding everything from civil rights law and affirmative action to access to mental and physical health care. When they are visible, Asian Americans are strategically used to dismantle progressive gain—putting them in a bizarre position opposite the interests of other racial minorities, though not as full members of the majority.

NOTE

Originally published in *Social Justice* 35 (2):134–144, 2008. ©2008 *Social Justice*, reprint by permission. All names are pseudonyms.

REFERENCES

Cheng, L., and P. Yang. 2000. "The 'Model Minority' Deconstructed." Pp. 449–458 in M. Zhou and J. Gatewood, eds., *Contemporary Asian America: A Multidisciplinary Reader*. New York: New York University Press.

Delgado, R. 1997. "Citizenship." Pp. 318–323 in J. Perea, ed., *Immigrants Out! The New Nativism and the Anti-immigrant Impulse in the United States*. New York: New York University Press.

Espiritu, Y. 2003. *Homebound: Filipino American Lives across Countries, Communities, and Countries*. Berkeley: University of California Press.

Kim, C. 2000. *Bitter Fruit: The Politics of Black-Korean Conflict in New York City*. New Haven, CT: Yale University Press.

Louie, V. 2004. *Compelled to Excel: Immigration, Education, and Opportunity among Chinese Americans*. Stanford, CA: Stanford University Press.

Maira, S. 2002. *Desis in the House: Indian American Youth Culture in New York City*. Philadelphia: Temple University Press.

Ong, A. 1987. *Spirits of Resistance and Capitalist Discipline*. Albany: State University of New York Press.

———. 1999. *Flexible Citizenship: The Cultural Logics of Transnationality*. Durham, NC: Duke University Press.

Osajima, K. 2000. "Asian Americans as the Model Minority: An Analysis of the Popular Press Image in the 1960s and 1980s." Pp. 459–482 in M. Zhou and J. Gatewood, eds., *Contemporary Asian America: A Multidisciplinary Reader*. New York: New York University Press.

Park, K. 1997. *The Korean American Dream: Immigrants and Small Business in New York City*. Ithaca, NY: Cornell University Press.

Park, L. 2005. *Consuming Citizenship: Children of Asian Immigrant Entrepreneurs*. Stanford, CA: Stanford University Press.

Park, R. 1950. *Race and Culture*. Glencoe, IL: Free Press.

Slotkin, R. 1973. *Regeneration through Violence: The Mythology of the American Frontier, 1600–1860*. Norman: University of Oklahoma Press.

Vivian, L. 2004. *Compelled to Excel: Immigration, Education, and Opportunity among Chinese Americans*. Stanford, CA: Stanford University Press.

Weiss, R. 1969. *The American Myth of Success*. New York: Basic Books.

Yoon, In-Jin. 1997. *On My Own: Korean Businesses and Race Relations in America*. Chicago: University of Chicago Press.

23

Racial Anxieties, Uncertainties, and Misinformation

A Complex Picture of Asian Americans and Selective College Admissions

OIYAN POON AND ESTER SIHITE

Entry and access to a college education at one of the nation's top postsecondary institutions has become a public concern only since the mid-twentieth century. Prior to the civil rights era, access to elite, and particularly private, institutions essentially remained an exclusive stronghold of upper-class white elites (Golden 2009; Karabel 2005). The civil rights movement, implementation of affirmative action policies, and the Higher Education Act of 1965 cracked open doors to higher education for the working classes and people of color, including Asian Americans. These developments, along with a public expectation for higher education to serve as a pathway of upward mobility (Haveman and Smeeding 2006), have brought public attention to questions of racial equity in college access. The expectation and trust in educational achievement as a key opportunity for upward mobility in the United States is particularly strong for Asian Americans, who often see few other options for mobility due to pervasive systemic inequalities (Lew 2006; Louie 2004; Sue and Okazaki 1990).

Emerging from the civil rights movement, affirmative action policies have addressed racial barriers and discrimination faced by people of color and women in education, employment, home and business ownership, and public procurement programs. Though less than a few decades old, affirmative action programs and policies have threatened centuries-old systems and practices that substantially privilege white men in wealth accumulation; and consequently, a backlash against these policies developed almost as soon as they were begun (Lipsitz 2006). Asian Americans, like other racially minoritized populations, have directly benefited from affirmative action policies and related diversity initiatives in higher education (Brest and Oshige 1995; Chang 2000; Park 2012, 2013).

However, some Asian Americans have exhibited a high level of anxiety and suspicion over affirmative action policies in selective college admissions that advance racial equity. For example, during the 2013–2014 California legislative session, vocal and politically organized groups consisting mostly of Chinese Americans halted efforts to overturn the state's ban on affirmative action in selective admissions at the state's public universities (Hing 2014). Yet, results from rigorous opinion polling reveal that the majority of Chinese Americans and other Asian Americans in California and across the United States support affirmative action (Ramakrishnan and Lee 2012, 2014). Moreover, according to electoral results in both California and Michigan's respective ballot referenda on affirmative action, the majority of Asian American voters in both states voted to support affirmative action policies ("Los Angeles Times Exit Poll" 1996; "Asian Americans for Affirmative Action" 2007).

The contradiction between a widespread assumption of Asian American opposition to affirmative action and empirical evidence of Asian American support for these policies leads us to examine the relationship among Asian Americans, affirmative action, and barriers to college access. For some Asian Americans, contentious discourse and the spread of misinformation over these issues have led to a high level of fear and anxiety over any consideration of race in selective admissions processes. This chapter argues that Asian American racial anxieties and uncertainties over selective college admissions are fueled by historical experiences with racial discrimination, misinformation, and discursive manipulation and, more important, by the realities of diminishing opportunities for all students to pursue high-quality and affordable postsecondary education.

In the first part of the chapter, we review the history of Asian American experiences with racial discrimination in US education. We pay particular attention to the period in the 1980s when the federal government investigated a handful of elite public and private institutions for allegedly practicing illegal anti-Asian quotas in admissions. This relatively recent event has understandably contributed toward a heightened sense of suspicion among some Asian Americans over selective admission policies and practices (Poon 2009b). Given this historical reality and context, misleading assumptions that falsely conflate quotas with affirmative action are easily spread, allowing uninformed fears and anxieties to take root among some Asian Americans. Therefore, we next confront contemporary myths about race-conscious affirmative action policies in selective college admissions often propagated by media and rumor. Both historical experiences and the propagation of misleading and false assumptions about race-conscious college admissions have contributed greatly toward Asian American anxieties and uncertainties over college access.

However as the second part of the chapter reveals, angst and frustrations targeting contemporary race-conscious admissions policies may be distracting critical attention away from key structural changes in higher education since the late twentieth century that have diminished access to high-quality and affordable higher education for all working- and middle-class families. Although it is important to recognize Asian American concerns and anxieties over access to high-quality postsecondary education as valid, this chapter highlights recent fundamental shifts in higher education that have significantly narrowed opportunities for all students. More specifically, we demonstrate how public divestment and budget cuts from higher education have precipitated substantial increases in the recruitment and institutional preferences for the admission of international students and others who can afford to pay full tuition, displacing many highly qualified students, including Asian Americans, from accessing higher education.

Given Asian American experiences with racism, it is no surprise that rigorous opinion polls have found this diverse population to be supportive of affirmative action, policies and programs meant to combat discriminatory barriers to education, employment, and general opportunities for upward mobility. Despite media portrayals and previous research suggesting deep divides among Asian Americans on affirmative action (Ong 2003; Ramakrishnan 2014), Asian Americans on both sides of the issue are generally committed to advancing racial equity. As such, this chapter concludes with a call for more public dialogue and discourse to identify shared Asian American community concerns over college access and collective strategies to advocate for racial justice and equity in college access for all students.

Historical Contexts Producing Mistrust and Anxiety

Contemporary Asian American concerns over educational discrimination must be understood within the context of a long history of anti-Asian policies in the United States. Like other students of color, Asian Americans, especially Chinese Americans, have been the targets of school segregation and exclusion policies (Low 1982; Wollenberg 1978). In the face of their experiences with racism in education, Asian Americans have also had a long history of fighting unjust policies, particularly through the court system (Ancheta 2006) and through political struggle (Lien 2001).

In this section, we present a summary of Asian American experiences with educational discrimination. We briefly discuss K–12 school segregation experienced by Asian Americans in the late nineteenth and early twentieth centuries. Then we turn our attention to the 1980s controversy over anti-Asian quotas, or negative action practices, at a small group of elite public and private universities. What happened in the 1980s, we argue, continues to haunt Asian Americans today, causing many to be highly suspicious of changes in public university admissions policy even when they seek to advance opportunities for the most marginalized Asian American and Pacific Islander populations, as exhibited in the University of California (UC) system in 2009. These historical and contemporary experiences provide a context for mistrust and anxiety among Asian American communities regarding government policies and institutional practices addressing race, access, and educational opportunities. Therefore, we conclude this section by deconstructing myths and misinformation held by some Asian Americans over what is and what is not affirmative action in selective admission.

Historical Contexts for Anxiety: Anti-Asian Discrimination in Education

To better understand the fear and anxiety over educational access among Asian Americans requires recognition of the ways Asian Americans have been racially marginalized in the US system of education, in both K–12 and higher education. While Asian Americans have been subjected to unjust laws excluding and segregating them from public education, they have also actively engaged in fighting back for educational equity.

In the 1800s, increasing immigration from Asia to the United States was met by a racist nativist backlash and a national movement to bar Asian immigration and exclude Asian Americans from fair civic and economic participation in the United States (Aarim-Heriot 2003; Chan 1991; Hing 1994; Takaki 1989). In addition to the 1882 Chinese Exclusion Act and restrictive covenants in property rights and civil rights, Asian Americans were also prohibited from attending public schools in some cases and forced to attend racially segregated schools in other cases. Until 1885, when Mamie Tape's family won a lawsuit against the San Francisco Board of Education, Chinese American children were prohibited from attending public schools in California. As a result of the court decision in *Tape v. Hurley* (1885), Asian American children were allowed to attend a public school separate from white students. The US Supreme Court legally reaffirmed racially segregated schooling for Asian Americans across the nation in *Lum v. Rice* (1927). In 1924, nine-year-old Martha Lum tried to enroll in a white school in Bolivar County, Mississippi. In this case, the US Supreme Court determined that Asian American students were not white and were therefore barred from attending school with white students. The little-known cases of Mamie Tape and Martha Lum contributed toward the momentum that led to the landmark US Supreme Court ruling in *Brown v. Board of Education of Topeka* (1954), by furthering public challenges to racially segregated schooling. Therefore, *Brown's* implications were significant for all communities of color.

The civil rights movement led not only to the decision in *Brown v. Board of Education*, but also to a national political climate that liberalized immigration policies and allowed for a rapid growth in the Asian American population after the Immigration and Nationality Act of 1965 was signed into law. By the 1980s, the growing population of Asian American children had reached college-going age, resulting in the expansion of this emerging population that few colleges were expecting. Some of these Asian American college students were being admitted and enrolling at the nation's top universities. Though they represented a very small, privileged percentage of the overall Asian American college-going population, Asian American students at some of the elite private and public universities and liberal arts colleges represented a conspicuous proportion of undergraduate enrollments. Soon, admissions and enrollment rates of Asian Americans at some of these campuses slowed down considerably.

Some Asian American college students began suspecting a handful of elite private and public institutions of implementing anti-Asian quotas that favored white applicants in their admissions practices, shortly after the US Supreme Court decision in *Regents of the University of California v. Bakke* (1978), which declared racial quotas and set-aside programs in selective admissions unconstitutional (Takagi 1993). Kang (1996) calls this practice "negative action," which privileges white applicants and directly contradicts racial justice tenets of affirmative action. By placing illegal quotas on Asian American students, university officials limited the admission of Asian Americans, defending white student admissions and enrollment from increasing numbers of Asian Americans entering selective colleges and universities (Nakanishi 1995). As a result of negative action allegations at UCLA, UC Berkeley, and Harvard, the US Department of Education Office of Civil Rights (OCR) conducted an extensive federal investigation. At the end of the inquiries, both UC campuses apologized for unfairly limiting Asian American admissions in favor of white applicants. Harvard was not found guilty of practicing anti-Asian quotas. Instead the OCR's findings implicated admissions preferences for children of alumni and student athletes, two groups that are overwhelmingly white, for the higher rates of acceptance of white applicants (Nakanishi 1995).

Although these cases of anti-Asian discrimination in the 1980s were an example of negative action, and not affirmative action, conservative white pundits manipulated the case to shift the debate's focus to disparage affirmative action, and advance an anti–affirmative action agenda. They wrongly argued that affirmative action was detrimental to Asian Americans and unfairly favored African Americans and Latinos (Robles 2006; Takagi 1993). Asian Americans were the perfect "racial mascot" for neoconservatives to begin dismantling affirmative action (Allred 2007). Legal scholar, Sumi Cho has defined racial mascotting as follows:

> The adoption of a racial [minority] group, or even an individual of color by a white political figure or constituency—a practice I refer to as mascotting—is necessary to deflect charges of racism and preserve the redeemed status of whiteness. Indeed, is it possible to imagine a winning campaign by the anti–affirmative action movement absent the conservative deployment of racial mascots? It hasn't happened. (cited in Allred 2007, 69)

By casting Asian Americans as a racial mascot, white anti–affirmative action activists countered claims of systemic racism with an image of minority hard work and success among Asian Americans. They also used Asian Americans as a mascot in their attacks on affirmative action to deflect charges of racism. In appropriating Asian American allegations of discrimination in admissions, these anti–affirmative action efforts were in direct contradiction with the values and aims of many Asian American community leaders involved in this case, who recognized the benefits of affirmative action for Asian Americans (Takagi 1993; Wang 1995).

The 1980s admissions controversy over negative action and subsequent manipulation of information remains embedded in the Asian American community's memory, perhaps predisposing many to be suspicious of changes to admissions policies especially at UC campuses (Poon 2009b). For example, in 2009 when the UC Board of Regents decided to amend its policy on undergraduate admission eligibility to allow more qualified students from California to have their applications reviewed, several vocal Asian American community advocates loudly expressed their opposition. Under the new policy slated to be implemented in 2012, about 30,000 more students were projected to have the opportunity to apply to the UC under the new policy, including about 5,686 who attend low-performing high schools and nearly 4,000 more Asian American and Pacific Islander students (Poon 2009b). Although the policy change was predicted to increase the number of applications from the most underrepresented Asian American and Pacific Islander populations eligible for review, some community leaders opposed the 2012 UC eligibility policy change. Many of these community leaders had been involved in the fight against anti-Asian quotas in the 1980s (Poon 2009a, 2009b). The experience with negative action in the 1980s contributed to a collective memory for Asian Americans and wariness of possible anti-Asian quotas.

Deconstructing Myths and Misinformation

The 1980s negative action controversy in selective college admissions also created significant confusion in the public's understanding of affirmative action and its effects on Asian Americans. Such a climate of confusion has easily produced misinformation and myths generating fear and anxiety among some Asian Americans over admissions policies at elite universities and colleges. For example, a variety of recent news articles and opinion pieces have made unsubstantiated claims of a penalty against Asian American applicants at elite colleges (Kiley 2012; Marcus 2011; Miller 2010). Misinformation and myths about affirmative action hinder opportunities for civil dialogue about strategies to remedy racial inequalities and injustices in the college admissions process. Therefore, we address three common myths about affirmative action in selective admissions and Asian Americans: (1) the misconception that grades and test scores alone indicate a student's "merit," (2) the notion that the relationship between affirmative action and Asian Americans in selective admissions today is equivalent to the ways Ivy League institutions in the 1920s discriminated against Jewish American applicants in favor of white Protestants from upper social echelons, and (3) the perception that affirmative action policies generally hurt Asian Americans.

Evidence of these fallacies can be found in recent public statements made by some Asian American leaders and in anti–affirmative action amicus briefs submitted in the *Fisher v. University of Texas* (2013) US Supreme Court case.[1] This section deconstructs these myths and paints a more accurate, albeit complex, picture of affirmative action as it relates to Asian Americans.

Myth 1: High Test Scores and Grades Are Trustworthy Indicators of "Merit"

One common misconception regarding affirmative action revolves around perceptions of "merit," which has been often equated solely with test scores and grades. Numerous passages in the anti–affirmative action amicus briefs by two Asian American organizations submitted to the US Supreme Court in the *Fisher* case argued that race-conscious affirmative action admissions policies unfairly penalize hardworking Asian American students with high test scores and grades. One of the anti–affirmative action Asian American organizations contended that race-conscious admissions policies harm Asian Americans "who demonstrate academic excellence at disproportionately high rates but often find the value of their work discounted on account of either their race, or nebulous criteria alluding to it" (Brief for the Louis D. Brandeis Center 2013, 3). Fundamental to this argument is the assumption that "merit" is most accurately measured by test scores, that selective colleges are interested only in student ability to achieve high grades and test scores, and that Asian Americans generally outscore other students. Asian American affirmative action opponents also assume that in many cases, if not most, rejected Asian Americans with high test scores and grades would have been admitted had they identified as some other race. Similar distortions of "merit" in college admissions have been echoed in other public discourse, including in the debate regarding State Constitutional Amendment (SCA) 5, an effort to restore affirmative action to higher education in California. Peter Kuo, a 2014 Republican candidate for the California State Senate fostered opposition against SCA 5 through claims such as the following: "determining the admission to our higher education should be based on individual merit and academic result; not based on sex, national origin nor race" on his campaign website (Peter Kuo for Senate 2014).

However, research demonstrates important limitations related to test scores and grades. In addition to being significantly limited in their ability to predict a student's potential for success in college and beyond (Sedlacek 2010), test score results and high school grade outcomes are often tainted by race and class biases (Conchas 2006; Tenenbaum and Ruck 2007). Studies have shown that SAT results, for example, correlate with students' racial identities (Freedle 2008; Jencks 1998; Santelices and Wilson 2010) and economic status (Briggs 2009), undermining the reliability of test scores to fairly evaluate academic achievement and potential (Geiser 2008; Santelices and Wilson 2010). Even the College Board, the organization that administers the SAT, in 2014 admitted that SAT scores are tainted by class inequalities and thus not reliable indicators of academic aptitude or potential (Balf 2014).

The questionable validity and reliability of the SAT and ACT have led some elite institutions to make test scores optional in their admissions processes (Hiss and Franks 2014; Poon 2014). Notably, over thirty top colleges and universities that stopped requiring the submission of test scores have experienced no difference in college GPA or graduation rates (Hiss and Franks 2014). In other words, if a college is interested in understanding students' merits, virtues, and potential contributions to a campus learning environment beyond their ability to achieve in high school classes and standardized tests, evaluating them based simply on grades and tests is extremely limiting.

US colleges and universities are institutions of learning and knowledge production applied to myriad world problems requiring leadership, strong cross-cultural communication skills, innovation, and creative thinking. Based on this mission, the nation's top colleges have developed and applied complex processes for holistic review that account for hundreds of factors and student characteristics in order to best understand the bigger picture of what a student, as a whole person, brings to a learning community. Applying their individual admissions review criteria and processes, they seek to identify potential students with a range of skills, interests, and potentials that can contribute toward these learning environments. Because they acknowledge the limitations of simple quantitative measures of students' qualities and strengths, colleges and universities have constructed complex, holistic review plans to account for a myriad of student characteristics.

However, affirmative action opponents have failed to acknowledge holistic review as a necessary part of the evaluation process, and have simultaneously overemphasized test scores and grades as indications of merit. Furthermore, the argument demonstrates a clear misunderstanding of what affirmative action is intended to foster and how it is legally applied to selective admissions processes. Based on the 2003 US Supreme Court decision in *Grutter v. Bollinger*, affirmative action allows race to be one of many factors considered in the comprehensive, holistic assessment of a student in the admissions process.

Myth 2: Asian Americans Are the New Jews

Early in the twentieth century, a number of elite institutions engaged in practices of overt exclusion of Jewish students. University leaders, including those at Harvard and Yale, openly expressed desires to address a "Jewish problem," an unwanted significant presence of Jewish students on their campuses (Karabel 2005). Robert Nelson Corwin, chairman of Yale's Board of Admissions from 1920 to 1933, articulated a strong bias against this population, writing that a large portion of Jews were an "alien and unwashed element . . . that graduates into the world as naked of all the attributes of refinement and honor as when born into it" (Karabel 2005, 12). A number of private elite institutions in the East had instituted measures to reduce the number of Jewish students. Harvard, especially, faced public scrutiny for its blatant policy of anti-Jewish restrictions. Strategically, then, Yale instituted practices in their admissions that were less explicit yet still had the same goals in mind. These practices included subjective screening for "qualities of personality and character . . . precisely the kind of subjective characteristics that were soon used to discriminate against Jewish applicants" (Karabel 2005, 114).

Some contemporary arguments opposing affirmative action have likened today's holistic admission practices to the exclusion of Jews in the early twentieth century. The comparison suggests that holistic review for affirmative action goals seek to discriminate against Asian American students with high test scores and high school grades. For example, one of the Asian American amicus briefs opposed to affirmative action submitted in the 2013 *Fisher* case presented a detailed history of anti-Jewish quotas at Ivy League institutions, concluding that "just as Asian Americans today sustain a disproportionate admissions burden in the name of 'diversity,' so too were Jews restricted at one time in the name of 'diversity' and 'balance'" (Brief for the Louis D. Brandeis Center 2013, 31). These arguments have unfortunately missed the inherent and stark differences between today's affirmative action policies and the anti-Jewish quotas of the early 1900s. While the main goal of affirmative action is to *affirm* and promote the participation of members of historically marginalized groups by confronting the realities of persistent racial barriers, anti-Jewish quotas explicitly served to maintain white Protestant social and political dominance through blatant discrimination. The inappropriate comparison between contemporary affirmative action policies and Ivy League exclusion of Jews in the early 1900s unfortunately contributes to continuing misunderstanding of the objectives of affirmative action. Holistic review today, seeking to increase diversity, is a rigorous evaluation of students to identify each applicant's unique characteristics and potential contributions to a college learning environment. Indeed, many Asian American students, who demonstrate a range of unique characteristics and talents, also benefit from this process.

Myth 3: Affirmative Action Harms Asian Americans

Suspicions of negative action against Asian Americans in selective admissions practices have persisted long after the 1980s (Poon 2009b). Since 2007, at least two Asian Americans rejected by their first choice Ivy League institution have filed legal complaints with the US Department of Education's OCR (Golden 2012; Liu 2007). In 2014, a white anti–affirmative action activist, Edward Blum, filed federal legal complaints against Harvard and the University of North Carolina alleging that holistic admissions practices interested in racial diversity and equity are anti-Asian (*Students for Fair Admissions v. Harvard* 2014; *Students for Fair Admissions v. UNC* 2014). These actions have been bolstered by a misinterpretation of a research finding by Espenshade and Chung (2005), who concluded that ending affirmative action would result in "[Asian Americans occupying] four out of every five seats created by accepting fewer African-American and Hispanic students" (304). Although the study did not account for complex holistic admission review processes, test for negative action, or show a direct correlation between Asian American admission and black and Latino student admissions at elite institutions, the study has effectively "[misled] many reasonable readers into believing that a strong causal claim about affirmative action has been made" (Kidder 2006, 614). The researchers also cautioned that "it would be a mistake to interpret [their data] as meaning that elite college admission officers are necessarily giving extra weight to black and Hispanic candidates just because they belong to underrepresented minority groups" because they were unable "to see behind the closed doors of admission offices" (Espenshade and Radford 2009, 94).

Moreover, as one pro–affirmative action Asian American amicus brief noted, Asian American applicants saw an increase of admission "with the highest percentages in the range [of years] occurring after UT Austin began considering race in 2005" (Brief for Asian Americans Advancing Justice 2013, 26). In addition, another pro–affirmative action Asian American amicus brief asserted that Asian American opponents of affirmative action

> conveniently ignore the fact that under UT's holistic admissions process, where race is one factor to be considered (and after the overwhelming majority of the freshman class was already admitted based on the Top Ten Percent law), Asian Americans are still consistently admitted and enrolled to UT in higher numbers than other minority groups. (Brief for the Asian Pacific American Legal Center [APALC] 2013, 13)

According to the brief for the Asian American Legal Defense and Education Fund (2013, 10), "the fact that the percentage of Asian American students at UT is five times larger than the percentage of Asian Americans in Texas is compelling evidence that no ceiling has been imposed" on Asian American students.

Nonetheless, some affirmative action opponents have pointed to the UC's large enrollments of Asian American undergraduates as evidence that Asian Americans benefit from the termination of affirmative action. In accordance with Proposition 209, a state ballot measure that amended the California state constitution in 1996, public universities in California cannot legally use race as a factor in their admission practices. The proportion of UC students who identify as Asian American has increased since the late 1990s, but they were already on the rise prior to the passage of Proposition 209. This demographic trend among undergraduates in the UC may also be attributed to a variety of factors including a general upsurge in the state's Asian American population at the end of the twentieth century and the unusually high level of enrollment yield among Asian Americans admitted to the UC (Poon 2012). It would be negligent to conclude, based on the current observation that Asian American students represent a large number of undergraduates in the UC, that affirmative action has harmed this population's opportunities for higher education. Moreover, it is important to remember that the majority of Asian American voters in California cast their ballots to preserve affirmative action ("Los Angeles Times Exit Poll" 1996).

In contrast to the false assumption that Asian Americans are harmed by affirmative action, research has demonstrated many ways in which Asian American students have benefited from, and can benefit from, affirmative action in selective college admissions. For one, underrepresented Asian American ethnic groups in higher education, such as Hmong, Cambodian, and Lao, experience severe educational disparities that warrant their inclusion in affirmative action admissions programs (Museus and Truong 2009; Park and Liu 2014; Teranishi 2010). In addition, because Asian American students exhibit a diversity of life experiences, backgrounds, accomplishments, and potential, many could benefit from holistic review that accounts for a multitude of characteristics including a consideration of ethnicity and race (APALC 2013). Furthermore, once Asian American students arrive on college campuses, they can benefit greatly from racially diverse learning environments resulting from affirmative action policies. These documented benefits include increased positive intergroup attitudes and improved levels of intellectual and civic engagement (Chang 2000; Park 2012).

Refocusing on Education Access for All

History and misinformation have contributed significantly to Asian American anxieties over college access. However, the concerns felt by many Asian Americans over college access, as for many Americans, can be attributed to larger structural issues facing US higher education, particularly in terms of the availability of high-quality and affordable postsecondary education. In recent years, the rising price of higher education has far outpaced the ability of many low-income and middle-income families to pay for college, as factored by income, health care costs, debt burden, and personal savings rates (Martin and Gillen 2011; Perna and Li 2006). Concurrent with federal Pell Grant aid declining in value and unmet financial needs rising for students, greater numbers of middle-income and upper-families have utilized federal and nonfederal loans to pay college-related expenses since the mid-1990s (Perna and Li 2006). While college affordability still impacts lower- and lower-middle-income families to the greatest degree, findings suggest that issues of affordability have recently begun to impact Americans across a wider range of income levels (Martin and Gillen 2011; Perna and Li 2006). In light of these issues, it is understandable for many to be anxious over diminishing opportunities in higher education. However, it is important that Asian Americans are not derailed from recognizing greater issues of declining affordability of and access to higher education for a growing proportion of Americans across races.

Notably, average amounts of financial need and associated loans differ among institutional types. The US Department of Education (Choy and Berker 2003) reported that unmet need is significantly greater for students at four-year private colleges and universities than for those at public four-year institutions. Thus, while a majority of Americans believe that "a college education is necessary for a person to be successful in today's working world" (Immerwahr et al. 2010, 4), widening disparities between cost and ability to pay may increasingly impact families' choice around higher education. That is, it is reasonable to assume that students and families are increasingly opting for higher education opportunities of lower cost (Martin and Gillen 2011).

An institutional type that bears a strong national profile but a generally lower financial burden for its students than its private counterpart is the four-year research and doctoral public institution. Accessibility to these institutions to many students in the United States, however, has been limited by shifting public financing and enrollment priorities. Relying historically on state support, these public institutions have in recent years felt the extreme reductions in state appropriations and funding (Jacquette and Curs 2013). In response to declining state support, a growing trend at public institutions, such as the UC system and the University of North Carolina, has been to pursue greater enrollments of out-of-state and international students, who are ineligible for in-state subsidies and therefore pay higher tuition than resident students (Jacquette and Curs 2013). UC Berkeley chancellor Nicholas Dirks stated in April 2014, after years of severe state budget cuts, that "tuition from out-of-state and international students [was] crucial" (Pratt 2014, para. 12). Preceding this comment was a 23.6 percent decrease in the number of California residents who had been admitted to the institution, falling from 3,822 to 3,091 between 2006 and 2013 (Pratt 2014). It can be deduced that many California residents, including many Asian Americans, experienced increased competition for admittance to the UC, and that this trend occurred at selective public institutions in other states, which also experienced significant decreases in state funding appropriations.

Therefore, a focus on access to higher education would likely be more effective if shifted to the affordability and public funding of higher education for all. Anxieties are warranted about accessing higher education because many selective state institutions are, in fact, becoming more difficult for students of lower- and middle-class families to get into. Misconceptions regarding affirmative action have effectively derailed many Asian Americans from the greater issues impacting all groups regarding affordability and access. Conservative interests have propelled these misunderstandings via the racial mascotting of Asian Americans. Ironically, though, energy and resources spent on trying to end affirmative action do not benefit the goals of access to quality higher education that families desire. Toward this set of broader goals, resources seem much better utilized toward striving for increased public support and affordability of higher education.

Implications and Conclusion

There is evidence suggesting that political figures with neoconservative agendas, such as Edward Blum, have capitalized on misunderstandings of affirmative action to effectively use Asian Americans as racial mascots in an effort to undo racial justice efforts in higher education. Although Asian Americans have benefited from affirmative action policies and other diversity initiatives in higher education, some individual Asian Americans have become apprehensive to support or even adamantly opposed to these policies. Following negative action allegations in the 1980s at a few elite institutions, white anti–affirmative action activists appropriated Asian American concerns of discrimination and negative action in admissions toward a rhetoric of affirmative action harming whites and Asian Americans, while using the latter group as racial mascots. This mascotting has arisen and become more evident in the wake of the *Fisher v. University of Texas* case. In early 2014 Blum, the executive director of the Project on Fair Representation, which initiated and led the legal actions resulting in the *Fisher* case, began searching for the next plaintiffs to feature in the ongoing legal battles over affirmative action with a particular appeal to Asian Americans denied admission to Harvard, the University of Wisconsin–Madison, or the University of North Carolina at Chapel Hill (Hing 2014). It is unsettling to see Blum, a white affirmative action opponent, blatantly engage in racially manipulative imagery, distorting both the positive impacts that affirmative action has for Asian Americans and the supportive majority opinion that this population holds on such policies.

What these contemporary racial dynamics call for, therefore, are affirmative action advocates to account for the complex experiences and demographics of Asian Americans to strengthen the defense of affirmative action through a framework of inclusive racial justice. To address the anxiety and suspicion expressed by some, constructive dialogue is needed to address the myths regarding affirmative action, and to speak to the individual and societal benefits that race-conscious policies can garner for all. Furthermore, in the public discourse and debate over college access, the racial equity and justice values held by many Asian Americans must be more clearly represented. Instead of a monolithic picture that depicts Asian Americans as being harmed by and opposing affirmative action, it must be made clear that the historical and educational experiences within this community vary significantly, but that across these differences the majority of Asian Americans support affirmative action (Ramakrishnan and Lee 2014). Last, it is imperative that the focus on higher education accessibility shift to issues of affordability and public investment in higher education, which have impacted accessibility for a greater and greater proportion of individuals in the United States in the twenty-first century. Ultimately a shift in attention and resources will better promote the opportunities for all students to pursue high-quality postsecondary education, much like affirmative action has, from the start, been working to do.

NOTE

1 Amicus briefs are legal briefs submitted by "friends of the court" who are not named in a lawsuit. Authors of these briefs are interested in the outcomes of the court decision and submit their briefs with hopes of influencing the decision. A total of five amicus briefs by Asian American and Pacific Islander interest organizations were submitted to the Court in *Fisher v. University of Texas* (2013). Two briefs argued against affirmative action, supporting Abigail Fisher. Three briefs supported affirmative action, offering supporting arguments in favor of the University of Texas.

REFERENCES

Aarim-Heriot, Najia. 2003. *Chinese Immigrants, African Americans, and Racial Anxiety in the United States, 1848–82*. Urbana: University of Illinois Press.

Allred, Nancy C. 2007. "Asian Americans and Affirmative Action: From Yellow Peril to Model Minority and Back Again." *Asian American Law Journal* 14 (1): 57–84. http://scholarship.law.berkeley.edu/aalj/vol14/iss1/3.

Ancheta, Angelo N. 2006. *Race, Rights, and the Asian American Experience*. 2nd ed. New Brunswick, NJ: Rutgers University Press.

"Asian Americans for Affirmative Action." 2007. *Nation*, January 8. http://www.thenation.com/blog/asian-americans-affirmative-action.

Balf, Todd. 2014. "The Story Behind the SAT Overhaul." *New York Times*, March 6. http://www.nytimes.com/2014/03/09/magazine/the-story-behind-the-sat-overhaul.html.

Brest, Paul, and Miranda Oshige. 1995. "Affirmative Action for Whom?" *Stanford Law Review* 47 (5): 855–900. doi:10.2307/1229177.

Brief for the Asian American Legal Defense and Education Fund. 2013. *Fisher v. University of Texas*, 570 US. http://www.advancingjustice-aajc.org/news-media/news/asian-american-civil-rights-groups-file-amicus-briefs-urging-supreme-court-uphold-0 (accessed October 3, 2015).

Brief for Asian Americans Advancing Justice. 2013. *Fisher v. University of Texas*, 570 US. http://www.advancingjustice-aajc.org/tags/fisher-v-university-texas-austin (accessed October 3, 2015).

Brief for the Asian Pacific American Legal Center. 2013. *Fisher v. University of Texas*, 570 US. http://advancingjustice-la.org/media-and-publications/publications/fisher-v-university-texas-austin-amicus-brief (accessed October 3, 2015).

Brief for the Louis D. Brandeis Center for Human Rights under Law, the 80–20 National Asian-American Educational Foundation, et al. 2013. *Fisher v. University of Texas*, 570 US. http://sblog.s3.amazonaws.com/wp-content/uploads/2012/05/12–05–29_Gura_Final_Fisher_Brief.pdf (accessed October 3, 2015).

Briggs, Derek C. 2009. "Preparation for College Admission Exams." Arlington, VA: National Association for College Admission Counseling. http://www.nacacnet.org/research/ PublicationsResources/Marketplace/Documents/TestPrepDiscussionPaper.pdf.

Brown v. Board of Education of Topeka, 347 US 483 (1954).

Chan, Sucheng. 1991. *Asian Americans: An Interpretive History*. Boston: Twayne.

Chang, Mitchell J. 2000. "The Educational Implications of Affirmative Action and Crossing the Color Line." *Amerasia Journal* 26 (3): 67–84.

Choy, Susan P., and Ali M. Berker. 2003. "How Families of Low- and Middle-Income Undergraduates Pay for College: Full-Time Dependent Students in 1999–2000." NCES 2003–162. Washington, DC: US Department of Education, National Center for Education Statistics. http://www.nyu.edu/classes/jepsen/ncess2003–162.pdf.

Conchas, Gilberto Q. 2006. *The Color of Success: Race and High-Achieving Urban Youth*. New York: Teachers College Press.

Espenshade, Thomas J., and Chang Y. Chung. 2005. "The Opportunity Cost of Admission Preferences at Elite Universities." *Social Science Quarterly* 86 (2): 293–305.

Espenshade, Thomas J., and Alexandria W. Radford. 2009. *No Longer Separate, Not Yet Equal: Race and Class in Elite College Admission and Campus Life*. Princeton: Princeton University Press.

Fisher v. University of Texas, 570 US (2012). http://www.supremecourt.gov/ opinions/12pdf/11–345_l5gm.pdf (accessed October 3, 2015).

Freedle, Roy O. 2008. "Correcting the SATs Ethnic and Social-Class Bias: A Method for Reestimating SAT Scores." *Harvard Educational Review* 73 (1): 1–43.

Geiser, Saul. 2008. "Not So Fast! A Second Opinion on a University of California Proposal to Endorse the New SAT." Center for Studies in Higher Education Research and Occasional Papers Series, CSHI.16.2008. http://www.cshe.berkeley.edu/sites/default/files/shared/publications/docs/ROPS-Geiser-SAT-11–12.pdf.

Golden, Daniel. 2009. *The Price of Admission: How America's Ruling Class Buys Its Way into Elite Colleges—And Who Gets Left Outside the Gates*. New York: Crown.

———. 2012. "Harvard Targeted in U.S. Asian-American Discrimination Probe." *Bloomberg*, February 2. http://www.bloomberg.com/news/2012–02–02/harvard-targeted-in-u-s-asian-american-discrimination-probe.html.

Grutter v. Bollinger, 539 US 306 (2003).

Haveman, Robert, and Timothy Smeeding. 2006. "The Role of Higher Education in Social Mobility." *Future of Children* 16 (2): 125–150.

Hing, Bill Ong. 1994. *Making and Remaking Asian America through Immigration Policy, 1850–1990*. Stanford, CA: Stanford University Press.

Hing, Julianne. 2014. "The Chinese-American Community Grapples with Affirmative Action, and Itself." *Colorlines*, March 18. http://colorlines.com/archives/2014/03/the_ chinese-american_community_grapples_with_affirmative_action_and_itself.html.

Hiss, William C, and Valerie W. Franks. 2014. *Defining Promise: Optional Standardized Testing Policies in American College and University Admissions*. Arlington, VA: National Association for College Admission Counseling. http://www.nacacnet.org/research/research-data/nacac-research/Documents/DefiningPromise.pdf.

Immerwahr, John, Jean Johnson, Amber Ott, and Jonathan Rochkind. 2010. *Squeeze Play 2010: Continued Public Anxiety on Cost, Harsher Judgments on How Colleges Are Run*. New York: Public Agenda. http://www.publicagenda.org/pages/squeeze-play-2010.

Jacquette, Ozan, and Bradley R. Curs. 2013. "The Effect of State Financial Support on Non-resident Enrollments for Public Universities." Paper presented at the meeting of the Association for Educational Finance and Policy, New Orleans, March 14–16.

Jencks, Christopher. 1998. "Racial Bias in Testing." Pp. 55–85 in Christopher Jencks and Meredith Phillips, eds., *The Black-White Test Score Gap*. Washington, DC: Brookings Institution.

Kang, Jerry. 1996. "Negative Action against Asian Americans: The Internal Instability of Dworkin's Defense of Affirmative Action." *Harvard Civil Rights-Civil Liberties Law Review* 31: 1–32.

Karabel, Jerome. 2005. *The Chosen: The Hidden History of Admission and Exclusion at Harvard, Yale, and Princeton*. New York: Houghton Mifflin Harcourt.

Kidder, William C. 2006. "Negative Action versus Affirmative Action: Asian Pacific Americans Are Still Caught in the Crossfire." *Michigan Journal of Race & Law* 11: 605–624.

Kiley, Kevin. 2012. "Think Outside 'the Box': Asian-American Students Perceive Bias in University Admissions and Counselors Want Clarification." *Inside Higher Ed*, October 12. https://www.insidehighered.com/news/2012/10/12/asian-american-students-perceive-bias-university-admissions-and-counselors-want.

Lew, Jamie. 2006. *Asian Americans in Class: Charting the Achievement Gap among Korean American Youth*. New York: Teachers College Press.

Lien, Pei-Te. 2001. *Making of Asian America through Political Participation*. Philadelphia: Temple University Press, 2001.

Lipsitz, George. 2006. *The Possessive Investment in Whiteness: How White People Profit from Identity Politics*. Rev. ed. Philadelphia: Temple University Press.

Liu, Adrian. 2007. "Affirmative Action and Negative Action: How Jian Li's Case Can Benefit Asian Americans." *Michigan Journal of Race & Law* 13: 391–432.

"Los Angeles Times Exit Poll: The General Election." 1996. *Los Angeles Times*, November 5. http://media.trb.com/media/acrobat/2008-10/43120439.pdf.

Louie, Vivian S. 2004. *Compelled to Excel: Immigration, Education, and Opportunity among Chinese Americans*. Stanford, CA: Stanford University Press.

Low, Victor. 1982. *The Unimpressible Race: A Century of Educational Struggle by the Chinese sin San Francisco*. San Francisco: East/West Publishing.

Lum v. Rice, 278 US 78 (1927).

Marcus, Jon. 2011. "Competitive Disadvantage." *Boston Globe*, April 17. http://www.boston.com/news/education/higher/articles/2011/04/17/high_achieving_asian_americans_are_being_shut_out_of_top_schools/?page=3.

Martin, Robert E., and Andrew Gillen. 2011. "Measuring College Affordability." SSRN 1734914. http://papers.ssrn.com/sol3/papers.cfm?abstract_id=1734914.

Miller, Kara. 2010. "Do Colleges Redline Asian-Americans?" *Boston Globe*, February 8. http://www.boston.com/bostonglobe/editorial_opinion/oped/articles/2010/02/08/do_colleges_redline_asian_americans/.

Museus, Samuel D., and Kimberly A. Truong. 2009. "Disaggregating Qualitative Data from Asian American College Students in Campus Racial Climate Research and Assessment." *New Directions for Institutional Research* 2009 (142): 17–26. doi:10.1002/ir.293.

Nakanishi, Don T. 1995. "A Quota on Excellence? The Asian American Admissions Debate." Pp. 273–284 in Don T. Nakanishi and Tina Y. Nishida, eds., *The Asian American Educational Experience: A Sourcebook for Teachers and Students*. New York: Routledge.

Ong, Paul M. 2003. "The Affirmative Action Divide." Pp. 377–406 in Don T. Nakanishi and James S. Lai, eds., *Asian American Politics: Law, Participation, and Policy*. Lanham, MD: Rowman & Littlefield.

Park, Julie J. 2012. *Asian Americans and the Benefits of Campus Diversity: What the Research Says*. Los Angeles: National Commission on Asian American and Pacific Islander Research in Education. http://care.gseis.ucla.edu/assets/care-asian_am_diversity _d4.pdf.

———. 2013. *When Diversity Drops: Race, Religion, and Affirmative Action in Higher Education*. New Brunswick, NJ: Rutgers University Press.

Park, Julie J., and Amy Liu. 2014. "Interest Convergence or Divergence? A Critical Race Analysis of Asian Americans, Meritocracy, and Critical Mass in the Affirmative Action Debate." *Journal of Higher Education* 85 (1): 36–64. doi:10.1353/jhe.2014.0001.

Perna, Laura W., and Chunyan Li. 2006. "College Affordability: Implications for College Opportunity." *Journal of Student Financial Aid* 36 (1): 7–24. http://publications. nasfaa.org/jsfa/vol36/iss1/1.

Peter Kuo for Senate. 2014. "We Must Stop SCA 5." http://www.kuoforsenate.com/forms/shares/new?page_id=46 (accessed October 3, 2015).

Poon, OiYan. 2009a. "Generational and Communication Gaps in the AAPI Education Agenda: AAPIs in the College Access Debate." *AAPI Nexus: Asian Americans & Pacific Islanders Policy, Practice and Community* 7 (2): 83–106.

———. 2009b. "Haunted by Negative Action: Asian Americans, Admissions, and Race in the 'Color-Blind Era.'" *Asian American Policy Review* 18: 81–90.

———. 2012. *Do Asian Americans Benefit from Race-Blind College Admissions Policies?* Los Angeles: National Commission on Asian American and Pacific Islander Research in Education. http://care.gseis.ucla.edu/assets/care-brief-raceblind.pdf.

———. 2014. "'I Had a Friend Who Had Worse Scores Than Me and He Got into a Better College': The Legal and Social Realities of the College Admissions Process." Pp. 179–194 in Stephanie M. McClure and Cherise A. Harris, eds., *What White People Think They Know: Questioning Conventional Wisdom on Race in the United States*. Thousand Oaks, CA: Sage.

Pratt, Timothy. 2014. "Residents Are Crowded Out of College by Out-of-State and Foreign Students." *Hechinger Report*, June 13. http://hechingerreport.org/content/residents-crowded-college-state-foreign-students_16363/.

Ramakrishnan, Karthick. 2014. "California Needs to Look Again at Asian Stance on Affirmative Action." *Los Angeles Times*, September 25. http://www.latimes.com/opinion/ commentary/la-oe-0925-ramakrishnan-affirmative-action-asians—20140925-story.html.

Ramakrishnan, Karthick, and Taeku Lee. 2012. "The Policy Priorities and Issue Preferences of Asian Americans and Pacific Islanders." National Asian American Survey. http://www.naasurvey.com/resources/Home/NAAS12-sep25-issues.pdf.

———. 2014. "Views of a Diverse Electorate: Opinions of California Registered Voters in 2014." National Asian American Survey. http://www.naasurvey.com/resources/Home/ NAAS-Field-2014-final.pdf.

Regents of the University of California v. Bakke, 438 US 265 (1978).

Robles, Rowena. 2006. *Asian Americans and the Shifting Politics of Race: The Dismantling of Affirmative Action at an Elite Public High School*. New York: Routledge.

Santelices, Maria V., and Mark Wilson. 2010. "Unfair Treatment? The Case of Freedle, the SAT, and the Standardization Approach to Differential Item Functioning." *Harvard Educational Review* 80 (1): 106–134.

Sedlacek, William E. 2010. "Noncognitive Measures for Higher Education Admissions." Pp. 845–849 in Penelope Peterson, Eva Baker, and Barry McGaw, eds., *The International Encyclopedia of Education*. 3rd ed.,. Amsterdam: Elsevier.

Smeeding, Timothy M., and Robert H. Haveman. 2006. "The Role of Higher Education in Social Mobility." *Future of Children* 16 (2): 125–150. doi:10.1353/foc.2006.0015.

Students for Fair Admissions. 2014a. *Students for Fair Admissions, Inc. v. President and Fellows of Harvard College (Harvard Corporation); and The Honorable and Reverend the Board of Overseers*. Case File. https://studentsforfairadmissions.org/wp-content/uploads/2014/11/SFFA-v.-Harvard-Complaint.pdf (accessed November 1, 2014).

———. 2014b. *Students for Fair Admissions, Inc. v. University of North Carolina*. Case File. https://studentsforfairadmissions.org/wp-content/uploads/ 2014/11/SFFA-v.-UNC-Complaint.pdf (accessed November 1, 2014).

Sue, Stanley, and Sumie Okazaki. 1990. "Asian-American Educational Achievements: A Phenomenon in Search of an Explanation." *American Psychologist* 45 (8): 913–920. doi:10.1037/0003-066X.45.8.913.

Takagi, Dana Y. 1993. *The Retreat from Race: Asian-American Admissions and Racial Politics*. New Brunswick, NJ: Rutgers University Press.

Takaki, Ronald T. 1989. *Strangers from a Different Shore: A History of Asian Americans*. New York: Penguin.

Tape v. Hurley, 66 Cal. 473 (1885).

Tenenbaum, Harriet R., and Martin D. Ruck. 2007. "Are Teachers' Expectations Different for Racial Minority Than for European American Students? A Meta-Analysis." *Journal of Educational Psychology* 99 (2): 253–273. doi:10.1037/0022-0663.99.2.253.

Teranishi, Robert T. 2010. *Asians in the Ivory Tower: Dilemmas of Racial Inequality in American Higher Education*. New York: Teachers College Press.

Wang, Ling-Chi. 1995. "Meritocracy and Diversity in Higher Education." Pp. 285–302 in Don T. Nakanishi and Tina Y. Nishida, eds., *The Asian American Educational Experience: A Sourcebook for Teachers and Students*. New York: Routledge.

Wollenberg, Charles. 1978. *All Deliberate Speed: Segregation and Exclusion in California Schools, 1855–1975*. Berkeley: University of California Press.

STUDY QUESTIONS

(1) According to Leung, how do stereotypes of Asian Americans vary between men and women? In light of these gendered stereotypes, how was Jeremy Lin's success in the NBA significant? In what way did stereotypes of Asian American men hamper Lin's trajectory as a basketball player?

(2) Although it lasted only a few weeks, "Linsanity" illustrated to the nation the way in which Asian Americans are racialized differently from other minorities. How did news coverage of Jeremy Lin differ from that of African American athletes? How does the difference in coverage demonstrate the distinction in how Asian Americans and African Americans are stereotyped in the United States? In your opinion, does one group have it worse than the other?

(3) To what extent—if any—does the model minority myth factor into contemporary debates about Asian American identity? Can you think of any ways in which the media continue to perpetuate this stereotype? What negative effects does it continue to perpetuate for contemporary Asian Americans?

(4) According to Park, what are the consequences for Asian Americans who do not adhere to the model minority stereotype? In what way does the narrative of the "forever foreigner" feed into the model minority stereotype? In what way does the model minority stereotype contribute to a "quintessential American tale"?

(5) Park's chapter argues that the immigrant narratives of second-generation Asian Americans are remarkably similar, regardless of country of origin, age, or socioeconomic status. What were some of the essential components of this universal immigrant narrative? How were the narratives of immigration similar in terms of their tone? What explains why the narratives were so similar?

(6) What discriminatory events prompted Asian American communities to develop a distrust of higher education institutions? In what ways have these historical acts of discrimination created a complicated relationship between Asian Americans and affirmative action policies?

(7) Why would people assume that Asian Americans would oppose affirmative action? In what ways have neoconservatives benefited from the belief that Asian Americans oppose affirmative action? What are the three primary myths about Asian Americans and their beliefs on affirmative action? Are these assumptions valid according to public opinion polls of Asian Americans?

SUGGESTED READINGS

Bonus, Rick, and Dina C. Maramba, eds. 2013. *The "Other" Students: Filipino Americans, Education, and Power.* Charlotte, NC: Information Age.

Byun, Soo-yung, and Hyunjoon Park. 2012. "The Academic Success of East Asian American Youth: The Role of Shadow Education." *Sociology of Education* 85 (1): 40–60.

Ecklund, Elaine H. 2005. "'Us' and 'Them': The Role of Religion in Mediating and Challenging the 'Model Minority' and Other Civic Boundaries." *Ethnic and Racial Studies* 28 (1): 132–150.

Eguchi, Shinsuke, and William Starosta. 2012. "Negotiating the Model Minority Image: Performative Aspects of College-Educated Asian American Professional Men." *Qualitative Research Reports in Communication* 13 (1): 88–97.

Fung, Richard. 1994. "Seeing Yellow: Asian Identity in Film and Video." Pp. 161–172 in Karin Aguilar-San Juan, ed., *The State of Asian America: Activism and Resistance in the 1990s.* Boston: South End.

Hanson, Sandra L., and Yu Meng. 2008. "Science Majors and Degrees among Asian American Students: Influences of Race and Sex in 'Model Minority' Experiences." *Journal of Women and Minorities in Science and Engineering* 14: 225–252.

Ho, Pensri. 2003. "Performing the 'Oriental': Professionals and the Asian Model Minority Myth." *Journal of Asian American Studies* 6 (2): 149–175.

Hsin, Amy, and Yu Xie. 2014. "Explaining Asian Americans' Academic Advantage over Whites." *Proceedings of the National Academy of Sciences of the United States of America* 111: 8416–8421.

Inkelas, Karen Kurotsuchi. 2003. "Caught in the Middle: Understanding Asian Pacific American Perspectives on Affirmative Action through Blumer's Group Position Theory." *Journal of College Student Development* 44 (5): 625–643.

John, D. A., A. B. de Castro, D. P. Martin, B. Duran, and D. T. Takeuchi. 2012. "Does an Immigrant Health Paradox Exist among Asian Americans? Associations of Nativity and Occupational Class with Self-Rated Health and Mental Disorders." *Social Science & Medicine* 75 (12): 2085–2098.

Kim, Chang Hwan, and Arthur Sokamoto. 2014. "The Earnings of Less Educated Asian American Men: Educational Selectivity and the Model Minority Image." *Social Problems* 61 (2): 283–304.

Lau, Anna S., William Tsai, Josephine Shih, Lisa L. Liu, Wei-Chin Hwang, and David T. Takeuchi. 2013. "The Immigrant Paradox among Asian American Women: Are Disparities in the Burden of Depression and Anxiety Paradoxical or Explicable?" *Journal of Consulting and Clinical Psychology* 81 (5): 901–911.

Lee, Robert. 1999. *Orientals: Asian Americans in Popular Culture.* Philadelphia: Temple University Press.

Lee, Sharon M. 2002. "Do Asian American Faculty Face a Glass Ceiling in Higher Education?" *American Educational Research Journal* 39 (3): 695–724.

Lee, Stacey J. 1996. *Unraveling the "Model Minority" Stereotype: Listening to Asian American Youth.* New York: Teachers College, Columbia University.

Lee, Wen Ho, with Helen Zia. 2001. *My Country versus Me: The First-Hand Account by the Los Alamos Scientist Who Was Falsely Accused.* New York: Hyperion.

Lew, J. 2007. "A Structural Analysis of Success and Failure of Asian Americans: A Case of Korean Americans in Urban Schools." *Teachers College Record* 109: 369–390.

Louie, Andrea. 2004. *Chineseness across Borders: Renegotiating Chinese Identities in China and the United States.* Durham, NC: Duke University Press.

Ng, Wendy. L. 2002. *Japanese American Internment during World War II: A History and Reference Guide.* Westport, CT: Greenwood.

Ngai, Mae. 2005. "Transnationalism and the Transformation of the Other." *American Quarterly* 57: 59–65.

Ono, Kent A. 2005. "Guilt without Evidence: Informal Citizenship and the Limits of Rationality in the Case of Wen Ho Lee." Pp. 76–88 in G. Thomas Goodnight, ed., *Proceedings of the Twelfth NCA/AFA Conference on Argumentation.* Annandale, VA: National Communication Association.

Park, Julie J. 2012. "It Takes a Village (or an Ethnic Economy): The Varying Roles of Socioeconomic Status, Religion, and Social Capital in SAT Preparation for Chinese and Korean American Students." *American Educational Research Journal* 49 (4): 624–650.

Park, Julie J., and Amy Liu. 2014. "Interest Convergence or Divergence? A Critical Race Analysis of Asian Americans, Meritocracy, and Critical Mass in the Affirmative Action Debate." *Journal of Higher Education* 85 (1): 36–64.

Park, Jung-Sun. 2004. "Korean American Youth and Transnational Flows of Popular Culture across the Pacific." *Amerasia Journal* 30 (1): 147–169.

Petersen, William. 1966. "Success Story: Japanese-American Style." *New York Times Magazine,* January 9.

Pyke, Karen, and Tran Dang. 2003. "'FOB' and 'Whitewashed': Identity and Internalized Racism among Second Generation Asian Americans." *Qualitative Sociology* 26 (2): 147–172.

Sue, Stanley, and Sumie Okazaki. 1990. "Asian American Educational Achievement: A Phenomenon in Search of an Explanation." *American Psychologist* 45: 913–920.

Takagi, Dana Y. 1990. "From Discrimination to Affirmative Action: Facts in the Asian American Admissions Controversy." *Social Problems* 37: 578–592.

Trueba, H. T., L. R. L. Cheng, and K. Ima. 1993. *Myth or Reality: Adaptive Strategies of Asian Americans in California*. London: Falmer Press.

Tuan, Mia. 1998. *Forever Foreigners or Honorary Whites? The Asian Ethnic Experience Today*. New Brunswick, NJ: Rutgers University Press.

Walker-Moffat, Wendy. 1995. *The Other Side of the Asian American Success Story*. San Francisco: Jossey-Bass.

Wolf, Diane L. 1997. "Family Secrets: Transnational Struggles among Children of Filipino Immigrants." *Sociological Perspectives* 40 (3): 457–482.

Wollenberg, Charles M. 1995. "'Yellow Peril' in Schools (I & II)." Pp. 3–29 in Don T. Nakanishi and Tina Yamano Nishida, eds., *The Asian American Educational Experience: A Sourcebook for Teachers and Students*. New York: Routledge.

Wu, Ellen D. 2013. *The Color of Success: Asian Americans and the Origins of the Model Minority*. Princeton: Princeton University Press.

Yoo, H. C., G. C. Gee, and D. T. Takeuchi. 2009. "Discrimination and Health among Asian American Immigrants: Disentangling Racial from Language Discrimination." *Social Science & Medicine* 68 (4): 726–732.

Zhou, Min. 2009. "How Neighbourhoods Matter for Immigrant Children: The Formation of Educational Resources in Chinatown, Koreatown and Pico Union, Los Angeles." *Journal of Ethnic and Migration Studies* 35 (7): 1153–1179.

FILMS

Berges, Paul Mayeda (producer/director). 1991. *En Ryo Identity* (23-minute documentary).

Ding, Loni (producer/director). 1982. *On New Ground* (30-minute documentary).

Dong, Arthur (director). 1989. *Forbidden City, U.S.A.* (56-minute documentary).

Gee, Deborah (director). 1988. *Slaying the Dragon* (60-minute documentary).

Huang, Renanta (director). 2003. *Tribute and Remembrance: Asian Americans after 9/11* (69-minute documentary).

Lau, Eunice (director). 2013. *A-Town Boyz* (90-minute documentary).

Lee, Joyce (producer/director). 1993. *Foreign Talk* (11-minute drama).

Nakamura, Robert A. (director), and Karen Ishizuka (producer). 1996. *Looking Like the Enemy* (52-minute documentary).

Nakasako, Spencer (producer/director). 1984. *Talking History* (30-minute documentary).

Okazaki, Steven (producer/director/writer). 1995. *American Sons* (28-minute documentary).

Soe, Valerie (director). 1992. *Picturing Oriental Girls* (15-minute experimental).

Tajiri, Rea (producer/director/writer). 1991. *History and Memory* (30-minute documentary).

Tanaka, Janice (director). 1999. *When You Are Smiling: The Deadly Legacy of Internment* (60-minute documentary).

Wong, Kristina (writer), Michael Closson (director/producer), and J. Elizabeth Martin (producer). 2010. *Wong Flew over the Cuckoo's Nest* (80-minute performance).

PART X

Multiplicity and Interracial Politics

24

Heterogeneity, Hybridity, Multiplicity

Marking Asian American Differences

LISA LOWE

In a poem by Janice Mirikitani ([1987] 2003), a Japanese American nisei woman describes her sansei daughter's rebellion.[1] The daughter's denial of Japanese American culture and its particular notions of femininity reminds the nisei speaker that she, too, has denied her antecedents, rebelling against her own more traditional issei mother:

> I want to break tradition—unlock this room
>   where women dress in the dark.
>   Discover the lies my mother told me.
>   The lies that we are small and powerless
>   that our possibilities must be compressed
>   to the size of pearls, displayed only as
>   passive chokers, charms around our neck.
> Break Tradition.
>   I want to tell my daughter of this room
>
>   of myself
>   filled with tears of shakuhatchi,
>
>   poems about madness,
>   sounds shaken from barbed wire and
>   goodbyes and miracles of survival.
>   This room of open window where daring ones escape.
>
> My daughter denies she is like me ...
>   her pouting ruby lips, her skirts
>   swaying to salsa, teena marie and the stones,
>   her thighs displayed in carnivals of color.
>   I do not know the contents of her room.
> She mirrors my aging.
> She is breaking tradition. (663)

The nisei speaker repudiates the repressive confinements of her issei mother: the disciplining of the female body, the tedious practice of diminution, the silences of obedience. In turn, the crises that have shaped the nisei speaker— internment camps, sounds of threatening madness—are unknown to, and unheard by, her sansei teenage daughter. The three generations of Japanese immigrant women in this poem are separated by their different histories and by different conceptions of what it means to be female and Japanese. The poet who writes "I do not know the contents of her room" registers these separations as "breaking tradition."

In another poem, by Lydia Lowe, Chinese women workers are divided also by generation, but even more powerfully by class and language. The speaker is a young Chinese American who supervises an older Chinese woman in a textile factory.

> The long bell blared,
> and then the *lo-ban*
> made me search all your bags
> before you could leave.
> Inside he sighed
> about slow work, fast hands,
> missing spools of thread—
> and I said nothing.
> I remember that day
> you came in to show me
> I added your tickets six zippers short.
> It was just a mistake.
> You squinted down
> at the check in your hands
> like an old village woman peers
> at some magician's trick.
> That afternoon
> when you thrust me your bags
> I couldn't look or raise my face.
> *Doi m-jyu.*
> Eyes on the ground,
> I could only see
> one shoe kicking against the other. (29)

This poem, too, invokes the breaking of tradition, although it thematizes another sort of stratification among Asian women: the structure of the factory places the English-speaking younger woman above the Cantonese-speaking older one. Economic relations in capitalist society force the young supervisor to discipline her elders, and she is acutely ashamed that her required behavior does not demonstrate the respect traditionally owed to parents and elders. Thus, both poems foreground commonly thematized topoi of diasporan cultures: the disruption and distortion of traditional cultural practices—like the practice of parental sacrifice and filial duty, or the practice of respecting hierarchies of age—not only as a consequence of immigration to the United States but as a part of entering a society with different class stratifications and different constructions of gender roles. Some Asian American discussions cast the disruption of tradition as loss and represent the loss in terms of regret and shame, as in the latter poem. Alternatively, the traditional practices of family continuity and hierarchy may be figured as oppressively confining, as in Mirikitani's poem, in which the two generations of daughters contest the more restrictive female roles of the former generations. In either case, many Asian American discussions portray immigration and relocation to the United States in terms of a loss of the "original" culture in exchange for the new "American" culture.

In many Asian American novels, the question of the loss or transmission of the "original" culture is frequently represented in a family narrative, figured as generational conflict between the Chinese-born first generation and the American-born second generation.[2] Louis Chu's 1961 novel *Eat a Bowl of Tea*, for example, allegorizes in the conflicted relationship between father and son the differences between "native" Chinese values and the new "Westernized" culture of Chinese Americans. Other novels have taken up this generational theme; one way to read Maxine Hong Kingston's *The Woman Warrior* (1975) or Amy Tan's *The Joy Luck Club* (1989) is to understand them as versions of this generational model of culture, refigured in feminine terms, between mothers and daughters. However, I will argue that interpreting Asian American culture exclusively in terms of the master narratives of generational conflict and filial relation essentializes Asian American culture, obscuring the particularities and incommensurabilities of class, gender, and national diversities among Asians; the reduction of ethnic cultural politics to struggles between first and second generations displaces (and privatizes) intercommunity differences into a familial opposition. To avoid this homogenizing of Asian Americans as exclusively hierarchical and familial, I would contextualize the "vertical" generational model of culture with the more "horizontal" relationship represented in Diana Chang's "The Oriental Contingent." In Chang's short story, two young women avoid the discussion of their Chinese backgrounds because each desperately fears that the other is "more Chinese," more "authentically" tied to the original culture. The narrator, Connie, is certain that her friend Lisa "never referred to her own background because it was more Chinese than Connie's, and therefore of a higher order. She was tact incarnate. All along, she had been going out of her way not to embarrass Connie. Yes, yes. Her assurance was definitely uppercrust (perhaps her father had been in the diplomatic service), and her offhand didacticness, her lack of self-doubt, was indeed characteristically Chinese-Chinese" (173). Connie feels ashamed because she assumes herself to be "a failed Chinese"; she fantasizes that Lisa was born in China, visits there frequently, and privately disdains Chinese Americans. Her assumptions about Lisa prove to be quite wrong, however; Lisa is even more critical of herself for "not being genuine." For Lisa, as Connie eventually discovers, was born in Buffalo and was adopted by non–Chinese American parents; lacking an immediate connection to Chinese culture, Lisa projects upon all Chinese the authority of being "more Chinese." Lisa confesses to Connie at the end of the story: "The only time I feel Chinese is when I'm embarrassed I'm not more Chinese—which is a totally Chinese reflex I'd give anything to be rid of!" (176). Chang's story portrays two women polarized by the degree to which they have each internalized a cultural definition of "Chineseness" as pure and fixed, in which any deviation is constructed as less, lower, and shameful. Rather than confirming the cultural model in which "ethnicity" is passed from generation to generation, Chang's story explores the "ethnic" relationship between women of the same generation. Lisa and Connie are ultimately able to reduce one another's guilt at not being "Chinese enough"; in one another they are able to find a common frame of reference. The story suggests that the making of Chinese American culture—how ethnicity is imagined, practiced, continued—is worked out as much between ourselves and our communities as it is transmitted from one generation to another.

In this sense, Asian American discussions of ethnicity are far from uniform or consistent; rather, these discussions contain a wide spectrum of articulations that includes, at one end, the desire for an identity represented by a fixed profile of ethnic traits and, at another, challenges to the very notions of identity and singularity which celebrate ethnicity as a fluctuating composition of differences, intersections, and incommensurabilities. These latter efforts attempt to define ethnicity in a manner that accounts not only for cultural inheritance but for active cultural construction, as well. In other words, they suggest that the making of Asian American culture may be a much "messier" process than unmediated vertical transmission from one generation to another, including practices that are partly inherited and partly modified, as well as partly invented.[3] As the narrator of *The Woman Warrior* suggests, perhaps one of the more important stories of Asian American experience is about the process of receiving, refiguring, and rewriting cultural traditions. She asks, "Chinese-Americans, when you try to understand what things in you are Chinese, how do you separate what is peculiar to childhood, to poverty, insanities, one family, your mother who marked your growing with stories, from what is Chinese? What is Chinese tradition and what is the movies?" (6). Or the dilemma of cultural syncretism might be posed in an interrogative version of the uncle's impromptu proverb in Wayne Wang's film *Dim Sum*: "You can take the girl out of Chinatown, but can you take the Chinatown out of the girl?" For rather than representing a fixed, discrete culture, "Chinatown" is itself the very emblem of fluctuating demographics, languages, and populations.[4]

I begin my chapter with these particular examples drawn from Asian American cultural texts in order to observe that what is referred to as "Asian America" is clearly a heterogeneous entity. From the perspective of the majority culture, Asian Americans may very well be constructed as different from, and other than, Euro-Americans. But from the perspectives of Asian Americans, we are perhaps even more different, more diverse, among ourselves: being men and women at different distances and generations from our "original" Asian cultures—cultures as different as Chinese, Japanese, Korean, Filipino, Indian, and Vietnamese—Asian Americans are born in the United States and born in Asia; of exclusively Asian parents and of mixed race; urban and rural; refugee and nonrefugee; communist-identified and anticommunist; fluent in English and non-English-speaking; educated and working-class. As with other diasporas in the United States, the Asian immigrant collectivity is unstable and changeable, with its cohesion complicated by intergenerationality, by various degrees of identification and relation to a "homeland," and by different extents of assimilation to and distinction from "majority culture" in the United States. Further, the historical contexts of particular waves of immigration within single groups contrast with one another; the Japanese Americans who were interned during World War II encountered quite different social and economic barriers than those from Japan who arrive in Southern California today. And the composition of different waves of immigrants differs in gender, class, and region. For example, the first groups of Chinese immigrants to the United States in 1850 were from four villages in Canton province, male by a ratio of ten to one, and largely of peasant backgrounds; the more recent Chinese immigrants are from Hong Kong, Taiwan, or the People's Republic (themselves quite heterogeneous and of discontinuous "origins"), or from the Chinese diaspora in other parts of Asia, such as Macao, Malaysia, or Singapore, and they are more often educated and middle-class men and women.[5] Further, once arriving in the United States, very few Asian immigrant cultures remain discrete, impenetrable communities. The more recent groups mix, in varying degrees, with segments of the existing groups; Asian Americans may intermarry with other ethnic groups, live in neighborhoods adjacent to them, or work in the same businesses and on the same factory assembly lines. The boundaries and definitions of Asian American culture are continually shifting and being contested from pressures both "inside" and "outside" the Asian-origin community.

I stress heterogeneity, hybridity, and multiplicity in the characterization of Asian American culture as part of a twofold argument about cultural politics, the ultimate aim of that argument being to disrupt the current hegemonic relationship between "dominant" and "minority" positions. On the one hand, my observation that Asian Americans are heterogeneous is part of a strategy to destabilize the dominant discursive construction and determination of Asian Americans as a homogeneous group. Throughout the late nineteenth and early twentieth centuries, Asian immigration to the United States was managed by exclusion acts and quotas that relied upon racialist constructions of Asians as homogeneous;[6] the "model minority" myth and the informal quotas discriminating against Asians in university admissions policies are contemporary versions of this homogenization of Asians.[7] On the other hand, I underscore Asian American heterogeneities (particularly class, gender, and national differences among Asians) to contribute to a dialogue within Asian American discourse, to negotiate with those modes of argumentation that continue to uphold a politics based on ethnic "identity." In this sense, I argue for the Asian American necessity—politically, intellectually, and personally—to organize, resist, and theorize *as* Asian Americans, but at the same time I inscribe this necessity within a discussion of the risks of a cultural politics that relies upon the construction of sameness and the exclusion of differences.

The first reason to emphasize the dynamic fluctuation and heterogeneity of Asian American culture is to release our understandings of either the "dominant" or the emergent "minority" cultures as discrete, fixed, or homogeneous, and to arrive at a different conception of the general political terrain of culture in California, a useful focus for this examination since it has become commonplace to consider it an "ethnic state," embodying a new phenomenon of cultural adjacency and admixture.[8] For if minority immigrant cultures are perpetually changing—in their composition, configuration, and signifying practices, as well as in their relations to one another—it follows that the "majority" or dominant culture, with which minority cultures are in continual relation, is also unstable and unclosed. The suggestion that the general social terrain of culture is open, plural, and dynamic reorients our understanding of what "cultural hegemony" is and how it works in contemporary California. It permits us to theorize about the roles that ethnic immigrant groups play in the making and unmaking of culture—and how these minority discourses challenge the existing structure of power, the existing hegemony.[9] We should remember that Antonio Gramsci writes about hegemony as not simply political or economic forms of rule but as the entire process of dissent and compromise through which a particular group is able to determine the political, cultural, and ideological character of a state (1971b). Hegemony does not refer exclusively to the process by which a dominant formation exercises its influence but refers equally to the process through which minority groups organize and contest any specific hegemony.[10] The reality of any specific hegemony is that, while it may be for the moment dominant, it is never absolute or conclusive. Hegemony, in Gramsci's thought, is a concept that describes both the social processes through which a particular dominance is maintained and those through which that dominance is challenged and new forces are articulated. When a hegemony representing the interests of a dominant group exists, it is always within the context of resistances from emerging "subaltern" groups.[11] We might say that hegemony is not only the political process by which a particular group constitutes itself as "the one" or "the majority" in relation to which "minorities" are defined and know themselves to be "other," but it is equally the process by which positions of otherness may ally and constitute a new majority, a "counterhegemony."[12]

The subaltern classes are, in Gramsci's definition, prehegemonic, not unified groups, whose histories are fragmented, episodic, and identifiable only from a point of historical hindsight. They may go through different phases when they are subject to the activity of ruling groups, may articulate their demands through existing parties, and then may themselves produce new parties; in *The Prison Notebooks*, Gramsci describes a final phase at which the "formations [of the subaltern classes] assert integral autonomy" (1971a, 52). The definition of the subaltern groups includes some noteworthy observations for our understanding of the roles of racial and ethnic immigrant groups in the United States. The assertion that the significant practices of the subaltern groups may not be understood as hegemonic until they are viewed with historical hindsight is interesting, for it suggests that some of the most powerful practices may not always be the explicitly oppositional ones, may not be understood by contemporaries, and may be less overt and recognizable than others. Provocative, too, is the idea that the subaltern classes are by definition "not unified"; that is, the subaltern is not a fixed, unified force of a single character. Rather, the assertion of "integral autonomy" by not unified classes suggests a coordination of distinct, yet allied, positions, practices, and movements—class-identified and not class-identified, in parties and not, ethnic-based and gender-based—each in its own not necessarily equivalent manner transforming and disrupting the apparatuses of a specific hegemony. The independent forms and locations of cultural challenge—ideological, as well as economic and political—constitute what Gramsci calls a "new historical bloc," a new set of relationships that together embody a different hegemony and a different balance of power. In this sense, we have in the growing and shifting ethnic minority populations in California an active example of this new historical bloc described by Gramsci; and in the negotiations between these ethnic groups and the existing majority over what interests precisely constitute the "majority," we have an illustration of the concept of hegemony, not in the more commonly accepted sense of "hegemony-maintenance," but in the often ignored sense of "hegemony-creation."[13] The observation that the Asian American community and other ethnic immigrant communities are heterogeneous lays the foundation for several political operations: First, by shifting, multiplying, and reconceiving the construction of society as composed of two numerically overdetermined camps called the majority and the minority, cultural politics is recast so as to account for a multiplicity of various, nonequivalent groups, one of which is Asian Americans. Second, the conception of ethnicity as heterogeneous provides a position for Asian Americans that is both ethnically specific, yet simultaneously uneven and unclosed; Asian Americans can articulate distinct group demands based on our particular histories of exclusion, but the redefined lack of closure—which reveals rather than conceals differences—opens political lines of affiliation with other groups (labor unions, other racial and ethnic groups, and gay, lesbian, and feminist groups) in the challenge to specific forms of domination insofar as they share common features.

In regard to the practice of "identity politics" within Asian American discourse, the articulation of an "Asian American identity" as an organizing tool has provided a concept of political unity that enables diverse Asian groups to understand our unequal circumstances and histories as being related; likewise, the building of "Asian American culture" is crucial, for it articulates and empowers our multicultural, multilingual Asian-origin community vis-à-vis the institutions and apparatuses that exclude and marginalize us. But I want to suggest that essentializing Asian American identity and suppressing our differences—of national origin, generation, gender, party, class—risks particular dangers: not only does it underestimate the differences and hybridities among Asians, but it also inadvertently supports the racist discourse that constructs Asians as a homogeneous group, that implies we are "all alike" and conform to "types"; in this respect, a politics based exclusively on ethnic identity willingly accepts the terms of the dominant logic that organizes the heterogeneous picture of racial and ethnic diversity into a binary schema of "the one" and "the other." The essentializing of Asian American identity also reproduces oppositions that subsume other nondominant terms in the same way that Asians and other groups are disenfranchised by the dominant culture: to the degree that the discourse generalizes Asian American identity as male, women are rendered invisible; or to the extent that Chinese are presumed to be exemplary of all Asians, the importance of other Asian groups is ignored. In this sense, a politics based on ethnic identity facilitates the displacement of intercommunity differences—between men and women, or between workers and managers—into a false opposition of "nationalism" and "assimilation." We have an example of this in recent debates where Asian American feminists who challenge Asian American sexism are cast as "assimilationist," as betraying Asian American "nationalism."

To the extent that Asian American discourse articulates an identity in reaction to the dominant culture's stereotype, even to refute it, I believe the discourse may remain bound to, and overdetermined by, the logic of the dominant culture. In accepting the binary terms ("white" and "nonwhite," or "majority" and "minority") that structure institutional policies about ethnicity, we forget that these binary schemas are not neutral descriptions. Binary constructions of difference use a logic that prioritizes the first term and subordinates the second; whether the pair "difference" and "sameness" is figured as a binary synthesis that considers "difference" as always contained within the "same," or that conceives of the pair as an opposition in which "difference" structurally implies "sameness" as its complement, it is important to see each of these figurations as versions of the same binary logic. My argument for heterogeneity seeks to challenge the conception of difference as exclusively structured by a binary opposition between two terms by proposing instead another notion of difference that takes seriously the conditions of heterogeneity, multiplicity, and nonequivalence. I submit that the most exclusive construction of Asian American identity—which presumes masculinity, American birth, and speaking English—is at odds with the formation of important political alliances and affiliations with other groups across racial and ethnic, gender, sexuality, and class lines. An essentialized identity is an obstacle to Asian American women allying with other women of color, for example, and it can discourage laboring Asian Americans from joining unions with workers of other colors. It can short-circuit potential alliances against the dominant structures of power in the name of subordinating "divisive" issues to *the* national question.

Some of the limits of identity politics are discussed most pointedly by Frantz Fanon in his books about the Algerian resistance to French colonialism. Before ultimately turning to some Asian American cultural texts in order to trace the ways in which the dialogues about identity and difference are represented within the discourse, I would like to briefly consider one of Fanon's most important texts, *The Wretched of the Earth* (*Les damnés de la terre* 1961). Although Fanon's treatise was cited in the 1960s as the manifesto for a nationalist politics of identity, rereading it today we find his text, ironically, to be the source of a serious critique of nationalism. Fanon argues that the challenge facing any movement dismantling colonialism (or a system in which one culture dominates another) is to provide for a new order that does not reproduce the social structure of the old system. This new order, he argues, must avoid the simple assimilation to the dominant culture's roles and positions by the emergent group, which would merely caricature the old colonialism, and it should be equally suspicious of an uncritical nativism, or racialism, appealing to essentialized notions of precolonial identity. Fanon suggests that another alternative is necessary, a new order, neither an assimilationist nor a nativist inversion, which breaks with the structures and practices of cultural domination and which continually and collectively criticizes the institutions of rule. One of the more remarkable turns in Fanon's argument occurs when he identifies both bourgeois assimilation and bourgeois nationalism as conforming to the same logic, as responses to colonialism that reproduce the same structure of cultural domination. It is in this sense that Fanon warns against the nationalism practiced by bourgeois neocolonial governments. Their nationalism, he argues, can be distorted easily into racism, territorialism, separatism, or ethnic dictatorships of one tribe or regional group over others; the national bourgeois replaces the colonizer, yet the social and economic structure remains the same.[14] Ironically, he points out, these separatisms, or "micro-nationalisms" (Mamadou Dia, quoted in Fanon 1961, 158), are themselves legacies of colonialism. He writes, "By its very structure, colonialism is regionalist and separatist. Colonialism does not simply state the existence of tribes; it also reinforces and separates them" (94). That is, a politics of ethnic separatism is congruent with the divide-and-conquer logic of colonial domination. Fanon links the practices of the national bourgeoisie that has assimilated colonialist thought and practice with nativist practices that privilege one tribe or ethnicity over others; nativism and assimilationism are not opposites but similar logics both enunciating the old order.

Fanon's analysis implies that an essentialized bourgeois construction of "nation" is a classification that excludes other subaltern groups that could bring about substantive change in the social and economic relations, particularly those whose social marginalities are due to class: peasants, workers, transient populations. We can add to Fanon's criticism that the category of nation often erases a consideration of women and the fact of difference between men and women and the conditions under which they live and work in situations of cultural domination. This is why the concentration of women of color in domestic service or reproductive labor (child care, home care, nursing) in the contemporary United States is not adequately explained by a nation-based model of analysis (see Glenn 1981). In light of feminist theory, which has gone the furthest in theorizing multiple inscription and the importance of positionalities, we can argue that it may be less meaningful to act exclusively in terms of a single valence or political interest—such as ethnicity or nation—than to acknowledge that social subjects are the sites of a variety of differences.[15] An Asian American subject is never purely and exclusively ethnic, for that subject is always of a particular class, gender, and sexual preference and may therefore feel responsible to movements that are organized around these other designations. This is not to argue against the strategic importance of Asian American identity, nor against the building of Asian American culture. Rather, I am suggesting that acknowledging class and gender differences among Asian Americans does not weaken us as a group; to the contrary, these differences represent greater political opportunity to affiliate with other groups whose cohesions may be based on other valences of oppression.

As I have already suggested, within Asian American discourse there is a varied spectrum of discussion about the concepts of ethnic identity and culture. At one end, there are discussions in which ethnic identity is essentialized as the cornerstone of a nationalist liberation politics. In these discussions, the cultural positions of nationalism (or ethnicism, or nativism) and of assimilation are represented in polar opposition: nationalism affirming the separate purity of its ethnic culture is opposed to assimilation of the standards of dominant society. Stories about the loss of the "native" Asian culture tend to express some form of this opposition. At the same time, there are criticisms of this essentializing position, most often articulated by feminists who charge that Asian American nationalism prioritizes masculinity and does not account for women. At the

other end, there are interventions that refuse static or binary conceptions of ethnicity, replacing notions of identity with multiplicity and shifting the emphasis
for ethnic "essence" to cultural hybridity. Settling for neither nativism nor assimilation, these cultural texts expose the apparent opposition between the two as
a constructed figure (as Fanon does when he observes that bourgeois assimilation and bourgeois nationalism often conform to the same colonialist logic). In
tracing these different discussions about identity and ethnicity through Asian
American cultural debates, literature, and film, I choose particular texts because
they are accessible and commonly held. But I do not intend to limit *discourse*
to only these particular textual forms; by *discourse*, I intend a rather extended
meaning—a network that includes not only texts and cultural documents but
social practices, formal and informal laws, policies of inclusion and exclusion,
and institutional forms of organization, for example, all of which constitute and
regulate knowledge about the object of that discourse, Asian America.

The terms of the debate about nationalism and assimilation become clearer
if we look first at the discussion of ethnic identity in certain debates about the
representation of culture. Readers of Asian American literature are familiar
with attacks by Frank Chin, Ben Tong, and others on Maxine Hong Kingston,
attacks that have been cast as nationalist criticisms of Kingston's "assimilationist" works. Her novel/autobiography *The Woman Warrior* is the primary target
of such criticism, since it is virtually the only "canonized" piece of Asian American literature; its status can be measured by the fact that the Modern Language
Association is currently publishing *A Guide to Teaching "The Woman Warrior"*
in its series that includes guides to Cervantes's *Don Quixote* and Dante's *Inferno*.
A critique of how and why this text has become fetishized as the exemplary
representation of Asian American culture is necessary and important. However, Chin's critique reveals other kinds of tensions in Asian American culture
that are worth noting. He does more than accuse Kingston of having exoticized
Chinese American culture; he argues that she has "feminized" Asian American
literature and undermined the power of Asian American men to combat the
racist stereotypes of the dominant white culture. Kingston and other women
novelists such as Amy Tan, he says, misrepresent Chinese history in order to
exaggerate its patriarchal structure; as a result, Chinese society is portrayed as
being even more misogynistic than European society. While Chin and others
have cast this conflict in terms of nationalism and assimilationism, I think it
may be more productive to see this debate, as Elaine Kim does in a recent essay
("'Such Opposite'" 1990), as a symptom of the tensions between nationalist and
feminist concerns in Asian American discourse. I would add to Kim's analysis
that the dialogue between nationalist and feminist concerns animates precisely
a debate about identity and difference, or identity and heterogeneity, rather than
a debate between nationalism and assimilationism; it is a debate in which Chin
and others stand at one end insisting upon a fixed masculinist identity, while

Kingston, Tan, or feminist literary critics like Shirley Lim and Amy Ling, with their representations of female differences and their critiques of sexism in Chinese culture, repeatedly cast this notion of identity into question. Just as Fanon points out that some forms of nationalism can obscure class, Asian American feminists point out that Asian American nationalism—or the construction of an essentialized, native Asian American subject—obscures gender. In other words, the struggle that is framed as a conflict between the apparent opposites of nativism and assimilation can mask what is more properly characterized as a struggle between the desire to essentialize ethnic identity and the fundamental condition of heterogeneous differences against which such a desire is spoken. The trope that opposes nativism and assimilationism can be itself a colonialist figure used to displace the challenges of heterogeneity, or subalternity, by casting them as assimilationist or antiethnic.

The trope that opposes nativism and assimilation not only organizes the cultural debates of Asian American discourse but figures *in* Asian American literature, as well. More often than not, however, this symbolic conflict between nativism and assimilation is figured in the topos with which I began, that of generational conflict. Although there are many versions of this topos, I will mention only a few in order to elucidate some of the most relevant cultural tensions. In one model, a conflict between generations is cast in strictly masculinist terms, between father and son; in this model, mothers are absent or unimportant, and female figures exist only as peripheral objects to the side of the central drama of male conflict. Louis Chu's *Eat a Bowl of Tea* (1961) exemplifies this masculinist generational symbolism, in which a conflict between nativism and assimilation is allegorized in the relationship between the father, Wah Gay, and the son, Ben Loy, in the period when the predominantly Cantonese New York Chinatown community changes from a "bachelor society" to a "family society."[16] Wah Gay wishes Ben Loy to follow Chinese tradition, and to submit to the father's authority, while the son balks at his father's "old ways" and wants to make his own choices. When Wah Gay arranges a marriage for Ben Loy, the son is forced to obey. Although the son had had no trouble leading an active sexual life before his marriage, once married, he finds himself to be impotent. In other words, Chu's novel figures the conflict of nativism and assimilation in terms of Ben Loy's sexuality: submitting to the father's authority, marrying the "nice Chinese girl" Mei Oi and having sons, is the so-called traditional Chinese male behavior. This path represents the nativist option, whereas Ben Loy's former behavior— carrying on with American prostitutes, gambling, etc.—represents the alleged path of assimilation. At the nativist Chinese extreme, Ben Loy is impotent and is denied access to erotic pleasure, and at the assimilationist American extreme, he has great access and sexual freedom. Allegorizing the choice between cultural options in the register of Ben Loy's sexuality, Chu's novel suggests that resolution lies at neither pole but in a third "Chinese American" alternative, in which Ben

Loy is able to experience erotic pleasure with his Chinese wife. This occurs only when the couple moves away to another state, away from the father; Ben Loy's relocation to San Francisco's Chinatown and the priority of pleasure with Mei Oi over the begetting of a son (which, incidentally, they ultimately do have) both represent important breaks from his father's authority and from Chinese tradition. Following Fanon's observations about the affinities between nativism and assimilation, we can understand Chu's novel as an early masculinist rendering of culture as conflict between the apparent opposites of nativism and assimilation, with its oedipal resolution in a Chinese American male identity; perhaps only with hindsight can we propose that the opposition itself may be a construction that allegorizes the dialectic between an articulation of essentialized ethnic identity and the context of heterogeneous differences.

Amy Tan's much more recent *The Joy Luck Club* (1989) refigures this topos of generational conflict in a different social context, among first- and second-generation Mandarin Chinese in San Francisco and, more importantly, between women. Tan's *Joy Luck* displaces *Eat a Bowl* not only because it deviates from the figuration of Asian American identity in a masculine oedipal dilemma by refiguring it in terms of mothers and daughters but also because *Joy Luck* multiplies the sites of cultural conflict, positing a number of struggles—familial and extra-familial—as well as resolutions, without privileging the singularity or centrality of one. In this way, *Joy Luck* ultimately thematizes and demystifies the central role of the mother-daughter relationship in Asian American culture.

Joy Luck represents the first-person narratives of four sets of Chinese-born mothers and their American-born daughters. The daughters attempt to come to terms with their mothers' demands, while the mothers simultaneously try to interpret their daughters' deeds, expressing a tension between the "Chinese" expectation of filial respect and the "American" inability to fulfill that expectation. By multiplying and subverting the model of generational discord with examples of generational concord, the novel calls attention to the heterogeneity of Chinese American family relations. On the one hand, mothers like Ying-ying St. Clair complain about their daughters' Americanization:

> For all these years I kept my mouth closed so selfish desires would not fall out. And because I remained quiet for so long now my daughter does not hear me. She sits by her fancy swimming pool and hears only her Sony Walkman, her cordless phone, her big, important husband asking her why they have charcoal and no lighter fluid.
>
> ... because I moved so secretly now my daughter does not see me. She sees a list of things to buy, her checkbook out of balance, her ashtray sitting crooked on a straight table.
>
> And I want to tell her this: We are lost, she and I, unseen and not seeing, unheard and not hearing, unknown by others. (67)

The mother presents herself as having sacrificed everything for a daughter who has ignored these sacrifices. She sees her daughter as preoccupied with portable, mobile high-tech commodities which, characteristically, have no cords, no ties, emblematizing the mother's condemnation of a daughter who does not respect family bonds. The mother implies that the daughter recognizes that something is skewed and attempts to correct it—balancing her checkbook, straightening her house—but, in the mother's eyes, she has no access to the real problems; being in America has taken this understanding away. Her daughter, Lena, however, tends to view her mother as unreasonably superstitious and domineering. Lena considers her mother's concern about her failing marriage as meddlesome; the daughter's interpretation of their antagonism emphasizes a cultural gap between the mother who considers her daughter's troubles her own and the daughter who sees her mother's actions as intrusive, possessive, and, worst of all, denying the daughter's own separate individuality.

On the other hand, in contrast to this and other examples of disjunction between the Chinese mothers and the Chinese American daughters, *Joy Luck* also includes a relationship between mother and daughter in which there is an apparent coincidence of perspective; tellingly, in this example the mother has died, and it is left to the daughter to "eulogize" the mother by telling the mother's story. Jing-mei Woo makes a trip to China, to reunite with her recently deceased mother's two daughters by an earlier marriage, whom her mother had been forced to abandon almost forty years before when fleeing China during the Japanese invasion. Jing-mei wants to fulfill her mother's last wish to see the long-lost daughters; she wishes to inscribe herself in her mother's place. Her narration of the reunion conveys her utopian belief in the possibility of recovering the past, of rendering herself coincident with her mother, narrating her desire to become again "Chinese."

> My sisters and I stand, arms around each other, laughing and wiping the tears from each other's eyes. The flash of the Polaroid goes off and my father hands me the snapshot. My sisters and I watch quietly together, eager to see what develops.
>
> The gray-green surface changes to the bright colors of our three images, sharpening and deepening all at once. And although we don't speak, I know we all see it: Together we look like our mother. Her same eyes, her same mouth, open in surprise to see, at last, her long-cherished wish. (288)

Unlike Lena St. Clair, Jing-mei does not seek greater autonomy from her mother; she desires a lessening of the disparity between their positions that is accomplished through the narrative evocation of her mother after she has died. By contrasting different examples of mother-daughter discord and concord, *Joy Luck* allegorizes the heterogeneous culture in which the desire for identity and sameness (represented by Jing-mei's story) is inscribed within the context of Asian American differences and disjunctions (exemplified by the other three pairs of mothers and daughters). The novel formally illustrates that the articulation of one, the desire for identity, depends upon the existence of the others, or the fundamental horizon of differences.

Further, although *Joy Luck* has been heralded and marketed as a novel about mother-daughter relations in the Chinese American family (one cover review characterizes it as a "story that shows us China, Chinese American women and their families, and the mystery of the mother-daughter bond in ways that we have not experienced before"), I would suggest that the novel also represents antagonisms that are not exclusively generational but are due to different conceptions of class and gender among Chinese Americans.

Toward the end of the novel, Lindo and Waverly Jong reach a climax of misunderstanding, in a scene that takes place in a central site of American femininity: the beauty parlor. After telling the stylist to give her mother a "soft wave," Waverly asks her mother, Lindo, if she is in agreement. The mother narrates,

> I smile. I use my American face. That's the face Americans think is Chinese, the one they cannot understand. But inside I am becoming ashamed. I am ashamed she is ashamed. Because she is my daughter and I am proud of her, and I am her mother but she is not proud of me. (255)

The American-born daughter believes she is treating her mother, rather magnanimously, to a day of pampering at a chic salon; the Chinese-born mother receives this gesture as an insult, clear evidence of a daughter ashamed of her mother's looks. The scene marks not only the separation of mother and daughter by generation but, perhaps less obviously, their separation by class and cultural differences that lead to different interpretations of how female identity is signified. On the one hand, the Chinese-born Lindo and American-born Waverly have different class values and opportunities; the daughter's belief in the pleasure of a visit to an expensive San Francisco beauty parlor seems senselessly extravagant to the mother whose rural family had escaped poverty only by marrying her to the son of a less humble family in their village. On the other hand, the mother and daughter also conflict over definitions of proper female behavior. Lindo assumes female identity is constituted in the practice of a daughter's deference to her elders, while for Waverly, it is determined by a woman's financial independence from her parents and her financial equality with men and by her ability to speak her desires, and it is cultivated and signified in the styles and shapes that represent middle-class feminine beauty. In this sense, I ultimately read *Joy Luck* not as a novel that exclusively depicts generational conflict among Chinese American women but rather as a text that thematizes the trope of the mother-daughter relationship in Asian American culture; that is, the novel comments upon the idealized construction of mother-daughter relationships (both in the majority culture's discourse about Asian Americans and in the Asian American discourse about ourselves), as well as upon the kinds of differences—of class and culturally specific definitions of gender—that are rendered invisible by the privileging of this trope.[17]

Before concluding, I want to turn to a final cultural text which not only restates the Asian American narrative that opposes nativism and assimilation but articulates a critique of that narrative, calling the nativist/assimilationist dyad into question. If *Joy Luck* poses an alternative to the dichotomy of nativism and assimilation by multiplying the generational conflict and demystifying the centrality of the mother-daughter relationship, then Peter Wang's film *A Great Wall* (1985)—both in its emplotment and in its very medium of representation—offers yet another version of this alternative. Wang's film unsettles both poles in the antinomy of nativist essentialism and assimilation by performing a continual geographical juxtaposition and exchange between a variety of cultural spaces. *A Great Wall* portrays the visit of Leo Fang's Chinese American family to the People's Republic of China and their monthlong stay with Leo's sister's family, the Chao family, in Beijing. The film concentrates on the primary contrast between the habits, customs, and assumptions of the Chinese in China and the Chinese Americans in California by going back and forth between shots of Beijing and Northern California, in a type of continual filmic "migration" between the two, as if to thematize in its very form the travel between cultural spaces. From the first scene, however, the film foregrounds the idea that in the opposition between native and assimilated spaces, neither begins as a pure, uncontaminated site or origin; and as the camera eye shuttles back and forth between, both poles of the constructed opposition shift and change. (Indeed, the Great Wall of China, from which the film takes its title, is a monument to the historical condition that not even ancient China was "pure," but coexisted with "foreign barbarians" against which the Middle Kingdom erected such barriers.) In this regard, the film contains a number of emblematic images that call attention to the syncretic, composite quality of all cultural spaces: when the young Chinese Liu finishes the university entrance exam his scholar-father gives him a Coca-Cola; children crowd around the single village television to watch a Chinese opera singer imitate Pavarotti singing Italian opera; the Chinese student learning English recites the Gettysburg Address. Although the film concentrates on both illustrating and dissolving the apparent opposition between Chinese Chinese and American Chinese, a number of other contrasts are likewise explored: the differences between generations both within the Chao and the Fang families (daughter Lili noisily drops her bike while her father practices tai chi; Paul kisses his Caucasian girlfriend and later tells his father that he believes all Chinese are racists when Leo suggests that he might date some nice Chinese girls); differences between men and women (accentuated by two scenes, one in which Grace Fang and Mrs. Chao talk about their husbands and children, the other in which Chao and Leo get drunk together); and, finally, the differences between capitalist and communist societies (highlighted in a scene in which the Chaos and Fangs talk about their different attitudes toward "work"). The representations of these other contrasts complicate and diversify the ostensible focus on cultural differences between Chinese and Chinese Americans, as if to testify to the condition that there is never only one exclusive valence of difference, but rather cultural difference is always simultaneously bound up with gender, economics, age, and other distinctions. In other words, when Leo says to his wife that the Great Wall makes the city "just as difficult to leave as to get in," the wall at once signifies the construction of a variety of barriers—not only between Chinese and Americans but between generations, men and women, capitalism and communism—as well as the impossibility of ever remaining bounded and impenetrable, of resisting change, recomposition, and reinvention. We are reminded of this impossibility throughout the film, but it is perhaps best illustrated in the scene in which the Fang and Chao families play a rousing game of touch football on the ancient immovable Great Wall.

The film continues with a series of wonderful contrasts: the differences in the bodily comportments of the Chinese American Paul and the Chinese Liu playing ping-pong, between Leo's jogging and Mr. Chao's tai chi, between Grace Fang's and Mrs. Chao's ideas of what is fitting and fashionable for the female body. The two families have different senses of space and of the relation between family members. In one subplot, the Chinese American cousin Paul is outraged to learn that Mrs. Chao reads her daughter Lili's mail; he asks Lili if she has ever heard of "privacy." This later results in a fight between Mrs. Chao and Lili in which Lili says she has learned from their American cousins that "it's not right to read other people's mail." Mrs. Chao retorts, "You're not 'other people,' you're my daughter. What is this thing, 'privacy'?" Lili explains to her that "privacy" can't be translated into Chinese. "Oh, so you're trying to hide things from your mother and use western words to trick her!" exclaims Mrs. Chao. Ultimately, just as the members of the Chao family are marked by the visit from their American relatives, the Fangs are altered by the time they return to California, each bringing back a memento or practice from their Chinese trip. In other words, rather than privileging either a nativist or assimilationist view, or even espousing a "Chinese American" resolution of differences, A Great Wall performs a filmic "migration" by shuttling between the various cultural spaces; we are left, by the end of the film, with a sense of culture as dynamic and open, the result of a continual process of visiting and revisiting a plurality of cultural sites.

In keeping with the example of A Great Wall, we might consider as a possible model for the ongoing construction of ethnic identity the migratory process suggested by Wang's filming technique and emplotment: we might conceive of the making and practice of Asian American culture as nomadic, unsettled, taking place in the travel between cultural sites and in the multivocality of heterogeneous and conflicting positions. Taking seriously the heterogeneities among Asian Americans in California, we must conclude that the grouping "Asian

American" is not a natural or static category; it is a socially constructed unity, a situationally specific position that we assume for political reasons. It is "strategic" in Gayatri Spivak's sense of a "strategic use of a positive essentialism in a scrupulously visible political interest" (1987, 205). The concept of "strategic essentialism" suggests that it is possible to utilize specific signifiers of ethnic identity, such as Asian American, for the purpose of contesting and disrupting the discourses that exclude Asian Americans, while simultaneously revealing the internal contradictions and slippages of Asian American so as to ensure that such essentialisms will not be reproduced and proliferated by the very apparatuses we seek to disempower. I am not suggesting that we can or should do away with the notion of Asian American identity, for to stress only our differences would jeopardize the hard-earned unity that has been achieved in the last two decades of Asian American politics, the unity that is necessary if Asian Americans are to play a role in the new historical bloc of ethnic Californians. In fact, I would submit that the very freedom, in the 1990s, to explore the hybridities concealed beneath the desire of identity is permitted by the context of a strongly articulated essentialist politics. Just as the articulation of the desire for identity depends upon the existence of a fundamental horizon of differences, the articulation of differences dialectically depends upon a socially constructed and practiced notion of identity. I want simply to remark that in the 1990s, we can afford to rethink the notion of ethnic identity in terms of cultural, class, and gender differences, rather than presuming similarities and making the erasure of particularity the basis of unity. In the 1990s, we can diversify our political practices to include a more heterogeneous group and to enable crucial alliances with other groups— ethnicity based, class based, gender based, and sexuality based—in the ongoing work of transforming hegemony.

NOTES

Originally published in *Diaspora* 1 (1): 24–44, 1991. ©1991 University of Toronto Press, reprint by permission. Many thanks to Elaine Kim for her thought-provoking questions and for asking me to deliver portions of this essay as papers at the 1990 meetings of the Association of Asian American Studies and of the American Literature Association; to James Clifford, who also gave me the opportunity to deliver a version of this essay at a conference sponsored by the Center for Cultural Studies at UC Santa Cruz; to the audience participants at all three conferences who asked stimulating questions which have helped me to rethink my original notions; and to Page duBois, Barbara Harlow, Susan Kirkpatrick, George Mariscal, Ellen Rooney, and Kathryn Shevelow, who read drafts and offered important comments and criticism.

1 "Nisei" refers to a second-generation Japanese American, born to immigrant parents in the United States, "sansei" a third-generation Japanese American. "Issei" refers to a first-generation immigrant.

2 See Kim (1982) for the most important book-length study of the literary representations of multigenerational Asian America.

3 Recent anthropological discussions of ethnic cultures as fluid and syncretic systems echo these concerns of Asian American writers. See, for example, Fischer (1986) and Clifford

(1988). For an anthropological study of Japanese American culture that troubles the paradigmatic construction of kinship and filial relations as the central figure in culture, see Yanagisako (1985).

4 We might think, for example, of the shifting of the Los Angeles "Chinatown" from its downtown location to the suburban community of Monterey Park. Since the 1970s, the former Chinatown has been superseded demographically and economically by Monterey Park, the home of many Chinese Americans as well as newly arrived Chinese from Hong Kong and Taiwan. The Monterey Park community of sixty-three thousand residents is currently over 50 percent Asian. On the social and political consequences of these changing demographics, see Fong (1994).

5 Chan's history of the Chinese immigrant populations in California, *Bittersweet* (1986), and her history of Asian Americans (1991) are extremely important in this regard. Numerous lectures by Ling-chi Wang at UC San Diego in 1987 and at UC Berkeley in 1988 have been very important to my understanding of the heterogeneity of waves of immigration across different Asian-origin groups.

6 The Chinese Exclusion Act of 1882 barred Chinese from entering the United States, the National Origins Act prohibited the entry of Japanese in 1924, and the Tydings-McDuffie Act of 1934 limited Filipino immigrants to fifty people per year. Finally, the most tragic consequence of anti-Asian racism occurred during World War II, when 120,000 Japanese Americans (two-thirds of whom were American citizens by birth) were interned in camps. For a study of the anti-Japanese movement culminating in the Immigration Act of 1924, see Daniels (1962). Takaki (1989) offers a general history of Asian-origin immigrant groups in the United States.

7 The model minority myth constructs Asians as aggressively driven overachievers; it is a homogenizing fiction that relies upon two strategies common in the subordinating construction of racial or ethnic otherness—the racial other as knowable, familiar ("like us"), and as incomprehensible, threatening ("unlike us"); the model minority myth suggests both that Asians are overachievers and "unlike us" and that they assimilate well and are thus "like us." Asian Americans are continually pointing out that the model minority myth distorts the real gains, as well as the impediments, of Asian immigrants; by leveling and homogenizing all Asian groups, it erases the different rates of assimilation and the variety of class identities among various Asian immigrant groups. Claiming that Asians are "overrepresented" on college campuses, the model minority myth is one of the justifications for the establishment of informal quotas in university admissions policies, similar to the university admission policies that discriminated against Jewish students from the 1930s to the 1950s.

8 In the past two decades, greatly diverse new groups have settled in California; demographers project that by the end of the century, the "majority" of the state will be composed of ethnic "minority" groups. Due to recent immigrants, this influx of minorities is characterized also by greater diversity within individual groups: the group we call Asian Americans no longer denotes only Japanese, Chinese, Koreans, and Filipinos but now includes Indian, Thai, Vietnamese, Cambodian, and Laotian groups; Latino communities in California are made up not only of Chicanos but also Guatemalans, Salvadorans, and Colombians. It is not difficult to find Pakistani, Armenian, Lebanese, and Iranian enclaves in San Francisco, Los Angeles, and even San Diego. While California's "multiculturalism" is often employed to support a notion of the "melting pot," to further an ideological assertion of equal opportunity for California's different immigrant groups, I am, in contrast, pursuing the ignored implications of this characterization of California as an ethnic state: that is, despite the increasing numbers of ethnic immigrants apparently racing to enjoy California's opportunities, for racial and ethnic immigrants there is no equality but uneven development, nonequivalence, and cultural heterogeneities, not only between but within groups.

9 For an important elaboration of the concept of "minority discourse," see JanMohamed and Lloyd (1990).

10 This notion of "the dominant"—defined by Williams (1977, 121) in a chapter discussing the "Dominant, Residual, and Emergent" as "a cultural process . . . seized as a cultural system, with determinate dominant features: feudal culture or bourgeois culture or a transition from one to the other"—is often conflated in recent cultural theory with Gramsci's concept of hegemony. Indeed, Williams writes, "We have certainly still to speak of the 'dominant' and the 'effective,' and in these senses of the hegemonic" (121), as if the dominant and the hegemonic are synonymous.

11 See Gramsci (1971a, 54–55). Gramsci describes "subaltern" groups as by definition not unified, emergent, and always in relation to the dominant groups:

> The history of subaltern social groups is necessarily fragmented and episodic. There undoubtedly does exist a tendency to (at least provisional stages of) unification in the historical activity of these groups, but this tendency is continually interrupted by the activity of the ruling groups; it therefore can only be demonstrated when an historical cycle is completed and this cycle culminates in a success. Subaltern groups are always subject to the activity of ruling groups, even when they rebel and rise up: only "permanent" victory breaks their subordination, and that not immediately. In reality, even when they appear triumphant, the subaltern groups are merely anxious to defend themselves (a truth which can be demonstrated by the history of the French Revolution at least up to 1830). Every trace of independent initiative on the part of subaltern groups should therefore be of incalculable value for the integral historian.

12 "Hegemony" remains a suggestive construct in Gramsci, however, rather than an explicitly interpreted set of relations. Contemporary readers are left with the more specific task of distinguishing which particular forms of challenge to an existing hegemony are significantly transformative and which forms may be neutralized or appropriated by the hegemony. Some cultural critics contend that counterhegemonic forms and practices are tied by definition to the dominant culture and that the dominant culture simultaneously produces and limits its own forms of counterculture. I am thinking here of some of the "new historicist" studies that use a particular notion of Foucault's discourse to confer authority to the "dominant," interpreting all forms of "subversion" as being ultimately "contained" by dominant ideology and institutions. Other cultural historians, such as Williams, suggest that because there is both identifiable variation in the social order over time, as well as variations in the forms of the counterculture in different historical periods, we must conclude that some aspects of the oppositional forms are not reducible to the terms of the original hegemony. Still other theorists, such as Ernesto Laclau and Chantal Mouffe, have expanded Gramsci's notion of hegemony to argue that in advanced capitalist society, the social field is not a totality consisting exclusively of the dominant and the counterdominant but rather that "the social" is an open and uneven terrain of contesting articulations and signifying practices. Some of these articulations and practices are neutralized, while others can be linked to build important pressures against an existing hegemony. See Laclau and Mouffe (1985, esp. 134–145). They argue persuasively that no hegemonic logic can account for the totality of "the social" and that the open and incomplete character of the social field is the precondition of every hegemonic practice. For if the field of hegemony were conceived according to a "zero-sum" vision of possible positions and practices, then the very concept of hegemony, as plural and mutable formations and relations, would be rendered impossible. Elsewhere, in "Hegemony and New Political Subjects," Mouffe (1988) goes even further to elaborate the practical dimensions of the hegemonic principle in terms of contemporary social movements.

13 Adamson (1980) reads *The Prison Notebooks* as the postulation of Gramsci's activist and educationalist politics; in chapter 6, he discusses Gramsci's two concepts of hegemony: hegemony as the consensual basis of an existing political system in civil society, as opposed to violent oppression or domination, and hegemony as a historical phase of bourgeois development in which class is understood not only economically but also in terms of a common intellectual and moral awareness, an overcoming of the "economic-corporative" phase. Adamson associates the former (hegemony in its contrast to domination) with "hegemony-maintenance," and the latter (hegemony as a stage in the political moment) as "hegemony-creation." Sassoon (1982) provides an excellent discussion of Gramsci's key concepts; she both historicizes the concept of hegemony and discusses the implications of some of the ways in which hegemony has been interpreted. Sassoon emphasizes the degree to which hegemony is opposed to domination to evoke the way in which one social group influences other groups, making certain compromises with them in order to gain their consent for its leadership in society as a whole.

14 Amilcar Cabral, the Cape Verdean African nationalist leader and theorist, echoes some fundamental observations made by Fanon: that the national bourgeoisie will collaborate with the colonizers and that tribal fundamentalism must be overcome or it will defeat any efforts at unity. In 1969, Cabral wrote ironically in "Party Principles and Political Practice" of the dangers of tribalism and nativism: "No one should think that he is more African than another, even than some white man who defends the interests of Africa, merely because he is today more adept at eating with his hand, rolling rice into a ball and putting it into his mouth" (Cabral 1979, 57).

15 I am thinking here especially of de Lauretis, Spivak, and Minh-ha. The last explains the multiple inscription of women of color:

> [M]any women of color feel obliged [to choose] between ethnicity and woman-hood: how can they? You never have/are one without the other. The idea of two illusorily separated identities, one ethnic, the other woman (or more precisely female), partakes in the Euro-American system of dualistic reasoning and its age-old divide-and-conquer tactics. . . . The pitting of anti-racist and anti-sexist struggles against one another allows some vocal fighters to dismiss blatantly the existence of either racism or sexism within their lines of action, as if oppression only comes in separate, monolithic forms. (Minh-ha 1989, 105)

16 For a more extensive analysis of generational conflict in Chu's novel, see Gong (1980). Gong asserts that "[t]he father/son relationship represents the most critical juncture in the erosion of a traditional Chinese value system and the emergence of a Chinese American character. Change from Chinese to Chinese American begins here" (74–75).

17 There are many scenes that resonate with my suggestion that generational conflicts cannot be isolated from either class or the historicity of gender. In the third section of the novel, it is class difference in addition to generational strife that founds the antagonism between mother and daughter: Ying-ying St. Clair cannot understand why Lena and her husband, Harold, have spent an enormous amount of money to live in a barn in the posh neighborhood of Woodside. Lena says, "My mother knows, underneath all the fancy details that cost so much, this house is still a barn" (151). In the early relationship between Suyuan Woo and her daughter, Jing-mei, the mother pushes her daughter to become a success, to perform on the piano; we can see that such desires are the reflection of the mother's former poverty, her lack of opportunity as both a poor refugee and a woman, but the daughter, trapped within a familial framework of explanation, sees her mother as punishing and invasive. Finally, the mother-and-daughter pair An-mei and Rose Hsu dramatize a conflict between the mother's belief that it is more honorable to keep personal problems within the Chinese family and

the daughter's faith in Western psychotherapy: the mother cannot understand why her daughter would pay a psychiatrist, a stranger, to talk about her divorce, instead of talking to her mother: the mother who was raised believing one must not show suffering to others because they, like magpies, would feed on your tears says of the daughter's psychiatrist, "really, he is just another bird drinking from your misery" (241).

REFERENCES

Adamson, Walter. 1980. *Hegemony and Revolution: A Study of Antonio Gramsci's Political and Cultural Theory*. Berkeley: University of California Press.

Cabral, Amílcar. 1979. *Unity and Struggle: Speeches and Writings of Amílcar Cabral*. Translated by Michael Wolfers. New York: Monthly Review.

Chan, Sucheng. 1986. *This Bittersweet Soil: The Chinese in California Agriculture, 1860–1910*. Berkeley: University of California Press.

———. 1991. *Asian Americans: An Interpretive History*. Boston: Twayne.

Chang, Diana. 1989. "The Oriental Contingent." Pp. 171–177 in Shirley Geok-Lin Lim, Mayumi Tsutakawa, and Margarita Donnelly, eds., *The Forbidden Stitch*. Corvallis, OR: Calyx.

Chu, Louis. 1961. *Eat a Bowl of Tea*. Seattle: University of Washington Press.

Clifford, James. 1988. *The Predicament of Culture: Twentieth Century Ethnography, Literature, and Art*. Cambridge, MA: Harvard University Press.

Daniels, Roger. 1962. *The Politics of Prejudice*. Berkeley: University of California Press.

Fanon, Frantz. 1961. *The Wretched of the Earth*. Translated by Constance Farrington. New York: Grove.

Fischer, Michael M. J. 1986. "Ethnicity and the Post-modern Arts of Memory." Pp. 194–233 in James Clifford and George Marcus, eds., *Writing Culture*. Berkeley: University of California Press.

Fong, Timothy P. 1994. *The First Suburban Chinatown: The Remaking of Monterey Park, California*. Philadelphia: Temple University Press.

Glenn, Evelyn Nakano. 1981. "Occupational Ghettoization: Japanese-American Women and Domestic Service, 1905–1970." *Ethnicity* 8: 352–386.

Gong, Ted. 1980. "Approaching Cultural Change through Literature: From Chinese to Chinese-American." *Amerasia* 7: 73–86.

Gramsci, Antonio. 1971a. "History of the Subaltern Classes: Methodological Criteria." Pp. 52–60 in Quinton Hoare and Geoffrey Nowell Smith, eds. and trans., *Selections from the Prison Notebooks*. New York: International.

———. 1971b. *Selections from the Prison Notebooks*. Edited and translated by Quinton Hoare and Geoffrey Nowell Smith. New York: International.

A Great Wall. 1985. Directed by Peter Wang. New Yorker Films.

JanMohamed, Abdul, and David Lloyd, eds. 1990. *The Nature and Context of Minority Discourse*. New York: Oxford University Press.

Kim, Elaine. 1982. *Asian American Literature: An Introduction to the Writings and Their Social Context*. Philadelphia: Temple University Press.

———. 1990. "'Such Opposite Creatures': Men and Women in Asian American Literature." *Michigan Quarterly Review* 29: 68–93.

Kingston, Maxine Hong. 1975. *The Woman Warrior*. New York: Random House.

Laclau, Ernesto, and Chantal Mouffe. 1985. *Hegemony and Socialist Strategy*. London: Verso.

Lauretis, Teresa de. 1987. *Technologies of Gender*. Bloomington: Indiana University Press.

Lowe, Lydia. 1988. "Quitting Time." *Ikon* 9: 29.

Minh-ha, Trinh T. 1989. *Woman, Native, Other: Writing Postcoloniality and Feminism*. Bloomington: Indiana University Press.

Mirikitani, Janice. 2003 [1987]. "Breaking Tradition." Pp. 663–666 in Harriet Sigerma, ed., *The Columbia Documentary History of American Women since 1941*. New York: Columbia University Press.

Mouffe, Chantal. 1988. "Hegemony and New Political Subjects: Toward a New Concept of Democracy." Pp. 89–104 in Cary Nelson and Lawrence Grossberg, eds., *Marxism and the Interpretation of Culture*. Urbana: University of Illinois Press.

Sassoon, Anne Showstack. 1982. "Hegemony, War of Position and Political Intervention." Pp. 94–115 in Anne Showstack Sassoon, ed., *Approaches to Gramsci*. London: Writers and Readers.

Spivak, Gayatri. 1987. *In Other Worlds*. London: Routledge.

Takaki, Ronald. 1989. *Strangers from a Different Shore: A History of Asian Americans*. Boston: Little, Brown.

Tan, Amy. 1989. *The Joy Luck Club*. New York: Putnam.

Williams, Raymond. 1977. *Marxism and Literature*. Oxford: Oxford University Press.

Yanagisako, Sylvia. 1985. *Transforming the Past: Kinship and Tradition among Japanese Americans*. Stanford, CA: Stanford University Press.

25

Critical Thoughts on Asian American Assimilation in the Whitening Literature

NADIA Y. KIM

In recent years the idea that Asian Americans, as well as Latinos, are becoming white or aligning with whites has become almost a priori among sociologists. This idea has been popularized by the forecast of a new black/nonblack divide (Bean and Stevens 2003; Gans 1999; J. Lee and Bean 2004; Yancey 2003). While the overall literature draws on the historical model of European immigrant "whitening" and on demographic data to support the racial assimilation thesis on Asian Americans, these works also rest on different core ideas. Warren and Twine (1997), for example, emphasize that today's "white" category seems to be expanding in ways akin to Euro-American history, while J. Lee and Bean (2004) rely on intermarriage and multiracial identification patterns to proffer an emerging black/nonblack divide. Yancey (2003) draws especially on racial attitudes toward and among Asian Americans and Latinos to evince his thesis of blacks' alienation from nonblack groups. Gans (1999) and Bonilla-Silva (2002) point to an emerging tri-racial hierarchy based on relational "race," color, and class phenomena.[1]

While the above literature insightfully portends the future and forces all race scholars to think seriously about these issues, this critical essay problematizes the forecast that Asian Americans are "whitening" (Warren and Twine 1997), experiencing "honorary whitening" (Bonilla-Silva 2002), joining a "residual" group (Gans 1999), and/or aligning with whites and Latinos as nonblacks (Bean and Stevens 2003; Gans 1999; J. Lee and Bean 2004; Yancey 2003; Waters 1999). The central argument of this essay is that Asian groups have been racially subordinated along lines of citizenship even if many of them have not been subordinated in the same way as blacks along color and socioeconomic lines. In other words, the racialization of Asian ethnics as "not-Americans" across historical periods irrespective of light skin, wealth, and fifth-generation status underscores the need to problematize the racial assimilation theses. The question pursued here is this: how can a group racialized as foreigners bask in the full privilege of whiteness if a central privilege of being white is to be an authentic American—*the* American (Lipsitz 1998)? This conundrum begs for a scholarly focus on racialization processes specific to Asian Americans and Latinos as well as those of whites and blacks. Rather than do so, however, much of the sociology of race and immigration has imposed on Asian Americans concepts derived from the traditional white-black color line (Ancheta 1998; Chan 1990; C. Kim 1999; T. Lee 2000; Okihiro 1994; Takaki 1998). Not only does this imposition on a neither-white-nor-black group inadvertently uphold binary classifications (e.g., white-black)—those upon which societal inequalities depend (P. Collins 2000; Glenn 2002)—but it underappreciates the foundations of anti-Asian subjugation: United States–Asia relations and citizenship (as linked to immigration). Apt here, then, is Cherrie Moraga's (1981, 29) oft-quoted phrase referring to men of color's seventies activist focus on race/nation at the expense of gender (Moya 1996): "*[t]he danger lies in failing to acknowledge the specificity of the oppression.*" Through a critical reevaluation of the sociological literature, this essay introduces the *specificity* of the oppression of Asian Americans and its implications for understanding the larger hegemonic project of white racial dominance over *all* nonwhites. That is, while *some* Asian American groups might be assimilating socioeconomically, Asian Americans at large are not whitening per se because such a move would hinge on racially assimilating into a status as *authentic Americans*. In other words, Asian Americans would need to be granted the full privilege of social citizenship to change from one race (Asian) to the dominant alternative (white).

Conceptualized thus, Asian Americans' racial positioning as forever foreigners, that is, inauthentic Americans (Tuan 1998), belies the core assumptions on which many of the racial assimilation theories rest. All of these theories use a US-bound framework to understand a population with a past and present harnessed to global inequalities. In addition, I question the core assumption that South-East European and Irish immigrants' path from "not-quite-white to white" is a harbinger of Asian Americans' futures. This prediction overlooks the fact that, contrary to wide acceptance among sociologists and to popular wisdom, European immigrants' expansion of the "white" category remains a debated question among historians of whiteness themselves (e.g., Arnesen 2001; Frank 1998; Guglielmo 2003; Kolchin 2002; Roediger 2006).

I also question the methodologies that racial assimilation theses employ to forecast the racial future of the United States. To be sure, scholars such as Gans (1999, 372–373) readily concede that the weakness of a predictive analysis "is its empirical reliance on the extrapolation of too many current trends and the assumed persistence of too many current phenomena." But even beyond that, most predictive studies do not empirically interview or systematically observe Asian Americans (or Latinos) in the United States to capture if and how "race" might matter; nor do they draw on the many qualitative/historical studies that have already done so (e.g., Espiritu 1992, 2003; Kibria 2002; C. Kim 1999; N. Kim 2003; Lowe 1996; Palumbo-Liu 1999; Park 2005; Purkayastha 2005; Pyke and Dang 2003; Rudrappa 2004; Tuan 1998, 1999). In addition, predictive studies do not draw on data from representative surveys that tap Asian Americans' experiences with racial bias and discrimination, especially pertaining to global inequalities, immigration, and social citizenship.

Citizenship: Racially Not American

US history reveals that citizenship was initially the province of white men of property (Glenn 2002). Later, white women were granted the right to naturalize and all blacks received it by way of the Fourteenth Amendment to the Constitution in 1868. Of course, the United States had rooted its nation building and ideology of the national family in the relegation of black and Native Americans to second-class citizenship, both before and after the Fourteenth Amendment (P. Collins 2001). Southern blacks in particular would be disenfranchised through the 1960s and, among the more coded parallels in the present day, black males constitute a disproportionate number of convicted felons who thus cannot vote, while the Motor Voter laws hark back to voter suppression under Jim Crow.[2] Yet, precisely because of the white-over-black racial model of the United States that has pivoted on the color line and its ideologies of racial superiority-inferiority, Asian Americans have been subordinated in a different manner as not second-class Americans but as the *not*-Americans. Multiple versions of this *conflation of Asia and Asian America*, the former often looming as "the enemy," persist in the present day. No group has been excluded from the country because of their "race" to the extent that Asian Americans have been. Starting in 1875, to forbid the entry of Chinese and other "Mongolian" prostitutes, felons, and contract laborers, Congress passed the Page Law—a law that effectively reduced the entry of all Chinese women. Because all women were suspected of prostitution, the growth of the Chinese American population was profoundly stunted (Espiritu 1997). Thereafter, federal laws excluded the immigration of Chinese male laborers (and their wives) in 1882 as well as those from India in 1917, from Korea and Japan in 1924, and from the Philippines in 1934. In brief, most Asians could not pass through the "golden door" because of their race.

Even those who lived in the United States could not be legal citizens, no matter how culturally and loyally American they were. Citizenship, then, has been not only the Achilles' heel of Asian Americans, but the shackle on the heel. In a landmark case Takao Ozawa was told by the Supreme Court in 1922 that Japanese people like him could not be citizens because they were not white. Learning from the Ozawa case, Bhagat Singh Thind petitioned the same court for citizenship a year later on the premise that ethnologists of the time classified Asian Indians as Caucasians. While the Supreme Court justices conceded his Caucasian status, they dismissed their previous logic by denying Thind citizenship on the grounds that the "common man" did not see him as white. By the time the last laws barring Asian American naturalization were lifted in the 1950s, many Asian Americans had been cumulatively disadvantaged by the many years without legal citizenship. Had it not been for the exclusion and antinaturalization laws, Asian Americans would likely be a much larger and dominant force in US politics, corporations, and national culture today. But even with legal citizenship in hand, Asian Americans have been denied the more crucial promise of civilized existence and membership in the nation, that is, *social* citizenship (Marshall 1973; Lowe 1996).[3]

At the heart of the exclusion acts and citizenship hierarchies is "nativistic racism." (Ancheta 1998, 11) Historically, as Ancheta (1998) has written, nativistic racism has relied on several ideologies and stereotypes: economic competitor, organized criminal, "illegal alien," and unwelcome immigrant; to that I would add military enemy ("yellow peril"). For example, white Americans' resentment of alleged economic competition from the "yellow hordes" secured the exclusion acts. And the alarmist "yellow peril" stereotype, often couched as "American patriotism," emerged from World War II and was entrenched by the conflict with Koreans and Chinese in the Korean Conflict, in Vietnam with the Vietnamese ("gooks"), and with most of these nations during the Cold War. Arguably, the most pernicious form of anti-Asian racism on US soil was the World War II mass incarceration of Japanese Americans (Ancheta 1998, 11), a group composed predominantly of US citizens, and law-abiding ones at that. Since Franklin D. Roosevelt's executive order to mass incarcerate Japanese Americans, Japanese ethnics and anyone confused for Japanese continue to suffer intimidation, violence, and other hate crimes on December 7, the anniversary of Japan's bombing of Pearl Harbor (Ancheta 1998, 11–12). More contemporary examples include the baseball bat murder of Vincent Chin in 1982 by two white males who scapegoated him for the US auto industry meltdown; to date, the two men have never spent a night in jail. The forever foreigner is evident in the many racial foreigner epithets hurled at Judge Lance Ito during the O. J. Simpson trial, despite his iconic symbol as a model minority. Then New York Senator Alfonse D'Amato mocked Ito's alleged accent (undetectable to everyone else) on the Don Imus show, Howard Stern branded him a "nip," and a book titled *O.J.'s Legal Pad* had sketches of a slant-eyed "samurai/kamikaze" warrior next to a caption that read, "Hiroshima, Nuke Judge Ito/Banzai, Banzai, Nagasaki/Use his head for backyard hockey!" (C. Kim 1999, 127). Owing to the 1996 Clinton campaign finance scandal involving John Huang and Charlie Yah-lin Trie, the Democratic National Committee telephoned all donors with Asian-sounding names to interrogate their citizenship status. It would be hard to imagine the same kind of treatment of white Americans if Bill Clinton had potentially taken money from someone in Europe. The examples are endless, but not only has anti-Asian violence remained high (an unrecognized social problem), but at the end of 2006 Rosie O'Donnell mocked the Chinese language and showed little remorse until Asian American organizations protested and lobbied for an apology. In 2007, the mass media, politicians, and pundits "foreignized" the Virginia Tech school shooter Seung-Hui Cho as a "South Korean" or "South Korean national" when in fact he was an American (he had lived in the United States since he was eight years old); they usually reported his name in the South Korean fashion as well: family name first.

In response to these issues, sociologists, political scientists, legal scholars, and Ethnic/American studies scholars have examined the ways in which Asian Americans (and Latinos) are subordinated along the citizenship line. Scholars have called this line the "insider-foreigner" axis, one rooted in a macro process of civic ostracism (C. Kim 1999), and/or have broadly focused on its legal (Ancheta 1998), national (T. Lee 2005), and political dimensions (Lie 2004). Most of these scholars agree that while some (or all) Asian American groups are valorized above blacks along class and color hierarchies, they are not "Americans" in the same manner that blacks are. In large part because of America's white-black legacy, black Americans are not constantly conflated with Ghana, Guinea, or Niger.

The Racialization of Asian Americans across Borders

Racial assimilation theories focus only on what happens to immigrants within US society and its institutions, excising global inequalities such as US foreign relations with the countries from whence the immigrants came. These accounts thereby underappreciate the importance of US rule over immigrants' home countries. Yet such dominance has institutionalized racial subordination over Asians abroad and has carried over to treatment of Asian Americans on "the home front." As Chan and Hune (1995, 213) aptly write, such transnational dominance matters:

> [T]hroughout U.S. history each Asian American community continued to have its image and well-being defined not by its activities in the United States but by a racial order that was both domestic and international. No other American immigrant community has had its domestic relations with the U.S. government so determined by the nation's foreign policies with homeland states.

In other words, Asian Americans' racial marginalization, in Yen Le Espiritu's (2003, 210) words, has been "shaped not only by the social location of their group within the United States but also by the position of their home country within the global racial order."

Yet racial assimilation theories have not integrated the transnational racialization of Asian immigrants into their analyses. This is despite the fact that Asian studies, Asian American studies, and global racism scholarship have long documented such phenomena or have pointed in that direction. Pioneering Asian American studies scholar Lisa Lowe (1996, 17) asserts, for example, that US intervention in Asia during and after World War II was part of a larger project to assume global hegemony, especially over Japan. Not just in the name of staving off communism, the United States, she writes, also sought to use Asia as a "brutal theater" on which to "perform its technological modernity and military force in relation to the Asiatic world."

On the level of "race," the United States justified its globalization projects in Asia by deploying Orientalist ideologies of Asians as foreign, other, or feminine (Said 1979). Certainly, the US role in Asia has engendered contradictions (Ong 1999) insofar as US capital investment helped create the "Asian Tiger" economies we know today (Lie 1998). Yet Asian capitalism has also served to *reinforce* racial subordination, as Asian nations and peoples morph into the "yellow peril" when they become too good at what they do (Ong 1999, 174–180). That is, the specters of the inferior and child-like Filipino "little brown brother" (Espiritu 2003), of the evil enemy "gook" of Vietnam and North Korea, and of the feminized dependents in South Korea all haunt Asian Americans in the United States today (Lowe 1996). No matter their light skin, wealth, or cultural literacy, they must contend with being forever not-American.

Reexamining Demographic Data on Asian Americans

Beyond the lack of a global lens on Asian America, racial assimilation theories have harnessed too much explanatory power to certain demographic data, namely data on socioeconomic attainment, intermarriage, and racial attitudes. Data on all of these areas are themselves more contextually and historically contingent and complex than forecasts of Asian American racial assimilation allow. In discussing these three areas I embed other key critiques, first, that most of these predictions, excepting Bonilla-Silva (2002) and Gans (1999), homogenize diverse Asian ethnics (as well as Latino ethnics). Second, they do not acknowledge the circular relationship between the model minority and the foreigner ideologies (Okihiro 1994). Finally, they presume European immigrants' "whitening" despite historians' debates about whether the white category ever in fact "expanded" (Arnesen 2001; Frank 1998; Guglielmo 2003; Kolchin 2002).

Reexamining the Socioeconomic Picture

I contend that social class mobility for Asian Americans is not a ticket out of racial subordination. That is, so long as Asian Americans continue to be conflated with (enemy) Asian nations and presumed to be not-American, they do not escape racial bias just because they have Yale degrees and expensive homes. To be sure, most East/South Asian Americans have been valorized for their socioeconomic successes as compared to black Americans who are often monolithically derogated the "underclass." In this way, Asian Americans can and do benefit from their "model minority" status, especially in light of whites' greater willingness to live beside (and marry) Asian Americans than blacks (Yancey 2003). Yet, the fact that model minority acclaim has not been enough to grant Asian groups "authentic American" status is reminiscent of black Americans' experiences of class. In the same way that a high class profile has not spared black Americans from institutionalized and everyday racism (e.g., S. Collins 1997; Cose 1993; Feagin and Sikes 1994), class status has not spared, and actually *has exacerbated*, nativistic racism against Asian Americans. A similar class parallel has been drawn between Asian Americans and Jewish people (Karabel 2005) for sharing a liminal position as honorary whites. While these two groups can be compared for suffering discrimination on account of their being successful, especially in the realm of higher education, they do not share a European background or phenotype. Anti-Semitism is thus racialized and ethnic-religious discrimination, whereas anti-Asianism is more squarely in the "race" camp. The fact that Asian Americans are often described in biological/essentialist ways, whether the stereotype is positive and negative, illustrates the point.

High class status as a catalyst for nativistic racism sharpens into relief the circularity between the "model minority" and the "foreigner" ideologies. As Gary Okihiro (1994, 142) aptly states, the model minority and the yellow peril are not poles, but "form a circular relationship that moves in either direction." That is, while Asian Americans' success can incite "yellow peril" discrimination (Ancheta 1998; Newman 1993), the feminized model minority image can assuage fears of Asian Americans as the masculinized yellow peril. This dialectic allows both representations to exist side-by-side (Okihiro 1994; Espiritu 1997).

Although high social class status has not spared Asian Americans from racial marginalization, I believe that the socioeconomic data on the group (which usually refer to East and South Asians) require further analysis. To be sure, in censuses from 1970 to 2000, it would appear that one could proclaim Asian Americans' socioeconomic glory. In 2000, Asian Americans had the highest education levels, the highest household and median family incomes, and the most expensive homes. Since 1980, they have even surpassed white Americans along all of these dimensions.[4] Yet, these data need to be understood in context. While some pundits claim that Asians are inherently more intelligent in mathematics and science than other groups, such a biological, essentialist conclusion ignores the social phenomenon of US policies favoring highly educated, professional Asian immigrants. That is, the US government's immigration policy since 1965 has mostly granted entrance to Asian immigrants with advanced education, advanced technical backgrounds, and/or other professional skills, as if to engineer a model minority (Park and Park 2005).

Socioeconomic data on Asian Americans need also be *disaggregated*. Asian Americans—consisting of Bangladeshi, Cambodian, Chinese, Filipino, Indian, Japanese, Korean, Laotian, Pakistani, Vietnamese, Pacific Islander ethnics, and so on—are among the most diverse of the racialized groups and are internally stratified in profound ways. Yet, social scientists tend to lump all of these groups together, not differentiating between ethnic/national groups that are highly dissimilar. One must consider the social class disparities *within* the Asian American group. In so doing, we find that many Asian American groups are, in fact, not middle-class. As Bonilla-Silva (2002) and Gans (1999) point out, Asian ethnics such as Vietnamese, Cambodian, and Laotian Americans (as well as Pacific Islander groups) tend to live in poverty, to be unemployed, and to be less educated than the average American (Xie and Goyette 2004). In fact, Xie and Goyette's (2004) analysis of 2000 census estimates found the Asian American poverty rate to be 10 to 13 percent, a rate considerably higher than that for white Americans. They found that not only is the poverty rate high among Southeast Asian groups like the Vietnamese, but it is high among certain East Asian groups as well, such as Chinese and Korean Americans. Indeed, Asian Americans could be considered one of the most stratified populations in the United States (Nishioka 2003).

In addition, Asian Americans' *individual* incomes lag more than 10 percent behind the individual incomes of white Americans; those of Pacific Islanders lag roughly 40 percent behind (Nishioka 2003). The difference between Asian Americans' *household* incomes (higher than that of whites) and their *individual* incomes (lower than that of whites) is partly explained by the larger number of earners in Asian immigrant households (Nishioka 2003; Takaki 1998). This extended family or multiple immigrant household differs markedly from most white American household structures. In addition, Asian Americans' higher household values can be largely explained by the propensity of Asian Americans to live in immigrant-receiving states with high costs of living, namely Hawaii, California, and New York (Nishioka 2003).

And despite being glorified as a model minority group "becoming white," Asian Americans' heads have certainly been bruised by the infamous glass ceiling. The clearest indicator that socioeconomic discrimination exists is the discrepancy between the earnings of Japanese Americans and their levels of education (Feagin and Feagin 1993, 354). Furthermore, despite Asian Americans' overall higher educational attainment than white Americans they are underrepresented in two major high-status occupations: (1) lawyers and judges (2.7 percent) as well as (2) administrators and public officers (2.4 percent) (Xie and Goyette 2004). Xie and Goyette also find that Asian Americans are greatly underrepresented as managers in several occupational sectors: government, private employment, and both public and private institutions of higher learning. In addition, although Asian American women currently earn more than white women on average, studies have found that at universities across the country Asian American women faculty disproportionately suffer from harassment in a hostile environment (Hune 1998).

In the civil service sector Asian Americans have filed many formal complaints about being passed over for managerial positions by those with far less training, education, and years of experience. Indeed, 75 percent expressed interest in managerial positions as opposed to technical work in the electronics industry (Asian Americans for Community Involvement 1993), while many others lodged glass ceiling complaints. The same study also found that the exclusion of Asian Americans from managerial positions could not be attributed to their poor English proficiency, time of arrival, cultural differences, work experience, formal training, or greater job concentration in low-status sectors of the economy. In brief, the fact that some Asian American groups are assimilating along social class lines is *part* of the story, but not the story itself.

Reexamining Asian Americans' Intermarriage Trends

While all of the studies invoke high rates of intermarriage to support their predictions of racial assimilation, none of them discusses the global inequalities that first spawned these marriages. As noted earlier, US relationships with Asian countries have had profound effects on Asians in the United States, including whom they marry. US imperialist rule in Asian countries points to why, historically, the rate of Asian female-white male marriages has been so much higher than that of Asian males-white females. America's colonization of the Philippines (1898–1944) and its continued military presence up to 1991 explains why the Philippines has sent more immigrants as wives of US servicemen than any other Asian nation (Min 2006, 46). Min reports that an estimated 343,000 brides of "US citizens" came from 1950 through 2003; most of these were the wives of servicemen. When the United States occupied Japan from the end of World War II until 1952, a sizeable portion of the armed forces remained behind in Japan, thus spurring a large number of Japanese emigrant brides in the 1950s and early 1960s (between 1950 and 1979 alone, about 71,000 wives immigrated) (Min 2006, 46). In South Korea where an even greater number of US troops have been stationed since 1945, approximately 96,000 Korean women married US soldiers and immigrated to the United States from 1950 through 1989. Asian-white intermarriages therefore cannot be understood apart from the larger context of US (neo)colonial and imperial rule.

In addition, most forecasts of Asian racial assimilation do not cite the studies that reveal a noticeable decrease in Asian-white pairings since 1980. For example, J. Lee and Bean (2004, 228) draw on Asian Americans' and Latinos' high rates of marriage with whites to affirm a growing black/nonblack divide, yet they cite mostly statistics for native-born and young Asian Americans rather than for the population at large. Asian Americans are a predominantly foreign-born populace (Lai and Arguelles 2003) and are also a group in which the first generation serves as leaders and elders.[5] I believe that the marital patterns of the entire group are important. Xie and Goyette's (2004) aggregate analysis reveals that most Asian

Americans are married to members of their own ethnic group. To illustrate, their comparison of recent censuses revealed that Filipino and Vietnamese Americans have dramatically shifted to coethnic marriage. And contrary to popular wisdom, the second largest proportion of marriages is not Asian-white couplings but *interethnic* marriages, that is, marriages *between* different Asian ethnic groups (Xie and Goyette 2004). According to the US Census Bureau's 5 percent Public Use Microdata Sample data, Asian-white marriage declined from 18 percent in 1980 to 15.3 percent in 1990 to 12.7 percent in 2000 (Min 2006). Not only has the proportion of Asian-white marriages dropped, rates of interethnic marriage *have risen* dramatically (S. Lee and Fernandez 1998; Min 2006; Qian and Lichter 2007; Shinagawa and Pang 1996). From 1980 through 1990 Asian interethnic marriages doubled from 11 to 21 percent and eclipsed marriages between Asian and white Americans; broken down by gender, 18.9 percent of Asian American men and 16.3 percent of women were interethnically married (S. Lee and Fernandez 1998).

In states with high concentrations of Asian Americans, such as California, the rate of interethnic marriage is even higher. While in 1990, 21.1 percent of Asian American men in California were interethnically married, by 2000, 64 percent were so married (S. Lee and Fernandez 1998). A gender breakdown reveals that, in 1980, 10.8 percent of Asian American women were married to Asian-descent men, while in 1990, 45.5 percent of women were so married (Shinagawa and Pang 1996). Given most Asian American women's consistently higher rates of marriage to whites than their male counterparts, a figure of 45.5 percent constitutes a dramatic increase. These jumps indicate that interethnic marriages will likely remain a trend for some time, having increased 400 to 500 percent between 1980 and 1990 alone.

What are the reasons for Asian Americans' growing preference for intra- and interethnic marriage over marriage with whites? Many speculate that the growing size of the Asian American population has largely contributed to the shift toward intra-Asian marriage. When the Asian American population was smaller, and many brides of US soldiers were immigrating, their rates of marriage with whites were rather high (this trend was also true of Native Americans). As the Asian population has grown, the larger group size itself has depressed outmarriage rates (Qian and Lichter 2007). Qian and Lichter add that such growth has consequently promoted in-group interaction and solidarity, hence endogamy. Overall, they find that increased immigration has slowed native-born Asian Americans' and Latinos' marital assimilation, results that stand in stark contrast to the marital assimilation patterns of various European immigrants in the early twentieth century. As Asian Americans constitute one of the fastest growing groups in the United States, endogamous marriage does not look as if it will abate in the foreseeable future.

Several studies contend that Asian Americans' choice of other Asian mates reveals a growing racial (panethnic) consciousness, especially among the second generation-plus (Kibria 1997; S. Lee and Fernandez 1998; Shinagawa and Pang 1996). For one, Asian Americans are keenly aware that they are treated as a monolith, thereby fostering their racial affinity and solidarity (Shinagawa and Pang 1996; S. Lee and Fernandez 1998). Such a move beyond solely an ethnic consciousness is especially acute in areas with large Asian American populations, such as California. And within states like California, the importance of Asian American populations on college campuses cannot be overstated. Because college is the site of the most interethnic contact, it is also the place where many Asian Americans forge and develop a panethnic consciousness. Interestingly, this trend further affirms the unpredictable outcomes of Asian Americans' ascent into the middle class insofar as middle-class status has fostered pan-Asian identification rather than identification with whiteness. To be sure, class is not the only determinant of intra- or interethnic marriages. Other influential factors could be the shared experiences of being American-born Asians (Kibria 2002). Finally, recent marital trends may be pointing to a broader "people of color" consciousness. As an example, Asian Americans' marriages to Latinos have risen from 3 percent in 1980 to 11 percent in 1990. Some attribute this change to the shared immigrant experience of many members of these groups as well as their common residence in states like California (S. Lee and Fernandez 1998).

Racial Attitudes and Ideology

Some of the scholarly predictions stress that Asian Americans' (and Latinos') antiblack attitudes parallel South-East Europeans' and the Irish's prejudicial dissociation from blacks in the early twentieth century (e.g., Bonilla-Silva 2002; Ignatiev 1995; Warren and Twine 1997; Yancey 2003). Although no group, including those of color, can escape the pull of racial prejudice, I believe that knowledge of the global and cultural context of Asian Americans' racial attitudes is necessary. That is, globally, the United States introduced its anti-Asian and antiblack racial ideologies to Asia as part of its imperialist expansion (N. Kim 2003; Feagin 2000). On a related cultural level, those Asians who have come to the United States have not been conditioned by norms of social desirability on issues of race that longtime Americans have been. Yet, survey analyses of Asian Americans—a predominantly non-US-born population—do not consider how the first generation's lack of exposure to norms of social desirability may shape their overall response patterns. Schuman et al.'s (1997) classic study, however, found that social desirability was palpable among white Americans, many of whom supported the *abstract principle* of racial equality, but were less enamored by the literal *implementation* of it. Although it is true that both Asian and European immigrants faced virulent and violent nativism, Asian Americans have not, to my knowledge, waged the kinds of mass organized riots that European immigrants exacted upon blacks in a bid for whiteness/nonblackness. This distancing and discrimination, however, was one of the key processes that enabled European immigrants to shore up the various dimensions of their whiteness. To be sure, most Asian Americans arrived in the mid-1900s, after the era in which these kinds of acts were more common, but there were certainly Asian Americans on both coasts at the same time European immigrants were proliferating in the East. These kinds of differences need to be considered and made clear whenever the historical records of Asian Americans and of South-East European and Irish Americans are made analogous.

A more fundamental problem is the racial assimilation account's reliance on the claim that European immigrants were once not white but later *became* white. Such a claim has not been conclusively supported by historians themselves. While historians have generally agreed that the United States always categorized South-East European and Irish immigrants as "white," they disagree on whether these immigrants were white on the ground (Arnesen 2001; Frank 1998; Guglielmo 2003; Kolchin 2002; Roediger 2006). Thomas Guglielmo's (2003) most comprehensive primary source research on Italian Americans, however, found that they were always categorized as white along the color line and were thus granted citizenship and all the other rights that attended such a privilege. He found that what was more ambiguous was the categorization of Italians as a race: southern Italian, northern Italian, and so on. Irrespective of where one stands in the historical debate, however, the larger take-home point is that social scientists cannot claim unequivocally that Asian Americans will expand the white category *again*, as it is not clear that the category has ever expanded before.

If we assume, however, that whiteness *did* expand to include "nonwhite" European immigrants, one of the necessary components was immigrants' eventual desire for a white identity. There is strong evidence, however, that Asian Americans across generations do not desire to blend in with whiteness or unhyphenated Americanness (e.g., Espiritu 2003; Kibria 2002; N. Kim 2003; Ong and Azores 1994; Rudrappa 2004). In further contrast to the South-East European and Irish immigrants at the turn of the century, contemporary Asian groups' retention of their ethnonational identity is further encouraged by America's multiculturalist era in which they live, an era that recognizes and hegemonically celebrates difference (Rudrappa 2004). While Asian immigrants might welcome the privileges and resources that attend whiteness, they do not desire a white identity, a variant thereof, or any kind of blending with other groups that would dilute their ethnonational difference. In this light, some of the key forces that secured European immigrant whitening—assuming that they were not white at the outset—are not paralleled in the Asian American (and Latino) experience of the latter twentieth century. In fact, some scholars believe that the stress on ethnicity/nationality among post-1965 immigrants and their progeny (Kibria 2002) signals a move toward ethnicity's increasing importance in race-centered America (Ong and Azores 1994).

Another key point it that as US exclusion laws against Asians, denial of citizenship to the group, and wartime incarceration bear out, Americanness has been, and continues to be, synonymous with whiteness (Lipsitz 1998). Whiteness, therefore, has several key dimensions beyond social class and racial attitudes. It is also anchored in nationality, a status claim that Asian Americans were denied legally and continue to be denied socially. Therefore, it seems optimistic at best and contradictory at worst to dub Asians as whitening or racially assimilating if they are denied one of the most crucial tenets of being white: authentic Americanness. Such concerns about social citizenship seem to get lost when the *specificity* of Asian American racialization is peripheral to the inquiry at hand.

Racial Stories Surveys Tell

Although the racial subordination of Asian Americans is obscured by the model minority stereotype, national public opinion often tells a different story. Two national surveys of Americans' racial attitudes by the National Conference for Community and Justice titled "Taking America's Pulse" found that whites reported many negative stereotypes of Asian Americans, particularly ones that constellate around the "forever foreigner" ideology (phrase from Tuan 1998).[6] A 2001 national survey study led by a professional Chinese American organization called the Committee of 100 found that, of the most prejudiced Americans, 18 percent reported that they would be uncomfortable with an Asian American supervisor.[7] Yet only 9 percent of these Americans were uncomfortable with a black supervisor, 5 percent with one who was female, and 7 percent with one who was Jewish. And consistent with foreigner stereotypes and Asian Americans' lack of political power, 23 percent of the nation stated that they were "uncomfortable" voting for an Asian American US presidential candidate. They were substantially less uncomfortable voting for an African American candidate (15 percent), a female candidate (14 percent), and a Jewish candidate (11 percent), most of whom, not surprisingly, are more prominent in politics than Asian Americans. To be sure, numbers also define this equation. Owing to the legacy of a white over black national history, black Americans constitute 13.1 percent of the US population while Asian Americans constitute 5 percent. At the same time, precisely because the hegemonic racial binary renders Asian Americans invisible, which suppresses the group's entrance into elected public service, and precisely because of the anti-Asian foreigner racialization, they are nowhere near 5 percent of elected officials in the United States. In striking terms, the Committee of 100 survey evidences the power of the not-American/foreigner racialization. Interested particularly in the American public's perceptions of *Chinese* Americans, the Committee of 100 was disturbed to find that anywhere between 68 and 73 percent of the nation believed that Chinese Americans were "taking away too many jobs from Americans," insinuating that Chinese Americans were themselves not American. Moreover, 68 to 73 percent of the public also believed that Chinese Americans had "too much power in the business world," invoking the stereotype of Asian Americans as foreign economic competitors. Another dimension of the foreigner racial ideology is to collapse Asians in the United States and Asians in Asia, as evidenced by the World War II mass incarceration of Japanese Americans. In fact, 46 percent of the country reported that "Chinese Americans passing on information to the Chinese government [was] a problem."

As further evidence that model minority stereotypes exist alongside foreigner ones, a large portion of the public also noted that Chinese Americans "have strong family values" and "place a higher value on education than do most other groups in America." Yet, studies like the 2000 "Taking America's Pulse" national survey found that it is precisely the success of some Asian Americans that has sparked negative foreigner stereotypes. Indeed, the positive stereotypes of Chinese Americans as valuing family and education were common even among those reporting the *most negative* attitudes toward Chinese Americans. A 1993 *Los Angeles Times* survey of Southern Californians found that Asian Americans were thought to be too successful and too enamored of material success.[8] Specifically, this survey asked whether any group "is getting more economic power than is good for Southern California" and whether any group "is working harder than the others to succeed in Southern California." Asian Americans were considered to be endangering the state with their growing economic prowess. In addition, survey analyses revealed a statistical linkage between the view of Asian Americans as too economically powerful and as the most prejudiced group in California. Counter to classic assimilation theory, then, Asian Americans' economic mobility often engenders less social acceptance and intensifies racism toward them (T. Lee 2000; Newman 1993). This link between model minority and foreigner stereotypes suggests that, irrespective of whether stereotypes are positive or negative, stereotypes are stereotypes nonetheless. Judging and homogenizing a group as having particular traits, traits that are often seen as inherent, effectively dehumanizes a group.

Paradoxically, Asian Americans are the only group that attributes the racial discrimination it faces to *success* in the United States. Moreover, Asian Americans are the only ones who consistently recognize that their lack of political power—their invisibility and unmet needs—is a major obstacle for them. It is thus not surprising that among all groups, Asian Americans have most strongly opposed a moratorium on immigration and the deportation of Chinese who seek US asylum. They also most ardently support the reparations for Japanese American internees and a University of California admissions policy that is meritocratic (T. Lee 2000, 135).

Beyond the good stereotype–bad stereotype paradox, multiple survey studies have revealed another paradox. It shows that while Asian Americans report experiencing discrimination at levels close to those of black Americans, most

Americans see Asian groups as experiencing little discrimination to none at all.[9] In two national polls of the four largest racial/ethnic groups in the United States—a 1995 *Washington Post*/Kaiser Foundation/Harvard University poll and a 1993 *Los Angeles Times* poll—Asian Americans were just behind African Americans in reporting experiences of discrimination. Polling only Asian American groups, the *Los Angeles Times* yielded similar results: 57 percent of those of Chinese descent, 46 percent of Filipino and Korean descent, and 41 percent of Vietnamese Americans reported discrimination. Even a 1998 University of Massachusetts poll that restricted Asian Americans' reports of discrimination to experiences *within the last three months of the survey* still found that fully 25 percent of Asian Americans reported bouts with discrimination. Still, only 10 to 15 percent of the American public considered racism to be an obstacle for Asian Americans, while the above *Washington Post* and *Los Angeles Times* polls revealed that 40 to 60 percent of Asian Americans reported thus. When the nation does indeed acknowledge racism against Asian Americans, they often use "blame the victim" reasoning, pointing to the group's supposed cultural distinctiveness, clannishness, and language problems (stereotypes linked to the foreigner ideology) (T. Lee 2000).

Why do Asian Americans report so much racial discrimination while non-Asians believe that they experience very little to none at all? One reason for the discrepancy may stem from the fact that Asian Americans who report discrimination tend to be those who are more successful and upwardly mobile. As Bobo and Suh (2000) found, Asian Americans face much of their racial discrimination in institutional contexts. The larger American public, however, would likely not think of professional Asian Americans as facing any racial barriers. Again, "model minority" success also breeds "majority" resistance. A second reason may be that survey items on race tend to be centered on the black American experience (T. Lee 2000). Despite the conspicuous diversification of the United States since 1965, surveys have been slow to modify and add questions to address the experiences of Asian Americans, Native Americans, Latinos, Arab Americans, and other groups. As such, the unique form of discrimination that Asian Americans experience—specifically along lines of citizenship—is not captured by survey questions on race generally. Rather, Taeku Lee finds that survey researchers continue to assess Asian Americans based on stereotypes mostly associated with black Americans, such as those pertaining to intelligence, family, criminality, and cultural community patterns. Yet studies of Asian Americans should focus on immigration, citizenship, the glass ceiling, entrepreneurship, and US relations with Asian nations, including imperialism and war. Indeed, survey respondents in the *Los Angeles Times* poll did not stereotype Asian Americans as welfare-dependent, but they did stereotype them as inscrutable and as perpetual foreigners. The public also expressed feelings of hostility toward Japan and other Asian nations. Interestingly, whites and Latinos who stereotyped Asian Americans as not properly integrated into American culture were more likely to hold anti-Asian attitudes (T. Lee 2000).

Finally, not only have surveys been inattentive to the specific struggles of Asian Americans, but so have the criminal justice system and the mass media. Although anti-Asian violence rose steadily in the 1990s and has been spiking in the years following 9/11, the American public is largely unaware of the high rates of anti-Asian violence and other hate crimes. For example, the middle to late 1990s witnessed high rates of anti-Asian violence, those that remained steady. The rates are indeed most likely higher, as reports are plagued by problems of underreporting.

Despite the nationwide decline in general hate crimes in recent years—hence, a decline in anti-Asian crimes—violence against Asian Americans has increased sharply in various states like Connecticut, Michigan, Nevada, and Wyoming; murders on the whole have also increased (National Asian Pacific American Legal Consortium 1994–2002). Also troubling is that the National Asian Pacific American Legal Consortium found that Asian Americans are increasingly subject to racially motivated crimes in their homes, workplaces, and schools (those who lived in public housing tended to suffer crimes at home). They also reported that in Asian Americans' places of employment, hate crimes increased 117 percent between 1995 and 1996. In school settings the FBI found a similar increase in school-based hate crimes against Asian Americans. That includes college campuses. There, Asian Americans have experienced a disturbing 100 percent increase in hate incidents. A 2000 report by the National Asian Pacific American Legal Consortium found that anti-Asian crimes on college campuses were a formidable problem, one that had not been adequately addressed. In the same year an online survey by *aMagazine*, an Asian American interest magazine, found that a third of the 559 college students had suffered racial epithets and similar verbal attacks on their campuses. Another 5 percent had been the victims of race-based physical attacks.

More tragically, countless Asian Americans have been murdered because of their race since they first arrived in the country centuries ago, from the bloodthirsty white male tax collectors in California to perpetrators of race hate at the dawn of the new millennium. Despite the poison of racism that took the lives of such Asian Americans as Thien Ly, Kuan Chung Kao, Won Joon Yoon, Joseph Ileto, and Balbir Singh Sodhi, to name a few, these murders have received very little public, media, or scholarly attention. While I can provide only a small snapshot of the murders here, I believe that they merit a brief summary. In 1996 Thien Ly, a young Vietnamese American with degrees from UCLA and Georgetown University, was gruesomely stabbed to death by two white male supremacists while he was exercising in Tustin, California. In 1997, Rohnert Park, California, police shot a thirty-three-year-old Chinese American engineer named Kuan Chung Kao, intoxicated at the time, for carrying a stick that they presumed to be a martial arts weapon. The officers shot Kao within *thirty-four seconds* of arriving at his home, immediately handcuffing him and preventing his wife, a registered nurse, from administering potentially life-saving CPR to him on the driveway where he lay bleeding. Kao died shortly thereafter. Despite mass protests, neither of the police officers has been punished for any misconduct. During a California summer in 1999, white supremacist Buford Furrow asked Filipino American postal worker Joseph Ileto to mail a letter for him. As Ileto obliged, Furrow shot him a total of nine times, firing at Ileto as he attempted to flee for his life. After the murder, Furrow admitted to shooting Ileto because he was "Hispanic or Asian" as well as a federal employee. Finally, one of the first-known racially motivated murders in the wake of 9/11 cost Balbir Singh Sodhi, a South Asian American, his life. In Mesa, Arizona, four days after 9/11, Sodhi was landscaping at his Chevron gas station when Frank Roque shot him dead because of his so-called resemblance to al-Qaeda members. Roque was finally arrested after attempting to murder Afghani and Lebanese Americans, all the while justifying his actions as patriotic. All of these incidents reveal that this silent dilemma of hate crimes against Asian Americans requires greater public awareness and, more important, solutions. Reaching solutions will require, however, a much better understanding of the racial subordination of Asian Americans in the first place.

Conclusion

Concerning the fate of the American racial landscape, this essay challenged the increasingly accepted sociological forecast that Asian Americans (and Latinos) are whitening or aligning with whites in a new black/nonblack divide. As noted, these studies do not incorporate the dimensions along which Asian Americans' racial status depends, namely hierarchies of citizenship within a context of global inequalities (i.e., US-Asian relations). As such, scholars need to address both the limits and dangers of Asian Americans' high social class status and an American national identity as a cornerstone of whiteness. Methodologically, this essay questioned why the racial assimilation literature does not engage the qualitative and quantitative studies that directly investigate issues of racialized citizenship. To support the point, the data presented here problematized and contextualized three major predicates of the thesis on Asian Americans' racial mobility: high socioeconomic status, high rates of intermarriage with whites, and racial attitudes and ideology.

Taken together, these arguments yield to a larger and more pressing point: the need to consider how white American dominance has been secured for about four hundred years by exercising racial power over *all* nonwhites. Of the racial assimilation studies on Asian Americans, Bonilla-Silva (2002) and Gans (1999) acknowledge this larger project of racial hegemony. Both contend that lighter

skinned and higher class Asian Americans could, respectively, join an honorary white and residual category (while darker skinned, lower income Asian
ethnics would "blacken"). These "middle" Asian ethnics would thereby shore
up white racial dominance by being politically palatable and serving as a buffer for black countermovements, a purpose that "in between" groups have often
served. While these studies should be applauded for their claims about tripartite
models, they need also investigate, and act on, the *specificity* of Asian American
racialization—to take seriously the denial of social citizenship to Asian groups
on a racial basis and to capture how it is linked to antiblack subordination and
the racial system writ large. In other words, Asian and black Americans have
been played off of one another, respectively, as "harder working than blacks" and
"more American than Asians" and, at different points in time, "more like those
blacks" ("Filipino brown brothers") and "more like us" (whites and blacks after
9/11) (Almaguer 1994; C. Kim 1999). While it does matter that white America
ideologically valorizes Asian ethnics above blacks in the color order, this tripartite arrangement also reveals a citizenship order in which Asian Americans
experience their most profound subordination. This white-led racial system,
then, has racialized Asian and black Americans vis-à-vis one another not only to
ensure an internecine minority war, but to legitimize the "foolproof" existence
of American meritocracy. That is, if the system can racially lump and stereotype
all Asian Americans as model minorities, then blacks have only themselves, not
the system, to blame. This point is also crucial insofar as it shows that Asian
Americans have been valorized for their success as a *racial minority* group, not
as a white majority. They have also experienced the highest rates of discrimination and violence precisely for being *too model* a minority, from the Chinese
gold miners to engineer Vincent Chin to the college students who systematically
face racial animus. While it matters, then, that Asian Americans are nonblack,
what matters most is that Asian and black people in the United States are both
nonwhite.

Much of the social scientific literature on race and immigration, however,
seems to have been swayed by the model minority ideology to the extent that it
does not examine the origins of the ideology or, more urgently, critically interrogate the hegemonic purpose that it serves. This is crucial, in my view, for just as
James McKee (1993) lamented the failure of assimilation-minded sociologists to
predict the racial upheavals of the 1960s and 1970s, I fear that like-minded sociologists are not grasping the centrality of race in Asian and Latino groups' lives
and thus not considering the big picture that is America's racialized system. As I
have argued, US relations with Asian nations have profoundly shaped the social
treatment of Asian Americans (e.g., Espiritu 1997, 2003); therefore, the bubbling
tensions with "evil" North Korea and the threat of China's and India's global
dominance will likely bring renewed attention to the yellow peril and Asian
menace. But if we sociologists neglect this historical and perpetual inequality,

then we have failed to grasp the fullness of our reality. Similarly, if we do not grasp how white racial dominance has depended on racializing *all* nonwhite groups in different and related ways (C. Kim 1999), we as a society will never get past ranking each other's oppressions to meet the core need of dismantling the racial system that ultimately hurts us all.

NOTES

Originally published in *Social Forces* 86 (2): 561–574, 2007. ©2007 *Social Forces*, reprint by permission.

1 I put "race" in quotes to denote its socially constructed character.
2 I thank Charles Gallagher for this point.
3 At the same time, Yen Espiritu (2003, 47) makes clear that marginalized groups like Asian Americans in the United States have never been fully excluded. Rather, she believes that US groups of color have undergone "differential inclusion" at the hands of elite white America.
4 Much of these data come from Lai and Arguelles (2003).
5 In addition, many Asian groups conform to age hierarchies whereby the first-generation members are the leaders of the communities, even if they are not as English-fluent and able to navigate US society as their offspring. The first generation is therefore central, not peripheral, to the fate of Asian America more broadly.
6 "Taking America's Pulse Survey" (2000, 2005).
7 "American Attitudes toward Chinese Americans & Asian Americans: A Committee of 100 Survey" (2001).
8 *Los Angeles Times* poll (1993), cited in Taeku Lee (2000).
9 The information in this paragraph comes from Taeku Lee (2000).

REFERENCES

Abelmann, Nancy, and John Lie. 1995. *Blue Dreams: Korean Americans and the Los Angeles Riots.* Cambridge, MA: Harvard University Press.
Almaguer, Tomás. 1994. *The Racial Faultline: The Historical Origin of White Supremacy in California.* Berkeley: University of California Press.
Ancheta, Angelo N. 1998. *Race, Rights, and the Asian American Experience.* New Brunswick, NJ: Rutgers University Press.
Arnesen, Eric. 2001. "Whiteness and the Historians' Imagination." *International Labor and Working-Class History* 60: 3–32.
Asian Americans for Community Involvement. 1993. "Qualified but . . . : A Report on Glass Ceiling Issues Facing Asian Americans in Silicon Valley." San Jose, CA: Asian Americans for Community Involvement.
Bean, Frank D., and Gillian Stevens. 2003. *America's Newcomers and the Dynamics of Diversity.* New York: Russell Sage Foundation.
Bobo, Lawrence, and Susan A. Suh. 2000. "Surveying Racial Discrimination: Analyses from a Multiethnic Labor Market." Pp. 527–564 in Lawrence D. Bobo, Melvin L. Oliver, James H. Johnson, and Abel Valenzuela, eds., *Prismatic Metropolis: Inequality in Los Angeles.* New York: Russell Sage Foundation.
Bonilla-Silva, Eduardo. 2002. "We Are All Americans! The Latin Americanization of Racial Stratification in the USA." *Race and Society* 5 (1): 3–16.
Chan, Kenyon, and Shirley Hune. 1995. "Racialization and Panethnicity: From Asians in America to Asian Americans." Pp. 205–233 in W. Hawley and A. Jackson, eds., *Toward a Common Destiny: Race and Ethnic Relations in American Schools.* San Francisco: Jossey-Bass.

Chan, Sucheng. 1990. "Introduction." Pp. xxi–lx in Mary P. Lee, *Quiet Odyssey: A Pioneer Korean Woman in America*. Seattle: University of Washington Press.

Collins, Patricia Hill. 2000. *Black Feminist Thought: Knowledge, Consciousness, and the Politics of Empowerment*. 2nd ed. New York: Routledge.

——. 2001. "'Like One of the Family': Race, Ethnicity, and the Paradox of US National Identity." *Ethnic and Racial Studies* 24 (1): 3–28.

Collins, Sharon M. 1997. *Black Corporate Executives: The Making and Breaking of a Black Middle Class*. Philadelphia: Temple University Press.

Cose, Ellis. 1993. *The Rage of a Privileged Class*. New York: HarperCollins.

Espiritu, Yen L. 1992. *Asian American Panethnicity: Bridging Institutions and Identities*. Philadelphia: Temple University Press.

——. 1997. *Asian American Women and Men: Labor, Laws and Love*. Walnut Creek, CA: AltaMira Press.

——. 2003. *Homebound: Filipino American Lives across Cultures, Communities, and Countries*. Berkeley: University of California Press.

Feagin, Joe R. 2000. *Racist America: Roots, Current Realities, and Future Reparations*. New York: Routledge.

Feagin, Joe R., and Clairece B. Feagin. 1993. *Racial and Ethnic Relations*. 4th ed. New York: Prentice Hall.

Feagin, Joe R., and Melvin Sikes. 1994. *Living with Racism: The Black Middle-Class Experience*. Boston: Beacon.

Frank, Dana. 1998. "White Working-Class Women and the Race Question." *International Labor and Working-Class History* 54: 80–102.

Gans, Herbert. 1999. "The Possibility of a New Racial Hierarchy in the Twenty-First Century United States." Pp. 371–390 in Michèle Lamont, ed., *The Cultural Territories of Race: Black and White Boundaries*. Chicago: University of Chicago Press.

Glenn, Evelyn N. 2002. *Unequal Freedom: How Race and Gender Shaped American Citizenship and Labor*. Cambridge, MA: Harvard University Press.

Guglielmo, Thomas A. 2003. *White on Arrival: Italians, Race, Color, and Power in Chicago, 1890–1945*. Oxford: Oxford University Press.

Hune, Shirley. 1998. *Asian Pacific American Women in Higher Education: Claiming Visibility and Voice*. Washington, DC: Association of American Colleges and Universities.

Ignatiev, Noel. 1995. *How the Irish Became White*. New York: Routledge.

Karabel, Jerome. 2005. *The Chosen: The Hidden History of Admission and Exclusion at Harvard, Yale, and Princeton*. Boston: Houghton Mifflin.

Kibria, Nazli. 1997. "The Construction of Asian American: Reflection on Interracial Marriage and Ethnic Identity among Second-generation Chinese and Korean Americans." *Ethnic and Racial Studies* 20 (3): 523–544.

——. 2002. *Becoming Asian American: Second-Generation Chinese and Korean American Identities*. Baltimore: Johns Hopkins University Press.

Kim, Claire J. 1999. "The Racial Triangulation of Asian Americans." *Politics and Society* 27 (1): 105–138.

Kim, Nadia Y. 2003. *Imperial Citizens: Koreans and Race from Seoul to LA*. Stanford, CA: Stanford University Press.

Kolchin, Peter. 2002. "Whiteness Studies: The New History of Race in America." *Journal of American History* 81 (1): 154–173.

Lai, Eric, and Dennis Arguelles. 2003. "Introduction." Pp. 1–6 in Eric Lai and Dennis Arguelles, eds., *The New Face of Asian Pacific America: Numbers, Diversity and Change in the 21st Century*. San Francisco: Asian Week and UCLA Asian American Studies Center Press.

Lee, Jennifer, and Frank D. Bean. 2004. "America's Changing Color Lines: Race/Ethnicity, Immigration, and Multiracial Identification." *Annual Review of Sociology* 30: 221–242.

Lee, Sharon, and Marilyn Fernandez. 1998. "Trends in Asian American Racial/Ethnic Intermarriage." *Sociological Perspectives* 41 (2): 323–342.

Lee, Taeku. 2000. "Racial Attitudes and the Color Lines at the Close of the Twentieth Century." Pp. 103–158 in Paul Ong, ed., *The State of Asian Pacific America: Transforming Race Relations: A Public Policy Report*. Los Angeles: Asian Pacific American Public Policy Institute, LEAP and UCLA Asian American Studies Center.

———. 2005. "Bringing Class, Ethnicity, and Nation Back to Race: The Color Lines in 2015." *Perspectives on Politics* 3 (3): 557–561.

Lie, John. 1998. *Han Unbound: The Political Economy of South Korea*. Stanford, CA: Stanford University Press.

———. 2004. *Modern Peoplehood*. Cambridge, MA: Harvard University Press.

Lipsitz, George. 1998. *The Possessive Investment in Whiteness: How White People Profit from Identity Politics*. Philadelphia: Temple University Press.

Lowe, Lisa. 1996. *Immigrant Acts: On Asian American Cultural Politics*. Durham, NC: Duke University Press.

Marshall, T. H. 1973. *Citizenship and Social Development*. Westport, CT: Greenwood.

Massey, Douglas. 1995. "The New Immigration and Ethnicity in the United States." *Population and Development Review* 21 (3): 631–652.

McKee, James B. 1993. *Sociology and the Race Problem: The Failure of a Perspective*. Urbana: University of Illinois Press.

Min, Pyong Gap. 2006. *Asian Americans: Contemporary Trends and Issues*. Thousand Oaks, CA: Pine Forge Press.

Moraga, Cherrie. 1981. "La Guera." Pp. 27–34 in Cherrie Moraga and Gloria Anzaldua, eds., *This Bridge Called My Back: Writings by Radical Women of Color*. Boston: Kitchen Table Press.

Moya, Paula. 1996. "Postmodernism, Realism, and the Politics of Identity: Cherrie Moraga and Chicana Feminism." Pp. 125–150 in C. T. Mohanty and M. J. Alexander, eds., *Feminist Genealogies, Colonial Legacies, Democratic Futures*. New York: Routledge.

National Asian Pacific American Legal Consortium. 1994–2002. *Audit of Violence Against Asian Pacific Americans*. Washington, DC: NAPALC.

Newman, Katherine. 1993. *Declining Fortunes*. New York: Basic Books.

Nishioka, Joyce. 2003. "The Model Minority?" Pp. 29–35 in Eric Lai and Dennis Arguelles, eds., *The New Face of Asian Pacific America: Numbers, Diversity and Change in the 21st Century*. San Francisco: Asian Week and UCLA Asian American Studies Center Press.

Okihiro, Gary Y. 1994. *Margins and Mainstreams: Asians in American History and Culture*. Seattle: University of Washington Press.

Ong, Aihwa. 1999. *Flexible Citizenship: The Cultural Logics of Transnationality*. Durham, NC: Duke University Press.

Ong, Paul M., and Tania Azores. 1994. "Asian Immigrants in Los Angeles: Diversity and Divisions." Pp. 100–129 in Paul M. Ong, Edna Bonacich, and Lucie Cheng, eds., *The New Asian Immigration in Los Angeles and Global Restructuring*. Philadelphia: Temple University Press.

Palumbo-Liu, David. 1999. *Asian/American: Historical Crossings of a Racial Frontier*. Stanford, CA: Stanford University Press.

Park, Edward J. W., and John S. W. Park. 2005. *Probationary Americans: Contemporary Immigration Policies and the Shaping of Asian American Communities*. New York: Routledge.

Park, Lisa Sun-hee. 2005. *Consuming Citizenship: Children of Asian Immigrant Entrepreneurs*. Stanford, CA: Stanford University Press.

Purkayastha, Bandana. 2005. *Negotiating Ethnicity: Second-Generation South Asian Americans Traverse a Transnational World.* New Brunswick, NJ: Rutgers University Press.

Pyke, Karen, and Tran Dang. 2003. "'FOB' and 'Whitewashed': Identity and Internalized Racism among Second Generation Asian Americans." *Qualitative Sociology* 26 (2): 147–172.

Qian, Zhenchao, and Daniel T. Lichter. 2007. "Social Boundaries and Marital Assimilation: Interpreting Trends in Racial and Ethnic Intermarriage." *American Sociological Review* 72: 68–94.

Roediger, David R. 2006. *Working Toward Whiteness: How America's Immigrants Became White: The Strange Journey from Ellis Island to the Suburbs.* New York: Perseus.

Rudrappa, Sharmila. 2004. *Ethnic Routes to Becoming American: Indian Immigrants and the Cultures of Citizenship.* New Brunswick, NJ: Rutgers University Press.

Said, Edward W. 1979. *Orientalism.* New York: Vintage.

———. 1993. *Culture and Imperialism.* New York: Knopf.

Schuman, Howard, Charlotte Steeh, Lawrence Bobo, and Maria Krysan. 1997. *Racial Attitudes in America: Trends and Interpretations.* Rev. ed. Cambridge, MA: Harvard University Press.

Shinagawa, Larry, and Gin Yong Pang. 1996. "Asian American Panethnicity and Intermarriage." *Amerasia Journal* 22 (2): 127–152.

Takaki, Ronald T. 1998. *Strangers from a Different Shore: A History of Asian Americans.* 2nd ed. New York: Penguin.

Tuan, Mia. 1998. *Forever Foreigners or Honorary Whites? The Asian Ethnic Experience Today.* New Brunswick, NJ: Rutgers University Press.

———. 1999. "Neither *Real* Americans nor *Real* Asians? Multigeneration Asian Ethnics Navigating the Terrain of Authenticity." *Qualitative Sociology* 22 (2): 105–125.

Warren, Jonathan W., and France W. Twine. 1997. "White Americans, the New Minority? Nonblacks and the Ever-Expanding Boundaries of Whiteness." *Journal of Black Studies* 28 (2): 200–218.

Waters, Mary C. 1999. *Black Identities: West Indian Immigrant Dreams and American Realities.* Cambridge, MA: Harvard University Press.

Xie, Yu, and Kimberly Goyette. 2004. *A Demographic Portrait of Asian Americans.* New York: Russell Sage Foundation.

Yancey, George. 2003. *Who Is White? Latinos, Asians, and the New Black/Nonblack Divide.* Boulder, CO: Lynne Rienner.

26

Beyond the Perpetual Foreigner and Model Minority Stereotypes

A Critical Examination of How Asian Americans Are Framed

JENNIFER NG, YOON PAK, AND XAVIER HERNANDEZ

Mainstream as well as academic discussions of race in the United States have long been framed in terms of black and white. This has had critical implications for the racialization of Asian Americans. Such a simplistic binary, for instance, obscures the very existence of Asians in America so that after many generations, even native-born Asian Americans are viewed as *perpetual foreigners* whose origins, identities, and status as citizens lie outside the scope of racial relevance. Or, when Asian Americans have been included on the continuum where white norms set a standard against which black and other minority group struggles for equality are measured, then select indicators have fortified their designation as a *model minority* whose achievements have been used as proof to all others that discrimination can be overcome with hard work and persistence.

How have Asian American experiences in education been shaped by the perpetual foreigner and model minority stereotypes? And, what are their contemporary effects? After all, "civic ostracism" as alien Others in regard to whites and "relative valorization" in stark contrast to nonwhites (Kim 1999) are two of the primary means by which Asian Americans have been racialized (Ancheta 2000). And though it is not uncommon for people—including some Asian Americans—to assume these stereotypes are harmless or even flattering, scholars in such varied fields as history (Takaki 1998), English (Lowe 2000), anthropology (Manalansan 2000, 2003), sociology (Kibria 2002; C. Kim 1999; Min 1996; Tuan 1998), ethnic and gender studies (Espiritu 1997; R. Lee 1999), and law (Ancheta 2000; Wu 1995) have suggested otherwise. Similarly, our examination of research on Asian Americans in education underscores the enduring significance of the perpetual foreigner and model minority stereotypes as well as their problematic effects (Ng, Lee, and Pak 2007; Pak, Maramba, and Hernandez 2014; see also Hartlep 2013).

What Happens When the Perpetual Foreigner and Model Minority Go to School?

In 1988, Garry Trudeau published a *Doonesbury* cartoon that illustrates the direct, educational relevance of the perpetual foreigner and model minority stereotypes about Asian Americans:

STUDENT: "Asians are threatening our economic future. . . . We can see it
   right here in our own school. Who are getting into the best colleges in disproportionate numbers? Asian kids! It's not fair."
TEACHER: "Uh. . . . That certainly was an unusual essay. . . . Unfortunately,
   it's racist."
STUDENT: "Um . . . are you sure? My parents helped me."

Set against the backdrop of the 1980s admissions scandal at elite universities where Asian Americans were perceived to be taking over college campuses (R. Takagi 1998), the sentiments captured in Trudeau's cartoon still warrant our consideration today as a basis for not only understanding how Asian Americans have been racially constructed but also demonstrating that those constructs continue to matter. In the sections to come, we first examine how Asian Americans are commonly framed in research intended to help educators learn about their Asian American students. With an almost exclusive focus on how newly arrived immigrants and refugees are culturally distinct, this work can be informative yet essentialize groups and reinforce assumptions of Asian Americans' infinite foreignness. In the two sections that follow, we discuss the importance of research that helps reframe our understanding of Asian Americans more meaningfully by (1) attending to the diversity that exists within this varied group and (2) considering how race intersects with other dimensions of difference in the situated complexities of people's lives.

Framing Asian Americans

It is not entirely surprising that the student in Trudeau's cartoon draws a distinction between the Asians who attend her school and those like herself who are entitled to claim it as "our own school." After all, Said's (1978) influential work on Orientalism illuminates what has become a normalized "discourse that both assumes and promotes a fundamental difference between the Western 'us' and Oriental 'them'" (Rizvi and Lingard 2006, 296). Indeed, a great deal of educational literature meant to help educators understand Asian Americans adopts a lens of "cultural difference" (Sleeter and Grant 2009) that reinforces a sense of their profound foreignness and membership in categorically separate and static groups.

Detailing the sociocultural and linguistic backgrounds of seven different ethnic groups, for instance, C. C. Park and Chi's (1999, viii) *Asian American Education: Prospects and Challenges* is designed to "provide a sense of how each groups is faring," illuminate the "unique educational issues, needs, and challenges faced by the group," and provide "practical and insightful suggestions" for individuals who work with Asian American students. Mathews's (2000) review of the cultural patterns of South and Southeast Asians typifies a related sort of description that covers family relationships, respect for age, social interaction, communication style, family expectations of success, humility, school situations, decision making, and socialization barriers, as well as their accompanying implications for teachers. And upon such foundations of understanding Asian Americans' cultural distinctiveness, G. Lee and Manning (2001a and 2001b) suggest teachers accommodate Asian parents and families by showing respect for immediate and extended family members, providing opportunities to share differences in US and Asian schools and society, and being considerate of Asian parents' English proficiency. Other scholars like Chiang (2000), for example, have also recommended specific instructional strategies and curricular materials that might be especially well suited for the "cultural characteristics and learning styles" of Asian American children in contrast to their mainstream, Caucasian peers.

Although this type of literature can provide educators with straightforward information and clear prescriptions for practice, it tends to treat groups monolithically and overlooks the more complicated realities of Asian American identities and experiences. Some authors express their awareness of this and offer caveats, such as G. Lee and Manning (2001b, 23):

> Prototypic Asian American parents and families do not exist. Just as all parents and families differ, Asian American parents differ by educational backgrounds, linguistic ability, socioeconomic status, acculturation, and demographic region, just to name representative examples. Educators need to be wary when referring to "Asian American" parents and families.

Nonetheless, the essentializing effects of these approaches taken in sum reify notions of Asian American foreignness (Lei 2006). With an almost exclusive focus on recent immigrant students and characterizations of them as members of static and culturally circumscribed groups, the normalization of Asian American difference soon follows. As Mathews concludes, for example, "Obedience, silence, and nonassertiveness are *normal* traits for most South Asian and Southeast Asian school children," "they do not *normally* initiate conversation, and they are comfortable with silence," and "behaviors such as timidity, overdependence, and lack of initiative can be manifestations of the *cultural* traits of students from South Asian and Southeast Asian families" (Mathews 2000, 103–104, emphasis added).

Interestingly, the construction of Asian Americans as markedly different has been central to explanations for their notable achievement and resulting model minority designation, too. With their Confucian ideals and emphases on family cohesion, deference to authority, and valuing of education (Pearce 2006), for example, frequent reference to their cultural distinctiveness has made the story of Asian American triumph appear almost certain and incontrovertible. In addition to culture, the scope of difference related to Asian American success has included their biological peculiarities as well, with Bracey citing in a 1999 *Phi Delta Kappan* essay an "Asian math gene" and later in 2005 an "Indian spelling gene." And still further, Asian American success has been attributed to the pathology of Asian parents whose single-minded, "mono-maniacally obsessive" involvement borders on child abuse (Bracey 2005, 92; see also Richwine 2009) and extreme Tiger mothering (Chua 2011).

Ultimately, framing Asian Americans as the model minority has desensitized individuals to a troubling history of race relations in the United States and served as powerful hegemonic device between groups (S. J. Lee 2009). On the one hand, the stereotype heralds Asian Americans as worthy of praise for accomplishments so remarkable they can be deemed "honorary Whites" (Kim 1999). Positioning the supposed quiet determination of Asian Americans against the outspoken protests and institutional critiques of African Americans seeking equality in the 1960s, for example, has resulted in fissures across these minority communities and coalitions that are evident still to this day. On the other hand, however, the associated threat of Asian American domination expressed by the student in Trudeau's cartoon has endured since the nineteenth century in what novelist Jack London popularized as the "yellow peril"; through similar fears provoked in a 1971 *Newsweek* headline proclaiming Asian Americans might in fact be "outwhiting the Whites" ("Success Story" 1971, 24); and in contemporary debates about such heated topics as diversity and affirmative action in higher education. If limited to the black/white binary of racial positions where "minority" and "high achievement" seem incompatible, then Asian Americans have arguably found themselves "de-minoritized" on the whole by discrete indicators of success (S. S. Lee 2006) and routinely ignored in discussions of race, discrimination, equality, and social justice (Inkelas 2003a, 2003b). Exceptions to the rule of Asian American accomplishment—Southeast Asians, for example (Depouw 2006; S. J. Lee 2006)—are subject to "ideological Blackening" (Ong 1996) and relegated alongside African Americans and other minorities who presumably do not share the value of education and hard work, despite historical evidence to the contrary (Anderson 1988, 2004a, 2004b; Span and Anderson 2005; Williams 2005). All the while, the model minority myth is left intact.

Asian Americans themselves are clearly underrepresented in the teaching profession, still barely above 1 percent of all K–12 teachers, public as well as private across the country, with an average enrollment of eight preservice teachers each in certification programs across the country (Gordon 2000; National Center for Education Statistics [NCES] 2007). Furthermore, Asian American teachers have far less average teaching experience and are far more likely to leave teaching positions to pursue careers outside of education than any other racial group (Teranishi 2010). These numbers are disproportionate to the participation of Asian Americans in the education system as well as the workforce at large, and they are problematic in various ways. For example, Asian American teachers are part of the growing diversity in the United States and can play key roles in increasing both students' and teachers' knowledge and positive interactions with members of different cultural groups (Jorgenson 2000). Given the heterogeneity within the community, Asian American teachers may also be especially able to identify with the needs and concerns of Asian American children, and their bicultural perspectives are a vital resource. This is not to say that Asian American students can or should interact only with Asian American teachers. However, the invisibility of Asian Americans across the spectrum of roles in public education fosters the neglect of Asian American students' complex identities, experiences, and educational needs, and it normalizes their absence.

Kiang (2004) notes that K–12 curriculum lacks significant content on Asia and Asian Pacific American history. Exacerbating this situation is the movement for high-stakes testing that has officially defined and standardized the curriculum students should learn, formalizing the exclusion of content about Asian Americans. These omissions affect all students and can reinforce Asian American stereotypes. S. J. Lee and Kumashiro (2005, 15–16) note,

> All students pick up social messages from what is included and what is excluded from the curriculum. Both AAPI and non-AAPI students are affected when issues related to AAPI history and culture are not taught in our schools. When Asian American and Pacific Islander histories are not taught as part of U.S. history the implicit message is that AAPIs are not real Americans, thereby contributing to the stereotype that AAPIs are perpetual foreigners.

Coloma (2013) expands on this point by emphasizing the importance of schooling and educational materials in establishing the boundaries of legitimate knowledge and truth. Simply put, schools do more than merely communicate impartial knowledge bases. They have an active part in determining the knowledge that is worthy of preservation and transmission to future generations of citizens. Thus, to place Asian Americans outside of this intellectual process renders them invisible within American culture and history.

Asian American studies (AAS) programs in higher education are a valuable—albeit underutilized—educational, cultural, and institutional asset that can contribute to improving the quality of K–12 educational curriculum and practice. At a minimum, they can provide assistance in curriculum development, raise awareness through teacher professional development, facilitate classroom research and advocacy, examine the long-term effects of AAS on teachers, support the involvement of Asian American parents and families, and mentor Asian American youth in school and community settings (Kiang 2004). But to rely solely on these programs, which are concentrated mainly in four-year universities, adds an expectation of collaboration to the heavy occupational responsibilities K–12 and higher education faculty already assume. It also naively overlooks the challenge of access and information sharing across organizations. And for students to have to wait until they are attending college themselves to benefit from these educational resources is incredibly unjust since so many will not have the privilege of such postsecondary experiences. Intervention is needed much earlier in the educational pipeline and across a wider range of institutions.

The impact of multicultural education in teacher preparation programs also must be considered because most teachers are white and have limited prior experience with Asian American children, whose numbers have doubled to 4.5 percent of the total student population (Goodwin 2002; NCES 2010). Whereas certain multicultural approaches can reinforce teachers' beliefs about distinct group differences or merely focus on the feel-good outcomes of human relations, other approaches can foster deeper knowledge about the historical and contemporary experiences of a racial/ethnic group, promote the individual and collective diversity that exists in society, and foster critical examination and transformation of existing systems that perpetuate discrimination and inequality (Sleeter and Grant 2009). An essential first step is that teachers must be trained to recognize the presence and range of experiences Asian American children have in schools. In reviewing teacher education textbooks, Goodwin (2002) found that terms such as "children of color," "diverse children," "culturally and linguistically diverse students," and "minority children" tended to be used interchangeably with "immigrant children." Each of these designations shapes a teacher's relationship to a student, as well as the student's relationship to the educational system in a markedly different way. This conflation of terms makes it nearly impossible for teachers to really understand or begin to address Asian American students' education identities and needs, let alone those of all underrepresented students.

Framing Asian Americans as perpetual foreigners and model minorities curtails genuine progress for both students and educators. Pang (1997) emphasizes the need for teachers who work with Asian American students to care about the whole child, including not only their educational but also social and psychological needs. Achieving such an end requires helping educators critically examine their own racial identity development (Carter 2000; Carter and Goodwin 1994), be insightful about their privileges and prejudices (Pang and Park 2003), and also recognize the need to continuously revise their pedagogical practices in order to adapt to the perennially changing demographics of students. Rather than categorically framing Asian Americans as perpetual foreigners irrelevant to existing conversations or as model minorities who can be dismissed without further regard, it is important to understand that incorporating Asian American perspectives meaningfully into the educational environment is also a means of achieving rightful incorporation into American society. The fact that AAS is so commonly mistaken for Asian studies but almost never confused for American studies is a prime example of this point.

Reframing Asian American Educational Experiences: Deliberately Disaggregating to Consider the Diversity Within

How can the educational experiences of Asian Americans be more meaningfully understood? As we have argued elsewhere (Ng, Lee, and Pak 2007), one important effort is to account carefully for the diversity that exists within the broad term "Asian American" along such lines of ethnicity, gender, and a host of other variables. This can be done by purposefully disaggregating the data that form the bases for our conclusions and actively seeking the varied circumstances of Asian Americans for what more nuanced insights can be gleaned. Though some Asian Americans are, of course, foreign-born and recent immigrants while others are high-achieving and quite accomplished, this does not adequately capture the realities of all Asian Americans. Creating monolithic truths about a group based on the performance of select subgroups can hardly be considered truthful at all.

Baker, Keller-Wolff, and Wolf-Wendel (2000) demonstrate the explanatory value of statistical models that disaggregate. While recognizing the constraints of available large-scale data sets and the need to maintain subgroup sample sizes, Baker et al. used 1998 National Educational Longitudinal Study data to assess the extent to which commonly used racial/ethnic classifications appropriately represented their constituent subgroups with respect to academic achievement. They concluded that some subgroups may not be accurately represented by their common aggregate classification. For example, the high mathematics achievement of Asian Americans overall was problematized when disaggregation indicated there was a range in outcomes from Pacific Islanders who performed 6.83 points below white students to West Asian students who performed 8.45 points above white students (524). Not only was the variation in outcomes across subgroups wide, but the inclusion of West Asian individuals from Iranian, Afghan, and Turkish backgrounds under the classification "Asian" in this data set reveals difficulties at the core of even conceptualizing Asian Americans. West Asian students' experiences are arguably quite distinct from those of Chinese, Japanese, Korean, Filipino, and Indian students, for instance, who have a shared history of being racialized as nonwhite.

In an era of high-stakes testing and accountability when disaggregation by race is a key feature, Asian American students continue to be considered in the aggregate, however. The 2001 No Child Left Behind Act (NCLB) does not require ethnic disaggregation of student performance, thus masking Asian American ethnic and socioeconomic variation. Kiang (2004) discusses these issues in regard to the Massachusetts Comprehensive Assessment System, the mandatory standardized tests assessing English, math, and science/technology. In schools with the highest concentrations of Southeast Asian students, the mean scaled scores for Asian students at the tenth grade level was failing compared to other districts where Chinese and Indian students were passing. As Pang, Han, and Pang (2011) similarly demonstrate, such realities remain hidden in the aggregate.

The struggles of nonnative English speakers are also obscured when NCLB requires students with limited English proficiency to still take the math portions of the test, with no hiatus. While language proficiency may seem at first unrelated to math performance, Wright (2006) documents a number of ways language is implicated. For example, students may be entitled to language support services that their schools are unable to adequately provide, and the vocabulary students need to engage many story problems requires more advanced cultural and linguistic proficiency than native-English speakers presume.

Disaggregation is a common mantra in postsecondary research as well. Researchers like Escueta and O'Brien (1991), Hsia (1988), Hsia and Hirano-Nakanishi (1995), and Hune and Chan (1997) found ethnic disparities in student achievement that remain salient still, with Southeast Asian and Pacific Islander students faring less well than their peers. Indeed, Hune and Chan (1997) document the bimodal nature of Asian American educational achievement overall, with high rates of students both dropping out of high school and completing college. They also identify differences by gender and academic discipline. Taken together, these studies contest the model minority myth of unilateral excellence and point to structural reasons why Asian Americans have excelled in some areas of higher education but not in others.

Studies of Asian American students' choices of major demonstrate a host of influential factors as well, including ethnicity, gender, and psychological measures such as locus of control (Song and Glick 2004). Simpson (2001) also found that Asian American students were more influenced by maternal guidance and high school English courses in choosing between a technical or public service/liberal arts program. And Teranishi et al. (2004) examined the impact of class and ethnicity on college choice for Asian Pacific American (APA) students using data from UCLA's Cooperative Institutional Research Program in 1997. The authors found that Southeast Asian and Chinese students were more often from families earning less than $24,999 a year. In addition, larger proportions of Chinese and Korean than Filipinos or Southeast Asians students attended highly selective colleges. Filipinos and Southeast Asians from the lowest income brackets were more likely to choose a college because it was close to home, and they expressed more major financial concerns about college than did other groups. Along with Japanese students, they were also twice as likely to apply to only one campus, in contrast to the Chinese and Korean students in the sample who were likely to apply to five or more colleges.

As a consequence of the near exclusive attention given to Asian Americans as model minorities attending elite universities, Asian Americans enrolled in community colleges are what Lew, Chang, and Wang (2005) have called an "overlooked minority." According to NCES (2014), one-third of Asian American/Pacific Islander students are enrolled in two-year institutions. Kiang's (1992) study of Asian American students in community college settings points to a number of significant barriers these students face, including their high rates of part-time work, lower retention rates compared to white students, frustration with language difficulties, family obligations, and struggles with anti-Asian racism. Makuakane-Drechsel and Hagedorn (2000) examined Hawaiian students at four community colleges in Oahu and identified such predictive variables for their academic persistence as cumulative grade point average, financial aid, and average credit hours. These findings illuminate specific challenges for ensuring wider access to—and persistence in—community colleges for Asian American students. And this particular study is notable also because it details the many difficulties students face even when they are not numerically the racial minority in an educational setting. Taken in sum, studies across the spectrum of higher education serve as important reminders that significant numbers of Asian American college students are overlooked when the prevailing characterization of Asian Americans is as the model minority attending only the most selective colleges and universities.

Reframing Asian American Educational Experiences, Again: The Importance of Intersectional Approaches

As we have argued before (Ng, Lee, and Pak 2007), research that takes an intersectional approach (Coloma 2006) to examining how race relates to other dimensions of difference in the situated complexities of people's actual lives is also vital in efforts to reframe Asian Americans as more than just perpetual foreigners and model minorities. After all, as Lowe (2000) points out, Asian Americans are a heterogeneous and hybrid group who defy easy categorization. And stereotypical labels placed upon Asian Americans are not merely empirical data markers; they are laden with sociocultural meaning and shape how people are treated by governing institutions and peer groups. Intersectional research thus defies the reduction of Asian Americans into simplistic caricatures and instead demonstrates how the myriad factors of ethnicity, language, gender, culture, socioeconomic status, sexuality, and the like affect Asian Americans' experiences.

Identity Development

Studies on Asian American identity formation as a dynamic process shaped by intergroup relations exemplify the possibilities of such work, especially because identity is a developmental concept reflecting an individual's sense of self derived from a feeling of belonging or commitment to one's own group as well as an acculturative concept indicating the way an individual relates to other groups and society at large (Shrake and Rhee 2004). S. J. Lee's (2009) study of Academic High provides this sort of rich depiction by exploring the varied identifications Asian American students constructed as they sought to make sense of their positions in the racial minefield of their school. Korean-identified students who socialized primarily with other Korean-identified students tried to befriend white students and adopt white-normed behaviors for status while avoiding contact with African American students; Asian-identified students who adhered firmly to a belief in fairness and meritocracy admired, but remained socially distant from, white students and rationalized their experiences with racism as temporary difficulties; "new wavers" who adopted an oppositional stance to school engaged the racially charged exchange of insults with African American students who were tracked in the same classes and lived in the same neighborhoods as they did while incorporating some displays of street culture; and Asian American–identified students who challenged the supposed superiority of whites questioned the truthfulness of the model minority stereotype and sought alliances with students of other racial groups.

In research similar to S. J. Lee's (2009) study, Goto (1997) situated the seemingly inconsistent and contradictory social and academic behavior of Chinese American high school students in a web of peer relationships including "nerds," "normal people," and "homeboys." Rather than endure the racialized stereotype of being nerds singularly focused on their academic achievement, these students positioned themselves strategically so as not to be too popular or too high-performing and, instead, remain comfortably anonymous. In this way, students lived up to their expressed preference for maintaining harmonious friendships with others rather than foster relationships characterized by individual competition and status. Considering the significance students of Asian descent attached to different reference subgroups at Academic High (S. J. Lee 1996) as well as the ways that students in Goto's (1997) study managed their academic personas and social positions, studies of this sort yield great insight into the varied dimensions of their identifiers (see also S. J. Lee 2001, 2005).

Identity continues to matter in higher education, and Kawaguchi (2003), Alvarez (2002), and Kodama et al. (2002) have proposed various identity development models for Asian American students that allow for the diversity and difference within the group to be considered further. In addition, Yang et al. (2002) demonstrate the processes by which Asian American students might internalize the model minority stereotype and also conclude that students who have internalized it are less likely to utilize Asian American–targeted services. Similar patterns were found for Asian American students who disidentified with their cultural heritage in comparison to those who reported valuing their family backgrounds. The latter group used ethnic-specific campus services more often. Research demonstrates, too, that pan-Asian identity and student activism help Asian American students better cope with discrimination, combat ignorance, and develop stronger commitments to their communities (Inkelas 2004; Rhoads, Lee, and Yamada 2002). These are important insights for campus staff members who implement student programs because, as Liang and Sedlacek (2003) found in their study of white student affairs practitioners, many hold stereotypical views of Asian American students as nonthreatening, technically inclined, and hardworking without due sensitivity to such challenges as family obligation or academic pressure, for example. School leaders in Delucchi and Do's (1996) case study of harassment at a University of California campus were hard-pressed to even recognize the treatment of a Vietnamese American student as being racially motivated, in contrast to incidents against African Americans, which were quickly characterized as racist.

Socioeconomic Status

The intersectionally varied experiences of particular ethnic groups also enrich existing literature by emphasizing the role of socioeconomic status on Asian American educational experiences. For example, Lew's (2004) work examines the relationship between ethnicity and class, documenting the effects of limited social capital and weak ethnic ties on working-class Korean students' decisions to drop out of high school. Respondents in her study reported feeling isolated and ill equipped to make decisions about their academic futures because their parents worked long hours and were unable to provide them with the firsthand guidance necessary to do well in school. Furthermore, they attended under-resourced schools where their teachers and counselors provided minimal and sometimes inaccurate advice. By internalizing feelings of their low status, Lew found that these students negotiated their racial and ethnic identities differently than other Asian American students who maintained strong ethnic community connections or had wealth. Instead, most Korean dropouts in Lew's study developed oppositional perspectives and "aligned their shared experiences of racism and low socio-economic status with other low-income minority peers—Blacks, Hispanics, and Asians" (Lew 2004, 318).

In her study of Filipino American educational experiences, Buenavista (2013) contextualizes the aspirations of youth and their parents historically against the Philippines' colonial relationship with the United States. As college-educated products of a heavily American-influenced education system in the Philippines, these immigrant Filipino parents instilled the liberal ideals of American higher education to their American-born children. However, as victims of discriminatory hiring practices and immigration policies, these parents also became underemployed, working-class individuals whose involvement with their children's education was limited. They struggled to provide their children with the same cultural capital that benefits others whose parents have gone to college before. And thus, Buenavista suggests many Filipino American students are more appropriately termed "1.5"-generation college students, neither completely unfamiliar with higher education as are some first-generation college students nor completely able to derive the economic, social, and academic advantages of their parents' prior college and later life experiences.

Louie (2001) found similar effects of distinct, conflicting immigrant experiences in her study of Chinese immigrant parents' expectations, strategies, and investments in their children's education. Whether middle or low income, the parents in Louie's study reported emphasizing the value of education not only because of their traditional cultural values but also because of the availability of postsecondary education in the United States compared to their respective countries of origin and the potential monetary returns for a college degree in the American labor market, and as a form of protection against the effects of perceived racial discrimination. However, middle-class Chinese parents whose livelihood was derived through their participation in the mainstream economy secured information about different educational options from their friends, teachers, and other school administrators. As a result, they were able to enroll their children in private schools, secure financial aid if necessary, or even move to neighborhoods with reportedly excellent schools. In contrast, the low-income Chinese parents in Louie's study worked primarily within the more limited ethnic economy of restaurants and garment factories and therefore relied on informal ethnic networks to learn about school reputations and specialized entrance examinations. Typically, these informants were also immigrants who had resided in the United States longer and were economically more secure.

Gender and Sexuality

Although advances are being made in educational scholarship, thorough consideration of issues related to the intersection of race, gender, and sexuality is still relatively scant (Mayo 2014). For example, Lei (2003) documents how the identities of Southeast Asian male students were constructed at Hope High School through racialized and gendered regulatory discourses and normative representations. Because these students were often quiet, teachers viewed them variously as model students, secretive, gang-like, and clannish. Compared to the masculine ideal of white, European American men, these students were viewed as small and weak. As a result, students typically socialized in groups with other Southeast

Asian young men who could provide them with protection from harassment if needed, and they all appeared tough to outside observers because they adopted markers of urban hip-hop culture. The result, as Lei (2003, 176) points out, is that

> [b]y being in a group, the Southeast Asian American males created a defense barrier that protected them from potential harassment. The same barrier, however, served to maintain a lack of communication and understanding between the Southeast Asian American male students and the rest of the school.

In describing her earlier study, S. J. Lee (2006, 24) also found that "the messages [boys] receive from school, popular culture, and society at large is that they are too short, too quiet, and too Asian. In short, they learn that they lack the qualities associated with hegemonic masculinity." Shrake and Rhee (2004) explain, however, that Asian American adolescent girls may become quickly assimilated into a more egalitarian American culture and society, thereby heightening the tensions between familial and societal expectations and leading to psychologically internalized distress such as depression or anxiety. The extent of Asian American students' acculturation also seems to be related to their level of personal self-esteem (Rhee, Chang, and Rhee 2003). These issues warrant further consideration because they not only affect Asian American students' self-concepts but also shape significant social and familial interactions.

Espiritu's (2001) research on gender dynamics within Filipino American families illustrates how key linkages between gender and racial/ethnic identity are uniquely felt by Filipino American girls. Instilled with values of sexual abstinence and purity as more than just abstract ideals but rather actual markers of their Filipino identity, the opinion among Filipino American girls that "we don't sleep around like White girls do" demonstrates how gender and ethnic identity were equated with one another. In other words, Filipina sexuality functioned as the gatekeeper of Filipino culture within an American context. The juxtaposition of Asian American female hypersexuality that needs to be controlled versus Asian American male asexuality that refuses to recognize the very humanity of young men is indicative of the need to acknowledge the varied ways that gender and racial identity intersect to create increasingly divergent outcomes for Asian American youth.

Family

Representations of Asian Americans as the model minority and perpetual foreigner support a simplistic discourse about the Asian family. Specifically, families are characterized as influential hubs of distinct and positive cultural values, promoting such values as education, hard work, and family cohesion. However, the issue of a culture gap is particularly relevant between immigrant parents and their US-born children. For example, the student respondents in Louie's (2001) study from working-class families reported that their parents utilized more authoritarian styles of interaction, which they believe fostered ineffective communication. Qin (2006) further explored the parent-child relations of two Chinese immigrant families, one from the middle class and one from the working class. Although the family relationships differed according to how much time parents were able to spend with their children instead of working outside the home and the quality of direct assistance given to support their children's educations, the children ultimately became alienated from their parents in both cases. Qin (2006, 163) attributes this estrangement to "dissonant acculturation" whereby

> [p]arents tend to compare their children's behaviors with those of children in China or their own experiences growing up, immigrant children increasingly compare their parents with the American parents they see in movies or parents of their friends, who emphasize more communication and freedom and less control in their relationship with children.

Parent-child alienation was most acute during adolescence, and the financial demands placed on low-income parents further exacerbated the problem.

S. J. Lee's (2001) study of Hmong American high school students provides additional detail about the ensuing difficulties involved in bridging cultural gaps between parents and their children. Examining 1.5-generation (those born abroad but residing in the United States for three to eight years) and second-generation (US-born) students, Lee found that both teachers and parents perceived 1.5-generation children to be model students. This view stemmed from the belief that Hmong culture provided children with a type of protection against becoming too Americanized and that "[a] good kid will go back to the culture." These 1.5-generation children remained relatively isolated from other children in school, and because they were able to compare their experiences of discrimination in the United States with the difficulties they endured in their native country, they were more willing to overlook instances of racism and focus on the positive aspects of living in their new homeland. American-born, second-generation Hmong students in Lee's study, however, were seen as bad kids because they wore baggy clothes reminiscent of gang attire, insisted on exercising their independence from authority, and rebelled against their parents' strict rules forbidding dating. In these instances, parents lamented what they saw as the loss of their children to (white) American ways. Conversely, the children expressed skepticism with the idea that education would lead to upward social mobility because they saw discrimination as a persistent feature of living in the United States. These children struggled to make sense of their experiences amid competing cultural messages and racialized realities.

In pursuit of higher education, family expectations can also be a source of intergenerational conflict. For instance, Gloria and Ho (2003) found that Asian American students might not view their family support as completely positive given the pressures that parental expectations can bring. Instead, Asian American students relied more often upon peer support. Osajima (1991) also found these pressures in his qualitative study of Asian American college students and the "hidden injuries of race." Osajima documents how Asian American students had persistent experiences with racism and highly complicated family relationships that challenge a model minority image of strong Asian families aligned agreeably around uniform, high educational expectations. Although students credited family support and expectations as influencing their educational aspirations, they also expressed frustration and compromised familial relationships due to these expectations. Work by R. Lee, Su, and Yoshida (2005) examines the various strategies Asian American college students use to cope with intergenerational conflict, and this research complicates the idea of perfect Asian American families.

Language

Related to issues of family and generational status, language differences and language loss between Asian immigrant parents and their children may have significant negative effects on family relations and other aspects of children's health and social development since language is a measure of acculturation. Using data from the 1997–1998 World Health Organization Study of Health Behavior in School Children, S. M. Yu, Huang, and Schwalberg (2002) documented the association between students who did not speak English at home and higher health risks (not wearing seat belts, for example), higher psychosocial risks (feeling marginalized at school and experiencing difficulty making new friends), and higher parental risks (feeling unsupported when trying to deal with school and personal problems). These adolescents also reported more frequent incidents of illness including dizziness, headaches, and stomach aches.

Language loss typically occurs in three generations or less, resulting in children who have little or no working knowledge of their parents' and grandparents' native language and cultural traditions. Researchers have attributed this phenomenon to the assimilative pressures of culturally and linguistically dominant groups over others as well as perceptions of linguistic inferiority internalized by minority individuals themselves that affect their social identity. Given the adverse direct and indirect effects of language loss and accompanying denigration of bilingual and bicultural identities, it is important to consider possible strategies for fostering language resilience among native, biliterate Asian American youth. Tse (2001) argues that schools alone have limited ability to revitalize threatened languages because resisting the process requires broader involvement with peer groups who use the heritage language, institutions that value the language, and parents who speak the language and encourage its use. Reinforcing the vitality of a language—its status and prestige as shaped by various social, political, cultural, and psychological influences—and involvement with rich literacy environments and experiences are essential.

School's Out: What Have We Ultimately Learned?

How Asian Americans are framed—and continuously reframed, as we have demonstrated in this chapter—matters. In the highly publicized and controversial debates on affirmative action at elite universities through the 1980s, for example, the model minority image of Asian Americans was erected alongside whites to represent the twin victims of preferential admissions by those seeking to repeal race-conscious policies (Takaki 1998). So on the one hand, they were portrayed as underrepresented due to the fact that less qualified students were being admitted at their expense. But simultaneously on the other hand, the image of Asian American students as foreign agents taking over college campuses invoked the discourse of yellow peril and accompanying sentiments of Asian American overrepresentation. As Omi and Takagi (1996) show through the 1990s, Asian Americans in California were both claimed by the political Right as victims of affirmative action and abandoned by the political Left, who were uncertain what to do with a minority group that seemed to be faring too well.

Rendered invisible in a racial "no-man's land," Inkelas (2003a, 2003b) argues that Asian Americans have become "diversity's missing minority." This cannot be taken as an indication that Asian Americans are fine, however. Studies continue to report that minority students (including Asian Americans) report greater social alienation than white students at both predominantly white institutions (Jones, Castellanos, and Cole 2002; Loo and Rolison 1986) and "majority minority" institutions (J. J. Park 2013; Poon 2011). Asian American students who experienced racism on campus had lower social adjustment (LeSure 1994), and Asian Americans' negative perceptions of campus were correlated with self-reported levels of depression (Cress and Ikeda 2003). And despite measures of academic satisfaction and persistence, Asian American students face stereotypes, prejudice, and harassment at rates that are significantly higher than those of whites (Ancis, Sedlacek, and Mohr 2000; Asian Pacific American Education Advisory Committee 1990; Mack, Tucker, and Cha 2000). Ranging from subtle comments that single out Asian Americans or ignore them (Woo 1997) to racial provocations and fights (Alvarez and Yeh 1999), such incidents are also likely to be underreported by Asian American students (Kotori and Malaney 2003). In their study at the University of Michigan where Asian Pacific American students reported gaining less from their education, experiencing a less favorable campus climate than their white peers, and feeling less overall satisfaction with campus life, Rohrlick et al. (1998, 9, emphasis added) conclude,

When measured by enrollment, retention, college grades, and graduation rates, Asian/APA students appear to be among the most successful students on our campus. It is incongruous, then, to find that their assessment of their undergraduate experience is less positive than other students, and troubling that their greatest differences occur in areas central to the University's mission. ... The initial comparison of responses suggests that APA students have a different experience on our campus than do White students—and one that is less positive. *If that is true, then it certainly challenges the myth that has grown out of the model minority image: that is, all we have to do is enroll APA students, and they will thrive on campus.* These results suggest that we need to revisit that assumption.

When educational attainment is viewed primarily in terms of individual advancement and occupational decision making mainly a matter of one's own preferences, research on Asian Americans compels continued, critical engagement. As Louie (2004) found in her study of how Chinese families convey messages to their children about higher education, race is highly salient, and education is a means to buffer the effects of racial discrimination. Kibria's (2002) study of second-generation Chinese and Korean American young adults concluded similarly that education can be a strategy for coping with racism. Research by Gordon (1997, 2000, 2005) and Asher (2002) suggests that the fear of ridicule and discrimination are among the varied reasons Asian Americans opt not to become teachers. And Rong and Preissle (1997) elaborate that in those occupations where Asian Americans are well represented—engineering, computer science, medicine, and other hard sciences, for example—their social interactions with others to "save face" against cultural awkwardness can be limited. Instead of simply viewing the involvement of Asian Americans in science, technology, engineering, and math (STEM) fields as evidence of their success securing well-paid, high-status jobs, the choices Asian Americans make with respect to their college majors and occupational futures are, in fact, constrained in an effort to guard against racial and gender discrimination in the workplace and limited future advancement (George-Jackson 2011).

Even in the ivory towers of academe, Asian American faculty and administrators are subject to other's assumptions that they are passive, hardworking, and nonconfrontational model minorities as well as foreigners whose cultural differences are so great they are incapable of much advancement or leadership. According to Teranishi (2010), Asian Americans are overrepresented in non-tenure-track faculty roles, while only 36 percent have tenure (compared to 43 percent of the professoriate at large). And Asian Americans represent only 2.8 percent of higher education administration and 1 percent of college presidents. Nakanishi (1993) and Hune and Chan (1997) highlight select issues that Asian Americans working in these capacities face, including the underrepresentation of APA faculty members as administrators (see also the 2005 Committee of 100 report), the concentration of faculty in sciences and engineering, and the greater concentration of Asian foreign nationals among faculty than native-born Asian Americans (a finding that points more to educational privilege and opportunity abroad than in the United States for Asians). Asian American faculty members who conduct research in AAS or other ethnic and gender studies fields face marginalization for work that is seen as not objective or rigorous (Chan 2005; Nakanishi 1993). And Asian American faculty struggle with glass ceilings (S. M. Lee 2002) and lower tenure rates (Minami 1990; Nakanishi 1990)—a problem especially true for Asian American women who are fewer in number than their male counterparts and objectified through sexist stereotypes as exotic and submissive (TuSmith and Reddy 2002; Vargas 2002). In comparison, several contributors to Li and Beckett's (2006) collection of studies and personal narratives by Asian and Asian American women highlight the advantage nativity brings foreign-born professors working in the largely white field of teachers of English to speakers of other languages (TESOL), for example.

History shows how complicated it can be to adequately understand the experiences of Asian Americans. During the early twentieth century, for example, sociologist Robert Park spearheaded academic studies on Asian immigrants and Asian Americans that fueled scholars' obsessions with Oriental success and drove a subsequent generation of researchers to seek explanations for a phenomenon instead of asking if the phenomenon actually existed (H. Yu, 2001). Juxtaposed with more recent efforts to amend the Higher Education Act and designate "Asian American and Pacific Islander-serving institutions" with accompanying federal dollars for recruiting and retaining AAPI students (Laanan and Starobin 2004), or to examine how diversity has been narrowly defined in legal terms to exclude Asian American students in the wake of such Supreme Court cases as *Gratz v. Bollinger* and *Grutter v. Bollinger* (Choy 2005; Gee 2004; Wu 1995), it is clear that opportunities for new insight exist. However, the problematic legacy and enduring impact of the model minority and perpetual foreigner stereotypes will require broad reeducation and active reframing.

REFERENCES

Alvarez, A. 2002. "Racial Identity and Asian Americans: Supports and Challenges." Pp. 33–43 in M. McEwan, C. Kodama, A. Alvarez, S. Lee, and C. Liang, eds., *Working with Asian American College Students: New Directions for Student Services*, vol. 97. San Francisco: Jossey-Bass.

Alvarez, A., and T. Yeh. 1999. "Asian Americans in College: A Racial Identity Perspective." Pp. 105–119 in D. Sandhu, ed., *Asian and Pacific Islander Americans' Issues and Concerns for Counseling and Psychotherapy*. Commack, NY: Nova Science.

Ancheta, A. 2000. *Race, Rights and the Asian American Experience*. New Brunswick, NJ: Rutgers University Press.

Ancis, J., W. Sedlacek, and J. Mohr. 2000. "Student Perceptions of Campus Cultural Climate by Race." *Journal of Counseling and Development* 78 (2): 180–185.

Anderson, J. D. 1988. *The Education of Blacks in the South, 1860–1935*. Chapel Hill: University of North Carolina Press.

———. 2004a. "Crosses to Bear and Promises to Keep: The Jubilee Anniversary of *Brown v. Board of Education*." *Urban Education* 39 (4): 359–372.

———. 2004b. "The Historical Context for Understanding the Test Score Gap." *Journal of Public Management and Social Policy* 10 (1): 2–22.

Asher, N. 2002. "Class Acts: Indian American High School Students Negotiate Professional and Ethnic Identities." *Urban Education* 37 (2): 267–295.

Asian Pacific American Education Advisory Committee. 1990. "Enriching California's Future: Asian Pacific Americans in the CSU." Report of the APA Education Advisory Committee, Office of the Chancellor, California State University.

Baker, B. D., C. Keller-Wolff, and L. Wolf-Wendel. 2000. "Two Steps Forward, One Step Back: Race/Ethnicity and Student Achievement in Education Policy Research." *Educational Policy* 14 (4): 511–529.

Bracey, G. W. 1999. "The Demise of the Asian Math Gene." *Phi Delta Kappan* 80 (8): 619–620.

———. 2005. "And Now, the Indian Spelling Gene." *Phi Delta Kappan* 87 (1): 92.

Buenavista, T. L. 2013. "Pilipinos in the Middle: Higher Education and a Sociocultural Context of Contradictions." Pp. 259–276 in D. C. Maramba and R. Bonus, eds., *The "Other" Students: Filipino Americans, Education, and Power* . Charlotte, NC: Information Age.

Carter, R. 2000. "Reimagining Race in Education: A New Paradigm from Psychology." *Teachers College Record* 102 (5): 864–897.

Carter, R. T., and A. L. Goodwin. 1994. "Racial Identity and Education." *Review of Research in Education* 20: 291–336.

Chan, S. 2005. *In Defense of Asian American Studies: The Politics of Teaching and Program Building*. Urbana: University of Illinois Press.

Chiang, L. H. 2000. "Teaching Asian American Students." *Teacher Educator* 36 (1): 58–69.

Choy, V. 2005. "Perpetuating the Exclusion of Asian Americans from the Affirmative Action Debate: An Oversight of the Diversity Rationale in *Grutter v. Bollinger*. *U.C. Davis Law Review* 38: 545–571.

Chua, A. 2011. *Battle Hymn of the Tiger Mother*. New York: Penguin.

Coloma, R. 2006. "Disorienting Race and Education: Changing Paradigms on the Schooling of Asian Americans and Pacific Islanders." *Race, Ethnicity, and Education* 9 (1): 1–15.

———. 2013. "Invisible Subject: Filipina/os in Secondary History Textbooks." Pp. 165–182 in D. C. Maramba and R. Bonus, eds., *The "Other" Students: Filipino Americans, Education and Power*. Charlotte, NC: Information Age.

Committee of 100. 2005. "Asian Pacific American (APAs) in Higher Education Report Card." http://www.committee100.org/publications/publications_edu.htm (accessed August 24, 2006).

Cress, C., and E. Ikeda. 2003. "Distress under Duress: The Relationship between Campus Climate and Depression in Asian American College Students." *NASPA Journal* 40 (2): 74–97.

Delucchi, M., and H. Do. 1996. "The Model Minority Myth and Perceptions of Asian Americans as Victims of Racial Harassment." *College Student Journal* 30 (3): 411–414.

Depouw, C. 2006. "Negotiating Race, Navigating School: Situating Hmong American University Student Experiences." Doctoral dissertation, University of Illinois at Urbana-Champaign.

Escueta, E., and E. O'Brien. 1991. "Asian Americans and Higher Education: Trends and Issues." *Research Briefs* 2 (4): 1–10. ERIC document ED381103.

Espiritu, Y. L. 1997. *Asian American Women and Men: Labor, Laws, and Love*. Thousand Oaks, CA: Sage.

———. 2001. "'We Don't Sleep Around Like White Girls Do': Family, Culture, and Gender in Filipina American Lives." *Signs: Journal of Women in Culture and Society* 26 (2): 415–440.

Gee, H. 2004. "From Bakke to Grutter and Beyond: Asian Americans and Diversity in America." *Texas Journal on Civil Liberties and Civil Rights* 9: 129–158.

George-Jackson, C. E. 2011. "STEM Switching: Examining Departures of Undergraduate Women in STEM Fields." *Journal of Women and Minorities in Science and Engineering* 17 (2): 149–171.

Gloria, A., and T. Ho. 2003. "Environmental, Social, and Psychological Experiences of Asian American Undergraduates: Examining Issues of Academic Persistence." *Journal of Counseling and Development* 81 (1): 93–105.

Goodwin, A. L. 2002. "Teacher Preparation and the Education of Immigrant Children." *Education and Urban Society* 34 (2): 156–172.

Gordon, J. A. 1997. "Teachers of Color Speak to Issues of Respect and Image." *Urban Review* 29 (1): 41–66.

———. 2000. "Asian American Resistance to Selecting Teaching as a Career: The Power of Community and Tradition." *Teachers College Record* 102 (1): 173–196.

———. 2005. "In Search of Educators of Color." *Leadership* 35 (2): 30–35.

Goto, S. T. 1997. "Nerds, Normal People, and Homeboys: Accommodation and Resistance among Chinese American Students." *Anthropology and Education Quarterly* 28 (1): 70–84.

Hartlep, N. D. 2013. *The Model Minority Stereotype: Demystifying Asian American Success*. Charlotte, NC: Information Age.

Hsia, J. 1988. *Asian Americans in Higher Education and at Work*. Hillsdale, NJ: Lawrence Erlbaum.

Hsia, J., and M. Hirano-Nakanishi. 1995. "The Demographics of Diversity: Asian Americans and Higher Education." Pp. 249–258 in D. Nakanishi and T. Nishida, eds., *The Asian American Educational Experience: A Sourcebook for Teachers and Students*. New York: Routledge.

Hune, S., and K. Chan. 1997. "Special Focus: Asian Pacific American Demographic and Educational Trends." Pp. 39–67 and 103–107 in D. Carter and R. Wilson, eds., *Minorities in Higher Education: Fifteenth Annual Status Report: 1996–1997*. Washington, DC: American Council on Education.

Inkelas, K. 2003a. "Caught in the Middle: Understanding Asian Pacific American Perspectives on Affirmative Action through Blumer's Group Position Theory." *Journal of College Student Development* 44 (5): 625–643.

———. 2003b. "Diversity's Missing Minority: Asian Pacific American Undergraduates' Attitudes towards Affirmative Action." *Journal of Higher Education* 74 (6): 601–639.

———. 2004. "Does Participation in Ethnic Cocurricular Activities Facilitate a Sense of Ethnic Awareness and Understanding? A Study of Asian Pacific American Undergraduates." *Journal of College Student Development* 45 (3): 285–302.

Jones, L., J. Castellanos, and D. Cole. 2002. "Examining the Ethnic Minority Student Experience at Predominantly White Institutions: A Case Study." *Journal of Hispanic Higher Education* 1 (1): 19–39.

Jorgenson, O. 2000. "The Need for More Ethnic Teachers: Addressing the Critical Shortage in American Public Schools." ID No. 10551. http://www.tcrecord.org (accessed August 28, 2000).

Kawaguchi, S. 2003. "Ethnic Identity Development and Collegiate Experience of Asian Pacific American Students: Implications for Practice." *NASPA Journal* 40 (3): 13–29.

Kiang, P. 1992. "Issues of Curriculum and Community for First-Generation Asian Americans in College." *New Directions for Community Colleges* 80: 97–113.

———. 2004. "Linking Strategies and Interventions in Asian American Studies to K–12 Classrooms and Teacher Preparation." *International Journal of Qualitative Studies in Education* 17 (2): 199–225.

Kibria, N. 2002. *Becoming Asian American: Second-Generation Chinese and Korean American Identities*. Baltimore: Johns Hopkins University Press.

Kim, C. 1999. "The Racial Triangulation of Asian Americans." *Politics and Society* 27 (1): 105–138.

Kodama, C., M. McEwen, C. Liang, and S. Lee. 2002. "An Asian American Perspective on Psychosocial Student Development Theory." Pp. 45–60 in M. McEwan, C. Kodama, A. Alvarez, S. Lee, and C. Liang, eds., *Working with Asian American College Students: New Directions for Student Services*, vol. 97. San Francisco: Jossey-Bass.

Kotori, C., and G. Malaney. 2003. "Asian American Students' Perceptions of Racism, Reporting Behaviors, and Awareness of Legal Rights and Procedures." *NASPA Journal* 40 (30): 56–76.

Laanan, F., and S. Starobin. 2004. "Defining Asian American and Pacific Islander–Serving Institutions." *New Directions for Community Colleges* 127: 49–59.

Lee, G., and M. L. Manning. 2001a. "Treat Asian Parents and Families Right." *Education Digest* 67 (4): 39–45.

———. 2001b. "Working with Asian Parents and Families." *Multicultural Education* 9 (1): 23–25.

Lee, R. 1999. *Orientals: Asian Americans in Popular Culture*. Philadelphia: Temple University Press.

Lee, R., J. Su, and E. Yoshida. 2005. "Coping with Intergenerational Family Conflict among Asian American College Students." *Journal of Counseling Psychology* 52 (3): 389–399.

Lee, S. J. 2001. "More Than 'Model Minorities' or 'Delinquents': A Look at Hmong American High School Students." *Harvard Educational Review* 71 (3): 505–529.

———. 2005. *Up Against Whiteness: Race, School, and Immigrant Youth*. New York: Teachers College Press.

———. 2006. "Additional Complexities: Social Class, Ethnicity, Generation, and Gender in Asian American Student Experiences." *Race, Ethnicity, and Education* 9 (1): 17–28.

———. 2009. *Unraveling the Model Minority Stereotype: Listening to Asian American Youth*. 2nd ed. New York: Teachers College Press.

Lee, S. J., and K. Kumashiro. 2005. "A Report on the Status of Asian American and Pacific Islanders in Education: Beyond the 'Model Minority' Stereotype." Washington, DC: National Education Association of the United States Human and Civil Rights.

Lee, S. M. 2002. "Do Asian American Faculty Face a Glass Ceiling in Higher Education?" *American Educational Research Journal* 39 (3): 695–724.

Lee, S. S. 2006. "Over-represented and De-minoritized: The Racialization of Asian Americans in Higher Education." *InterActions: UCLA Journal of Education and Information Studies* 2 (2): Article 4. http://repositories.cdlib.org/gseis/interactions/vol2/iss2/art4.

Lei, J. 2003. "(Un)necessary Toughness? Those 'Loud Black Girls' and Those 'Quiet Asian Boys.'" *Anthropology and Education Quarterly* 34 (2): 158–181.

———. 2006. "Teaching and Learning with Asian American and Pacific Islander Students." *Race, Ethnicity, and Education* 9 (1): 85–101.

LeSure, G. 1994. "Ethnic Differences and the Effects of Racism on College Adjustment." Paper presented at the annual convention of the American Psychological Association, Toronto, August 22.

Lew, J. 2004. "The 'Other' Story of Model Minorities: Korean American High School Dropouts in an Urban Context." *Anthropology and Education Quarterly* 35 (3): 303–323.

Lew, J., J. Chang, and W. Wang. 2005. "UCLA Community College Review: The Overlooked Minority. Asian Pacific American Students at Community Colleges." *Community College Review* 33 (2): 64–84.

Li, G., and G. Beckett. 2006. *"Strangers" of the Academy: Asian Women Scholars in Higher Education*. Sterling, VA: Stylus.

Liang, C., and W. Sedlacek. 2003. "Attitudes of White Student Services Practitioners toward Asian Americans." *NASPA Journal* 40 (3): 30–42.

Loo, C., and G. Rolison. 1986. "Alienation of Ethnic Minority Students at a Predominantly White University." *Journal of Higher Education* 57 (1): 58–77.

Louie, V. 2001. "Parents' Aspirations and Investment: The Role of Social Class in the Educational Experiences of 1.5- and Second-Generation Chinese Americans." *Harvard Educational Review* 71 (3): 438–474.

———. 2004. *Compelled to Excel: Immigration, Education, and Opportunity among Chinese Americans*. Stanford, CA: Stanford University Press.

Lowe, L. 2000. "Heterogeneity, Hybridity, Multiplicity: Marking Asian American Differences." Pp. 677–696 in M. Zhou and J. Gatewood, eds., *Contemporary Asian America: A Multidisciplinary Reader*. New York: New York University Press.

Mack, D., T. Tucker, and S. Cha. 2000. "Inter-ethnic Relations on Campus: The Color of Hatred." Paper presented at the annual conference of the American Psychological Association, Washington, DC, August 4–8.

Makuakane-Drechsel, T., and Hagedorn, L. 2000. "Correlates of Retention among Asian Pacific Americans in Community Colleges: The Case for Hawaiian Students." *Community College Journal of Research and Practice* 24: 639–655.

Manalansan, M., ed. 2000. *Cultural Compass: Ethnographic Explorations of Asian America*. Philadelphia: Temple University Press.

———. 2003. *Global Divas: Filipino Gay Men in the Diaspora*. Durham, NC: Duke University Press.

Mathews, R. 2000. "Cultural Patterns of South Asian and Southeast Asian Americans." *Intervention in School and Clinic* 36 (2): 101–104.

Mayo, C. S. 2014. *LGBTQ Youth and Education: Policies and Practices*. New York: Teachers College Press.

Min, P. G. 1996. *Caught in the Middle: Korean Communities in New York and Los Angeles*. Berkeley: University of California Press.

Minami, D. 1990. "Guerilla War at UCLA: Political and Legal Dimensions of the Tenure Battle." *Amerasia Journal* 16 (1): 81–107.

Nakanishi, D. 1990. "Why I Fought." *Amerasia Journal* 16 (1): 139–158.

———. 1993. "Asian Pacific Americans in Higher Education: Faculty and Administrative Representation and Tenure." Pp. 370–375 in C. Turner, M. Garcia, A. Nora, and L. Rendon, eds., *Racial and Ethnic Diversity in Higher Education*. Needham Heights, MA: Simon & Schuster.

National Center for Education Statistics. 2007. "Table 2. Percentage Distribution of School Teachers, by Race/Ethnicity, School Type, and Selected School Characteristics: 2007–08." http://nces.ed.gov/pubs2009/2009324/tables/sass0708_2009324_t12n_02.asp (accessed October 20, 2014).

———. 2010. "Status and Trends in the Education of Racial and Ethnic Groups." Washington, DC: US Department of Education.

———. 2014. "Table 306.20. Total Fall Enrollment in Degree-Granting Postsecondary Institutions, by Level and Control of Institution and Race/Ethnicity of Student: Selected Years, 1976 through 2012." http://nces.ed.gov/programs/digest/d13/tables/dt13_306.20.asp (accessed September 29, 2015).

Ng, J. C., S. S. Lee, and Y. K. Pak. 2007. "Contesting the Model Minority and Perpetual Foreigner Stereotypes. A Critical Review of Literature on Asian Americans in Education." *Review of Research in Education* 31 (1): 95–130.

Omi, M., and D. Takagi. 1996. "Situating Asian Americans in the Political Discourse on Affirmative Action." *Representations* 55: 155–162.

Ong, A. 1996. "Cultural Citizenship as Subject-Making: Immigrants Negotiate Racial and Cultural Boundaries in the United States." *Current Anthropology* 37 (5): 737–762.

Osajima, K. 1991. "Breaking the Silence: Race and the Educational Experiences of Asian American College Students." Pp. 115–134 in M. Foster, ed., *Readings on Equal Education: Qualitative Investigations into Schools and Schooling*, vol. 11. New York: AMS Press.

Pak, Y. K., D. C. Maramba, and X. J. Hernandez. 2014. *Asian Americans in Higher Education: Charting New Realities*. ASHE Higher Education Report 40(1). Edited by K. Ward and L. E. Wolf-Wendel. San Francisco: Jossey-Bass.

Pang, V. O. 1997. "Caring for the Whole Child: Asian Pacific American Students." Pp. 149–188 in J. J. Irvine, ed., *Critical Knowledge for Diverse Teachers and Learners*. Washington, DC: AACTE Publications.

Pang, V. O., P. P. Han, and J. M. Pang. 2011. "Asian American and Pacific Islander Students: Equity and the Achievement Gap." *Educational Researcher* 40 (8): 378–389.

Pang, V. O., and C. D. Park. 2003. "Examination of the Self-Regulation Mechanism: Prejudice Reduction in Pre-service Teachers." *Action in Teacher Education* 25 (3): 1–12.

Park, C. C., and M. M. Chi, eds. 1999. *Asian American Education: Prospects and Challenges*. Westport, CT: Bergin and Garvey.

Park, J. J. 2013. *When Diversity Drops: Race, Religion, and Affirmative Action in Higher Education*. New Brunswick, NJ: Rutgers University Press

Pearce, R. R. 2006. "Effects of Cultural and Social Structural Factors on the Achievement of White and Chinese American Students at School Transition Points." *American Educational Research Journal* 43 (10): 75–101.

Poon, O. A. 2011. "A Critical Race Theory Case Study of Asian Americans, 'Critical Mass,' and Campus Racial Climate." Pp. 101–130 in R. Endo and X. L. Rong, eds., *Asian American Education: Identities, Racial Issues, and Languages*, 6th ed. Charlotte, NC: Information Age.

Qin, D. B. 2006. "'Our Child Doesn't Talk to Us Anymore': Alienation in Immigrant Chinese Families." *Anthropology and Education Quarterly* 37 (2): 162–179.

Rhee, S., J. Chang, and J. Rhee. 2003. "Acculturation, Communication Patterns, and Self-Esteem among Asian and Caucasian American Adolescents." *Adolescence* 38 (152): 749–768.

Rhoads, R., J. Lee, and M. Yamada. 2002. "Panethnicity and Collective Action among Asian American Students: A Qualitative Case Study." *Journal of College Student Development* 43 (6): 876–891.

Richwine, J. 2009. *IQ and Immigration Policy*. Cambridge, MA: Harvard University Press.

Rizvi, F., and B. Lingard. 2006. "Edward Said and the Cultural Politics of Education." *Discourse: Studies in the Cultural Politics of Education* 27 (3): 293–308.

Rohrlick, J., D. Alvarado, K. Zaruba, and R. Kallio. 1998. "From the Model Minority to the Invisible Minority: Asian and Pacific American Students in Higher Education Research." Paper presented at the annual forum of the Association for Institutional Research, Minneapolis, May 17–20.

Rong, X. L., and J. Preissle. 1997. "The Continuing Decline in Asian American Teachers." *American Educational Research Journal* 34 (2): 267–293.

Said, E. 1978. *Orientalism*. New York: Vintage.

Shrake, E. K., and S. Rhee. 2004. "Ethnic Identity as a Predictor of Problem Behaviors among Korean American Adolescents." *Adolescence* 39 (155): 601–622.

Simpson, J. 2001. "Segregated by Subject: Racial Differences in the Factors Influencing Academic Major between European Americans, Asian Americans, and African, Hispanic and Native Americans." *Journal of Higher Education* 72 (1): 63–100.

Sleeter, C., and C. Grant. 2009. *Making Choices for Multicultural Education: Five Approaches to Race, Class, and Gender*. 6th ed. New York: John Wiley.

Song, C., and J. Glick. 2004. "College Attendance and Choice of College Majors among Asian American Students." *Social Science Quarterly* 85 (5): 1401–1421.

Span, C., and J. D. Anderson. 2005. "The Quest for 'Book Learning': African American Education in Slavery and Freedom." Pp. 295–311 in A. Hornsby, Jr., D. P. Aldridge, and A. M. Hornsby, eds., *A Companion to African American History*. Malden, MA: Blackwell.

"Success Story: Outwhiting the Whites." 1971. *Newsweek*, June 21, 24–25.

Takagi, D. 1993. *The Retreat from Race: Asian American Admissions and Racial Politics*. New Brunswick, NJ: Rutgers University Press.

Takaki, R. 1998. *Strangers from a Different Shore: A History of Asian Americans*. Boston: Little, Brown.

Teranishi, R. 2010. *Asians in the Ivory Tower: Dilemmas of Racial Inequality in American Higher Education*. New York: Teachers College Press.

Teranishi, R., M. Ceja, A. Antonio, W. Allen, and P. McDonough. 2004. "The College-Choice Process for Asian Pacific Americans: Ethnicity and Socioeconomic Class in Context." *Review of Higher Education* 27 (4): 527–551.

Tse, L. 2001. "Resisting and Reversing Language Shift: Heritage-Language Resilience among U.S. Native Biliterates." *Harvard Educational Review* 71 (4): 676–707.

Tuan, M. 1998. *Forever Foreigners or Honorary Whites? The Asian Ethnic Experience Today*. New Brunswick, NJ: Rutgers University Press.

TuSmith, B., and M. Reddy, eds. 2002. *Race in the College Classroom: Pedagogy and Politics*. New Brunswick, NJ: Rutgers University Press.

Vargas, L., ed. 2002. *Women Faculty of Color in the White Classroom: Narratives on the Pedagogical Implications of Teacher Diversity*. New York: Peter Lang.

Williams, H. 2005. *Self-Taught: African American Education in Slavery and Freedom*. Chapel Hill: University of North Carolina Press.

Woo, D. 1997. "Asian Americans in Higher Education: Issues of Diversity and Engagement." *Race, Gender and Class* 4 (3): 122–143.

Wright, W. 2006. "Catching Up in Math? The Case of Newly-Arrived Cambodian Students in a Texas Intermediate School." *Texas Association for Bilingual Education Journal* 9 (1): 1–22.

Wu, F. 1995. "Neither Black nor White: Asian Americans and Affirmative Action." *Third World Law Journal* 15: 225–284.

Yang, R., S. Byers, L. Ahuna, and K. Castro. 2002. "Asian American Students' Use of a University Student-Affairs Office." *College Student Journal* 36 (3): 448–470.

Yu, H. 2001. *Thinking Orientals: Migration, Contact, and Exoticism in Modern America*. Oxford: Oxford University Press.

Yu, S. M., Z. J. Huang, and R. H. Schwalberg. 2002. "Association of Language Spoken at Home with Health and School Issues among Asian American Adolescents." *Journal of School Health* 72 (5): 192–198.

27

Race-Based Considerations and the Obama Vote

Evidence from the 2008 National Asian American Survey

S. KARTHICK RAMAKRISHNAN, JANELLE WONG, TAEKU LEE, AND JANE JUNN

Well before the dust of the 2008 Democratic Party nomination process settled, Senator Hillary Clinton had garnered a hard-fought and decisive victory in the California primary. In some respects, the contours of the California vote were unsurprising. As in other state primaries and caucuses, African Americans were beginning to support Senator Barack Obama over Clinton in overwhelming numbers. What surprised many observers, however, was the similarly overwhelming support for Clinton over Obama among Asian Americans. This lopsided margin in the Asian American vote was also evident in exit polls from other Super Tuesday states such as New York and New Jersey. This led many media observers to ask, in the words of *Time* magazine's Lisa Takeuchi Cullen, "Does Obama Have an Asian Problem?" (Cullen 2008), with feature stories and anecdotal evidence suggesting that he did.

Such pronouncements were problematic, however, because they were drawn from a limited set of data. The California exit poll interviews were conducted only in English or Spanish, the ones in New York and New Jersey were conducted in a handful of cities, and none of the surveys weighted for the differential residential patterns of Asian Americans versus other primary voters. In addition to the limitations of the exit poll sampling and interview methods, the subsequent analysis of marginal vote totals failed to show the relative importance of racial attitudes versus other factors such as partisanship and political interest. The use of qualitative data via "person in the street" interviews did nothing to shed light on the generality of the problem or its magnitude.

In this article, we bring evidence from the 2008 National Asian American Survey (NAAS) to bear on the question of whether, and to what extent, race-related attitudes shaped the Asian American vote. The NAAS is the most comprehensive survey to date of Asian Americans' civic and political life in the United States, with 5,159 interviews conducted over two months in 2008 in eight languages (English, Cantonese, Mandarin, Korean, Vietnamese, Tagalog, Japanese, and Hindi) and with large numbers of respondents from the six largest Asian national-origin groups (Asian Indians, Chinese, Filipinos, Japanese, Koreans, and Vietnamese). We focus on the vote choice of Asian Americans to examine the extent to which race-related attitudes account for variations in Asian American support for Obama over Clinton in the 2008 primary. We examine the relationship between vote choice and attitudes toward blacks after controlling for a host of standard factors that have been shown to be predictive of vote choice. Finally, we uncover the extent to which these race-related considerations account for the relatively high level of "undecideds" among Asian American voters in the summer and fall of 2008.

Conventional Wisdom about Asian Americans in the 2008 Election

The Democratic primaries in 2008 attracted a high level of attention from news media and voters alike. Not only did the contest feature a compelling story of an insurgent candidate taking on a formidable political dynasty, it was also deemed historic because of the likely nomination of either the first female or the first African American on a major-party presidential ballot. Given the competitiveness of the race even after Super Tuesday, all eyes focused on the contest for delegates, especially in some of the remaining large states such as Texas, Ohio, Virginia, and Washington. Some mainstream news outlets saw that, perhaps for the first time, Asian Americans held the potential to shape the momentum of a presidential primary, especially if they had a large turnout in states such as Washington and Virginia, which held their nominating contests less than a week after Super Tuesday.

In trying to assess each candidate's chance at winning these states, reporters and news analysts turned to data on Asian American voters in states such as California and New York. The sources may have been disparate (the National Election Pool sample of about 150 Asian Americans in California and a sample of 700 voters interviewed by the Asian American Legal Defense and Education Fund in New York City and three cities in New Jersey), but the picture that emerged was the same: Asian Americans supported Clinton over Obama in the primaries by the strongest margin recorded for any racial or ethnic group (Cullen 2008). Underlying many media treatments of Asian American primary voting patterns were questions about whether Clinton's popularity with Asian Americans reflected antipathy or at least a discomfort with black Americans.

The first prominent story suggesting racial attitudes as a significant factor in the Asian American vote was a segment by reporter Gary Tuchman on the popular CNN show *Andersen Cooper 360°* on the eve of the Washington state caucuses. The reporter started the segment in a Chinatown grocery store, where an informal canvass revealed no support for Obama. The story followed with a comment from a fourth-generation Japanese American that many Asian Americans would vote for a Caucasian because "they don't like change," and concluded with a few words from a shopper at the Chinese store:

TUCHMAN: This woman actually refers to Hillary Clinton's skin color.

UNIDENTIFIED FEMALE: The white lady.

TUCHMAN [ON CAMERA]: So do you like Hillary Clinton?

UNIDENTIFIED FEMALE: Yes. I like her.

TUCHMAN: Do you like Obama?

UNIDENTIFIED FEMALE: Not really.

TUCHMAN [VOICE-OVER]: Obama had a large number of Asian-Americans at this huge Seattle rally but didn't appear to be near the percentage of the rally for the senator from New York. Advantage, Clinton. ("Asian American Voters" 2008)

Academic observers also speculated that racial attitudes were at play. In a *Time* magazine article titled "Does Obama Have an Asian Problem?" Oliver Wang, a sociology professor at California State University, commented that "on a gut level my reaction is that at least some Asian Americans are uncomfortable voting for a Black candidate." His explanation rested squarely on assumptions about foreign-born Asian Americans, hypothesizing that new immigrants may have little direct experience with African Americans and that lack of contact may lead to racial bias (Cullen 2008).

Asian American advocacy organizations and the ethnic media disputed this perspective, citing Clinton's strong name recognition and better, more targeted outreach to Asian American communities as key explanations for the Asian American vote. In addition, scholars and community leaders suggested that Clinton benefited from immigrants' nostalgia for her husband's administration. Matt Barreto, a political scientist at the University of Washington, argued,

> They remember the good times in the 1990s. There was [*sic*] a lot of benefits; not only the economy, but other policies that benefited immigrants and, in particular, Asian Americans that would cause them to remember the Clintons in fondness. ("Asian American Voters" 2008)

Others noted that many Asian American voters were naturalized during Bill Clinton's administration and thus came of political age under "the Clintons" (Kim 2008). In addition, commentators speculated that Asian Americans, particularly recent immigrants, might be wary of change and more comfortable voting for a known entity ("Asian American Voters" 2008).[1]

If Obama indeed had an Asian American problem in the Democratic primary, he seemed to have overcome it by the general election. The NAAS showed that, as early as August 2008, Obama enjoyed a nearly two-to-one advantage over John McCain among Asian American likely voters. Still, nearly one-third of Asian American likely voters remained undecided, higher than for any other racial or ethnic group. Exit polls in November suggested that most of these undecided voters broke in favor of Obama, with the National Exit Poll survey showing that Asian American voters favored Obama over McCain by 62 percent to 35 percent ("Exit Polls" 2008), while an Election Day exit poll of over 16,000 voters in eleven states by the Asian American Legal Defense and Education Fund (AALDEF 2009) suggested an even greater margin of 76 percent to 22 percent.

Still, many questions about the role of race in the vote choice of Asian Americans remain unanswered. For instance, while Asian Americans largely supported Obama in the general election, racial attitudes may still have played a significant role in their support for Clinton over Obama in the primaries. Furthermore, racial attitudes may have continued to play a significant role in the general election campaign, perhaps accounting for the relatively high proportion of Asian American voters declaring themselves to be "undecided" even as late as October 2008. Using the 2008 NAAS, we focus on the following questions:

1. Did racial attitudes play a role in Asian American primary and caucus voters' choice of Clinton over Obama, and how did racial attitudes compare with the effects of other factors such as issue preferences and party identification?
2. To what extent did racial attitudes play a role in boosting the proportion of Asian American voters who said they were undecided between McCain and Obama?
3. To what extent did racial attitudes account for variations in individual-level shifts, from supporting Clinton in the primary to Obama in the general election?

Race and Asian Americans

Because race relations in the United States have long been framed in terms of the "black-white paradigm" (Blackwell, Kwoh, and Pastor 2002, 37), it is not surprising that commentators confronted with exit poll data on Asian American primary voters began to speculate about the group's racial loyalties. With which group would Asian Americans find common political ground? Mia Tuan (1999) posed the question more provocatively in her book, *Forever Foreigners or Honorary Whites?* Like white Americans, on average, Asian Americans enjoy high levels of economic and educational achievement in the United States. Asian Americans are also the most residentially integrated minority group in the United States. Such trends might suggest that Asian Americans would link their political fortunes with similarly situated white Americans and perhaps a white candidate. Dana Takagi (1993) provided a compelling account of how some Asian American students coalesced with conservative whites in the battle over affirmative action, for example.

Yet Asian Americans share much in common with black Americans as well. Like many African Americans, Asian Americans compose a phenotypically distinct population sometimes subject to racial stereotyping, discrimination, or even violence rooted in perceived racial difference. Janine Young Kim's (1999) article, "Are Asians Black?" presented a nuanced argument for considering seriously shared histories and experiences of racialization between black Americans and Asian Americans. Although scholars of Asian American studies have made forceful arguments for moving "beyond the black-white paradigm" (Chang 1999; Wu 2001; Ancheta 1998), Kim argued that "Blackness," as defined by the paradigm properly understood, serves to explain the racial positioning of both blacks and Asian Americans. In fact, like Claire Jean Kim who accounted for the "racial triangulation" of Asian Americans (1999), Janine Kim (1999) suggested an intimate relationship between the racial position of black Americans and that of Asian Americans. Furthermore, Janine Kim (1999) argued that "situating Asian Americans as a buffer between Black and White does not position Asian Americans outside the Black-White paradigm, but rather in a dominant place where they can be manipulated to serve the interests of the dominant group" (2409).

Although Asian Americans have joined in coalition with other groups of racial minorities to fight for worker rights, push for greater civil rights protections, and elect candidates of color, examples of intergroup conflict between Asian Americans and other groups more often make headlines. Media coverage over the past two decades has emphasized tensions between Asian Americans and other minority groups. News stories following the greengrocers boycott in Brooklyn in 1990 and the urban unrest in Los Angeles in 1992, for instance, were especially keen to highlight "black-Korean conflict." These media accounts, more often than not, distort and overplay the extent of this conflict, ignore the agency and voice of Asian Americans themselves, and portray such events in terms of "episodic frames" that point to individual-level prejudices rather than "thematic frames" that underscore structural factors that precipitate intergroup competition (Cho 1993; Abelmann and Lie 1995; Yoon 1995; Kim 2000; Lee 2002; see Iyengar 1994 on media framing).

In fact, just a handful of scholars have investigated Asian Americans' racial attitudes systematically (Johnson, Farrell, and Guinn 1997; see also Bobo and Johnson 2000; Bobo and Suh 2000). Using data from the 1992–1994 Los Angeles Survey of Urban Inequality, Johnson, Farrell, and Guinn (1997, 1064) found that a majority of Asian Americans in their sample viewed blacks and Latinos as "less intelligent" and "more welfare dependent" than their own group. Using data from the 1992 Los Angeles County Social Survey, Taeku Lee (2000, 109, 114) found that Asian Americans exhibited distinct attitudinal preferences for intermarriage and residential integration with whites over blacks. Beyond this limited scholarship, however, we know little about Asian Americans' racial attitudes, and we know even less about how those perspectives influence political behavior. New data from the NAAS allow us to investigate these relationships. In particular, we examine the relationship between various race-related considerations among Asian Americans and their presidential vote choice.

Presidential Vote Choice among Asian Americans

The literature on presidential vote choice is vast (e.g., Lazarsfeld, Berelson, and Gaudet 1944; Berelson, Lazarsfeld, and McPhee 1954; Campbell et al. 1960; Nie, Verba, and Petrocik 1976; Wolfinger and Rosenstone 1980; Fiorina 1981; Lewis-Beck et al. 2007). Much of the research in this area over the past fifty years has concentrated on the ways individual-level attributes and political attitudes predict voting turnout. Among the most important predictors of the act of voting are affiliation with a political party (e.g., Campbell et al. 1960; Bartels 2000) and socioeconomic status (Converse 1966; Wolfinger and Rosenstone 1980; Markus 1988), including education (Axelrod 1986; Erikson 1989), religious identity and religiosity (Layman 2001; Pew Forum on Religion and Public Life 2008), and group identity (Wolfinger 1965; Mutz and Mondak 1997; for a related study, see Barreto and Pedraza 2008). Age and life cycle effects have also been identified as important predictors of voting behavior (e.g., Erikson 1989; Jennings and Niemi 1981; Highton and Wolfinger 2001). Beyond individual-level demographic factors, scholars have also highlighted the significance of issue positions (Page and Brody 1972; Nie, Verba, and Petrocik 1976; Carmines and Stimson 1989; Abramowitz 1994), ideology (Hinich and Munger 1994), political mobilization (Rosenstone and Hansen 1993; Gerber and Green 2000), and economic conditions (Markus 1988).

The past decade has also seen some periodic attempts to examine the presidential vote choice of Asian Americans. Past research using a multicity study of Asian Americans, the 2000–2001 Pilot National Asian American Political Survey, suggested that the strongest predictor of Asian Americans' vote for Democratic candidate Al Gore in 2000 was party identification. Democrats were much more likely to vote for Gore and Republicans were much less likely to vote for Gore than those who did not identify with a major US party (Lien, Conway, and Wong 2004). In addition, Lien, Conway, and Wong (2004) found that geography and national origin mattered for Asian American vote choice in 2000. Controlling for other factors, those residing in Honolulu were less likely to support Gore than those from Los Angeles, San Francisco, New York, and Chicago. Those of Korean and South Asian national origin were more likely to favor Bush over Gore than those of Chinese national origin.[2] Finally, factors such as socioeconomic status, having a sense of linked fate with other Asian Americans, and experience with racial discrimination were not associated strongly with vote choice among Asian Americans. These past studies help focus our attention on key variables likely to affect Asian American voting behavior in the 2008 presidential election.

Finally, very little is known about Asian American support for candidates of different racial backgrounds. A long history of research suggests that racial prejudice among white voters hurts black candidates, especially in statewide races or in majority white districts (Terkildsen 1993). Data from experiments consistently show that when whites are presented with a white and a black candidate, they will evaluate the former more favorably than the latter (Sigelman et al. 1995; Terkildsen 1993). Nayda Terkildsen found that when presented with candidates that were identical except for their racial backgrounds, white subjects preferred the white candidate (Terkildsen 1993, 1041). Carol Sigelman and colleagues' (1995) experimental results suggested that white respondents judge black candidates and Latino candidates to be less competent than white candidates with otherwise identical characteristics. However, studies from actual elections point to mixed findings about racial voting, with some suggesting that voter stereotypes and discrimination decline after an electorate has experience with a black incumbent (Hajnal 2001), others indicating that white voters no longer discriminate against black candidates (Highton 2004), and still others suggesting that white voters choose to express an enthusiasm for a black candidate that is not reflected in the privacy of the voting booth (Bullock 1984).[3] Studies have also diverged over whether an unusually high proportion of undecided voters in elections featuring a white candidate and a nonwhite candidate is evidence for racial voting (Citrin, Green, and Sears 1990; Reeves 1997). One notable limitation to the literature on racial voting is that it has concentrated primarily on the vote choice of whites and, to a lesser extent, blacks. Although some scholars have studied Latino support for black candidates (Kaufmann 2003), very little is known about Asian American voters' support for black or non-Asian candidates.

Data and Variable Construction

The NAAS is the most comprehensive survey to date of the civic and political life of Asians in the United States. Based on 5,159 interviews conducted from August 18, 2008 to October 29, 2008, the NAAS included adults in the United States who identified any family background from countries in Asia.[4] Survey interviews were conducted in eight languages (English, Cantonese, Mandarin, Korean, Vietnamese, Tagalog, Japanese, and Hindi) and yielded sample sizes of at least 500 adult residents for Asian Americans in the six largest national-origin groups. The registered voters in our sample included 784 Asian Americans of Indian origin, 748 of Chinese origin, 521 of Vietnamese origin, 406 of Filipino origin, 388 of Korean origin, and 340 of Japanese origin.[5] We weighted our sample, using a raking procedure and population characteristics from the American Community Survey, to reflect the balance of gender, nativity, citizenship status, and educational attainment of the six largest Asian national-origin groups in the United States, as well as the proportion of these national-origin groups within each state.

For this article, we focused on two dependent variables: Asian American vote choice between Clinton and Obama during the Democratic primaries and caucuses (hereafter "primaries") and the *intended* vote choice between McCain and Obama in the general election. Our survey did not include any self-reported measures of racial prejudice. We excluded such measures because of the difficulty in using telephone surveys to obtain reliable measures of intergroup prejudice, including problems associated with misreporting attitudes and testing effects from asking the same measure of prejudice with more than one reference group, the extensive number of items required in the most commonly used measure—the racial resentment scale—as well as the controversy about its general external validity (see, e.g., Kinder and Sanders 1996; Fazio et al. 1995; Blank, Dabady, and Citro 2004).[6] In its stead, our survey asked respondents, "Thinking about government services, political power and representation, would you say Asian Americans have a lot in common, some, little in common, or nothing at all in common with [African Americans or blacks]/[Latinos or Hispanics]/[whites] (*rotated*)?" We used respondent rankings on these three reference groups to come up with two measures: (1) a measure of *general group distance*, where the variable took on a value of 1 if the respondent stated that Asian Americans had little or nothing in common politically with any other racial or ethnic group, and (2) a measure of *Latino-Black proximity* that captured the extent to which respondents saw more political commonality with Latinos than with African Americans. This measure is theoretically interesting because it allows us to identify those respondents who saw the potential for political coalitions with Latinos but not with blacks.[7] It does not allow us to test specifically for the influence of anti-black prejudice per se on Asian American vote choice, but it did allow us to assess the effect of racial considerations on this choice.

In our attempt to ascertain the role of race-based political considerations for Asian American voters in the primary and general elections, we also included several other factors that have traditionally been significant predictors of presidential vote choice. These included *party identification, issue positions* on important policy questions such as government provision of health care and restrictions on abortion, the frequency of *religious attendance*, and other demographic factors such as age, gender, and educational attainment.[8] In addition to these standard sets of factors, we added two other factors that were potentially important in explaining the vote choice of Asian Americans: national origin and past experience with discrimination.

Findings

How did Asian Americans vote in the 2008 presidential primaries? In Table 27.1, we present the self-reported vote preferences of Asian American registered voters. Since several states had open primaries, or modified open primaries where "decline-to-state" voters could still choose a primary candidate, we present the results for all registered voters, regardless of their party registration. As Table 27.1 indicates, Asian Americans did favor Clinton over Obama by a substantial margin (45 percent to 27 percent overall, or 61 percent to 36 percent among Democratic primary voters). However, these margins in our national survey appear to be smaller than those reported in exit polls from California (71 percent to 25 percent among Democratic primary voters) and New York (86 percent to 14 percent among Democratic primary voters).[9]

TABLE 27.1. Asian American Vote Choice in the 2008 Primaries, among Registered Voters

	Total	Asian Indian	Chinese	Filipino	Japanese	Korean	Vietnamese
Clinton	45	44	57	41	37	29	49
Obama	27	36	20	32	42	28	5
Other Democrat	2	1	0	4	3	1	0
McCain	17	13	10	17	15	24	39
Other Republican	4	4	8	2	1	6	1
Other (unknown)	5	3	5	4	2	12	7

Note: Values are percentages.
Source: National Asian American Survey (2008).

Vote choice varied dramatically by national origin. Chinese Americans were the group most likely to vote for Clinton in the primaries (57 percent), and they had the lowest proportion of primary voters for Obama (20 percent). By contrast, Korean American primary voters were equally likely to support the two major Democratic candidates, and Japanese Americans were more likely to support Obama over Clinton. Vietnamese Americans, traditionally the most Republican-leaning Asian American group, actually showed stronger support for Clinton (49 percent) than McCain (39 percent) and very weak support for Obama (5 percent).[10]

Despite the tepid support for Obama in the primaries, Asian Americans appeared to be leaning strongly toward Obama in the weeks leading up to the general election. When asked whom they planned to vote for in the general election, 40 percent of registered Asian Americans said Obama, 23 percent said McCain, and 36 percent said they were undecided about their vote choice. As Table 27.2 indicates, Asian Americans heavily favored Obama over McCain throughout the last months of the campaign. The most striking trend observed over that period, however, is the large proportion of Asian Americans who claimed to be undecided between the candidates. In September 2008, over one-third of registered voters described themselves as "undecided," and even in October, more than one in four did so. By contrast, most polls showed that about 8 percent of registered voters nationally were undecided over the same period (Cost 2008). National-origin differences persisted in the general election. When asked whom they planned to vote for in the presidential contest, Indian, Chinese, Japanese, and Korean Americans expressed strong support for Obama over McCain. Filipino Americans expressed weaker levels of support for Obama, while Vietnamese Americans were the only group likely to favor McCain over Obama. It is striking to note, however, that substantial proportions of each of these groups (22 percent to 42 percent) remained undecided even as the election drew to a close (national origin differences in intended vote choice are shown in Table 27.A.1 in the appendix).

TABLE 27.2. Asian American Vote Choice in the 2008 General Election, among Registered Voters, by Month of Interview

	Overall	August	September	October
Obama	40	38	40	47
McCain	23	21	25	21
Other	1	1	1	5
Undecided	36	40	34	28

Note: Values are percentages.
Source: National Asian American Survey (2008).

Did Asian American support for Clinton in the primaries have anything to do with the relatively high level of undecided voters in the general election campaign? Table 27.3 shows the relationship between vote choices in the primary and general election among Asian Americans. We found that the proportion of undecided voters in the general election was indeed higher for those who voted for Clinton than for those who had voted for anyone else during the primaries. Nearly one-third (32 percent) of Clinton primary voters remained undecided about the presidential vote, while only 19 percent of Obama primary voters and 13 percent of McCain primary voters were undecided.[11] Still, it is important to note that a majority of Clinton voters intended to vote for Obama, and only 16 percent of them declared a preference for McCain. Furthermore, the proportion of undecided voters was even higher among those who had not voted in the primaries (40 percent) than among those who had voted for Clinton (32 percent). Thus, continued attachment to Clinton provides only a partial explanation for Asian American indecision during the general election. Furthermore, as we shall see in the multivariate analysis that follows, prior support for Clinton played only a marginal role in explaining vote indecision among Asian Americans in the general election.

TABLE 27.3. Asian American Vote Choice in the 2008 General Election, among Registered Voters, by Primary Vote Choice

	Clinton	Obama	McCain	Did Not Vote in the Primaries
Obama	50	82	4	34
McCain	16	0	82	24
Other	2	0	0	2
Undecided	32	18	14	40

Note: Values are percentages.
Source: National Asian American Survey (2008).

So far, we have focused on the descriptive findings that related to our dependent variables. Before proceeding with the multivariate analysis, however, it is important to examine the distribution of Asian American voters on our measures of general group distance and Latino-black proximity. As the first column in Table 27.4 shows, about one in four Asian Americans indicated that on matters of political power and representation, Asian Americans had little or nothing in common with any other racial group. There were some significant national-origin differences, with Vietnamese American voters expressing the greatest levels of general group distance (45 percent), and Korean Americans expressing the least (19 percent). Finally, when comparing the degree of political commonality with Latinos and African Americans, we found that two-thirds of the Asian American electorate saw no difference between the two groups. Among the remainder, however, about twice as many Asian Americans felt more political commonality with Latinos than with blacks.

TABLE 27.4. Group Distance and the Black-Latino Divide among Asian American Registered Voters

	Group Distance	Closer to Blacks	No Difference	Closer to Latinos
Asian Indian	36	13	73	14
Chinese	25	11	70	19
Filipino	23	10	58	32
Japanese	30	11	74	15
Korean	19	14	65	21
Vietnamese	45	10	74	16
Overall	28	11	68	21

Note: Values are percentages. Group distance = o if "little" or "nothing" in common with blacks, Latinos, and whites on matters of government services, political power, and representation; 1 otherwise.

To what extent were these race-related considerations associated with the Asian American vote for Clinton over Obama, and how did they compare with other competing explanations? We addressed these questions with a logit model that regressed a dummy variable measuring support for Obama over Clinton in the primary on party identification, important issue positions, frequency of religious attendance, past experience with discrimination, and various demographic factors including age, gender, education, and national origin (see Table 27.A.2 in the appendix). Our regression analysis showed that proximity to Latinos over blacks does indeed predict a vote for Clinton over Obama, and that this relationship is statistically significant at the .10 level. In other words, we found Asian American primary voters who felt more political commonality with Latinos than with blacks were more likely to vote for Clinton over Obama, even after controlling for generalized levels of group distance and a host of other factors.

At the same time, it is important to note that other factors such as age and gender bore an even stronger relationship to the primary vote choice of Asian Americans. Just as the rest of the electorate, older voters and women were more likely to favor Clinton over Obama in the primary. Other factors, such as party identification and issue preferences, played a relatively marginal role in the choice between Clinton and Obama. Finally, there were sizable national-origin differences in the primary vote choice, and these remained even after we controlled for factors such as age, gender, and issue preferences. Thus, while race-based considerations played a significant role in the vote choice of Asian Americans in the Democratic primary, other factors such as age and gender delivered more explanatory power.

We turned next to consider the relationship between race-based considerations and the general election choice between McCain and Obama. As we have seen, more than one in three Asian American registered voters in our sample were undecided between McCain and Obama, and nearly one in four remained undecided even in the last month of the presidential campaign. Were these "undecided" Asian American registered voters hiding their true feelings about the race of the candidates by claiming to be undecided rather than admitting that they were not voting for Obama? To what extent did feelings about African Americans underlie the "undecided" vote among Asian Americans? To answer these questions, we relied on the same set of explanatory factors as in the analysis of the Democratic primary vote, with one important addition: we added a variable for whether or not the respondent voted for Clinton in the primary, to control for the possibility that a residual attachment to Clinton prompted greater feelings of ambivalence among Asian American voters, regardless of other factors such as issue preferences and race-based considerations.

There were different ways to model intended vote choice: as a logit regression between undecided voters and Obama supporters, as an ordered logit regression going from McCain supporters to undecideds to Obama supporters, and as a multinomial logit that did not presume any ordering in the vote choice among Obama, McCain, and undecideds. For ease of interpretation, we present standardized effects based on the logit regression, and discuss instances where alternative modeling techniques lead to different outcomes for our variables of interest. The results from our regressions indicated that Asian Americans who felt closer politically to Latinos than to blacks were more likely to claim they were undecided about their presidential pick, a finding that was statistically significant at the 10 percent level. We also found that those who had personally experienced racial or ethnic discrimination were less likely to be undecided.

However, the effects of these race-based attitudes and experiences paled in comparison to other factors, most notably party identification, issue preferences, and gender. While partisanship and issue preferences played a small role in the primary season, it is not surprising that they played a much larger role in the general election. Party identification played the biggest role, by far. Even though a third of Asian American registered voters identified as "pure Independents," meaning they did not claim to lean toward either party, 45 percent identified with the Democratic Party, with 21 percent strongly doing so. Nearly a quarter of Asian American voters identified with the Republican Party (22 percent), with 10 percent strongly doing so.

Given the differentiation of Asian American voters along this important dimension of vote choice, it is not surprising, then, that it played the strongest role in whether a respondent was undecided or had made up his or her mind.[12] Issue preferences also played a strong role. McCain and Obama staked out strongly contrasting positions on issues such as abortion rights and the government provision of health care, and our analysis indicated that such issue differentiation played a significant role in the vote choice of Asian Americans. Gender also played a significant role, with female voters more likely to be undecided than male voters. By contrast, other factors such as religious attendance, educational attainment, and prior support for Clinton in the primary bore no significant relationship to whether or not Asian American voters declared themselves as undecided.

In order to ensure that our findings about the modest effects of race-based considerations were not subject to variations in our modeling choice, we tested for various interaction effects and for alternative ways of modeling the presidential vote choice. Two important findings turned up when we tested for interactive effects, with respect to gender and partisanship. The role of Latino-black proximity was stronger among women than among men; indeed, among men the relationship was close to nil. Furthermore, we found that race-based considerations played a varying role according to party identification, with certain components mattering for some groups but not others. Among Democrats, the relative proximity to blacks played an important role, while for Republicans, general group distance played a significant role, and among Independents, group distance and past experiences with discrimination played an important role. We found no interactive effects between prior support for Clinton and race-based considerations in terms of Asian American voter intention in the general election. Finally, in terms of alternative ways of modeling the intended vote for president, we found that proximity to Latinos over blacks remains statistically significant at the .10 level using an ordered logit model (going from McCain to undecided to Obama), but the variable is not significant in a multinomial logit model (Table 27.A.3 in the appendix).[13]

Implications and Conclusions

Was race an important factor in the Asian American vote in 2008? Media accounts of the presidential primaries, based on a limited set of exit poll survey data and a few interviews with experts and "persons on the street," suggested that race-based attitudes played an important role in the lopsided support among Asian Americans for Clinton over Obama. Our findings, based on the NAAS, partially support these hypotheses, but situate them within a more comprehensive account of Asian American vote choice in 2008. We find, first of all, that Asian American support for Clinton over Obama was not as large as previously thought: instead of margins approximating 85 to 15 percent in the Democratic primary, as suggested in exit polls, we find margins closer to 60 to 30 percent. Furthermore, when we assess the relative importance of race-based considerations and other factors, we find that national origin, age, and gender played a markedly greater role in shaping the primary vote choice of Asian Americans than factors such as prior experiences with racial discrimination and feelings of political commonality with African Americans.

We also find that the role of race-based considerations grew much weaker in the general election than in the primaries. Party identification and issue preferences played such a strong role in shaping the vote choice of Asian Americans that the effects of race-based considerations were comparatively very weak. This points to the importance of context in shaping whether or not race-based considerations were relevant to vote choice. In the primary election, Clinton and Obama did not vary substantially on issue positions such as health care and abortion rights. Furthermore, low-information voters could not rely on differences in the party affiliation of candidates to guide their vote choices in the primary (Rahn 1993; Popkin 1991). In the general election, however, voters could rely both on partisan cues and on substantive issue differences between McCain and Obama, relegating factors such as age, gender, and race-based attitudes to a more subordinate role.

While the varying importance of race-based considerations between the primary and general election is relatively easy to explain, other findings require further exploration. In particular, we need to understand why the effects of race-based considerations seem to have been stronger among Asian American women than men, and why they had a varying effect across party identification. It is possible that the interaction effect we find by gender is a "Hillary Clinton effect," one that is particular to the dynamics of a historic presidential primary that featured a prominent and competitive female candidate. We need data from other points in time, and possibly other types of races, to see if these gendered effects are more generally true.

As for party identification, one may be tempted to argue that our finding about the significance of race-based considerations among Democrats is in line with Paul Sniderman's work on white public opinion toward affirmative action programs, with race-related factors playing a stronger role independent of ideology among Democratic identifiers than Republicans (Sniderman, Crosby, and Howell 2000). A similar logic could apply in this case, where race-based considerations operated in a direction opposite to the role of party identification among Democrats, but in the same direction for Republicans. What we find, however, is a more complicated story: a different set of race-based considerations seems to have mattered for Republicans and Independents, with general group distance mattering more for non-Democrats, and proximity to blacks in particular making more of a difference for Democrats.

It is possible that these puzzles are an artifact of the way we measure race-based considerations. For instance, the NAAS does not have any direct measures of racial prejudice or stereotyping with respect to African Americans and other groups. Nor does it contain measures about social networks, residential contexts, and work contexts to know more about the interactions of Asian Americans with in-group and out-group members. Thus, we cannot rule out the possibility that our measures of race-based considerations are standing in for other factors such as racial prejudice or social distance. Finally, it is important to note that the distribution of our race-related factors is highly uneven: only 26 percent see Asian Americans as having little or nothing in common with other groups, and only 19 percent see Asian Americans as having more political commonality with Latinos than with blacks. Thus, the distribution on our independent variables cannot be interpreted as evidence of hostile feelings toward African Americans or other racial and ethnic groups.

Still, our findings shed some much-needed light on the question of whether race was the primary factor in the vote choice of Asian Americans in the primary and general elections of 2008. Our analysis finds that race-based considerations do help to explain why Asian Americans supported Clinton over Obama and why individuals claimed to be "undecided" about their candidate choice in the general election. However, these factors played a relatively limited role when compared with other factors such as party identification, issue preferences, age, and gender.

This was especially true in the general election, where our preelection survey as well as exit polls both suggest that Asian Americans heavily favored Obama over McCain, even though their support for Obama was more tepid during the primary season. It remains an open question whether our findings from the presidential election in 2008 will apply to other electoral contests. Given the growing share of Asian American voters in many states, cities, and congressional districts, and given the increasing number of minority candidates for elected office, it is clear that questions about the role of race in vote choice will increasingly require research that breaks the traditional black-white paradigm, to include the opinions and voting behavior of Asian Americans and Latinos.

Appendix

TABLE 27.A.1. Asian American Vote Choice in the 2008 General Election, among Registered Voters, by Ethnicity

	Total	Asian Indian	Chinese	Filipino	Japanese	Korean	Vietnamese
Obama	40	51	42	31	62	41	16
McCain	23	16	14	26	16	22	53
Other	1	1	2	1	0	3	1
Undecided	36	32	42	42	22	34	30

Note: Values are percentages.
Source: National Asian American Survey (2008).

TABLE 27.A.2. Logit Regressions of Vote Choice in the 2008 Primary and General Election

	Obama vs. Clinton Voter	Undecided vs. Obama Supporter
Group distance	−0.39	0.186
	[0.225]*	[0.137]
Proximity to Latinos versus blacks	−0.229	0.151
	[0.118]*	[0.078]*
Democrat	0.217	−1.614
	[0.204]	[0.127]***
Republican	0.15	0.512
	[0.497]	[0.250]**

TABLE 27.A.2. (*cont.*)

	Obama vs. Clinton Voter	Undecided vs. Obama Supporter
Religious services frequency	−0.075	0.005
	[0.047]	[0.030]
Any experience with discrimination	−0.022	−0.302
	[0.185]	[0.124]**
Age	−0.015	0.009
	[0.006]**	[0.004]**
Liberal: government services	0.088	−0.204
	[0.091]	[0.057]***
Liberal: abortion rights	0.077	−0.16
	[0.067]	[0.043]***
Education	0.023	−0.066
	[0.091]	[0.057]
Female	−0.408	0.408
	[0.187]**	[0.124]***
South Asian	0.61	0.003
	[0.266]**	[0.061]
Filipino	0.094	0.168
	[0.115]	[0.068]**
Japanese	0.27	−0.214
	[0.077]***	[0.055]***
Korean	0.157	0.023
	[0.075]**	[0.041]
Vietnamese	−0.136	0.048
	[0.078]*	[0.038]
Other Asian	0.079	−0.053
	[0.085]	[0.049]
Clinton primary voter		−0.098
		[0.150]
Constant	−0.548	1.447
	[0.714]	[0.453]***
Observations	586	1,491
Pseudo-R^2	.08	.18

Note: Standard errors are in brackets.

*$p < .10$. **$p < .05$. ***$p < .01$.

TABLE 27.A.3. Ordered Logit Regression of Intended Vote Choice in the 2008
General Election

	McCain to Undecided to Obama
Group distance	−0.222
	[0.107]**
Proximity to Latinos versus blacks	−0.138
	[0.062]**
Democrat	1.616
	[0.113]***
Republican	−1.955
	[0.144]***
Religious services frequency	−0.035
	[0.024]
Any experience with discrimination	0.094
	[0.100]
Age	−0.013
	[0.003]***
Liberal: government services	0.316
	[0.041]***
Liberal: abortion rights	0.142
	[0.035]***
Education	0.064
	[0.046]
Female	−0.157
	[0.099]
South Asian	−0.004
	[0.056]
Filipino	−0.07
	[0.053]
Japanese	0.16
	[0.046]***
Korean	0
	[0.033]
Vietnamese	−0.157
	[0.028]***
Other Asian	0.04
	[0.040]

TABLE 27.A.3. (*cont.*)

	McCain to Undecided to Obama
Clinton primary supporter	0.179
	[0.130]
Observations	1,979
Pseudo-R^2	.26

Note: Standard errors are in brackets.
**$p < .05$. ***$p < .01$.

NOTES

Originally published in *Du Bois Review: Social Science Research on Race* 6 (1): 219–238, 2009. ©2009 *Du Bois Review*, reprinted by permission.

1 It is important to note that immigrant communities are made up of people willing to risk a move from their homeland to another country. As such, they may be less averse to risk than this perspective assumes.

2 National origin figures prominently in presidential vote choice among Latinos as well (Stokes-Brown 2006; Nuño 2007).

3 Highton acknowledges that his study is limited by the fact that there are few black candidates who seek open seats in majority-white districts (Highton 2004, 14).

4 More specifically, we include people with family backgrounds from countries in East Asia, South Asia, Southeast Asia, and the Philippines.

5 In our survey, 120 registered voters are categorized as "Other Asian American," which includes multiracial respondents as well as those outside the six largest ethnic origin groups.

6 Online experiments, such as Project Implicit (http://implicit.harvard.edu/), and online survey experiments offer the promise of providing a better controlled setting for testing racial prejudice than telephone surveys asking respondents the extent to which they agree or disagree with various stereotypes.

7 The measure of relative commonality with blacks, rather than absolute commonality with blacks, also had the added benefit of not being highly correlated with our measure of general group distance. Using the absolute measure of commonality in our multivariate model showed the effect to be statistically insignificant in the primary election model, but not in the general election model.

8 Given the high proportion of "refuse" responses on our household income question (25 percent), we exclude it from the models presented in this article. Running the same model on the smaller N of those who reported their household incomes does not change the substance of our findings about the relative importance of race-based considerations in the Asian American vote.

9 As noted earlier, the National Asian American Survey has several advantages over exit polls, including having interviews in multiple languages, drawing respondents from ethnic enclaves as well as more dispersed areas of settlement, and being able to weight survey respondents to known population characteristics of Asian Americans. The NAAS survey does face one relative limitation: problems with recalling vote choice in the primary election are likely greater in our survey conducted in the early fall than in exit polls conducted on Election Day.

10 Vietnamese American support for Clinton in the primary did not translate to support for the Democrats in the general election, as most indicated an intention to vote for McCain.

11 The proportion of undecided voters among those who voted for other Democratic and Republican candidates was lower than for Clinton primary voters, although the small sample sizes for these groups make these differences statistically insignificant.

12 Similar results hold when we operationalize party identification as a three-point or seven-point measure.

13 We also find that race-based considerations are insignificant in models that include income, and in the ordered logit regression when nativity is added to the mix. Adding these variables to the model may be problematic for several reasons. In the case of income, 25 percent of our sample refused to answer the question, and more may have misreported their income. In the case of nativity, we have no alternative explanation for why nativity would matter, apart from the factors already in the model.

REFERENCES

Abelmann, Nancy, and John Lie. 1995. *Blue Dreams: Korean Americans and the Los Angeles Riots.* Cambridge, MA: Harvard University Press.

Abramowitz, Alan I. 1994. "Issue Evolution Reconsidered: Racial Attitudes and Partisanship in the U.S. Electorate." *American Journal of Political Science* 38 (1): 1–24.

Ancheta, Angelo N. 1998. *Race, Rights, and the Asian American Experience.* New Brunswick, NJ: Rutgers University Press.

Asian American Legal Defense and Education Fund (AALDEF). 2009. "AALDEF: Press Release—AALDEF Exit Poll of over 16,000 Asian American Voters Shows Strong Support for Barack Obama in Historic 2008 Presidential Election." http://www.aaldef.org/article.php?article_id=388 (accessed February 1, 2009).

"Asian American Voters." 2008. On *Anderson Cooper 360°*, February 8–23. http://ac360.blogs.cnn.com/2008/02/08/the-asian-american-vote/.

Axelrod, Robert. 1986. "Presidential Election Coalitions in 1984." *American Political Science Review* 80 (1): 281–284.

Barreto, Matt, and Francisco Pedraza. 2008. "The Renewal and Persistence of Group Identification in American Politics." Paper presented at the Shambaugh Conference, Iowa City, May 9.

Bartels, Larry M. 2000. "Partisanship and Voting Behavior, 1952–1996." *American Journal of Political Science* 44 (1): 35–50.

Berelson, Bernard, Paul F. Lazarsfeld, and William McPhee. 1954. *Voting: A Study of Opinion Formation in a Presidential Campaign.* Chicago: University of Chicago Press.

Blackwell, Angela Glover, Stewart Kwoh, and Manuel Pastor. 2002. *Searching for Uncommon Ground: New Dimensions on Race in America.* New York: Norton.

Blank, Rebecca M., Marilyn Dabady, and Constance F. Citro, eds. 2004. *Measuring Racial Discrimination.* Washington, DC: National Research Council.

Bobo, Lawrence D., and Devon Johnson. 2000. "Racial Attitudes in a Prismatic Metropolis: Mapping Identity, Stereotypes, Competition, and Views on Affirmative Action." Pp. 81–166 in Lawrence D. Bobo, Melvin L. Oliver, James H. Johnson, Jr., and Abel Valenzuela, Jr., eds., *Prismatic Metropolis: Inequality in Los Angeles.* New York: Russell Sage Foundation.

Bobo, Lawrence D., and Susan Suh. 2000. "Surveying Racial Discrimination: Analyses from a Multiethnic Labor Market." Pp. 523–560 in Lawrence D. Bobo, Melvin L. Oliver, James H. Johnson, Jr., and Abel Valenzuela, Jr., eds., *Prismatic Metropolis: Inequality in Los Angeles.* New York: Russell Sage Foundation.

Bullock, Charles S., III. 1984. "Racial Crossover Voting and the Election of Black Officials." *Journal of Politics* 46 (1): 238–251.

Campbell, Angus, Philip E. Converse, Warren E. Miller, and Donald E. Stokes. 1960. *The American Voter*. New York: John Wiley.

Carmines, Edward G., and James A. Stimson. 1989. *Issue Evolution: Race and the Transformation of American Politics*. Princeton: Princeton University Press.

Chang, Robert. 1999. *Disoriented: Asian Americans, Law, and the Nation-State*. New York: New York University Press.

Cho, Sumi K. 1993. "Korean Americans vs. African Americans: Conflict and Construction." Pp. 196–214 in Robert Gooding-Williams, ed., *Reading Rodney King/Reading Urban Uprising*. New York: Routledge.

Citrin, Jack, Donald Philip Green, and David O. Sears. 1990. "Whites' Reactions to Black Candidates: When Does Race Matter?" *Public Opinion Quarterly* 54 (1): 74–96.

Converse, Philip E. 1966. "On the Possibility of Major Political Realignment in the South." Pp. 212–242 in Angus Campbell, Philip E. Converse, Warren E. Miller, and Donald E. Stokes, eds., *Elections and the Political Order*. New York: John Wiley.

Cost, Jay. 2008. "On the State of the Race." *RealClearPolitics.com*, HoreRaceBlog, September 30. http://www.realclearpolitics.com/horseraceblog/2008/09/ (accessed April 6, 2009).

Cullen, Lisa Takeuchi. 2008. "Does Obama Have an Asian Problem?" *Time*, February 18. http://www.time.com/time/politics/article/0,8599,1714292,00.html (accessed March 18, 2009).

Erikson, Robert S. 1989. "Economic Conditions and the Presidential Vote." *American Political Science Review* 83 (2): 567–573.

"Exit Polls—Election Results 2008—The New York Times." 2008. *New York Times*. http://elections.nytimes.com/2008/results/president/exit-polls.html (accessed November 20, 2008).

Fazio, Russell H., Joni R. Jackson, Bridget C. Dunton, and Carol J. Williams. 1995. "Variability in Automatic Activation as an Unobtrusive Measure of Racial Attitudes: A Bona Fide Pipeline?" *Journal of Personality and Social Psychology* 69 (6): 1013–1027.

Fiorina, Morris P. 1981. *Retrospective Voting in American National Elections*. New Haven, CT: Yale University Press.

Gerber, Alan S., and Donald P. Green. 2000. "The Effects of Canvassing, Telephone Calls, and Direct Mail on Voter Turnout: A Field Experiment." *American Political Science Review* 94 (3): 653–663.

Hajnal, Zoltan L. 2001. "White Residents, Black Incumbents, and a Declining Racial Divide." *American Political Science Review* 95 (3): 603–617.

Highton, Benjamin. 2004. "White Voters and African American Candidates for Congress." *Political Behavior* 26 (1): 1–25.

Highton, Benjamin, and Raymond E. Wolfinger. 2001. "The Political Implications of Higher Turnout." *British Journal of Political Science* 31 (1): 179–223.

Hinich, Melvin J., and Michael C. Munger. 1994. *Ideology and the Theory of Political Choice*. Ann Arbor: University of Michigan Press.

Iyengar, Shanto. 1994. *Is Anyone Responsible? How Television Frames Political Issues*. Chicago: University of Chicago Press.

Jennings, M. Kent, and Richard G. Niemi. 1981. *Generations and Politics: A Panel Study of Young Adults and Their Parents*. Princeton: Princeton University Press.

Johnson, James, Jr., Walter Farrell, Jr., and Chandra Guinn. 1997. "Immigration Reform and the Browning of America: Tensions, Conflicts, and Community Instability in Metropolitan Los Angeles." *International Migration Review* 31 (4): 1055–1095.

Kaufmann, Karen. 2003. "Black and Latino Voters in Denver: Responses to Each Other's Political Leadership." *Political Science Quarterly* 118 (1): 107–125.

Kim, Claire Jean. 1999. "The Racial Triangulation of Asian Americans." *Politics and Society* 27 (1): 105–138.

———. 2000. *Bitter Fruit: The Politics of Black-Korean Conflict in New York City*. New Haven, CT: Yale University Press.

Kim, Janine Young. 1999. "Are Asians Black? The Asian-American Civil Rights Agenda and the Contemporary Significance of the Black/White Paradigm." *Yale Law Journal* 108 (8): 2385–2412.

Kim, Kenneth. 2008. "Did Asian Americans Swing California for Clinton?" *NewAmericaMedia. com*, February 7. http://news.newamericamedia.org/news/view_article.html?article_id=d7a4a 2a86575f4bfbc4e0e32a87a448d (accessed March 18, 2009).

Kinder, Donald R., and Lynn M. Sanders. 1996. *Divided by Color: Racial Politics and Democratic Ideals*. Chicago: University of Chicago Press.

Layman, Geoffrey. 2001. *The Great Divide: Religious and Cultural Conflict in American Party Politics*. New York: Columbia University Press.

Lazarsfeld, Paul, Bernard Berelson, and Hazel Gaudet. 1944. *The People's Choice*. New York: Duell, Sloane, and Pierce.

Lee, Jennifer. 2002. *Civility in the City: Blacks, Jew, and Koreans in Urban America*. Cambridge, MA: Harvard University Press.

Lee, Taeku. 2000. "Racial Attitudes and the Color Line(s) at the Close of the Twentieth Century." Pp. 103–158 in Paul M. Ong, ed., *Transforming Race Relations: A Public Policy Report*. Los Angeles: LEAP Asian Pacific American Public Policy Institute and UCLA Asian American Studies Center

Lewis-Beck, Michael S., William G. Jacoby, Helmut Norpoth, and Herbert F. Weisberg. 2007. *The American Voter Revisited*. Ann Arbor: University of Michigan Press.

Lien, Pei-te, M. Margaret Conway, and Janelle Wong. 2004. *The Politics of Asian Americans: Diversity and Community*. New York: Routledge.

Markus, Gregory B. 1988. "The Impact of Personal and National Economic Conditions on the Presidential Vote: A Pooled Cross-Sectional Analysis." *American Journal of Political Science* 32 (1): 137–154.

Mutz, Diana C., and Jeffery J. Mondak. 1997. "Dimensions of Sociotropic Behavior: Group-Based Judgments of Fairness and Well-Being." *American Journal of Political Science* 41 (1): 284–308.

Nie, Norman H., Sidney Verba, and John Petrocik. 1976. *The Changing American Voter*. Cambridge, MA: Harvard University Press.

Nuño, Stephen. 2007. "Latino Mobilization and Vote Choice in the 2000 Presidential Election." *American Politics Research* 35 (2): 273–293.

Page, Benjamin I., and Richard A. Brody. 1972. "Policy Voting and the Electoral Process: The Vietnam War Issue." *American Political Science Review* 66 (3): 979–995.

Pew Forum on Religion and Public Life. 2008. *U.S. Religious Landscape Survey. Religious Beliefs and Practices: Diverse and Politically Relevant*. Washington, DC: Pew Forum on Religion and Public Life. http://religions.pewforum.org/pdf/report2-religious-landscape-study-full.pdf (accessed March 19, 2009).

Popkin, Samuel. 1991. *The Reasoning Voter: Communication and Persuasion in Presidential Campaigns*. Chicago: University of Chicago Press.

"President: National Exit Poll." 2008. CNN. http://www.cnn.com/ELECTION/2008/results/ polls/#USP00p1 (accessed March 18, 2009).

Rahn, Wendy M. 1993. "The Role of Partisan Stereotypes in Information Processing about Political Candidates." *American Journal of Political Science* 37 (2): 472–496.

Reeves, Keith. 1997. *Voting Hopes or Fears: White Voters, Black Candidates, and Racial Politics in America*. New York: Oxford University Press.

Rosenstone, Steven J., and John Mark Hansen. 1993. *Mobilization, Participation, and Democracy in America*. New York: Macmillan.

Sigelman, Carol K., Lee Sigelman, Barbara J. Walkosz, and Michael Nitz. 1995. "Black Candidates, White Voters: Understanding Racial Bias in Political Perceptions." *American Journal of Political Science* 39 (1): 243–265.

Sniderman, Paul M., Gretchen C. Crosby, and William G. Howell. 2000. "The Politics of Race." Pp. 236–279 in David O. Sears, Jim Sidanius, and Lawrence D. Bobo, eds., *Racialized Politics: The Debate about Racism in America*. Chicago: University of Chicago Press.

Stokes-Brown, Atiya. 2006. "Racial Identity and Latino Vote Choice." *American Politics Research* 34 (5): 627–652.

Takagi, Dana Y. 1993. *The Retreat from Race: Asian-American Admissions and Racial Politics*. New Brunswick, NJ: Rutgers University Press.

Terkildsen, Nayda. 1993. "When White Voters Evaluate Black Candidates: The Processing Implications of Candidate Skin Color, Prejudice, Self-Monitoring." *American Journal of Political Science* 37 (4): 1032–1053.

Tuan, Mia. 1999. *Forever Foreigners or Honorary Whites? The Asian Ethnic Experience Today*. New Brunswick, NJ: Rutgers University Press.

Wolfinger, Raymond E. 1965. "The Development and Persistence of Ethnic Voting." *American Political Science Review* 59 (4): 896–908.

Wolfinger, Raymond E., and Steven J. Rosenstone. 1980. *Who Votes?* New Haven, CT: Yale University Press.

Wu, Frank. 2001. *Yellow: Race in America beyond Black and White*. New York: Basic Books.

Yoon, In-Jin. 1995. *On My Own: Korean Businesses and Race Relations in America*. Chicago: University of Chicago Press.

STUDY QUESTIONS

(1) What does Lowe identify as the "master narratives" of Asian American culture? In what ways do these master narratives obscure the heterogeneity of Asian American communities? How is this evident in the poetry and novels she includes in her chapter? Are these master narratives present in your experiences with Asian American families and communities?

(2) What are the different dangers of essentializing Asian American identity and culture? How does essentialism reinforce dominant frameworks of racism? How does it hinder less powerful voices within the Asian American collective? In what ways does it function as an obstacle to cross-racial alliances?

(3) What are the different sociological arguments and measures that scholars have used to argue that Asian Americans are becoming white? What are the limitations of these arguments, according to Kim? In what ways does Kim's focus on citizenship and authenticity dispel the argument that Asian Americans are becoming white?

(4) Why does Kim argue that racial assimilation theories must be more transnational, particularly for Asian Americans? What relevance do America's economic and political relationships to Asian nations have on the racialization of different Asian American communities living on US soil? How does this approach help us disaggregate the heterogeneous experiences of Asian immigrant groups in the United States?

(5) What are some of the disadvantages that Asian American students face in their K–12 experiences, especially with respect to teachers and curriculum? How do Asian American studies programs in colleges address these problems? How do Asian American studies programs continue to fall short?

(6) Throughout this book, we have read about the political impact of uniting under a single Asian American identity. However, Ng and her colleagues argue for the "deliberate disaggregation" of Asian American groups. What are the potential advantages of disaggregating the different ethnicities within the Asian American umbrella? In other words, what might we uncover when we do this? Do you feel there are any disadvantages to doing this?

(7) According to Ramakrishnan and his colleagues, how did the media explain Barack Obama's lack of support among Asian Americans during the Democratic primary race against Hillary Clinton? How did media explanations differ from Asian American advocacy organizations? What did the results from the National Asian American Survey show? How did support for Obama change during the general election against John McCain?

(8) How did Ramakrishnan and his colleagues measure "race-based considerations" in their analysis of the National Asian American Survey? What impact did race-based considerations have on the Democratic primary and general election, respectively? In what other ways could political scientists and other researchers effectively measure race-based considerations in future studies?

SUGGESTED READINGS

Aoki, Andrew L., and Don Nakanishi. 2001. "Asian Pacific Americans and the New Minority Politics." *PS: Political Science and Politics* 34 (3): 605–610.

Chang, Jeff. 1994. "Race, Class, Conflict and Empowerment: On Ice Cube's 'Black Korea.'" Pp. 87–107 in Edward T. Change and Russell C. Leong, eds., *Los Angeles: Struggles toward Multiethnic Community*. Seattle: University of Washington Press.

Chung, Angie. 2001. "The Powers That Bind: A Case Study of the Collective Bases of Coalition Building in Post–Civil Unrest Los Angeles." *Urban Affairs Review* 37: 205–226.

Diaz-Veizades, J., and E. Chang. 1996. "Building Cross-Cultural Coalitions: A Case-Study of the Black-Korean Alliance and the Latino-Black Roundtable." *Ethnic and Racial Studies* 19 (3): 680–700.

Fujita, Rony. 2000. "Coalitions, Race, and Labor: Rereading Philip Vera Cruz." *Journal of Asian American Studies* 3 (2): 139–162.

Hirabayashi, Lane. 1995. "Back to the Future: Reframing Community-Based Research." *Amerasia Journal* 21 (1–2): 103–118.

Horton, John. 1995. *The Politics of Diversity: Immigration, Resistance, and Change in Monterey Park, California*. Philadelphia: Temple University Press.

Joyce, Patrick. 2003. *No Fire Next Time: Black-Korean Conflicts and the Future of America's Cities*. Ithaca, NY: Cornell University Press.

Kim, Clarie. 2000. *Bitter Fruit: The Politics of Black-Korean Conflict in New York City*. New Haven, CT: Yale University Press.

Kim, Elaine H. 1995. "Beyond Railroads and Internment: Comments on the Past, Present, and Future of Asian American Studies." Pp. 11–21 in Gary Y. Okihiro, Marilyn Alquizola, Dorothy Fujita-Rony, and K. Scott Wong, eds., *Privileging Positions: The Sites of Asian American Studies*. Pullman: Washington State University Press.

Lien, Pei-te. 2002. "The Participation of Asian Americans in U.S. Elections." *Asian Pacific American Law Journal* 8: 55–99.

Lowe, Lisa. 1996. *Immigrant Acts: On Asian Cultural Practices*. Durham, NC: Duke University Press.

McGregor, Davianna Pomaika'i. 2004. "Engaging Hawaiians in the Expansion of the U.S. Empire." *Journal of Asian American Studies* 7 (3): 209–222.

Naber, Nadine. 2002. "So Our History Doesn't Become Your Future: The Local and Global Politics of Coalition Building Post September 11th." *Journal of Asian American Studies* 5 (3): 217–242.

Nakanishi, Don, and James S. Lai, eds. 2003. *Asian American Politics: Law, Participation, and Policy*. Lanham, MD: Rowman & Littlefield.

Okamoto, Dina. 2010. "Organizing Across Ethnic Boundaries in the Post–Civil Rights Era: Asian American Panethnic Coalitions." Pp. 143–169 in N. Van Dyke and H. McCammon, eds., *Strategic Alliances: Coalition Building and Social Movements*. Minneapolis: University of Minnesota Press.

Omi, Michael, and Howard Winant. 1994. *Racial Formation in the United States: From the 1960s to the 1990s*. 2nd ed. New York: Routledge.

Ong, Paul. 2003. "The Affirmative Action Divide." Pp. 377–406 in Don Nakanishi and James S. Lai, eds., *Asian American Politics: Law, Participation, and Policy*. Lanham, MD: Rowman & Littlefield.

Park, Edward. 1998. "Competing Visions: Political Formation of Korean Americans in Los Angeles, 1992–1997." *Amerasia Journal* 24: 41–57.

Park, Kyeyoung. 1996. "Use and Abuse of Race and Culture: Black/Korean Tension in America." *American Anthropologist* 98 (3): 492–499.

Rodriguez, Robyn, and Nerissa S. Balce. 2004. "American Insecurity and Racial Filipino Community Politics." *Peace Review* 16 (2): 131–140.

Saito, Leland. 2009. *The Politics of Exclusion: The Failure of Race-Neutral Policies in Urban America*. Stanford, CA: Stanford University Press.

Seshagiri, Urmila. 2003. "At the Crossroads of Two Empires: Mira Nair's Mississippi Masala and the Limits of Hybridity." *Journal of Asian American Studies* 6 (2): 177–198.

Vo, Linda. 2004. *Mobilizing an Asian American Community*. Philadelphia: Temple University Press.

Wang, L. Ling-Chi. 1995. "The Structure of Dual Domination: Toward a Paradigm for the Study of the Chinese Diaspora in the United States." *Amerasia Journal* 21 (1–2): 149–169.

Wong, Janelle, Karthick Ramakrishnan, Taeku Lee, and Jane Junn. 2011. *Asian American Political Participation: Emerging Constituents and Their Political Identities*. New York: Russell Sage Foundation.

Yamamoto, Eric. 1999. *Interracial Justice: Conflict and Reconciliation in Post–Civil Rights America*. New York: New York University Press.

FILMS

Chiang, S. Leo (producer/director). 2012. *Mr. Cao Goes to Washington* (72-minute documentary).

Ding, Loni (producer/director). 1987. *The Color of Honor: Japanese American Soldiers in World War II* (101-minute documentary).

Griffith, C. A., and H. L. T. Quan (producers). 2009. *Mountains That Take Wing: Angela Davis & Yuri Kochiyama: A Conversation on Life, Struggles, and Liberation* (97-minute documentary).

Japanese American National Museum. 1997. *From Bullets to Ballots* (24-minute documentary).

Kim-Gibson, Dai Sil (director). 2003. *Wet Sand: Voices from L.A. Ten Years Later* (57-minute documentary).

Okino, Steve (producer). 2006. *A Most Unlikely Hero* (57-minute documentary).

Sakya, Sapana, Donald Young, and Kyung Yu (directors). 2003. *Searching for Asian America* (90-minute documentary).

ABOUT THE CONTRIBUTORS

Carl L. Bankston III, PhD, is Professor of Sociology at Tulane University.

Frank D. Bean, PhD, is Distinguished Professor of Sociology in the School of Social Sciences, and Director, Center for Research on International Migration, at the University of California, Irvine.

Jennifer Bucceri, PhD, received her doctorate from the Counseling and Clinical Psychology Department at Columbia University.

Melissa J. H. Corpus, PhD, received her doctorate from the Counseling and Clinical Psychology Department at Columbia University.

Pawan Dhingra, PhD, is Professor of Sociology and American Studies at Tufts University.

Susan Eckstein, PhD, is Professor of Sociology and International Relations at Boston University.

Yen Le Espiritu, PhD, is Professor in the Ethnic Studies Department at the University of California, San Diego.

J. V. Gatewood, PhD, received his doctorate in American Studies at Brown University in 2008. He is currently pursuing a new career as a nurse-practitioner.

C. Winter Han, PhD, is Assistant Professor in the Sociology and Anthropology Department at Middlebury College.

Xavier Hernandez is a doctoral student in the Department of Education Policy, Organization, and Leadership at the University of Illinois at Urbana-Champaign.

Danielle Antoinette Hidalgo, PhD, is Assistant Professor of Sociology at California State University, Chico.

Janine Young Kim, JD, is Professor of Law at Marquette University.

Nadia Y. Kim, PhD, is Associate Professor of Sociology at Loyola Marymount University.

Jane Junn, PhD, is Professor of Political Science at the University of Southern California.

Jennifer Lee, PhD, is Professor of Sociology at the University of California, Irvine.

Taeku Lee, PhD, is Professor of Political Science and Professor of Law at the University of California, Berkeley.

Maxwell Leung, PhD, is Assistant Professor in the Critical Studies Program at California College of the Arts.

Wei Li, PhD, is Professor at the School of Social Transformation and School of Geographical Sciences and Urban Planning at Arizona State University.

Annie I. Lin, PhD, received her doctorate in Counseling Psychology at Columbia University.

Lisa Lowe, PhD, is Professor of English at Tufts University, and a member of the Consortium of Studies in Race, Colonialism, and Diaspora.

Sunaina Maira, EdD, is Professor of Asian American Studies at the University of California, Davis.

Kevin L. Nadal, PhD, is Associate Professor of Psychology at John Jay College of Criminal Justice and Executive Director of the Center for LGBTQ Studies at CUNY Graduate Center.

Jennifer Ng, PhD, is Associate Professor in the Department of Educational Leadership and Policy Studies at the University of Kansas.

Thanh-Nghi Nguyen, PhD, earned her doctorate in Sociology at Boston University and currently lives in Hawaii.

Anthony C. Ocampo, PhD, is Assistant Professor of Sociology at California State Polytechnic University, Pomona, and Ford Foundation Postdoctoral Fellow at the University of California, Riverside, School of Public Policy.

Glenn Omatsu is Senior Lecturer in Asian American Studies at California State University, Northridge.

Yoon Pak, PhD, is Associate Professor in Education Policy, Organization, and Leadership and Asian American Studies at the University of Illinois at Urbana-Champaign.

Lisa Park (pseudonym) is a mixed-heritage Asian American writer.

Lisa Sun-Hee Park, PhD, is Professor of Sociology at the University of Minnesota–Twin Cities.

Kim Park Nelson, PhD, is Associate Professor of American Multicultural Studies at Minnesota State University–Moorhead.

Rhacel Salazar Parreñas, PhD, is Professor of Sociology and Gender Studies at the University of Southern California.

OiYan Poon, PhD, is Assistant Professor of Higher Education at Loyola University Chicago.

S. Karthick Ramakrishnan, PhD, is Professor of Political Science and Associate Dean of the School of Public Policy at the University of California, Riverside.

Ester Sihite is a doctoral student in the Higher Education Program at Loyola University Chicago.

Emily Skop, PhD, is Associate Professor of Geography in the Department of Geography and Environment Studies at the University of Colorado–Colorado Springs.

Derald Wing Sue, PhD, is Professor of Psychology and Education at Columbia University's Teachers College.

Gina C. Torino, PhD, received her doctorate in Counseling Psychology from Columbia University.

Karen Umemoto, PhD, is Professor in the Department of Urban and Regional Planning at the University of Hawaii at Manoa.

Janelle Wong, PhD, is Professor of American Studies and the Director of the Asian American Studies Program at the University of Maryland, College Park.

Yang Sao Xiong, PhD, is Assistant Professor in the School of Social Work and the Asian American Studies Program at the University of Wisconsin–Madison.

Wan Yu is a doctoral student in the School of Geographical Sciences and Urban Planning at Arizona State University.

Min Zhou, PhD, is Tan Lark Sye Chair Professor of Sociology and Director of the Chinese Heritage Centre at Nanyang Technological University, Singapore. She is also Professor of Sociology and Asian American Studies and Walter and Shirley Wang Endowed Chair in US-China Relations and Communications at the University of California, Los Angeles.

INDEX

Abelmann, N., 233, 572, 604, 619

Abraham, M., 212

Abrahamic religions: of Christianity, 230, 292, 406; of Islam, 453–60; of Judaism, 513, 515–16, 549, 560, 566

Abramowitz, A. I., 605, 619

Act on the Immigration and Legal Status of Overseas Koreans, 422

Activism, xiv, 2, 9, 25–28, 31, 38, 44, 48–49, 53, 61–70, 73, 75–77, 81–86, 88–96, 126, 317, 344, 350, 378, 383, 418, 421, 425, 448, 512, 516, 520, 551, 555

Adamson, W., 551

Adaptation, 121–23, 129, 141–42, 146, 148, 150, 232

Adler, S. R., 179

Admissions quotas, 55, 77, 509–516, 536, 549

Adolfson, N., 420

Adoption and Safe Families Act, 410

Advocacy Group, 76, 424, 492, 602

Aesthetics, 265

Affirmative action, 18, 55, 62, 76–82, 334–35, 340, 348, 351, 506, 508–28, 579, 591, 603, 614

Affirmative action, policies, 340, 506, 510, 513

African Americans, 2, 5, 17, 19, 25–26, 29, 30–32, 40, 47, 55–56, 64, 66, 70, 72–73, 75, 77–70, 82, 87, 91–92, 96, 121, 183, 223, 227, 264, 269, 285, 304, 310, 336, 339, 342–43, 344–46, 349–50, 352, 355, 364–66, 379, 396, 400, 409–10, 412–13, 424, 428, 445–45, 449, 454–55, 465, 466, 467–69, 472, 479, 483–84, 492, 494, 512, 517, 521, 526, 551, 566, 568, 579, 585–86, 598–604, 607, 610–14; community, 2, 17, 19, 29, 31, 66, 70, 72–73, 75, 78–79, 336, 332, 568, 602; ghetto, 344; movements, 2, 25–26, 31, 40, 64, 66, 73, 75, 91–92, 344, 345, 410, 466; neoconservatives, 77–79, 82, 91, 512; slavery, 396, 455

After-school programs, 382

Agbayani-Siewart, P., 157

Agger, B., 315

Agnew, S., 70

A Great Wall (film), 546–47, 552

Agricultural Workers Organizing Committee, 88

Aguirre, A., 340–41

Aid to Families with Dependent Children, 207

AIDS, 102, 350

Akbar, M., 468

Alba, R., 121, 391, 393, 396

Alexander, C., 229

Allen, J. P., 265

Allred, N. C., 512

Almaguer, T., 571

Almirol, E. B., 157

Alvarez, A., 585, 591

Alvarez, A. N., 307

Amerasian, 137

American: birth, 114, 539; Catholicism, 293; colonialism, 7, 15, 31, 236, 238–39, 244, 358, 367, 373; exceptionalism, 492; gay culture, 294, 307; individualism, 67, 90, 299, 453

American Community Survey, 141–42, 187, 205, 606

American dream, xvii, 17, 36, 64, 207, 343, 382, 435, 440–41, 452–53, 498, 501, 505

American Federation of Teachers, 50

American foreign policy, influence on migration of Southeast Asians, 104, 130, 175

American Indians, 77, 218, 221–22, 225, 227–28, 230, 233, 396, 409

Americanization, 252, 367, 543

American Puritanism, 499

Americans for Immigration Control, 161

American West, xiii, 93, 107, 110, 142, 144, 217, 380, 397, 399, 446

Ancheta, A. N, 348–49, 351, 510, 555, 557–58, 560, 576, 604

Anderson, J. D., 579

Anglo-American culture, 351

Anti-Asian: crimes, 557, 569; legislation, 106, 194, 415; violence, 81, 92, 120, 217, 557, 569

Anti-immigrant sentiment, 161

Antimiscegenation law, 159, 194, 340

Areza, P. D., 163

Arguelles, D., 562

Armenians, 549

9 781479 826223